Fixed Income Securities

Second Edition

Fixed Income Securities

Second Edition

Frank J. Fabozzi, Ph.D., CFA

JOHN WILEY & SONS

To my wife, Donna,
and my children, Karly, Patricia, and Francesco

Published by John Wiley & Sons, Inc.
Published simultaneously in Canada.

ISBN: 0-471-21830-8

Printed in the United States of America.

10 9 8 7 6 5 4 3 2 1

About the Author

Frank J. Fabozzi is editor of the *Journal of Portfolio Management* and an Adjunct Professor of Finance at Yale University's School of Management. He is a Chartered Financial Analyst and Certified Public Accountant. Dr. Fabozzi is on the board of directors of the Guardian Life family of funds and the BlackRock complex of funds. He earned a doctorate in economics from the City University of New York in 1972 and in 1994 received an honorary doctorate of Humane Letters from Nova Southeastern University. Dr. Fabozzi is a Fellow of the International Center for Finance at Yale University.

Preface

The objective of this book is to provide comprehensive coverage of the wide range of fixed income securities. This includes a description of each security and its investment features and characteristics. While the majority of *Fixed Income Securities: Second Edition* is devoted to the securities, there is also an explanation of how securities are valued, yield and yield spread measures, interest rate risk measures, tax treatment, collateralized borrowing, and an overview of fixed income portfolio management and strategies.

Chapter 1 provides an overview of the features and risks associated with fixed income securities. These features include maturity, par value, the various types of coupon rates (fixed and floating), accrued interest, yield, provisions for paying off bonds before maturity (call and refunding provisions), and options granted to bondholders (put provisions and conversion provisions). Coverage of the risks associated with investing in fixed income securities include interest rate risk, call and prepayment risk, credit risk, liquidity risk, exchange rate risk, and inflation risk.

Chapter 2 explains how fixed income securities are valued and the various measures of interest rate risk. Valuation of fixed income securities involves estimating the cash flow from a security and then computing the present value of the estimated cash flow. The difficulty of estimating the cash flow for certain types of fixed income securities is explained. The two methodologies for computing the present value of the estimated cash flow—the traditional approach (which uses only one discount rate) versus the arbitrage-free approach (which uses multiple discount rates)—is discussed and illustrated. The interest rate risk measures explained are modified duration, effective duration, dollar duration, portfolio duration, contribution to duration, spread duration for fixed-rate bonds, index and spread duration for a floating-rate security, and convexity.

Yield and yield spread measures are covered in Chapter 3. The sources of return from investing in a fixed income security are first explained. Yield measures covered are current yield, yield to maturity, yield to first call, yield to next call, yield to first par call, yield to refunding, yield to put, yield to worst, and cash flow yield. The yield spread measures explained are nominal spread, zero-volatility spread, and option-adjusted spread. The margin or spread measures for floating-rate securities covered are the spread for life and the discount margin. Each measure is not only illustrated, but the limitations are highlighted. Also in Chapter 3 is an explanation of spot rates. These rates are used for computing the present value of the estimated cash flow using the arbitrage-free approach to valuation.

Chapters 4 through 14 cover the securities. Chapter 4 explains U.S. Treasury securities. These securities include Treasury bills, fixed-rate Treasury notes and bonds, and stripped Treasury securities. Federal agency securities are covered in Chapter 5. Federal agencies are categorized as either federally related institutions (i.e., arms of the federal government) or government-sponsored enterprises

(i.e., privately owned but publicly chartered entities). The major issuer that falls into the federally related institutions category and whose securities are described in the chapter is the Tennessee Valley Authority. Government sponsored enterprises issue debentures and securities backed by loans. In Chapter 3 the various types of debentures are described. There are six government-sponsored enterprises that currently issue securities: Federal National Mortgage Association (Fannie Mae), Federal Home Loan Mortgage Corporation (Freddie Mac), Federal Home Loan Bank System, Federal Agricultural Mortgage Corporation (Farmer Mac), Federal Farm Credit System, and Student Loan Marketing Association (Sallie Mae). These entities are discussed in the chapter.

Chapter 6 covers securities issued by state and local governments, popularly referred to as municipal securities. The majority of these securities are exempt from federal income taxes and, as a result, appeal to investors that face a high marginal tax bracket. The tax provisions affecting municipal securities are discussed. The types of municipal securities include tax-backed debt (general obligation bonds, appropriation-backed obligations, dedicated tax-backed obligations, and debt obligations supported by public credit enhancement programs) and revenue bonds. Also described in Chapter 6 are hybrid municipal bond structures—insured bonds and refunded bonds—and municipal derivative securities.

Corporate debt obligations are covered in two chapters, Chapters 7 and 8. In Chapter 7 an overview of corporate bankruptcy and creditor rights is provided. After this overview there is a description of the various features of corporate debt obligations, including secured versus unsecured debt, indentures, and sinking fund provisions. The credit quality of corporate bonds are provided by organizations referred to as "rating agencies." Currently they include Fitch, Moody's Investors Service, and Standard & Poor's Corporation. These companies assess the credit quality of an issuer and cast their opinion in the form of a rating. These ratings are described in Chapter 7, along with an explanation of the rating process and the factors that are considered by rating agencies in assessing the credit risk of an issuer.

Speculative-grade corporate bonds (more popularly referred to as high-yield bonds or "junk" bonds), convertible bonds, medium-term notes, commercial paper, corporate bank loans, and preferred stock are described in Chapter 8. Default and recovery statistics, as well as the rights of creditors in bankruptcy versus what actually takes place in a bankruptcy, are also explained.

In Chapters 9, 10, and 11, securities backed by residential mortgages are described. These securities are popularly referred to as mortgage-backed securities. As explained in Chapter 9, the difficulty in analyzing any mortgage-backed security is due to prepayments. An investor who purchases a mortgage-backed security is exposed to prepayment risk. Chapter 9 describes various mortgage designs and the creation of the basic type of mortgage-backed product, the passthrough security. The passthrough securities issued by a federally related institution, the Government National Mortgage Association (Ginnie Mae), and

two government-sponsored enterprises (Fannie Mae and Freddie Mac) are referred to as agency passthrough securities. Passthrough securities backed by residential mortgages that are issued by any entity other than Ginnie Mae, Fannie Mae, or Freddie Mac are referred to as nonagency passthrough securities. The focus in Chapter 9 is on agency passthrough securities. Passthrough securities backed by agricultural real estate are issued by Farmer Mac and are referred to as agricultural mortgage-backed securities.

From a mortgage passthrough security, two derivative mortgage-backed securities can be created—stripped mortgage-backed securities and collateralized mortgage obligations (CMOs). Stripped mortgage-backed securities include principal-only mortgage strips and interest-only mortgage strips. These securities and their risk characteristics are discussed in Chapter 9. In Chapter 10, CMOs that are issued by Fannie Mae, Freddie Mac, or Ginnie Mae are described, as well as the motivation for creating these securities. There are many types of CMO products created. These securities or bond classes are referred to as "tranches." They include sequential-pay tranches, accrual tranches, floating-rate tranches, inverse floating-rate tranches, planned amortization class tranches, support tranches, support tranches with schedules, and notional IO tranches. Each type of tranche is explained, as well as the exposure of each tranche type to prepayment risk.

In Chapter 11, nonagency mortgage-backed securities are covered. While both agency and nonagency mortgage-backed securities expose investors to prepayment risk, nonagency mortgage-backed securities also expose investors to credit risk. As a result, to obtain a rating for the tranches in a nonagency mortgage-backed security, it is necessary for the issuer to enhance the credit quality of the issue. The various ways in which a nonagency mortgage-backed security are credit enhanced and the important role of the servicer are described in the chapter.

Asset-backed securities are securities backed by a pool of loans or receivables. While technically mortgage-backed securities are asset-backed securities, in the United States there is a separation between the two. In Chapter 12, the features of asset-backed securities are explained—credit enhancement, amortizing versus nonamortizing assets, floating rate versus fixed rate, passthrough versus paythrough, and optional clean-up call provisions. Then several types of products are reviewed—home equity loan-backed securities, manufactured housing-backed securities, commercial mortgage-backed securities, auto loan-backed securities, SBA loan-backed securities, and credit card receivable-backed securities. The unique risks associated with investing in asset-backed securities are asset risks, structural risks, the risks associated with the legal structure, and the risks associated with third-party providers. These risks are explained in the chapter.

A major sector of the asset-backed securities market is the market for collateralized debt obligations (CDOs). These are securities backed by a pool of debt obligations consisting of one or more of the following: high-yield corporate bonds, emerging market bonds, bank loans, special situation loans, distressed debt, or tranches of asset-backed or mortgage-backed deals. When a CDO includes only

bonds as collateral, the issue is referred to as a collateralized bond obligation; a CDO is referred to as a collateralized loan obligation if the collateral consists of only loans. Chapter 13 describes CDOs—their structure and the types of transactions (arbitrage versus balance sheet), and cash flow versus market value transactions.

Chapter 14 reviews the various types of international bonds. The chapter begins with foreign exchange rates and a classification of trading blocs. Then the different types of international bonds are described: foreign bonds, Eurobonds, and global bonds. Coverage of central government securities includes the methods of distribution, special structures in emerging market government bonds, accrued interest and market conventions, and credit risk.

An investor seeking to borrow funds to invest in the bond market can do so by means of a collateralized loan. This means that the collateral for the loan is a bond that is owned or one that is being purchased with the borrowed funds. The most common mechanism used by institutional investors is the repurchase agreement. A specialized type of repurchase agreement used for passthrough securities is the dollar roll. For retail investors, the most common type of collateralized borrowing is the purchase of securities on margin. In Chapter 15, these various forms of collateralized borrowing are explained. Since a collateralized borrowing may result in leveraging a portfolio, the chapter begins with the principles of leverage—the advantages and disadvantages of using leverage. Securities lending is a way in which an entity can borrow securities and is described in the chapter.

The federal income tax treatment of transactions in the fixed income securities market are reviewed in Chapter 16. Specifically, the following are covered: different definitions of income as specified in the tax code, tax basis, capital gain or loss, and tax treatment of capital gain or loss. The tax law dealing with the treatment of interest income is complex when securities are not purchased at par value. The rules are described in the chapter.

Chapters 17 and 18 provide an overview of fixed income portfolio management for institutional investors. An overview of the investment management process is provided in Chapter 17. The five steps in this process are (1) setting investment objectives, (2) establishing investment policy, (3) selecting the portfolio strategy, (4) selecting the assets, and (5) measuring and evaluating performance. In the discussion of the fifth step, there is coverage of the various methodologies for measuring the performance of a portfolio manager—arithmetic average rate of return, time-weighted rate of return, and dollar-weighted rate of return. The various types of bond indexes—broad-based U.S. bond market indexes, specialized U.S. bond market indexes, and global and international bond indexes—are then reviewed. The chapter concludes with a framework that should be used by portfolio managers in assessing the potential performance of a portfolio, total return.

An overview of fixed income portfolio strategies is the subject of Chapter 18. The strategy pursued by a manager will either be an active or passive strategy. The decision as to whether to pursue an active or passive strategy will be based on whether the manager (or client) believes that the bond market or a sector

of the bond market is price efficient. Consequently, the chapter begins with the concept of the pricing efficiency of a market and its implications for portfolio strategy selection. Then a classification of strategies that a portfolio manager can pursue given a benchmark, as suggested by Kenneth Volpert of the Vanguard Group, is provided—pure bond indexing, enhanced indexing/matching primary risk factors, enhanced indexing/minor risk factor mismatches, active management/large risk factor mismatches, and active management/full-blown active. The primary risk factors associated with an index are explained. Value-added strategies are then described—strategic strategies (interest rate expectations strategies, yield curve strategies, and inter- and intra-sector allocation strategies) and tactical strategies. The motivation for international bond investing is then provided, as well as a framework for formulating a strategy for international bond investing. The chapter concludes with a description of strategies that institutional investors employ to manage a portfolio where the objective is to satisfy liabilities. These strategies are referred to as structured portfolio strategies and include immunization and cash flow matching.

In preparing sections of some chapters, I have drawn from material that I coauthored with the following individuals: Anand Bhattacharya, Sylvan Feldstein, Michael Fleming, Frank J. Jones, J. Hank Lynch, Steven V. Mann, Chuck Ramsey, Richard Wilson, and David Yuen. I benefitted from discussions with the following individuals: Mark J.P. Anson, Laurie Goodman, Andrew Kalotay, George P. Kegler, Jack Malvey, Jan Mayl, Ron Ryan, Richard Shea, Christopher B. Stewart, and Kenneth E. Volpert.

I am grateful to Jack Malvey for granting me permission to use material from various publications of Lehman Brothers, to Laurie Goodman for allowing me to use a table appearing in a UBS/Warburg publication, to Professor Edward Altman for allowing me to use the results of some tables from his research on defaults and recoveries in one of my exhibits, and to Standard & Poor's Corporation for permitting me to use one of its rating transition tables.

Finally, I thank Megan Orem for her editorial assistance throughout this project.

Frank J. Fabozzi

Table of Contents

Chapter 1

Features and Risks of Fixed Income Securities

In its simplest form, a fixed income security is a financial obligation of an entity that promises to pay a specified sum of money at specified future dates. The entity that promises to make the payment is called the *issuer* of the security. Some examples of issuers are the U.S. government or a foreign government, a state or local government entity, a domestic or foreign corporation, and a supranational institution such as the World Bank.

Fixed income securities fall into two general categories: debt obligations and preferred stock. In the case of a debt obligation, the issuer is called the *borrower.* The investor who purchases such a fixed income security is said to be the *lender* or *creditor.* The promised payments that the issuer agrees to make at the specified dates consist of two components: interest payments and repayment of the amount borrowed. Fixed income securities that are debt obligations include bonds, mortgage-backed securities, and asset-backed securities.

In contrast to a fixed income security that represents a debt obligation, preferred stock represents an ownership interest in a corporation. The payments that are made to the preferred stockholder include dividends and repayment of a fixed amount to retire the obligation. The dividends paid represent a distribution of the corporation's profit. Unlike investors who own a corporation's common stock, investors who own the preferred stock can only realize a contractually fixed dividend payment. Moreover, the payments that must be made to preferred stockholders have priority over the payments that a corporation pays to common stockholders. In the case of a liquidation of a corporation, preferred stockholders are given preference over common stockholders. Consequently, preferred stock is a form of equity that has characteristics similar to bonds.

Prior to the 1980s, fixed income securities were simple investment products. Holding aside default by the issuer, the investor knew how much interest would be received periodically and when the amount borrowed would be repaid. Moreover, most investors purchased these securities with the intent of holding them to their maturity date. Beginning in the 1980s, the fixed income world changed. First, fixed income securities became more complex. There are features in many fixed income securities that make it difficult to determine when the amount borrowed will be repaid. For some securities it is difficult to project the amount of interest that will be received periodically. Second, the hold-to-maturity investor has been replaced by the institutional investor who actively trades fixed income securities.

The purpose of this book is to explain the wide range of fixed income securities and their investment characteristics. The major focus is on fixed income securities that are debt obligations. While fixed income securities include more than bonds, we will frequently use the terms *fixed income securities* and *bonds* interchangeably.

FEATURES OF BONDS

The promises of the issuer and the rights of the bondholders are set forth in great detail in the *indenture*. Bondholders would have great difficulty in determining from time to time whether the issuer was keeping all the promises made in the indenture. This problem is resolved for the most part by bringing in a *trustee* as a third party to the contract. The indenture is made out to the trustee as a representative of the interests of the bondholders; that is, a trustee acts in a fiduciary capacity for bondholders. A trustee is a bond or trust company with a trust department whose officers are experts in performing the functions of a trustee.

Maturity

The *term to maturity* of a bond is the number of years over which the issuer has promised to meet the conditions of the obligation. The maturity of a bond refers to the date that the debt will cease to exist, at which time the issuer will redeem the bond by paying the amount borrowed. The maturity date of a bond is always identified when describing a bond. For example, a description of a bond might state "due 12/1/2020."

The practice in the bond market is to refer to the "term to maturity" of a bond as simply its "maturity" or "term." As we explain later, there may be provisions in the indenture that allow either the issuer or bondholder to alter a bond's term to maturity.

Generally, bonds with a maturity between 1 and 5 years are considered "short-term." Bonds with a maturity between 5 and 12 years are viewed as "intermediate-term," and "long-term" bonds are those with a maturity of more than 12 years.

There are bonds of every maturity. Typically, the longest maturity is 30 years. However, Walt Disney Co. issued bonds in July 1993 with a maturity date of 7/15/2093, making them 100-year bonds at the time of issuance. In December 1993, the Tennessee Valley Authority issued bonds that mature on 12/15/2043, making them 50-year bonds.

There are three reasons why the term to maturity of a bond is important. The most obvious is that it indicates the time period over which the bondholder can expect to receive interest payments and the number of years before the principal will be paid in full. The second reason is that the yield on a bond depends on it. This will be explained in Chapter 4. Finally, the price of a bond will fluctuate over its life as interest rates in the market change. The price volatility of a bond is

dependent on its maturity. More specifically, as explained later, with all other factors constant, the longer the maturity of a bond, the greater the price volatility resulting from a change in interest rates.

Par Value

The *par value* of a bond is the amount that the issuer agrees to repay the bondholder by the maturity date. This amount is also referred to as the *principal*, *face value, redemption value*, or *maturity value*. Bonds can have any par value.

Because bonds can have a different par value, the practice is to quote the price of a bond as a percentage of its par value. A value of 100 means 100% of par value. So, for example, if a bond has a par value of $1,000 and the issue is selling for $900, this bond would be said to be selling at 90. If a bond with a par value of $5,000 is selling for $5,500, the bond is said to be selling for 110. The reason why a bond sells above or below its par value is explained in Chapter 3.

Coupon Rate

The *coupon rate*, also called the *nominal rate*, is the interest rate that the issuer agrees to pay each year. The annual amount of the interest payment made to bondholders during the term of the bond is called the *coupon*. The coupon is determined by multiplying the coupon rate by the par value of the bond. For example, a bond with an 8% coupon rate and a par value of $1,000 will pay annual interest of $80.

When describing a bond of an issuer, the coupon rate is indicated along with the maturity date. For example, the expression "6s of 12/1/2020" means a bond with a 6% coupon rate maturing on 12/1/2020.

In the United States, the usual practice is for the issuer to pay the coupon in two semiannual installments. Mortgage-backed securities and asset-backed securities typically pay interest monthly. For bonds issued in some markets outside the United States, coupon payments are made only once per year.

In addition to indicating the coupon payments that the investor should expect to receive over the term of the bond, the coupon rate also affects the bond's price sensitivity to changes in market interest rates. As illustrated later, all other factors constant, the higher the coupon rate, the less the price will change in response to a change in market interest rates.

Zero-Coupon Bonds

Not all bonds make periodic coupon payments. Bonds that are not contracted to make periodic coupon payments are called *zero-coupon bonds*. The holder of a zero-coupon bond realizes interest by buying the bond substantially below its par value. Interest then is paid at the maturity date, with the interest being the difference between the par value and the price paid for the bond. So, for example, if an investor purchases a zero-coupon bond for 70, the interest is 30. This is the difference between the par value (100) and the price paid (70).

The reason for the issuance of zero-coupon bonds is explained in Chapter 3.

There is another type of fixed income security that does not pay interest until the maturity date. This type has contractual coupon payments, but those payments are accrued and distributed along with the maturity value at the maturity date. These instruments are called *accrued coupon instruments* or *accrual securities*. There are municipal bonds and certain types of mortgage-backed securities that have this characteristic.

Floating-Rate Securities

The coupon rate on a bond need not be fixed over the bond's life. *Floating-rate securities*, sometimes called *variable-rate securities*, have coupon payments that reset periodically according to some *reference rate*. The typical formula for the coupon rate at the dates when the coupon rate is reset is:

Reference rate + Quoted margin

The *quoted margin* is the additional amount that the issuer agrees to pay above the reference rate. For example, suppose that the reference rate is the 1-month London interbank offered rate (LIBOR).[1] Suppose that the quoted margin is 100 basis points. Then the coupon reset formula is:

1-month LIBOR + 100 basis points

So, if 1-month LIBOR on the coupon reset date is 5%, the coupon rate is reset for that period at 6% (5% plus 100 basis points).

The quoted margin need not be a positive value. The quoted margin could be subtracted from the reference rate. For example, the reference rate could be the yield on a 5-year Treasury security and the coupon rate could reset every 6 months based on the following coupon reset formula:

5-year Treasury yield – 90 basis points

So, if the 5-year Treasury yield is 7% on the coupon reset date, the coupon rate is 6.1% (7% minus 90 basis points).

The reference rate for most floating-rate securities is an interest rate or an interest rate index. There are some issues where this is not the case. Instead, the reference rate is some financial index such as the return on the Standard & Poor's 500 or a nonfinancial index such as the price of a commodity. Through financial engineering, issuers have been able to structure floating-rate securities with almost any reference rate. In several countries, there are government bonds whose coupon reset formula is tied to an inflation index. As explained in Chapter 4, in 1997 the U.S. government began issuing such bonds.

---

[1] LIBOR is the interest rate at which major international banks offer each other on Eurodollar certificates of deposit (CDs) with given maturities. The maturities range from overnight to 5 years. Reference to "1-month LIBOR" means the interest rate that major international banks are offering to pay to other such banks on a CD that matures in 1 month.

Caps and Floors A floating-rate security may have a restriction on the maximum coupon rate that will be paid at a reset date. The maximum coupon rate is called a *cap*. For example, suppose for our hypothetical floating-rate security whose coupon rate formula is 1-month LIBOR plus 100 basis points, there is a cap of 11%. If 1-month LIBOR is 10.5% at a coupon reset date, then the coupon reset formula would give a value of 11.5%. However, the cap restricts the coupon rate to 11%. Thus, for our hypothetical security, once 1-month LIBOR exceeds 10%, the coupon rate is capped at 11%.

Because a cap restricts the coupon rate from increasing, a cap is an unattractive feature for the investor. In contrast, there could be a minimum coupon rate specified for a floating-rate security. The minimum coupon rate is called a *floor*. If the coupon reset formula produces a coupon rate that is below the floor, the floor is paid instead. Thus, a floor is an attractive feature for the investor.

Inverse Floaters Typically, the coupon reset formula on floating-rate securities is such that the coupon rate increases when the reference rate increases, and decreases when the reference rate decreases. There are issues whose coupon rate moves in the opposite direction from the change in the reference rate. Such issues are called *inverse floaters* or *reverse floaters*. A general formula for an inverse floater is:

$K - L \times$ (Reference rate)

For example, suppose that for a particular inverse floater K is 12% and L is 1. Then the coupon reset formula would be:

12% – Reference rate

Suppose that the reference rate is 1-month LIBOR, then the coupon reset formula would be:

12% – 1-month LIBOR

If in some month 1-month LIBOR at the coupon reset date is 5%, the coupon rate for the period is 7%. If in the next month 1-month LIBOR declines to 4.5%, the coupon rate increases to 7.5%.

Notice that if 1-month LIBOR exceeded 12%, then the coupon reset formula would produce a negative coupon rate. To prevent this, there is a floor imposed on the coupon rate. Typically, the floor is zero. While not explicitly stated, there is a cap on the inverse floater. This occurs if 1-month LIBOR is zero. In that unlikely event, the maximum coupon rate is 12% for our hypothetical inverse floater. In general, it will be the value of K in the coupon reset formula for an inverse floater.

Suppose instead that the coupon reset formula for an inverse floater whose reference rate is 1-month LIBOR is as follows:

28% – 3 × (1-month LIBOR)

If 1-month LIBOR at a reset date is 5%, then the coupon rate for that month is 13%. If in the next month 1-month LIBOR declines to 4%, the coupon rate increases to 16%. Thus, a decline in 1-month LIBOR of 100 basis points increases the coupon rate by 300 basis points.[2] This is because the value for L in the coupon reset formula is 3. Assuming neither the cap nor the floor is reached, for each one basis point change in 1-month LIBOR the coupon rate changes by three basis points.

Range Notes A *range note* is a floating-rate security whose coupon rate is equal to the reference rate as long as the reference rate is within a certain range at the reset date. If the reference rate is outside of the range, the coupon rate is zero for that period.

For example, a 3-year range note might specify that the reference rate is 1-year LIBOR and that the coupon rate resets every year. The coupon rate for the year will be 1-year LIBOR as long as 1-year LIBOR at the coupon reset date falls within the range as specified below:

	Year 1	Year 2	Year 3
Lower limit of range	4.5%	5.25%	6.00%
Upper limit of range	5.5%	6.75%	7.50%

If 1-year LIBOR is outside of the range, the coupon rate is zero. For example, if in Year 1 1-year LIBOR is 5% at the coupon reset date, the coupon rate for the year is 5%. However, if 1-year LIBOR is 6%, the coupon rate for the year is zero since 1-year LIBOR is greater than the upper limit for Year 1 of 5.5%.

Step-Up Notes

There are securities that have a coupon rate that increases over time. These securities are called *step-up notes* because the coupon rate "steps up" over time. For example, a 5-year step-up note might have a coupon rate that is 5% for the first 2 years and 6% for the last 3 years. Or, the step-up note could call for a 5% coupon rate for the first 2 years, 5.5% for the third and fourth years, and 6% for the fifth year. When there is only one change (or step up), as in our first example, the issue is referred to as a *single step-up note*. When there is more than one increase, as in our second example, the issue is referred to as a *multiple step-up note*.

Ratchet Bonds

A *ratchet bond* has a coupon rate that adjusts periodically at a fixed margin over a reference rate. However, it can only adjust downward based on a coupon formula. Once the coupon rate is adjusted down, it cannot be readjusted up if the reference rate subsequently increases. This type of bond was first introduced to the bond market in 1998 by the Tennessee Valley Authority.

---

[2] A basis point is equal to 0.0001 or 0.01%. Thus, 100 basis points are equal to 1%.

Deferred Coupon Bonds

There are issues whose coupon payment is deferred for a specified number of years. That is, there is no coupon payment for the deferred period and then a lump sum payment at some specified date and coupon payments until maturity.

Accrued Interest

Bond issuers do not disburse coupon interest payments every day. Instead, typically in the United States coupon interest is paid every 6 months. In some countries, interest is paid annually. For mortgage-backed and asset-backed securities, interest is usually paid monthly. The coupon interest payment is made to the bondholder of record. Thus, if an investor sells a bond between coupon payments and the buyer holds it until the next coupon payment, then the entire coupon interest earned for the period will be paid to the buyer of the bond since the buyer will be the holder of record. The seller of the bond gives up the interest from the time of the last coupon payment to the time until the bond is sold. The amount of interest over this period that will be received by the buyer even though it was earned by the seller is called *accrued interest.*

In the United States and in many countries, the bond buyer must pay the bond seller the accrued interest. The amount that the buyer pays the seller is the agreed-upon price for the bond plus accrued interest. This amount is called the *dirty price*. The agreed-upon bond price without accrued interest is called the *clean price*.

A bond in which the buyer must pay the seller accrued interest is said to be trading *cum-coupon*. If the buyer forgoes the next coupon payment, the bond is said to be trading *ex-coupon*. In the United States, bonds are always traded cum-coupon. There are bond markets outside the United States where bonds are traded ex-coupon for a certain period before the coupon payment date.

There are exceptions to the rule that the bond buyer must pay the bond seller accrued interest. The most important exception is when the issuer has not fulfilled its promise to make the periodic payments. In this case, the issuer is said to be in default. In such instances, the bond's price is sold without accrued interest and is said to be traded *flat*.

Calculating Accrued Interest When calculating accrued interest, three pieces of information are needed: (1) the number of days in the accrued interest period, (2) the number of days in the coupon period, and (3) the dollar amount of the coupon payment. The number of days in the accrued interest period represents the number of days over which the investor has earned interest. Given these values, the accrued interest (AI) assuming semiannual payments is calculated as follows:

$$\text{AI} = \frac{\text{Annual coupon}}{2} \times \frac{\text{Days in AI period}}{\text{Days in coupon period}}$$

For example, suppose that (1) there are 50 days in the accrued interest period, (2) there are 183 days in a coupon period, and (3) the annual coupon per $100 of par value is $8. Then the accrued interest is:

$$AI = \frac{\$8}{2} \times \frac{50}{183} = \$1.0929$$

It is not simple to determine the number of days in the accrued interest period and the number of days in the coupon period. The calculation begins with the determination of three key dates: trade date, settlement date, and value date. The *trade date* is the date on which the transaction is executed. The *settlement date* is the date a transaction is completed. The settlement date varies by the type of bond. For example, for Treasury securities, settlement is the next business day after the trade date; for corporate bonds it is normally 5 business days after the trade date. The *value date* is usually, but not always, the same as the settlement date. Unlike the settlement date, the value date is not constrained to fall on a business day.

Interest accrues on a bond from and including the date of the previous coupon up to but *excluding* the value date.[3] However, this may differ slightly in some non-U.S. markets. For example, in some countries interest accrues up to and *including* the value date. For a newly issued security, there is no previous coupon payment. Instead, the interest accrues from a date called the *dated date*.

The number of days in the accrued interest period and the number of days in the coupon period may not be simply the actual number of calendar days between two dates because there is a market convention for each type of security that specifies how to determine the number of days between two dates. These conventions are called *day count conventions*. We'll discuss these conventions in the appendix to the next chapter.

Yield

The most common measure to describe the *potential* return from investing in a fixed income security is its *yield*. A security's yield takes into consideration that the investor earns a return from the coupon payments and any capital gain or loss from holding the security. It also recognizes that an investor has the opportunity to reinvest any cash flow and therefore can earn interest on reinvesting those cash flows while the bond is held.

We will postpone our discussion of how to calculate a security's yield until Chapter 3. There we will see the different types of yields that can be calculated for fixed income securities. More important, we will see the limitations of using yield measures as an indication of the potential return that can be realized by investing in a fixed income security.

Provisions for Paying off Bonds

The issuer of a bond agrees to repay the principal by the stated maturity date. The issuer can agree to repay the entire amount borrowed in one lump sum payment at the maturity date. That is, the issuer is not required to make any principal repayments prior to the maturity date. Such bonds are said to have a *bullet maturity*.

[3] This is the definition used by the International Securities Market Association (ISMA).

There are bond issues that consist of a series of blocks of securities maturing in sequence. The blocks of securities are said to be *serial bonds*. The coupon rate for each block can be different. Bonds issued by municipalities are sometimes issued as serial bonds. For example, a $250 million par issue of The Port Authority of New York and New Jersey, Special Project Bonds, Series 4 issued on May 1, 1996, had the following serial bonds:

Installment	Par Amount	Coupon (%)	Maturity Date
First	$5,400,000	6.25	October 1, 1999
Second	6,800,000	6.50	October 1, 2001
Third	52,200,000	7.00	October 1, 2007
Fourth	48,600,000	6.75	October 1, 2011
Fifth	137,000,000	6.75	October 1, 2019

One type of corporate bond in which there are serial bonds is an equipment trust certificate. An investor in a serial bond knows when the bonds will mature.

Fixed income securities backed by pools of loans (mortgage-backed securities and asset-backed securities) often have a schedule of principal repayments. Such fixed income securities are said to be *amortizing securities*. For many loans, the payments are structured so that when the last loan payment is made, the entire amount owed is fully paid off.

Another example of an amortizing feature is a bond that has a sinking fund provision. This provision for repayment of a bond may be designed to liquidate all of an issue by the maturity date, or it may be arranged to repay only a part of the total by the maturity date. We discuss this provision later in this section.

Many issues have a call provision granting the issuer an option to retire all or part of the issue prior to the stated maturity date. Some issues specify that the issuer must retire a predetermined amount of the issue periodically. Various types of call provisions are discussed as follows.

Call and Refunding Provisions

An issuer generally wants the right to retire a bond issue prior to the stated maturity date because it recognizes that at some time in the future the general level of interest rates may fall sufficiently below the issue's coupon rate so that redeeming the issue and replacing it with another issue with a lower coupon rate would be economically beneficial. This right is a disadvantage to the bondholder since proceeds received must be reinvested at a lower interest rate. As a result, an issuer who wants to include this right as part of a bond offering must compensate the bondholder when the issue is sold by offering a higher coupon rate, or equivalently, accepting a lower price than if the right is not included.

The right of the issuer to retire the issue prior to the stated maturity date is referred to as a *call option*. If an issuer exercises this right, the issuer is said to "call the bond." The price that the issuer must pay to retire the issue is referred to as the *call price*. Typically, there is not one call price but a *call schedule,* which sets forth a call price based on when the issuer can exercise the call option.

When a bond is issued, typically the issuer may not call the bond for a number of years. That is, the issue is said to have a *deferred call*. The date at which the bond may first be called is referred to as the *first call date*. The first call date for the Walt Disney 7.55s due 7/15/2093 (the 100-year bonds) is 7/15/2023. For the 50-year Tennessee Valley Authority 6⅞s due 12/15/2043, the first call date is 12/15/2003.

Bonds can be called in whole (the entire issue) or in part (only a portion). When less than the entire issue is called, the specific bonds to be called are selected randomly or on a pro rata basis. When bonds are selected randomly, the serial number of the certificates called is published in *The Wall Street Journal* and major metropolitan dailies.

Call Schedule Generally, the call schedule is such that the call price at the first call date is a premium over the par value and scaled down to the par value over time. The date at which the issue is first callable at par value is referred to as the *first par call date*.

For example, the Becton Dickinson & Co. 8.70s due 1/15/2025 bonds were issued on 1/10/95. The first par call date is 1/15/2015. Thus, at issuance this corporate bond had a 10-year deferred call. The call schedule for this issue is as follows:

If redeemed during the 12 months beginning January 15:	Call price
2005	103.949
2006	103.554
2007	103.159
2008	102.764
2009	102.369
2010	101.975
2011	101.580
2012	101.185
2013	100.790
2014	100.395
2015 and thereafter	100.000

The $150 million Anheuser Busch Company 8⅝s due 12/1/2016 issued 11/20/1986 also had a 10-year deferred call and the following call schedule:

If redeemed during the 12 months beginning December 1:	Call price
1996	104.313
1997	103.881
1998	103.450
1999	103.019
2000	102.588
2001	102.156
2002	101.725
2003	101.294
2004	100.863
2005	100.431
2006 and thereafter	100.000

Not all issues have a call schedule in which the call price starts out as a premium over par. There are issues where the call price at the first call date and subsequent call dates is par value. In such cases, the first call date is the same as the first par call date. For example, the first par call date for the U.S. Treasury 12¾s due 11/15/2010 issued on 11/07/1980 is 11/15/2005, and this date is the first call date.

There are three call schedules for zero-coupon bonds found in the market. The first is a call schedule for which the call price is below par value at the first call date and scales up to par value over time. The Baker Hughes Inc. 0s due 5/5/2008, which had an initial sale price of about 58.088 at issuance on 4/28/1993, has the following call schedule:

If redeemed during the 12 months beginning May 5:	Call price
1998	70.683
1999	73.178
2000	75.762
2001	78.437
2002	81.206
2003	84.073
2004	87.042
2005	90.115
2006	93.296
2007	96.590

The second type of call schedule for a zero-coupon bond is one in which the call price at the first call date is above par and scales down to par. An example is the Bell Cable Media PLC 0s due 7/15/2004 that were initially sold at 54.2748 on 7/15/1994 with the following call schedule:

If redeemed during the 12 months beginning July 15:	Call price
1999	104.480
2000	102.990
2001	101.490
2002	100.000
2003	100.000

The third type of call schedule for a zero-coupon bond is one in which the call price is par value at the first call date and any subsequent call date.

Regular versus Special Redemption Prices The call prices in the call schedule are called the *regular* or *general redemption prices*. There are also *special redemption prices* for debt redeemed through the sinking fund and through other provisions, and the proceeds from the confiscation of property through the right of eminent domain. The special redemption price is usually par value, but in the case of some utility issues it initially may be the public offering price, which is amortized down to par value (if a premium) over the life of the bonds.

Noncallable versus Nonrefundable Bonds If a bond issue does not have any protection against early call, then it is said to be a *currently callable issue*. But most new bond issues, even if currently callable, usually have some restrictions against certain types of early redemption. The most common restriction is prohibiting the *refunding* of the bonds for a certain number of years. Refunding a bond issue means redeeming bonds with funds obtained through the sale of a new bond issue.

Many investors are confused by the terms *noncallable* and *nonrefundable*. Call protection is much more absolute than refunding protection. While there may be certain exceptions to absolute or complete call protection in some cases, it still provides greater assurance against premature and unwanted redemption than does refunding protection. Refunding prohibition merely prevents redemption only from certain sources of funds, namely the proceeds of other debt issues sold at a lower cost of money. The bondholder is only protected if interest rates decline, and the borrower can obtain lower-cost money to pay off the debt.

Beginning in early 1986, a number of industrial companies issued long-term debt with extended call protection, not refunding protection. A number are noncallable for the issue's life, such as Dow Chemical Company's 8⅝s due in 2006 and Atlantic Richfield's 9⅞s due in 2016. The prospectuses for both issues expressly prohibit redemption prior to maturity. These *noncallable-for-life issues* are referred to as *bullet bonds*.

Prepayments

For amortizing securities that are backed by loans and have a schedule of principal repayments, individual borrowers typically have the option to pay off all or part of their loan prior to the scheduled date. Any principal repayment prior to the scheduled date is called a *prepayment*. The right of borrowers to prepay is called the *prepayment option*.

Basically, the prepayment option is the same as a call option. However, unlike a call option, there is not a call price that depends on when the borrower pays off the issue. Typically, the price at which a loan is prepaid is par value.

Sinking Fund Provision

An indenture may require the issuer to retire a specified portion of an issue each year. This is referred to as a *sinking fund requirement*. The alleged purpose of the sinking fund provision is to reduce credit risk. This kind of provision for repayment of debt may be designed to liquidate all of a bond issue by the maturity date, or it may be arranged to pay only a part of the total by the end of the term. If only a part is paid, the remainder is called a *balloon maturity*. The $150 million Ingersoll Rand 7.20s issue due 6/1/2025 and issued on 6/5/1995 with a sinking fund schedule that begins on 6/1/2006 is an example of an issue with a balloon maturity. Each year the issuer must retire $7.5 million.

Generally, the issuer may satisfy the sinking fund requirement by either (1) making a cash payment of the face amount of the bonds to be retired to the trustee, who then calls the bonds for redemption using a lottery, or (2) delivering

to the trustee bonds purchased in the open market that have a total par value equal to the amount that must be retired. If the bonds are retired using the first method, interest payments stop at the redemption date.

Usually, the periodic payments required for sinking fund purposes will be the same for each period. A few indentures might permit variable periodic payments, where payments change according to certain prescribed conditions set forth in the indenture. Many indentures include a provision that grants the issuer the option to retire more than the amount stipulated for sinking fund retirement. This is referred to as an *accelerated sinking fund provision*. For example, the Anheuser Busch 8⅝s due 12/1/2016, whose call schedule was presented earlier, has a sinking fund requirement of $7.5 million per annum beginning on 12/01/1997. The issuer is permitted to retire up to $15 million each year.

Usually the sinking fund call price is the par value if the bonds were originally sold at par. When issued at a price in excess of par, the call price generally starts at the issuance price and scales down to par as the issue approaches maturity.

There is a difference between the amortizing feature for a bond with a sinking fund provision and the regularly scheduled principal repayment for a mortgage-backed and an asset-backed security. The owner of a mortgage-backed security and an asset-backed security knows that, assuming no default, there will be principal repayments. In contrast, the owner of a bond with a sinking fund provision is not assured that his or her particular holding will be called to satisfy the sinking fund requirement.

Options Granted to Bondholders

It is common for a bond issue to include a provision in the indenture that gives either the bondholder and/or the issuer an option to take some action against the other party. The most common type of option embedded in a bond is a call feature, which was discussed earlier. This option is granted to the issuer. There are two options that can be granted to the bondholder: the right to put the issue and the right to convert the issue.

Put Provision

An issue with a *put provision* included in the indenture grants the bondholder the right to sell the issue back to the issuer at a specified price on designated dates. The specified price is called the *put price*. Typically, a bond is putable at par if it is issued at or close to par value. For a zero-coupon bond, the put price is below par.

The advantage of the put provision to the bondholder is that if after the issue date market rates rise above the issue's coupon rate, the bondholder can force the issuer to redeem the bond at the put price and then reinvest the proceeds at the prevailing higher rate.

Conversion Privilege

A *convertible bond* is an issue giving the bondholder the right to exchange the bond for a specified number of shares of common stock. Such a feature allows the

bondholder to take advantage of favorable movements in the price of the issuer's common stock. An *exchangeable bond* allows the bondholder to exchange the issue for a specified number of shares of common stock of a corporation different from the issuer of the bond. These bonds are discussed in Chapter 7.

Currency Denomination

The payments that the issuer makes to the bondholder can be in any currency. For bonds issued in the United States, the issuer typically makes both coupon payments and principal repayments in U.S. dollars. However, there is nothing that forces the issuer to make payments in U.S dollars. The indenture can specify that the issuer may make payments in some other specified currency. For example, payments may be made in Japanese yen.

An issue in which payments to bondholders are in U.S. dollars is called a *dollar-denominated issue*. A *nondollar-denominated issue* is one in which payments are not denominated in U.S. dollars. There are some issues whose coupon payments are in one currency and whose principal payment is in another currency. An issue with this characteristic is called a *dual-currency issue*.

Some issues allow either the issuer or the bondholder the right to select the currency in which a payment will be paid. This option effectively gives the party with the right to choose the currency the opportunity to benefit from a favorable exchange rate movement.

RISKS ASSOCIATED WITH INVESTING IN FIXED INCOME SECURITIES

Bonds may expose an investor to one or more of the following risks: (1) interest rate risk; (2) call and prepayment risk; (3) credit risk; (4) liquidity risk; (5) exchange rate or currency risk; and (6) inflation or purchasing power risk. While these risks are discussed further in later chapters, we describe them briefly as follows. There are additional risks that are discussed in later chapters. Some of the risks discussed in later chapters pertain to the risks associated with fixed income portfolio strategies.

Interest Rate Risk

The price of a typical fixed income security will change in the opposite direction from a change in interest rates. That is, when interest rates rise, a fixed income security's price will fall; when interest rates fall, a fixed income security's price will rise. For example, consider a 6% 20-year bond. If the yield investors require to buy this bond is 6%, the price of this bond would be $100. However, if the required yield increased to 6.5%, the price of this bond would decline to $94.4479. Thus, for a 50 basis point increase in yield, the bond's price declines by 5.55%. If, instead, the yield declines from 6% to 5.5%, the bond's price will rise by 6.02% to $106.0195.

The reason for this inverse relationship between price and changes in interest rates or changes in market yields is as follows. Suppose investor X purchases our hypothetical 6% coupon 20-year bond at par value ($100). As explained in Chapter 3, the yield for this bond is 6%. Suppose that immediately after the purchase of this bond two things happen. First, market interest rates rise to 6.50%, so that if an investor wants to buy a similar 20-year bond, a 6.50% coupon rate would have to be paid by the bond issuer in order to offer the bond at par value. Second, suppose investor X wants to sell the bond. In attempting to sell the bond, investor X would not find an investor who would be willing to pay par value for a bond with a coupon rate of 6%. The reason is that any investor who wanted to purchase this bond could obtain a similar 20-year bond with a coupon rate 50 basis points higher, 6.5%. What can the investor do? The investor cannot force the issuer to change the coupon rate to 6.5%. Nor can the investor force the issuer to shorten the maturity of the bond to a point where a new investor would be willing to accept a 6% coupon rate. The only thing that the investor can do is adjust the price of the bond so that at the new price the buyer would realize a yield of 6.5%. This means that the price would have to be adjusted down to a price below par value. The new price must be $94.4469. While we assumed in our illustration an initial price of par value, the principle holds for any purchase price. Regardless of the price that an investor pays for a bond, an increase in market interest rates will result in a decline in a bond's price.

Suppose that instead of a rise in market interest rates to 6.5%, they decline to 5.5%. Investors would be more than happy to purchase the 6% coupon 20-year bond for par value. However, investor X realizes that the market is only offering investors the opportunity to buy a similar bond at par value with a coupon rate of 5.5%. Consequently, investor X will increase the price of the bond until it offers a yield of 5.5%. That price is $106.0195.

Since the price of a bond fluctuates with market interest rates, the risk that an investor faces is that the price of a bond held in a portfolio will decline if market interest rates rise. This risk is referred to as *interest rate risk* and is by far the major risk faced by investors in the bond market.

Bond Features that Affect Interest Rate Risk

The degree of sensitivity of a bond's price to changes in market interest rates depends on various characteristics of the issue, such as maturity and coupon rate. Consider first maturity. All other factors constant, the longer the maturity, the greater the bond's price sensitivity to changes in interest rates. For example, we know that for a 6% 20-year bond selling to yield 6%, a rise in the yield required by investors to 6.5% will cause the bond's price to decline from $100 to $94.4479, a 5.55% price decline. For a 6% 5-year bond selling to yield 6%, the price is $100. A rise in the yield required by investors from 6% to 6.5% would decrease the price to $97.8944. The decline in the bond's price is only 2.11%.

Now let's turn to the coupon rate. A property of a bond is that, all other factors constant, the lower the coupon rate, the greater the bond's price sensitivity

to changes in interest rates. For example, consider a 9% 20-year bond selling to yield 6%. The price of this bond would be $112.7953. If the yield required by investors increases by 50 basis points to 6.5%, the price of this bond would fall by 2.01% to $110.5280. This decline is less than the 5.55% decline for the 6% 20-year bond selling to yield 6%. An implication is that zero-coupon bonds have greater price sensitivity to interest rate changes than same-maturity bonds bearing a coupon rate and trading at the same yield.

Because of credit risk (discussed later), different bonds trade at different yields, even if they have the same coupon rate and maturity. How, then, holding other factors constant, does the level of interest rates affect a bond's price sensitivity to changes in interest rates? As it turns out, the higher the level of interest rates that a bond trades, the lower the price sensitivity.

To see this, we can compare a 6% 20-year bond initially selling at a yield of 6% and a 6% 20-year bond initially selling at a yield of 10%. The former is initially at a price of $100, and the latter carries a price of $65.68. Now, if the yield on both bonds increases by 100 basis points, the first bond trades down by 10.68 points (10.68%). After the assumed increase in yield, the second bond will trade at a price of $59.88, for a price decline of only 5.80 points (or 8.83%). Thus, we see that the bond that trades at a lower yield is more volatile in both percentage price change and absolute price change, as long as the other bond characteristics are the same. An implication of this is that, for a given change in interest rates, price sensitivity is lower when the level of interest rates in the market is high, and price sensitivity is higher when the level of interest rates is low.

We can summarize these three characteristics that affect the bond's price sensitivity to changes in market interest rates as follows:

Characteristic 1: For a given maturity and initial yield, the lower the coupon rate, the greater the bond's price sensitivity to changes in market interest rates.

Characteristic 2: For a given coupon rate and initial yield, the longer the maturity of a bond, the greater the bond's price sensitivity to changes in market interest rates.

Characteristic 3: For a given coupon rate and maturity, the lower the level of interest rates, the greater the bond's price sensitivity to changes in market interest rates.

A bond's price sensitivity bond will also depend on any options embedded in the issue. This is explained later when we discuss call risk.

Interest Rate Risk for Floating-Rate Securities

The change in the price of a fixed-rate coupon bond when market interest rates change is because the bond's coupon rate differs from the prevailing market interest rate. For a floating-rate security, the coupon rate is reset periodically based on the prevailing value for the reference rate plus the quoted margin. The quoted

margin is set for the life of the security. The price of a floating-rate security will fluctuate depending on three factors.

First, the longer the time to the next coupon reset date, the greater the potential price fluctuation. For example, consider a floating-rate security whose coupon resets every 6 months and the coupon formula is 6-month LIBOR plus 20 basis points. Suppose that on the coupon reset date 6-month LIBOR is 5.8%. If the next day after the coupon is reset, 6-month LIBOR rises to 6.1%, this means that this security is offering a 6-month coupon rate that is less than the prevailing 6-month rate for the remaining 6 months. The price of the security must decline to reflect this. Suppose instead that the coupon resets every month at 1-month LIBOR and that this rate rises right after a coupon rate is reset. Then, while the investor would be realizing a submarket 1-month coupon rate, it is for only a month. The price decline will be less than for the security that resets every 6 months.

The second reason why a floating-rate security's price will fluctuate is that the index spread that investors want in the market changes. For example, consider once again the security whose coupon reset formula is 6-month LIBOR plus 20 basis points. If market conditions change such that investors want a quoted margin of 30 basis points rather than 20 basis points, this security would be offering a coupon rate that is 10 basis points below the market rate. As a result, the security's price will decline.

Finally, as noted earlier, a floating-rate security may have a cap. Once the coupon rate as specified by the coupon reset formula rises above the cap rate, the security offers a below-market coupon rate and its price will decline. In fact, once the cap is reached, the security's price will react much the same way to changes in market interest rates as that of a fixed-rate coupon security.

Measuring Interest Rate Risk

Investors are interested in estimating the price sensitivity of a bond to changes in market interest rates. The measure commonly used to approximate the percentage price change is *duration*. Duration is the approximate percentage price change for a 100 basis point change in interest rates. In the next chapter, the procedure for calculating duration will be explained.

The duration for the 6% coupon 5-year bond trading at par to yield 6% is 4.27. Thus the price of this bond will change by approximately 4.27% if interest rates change by 100 basis points. For a 50 basis point change, this bond's price will change by approximately 2.14% (4.27% divided by 2). As explained earlier, this bond's price would actually change by 2.11%. Thus, duration does a good job of approximating the percentage price change. It turns out that the approximation is good the smaller the change in interest rates. The approximation is not as good for a large change in interest rates.

Call and Prepayment Risk

As explained earlier, a bond may include a provision that allows the issuer to retire or call all or part of the issue before the maturity date. From the investor's

perspective, there are three disadvantages to call provisions. First, the cash flow pattern of a callable bond is not known with certainty. Second, because the issuer will call the bonds when interest rates have dropped, the investor is exposed to reinvestment risk (i.e., the investor will have to reinvest the proceeds when the bond is called at relatively lower interest rates). Finally, the capital appreciation potential of a bond will be reduced because the price of a callable bond may not rise much above the price at which the issuer will call the bond. Because of these disadvantages faced by the investor, a callable bond is said to expose the investor to *call risk*. The same disadvantages apply to fixed income securities that can prepay. In this case the risk is referred to as *prepayment risk*.

Credit Risk

An investor who lends funds by purchasing a bond issue is exposed to three types of credit risk: (1) default risk, (2) credit spread risk, and (3) downgrade risk.

Default Risk

Traditionally, credit risk is defined as the risk that the issuer will fail to satisfy the terms of the obligation with respect to the timely payment of interest and repayment of the amount borrowed. This form of credit risk is called *default risk*. If a default does occur, this does not mean the investor loses the entire amount invested. There is a certain percentage of the investment that can be expected to be recovered. This is called the *recovery rate*.

Credit Spread Risk

Even in the absence of default, an investor is concerned that the market value of a bond will decline and/or the price performance of that bond will be worse than that of other bonds against which the investor is compared. To understand this, recall that the price of a bond changes in the opposite direction to the change in the yield required by the market. Thus, if yields in the economy increase, the price of a bond declines, and vice versa.

As explained later in this book, the yield on a bond is made up of two components: (1) the yield on a similar default-free bond issue and (2) a premium above the yield on a default-free bond issue necessary to compensate for the risks associated with the bond. The risk premium is referred to as a *spread*. In the United States, Treasury issues are the benchmark yields because they are believed to be default free, they are highly liquid, and Treasury issues are not callable (with the exception of some old issues). The part of the risk premium or spread attributable to default risk is called the *credit spread*.

The price performance of a non-Treasury bond issue and the return that the investor will realize by holding that issue over some time period will depend on how the credit spread changes. If the credit spread increases—investors say that the spread has "widened"—the market price of the bond issue will decline (assuming Treasury rates have not changed). The risk that an issuer's debt obligation will decline due to an increase in the credit spread is called *credit spread risk*.

This risk exists for an individual issue, for issues in a particular industry or economic sector, and for all non-Treasury issues in the economy. For example, in general during economic recessions investors are concerned that issuers will face a decline in cash flows that would be used to service their obligations. As a result, the credit spread tends to widen for non-Treasury issuers and the prices of all such issues throughout the economy will decline.

Downgrade Risk

While there are investors who seek to allocate funds among different sectors of the bond market to capitalize on anticipated changes in credit spreads, an investor investigating the credit quality of an individual issue is concerned with the prospects of the credit spread increasing for that particular issue. Market participants gauge the default risk of an issue by looking at the credit ratings assigned to issues by the rating agencies—Moody's Investors Service, Inc., Standard & Poor's Corporation, and Fitch. (We will discuss the ratings later in this book.) Once a credit rating is assigned to a debt obligation, a rating agency monitors the credit quality of the issuer and can reassign a different credit rating.

An improvement in the credit quality of an issue or issuer is rewarded with a better credit rating, referred to as an *upgrade*; a deterioration in the credit rating of an issue or issuer is penalized by the assignment of an inferior credit rating, referred to as a *downgrade*. An unanticipated downgrading of an issue or issuer increases the credit spread and results in a decline in the price of the issue or the issuer's bonds. This risk is referred to as *downgrade risk* and is closely related to credit spread risk.

Occasionally, the ability of an issuer to make interest and principal payments changes dramatically and unexpectedly because of factors including the following:

1. a natural disaster (such as an earthquake or hurricane) or an industrial accident that impairs an issuer's ability to meet its obligations
2. a takeover or corporate restructuring that impairs an issuer's ability to meet its obligations
3. political factors that alters a government's willingness or ability to repay its obligation

These events can result in a downgrading of an issue. A downgrade due to such events is referred to as *event risk.*

Liquidity Risk

When an investor wants to sell a bond prior to the maturity date, he or she is concerned whether the price that can be obtained from dealers is close to the true value of the issue. For example, if recent trades in the market for a particular issue have been between 97.25 and 97.75 and market conditions have not

changed, an investor would expect to sell the bond somewhere in the 97.25 to 97.75 area.

Liquidity risk is the risk that the investor will have to sell a bond below its true value where the true value is indicated by recent transactions. The primary measure of liquidity is the size of the spread between the bid price (the price at which a dealer is willing to buy a security) and the ask price (the price at which a dealer is willing to sell a security). The wider the bid-ask spread, the greater the liquidity risk.

A liquid market can generally be defined by "small bid-ask spreads which do not materially increase for large transactions."[4] Bid-ask spreads, and therefore liquidity risk, change over time.

For investors who plan to hold a bond until maturity and need not mark a position to market, liquidity risk is not a major concern. An institutional investor that plans to hold an issue to maturity but is periodically marked to market is concerned with liquidity risk. By marking a position to market, it is meant that the security is revalued in the portfolio based on its current market price. For example, mutual funds are required to mark to market at the end of each day the holdings in their portfolio in order to compute the net asset value (NAV). While other institutional investors may not mark to market as frequently as mutual funds, they are marked to market when reports are periodically sent to clients or the board of directors or trustees.

Moreover, there is a borrowing vehicle that investors can use in the bond market to purchase securities. This vehicle is a repurchase agreement and is effectively a collateralized borrowing. In Chapter 15, we will discuss this vehicle for borrowing and we will see that the bonds purchased are used as collateral. The bonds purchased are marked to market periodically in order to determine whether the collateral provides adequate protection for the lender of the funds. When liquidity in the market dries up, the investor who has borrowed the funds must rely solely on the prices determined by the dealer, and this under certain market conditions could have adverse consequences.

Exchange Rate or Currency Risk

A nondollar-denominated bond (i.e., a bond whose payments occur in a foreign currency) has unknown U.S. dollar cash flows. The dollar cash flows are dependent on the exchange rate at the time the payments are received. For example, suppose an investor purchases a bond whose payments are in Japanese yen. If the yen depreciates relative to the U.S. dollar, then fewer dollars will be received. The risk of this occurring is referred to as *exchange rate* or *currency risk*. Of course, should the yen appreciate relative to the U.S. dollar, the investor will benefit by receiving more dollars.

---

[4] Robert I. Gerber, "A User's Guide to Buy-Side Bond Trading," Chapter 16 in Frank J. Fabozzi (ed.), *Managing Fixed Income Portfolios* (New Hope, PA: Frank J. Fabozzi Associates, 1997), p. 278.

Inflation or Purchasing Power Risk

Inflation risk or *purchasing power risk* arises because of the variation in the value of cash flows from a security due to inflation, as measured in terms of purchasing power. For example, if an investor purchases a bond with a coupon rate of 7%, but the rate of inflation is 8%, the purchasing power of the cash flow has declined. For all but floating-rate securities and inflation-protection securities, an investor is exposed to inflation risk because the interest rate the issuer promises to make is fixed for the life of the issue. To the extent that interest rates reflect the expected inflation rate, floating-rate securities have a lower level of inflation risk.

SECONDARY MARKET AND ELECTRONIC TRADING IN BONDS

While a considerable amount of trading of common stocks takes place on organized exchanges, the dominant secondary market for bond trading is the over-the-counter (OTC) market. As such, trading is based on dealer trading desks, which take principal positions to fill customer buy and sell orders. Dealers are said to "make a market" in a security.

In recent years, however, there has been an evolution away from the traditional OTC market toward electronic trading. This trend is likely to continue. There are several related reasons for this transition. Because the fixed income business has been a principal rather than an agency business, the capital of the market makers is critical. And while the amount of capital of the broker/dealers has increased during the last several years, the amount of capital of U.S. institutional investors (pension funds, mutual funds, insurance companies, commercial banks) and international customers has increased much more, and the size of the orders has increased significantly. As a result, making markets has become riskier for market makers. Moreover, the increase in the volatility in the bond markets has increased the capital required of bond dealers. Finally, the profitability of fixed income market making has declined since many of the products have become more commodity-like and their bid-offer spreads have decreased.

The combination of the increased risk and the decreased profitability of market making in bonds has induced the major dealers to deemphasize this business in the allocation of capital. As a result, the liquidity of the traditionally OTC bond market has declined, and this decline in liquidity has opened the way for other market-making mechanisms, in particular electronic trading. In fact, the same dealer firms that have been the major market makers in bonds have also been the supporters of electronic trading in bonds.

There are a variety of types of electronic trading systems for bonds. The two major types are the *dealer-to-customer systems* and the *exchange systems*. With respect to dealer-to-customer systems, there can be a single dealer or multiple dealer systems. Single-dealer systems are based on a customer dealing with a

single, identified dealer over the computer. The single-dealer system simply computerizes the traditional customer/dealer market-making mechanism. Multidealer systems provide some advancement over the single-dealer method. A customer can select from any of several identified dealers whose bids and offers are provided on a computer screen. The customer knows the identity of the dealer, and the transaction is cleared through the dealer's procedures. Currently, a large share of U.S. Treasury securities are traded via the dealer-to-customer Tradeweb system.

The exchange system is quite different and has potentially significantly greater value added. According to the exchange system, dealer and customer bids and offers are entered into the system on an anonymous basis, and the clearing of the executed trades is done through a common process. Two exchange systems are scheduled to begin operations during 2001, Bondbook and another system sponsored by Bloomberg.

KEY POINTS

- *Basically, a fixed income security is a financial obligation of an entity (the issuer) who promises to pay a specified sum of money at specified future dates.*
- *Fixed income securities fall into two general categories: debt obligations and preferred stock.*
- *The promises of the issuer and the rights of the bondholders are set forth in the indenture.*
- *The term to maturity of a bond is the number of years over which the issuer has promised to meet the conditions of the obligation.*
- *The par value (principal, face value, redemption value, or maturity value) is the amount that the issuer agrees to repay the bondholder by the maturity date.*
- *Bond prices are quoted as a percentage of par value, with par value equal to 100.*
- *The interest rate that the issuer agrees to pay each year is called the coupon rate; the coupon is the annual amount of the interest payment and is found by multiplying the par value by the coupon rate.*
- *Zero-coupon bonds do not make periodic coupon payments; the bondholder realizes interest at the maturity date equal to the difference between the maturity value and the price paid for the bond.*
- *A floating-rate security is an issue whose coupon rate resets periodically based on some formula; the typical coupon reset formula is some reference rate plus an index spread.*
- *A floating-rate security may have a cap, which sets the maximum coupon rate that will be paid at a reset date.*
- *A cap is a disadvantage to the bondholder, whereas a floor is an advantage to the bondholder.*
- *An inverse floater is an issue whose coupon rate moves in the opposite direction from the change in the reference rate.*
- *A range note is a floating-rate security whose coupon rate is equal to the reference rate as long as the reference rate is within a certain range at the reset date and zero otherwise.*
- *A step-up note is a security whose coupon rate increases over time.*
- *Accrued interest is the amount of interest accrued since the last coupon payment, and in the United States (as well as in many countries), the bond buyer must pay the bond seller the accrued interest.*
- *The dirty price of a security is the agreed-upon price plus accrued interest; the clean price is the agreed-upon price without accrued interest.*

- ❑ *Interest accrues on a bond from and including the date of the previous coupon up to but excluding the value date; the value date is usually, but not always, the same as the settlement date.*
- ❑ *A bullet maturity means that the issuer agrees to pay the entire amount due at the maturity date.*
- ❑ *Bond issues consisting of a series of blocks of securities maturing in sequence are called serial bonds.*
- ❑ *An amortizing security is a security for which there is a schedule for the repayment of principal.*
- ❑ *A call provision grants the issuer an option to retire all or part of the issue prior to the stated maturity date.*
- ❑ *A call provision is an advantage to the issuer and a disadvantage to the bondholder.*
- ❑ *The call schedule specifies when the issuer can call the issue and the call price at each call date.*
- ❑ *When a callable bond is issued, typically the issuer may not call the bond for a number of years; that is, there is a deferred call.*
- ❑ *The call prices in the call schedule are the regular or general redemption prices, and there are special redemption prices for debt redeemed through the sinking fund and through other provisions.*
- ❑ *A currently callable bond is an issue that does not have any protection against early call.*
- ❑ *Most new bond issues, even if currently callable, usually have some restrictions against refunding.*
- ❑ *For an amortizing security backed by a pool of loans, the borrowers typically have the right to prepay in whole or in party prior to the scheduled principal repayment date; this provision is called a prepayment option.*
- ❑ *Call protection is much more absolute than refunding protection.*
- ❑ *A sinking fund requirement provision mandates that the issuer retire a specified portion of an issue each year.*
- ❑ *An accelerated sinking fund provision allows the issuer to retire more than the amount stipulated to satisfy the sinking fund requirement.*
- ❑ *A putable bond is one in which the bondholder has the right to sell the issue back to the issuer at a specified price on designated dates.*
- ❑ *A convertible bond is an issue giving the bondholder the right to exchange the bond for a specified number of shares of common stock.*
- ❑ *A nondollar-denominated issue is one in which payments are denominated in a foreign currency, and a dual-currency issue is one in which every coupon payment is in one currency and the principal payment is in another currency.*

- ❑ *The price of a bond changes inversely with a change in market interest rates.*
- ❑ *Interest rate risk refers to the adverse price movement of a bond as a result of a change in market interest rates; for the owner of a bond, it is the risk that interest rates will rise.*
- ❑ *The coupon rate and maturity of a bond affect its price sensitivity to changes in market interest rate.*
- ❑ *For a given coupon rate and initial yield, the longer the maturity, the greater a bond's price sensitivity to changes in market interest rates.*
- ❑ *For a given maturity and initial yield, the lower the coupon rate, the greater a bond's price sensitivity to changes in market interest rates.*
- ❑ *Price sensitivity to interest rate changes is less when yield levels in the market are high than when yield levels are low.*
- ❑ *A floating-rate security's price sensitivity depends on (1) the length of time to the next reset date, (2) changes in the market's requirement for the quoted margin, and (3) whether the cap is reached.*
- ❑ *The duration of a bond measures the approximate percentage price change for a 100 basis point change in interest rates.*
- ❑ *Call risk and prepayment risk refer to the risk that a security will be paid off before the scheduled principal repayment date.*
- ❑ *From an investor's perspective, the disadvantages to call and prepayment provisions are (1) the cash flow pattern is uncertain, (2) reinvestment risk because proceeds received will have to be reinvested at a relatively lower interest rate, and (3) the capital appreciation potential of a bond will be reduced.*
- ❑ *A bond investor is exposed to credit risk, and this risk can be categorized as default risk, credit spread risk, and downgrade risk.*
- ❑ *Liquidity risk depends on the ease with which an issue can be sold at or near its true value and is primarily gauged by the bid-ask spread quoted by dealers.*
- ❑ *From the perspective of a U.S. investor, exchange rate risk is the risk that a currency in which a security is denominated will depreciate relative to the U.S. dollar.*
- ❑ *Inflation risk or purchasing power risk arises because of the variation in the value of cash flows from a security due to inflation.*
- ❑ *Secondary bond trading is done primarily in the over-the-counter market, but in recent years electronic trading in bonds has increased.*

Chapter 2

Valuation of Fixed Income Securities and the Measurement of Interest Rate Risk

V*aluation* is the process of determining the fair value of a financial asset. The process is also referred to as "valuing" or "pricing" a financial asset. In this chapter, we explain the general principles of fixed income security valuation. Yields and yield spreads are often cited in the market and used as a measure of relative value. We postpone our discussion of yields and yield spread measures until the next chapter, where we discuss how they are calculated and their limitations as a measure of relative value. Also, in this chapter we show how one of the major risks discussed in the previous chapter, interest rate risk, is quantified. As we will see, without being able to value a security, the measurement of interest rate risk is not possible.

GENERAL PRINCIPLES OF VALUATION

The fundamental principle of valuation is that the value of any financial asset is the present value of the expected cash flows. This principle applies regardless of the financial asset. Thus, the valuation of a financial asset involves the following three steps:

Step 1: Estimate the expected cash flows.
Step 2: Determine the appropriate interest rate or interest rates that should be used to discount the cash flows.
Step 3: Calculate the present value of the expected cash flows found in step 1 by the interest rate or interest rates determined in step 2.

Estimating Cash Flows

Cash flow is simply the cash that is expected to be received at some time from an investment. In the case of a fixed income security, it does not make any difference whether the cash flow is interest income or repayment of principal. The *cash flows* of a security are the collection of each period's cash flow. Holding aside the risk of default, the cash flows for only a few fixed income securities is simple to project. In Chapter 4, we will see securities with this feature—Treasury securi-

ties. These securities have known cash flows.[1] One type of security issued by the U.S. Treasury is a coupon security. The cash flows for a Treasury coupon security are the coupon interest payments every 6 months up to the maturity date and the principal repayment at the maturity date.

Investors will find it difficult to estimate the cash flows when they purchase a fixed income security where

1. the issuer or the investor has the option to change the contractual due date of the repayment of the principal, or
2. the coupon payment is reset periodically based on a formula that depends on some value or values for reference rates, prices, or exchange rates, or
3. the investor has the choice to convert or exchange the security into common stock.

Callable bonds, putable bonds, mortgage-backed securities, and asset-backed securities are examples of (1). Floating-rate securities are an example of (2). Convertible bonds and exchangeable bonds are examples of (3).

For securities that fall into the first category, a key factor determining whether either the issuer of the security or the investor would exercise an option to alter the cash flows is the level of interest rates in the future relative to the security's coupon rate. Specifically, for a callable bond, if the prevailing market rate the issuer can realize by issuing a new security is sufficiently below the issue's coupon rate to justify the costs associated with refunding the issue, the issuer is likely to call the issue. Similarly, for a loan, if the prevailing refinancing rate available in the market is sufficiently below the loan's rate so that there will be savings by refinancing after considering the associated refinancing costs, then the borrower has an incentive to refinance. For a putable bond, if the interest rate on comparable securities rises such that the value of the putable bond falls below the value at which it must be repurchased by the issuer (i.e., the put price), then the investor will put the issue.

What this means is that to properly estimate the cash flows of a fixed income security, it is necessary to incorporate into the analysis how interest rates can change in the future and how such changes affect the cash flows. As we will see later, this is done in valuation models by introducing a parameter that reflects the expected volatility of interest rates.

Determining the Appropriate Rate or Rates

Once the cash flows for a fixed income security are estimated, the next step is to determine the appropriate interest rate. To do this, the investor must address the following three questions:

---

[1] As explained in Chapter 4, while the U.S. Treasury no longer issues callable securities, there are outstanding Treasury securities that are callable and therefore do not have simple cash flows. Our discussion regarding Treasury securities refers to noncallable Treasury securities.

1. What is the minimum interest rate the investor should require?
2. How much more than the minimum interest rate should the investor require?
3. Should the investor require the same interest rate for each estimated cash flow or a unique interest rate for each estimated cash flow?

Minimum Interest Rate

The minimum interest rate that an investor should require is the yield available in the marketplace on a default-free cash flow. In the United States, this is the yield on a U.S. Treasury security. This is one of the reasons that the Treasury market is closely watched by market participants. We discuss Treasury securities and yields on Treasury securities in Chapter 4. The minimum interest rate that investors want is referred to as the *base interest rate.* There is not one base interest rate. There is a base interest rate for each maturity.

Premium Over the Base Interest Rate

The premium over the base interest rate on a Treasury security that investors will require reflects the additional risks the investor faces by acquiring a security that is not issued by the U.S. government. We discussed these risks in Chapter 1. This premium is called a *risk premium* or a *spread over Treasuries*. Thus we can express the interest rate offered on a non-Treasury security as:

base interest rate + risk premium

or equivalently,

base interest rate + spread

The factors that affect the spread include (1) the issuer's perceived creditworthiness; (2) provisions that grant either the issuer or the investor the option to do something; (3) the taxability of the interest received by investors; and (4) the expected liquidity of the security.

Perceived Creditworthiness of Issuer *Default risk* refers to the risk that the issuer of a bond may be unable to make timely principal or interest payments. As explained in the previous chapter, most market participants rely primarily on the nationally recognized statistical rating organizations to assess the default risk of an issuer. The spread between Treasury securities and non-Treasury securities that are identical in all respects except for quality is referred to as a *quality spread* or *credit spread.*

Inclusion of Options As explained in Chapter 1, it is not uncommon for an issue to include a provision that gives either the bondholder and/or the issuer an

option to take some action against the other party. The presence of an embedded option has an effect on the spread of an issue relative to a Treasury security and the spread relative to otherwise comparable maturity issues that do not have an embedded option. In general, market participants will require a larger spread to a comparable-maturity Treasury security for an issue with an embedded option that is favorable to the issuer (e.g., a call option) than for an issue without such an option. In contrast, market participants will require a smaller spread to a comparable-maturity Treasury security for an issue with an embedded option that is favorable to the investor (e.g., put option or conversion option). In fact, for an issue with an option that is favorable to an investor, the coupon rate may be less than that on a comparable-maturity Treasury security.

Taxability of Interest Unless exempted under the federal income tax code, interest income is taxable at the federal level. In addition to federal income taxes, there may be state and local taxes on interest income. The federal tax code specifically exempts the interest income from qualified tax-exempt securities from taxation at the federal level. As explained in Chapter 5, most municipal securities are tax-exempt securities. Because of the tax-exempt feature of municipal bonds, the yield on a municipal bond is less than that on a Treasury security with the same maturity.

State and local governments are not permitted to tax the interest income from securities issued by the U.S. Treasury. Thus, part of the spread between Treasury securities and taxable non-Treasury securities of the same maturity reflects the value of the exemption from state and local income taxes.

Expected Liquidity of an Issue Bonds trade with different degrees of liquidity. The greater the expected liquidity, the lower the yield that investors would require. Treasury securities are the most liquid securities in the world. The lower yield offered on Treasury securities relative to non-Treasury securities of the same maturity reflects the difference in liquidity.

Single or Multiple Interest Rates

For each cash flow estimated, the same interest rate can be used to calculate the present value. Alternatively, it can be argued that each cash flow is unique and therefore it may be more appropriate to value each cash flow using an interest rate specific to that cash flow. In the traditional approach to valuation discussed later, we will see that a single interest rate is used. In the arbitrage-free valuation approach, multiple interest rates are used.

Discounting the Estimated Cash Flows

Given the estimated cash flows and the appropriate interest rate or interest rates that should be used to discount the estimated cash flows, the final step in the valuation process is to value the cash flows.

The value of a single cash flow to be received in the future is equal to the amount of money that must be invested today to generate that future value. The resulting value is called the *present value* of a cash flow. (It is also called the *discounted value.*) The present value of a cash flow will depend on when a cash flow will be received (i.e., the *timing* of a cash flow) and the interest rate used to calculate the present value. The interest rate used is called the *discount rate.*

A present value for each estimated cash flow is first calculated. The sum of the present values for all of a security's estimated cash flows is then the value of the security.

The present value of the expected cash flow to be received t years from now if a discount rate i can be earned on any sum invested today is:

$$\text{Present value} = \frac{\text{Expected cash flow}}{(1+i)^t}$$

To illustrate the present value formula, consider a simple bond that matures in 4 years, has a coupon rate of 10%, and has a maturity value of $100. For simplicity, let's assume for now that the bond pays interest annually, and the same discount rate of 8% should be used to calculate the present value of each cash flow. Then the cash flow for this bond is:

Year	Expected Cash Flow
1	$10
2	10
3	10
4	110

The present value of each cash flow is

Year 1: $\text{Present value}_1 = \frac{\$10}{(1.08)^1} = \$9.2593$

Year 2: $\text{Present value}_2 = \frac{\$10}{(1.08)^2} = \$8.5734$

Year 3: $\text{Present value}_3 = \frac{\$10}{(1.08)^3} = \$7.9383$

Year 4: $\text{Present value}_4 = \frac{\$110}{(1.08)^4} = \$80.8533$

The value of this security is then the sum of the present values of the four cash flows. That is, the present value is $106.6243 ($9.2593 + $8.5734 + $7.9383 + $80.8533).

Present Value Properties

An important property about the present value can be seen from the above illustration. For the first 3 years, the cash flow is the same ($10) and the discount rate is the same

(8%). The present value is lower the further into the future the cash flow will be received. *This is an important property of the present value: for a given discount rate, the further into the future a cash flow is received, the lower its present value.*

Suppose that instead of a discount rate of 8%, a 12% discount rate is used for each cash flow. Then, the present value of each cash flow is:

$$\textit{Year 1}\text{: Present value}_1 = \frac{\$10}{(1.12)^1} = \$8.9286$$

$$\textit{Year 2}\text{: Present value}_2 = \frac{\$10}{(1.12)^2} = \$7.9719$$

$$\textit{Year 3}\text{: Present value}_3 = \frac{\$10}{(1.12)^3} = \$7.1178$$

$$\textit{Year 4}\text{: Present value}_4 = \frac{\$110}{(1.12)^4} = \$69.9070$$

The value of this security is then $93.9253 ($8.9286 + $7.9719 + $7.1178 + $69.9070). The security's value is lower if a 12% discount rate is used compared to an 8% discount rate ($93.9253 versus $106.6243). This is a general property of present value. The higher the discount rate, the lower the present value. Since the value of a security is the present value of the cash flows, this property carries over to the value of a security: *the higher the discount rate, the lower a security's value.* The reverse is also true: *the lower the discount rate, the higher a security's value.*

Exhibit 1 shows for an option-free bond (i.e., a bond that is not callable, putable, or convertible) this inverse relationship between a security's value and the discount rate. The shape of the curve in Exhibit 1 is referred to as *convex.*

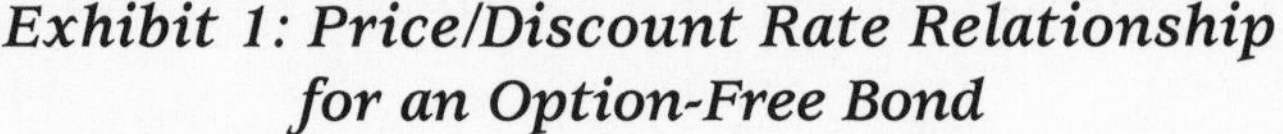

Exhibit 1: Price/Discount Rate Relationship for an Option-Free Bond

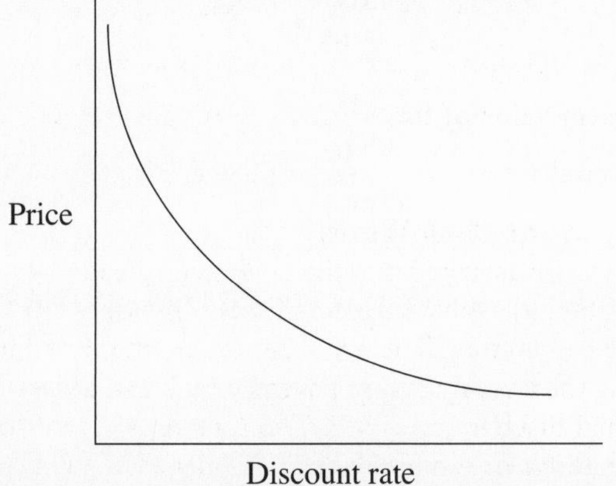

Relationship between Coupon Rate, Discount Rate, and Price Relative to Maturity Value

Another important property is worth noting. The coupon rate on our hypothetical security is 10%. When an 8% discount rate is used, the security's value ($106.6243) is greater than the maturity value ($100). A security whose value is greater than its maturity value is said to be trading at a *premium to maturity value* or *premium to par value*. In general, when the discount rate is less than the coupon rate, the security will trade at a premium to its maturity value. When a discount rate of 12% is used, the security's value is less than its maturity value ($93.9253). In such cases, the security is said to be trading at a *discount to maturity value* or *discount to par value*. In general, when the discount rate is greater than the coupon, the security will trade at a discount to its maturity value. A security's value will be equal to its maturity value when the discount rate is equal to the coupon rate. So, if a 10% discount rate is used to calculate the present value of the cash flows, it would be found that the security's value is $100.

Valuation Using Multiple Discount Rates

If instead of the same discount rate for each year, let's suppose that the appropriate discount rates are as follows: year 1, 6.8%; year 2, 7.2%; year 3, 7.6%; and year 4, 8%. Then the present value of each cash flow is:

$$\textit{Year 1}: \text{Present value}_1 = \frac{\$10}{(1.068)^1} = \$9.3633$$

$$\textit{Year 2}: \text{Present value}_2 = \frac{\$10}{(1.072)^2} = \$8.7018$$

$$\textit{Year 3}: \text{Present value}_3 = \frac{\$10}{(1.076)^3} = \$8.0272$$

$$\textit{Year 4}: \text{Present value}_4 = \frac{\$110}{(1.08)^4} = \$80.8533$$

The present value of this security assuming the various discount rates is $106.9456.

Valuing Semiannual Cash Flows

In our illustrations, we assumed that the coupon payments are paid once per year. For most bonds, the payments are semiannual. This does not introduce any complexities into the calculation. The procedure is to simply adjust the coupon payments by dividing the annual coupon payment by 2 and adjust the discount rate by dividing the annual discount rate by 2. The time period t in the present value formula is treated in terms of 6-month periods rather than years.

For example, consider once again the 4-year 10% coupon bond with a maturity value of $100. The cash flow for the first 3.5 years is equal to $5 ($10/2). The last cash flow is $105. If an annual discount rate of 8% is used, the semi-annual discount rate is 4%. The present value of each cash flow is then:

Period 1: $\text{Present value}_1 = \dfrac{\$5}{(1.04)^1} = \$4.8077$

Period 2: $\text{Present value}_2 = \dfrac{\$5}{(1.04)^2} = \$4.6228$

Period 3: $\text{Present value}_3 = \dfrac{\$5}{(1.04)^3} = \$4.4449$

Period 4: $\text{Present value}_4 = \dfrac{\$5}{(1.04)^4} = \$4.2740$

Period 5: $\text{Present value}_5 = \dfrac{\$5}{(1.04)^5} = \$4.1096$

Period 6: $\text{Present value}_6 = \dfrac{\$5}{(1.04)^6} = \$3.9516$

Period 7: $\text{Present value}_7 = \dfrac{\$5}{(1.04)^7} = \$3.7996$

Period 8: $\text{Present value}_8 = \dfrac{\$105}{(1.04)^8} = \$76.7225$

The security's value is equal to $106.7327

Valuing a Zero-Coupon Bond

For a zero-coupon bond, there is only one cash flow—the maturity value. The value of a zero-coupon bond that matures N years from now is

$$\frac{\text{Maturity value}}{(1 + i/2)^{2N}}$$

For example, a 5-year zero-coupon bond with a maturity value of $100 discounted at an 8% interest rate is $67.5564, as shown below:

$$\frac{\$100}{(1.04)^{10}} = \$67.5564$$

Valuing a Bond between Coupon Payments

For coupon-paying bonds, a complication arises when we try to price a bond between coupon payments. The amount that the buyer pays the seller in such cases is the present value of the cash flow. But one of the cash flows, the very

next cash flow, encompasses two components as shown below (assuming the buyer does not sell the bond prior to the next coupon payment date):

1. interest earned by the seller
2. interest earned by the buyer

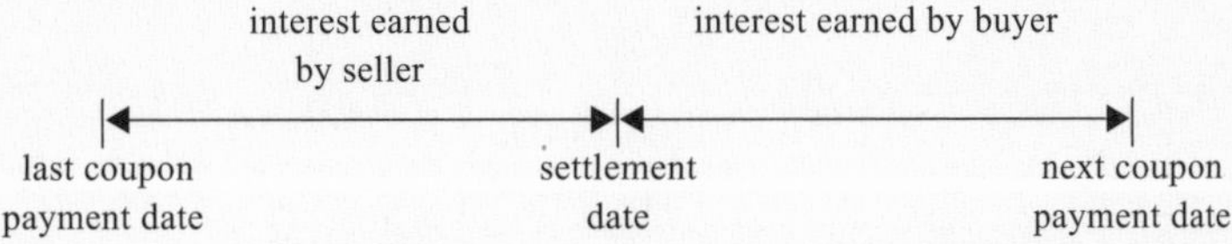

The interest earned by the seller is the interest that has accrued since the last coupon payment was made and the settlement date. This interest is called *accrued interest*. The buyer must compensate the seller for the accrued interest. The buyer recovers the accrued interest when the next coupon payment is received.

When the price of a bond is computed using the present value calculations described earlier, it is computed with accrued interest embodied in the price. This price is referred to as the *full price*. (Some market participants refer to it as the *dirty price*.) It is the full price that the buyer pays the seller. From the full price, the accrued interest must be deducted to determine the *price* of the bond, sometimes referred to as the *clean price*.

Below we show how the present value formula is modified to compute the full price when a bond is purchased between coupon periods.

Computing the Full Price To compute the full price, it is first necessary to determine the fractional periods between the settlement date and the next coupon payment date. This is determined as follows:

$$w \text{ periods} = \frac{\text{days between settlement date and next coupon payment date}}{\text{days in coupon period}}$$

Then the present value of the expected cash flow to be received t periods from now using a discount rate i, assuming the first coupon payment is w periods from now, is:

$$\text{present value}_t = \frac{\text{expected cash flow}}{(1+i)^{t-1+w}}$$

This procedure for calculating the present value when a security is purchased between coupon payments is called the "Street method."

To illustrate the procedure, we will use the hypothetical 4-year bond with a coupon rate of 10% and interest payable semiannually. Assume that this bond is purchased between coupon payments and that there are (1) 78 days between the settlement date and the next coupon payment date and (2) 182 days in the coupon

period. Then w is 0.4286. The present value of each cash flow assuming that each is discounted at 8% is

$$\textit{Period 1}: \text{Present value}_1 = \frac{\$5}{(1.04)^{0.4286}} = \$4.9167$$

$$\textit{Period 2}: \text{Present value}_2 = \frac{\$5}{(1.04)^{1.4286}} = \$4.7275$$

$$\textit{Period 3}: \text{Present value}_3 = \frac{\$5}{(1.04)^{2.4286}} = \$4.5457$$

$$\textit{Period 4}: \text{Present value}_4 = \frac{\$5}{(1.04)^{3.4286}} = \$4.3709$$

$$\textit{Period 5}: \text{Present value}_5 = \frac{\$5}{(1.04)^{4.4286}} = \$4.2028$$

$$\textit{Period 6}: \text{Present value}_6 = \frac{\$5}{(1.04)^{5.4286}} = \$4.0411$$

$$\textit{Period 7}: \text{Present value}_7 = \frac{\$5}{(1.04)^{6.4286}} = \$3.8857$$

$$\textit{Period 8}: \text{Present value}_8 = \frac{\$105}{(1.04)^{7.4286}} = \$78.4613$$

The full price is the sum of the present value of the cash flows, which is \$109.1517. Remember that the full price includes the accrued interest that the buyer is paying the seller.

Computing the Accrued Interest and the Clean Price To find the price without accrued interest, called the *clean price* or simply *price*, the accrued interest must be computed. To determine the accrued interest, it is first necessary to determine the number of days in the accrued interest period. The number of days in the accrued interest period is determined as follows:

$$\begin{aligned} &\text{days in accrued interest period} \\ &\quad = \text{days in coupon period} \\ &\qquad - \text{days between settlement and next coupon payment} \end{aligned}$$

The percentage of the next semiannual coupon payment that the seller has earned as accrued interest is then found as follows:

$$\frac{\text{days in accrued interest period}}{\text{days in coupon period}}$$

So, for example, returning to our illustration where the full price was computed, since there are 182 days in the coupon period and there are 78 days

from the settlement date to the next coupon payment, the number of days in the accrued interest period is 182 minus 78, or 104 days. Therefore, the percentage of the coupon payment that is accrued interest is:

$$\frac{104}{182} = 0.5714 = 57.14\%$$

This is the same percentage found by simply subtracting w from 1. In our illustration, w was 0.4286. Then $1 - 0.4286 = 0.5714$.

Given the value of w, the amount of accrued interest (AI) is equal to:

$$\text{AI} = \text{semiannual coupon payment} \times (1 - w)$$

So, for the 10% coupon bond whose full price we computed, since the semiannual coupon payment per $100 of par value is $5 and w is 0.4286, the accrued interest is:

$$\$5 \times (1 - 0.4286) = \$2.8571$$

The clean price is then:

full price – accrued interest

In our illustration, the clean price is[2]

$$\$109.1517 - \$2.8571 = \$106.2946$$

TRADITIONAL APPROACH TO VALUATION

The traditional approach to valuation has been to discount every cash flow of a fixed income security by the same interest rate (or discount rate). For example, consider the three hypothetical 10-year Treasury securities shown in Exhibit 2: a 12% coupon bond, an 8% coupon bond, and a zero-coupon bond. The cash flows for each security are shown in the exhibit. Since the cash flow of all three securities are viewed as default free, the traditional practice is to use the same discount rate to calculate the present value of all three securities and use the same discount rate for the cash flow for each period. For the three hypothetical bonds, suppose that the yield on a 10-year Treasury trading at par value is 10%. Then, the practice is to discount each cash flow using a discount rate of 10%.

---

[2] Notice that in computing the full price the present value of the next coupon payment is computed. However, the buyer pays the seller the accrued interest now although it will be recovered at the next coupon payment date.

Exhibit 2: Cash Flows for Three 10-Year Hypothetical Treasury Securities Per $100 of Par Value

Each period is 6 months

	Coupon Rate		
Period	12%	8%	0%
1	$6	$4	$0
2	6	4	0
3	6	4	0
4	6	4	0
5	6	4	0
6	6	4	0
7	6	4	0
8	6	4	0
9	6	4	0
10	6	4	0
11	6	4	0
12	6	4	0
13	6	4	0
14	6	4	0
15	6	4	0
16	6	4	0
17	6	4	0
18	6	4	0
19	6	4	0
20	106	104	100

For a non-Treasury security, a risk premium is added to the base interest rate (the Treasury rate). The risk premium is the same regardless of when a cash flow is to be received in the traditional approach. For a 10-year non-Treasury security, suppose that 90 basis points is the appropriate risk premium. Then all cash flows would be discounted at the base interest rate of 10% plus 90 basis points.

THE ARBITRAGE-FREE VALUATION APPROACH

The fundamental flaw of the traditional approach is that it views each security as the same package of cash flows. For example, consider a 10-year U.S. Treasury bond with an 8% coupon rate. The cash flows per $100 of par value would be 19 payments of $4 every 6 months and $104 for 20 6-month periods from now. The traditional practice would discount every cash flow using the same interest rate.

The proper way to view the 10-year 8% coupon bond is as a package of zero-coupon bonds. Each cash flow should be considered a zero-coupon bond whose maturity value is the amount of the cash flow and whose maturity date is the date that the cash flow is to be received. Thus, the 10-year 8% coupon bond should be viewed as 20 zero-coupon instruments. The reason this is the proper

way to value a fixed income security is that it does not allow a market participant to realize an arbitrage profit by taking apart or "stripping" a security and selling off the stripped securities at a higher aggregate value than it would cost to purchase the security in the market. This approach to valuation is referred to as the *arbitrage-free approach*.

By viewing any financial asset as a package of zero-coupon bonds, a consistent valuation framework can be developed. For example, under the traditional approach to the valuation of fixed income securities, a 10-year zero-coupon bond would be viewed as the same financial asset as a 10-year 8% coupon bond. Viewing a financial asset as a package of zero-coupon bonds means that these two bonds would be viewed as different packages of zero-coupon bonds and valued accordingly.

The difference between the traditional valuation approach and the arbitrage-free approach is depicted in Exhibit 3, which shows how the three bonds whose cash flows are depicted in Exhibit 2 should be valued. With the traditional approach, the base interest rate for all three securities is the yield on a 10-year U.S. Treasury security. With the arbitrage-free approach, the base interest rate for a cash flow is the theoretical rate that the U.S. Treasury would have to pay if it issued a zero-coupon bond with a maturity date equal to the maturity date of the estimated cash flow.

Exhibit 3: Comparison of Traditional Approach and Arbitrage-Free Approach in Valuing a Treasury Security

Each period is 6 months

	Discount (Base Interest) Rate		Cash Flows For*		
Period	Traditional Approach	Arbitrage-Free Approach	12%	8%	0%
1	10-year Treasury rate	1-period Treasury spot rate	$6	$4	$0
2	10-year Treasury rate	2-period Treasury spot rate	6	4	0
3	10-year Treasury rate	3-period Treasury spot rate	6	4	0
4	10-year Treasury rate	4-period Treasury spot rate	6	4	0
5	10-year Treasury rate	5-period Treasury spot rate	6	4	0
6	10-year Treasury rate	6-period Treasury spot rate	6	4	0
7	10-year Treasury rate	7-period Treasury spot rate	6	4	0
8	10-year Treasury rate	8-period Treasury spot rate	6	4	0
9	10-year Treasury rate	9-period Treasury spot rate	6	4	0
10	10-year Treasury rate	10-period Treasury spot rate	6	4	0
11	10-year Treasury rate	11-period Treasury spot rate	6	4	0
12	10-year Treasury rate	12-period Treasury spot rate	6	4	0
13	10-year Treasury rate	13-period Treasury spot rate	6	4	0
14	10-year Treasury rate	14-period Treasury spot rate	6	4	0
15	10-year Treasury rate	15-period Treasury spot rate	6	4	0
16	10-year Treasury rate	16-period Treasury spot rate	6	4	0
17	10-year Treasury rate	17-period Treasury spot rate	6	4	0
18	10-year Treasury rate	18-period Treasury spot rate	6	4	0
19	10-year Treasury rate	19-period Treasury spot rate	6	4	0
20	10-year Treasury rate	20-period Treasury spot rate	106	104	100

* Per $100 of par value.

Exhibit 4: Determination of the Theoretical Value of an 8% 10-Year Treasury

Period	Years	Cash Flow ($)	Spot Rate (%)	Present Value ($)
1	0.5	4	3.0000	3.9409
2	1.0	4	3.3000	3.8712
3	1.5	4	3.5053	3.7968
4	2.0	4	3.9164	3.7014
5	2.5	4	4.4376	3.5843
6	3.0	4	4.7520	3.4743
7	3.5	4	4.9622	3.3694
8	4.0	4	5.0650	3.2747
9	4.5	4	5.1701	3.1791
10	5.0	4	5.2772	3.0828
11	5.5	4	5.3864	2.9861
12	6.0	4	5.4976	2.8889
13	6.5	4	5.6108	2.7916
14	7.0	4	5.6643	2.7055
15	7.5	4	5.7193	2.6205
16	8.0	4	5.7755	2.5365
17	8.5	4	5.8331	2.4536
18	9.0	4	5.9584	2.3581
19	9.5	4	6.0863	2.2631
20	10.0	104	6.2169	56.3828
			Total	$115.2619

Therefore, to implement the arbitrage-free approach, it is necessary to determine the theoretical rate that the U.S. Treasury would have to pay to issue a zero-coupon Treasury bond for each maturity. Another name used for the zero-coupon Treasury rate is the *Treasury spot rate*. In the next chapter, we explain how the Treasury spot rate can be calculated. The spot rate for a Treasury security of some maturity is the base interest rate that should be used to discount a default-free cash flow with the same maturity.

Valuation Using Treasury Spot Rates

For the purposes of our discussion as follows, we take the Treasury spot rate for each maturity as given. To illustrate how Treasury spot rates are used to value a Treasury security, we use the hypothetical Treasury spot rates shown in the third column of Exhibit 4 to value an 8% 10-year Treasury security. The present value of each period's cash flow is shown in the last column. The sum of the present values is the theoretical value for the Treasury security. For the 8% 10-year Treasury, it is $115.2619.

Credit Spreads and the Valuation of Non-Treasury Securities

The Treasury spot rates can be used to value any default-free security. For a non-Treasury security, the theoretical value is not as easy to determine. The value of a

non-Treasury security is found by discounting the cash flows by the Treasury spot rates (i.e., the base interest rates) plus a risk premium to reflect the additional risks we noted earlier that are associated with investing in a non-Treasury security.

In practice, the spot rate used to discount the cash flow of a non-Treasury security is the Treasury spot rate plus a constant credit spread. For example, suppose the 6-month Treasury spot rate is 3% and the 10-year Treasury spot rate is 6%. Also suppose that a suitable credit spread is 90 basis points. Then a 3.9% spot rate is used to discount a 6-month cash flow of a non-Treasury bond and a 6.9% discount rate to discount a 10-year cash flow.

The drawback of this approach is that there is no reason to expect the credit spread to be the same regardless of when the cash flow is expected to be received. Instead, it might be expected that the credit spread increases with the maturity of the bond. That is, there is a *term structure for credit spreads.*

Dealer firms typically construct a term structure for credit spreads for a particular rating based on the input of traders. Generally, the credit spread increases with maturity. This is a typical shape for the term structure of credit spreads. In addition, the shape of the term structure is not the same for all credit ratings. The lower the credit rating, the steeper the term structure.

When the credit zero spreads for a given issuer are added to the Treasury spot rates, the resulting term structure is used to value bonds of issuers of the same credit quality. This term structure is referred to as the *benchmark spot rate curve* or *benchmark zero-coupon rate curve.*

For example, Exhibit 5 reproduces the Treasury spot rate curve in Exhibit 4. Also shown in the exhibit is a hypothetical credit spread for a non-Treasury security. The resulting benchmark spot rate curve is in the next-to-the-last column. This spot rate curve is used to value the securities of this issuer. This is done in Exhibit 5 for a hypothetical 8% 10-year issue for this issuer. The theoretical value is $108.4615. Notice that the theoretical value is less than that for an otherwise comparable Treasury security. The theoretical value for an 8% 10-year Treasury is $115.2619 (see Exhibit 4).

VALUATION MODELS

A *valuation model* provides the fair value of a security. Thus far, the two approaches to valuation we have presented have dealt with the valuation of simple securities. By simple we mean that it assumes the securities do not have an embedded option. Thus, a Treasury security and an option-free non-Treasury security can be valued using the procedures described previously.

More general valuation models handle securities with embedded options. In the fixed income area, two valuation models are commonly used—the binomial model and the Monte Carlo simulation model. The former model is used to value callable bonds, putable bonds, floating-rate notes, and structured notes in which the

coupon formula is based on an interest rate. The Monte Carlo simulation model is used to value mortgage-backed securities and certain types of asset-backed securities.

It is beyond the scope of this chapter to go into the details of these two models.[3] What is critical to understand is that valuation models use the principles of valuation described earlier in this chapter. Basically, these models look at possible paths that interest rates can take in the future and what the security's value would be on a given interest rate path. A security's value is then an averaging of these possible interest rate path values.

There are four features common to the binomial and Monte Carlo valuation models. First, each model begins with the yield on Treasury securities and generates the Treasury spot rates. Second, each model makes an assumption about the expected volatility of short-term interest rates. This is a critical assumption in both models since it can significantly affect the fair value estimated. Third, based on the volatility assumption, different paths that the short-term interest rate can take are generated. Fourth, the model is calibrated to the Treasury market. This means that if an "on-the-run" Treasury issue[4] is valued using the model, the model will produce the observed market price.

Exhibit 5: Calculation of Theoretical Value of a Hypothetical 8% 10-Year Non-Treasury Security Using Credit Term Structure

Period	Years	Cash flow ($)	Treasury spot rate (%)	Credit spread (%)	Benchmark spot (%)	Present value ($)
1	0.5	4	3.0000	0.20	3.2000	3.9370
2	1.0	4	3.3000	0.20	3.5000	3.8636
3	1.5	4	3.5053	0.25	3.7553	3.7829
4	2.0	4	3.9164	0.30	4.2164	3.6797
5	2.5	4	4.4376	0.35	4.7876	3.5538
6	3.0	4	4.7520	0.35	5.1020	3.4389
7	3.5	4	4.9622	0.40	5.3622	3.3237
8	4.0	4	5.0650	0.45	5.5150	3.2177
9	4.5	4	5.1701	0.45	5.6201	3.1170
10	5.0	4	5.2772	0.50	5.7772	3.0088
11	5.5	4	5.3864	0.55	5.9364	2.8995
12	6.0	4	5.4976	0.60	6.0976	2.7896
13	6.5	4	5.6108	0.65	6.2608	2.6794
14	7.0	4	5.6643	0.70	6.3643	2.5799
15	7.5	4	5.7193	0.75	6.4693	2.4813
16	8.0	4	5.7755	0.80	6.5755	2.3838
17	8.5	4	5.8331	0.85	6.6831	2.2876
18	9.0	4	5.9584	0.90	6.8584	2.1801
19	9.5	4	6.0863	0.95	7.0363	2.0737
20	10.0	104	6.2169	1.00	7.2169	51.1833
					Total	$108.4615

3 The details are provided in Frank J. Fabozzi, *Valuation of Fixed Income Securities and Derivatives, Third Edition* (New Hope, PA: Frank J. Fabozzi Associates, 1998).

4 What is meant by an "on-the-run" Treasury issue is explained in Chapter 4.

Interest Rate Volatility

One critical assumption in the two valuation models is the assumption about expected interest rate volatility. Here we give an intuitive idea of what is meant by interest rate volatility.

Interest rate volatility is a measure of how much interest rates can vary around an average value. The standard deviation is a measure of this volatility. Volatility is typically measured relative to the current level of rates. For example, suppose a volatility of the short-term interest rate of 15% is assumed and that the short-term rate is currently 6%. Then the volatility of the short-term interest rate can be translated into basis points by multiplying the volatility by the current level of the short-term rate. In our example, it is 0.15 times 0.06, which equals 0.0090 or 90 basis points. The greater the standard deviation, the greater the expected volatility of short-term interest rates. For example, a volatility of 20% means a standard deviation of 120 basis points when the short-term rate is 6%.

What does a standard deviation measured in basis points tell us? For those who have had a course in elementary statistics, a normal probability distribution was discussed. The normal probability distribution has the following properties: (1) there is a 66% probability that the outcome will be between one standard deviation below and above the mean; (2) there is a 96% probability that the outcome will be between two standard deviations below and above the mean; and (3) there is a 99.7% probability that the outcome will be between three standard deviations below and above the mean.

For example, suppose that the current value of the short-term interest rate is 6% and the standard deviation is 90 basis points. This means that there is a 66% probability that the short-term interest rate 1 year from now will be between 5.1% (= 6% – 90 basis points) and 6.9% (= 6% + 90 basis points). There is a 96% probability that the short-term interest rate 1 year from now will be between 4.2% (= 6% – 180 basis points) and 7.8% (= 6% + 180 basis points). There is a 99.7% probability that the short-term interest rate 1 year from now will be between 3.3% (= 6% – 270 basis points) and 8.7% (= 6% + 270 basis points).

Notice that the higher the volatility assumed (i.e., the larger the standard deviation), the wider the interval for the possible outcome of the short-term interest rate for a given probability.

Impact of Interest Rate Volatility Assumption on Value

The effect of the interest rate volatility assumption on a security's value is as follows. The greater the assumed interest rate volatility, the higher the value of the embedded option. For fixed income securities in which the issuer is given an option, the investor has given a more valuable option to the issuer. This results in a lower value for the security compared to a value for a lower assumed interest rate volatility. For example, when valued assuming a 12% interest rate volatility, suppose a callable bond's value is $108. If an interest rate volatility greater than 12% is assumed, the callable bond's value will be less than $108.

For fixed income securities in which the investor is given an option, the higher the interest rate volatility assumed, the higher the security's value. For example, for a putable bond, suppose that the security's value is $102 assuming 12% interest rate volatility. If an interest rate volatility greater than 12% is assumed, the putable bond's value will be greater than $102.

Modeling Risk

The user of any valuation model is exposed to *modeling risk*. This is the risk that the output of the model is incorrect because the assumptions on which it is based are incorrect. Consequently, it is imperative that the results of a valuation model be stress-tested for modeling risk by altering the assumptions.

MEASURING INTEREST RATE RISK

A major risk faced by investors is interest rate risk. In Chapter 1, we described the characteristics of a bond that affect its interest rate risk. However, to effectively control a portfolio's exposure to interest rate risk, it is necessary to quantify this risk. In the remainder of this chapter, we explain how this is done. The most popular measure of interest rate risk is duration. We explain this measure and discuss its limitations.

The most obvious way to measure the price sensitivity as a percentage of the security's current price to changes in interest rates is to change rates by a small number of basis points and calculate how a security's value will change as a percentage of the current price. The name popularly used to refer to the approximate percentage price change is *duration*. It can be demonstrated that the following formula gives the approximate percentage price change for a 100 basis point change in interest rates:

$$\text{Duration} = \frac{\text{Value if rates fall} - \text{Value if rates rise}}{2(\text{Current price})(\text{Change in rates in decimal})}$$

where "Value if rates fall" is the estimated value of the security if interest rates fall by a small number of basis points, "Value if rates rise" is the estimated value of the security if interest rates rise by a small number of basis points, and "Change in rates in decimal" is how much interest rates are changed to obtain the values in the numerator.

It is critical to understand that the two values in the numerator of the duration formula are the estimated values if interest rates change. These values are obtained from a valuation model. Consequently, *the resulting measure of the price sensitivity of a security to interest rate changes (i.e., duration) is only as good as the valuation model employed to obtain the estimated value of the security.* The more difficult it is to value a security, the less confidence an investor may have in the estimated duration. Because duration is dependent on a valuation model, we have introduced this measure in the same chapter as valuation.

To illustrate the duration calculation, consider the following option-free bond: a 6% coupon 5-year bond trading at par value to yield 6%. The initial value is $100. Suppose the yield is changed by 50 basis points. Thus, the change in interest rates in decimal is 0.005. If the yield is decreased to 5.5%, the value of this bond would be $102.1600. If the yield is increased to 6.5%, the value of this bond would be $97.8944. Substituting these values into the duration formula, we get:

$$\text{Duration} = \frac{\$102.1600 - \$97.8944}{2(\$100)(0.005)} = 4.27$$

Interpreting Duration

The duration of a security can be interpreted as the approximate percentage change in the price for a 100 basis point change in interest rates. Thus a bond with a duration of 4.8 will change by approximately 4.8% for a 100 basis point change in interest rates. For a 50 basis point change in interest rates, the bond's price will change by approximately 2.4%; for a 25 basis point change in interest rates, 1.2%, and so on.

An investor who anticipates a decline in interest rates will extend (i.e., increase) the portfolio's duration.[5] Suppose that a portfolio manager increases the present portfolio duration of 3 to 5. This means that for a 100 basis point change in interest rates, the portfolio will change by about 2% more than if the portfolio duration was left unchanged.

Dollar Duration

Duration is related to percentage price change. However, for two bonds with the same duration but trading at different prices, the dollar price change will not be the same. For example, consider two bonds, W and X. Suppose that both bonds have a duration of 5, but that W is trading at par value while X is trading at $90. A 100 basis point change for both bonds will change the price by approximately 5%. This means a price change of $5 (5% times $100) for W and a price change of $4.5 (5% times $90) for V.

The dollar price change of a bond can be measured by multiplying duration by the full dollar price and the number of basis points (in decimal form) and is called the *dollar duration*.[6] That is:

$$\text{Dollar duration} = \text{Duration} \times \text{Dollar price} \times \text{Change in rates in decimal}$$

The dollar duration for a 100 basis point change in rates is:

$$\text{Dollar duration} = \text{Duration} \times \text{Dollar price} \times 0.01$$

---

[5] How a portfolio's duration is calculated will be discussed later.

[6] For a one basis point change in yield, the dollar price change will give the same result as the price value of a basis point or dollar value of an 01.

So, for bonds W and X, the dollar duration for a 100 basis point change in rates is:

For bond W: Dollar duration = 5 × \$100 × 0.01 = \$5.0
For bond X: Dollar duration = 5 × \$90 × 0.01 = \$4.5

Modified Duration versus Effective Duration

A popular form of duration that is used by practitioners is *modified duration.* Modified duration is the approximate percentage change in a bond's price for a 100 basis point change in interest rates, assuming that the bond's cash flows do *not* change when interest rates change. What this means is that in calculating the values used in the numerator of the duration formula, the cash flows used to calculate the current price are assumed. Therefore, the change in the bond's value when interest rates change by a small number of basis points is due solely to discounting at the new yield level.

The assumption that the cash flows will not change when interest rates change makes sense for option-free bonds such as noncallable Treasury securities because the payments made by the U.S. Department of the Treasury to holders of its obligations do not change when interest rates change. However, the same cannot be said for callable and putable bonds and mortgage-backed securities. For these securities, a change in interest rates will alter the expected cash flows.

The price/yield relationship for callable bonds and securities is shown in Exhibit 6. As interest rates or yields in the market decline, the concern that they will decline further so that the issuer or homeowner will benefit from calling the bond increases. The exact yield level at which investors begin to view the issue likely to be called may not be known, but we do know that there is some level. In Exhibit 6, at yield levels below y^*, the price/yield relationship for the callable bond departs from the price/yield relationship for the option-free bond. If, for example, the market yield is such that an option-free bond would be selling for \$109, but since it is callable would be called at \$104, investors would not pay \$109. If they did and the bond is called, investors would receive \$104 (the call price) for a bond they purchased for \$109. Notice that for a range of yields below y^*, there is price compression (i.e., there is limited price appreciation as yields decline). The portion of the callable bond price/yield relationship below y^* is said to be *negatively convex.*

Negative convexity means that the price appreciation will be less than the price depreciation for a large change in yield of a given number of basis points. In contrast, a bond that is option-free exhibits *positive convexity.* This means that the price appreciation will be greater than the price depreciation for a large change in yield. The price changes resulting from bonds exhibiting positive convexity and negative convexity can be expressed as follows:

	Absolute value of percentage price change for:	
Change in interest rates	Positive convexity	Negative convexity
−100 basis points	*X*%	less than *Y*%
+100 basis points	less than *X*%	*Y*%

Exhibit 6: Price/Yield Relationship for an Option-Free Bond and a Callable Bond

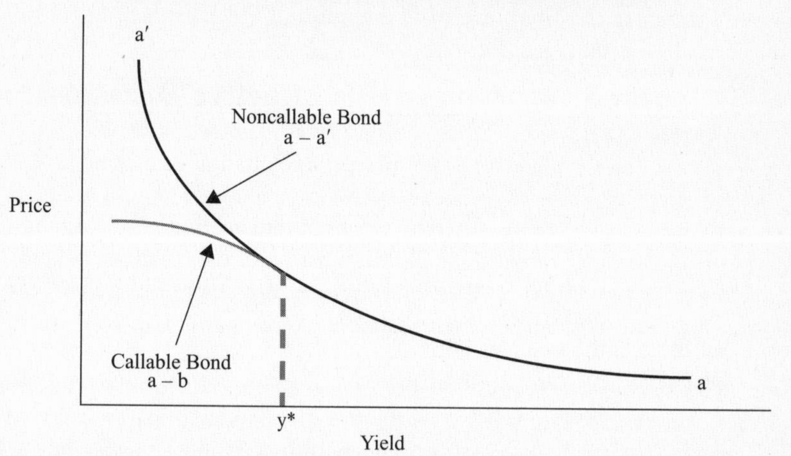

Exhibit 7: Modified Duration Versus Effective Duration

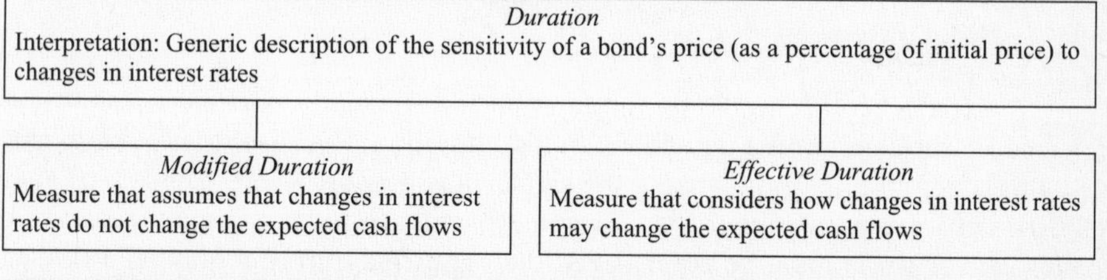

The two valuation models described earlier—binomial model and Monte Carlo simulation model—take into account how changes in interest rates will affect cash flows. Thus, when the values used in the numerator are obtained from these valuation models, the resulting duration takes into account both the discounting at different interest rates and how the cash flows can change. When duration is calculated in this manner, it is referred to as *effective duration* or *option-adjusted duration*. Exhibit 7 summarizes the distinction between modified duration and effective duration.

The difference between modified duration and effective duration for fixed income securities with an embedded option can be quite dramatic. For example, a callable bond could have a modified duration of 4 but an effective duration of only 3. For certain collateralized mortgage obligations described in Chapter 10, the modified duration could be 7 and the effective duration 20! Thus, using modified duration as a measure of the price sensitivity of a security to rate changes would be misleading. The more appropriate measure for any security with an embedded option is effective duration.

Macaulay Duration

It is worth comparing the modified duration formula presented previously to that commonly found in the literature. It is common in the literature to find the following formula for modified duration:[7]

$$\frac{1}{(1+\text{yield}/k)}\left[\frac{1\times \text{PVCF}_1 + 2\times \text{PVCF}_2 + \ldots + n\times \text{PVCF}_n}{k\times \text{Price}}\right]$$

where

k = number of periods, or payments, per year (e.g., $k = 2$ for semiannual-pay bonds and $k = 12$ for monthly-pay bonds)

n = number of periods until maturity (i.e., number of years to maturity times k)

yield = the bond's yield

PVCF_t = present value of the cash flow in period t discounted at the bond's yield

The expression in the bracket for the modified duration formula is a measure formulated in 1938 by an economist, Frederick Macaulay, and is popularly referred to as *Macaulay duration.*[8] Thus, modified duration is commonly expressed as:

$$\text{Modified duration} = \frac{\text{Macaulay duration}}{(1+\text{yield}/k)}$$

The general formulation for duration as given earlier provides a short-cut procedure for determining a bond's modified duration. Because it is easier to calculate the modified duration using the short-cut procedure, many vendors of analytical software use it rather than the long formula to reduce computation time. But, once again, it must be emphasized that modified duration may be a flawed measure of a bond's price sensitivity to interest rate changes for a bond with an embedded option.

Unfortunately, duration is too often interpreted by market participants as some measure of the weighted average time of the receipt of a security's cash flows. The interpretation is not incorrect, it is just not meaningful for purposes of managing a bond portfolio. For example, some bonds have a negative duration. How would that be interpreted? More important, some securities have a duration that exceeds the security's maturity.

Duration of a Floating-Rate Security

The price of a fixed-rate coupon bond fluctuates in the market because the prevailing market interest rate is different from the issue's coupon rate. For a floating-rate security, the coupon rate resets periodically to a rate that should be close

---

[7] More specifically, this is the formula for modified duration for a bond on a coupon anniversary date.

[8] Frederick Macaulay, *Some Theoretical Problems Suggested by the Movement of Interest Rates, Bond Yields, and Stock Prices in the U.S. Since 1856* (New York: National Bureau of Economic Research, 1938).

to the prevailing market interest rate. Recall that the coupon reset formula for a floating-rate security is the reference rate plus the quoted margin.

Assuming that the quoted margin that the market requires over the reference rate does not change, the greater the reset frequency, the smaller the duration because the coupon rate adjusts to the market rate and therefore the price stays near par value. When the coupon reset date is close, the duration is close to zero. If the quoted margin that the market requires changes, then a floating-rate security can trade at a premium or discount to maturity value even at a coupon reset date.

In addition, all of this assumes that there are no caps or floors (i.e., restrictions on how the coupon rate may reset). If there is a cap, then the floating-rate security's duration will take on the characteristics of a fixed-rate security if the coupon rate that would be set in the absence of the cap is significantly above the cap rate. The security in this case will trade at a discount from maturity value because the coupon rate is below the prevailing market rate. If there is a floor, the coupon rate will be fixed at a rate above the prevailing rate required by the market. In this case, the security will trade at a premium to maturity value.

Portfolio Duration

A portfolio's duration can be obtained by calculating the weighted average of the duration of the bonds in the portfolio. The weight is the proportion of the portfolio that a security comprises. Mathematically, a portfolio's duration can be calculated as follows:

$$W_1D_1 + W_2D_2 + W_3D_3 + \dots + W_KD_K$$

where

W_i = market value of bond i/market value of the portfolio
D_i = effective duration of bond i
K = number of bonds in the portfolio

To illustrate this calculation, consider the following three-bond portfolio:

Bond	Par amount owned	Price	Duration
1	$40 million	$40,000,000	3.4
2	50 million	42,313,750	5.0
3	10 million	13,785,860	0.6

The market value for the portfolio is $96,099,610.

In this illustration, K is equal to 3 and

$$W_1 = \$40{,}000{,}000/\$96{,}099{,}610 = 0.416 \qquad D_1 = 3.4$$
$$W_2 = \$42{,}313{,}750/\$96{,}099{,}610 = 0.440 \qquad D_2 = 5.0$$
$$W_3 = \$13{,}785{,}860/\$96{,}099{,}610 = 0.144 \qquad D_3 = 0.6$$

The portfolio's duration is:

$$0.416(3.4) + 0.440(5.0) + 0.144(0.6) = 3.7$$

A portfolio duration of 3.7 means that for a 100 basis point change in the yield for *all* three bonds, the market value of the portfolio will change by approximately 3.7%. But keep in mind, the yield on all three bonds must change by 100 basis points for the duration measure to be useful.

The assumption that all interest rates must change by the same number of basis points is a critical assumption, and its importance cannot be overemphasized. Market practitioners refer to this as the "parallel yield curve shift assumption." In Chapter 4, we show how the Treasury yield curve shifts. In Chapter 18, we show how two portfolios with the same duration can perform quite differently if the yield curve does not shift in a parallel fashion.

Contribution to Portfolio Duration

Investors commonly assess their exposure to an issue or to a sector in terms of the percentage of that issue or sector in the portfolio. A better measure of exposure of an individual issue or sector to changes in interest rates is in terms of its *contribution to portfolio duration*. This is found by multiplying the percentage that the individual issue or sector is of the portfolio by the duration of the individual issue or sector. That is,

$$\text{Contribution to portfolio duration} = \frac{\text{Market value of issue or sector}}{\text{Market value of portfolio}} \times \text{Duration of issue or sector}$$

Other Duration Measures

There are a variety of other measures of duration that relate to both fixed-rate bonds and floating-rate securities. We discuss these as follows.

Spread Duration for Fixed-Rate Bonds

Duration is a measure of the change in the value of a bond when rates change. The interest rate that is assumed to shift is the Treasury rate. However, for non-Treasury securities, the yield is equal to the Treasury yield plus a spread to the Treasury yield curve. The price of a bond exposed to credit risk can change even though Treasury yields are unchanged because the spread required by the market changes. A measure of how a non-Treasury issue's price will change if the spread sought by the market changes is called *spread duration*. For example, a spread duration of 2 for a security means that if the Treasury rate is unchanged but spreads change by 100 basis points, the security's price will change by approximately 2%.

Index and Spread Duration of a Floating-Rate Security

The price sensitivity of a floater will change depending on three factors: (1) time remaining to the next coupon reset date, (2) whether the cap is reached, and (3) whether the spread that the market wants changes. Two measures have been

developed to estimate the sensitivity of a floater to each component of the coupon reset formula: the reference rate and the spread. *Index duration* is a measure of the price sensitivity of a floater to changes in the reference rate (i.e., index) holding the spread constant. *Spread duration* measures a floater's price sensitivity to a change in the spread, assuming that the reference rate is unchanged.

Convexity Measure: Second-Order Approximation of Price Change

Notice that the duration measure indicates that regardless of whether interest rates rise or fall, the approximate percentage price change is the same. However, this is not a property of a bond's price volatility. While for small changes in interest rates the percentage price change will be the same for an increase or a decrease in interest rates, for a large change it is not. This suggests that duration is only a good approximation of the percentage price change for a small change in interest rates.

To see this, consider a 9% 20-year bond selling to yield 6% with a duration of 10.66. If yields increase instantaneously by 10 basis points (from 6% to 6.1%), then using duration the approximate percentage price change would be –1.066% (–10.66% divided by 10, remembering that duration is the percentage price change for a 100 basis point change in yield). The actual percentage price change is –1.07%. Similarly, if the yield decreases instantaneously by 10 basis points (from 6.00% to 5.90%), then the percentage change in price would be +1.066%. The actual percentage price change would be +1.07%. This example illustrates that for small changes in interest rates, duration does an excellent job of approximating the percentage price change.

Instead of a small change in interest rates, let's assume that yields increase by 200 basis points, from 6% to 8%. The approximate percentage price change is –21.32% (–10.66% times 2). The actual percentage change in price is only –18.40%. Moreover, if the yield decreases by 200 basis points from 6% to 4%, the approximate percentage price change based on duration would be +21.32%, compared to an actual percentage price change of +25.04%. Thus, the approximation is not as good for a 200 basis point change in interest rates because for an individual bond, duration is in fact only a first approximation of price change for a small change in interest rates. For a portfolio, duration is a first approximation of the change in the portfolio's value for a small parallel shift in the yield curve. The approximation can be improved by using a second approximation. This approximation is referred to as a bond's or portfolio's *convexity.*[9] The use of this term in the industry is unfortunate since the term convexity is also used to describe the shape or

---

[9] Mathematically, any function can be estimated by a series of approximations referred to as a Taylor series. Each approximation or term of the Taylor series is based on the corresponding derivative. For a bond, duration is the first approximation to price and is related to the first derivative of the bond's price. The convexity measure is the second approximation and is related to the second derivative of the bond's price. It turns out that in general the first two approximations do a good job of estimating the bond's price, so no additional derivatives are needed. The derivation is provided in Chapter 4 of Frank J. Fabozzi, *Bond Markets, Analysis, and Strategies* (Englewood Cliffs, NJ: Prentice Hall, 1993).

curvature of the price/yield relationship, as explained earlier in this chapter. We can better describe this approximation as the *convexity correction*.[10] The convexity correction of a bond can be used to approximate the change in price that is not explained by duration.

Convexity Measure

The convexity correction is obtained by first estimating the *convexity measure*, calculated using the following formula:

$$\text{Convexity measure} = \frac{\text{Value if rates fall} + \text{Value if rates rise} - 2(\text{Current price})}{2(\text{Current price})(\text{Change in rates in decimal})^2}$$

The values required to calculate the convexity measure are the same values needed to compute duration.

For our hypothetical 9% 20-year bond selling to yield 6%, if interest rates are changed by 20 basis points, we know that

Current price	=	$134.6722
Value if rates fall	=	$137.5888
Value if rates rise	=	$131.8439
Change in rates in decimal	=	0.002

Substituting these values into the convexity measure formula, we get

$$\text{Convexity measure} = \frac{\$137.5888 + \$131.8439 - 2(\$134.6722)}{2(\$134.6722)(0.002)^2} = 81.96$$

Convexity Correction

The convexity correction is the approximate percentage change adjustment to the duration estimate due to the bond's convexity (i.e., the percentage price change not explained by duration). Given the convexity measure, the convexity correction is:

$$\text{Convexity correction} = \text{Convexity measure} \times (\text{Change in rates in decimal})^2$$

For example, for the 9% coupon bond maturing in 20 years, the convexity correction if interest rates increase from 6% to 8% is

$$\text{Convexity correction} = 81.96 \times (0.02)^2 = 0.0328 = 3.28\%$$

If interest rates decrease from 6% to 4%, the convexity correction to the approximate percentage price change would also be 3.28%.

---

[10] It is a "correction" because duration attempts to approximate the price change using a straight line to the convex price/yield relationship in Exhibit 1.

The approximate percentage price change based on duration with the convexity correction is found by simply adding the two estimates. So, for example, if interest rates change from 6% to 8%, the estimated percentage price change would be:

Estimated change approximated by duration	=	−21.32%
Convexity correction	=	+ 3.28%
Total estimated percentage price change	=	−18.04%

The actual percentage price change is −18.40%.

For a decrease of 200 basis points, from 6% to 4%, the approximate percentage price change would be as follows:

Estimated change approximated by duration	=	+21.32%
Convexity correction	=	+3.28%
Total estimated percentage price change	=	+24.60%

The actual percentage price change is +25.04%.

Thus, duration with the convexity correction does a good job of estimating the sensitivity of a bond's price change to a large change in interest rates.

It is important to understand that the convexity measure as computed can be scaled in different ways. For our option-free bond where we computed the convexity measure to be 81.96, some vendors and dealers could report a value of 81.96, 163.92 (i.e., double 81.96), 0.8196 (i.e., 81.96 divided by 100), or 1.6392 (i.e., 81.96 divided by 50). That is, they can scale the convexity measure. All of these values are correct, but they mean nothing in isolation. To use them to obtain the convexity correction to the price change estimated by duration requires knowing how they are computed so that the convexity correction formula is scaled accordingly. For example, suppose that the convexity measure is such that in the convexity measure formula, the 2 is deleted from the formula. Hence, the convexity measure would be 163.92. Then the convexity correction formula would be adjusted as follows:

$$\text{Convexity correction} \\ = 0.5 \times \text{Convexity measure} \times (\text{Change in rates in decimal})^2$$

So, if the convexity measure is 163.92, then substituting this value into the above equation, for a 200 basis point change in rates one would obtain the same convexity correction as before.

Standard Convexity and Effective Convexity

The values used to calculate the convexity measure can be obtained by either assuming that when interest rates change the expected cash flows do not change or they do change. In the former case, the resulting convexity is referred to as *standard convexity*. Actually, in the industry, convexity is not qualified by the

adjective "standard." Thus, in practice the term *convexity* typically means that the cash flows are assumed not to change when interest rates change. *Effective convexity*, in contrast, assumes that the cash flows do change when interest rates change. This is the same distinction made for duration.

As with duration, for bonds with embedded options there could be quite a difference between the calculated standard convexity and effective convexity. In fact, for all option-free bonds, either convexity measure will have a positive value.[11] For callable bonds, mortgage-backed securities, and certain asset-backed securities, the calculated effective convexity can be negative when the calculated standard convexity gives a positive value.

APPENDIX: DAY COUNT CONVENTIONS

In Chapter 1, we explained that accrued interest (AI) assuming semiannual payments is calculated as follows:

$$\text{AI} = \frac{\text{Annual coupon}}{2} \times \frac{\text{Days in AI period}}{\text{Days in coupon period}}$$

In calculating the number of days between two dates, the actual number of days is not always the same as the number of days that should be used in the accrued interest formula. The number of days used depends on the day count convention for the particular security. Specifically, there are different day count conventions for Treasury securities than for government agency securities, municipal bonds, and corporate bonds.

For coupon-bearing Treasury securities, the day count convention used is to determine the actual number of days between two dates. This is referred to as the "actual/actual" day count convention. For example, consider a coupon-bearing Treasury security whose previous coupon payment was March 1. The next coupon payment would be on September 1. Suppose this Treasury security is purchased with a value date of July 17th. The actual number of days between July 17 (the value date) and September 1 (the date of the next coupon payment is 46 days) is shown below:

July 17 to July 31	14 days
August	31 days
September 1	1 day
	46 days

The number of days in the coupon period is the actual number of days between March 1 and September 1, which is 184 days. The number of days between the last coupon payment (March 1) to July 17 is therefore 138 days (184 days – 46 days).

For coupon-bearing agency, municipal, and corporate bonds, a different day count convention is used. It is assumed that every month has 30 days, that any

---

11 Hence, some dealer firms refer to the convexity adjustment as the "convexity gain."

6-month period has 180 days, and that there are 360 days in a year. This day count convention is referred to as "30/360." For example, consider once again the Treasury security purchased with a value date of July 17, the previous coupon payment on March 1, and the next coupon payment on September 1. If the security is an agency, municipal, or corporate bond instead, the number of days until the next coupon payment is 44 days as shown below:

July 17 to July 31	13 days
August	30 days
September 1	1 day
	44 days

The number of days from March 1 to July 17 is 136, which is the number of days in the accrued interest period.

KEY POINTS

- *Valuation is the process of determining the fair value of a financial asset.*

- *The fundamental principle of valuation is that the value of any financial asset is the present value of the expected cash flows, where a cash flow is the cash that is expected to be received at some time.*

- *The valuation process involves three steps: (1) estimating the expected cash flows, (2) determining the appropriate interest rate or interest rates that should be used to discount the cash flows, and (3) calculating the present value of the expected cash flows.*

- *For any fixed income security in which neither the issuer nor the investor can alter the repayment of the principal before its contractual due date, the cash flows can easily be determined assuming that the issuer does not default.*

- *The difficulty in determining cash flows arises for securities where either the issuer or the investor can alter the cash flows or the coupon rate is reset by a formula that depends on the future value of some reference rate, price, or exchange rate.*

- *The minimum interest rate or base rate that an investor should require is the yield available on Treasury securities since the cash flows of these securities are viewed as default-free cash flows.*

- *The risk premium over the interest rate on a Treasury security that investors will require reflects the additional risks the investor faces by acquiring a security that is not issued by the U.S. government.*

- *The interest rate offered on a non-Treasury security is the sum of the base interest rate plus the risk premium (or spread).*

- *The factors that affect the spread or risk premium include (1) the issuer's perceived creditworthiness; (2) provisions that grant either the issuer or the investor the option to do something; (3) the taxability of the interest; and (4) the expected liquidity of the security.*

- *In general, investors will require a larger spread to a comparable Treasury security for an issue with an embedded option that is favorable to the issuer (e.g., a call option) than for an issue without such an option.*

- *For a given discount rate, the present value of a single cash flow to be received in the future is the amount of money that must be invested today that will generate that future value.*

- *The present value of a cash flow will depend on when a cash flow will be received (i.e., the timing of a cash flow) and the discount rate (i.e., interest rate) used to calculate the present value.*

- *The sum of the present values for a security's estimated cash flows is the value of the security.*

- *The present value is lower the further into the future the cash flow will be received.*

- ❑ *The higher the discount rate, the lower a cash flow's present value and therefore since the value of a security is the present value of the cash flows, the higher the discount rate, the lower a security's value.*

- ❑ *A security whose value is greater than its maturity value is said to be trading at a premium to maturity value or premium to par value.*

- ❑ *In general, when the discount rate is less than the coupon rate, the security will trade at a premium to its maturity value and when the discount rate is higher than the coupon rate, the security will trade at a discount to its maturity value.*

- ❑ *The traditional valuation methodology is to discount every cash flow of a fixed income security by the same interest rate (or discount rate), thereby incorrectly viewing each security as the same package of cash flows.*

- ❑ *The arbitrage-free approach values a bond as a package of cash flows, with each cash flow viewed as a zero-coupon bond and each cash flow discounted at its own unique discount rate.*

- ❑ *The Treasury yield curve indicates the relationship between the yield on Treasury securities and maturity, and from this relationship the theoretical Treasury zero-coupon rates can be calculated.*

- ❑ *The theoretical Treasury zero-coupon rates are called Treasury spot rates.*

- ❑ *To value a security with credit risk, it is necessary to determine a term structure of credit risk.*

- ❑ *Adding a credit spread for an issuer to the Treasury spot rate curve gives the benchmark spot rate curve that should be used to value that issuer's security.*

- ❑ *Valuation models seek to estimate the fair or theoretical value of a bond and accommodate securities with embedded options.*

- ❑ *The two valuation models used to value bonds with embedded options are the binomial model and the Monte Carlo simulation model.*

- ❑ *The binomial model is used to value callable bonds, putable bonds, floating-rate notes, and structured notes in which the coupon formula is based on an interest rate.*

- ❑ *The Monte Carlo simulation model is used to value mortgage-backed securities.*

- ❑ *Basically, the binomial and Monte Carlo models look at possible paths that interest rates can take in the future and what the security's value would be on a given interest rate path, with the security's value being an average of the possible interest rate path values.*

- ❑ *In a valuation model, the uncertainty of future interest rates is captured by introducing the expected volatility of interest rates.*

- ❑ *The standard deviation is a statistical measure of volatility, and the assumed value has an important impact on the theoretical value of a bond with an embedded option.*

- ☐ *The user of a valuation model is exposed to modeling risk and should test the sensitivity of the model to alternative assumptions.*
- ☐ *The price/yield relationship for an option-free bond is convex.*
- ☐ *The percentage price change of a bond can be estimated by changing interest rates by a small number of basis points and observing how the price changes.*
- ☐ *The duration of a bond measures the approximate percentage price change for a 100 basis point change in interest rates.*
- ☐ *Dollar duration measures the dollar price change of a bond when interest rates change.*
- ☐ *Modified duration is the approximate percentage change in a bond's price for a 100 basis point change in interest rates, assuming that the bond's cash flows do not change when interest rates change.*
- ☐ *Callable bonds and mortgage passthrough securities exhibit negative convexity—the percentage price change for a rise in rates is greater than for a decline in rates by the same number of basis points.*
- ☐ *Modified duration may not be a useful measure of the price sensitivity for securities with embedded options.*
- ☐ *Effective duration or option-adjusted duration is the approximate percentage price change of a bond for a 100 basis point change in interest rates, allowing for the cash flows to change as a result of the change in interest rates.*
- ☐ *The difference between modified duration and effective duration for fixed income securities with an embedded option can be quite dramatic.*
- ☐ *Assuming the spread over the reference rate that the market requires does not change and that there are no caps or floors, the duration for a floating-rate security is smaller the greater the reset frequency.*
- ☐ *A portfolio's duration can be obtained by calculating the weighted average of the duration of the bonds in the portfolio.*
- ☐ *When using a portfolio duration, it is assumed that all interest rates change by the same number of basis points, an assumption referred to as the "parallel yield curve shift assumption."*
- ☐ *The contribution to portfolio duration is a better measure of exposure of an individual issue or sector to changes in interest rates and is found by multiplying the percentage that the individual issue or sector is of the portfolio by the duration of the individual issue or sector.*
- ☐ *Spread duration for a fixed-rate bond is a measure of how a non-Treasury issue's price will change if the spread sought by the market changes.*
- ☐ *For a floating-rate security, an index duration and a spread duration can be computed.*

- ❑ *Index duration is a measure of the price sensitivity of a floater to changes in the reference rate (i.e., index) holding the spread constant; spread duration measures a floater's price sensitivity to a change in the spread, assuming that the reference rate is unchanged.*

- ❑ *The estimate of the price sensitivity of a bond based on duration can be improved by using a bond's convexity measure.*

- ❑ *As with duration, the convexity measure of a bond can be measured, assuming that the cash flows do not change when interest rates change (standard convexity) or assuming that they do change when interest rates change (effective convexity).*

Chapter 3

Yield and Yield Spread Measures

In the previous chapter, we focused on the principles for valuing a fixed income security. Frequently, investors assess the relative value of a security by some yield or yield spread measure. There are various yield measures that are quoted in the market. These measures are based on assumptions that limit their use to gauge relative value. This chapter explains the various yield and yield spread measures and their limitations. In Chapter 17, we provide a better framework for assessing the potential performance of a security—total return. In addition, we explained in Chapter 2 how the value of a security should be calculated using theoretical spot rates. While we illustrated how spot rates are used to value a security, we did not explain how spot rates are obtained. In this chapter, we show how theoretical spot rates are obtained. Yields and spot rates are related to another important rate, forward rates. An explanation of this concept is provided in the appendix to this chapter.

SOURCES OF RETURN

When an investor purchases a fixed income security, he or she can expect to receive a dollar return from one or more of the following sources:[1]

1. the coupon interest payments made by the issuer
2. any capital gain (or capital loss – a negative dollar return) when the security matures, is called, or is sold
3. income from reinvestment of the interim cash flows

Any yield measure that purports to measure the potential return from a fixed income security should consider all three sources of return described above.

---

[1] The classification of the sources of return in our discussion in this chapter is different from the treatment under the U.S. tax code. For example, as explained in Chapter 16, for zero-coupon instruments purchased at issuance, the tax code treats the difference between the par value and the purchase price as interest income. More specifically, the discount from par value is called an *original interest discount*. In our discussion in this chapter, it would be classified as a capital gain. As a second example, the tax code has rules for the treatment of what it defines as a bond purchased below par value because of changes in market interest rates. The difference between the par value and market price is called a *market discount* and is treated as interest income under the tax code. In our discussion we would define the difference as a capital gain.

Coupon Interest Payments

The most obvious source of return is the periodic coupon interest payments. For zero-coupon instruments, the return from this source is zero, although the investor is effectively receiving interest by purchasing a security below its par value and realizing interest at the maturity date when the investor receives the par value.

Capital Gain or Loss

When the proceeds received when a bond matures, is called, or is sold are greater than the purchase price, a capital gain results. For a bond held to maturity, there will be a capital gain if the bond is purchased below its par value. A bond purchased below its par value is said to be purchased at a *discount*. For example, a bond purchased for $94.17 with a par value of $100 will generate a capital gain of $5.83 ($100 – $94.17) if held to maturity. For a callable bond, a capital gain results if the price at which the bond is called (i.e., the call price) is greater than the purchase price. For example, if the bond in our previous example is callable and subsequently called at $100.5, a capital gain of $6.33 ($100.5 – $94.17) will be realized. If the same bond is sold prior to its maturity or before it is called, a capital gain will result if the proceeds exceed the purchase price. So, if our hypothetical bond is sold prior to the maturity date for $103, the capital gain would be $8.83 ($103 – $94.17).

A capital loss is generated when the proceeds received when a bond matures, is called, or is sold are less then the purchase price. For a bond held to maturity, there will be a capital loss if the bond is purchased for more than its par value. A bond purchased for more than its par value is said to be purchased at a *premium*. For example, a bond purchased for $102.5 with a par value of $100 will generate a capital loss of $2.5 ($102.5 – $100) if held to maturity. For a callable bond, a capital loss results if the price at which the bond is called is less than the purchase price. For example, if the bond in our previous example is callable and subsequently called at $100.5, a capital loss of $2 ($102.5 – $100.5) will be realized. If the same bond is sold prior to its maturity or before it is called, a capital loss will result if the sale price is less than the purchase price. So, if our hypothetical bond is sold prior to the maturity date for $98.5, the capital loss would be $4 ($102.5 – $98.5).

Reinvestment Income

With the exception of zero-coupon instruments, fixed income securities make periodic payments of interest that can be reinvested until the security is removed from the portfolio. There are also instruments in which there are periodic principal repayments that can be reinvested until the security is removed from the portfolio. As explained in Chapter 1, repayment of principal prior to the maturity date occurs for amortizing instruments such as mortgage-backed securities and asset-backed securities. The interest earned from reinvesting the interim cash flows (interest and/or principal payments) until the security is removed from the portfolio is called *reinvestment income*.

TRADITIONAL YIELD MEASURES

There are several yield measures cited in the bond market. These include current yield, yield to maturity, yield to call, yield to put, yield to worst, and cash flow yield. For floating-rate securities, a measure called *discount margin* is computed. These yield measures are expressed as a percent return rather than a dollar return. Below we explain how each measure is calculated and its limitations.

Current Yield

The current yield relates the annual dollar coupon interest to the market price. The formula for the current yield is:

$$\text{Current yield} = \frac{\text{Annual dollar coupon interest}}{\text{Price}}$$

For example, the current yield for a 7% 8-year bond whose price is $94.17 is 7.43% as shown below:

$$\text{Annual dollar coupon interest} = 0.07 \times \$100 = \$7$$

$$\text{Price} = \$94.17$$

$$\text{Current yield} = \frac{\$7}{\$94.17} = 0.0743 \text{ or } 7.43\%$$

The current yield will be greater than the coupon rate when the bond sells at a discount; the reverse is true for a bond selling at a premium. For a bond selling at par, the current yield will be equal to the coupon rate.

The drawback of the current yield is that it considers only the coupon interest and no other source that will impact an investor's return. No consideration is given to the capital gain that the investor will realize when a bond is purchased at a discount and held to maturity; nor is there any recognition of the capital loss that the investor will realize if a bond purchased at a premium is held to maturity.

Yield to Maturity

The most popular measure of yield in the bond market is the yield to maturity. The *yield to maturity* is the interest rate that will make the present value of the cash flows from a bond equal to its market price plus accrued interest. Calculation of the yield to maturity of a bond is the reverse process of calculating the price of a bond. As explained in the previous chapter, to find the price of a bond we determine the cash flows and the required yield, then we calculate the present value of the cash flows to obtain the price. To find the yield to maturity, we first determine the cash flows. Then we search by trial and error for the interest rate that will make the present value of the cash flows equal to the market price plus accrued interest. In the illustrations presented in this chapter, we assume that the next coupon payment will be 6 months from now so that there is no accrued interest.

To illustrate, consider a 7% 8-year bond selling for $94.17. The cash flows for this bond are (1) 16 payments every 6 months of $3.50 and (2) a payment 16 6-month periods from now of $100. The present value using various discount (interest) rates is:

Interest rate	3.5%	3.6%	3.7%	3.8%	3.9%	4.0%
Present value	100.00	98.80	97.62	96.45	95.30	94.17

When a 4.0% interest rate is used, the present value of the cash flows is equal to $94.17, which is the price of the bond. Hence, 4.0% is the *semiannual* yield to maturity.

The market convention adopted is to double the semiannual yield and call that the yield to maturity. Thus, the yield to maturity for the above bond is 8% (2 times 4.0%). The yield to maturity computed using this convention—doubling the semiannual yield—is called a *bond-equivalent yield* or *coupon-equivalent yield*.

The following relationships between the price of a bond, coupon rate, current yield, and yield to maturity hold:

Bond selling at	Relationship
par	coupon rate = current yield = yield to maturity
discount	coupon rate < current yield < yield to maturity
premium	coupon rate > current yield > yield to maturity

The yield to maturity considers not only the coupon income but also any capital gain or loss that the investor will realize by holding the bond to maturity. The yield to maturity also considers the timing of the cash flows. It does consider reinvestment income; however, it assumes that the coupon payments can be reinvested at an interest rate equal to the yield to maturity. So, if the yield to maturity for a bond is 8%, for example, to earn that yield the coupon payments must be reinvested at an interest rate equal to 8%. The following illustration clearly demonstrates this point.

Suppose an investor has $94.17 and places the funds in a certificate of deposit that pays 4% every 6 months for 8 years or 8% per year (on a bond-equivalent basis). At the end of 8 years, the $94.17 investment will grow to $176.38. Instead, suppose an investor buys the following bond: a 7% 8-year bond selling for $94.17. The yield to maturity for this bond is 8%. The investor would expect that at the end of 8 years, the total dollars from the investment will be $176.38.

Let's look at what the investor will receive. There will be 16 semiannual interest payments of $3.50, which will total $56. When the bond matures, the investor will receive $100. Thus, the total dollars that the investor will receive is $156 by holding the bond to maturity. But this is less than the $176.38 necessary to produce a yield of 8% on a bond-equivalent basis by $20.38 ($176.38 minus $156). How is this deficiency supposed to be made up? If the investor reinvests the coupon payments at a semiannual interest rate of 4% (or 8% annual rate on a bond-equivalent basis), then the interest earned on the coupon payments will be $20.38. Consequently, of the $82.21 total dollar return ($176.38 minus $94.17) necessary to produce a yield of 8%, about 25% ($20.38 divided by $82.21) must be generated by reinvesting the coupon payments.

Clearly, the investor will only realize the yield to maturity that is stated at the time of purchase if (1) the coupon payments can be reinvested at the yield to maturity and (2) the bond is held to maturity. With respect to the first assumption, the risk that an investor faces is that future interest rates will be less than the yield to maturity at the time the bond is purchased. This risk is referred to as reinvestment risk—a risk we introduced in Chapter 1 in the context of callable bonds. If the bond is not held to maturity, it may have to be sold for less than its purchase price, resulting in a return that is less than the yield to maturity. The risk that a bond will have to be sold at a loss is referred to as interest rate risk. We discussed this risk in Chapter 1 and showed the factors that affect a bond's interest rate risk. In Chapters 1 and 2, we explained how this risk is measured using duration.

There are two characteristics of a bond that determine the degree of reinvestment risk. First, for a given yield to maturity and a given coupon rate, the longer the maturity the more the bond's total dollar return is dependent on reinvestment income to realize the yield to maturity at the time of purchase (i.e., the greater the reinvestment risk). The implication is that the yield to maturity measure for long-term coupon bonds tells little about the potential yield that an investor may realize if the bond is held to maturity. For long-term bonds, in high interest rate environments the reinvestment income component may be as high as 70% of the bond's potential total dollar return.

The second characteristic that determines the degree of reinvestment risk is the coupon rate. For a given maturity and a given yield to maturity, the higher the coupon rate, the more dependent the bond's total dollar return will be on the reinvestment of the coupon payments in order to produce the yield to maturity at the time of purchase. This means that holding maturity and yield to maturity constant, premium bonds will be more dependent on reinvestment income than bonds selling at par. In contrast, discount bonds will be less dependent on reinvestment income than bonds selling at par. For zero-coupons bonds, none of the bond's total dollar return is dependent on reinvestment income. So, a zero-coupon bond has no reinvestment risk if held to maturity.

The dependence of the total dollar return on reinvestment income for bonds with different coupon rates and maturities is shown in Exhibit 1.

Yield to Call

When a bond is callable, the practice has been to calculate a yield to call as well as a yield to maturity. A callable bond may have a call schedule. The yield to call assumes that the issuer will call the bond at some assumed call date and the call price is then the call price specified in the call schedule.

Typically, investors calculate a *yield to first call* or *yield to next call*, a *yield to first par call*, and *yield to refunding*. The yield to first call is computed for an issue that is not currently callable, while the yield to next call is computed for an issue that is currently callable.

Exhibit 1: Percentage of Total Dollar Return from Reinvestment Income

	Years to maturity				
	2	3	5	8	15
7% coupon					
Price	98.19	97.38	95.94	94.17	91.35
% of total	5.2%	8.6%	15.2%	24.8%	44.5%
8% coupon					
Price	100.00	100.00	100.00	100.00	100.00
% of total	5.8%	9.5%	16.7%	26.7%	46.5%
12% coupon					
Price	107.26	110.48	116.22	122.30	134.58
% of total	8.1%	12.9%	21.6%	31.0%	51.8%

Yield to refunding is used when bonds are currently callable but have some restrictions on the source of funds used to buy back the debt when a call is exercised. Namely, if a debt issue contains some refunding protection, bonds cannot be called for a certain period of time with the proceeds of other debt issues sold at a lower cost of money. As a result, the bondholder is afforded some protection if interest rates decline and the issuer can obtain lower-cost funds to pay off the debt. It should be stressed that the bonds can be called with funds derived from other sources (e.g., cash on hand) during the refunded-protected period. The refunding date is the first date the bond can be called using lower-cost debt.

The procedure for calculating any yield to call measure is the same as for any yield calculation: determine the interest rate that will make the present value of the expected cash flows equal to the price plus accrued interest. In the case of yield to first call, the expected cash flows are the coupon payments to the first call date and the call price. For the yield to first par call, the expected cash flows are the coupon payments to the first date at which the issuer can call the bond at par and the par value. For the yield to refunding, the expected cash flows are the coupon payments to the first refunding date and the call price at the first refunding date.

To illustrate the computation, consider a 7% 8-year bond with a maturity value of $100 selling for $106.36. Suppose that the first call date is 3 years from now and the call price is $103. The cash flows for this bond if it is called in 3 years are (1) six coupon payments of $3.50 and (2) $103 in six 6-month periods from now. The process for finding the yield to first call is the same as for finding the yield to maturity. The present value for several semiannual interest rates is shown in Exhibit 2. Since a semiannual interest rate of 2.8% makes the present value of the cash flows equal to the price, 2.8% is the yield to first call. Therefore, the yield to first call on a bond-equivalent basis is 5.6%.

Exhibit 2: Yield to Call for an 8-Year 7% Coupon Bond with a Maturity Value of $100, First Call Date is the End of Year 3, and Call Price of $103

Annual interest rate (%)	Semiannual rate (%)	Present value of 6 payments of $3.5	Present value of $103 6 periods from now	Present value of cash flows
5.0	2.5	$16.27	$91.83	$108.10
5.2	2.6	16.21	91.30	107.51
5.4	2.7	16.16	90.77	106.93
5.6	2.8	16.12	90.24	106.36

Limitations of Yield to Call Measures

Let's take a closer look at the yield to call as a measure of the potential return of a security. The yield to call does consider all three sources of potential return from owning a bond. However, as in the case of the yield to maturity, it assumes that all cash flows can be reinvested at the yield to call until the assumed call date. As we just demonstrated, this assumption may be inappropriate. Moreover, the yield to call assumes that (1) the investor will hold the bond to the assumed call date and (2) the issuer will call the bond on that date.

These assumptions underlying the yield to call are often unrealistic. They do not take into account how an investor will reinvest the proceeds if the issue is called. For example, consider two bonds, M and N. Suppose that the yield to maturity for bond M, a 5-year noncallable bond, is 7.5%, while for bond N the yield to call assuming the bond will be called in 3 years is 7.8%. Which bond is better for an investor with a 5-year investment horizon? It's not possible to tell for the yields cited. If the investor intends to hold the bond for 5 years and the issuer calls bond N after 3 years, the total dollars that will be available at the end of 5 years will depend on the interest rate that can be earned from investing funds from the call date to the end of the investment horizon.

Yield to Put

When a bond is putable, the yield to the first put date is calculated. The yield to put is the interest rate that will make the present value of the cash flows to the first put date equal to the price plus accrued interest. As with all yield measures (except the current yield), yield to put assumes that any interim coupon payments can be reinvested at the yield calculated. Moreover, the yield to put assumes that the bond will be put on the first put date.

Yield to Worst

A yield can be calculated for every possible call date and put date. In addition, a yield to maturity can be calculated. The lowest of all these possible yields is called the *yield to worst*. For example, suppose that there are only four possible call dates for a callable bond and that a yield to call assuming each possible call date is 6%, 6.2%, 5.8%, and 5.7%, and that the yield to maturity is 7.5%. Then the yield to worst is the minimum of these values, 5.7% in our example.

The yield to worst measure holds little meaning as a measure of potential return.

Cash Flow Yield

As we explain in Chapters 9 through 12, mortgage-backed securities and asset-backed securities are backed by a pool of loans. The cash flows for these securities include principal repayment as well as interest. The complication that arises is that the individual borrowers whose loans make up the pool typically can prepay their loan in whole or in part prior to the scheduled principal repayment date. Because of prepayment, in order to project the cash flows it is necessary to make an assumption about the rate at which prepayments will occur. This rate is called the *prepayment rate* or *prepayment speed*.

Given the cash flows based on the assumed prepayment rate, a yield can be calculated. The yield is the interest rate that will make the present value of the projected cash flows equal to the price plus accrued interest. A yield calculated is commonly referred to as a *cash flow yield*.

Typically, the cash flows for mortgage-backed and asset-backed securities are monthly. Therefore the interest rate that will make the present value of the projected principal repayment and interest payments equal to the market price plus accrued interest is a monthly rate. The bond-equivalent yield is found by calculating the effective 6-month interest rate and then doubling it. That is:

$$\text{Cash flow yield on a bond-equivalent basis (if monthly pay)} = 2[(1 + \text{Monthly yield})^6 - 1]$$

For example, if the monthly yield is 0.5%, then:

$$\text{Cash flow yield on a bond-equivalent basis} = 2[(1.005)^6 - 1] = 6.08\%$$

If, instead, the security pays quarterly rather than monthly, the yield is calculated as follows:

$$\text{Cash flow yield on a bond-equivalent basis (if quarterly pay)} = 2\,[(1 + \text{Quarterly yield})^2 - 1]$$

As we have noted, the yield to maturity has two shortcomings as a measure of a bond's potential return: (1) it is assumed that the coupon payments can be reinvested at a rate equal to the yield to maturity, and (2) it is assumed that the bond is held to maturity. These shortcomings are equally present in application of the cash flow yield measure: (1) the projected cash flows are assumed to be reinvested at the cash flow yield, and (2) the mortgage-backed or asset-backed security is assumed to be held until the final payoff of all the loans based on some prepayment assumption. The importance of reinvestment risk—the risk that the cash flows will be reinvested at a rate less than the cash flow yield—is particu-

larly important for mortgage-backed and asset-backed securities since payments are typically monthly and include principal repayments (scheduled and prepayments), as well as interest. Moreover, the cash flow yield is dependent on realization of the projected cash flows according to some prepayment rate. If actual prepayments differ significantly from the prepayment rate assumed, the cash flow yield will not be realized.

Margin Measures for Floating-Rate Securities

The coupon rate for a floating-rate security changes periodically according to a reference rate (such as LIBOR or a Treasury rate). Since the future value for the reference rate is unknown, it is not possible to determine the cash flows. This means that a yield to maturity cannot be calculated. Instead, "margin" measures are computed. By margin it is meant some spread above the floater's reference rate.

Several spread or margin measures are routinely used to evaluate floaters. Two margin measures commonly used are spread for life and discount margin.[2]

Spread for Life

When a floater is selling at a premium/discount to par, investors consider the premium or discount as an additional source of dollar return. *Spread for life* (also called *simple margin*) is a measure of potential return that accounts for the accretion (amortization) of the discount (premium) as well as the constant quoted margin over the security's remaining life. Spread for life (in basis points) is calculated using the following formula:

$$\text{Spread for life} = \left[\frac{100(100 - \text{Price})}{\text{Maturity}} + \text{Quoted margin}\right] \times \left(\frac{100}{\text{Price}}\right)$$

where

Price = market price per \$100 of par value
Maturity = number of years to maturity using the appropriate day-count convention
Quoted margin = quoted margin in the coupon reset formula measured in basis points

For example, suppose that a floater with a quoted margin of 80 basis points is selling for 99.3098 and matures in 6 years. Then,

Price = 99.3098
Maturity = 6
Quoted margin = 80

[2] Two others margin measures are adjusted simple margin and adjusted total margin. These measures are discussed and illustrated in Frank J. Fabozzi and Steven V. Mann, *Introduction to Fixed Income Analytics* (New Hope, PA: Frank J. Fabozzi Associates, 2001), pp. 219–221.

$$\text{Spread for life} = \left[\frac{100(100 - 99.3098)}{6} + 80\right] \times \left(\frac{100}{99.3098}\right)$$

$$= 92.14 \text{ basis points}$$

The limitations of the spread for life are that it considers only the accretion/amortization of the discount/premium over the floater's remaining term to maturity and does not consider the level of the coupon rate or the time value of money.

Discount Margin

Discount margin estimates the average margin over the reference rate that the investor can expect to earn over the life of the security. The procedure for calculating the discount margin is as follows:

Step 1. Determine the cash flows assuming that the reference rate does *not* change over the life of the security.

Step 2. Select a margin.

Step 3. Discount the cash flows found in Step 1 by the current value of the reference rate plus the margin selected in Step 2.

Step 4. Compare the present value of the cash flows as calculated in Step 3 to the price plus accrued interest. If the present value is equal to the security's price plus accrued interest, the discount margin is the margin assumed in Step 2. If the present value is not equal to the security's price plus accrued interest, go back to Step 2 and try a different margin.

For a security selling at par, the discount margin is simply the quoted margin in the coupon reset formula.

To illustrate the calculation, suppose that the coupon reset formula for a 6-year floating-rate security selling for $99.3098 is 6-month LIBOR plus 80 basis points. The coupon rate is reset every 6 months. Assume that the current value for the reference rate is 10%.

Exhibit 3 shows the calculation of the discount margin for this security. The second column shows the current value for 6-month LIBOR. The third column sets forth the cash flows for the security. The cash flow for the first 11 periods is equal to one-half the current 6-month LIBOR (5%) plus the semiannual quoted margin of 40 basis points multiplied by $100. At the maturity date (i.e., period 12), the cash flow is $5.4 plus the maturity value of $100. The top row of the last five columns shows the assumed margin. The rows below the assumed margin show the present value of each cash flow. The last row gives the total present value of the cash flows.

For the five assumed margins, the present value is equal to the price of the floating-rate security ($99.3098) when the assumed margin is 96 basis points. Therefore, the discount margin is 96 basis points. Notice that the discount margin is 80 basis points, the same as the quoted margin, when this security is selling at par.

Exhibit 3: Calculation of the Discount Margin for a Floating-Rate Security

Floating-rate security: Maturity = 6 years
Coupon formula = LIBOR + 80 basis points
Reset every 6 months

			Present value ($) at assumed margin of				
Period	LIBOR (%)	Cash flow ($)*	80 bp	84 bp	88 bp	96 bp	100 bp
1	10	5.4	5.1233	5.1224	5.1214	5.1195	5.1185
2	10	5.4	4.8609	4.8590	4.8572	4.8535	4.8516
3	10	5.4	4.6118	4.6092	4.6066	4.6013	4.5987
4	10	5.4	4.3755	4.3722	4.3689	4.3623	4.3590
5	10	5.4	4.1514	4.1474	4.1435	4.1356	4.1317
6	10	5.4	3.9387	3.9342	3.9297	3.9208	3.9163
7	10	5.4	3.7369	3.7319	3.7270	3.7171	3.7122
8	10	5.4	3.5454	3.5401	3.5347	3.5240	3.5186
9	10	5.4	3.3638	3.3580	3.3523	3.3409	3.3352
10	10	5.4	3.1914	3.1854	3.1794	3.1673	3.1613
11	10	5.4	3.0279	3.0216	3.0153	3.0028	2.9965
12	10	105.4	56.0729	55.9454	55.8182	55.5647	55.4385
		Present value	100.0000	99.8269	99.6541	99.3098	99.1381

* For periods 1–11: Cash flow = $100 (0.5) (LIBOR + Assumed margin)
For period 12: Cash flow = $100 (0.5) (LIBOR + Assumed margin) + $100

There are two drawbacks of the discount margin as a measure of the potential return from investing in a floating-rate security. First, the measure assumes that the reference rate will not change over the life of the security. Second, if the floating-rate security has a cap or floor, this is not taken into consideration.

THEORETICAL SPOT RATES

In Chapter 2, we explained the key role that theoretical spot rates play in valuation. Recall that a spot rate is a zero-coupon rate. The theoretical spot rates for Treasury securities represent the appropriate set of interest rates that should be used to value default-free cash flows.

A default-free theoretical spot rate curve can be constructed from the observed Treasury yield curve. Several approaches are used in practice. The approach that we describe as follows for creating a theoretical spot rate curve is called *bootstrapping*. To explain this approach, we use the price, annualized yield (yield to maturity), and maturity for the 20 hypothetical Treasury securities shown in Exhibit 4.

Throughout the analysis and illustrations to come, it is important to remember that the basic principle is that the value of the Treasury coupon security should be equal to the value of the package of zero-coupon Treasury securities that duplicates the coupon bond's cash flows.

Exhibit 4: Maturity and Yield to Maturity for 20 Hypothetical Treasury Securities

Period	Years	Yield to Maturity (%)	Price	Spot Rate (%)
1	0.5	3.00	—	3.0000
2	1.0	3.30	—	3.3000
3	1.5	3.50	100.00	3.5053
4	2.0	3.90	100.00	3.9164
5	2.5	4.40	100.00	4.4376
6	3.0	4.70	100.00	4.7520
7	3.5	4.90	100.00	4.9622
8	4.0	5.00	100.00	5.0650
9	4.5	5.10	100.00	5.1701
10	5.0	5.20	100.00	5.2772
11	5.5	5.30	100.00	5.3864
12	6.0	5.40	100.00	5.4976
13	6.5	5.50	100.00	5.6108
14	7.0	5.55	100.00	5.6643
15	7.5	5.60	100.00	5.7193
16	8.0	5.65	100.00	5.7755
17	8.5	5.70	100.00	5.8331
18	9.0	5.80	100.00	5.9584
19	9.5	5.90	100.00	6.0863
20	10.0	6.00	100.00	6.2169

Consider the 6-month and 1-year Treasury securities in Exhibit 4. As we explain in Chapter 4, these two securities are called Treasury bills and they are issued as zero-coupon instruments. Therefore, the annualized yield of 3.00% for the 6-month Treasury security is equal to the 6-month spot rate. Similarly, for the 1-year Treasury security, the cited yield of 3.30% is the 1-year spot rate. Given these two spot rates, we can compute the spot rate for a theoretical 1.5-year zero-coupon Treasury. The value of a theoretical 1.5-year Treasury should equal the present value of the three cash flows from the 1.5-year coupon Treasury, where the yield used for discounting is the spot rate corresponding to the time of the receipt of the cash flow. Since all the coupon bonds are selling at par, as explained in the previous section, the yield to maturity for each bond is the coupon rate. Using $100 as par, the cash flows for the 1.5-year coupon Treasury are:

0.5 year	0.035 × $100 × 0.5	= $1.75
1.0 year	0.035 × $100 × 0.5	= $1.75
1.5 years	0.035 × $100 × 0.5 + 100	= $101.75

The present value of the cash flows is then:

$$\frac{1.75}{(1+z_1)^1} + \frac{1.75}{(1+z_2)^2} + \frac{101.75}{(1+z_3)^3}$$

where

$$z_1 = \text{one-half the annualized 6-month theoretical spot rate}$$
$$z_2 = \text{one-half the 1-year theoretical spot rate}$$
$$z_3 = \text{one-half the 1.5-year theoretical spot rate}$$

Since the 6-month spot rate is 3% and the 1-year spot rate is 3.30%, we know that:

$$z_1 = 0.0150 \text{ and } z_2 = 0.0165$$

We can compute the present value of the 1.5-year coupon Treasury security as:

$$\frac{1.75}{(1+z_1)^1} + \frac{1.75}{(1+z_2)^2} + \frac{101.75}{(1+z_3)^3} = \frac{1.75}{(1.015)^1} + \frac{1.75}{(1.0165)^2} + \frac{101.75}{(1+z_3)^3}$$

Since the price of the 1.5-year coupon Treasury security is par, the following relationship must hold:

$$\frac{1.75}{(1.015)^1} + \frac{1.75}{(1.0165)^2} + \frac{101.75}{(1+z_3)^3} = 100$$

We can solve for the theoretical 1.5-year spot rate as follows:

$$1.7241 + 1.6936 + \frac{101.75}{(1+z_3)^3} = 100$$

$$\frac{101.75}{(1+z_3)^3} = 96.5822$$

$$(1+z_3)^3 = \frac{101.725}{96.5822}$$

$$z_3 = 0.0175265 = 1.75265\%$$

Doubling this yield, we obtain the bond-equivalent yield of 3.5053%, which is the theoretical 1.5-year spot rate. That rate is the rate that the market would apply to a 1.5-year zero-coupon Treasury security if, in fact, such a security existed.

Given the theoretical 1.5-year spot rate, we can obtain the theoretical 2-year spot rate. The cash flows for the 2-year coupon Treasury in Exhibit 4 are:

0.5 year	$0.039 \times \$100 \times 0.5$	=	\$1.95
1.0 year	$0.039 \times \$100 \times 0.5$	=	\$1.95
1.5 years	$0.039 \times \$100 \times 0.5$	=	\$1.95
2.0 years	$0.039 \times \$100 \times 0.5 + 100$	=	\$101.95

The present value of the cash flows is then:

$$\frac{1.95}{(1+z_1)^1} + \frac{1.95}{(1+z_2)^2} + \frac{1.95}{(1+z_3)^3} + \frac{101.95}{(1+z_4)^4}$$

where z_4 = one-half the 2-year theoretical spot rate.

Since the 6-month spot rate, 1-year spot rate, and 1.5-year spot rate are 3.00%, 3.30%, and 3.5053%, respectively, then:

$$z_1 = 0.0150 \quad z_2 = 0.0165 \quad z_3 = 0.017527$$

Therefore, the present value of the 2-year coupon Treasury security is:

$$\frac{1.95}{(1.0150)^1} + \frac{1.95}{(1.0165)^2} + \frac{1.95}{(1.017527)^3} + \frac{101.95}{(1+z_4)^4}$$

Since the price of the 2-year coupon Treasury security is par, the following relationship must hold:

$$\frac{1.95}{(1.0150)^1} + \frac{1.95}{(1.0165)^2} + \frac{1.95}{(1.017527)^3} + \frac{101.95}{(1+z_4)^4} = 100$$

We can solve for the theoretical 2-year spot rate as follows:

$$\frac{101.95}{(1+z_4)^4} = 94.3392$$

$$(1+z_4)^4 = \frac{101.95}{94.3392}$$

$$z_4 = 0.019582 = 1.9582\%$$

Doubling this yield, we obtain the theoretical 2-year spot rate bond-equivalent yield of 3.9164%.

One can follow this approach sequentially to derive the theoretical 2.5-year spot rate from the calculated values of z_1, z_2, z_3, and z_4 (the 6-month, 1-year, 1.5-year, and 2-year rates), and the price and coupon of the 2.5-year bond in Exhibit 4. Further, one could derive theoretical spot rates for the remaining 15 half-yearly rates.

The spot rates thus obtained are shown in the last column of Exhibit 4. They represent the term structure of default-free spot rate for maturities up to 10 years at the particular time to which the bond price quotations refer. In fact, the default-free spot rates shown in Exhibit 4 were used in the previous chapter in our illustrations.

YIELD SPREAD MEASURES

Traditional analysis of the yield spread for a non-Treasury bond involves calculating the difference between the bond's yield and the yield to maturity of a comparable-maturity Treasury coupon security. The latter is obtained from the Treasury yield curve. For example, consider the following 10-year bonds:

Issue	Coupon	Price	Yield to maturity
Treasury	6%	100.00	6.00%
Non-Treasury	8%	104.19	7.40%

The yield spread for these two bonds as traditionally computed is 140 basis points (7.4% minus 6%). We refer to this traditional yield spread as the *nominal spread*.

The drawbacks of the nominal spread measure are (1) for both bonds, the yield fails to take into consideration the term structure of the spot rates, and (2) in the case of callable and/or putable bonds, expected interest rate volatility may alter the cash flows of the non-Treasury bond. Let's focus on the first problem.

Zero-Volatility Spread

The *zero-volatility spread* or *Z-spread* is a measure of the spread that the investor would realize over the entire Treasury spot rate curve if the bond is held to maturity. It is not a spread off one point on the Treasury yield curve, as is the nominal spread. The Z-spread, also called the *static spread*, is calculated as the spread that will make the present value of the cash flows from the non-Treasury bond when discounted at the Treasury spot rate plus the spread equal to the non-Treasury bond's price. A trial-and-error procedure is required to determine the Z-spread.

To illustrate how this is done, let's use the non-Treasury bond in our previous illustration and the Treasury spot rate curve in Exhibit 4. The Treasury spot rates are reproduced in the fourth column of Exhibit 5. The third column in the exhibit shows the cash flows for the 8% 10-year non-Treasury issue. The goal is to determine the spread that, when added to all the Treasury spot rates, will produce a present value for the cash flows of the non-Treasury bond equal to its market price of $104.19.

Suppose we select a spread of 100 basis points. To each Treasury spot rate shown in the fourth column, 100 basis points is added. So, for example, the 5-year (period 10) spot rate is 6.2772% (5.2772% plus 1%). The spot rate plus 100 basis points is then used to calculate the present value of $107.5414. Because the present value is not equal to the non-Treasury issue's price ($104.19), the Z-spread is not 100 basis points. If a spread of 125 basis points is tried, it can be seen from the next-to-the-last column of Exhibit 5 that the present value is $105.7165; again, because this is not equal to the non-Treasury issue's price, 125 basis points is not the Z-spread. The last column of Exhibit 5 shows the present value when a 146 basis point spread is tried. The present value is equal to the non-Treasury issue's price. Therefore, 146 basis points is the Z-spread, compared to the nominal spread of 140 basis points.

Exhibit 5: Determination of the Z-Spread for an 8% 10-Year Non-Treasury Issue Selling at $104.19 to Yield 7.4%

		Cash	Spot	Present value ($) assuming a spread of		
Period	Years	flow ($)	rate (%)	100 bp	125 bp	146 bp
1	0.5	4.00	3.0000	3.9216	3.9168	3.9127
2	1.0	4.00	3.3000	3.8334	3.8240	3.8162
3	1.5	4.00	3.5053	3.7414	3.7277	3.7163
4	2.0	4.00	3.9164	3.6297	3.6121	3.5973
5	2.5	4.00	4.4376	3.4979	3.4767	3.4590
6	3.0	4.00	4.7520	3.3742	3.3497	3.3293
7	3.5	4.00	4.9622	3.2565	3.2290	3.2061
8	4.0	4.00	5.0650	3.1497	3.1193	3.0940
9	4.5	4.00	5.1701	3.0430	3.0100	2.9826
10	5.0	4.00	5.2772	2.9366	2.9013	2.8719
11	5.5	4.00	5.3864	2.8307	2.7933	2.7622
12	6.0	4.00	5.4976	2.7255	2.6862	2.6537
13	6.5	4.00	5.6108	2.6210	2.5801	2.5463
14	7.0	4.00	5.6643	2.5279	2.4855	2.4504
15	7.5	4.00	5.7193	2.4367	2.3929	2.3568
16	8.0	4.00	5.7755	2.3472	2.3023	2.2652
17	8.5	4.00	5.8331	2.2596	2.2137	2.1758
18	9.0	4.00	5.9584	2.1612	2.1148	2.0766
19	9.5	4.00	6.0863	2.0642	2.0174	1.9790
20	10.0	104.00	6.2169	51.1833	49.9638	48.9630
			Total	107.5414	105.7165	104.2145

Notice that the procedure for calculating the Z-spread is the same as for calculating the discount margin for a floating-rate security.

Typically, for standard coupon-paying bonds with a bullet maturity (i.e., a single payment of principal), the Z-spread and the nominal spread will not differ significantly. In our example it is only 6 basis points.

For short-term issues, there is little divergence. The main factor causing any difference is the shape of the spot rate curve. The steeper the spot rate curve, the greater the difference. To illustrate this concept, consider the two yield curves shown in Exhibit 6. The yield for the longest maturity of both spot rate curves is 6%. The first curve is steeper than the one used in Exhibit 5; the second curve is flat, with the yield for all maturities equal to 6%. It can be shown that for the first spot rate curve the Z-spread is 154. Thus, with this steeper spot rate curve, the difference between the Z-spread and the nominal spread is 14 basis points. For the flat curve the Z-spread is 140 basis points, the same as the nominal spread. This will always be the case.

The difference between the Z-spread and the nominal spread is greater for issues in which the principal is repaid over time rather than only at maturity. Thus the difference between the nominal spread and the Z-spread will be considerably greater for mortgage-backed securities and asset-backed securities in a steep yield curve environment.

Exhibit 6: Two Hypothetical Spot Rate Curves

Period	Years	Steep curve (%)	Flat curve (%)
1	0.5	2.00	6.00
2	1.0	2.40	6.00
3	1.5	2.80	6.00
4	2.0	2.90	6.00
5	2.5	3.00	6.00
6	3.0	3.10	6.00
7	3.5	3.30	6.00
8	4.0	3.80	6.00
9	4.5	3.90	6.00
10	5.0	4.20	6.00
11	5.5	4.40	6.00
12	6.0	4.50	6.00
13	6.5	4.60	6.00
14	7.0	4.70	6.00
15	7.5	4.90	6.00
16	8.0	5.00	6.00
17	8.5	5.30	6.00
18	9.0	5.70	6.00
19	9.5	5.80	6.00
20	10.0	6.00	6.00

Z-Spread Relative to Any Benchmark

In the same way that a Z-spread relative to a default-free spot rate curve can be calculated, a Z-spread to any benchmark spot rate curve can be calculated. To illustrate, suppose that a hypothetical non-Treasury security with a coupon rate of 8% and a 10-year maturity is trading at $105.5423. Assume that the benchmark spot rate curve for this issuer is the one given in Exhibit 5 of the previous chapter. The Z-spread relative to that issuer's benchmark spot rate curve is the spread that must be added to the spot rates shown in the next-to-last column of that exhibit that will make the present value of the cash flows equal to the market price. In our illustration, the Z-spread relative to this benchmark is 40 basis points.

Thus, when a Z-spread is cited, it must be cited relative to some benchmark spot rate curve. This is necessary because it indicates the credit and sector risks that are being considered when the Z-spread was calculated.

Option-Adjusted Spread

The Z-spread seeks to measure the spread over the spot rate curve. This overcomes the first problem of the traditional spread measure—the nominal spread—that we cited earlier. Now let's look at the second shortcoming—failure to take future interest rate volatility into account, which could change the cash flows.

What an investor seeks to do is to buy securities whose value is greater than their price. A valuation model allows an investor to estimate the value of a security, which at this point would be sufficient to determine the fairness of the

security's price. That is, the investor can say that a bond is 1 point cheap or 2 points cheap, and so on.

A valuation model need not stop here, however. Instead, it can convert the divergence between the market price for the security and the value derived from the model into a yield spread measure. This step is necessary since most market participants find it more convenient to think about yield spread than about price differences.

The *option-adjusted spread* (OAS) was developed as a measure of the yield spread that can be used to convert dollar differences between value and market price. Thus, basically, the OAS is used to reconcile value with market price. But what is it a "spread" over? The OAS is a spread over the issuer's spot rate curve or benchmark. The spot rate curve itself is not a single curve, but a series of spot rate curves that allow for changes in interest rates.

The resulting spread is referred to as "option-adjusted" because the cash flows of the security whose value we seek are adjusted to reflect the embedded option. In contrast, the Z-spread does not consider how the cash flows will change when interest rates change in the future. That is, the Z-spread assumes that interest rate volatility is zero. This is why the Z-spread is also referred to as the *zero-volatility OAS*.

Thus, the OAS is only as good as the valuation model.[3] In the case of the binomial model and Monte Carlo model, the OAS is the constant spread that when added to the interest rates on the possible interest rate paths that are used to value the security will produce the security's market price.

As we explained in the previous chapter, there are assumptions that underlie a valuation model. Consequently, these assumptions affect the calculated OAS. One critical assumption is interest rate volatility. Specifically, the higher the interest rate volatility assumed, the lower the OAS.

In comparing the OAS of dealer firms, it is critical to check on the volatility assumption made. Moreover, it is important to inquire as to the benchmark on-the-run yield curve used. Some dealers use the Treasury on-the-run issues. As a result, the OAS captures the credit spread. In contrast, some vendors and dealers use the issuer's on-the-run issue, which reflects the issuer's credit risk.

OAS for Floating-Rate Securities The OAS concept can also be used for floating-rate securities that have a restriction on the coupon rate (i.e., when there may be a cap and/or floor on the coupon rate). In fact, the OAS concept was initially developed to evaluate such securities. The spread is "option-adjusted" because the cash flows are altered along an interest rate path based on the restrictions on the coupon rate.

Option Cost The implied cost of the option embedded in any security can be obtained by calculating the difference between the OAS at the assumed volatility of interest rates and the Z-spread. That is,

---

[3] Valuation models are explained in the previous chapter.

Option cost = Z-spread – OAS

The reason that the option cost is measured in this way is as follows. In an environment in which interest rates are assumed not to change, the investor would earn the Z-spread. When future interest rates are uncertain, the spread is different because of the embedded option; the OAS reflects the spread after adjusting for this option. Therefore, the option cost is the difference between the spread that would be earned in a static interest rate environment (the Z-spread, or equivalently, the zero-volatility OAS) and the spread after adjusting for the option (the OAS).

For callable bonds and most mortgage-backed and asset-backed securities, the option cost is positive because the borrower's ability to alter the cash flows will result in an OAS that is less than the Z-spread. In the case of a putable bond, the OAS is greater than the Z-spread so that the option cost is negative. This occurs because of the investor's ability to alter the cash flows.

In general, when the option cost is positive, this means that the investor has sold an option to the issuer or borrower. This is true for callable bonds and most mortgage-backed and asset-backed securities. A negative value for the option cost means that the investor has purchased an option from the issuer or borrower. A putable bond is an example of this negative option cost. There are certain securities in the mortgage-backed securities market that also have an option cost that is negative.

Highlighting the Pitfalls of the Nominal Spread We can use the concepts presented in this chapter to highlight the pitfalls of the nominal spread. First, we can recast the relationship between the option cost, Z-spread, and OAS as follows:

Z-spread = OAS + Option cost

Next, recall that the nominal spread and the Z-spread may not diverge significantly. Suppose that the nominal spread is approximately equal to the Z-spread. Then, we can substitute nominal spread for Z-spread in the previous relationship, giving:

Nominal spread = OAS + Option cost

This relationship tells us that a high nominal spread could be hiding a high option cost (i.e., an investor is only compensated for the OAS). The option cost represents the portion of the spread that the investor has given to the issuer or borrower. Thus, while the nominal spread for a security that can be called or prepaid might be, say 200 basis points, the option cost may be 190 and the OAS only 10 basis points. An investor who relies on the nominal spread may not be adequately compensated for taking on the option risk associated with a security with an embedded option.

APPENDIX: FORWARD RATES

In the chapter, we saw how a default-free theoretical spot rate curve can be extrapolated from the Treasury yield curve. Additional information useful to market participants can be extrapolated from the Treasury yield curve: *forward rates*. Under certain assumptions, these rates can be viewed as the market's consensus of future interest rates.

Examples of forward rates that can be calculated from the Treasury yield curve are the:

- 6-month forward rate 6 months from now
- 6-month forward rate 3 years from now
- 1-year forward rate 1 year from now
- 3-year forward rate 2 years from now
- 5-year forward rates 3 years from now

Since the forward rates are extrapolated from the Treasury yield curve, these rates are sometimes referred to as *implicit forward rates*.

Deriving Six-Month Forward Rates

To illustrate the process of extrapolating 6-month forward rates, we will use the yield curve and corresponding spot rate curve from Exhibit 4 of this chapter.

Consider an investor who has a 1-year investment horizon and is faced with the following two alternatives:

- buy a 1-year Treasury bill, or
- buy a 6-month Treasury bill, and when it matures in 6 months buy another 6-month Treasury bill.

The investor will be indifferent toward the two alternatives if they produce the same return over the 1-year investment horizon. The investor knows the spot rate on the 6-month Treasury bill and the 1-year Treasury bill. However, he does not know what yield will be available on a 6-month Treasury bill that will be purchased 6 months from now. That is, he does not know the 6-month forward rate 6 months from now. Given the spot rates for the 6-month Treasury bill and the 1-year Treasury bill, the forward rate on a 6-month Treasury bill is the rate that equalizes the dollar return between the two alternatives.

To see how that rate can be determined, suppose that an investor purchased a 6-month Treasury bill for $X. At the end of 6 months, the value of this investment would be:

$$X(1 + z_1)$$

where z_1 is one-half the bond-equivalent yield (BEY) of the theoretical 6-month spot rate.

Exhibit A-1: Graphical Depiction of the 6-Month Forward Rate 6 Months from Now

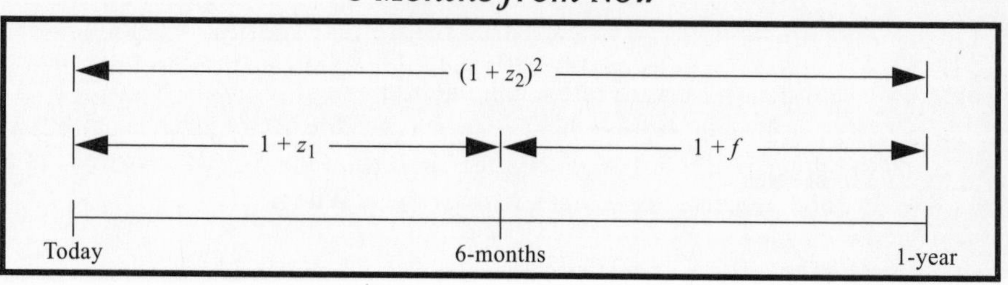

Let f represent one-half the forward rate (expressed as a BEY) on a 6-month Treasury bill available 6 months from now. If the investor were to rollover his investment by purchasing that bill at that time, then the future dollars available at the end of 1 year from the $\$X$ investment would be:

$$X(1 + z_1)(1 + f)$$

Now consider the alternative of investing in a 1-year Treasury bill. If we let z_2 represent one-half the BEY of the theoretical 1-year spot rate, then the future dollars available at the end of 1 year from the $\$X$ investment would be:

$$X(1 + z_2)^2$$

This is depicted in Exhibit A-1.

Now, we are prepared to analyze the investor's choices and what this says about forward rates. The investor will be indifferent toward the two alternatives confronting him if he makes the same dollar investment ($\$X$) and receives the same future dollars from both alternatives at the end of one year. That is, the investor will be indifferent if:

$$X(1 + z_1)(1 + f) = X(1 + z_2)^2$$

Solving for f, we get:

$$f = \frac{(1 + z_2)^2}{(1 + z_1)} - 1$$

Doubling f gives the BEY for the 6-month forward rate 6 months from now.

We can illustrate the use of this formula with the theoretical spot rates shown in Exhibit 4. From that exhibit, we know that:

6-month bill spot rate = 0.030, therefore $z_1 = 0.0150$
1-year bill spot rate = 0.033, therefore $z_2 = 0.0165$

Substituting into the formula, we have:

$$f = \frac{(1.0165)^2}{(1.0150)} - 1 = 0.0180 = 1.8\%$$

Therefore, the 6-month forward rate 6 months from now is 3.6% (1.8% × 2) BEY.

Let's confirm our results. If $X is invested in the 6-month Treasury bill at 1.5% and the proceeds then reinvested for 6 months at the 6-month forward rate of 1.8%, the total proceeds from this alternative would be:

$$X(1.015)(1.018) = 1.03327\,X$$

Investment of $X in the 1-year Treasury bill at one-half the 1-year rate, 1.0165%, would produce the following proceeds at the end of 1 year:

$$X(1.0165)^2 = 1.03327\,X$$

Both alternatives have the same payoff if the 6-month Treasury bill yield 6 months from now is 1.8% (3.6% on a BEY). This means that, if an investor is guaranteed a 1.8% yield (3.6% BEY) on a 6-month Treasury bill 6 months from now, he will be indifferent toward the two alternatives.

The same line of reasoning can be used to obtain the 6-month forward rate beginning at any time period in the future. For example, the following can be determined:

- the 6-month forward rate 3 years from now
- the 6-month forward rate 5 years from now

The notation that we use to indicate 6-month forward rates is ${}_1f_m$ where the subscript 1 indicates a one-period (6-month) rate and the subscript *m* indicates the period beginning *m* periods from now. When *m* is equal to zero, this means the current rate. Thus, the first 6-month forward rate is simply the current 6-month spot rate. That is, ${}_1f_0 = z_1$.

The general formula for determining a 6-month forward rate is:

$${}_1f_m = \frac{(1 + z_{m+1})^{m+1}}{(1 + z_m)^m} - 1$$

For example, suppose that the 6-month forward rate 4 years (eight 6-month periods) from now is sought. In terms of our notation, *m* is 8 and we seek ${}_1f_8$. The formula is then:

$${}_1f_8 = \frac{(1 + z_9)^9}{(1 + z_8)^8} - 1$$

Exhibit A-2: Six-Month Forward Rates: The Short-Term Forward Rate Curve

Notation	Forward Rate
${}_1f_0$	3.00
${}_1f_1$	3.60
${}_1f_2$	3.92
${}_1f_3$	5.15
${}_1f_4$	6.54
${}_1f_5$	6.33
${}_1f_6$	6.23
${}_1f_7$	5.79
${}_1f_8$	6.01
${}_1f_9$	6.24
${}_1f_{10}$	6.48
${}_1f_{11}$	6.72
${}_1f_{12}$	6.97
${}_1f_{13}$	6.36
${}_1f_{14}$	6.49
${}_1f_{15}$	6.62
${}_1f_{16}$	6.76
${}_1f_{17}$	8.10
${}_1f_{18}$	8.40
${}_1f_{19}$	8.72

From Exhibit 4, since the 4-year spot rate is 5.065% and the 4.5-year spot rate is 5.1701%, z_8 is 2.5325% and z_9 is 2.58505%. Then,

$$ {}_1f_8 = \frac{(1.0258505)^9}{(1.025325)^8} - 1 = 3.005\% $$

Doubling this rate gives a 6-month forward rate 4 years from now of 6.01%

Exhibit A-2 shows all of the 6-month forward rates for the Treasury yield curve and corresponding spot rate curve shown in Exhibit 4. The set of these forward rates is called the *short-term forward-rate curve.*

Relationship between Spot Rates and Short-Term Forward Rates

Suppose an investor invests $X in a 3-year zero-coupon Treasury security. The total proceeds 3 years (six periods) from now would be:

$$ X(1 + z_6)^6 $$

The investor could instead buy a 6-month Treasury bill and reinvest the proceeds every 6 months for 3 years. The future dollars or dollar return will depend on the 6-month forward rates. Suppose that the investor can actually reinvest the proceeds maturing every 6 months at the calculated 6-month forward

rates shown in Exhibit A-2. At the end of 3 years, an investment of \$$X$ would generate the following proceeds:

$$X(1 + z_1)(1 + {}_1f_1)(1 + {}_1f_2)(1 + {}_1f_3)(1 + {}_1f_4)(1 + {}_1f_5)$$

Since the two investments must generate the same proceeds at the end of 4 years, the two previous equations can be equated:

$$X(1 + z_6)^6 = X(1 + z_1)(1 + {}_1f_1)(1 + {}_1f_2)(1 + {}_1f_3)(1 + {}_1f_4)(1 + {}_1f_5)$$

Solving for the 3-year (6-period) spot rate, we have:

$$z_6 = [(1 + z_1)(1 + {}_1f_1)(1 + {}_1f_2)(1 + {}_1f_3)(1 + {}_1f_4)(1 + {}_1f_5)]^{1/6} - 1$$

This equation tells us that the 3-year spot rate depends on the current 6-month spot rate and the five 6-month forward rates. In fact, the right-hand side of this equation is a geometric average of the current 6-month spot rate and the five 6-month forward rates.

Let's use the values in Exhibits 4 and A-2 to confirm this result. Since the 6-month spot rate in Exhibit 4 is 3%, z_1 is 1.5%, and therefore

$$\begin{aligned} z_6 &= [(1.015)(1.018)(1.0196)(1.02575)(1.0327)(1.03165)]^{1/6} - 1 \\ &= 0.023761 = 2.3761\% \end{aligned}$$

Doubling this rate gives 4.7522%. This agrees with the spot rate shown in Exhibit 4.

In general, the relationship between a T-period spot rate, the current 6-month spot rate, and the 6-month forward rates is as follows:

$$z_T = [(1 + z_1)(1 + {}_1f_1)(1 + {}_1f_2)\ldots(1 + {}_1f_{T-1})]^{1/T} - 1$$

Therefore, discounting at the forward rates will give the same present value as discounting at spot rates. This means that calculating the Z-spread over the Treasury spot rate curve is the same as calculating the Z-spread over the Treasury forward rate curve.

KEY POINTS

- *The sources of return from holding a bond to maturity are the coupon interest payments, any capital gain or loss, and reinvestment income.*

- *Reinvestment income is the interest income generated by reinvesting coupon interest payments and any principal repayments from the time of receipt to the bond's maturity.*

- *The current yield relates the annual dollar coupon interest to the market price and fails to recognize any capital gain or loss and reinvestment income.*

- *The yield to maturity is the interest rate that will make the present value of the cash flows from a bond equal to the price plus accrued interest.*

- *The market convention to annualize a semiannual yield is to double it, and the resulting annual yield is referred to as a bond-equivalent yield.*

- *The yield to maturity takes into account all three sources of return but assumes that the coupon payments and any principal repayments can be reinvested at an interest rate equal to the yield to maturity.*

- *The yield to maturity will only be realized if the interim cash flows can be reinvested at the yield to maturity and the bond is held to maturity.*

- *The risk an investor faces that future reinvestment rates will be less than the yield to maturity at the time a bond is purchased is called reinvestment risk.*

- *Price or interest rate risk is the risk that if a bond is not held to maturity, an investor may have to sell it for less than the purchase price.*

- *The longer the maturity and the higher the coupon rate, the more a bond's return is dependent on reinvestment income to realize the yield to maturity at the time of purchase.*

- *The yield to call is the interest rate that will make the present value of the expected cash flows to the assumed call date equal to the price plus accrued interest.*

- *Yield measures for callable bonds include yield to first call, yield to next call, yield to first par call, and yield to refunding.*

- *The yield to call does consider all three sources of potential return but assumes that all cash flows can be reinvested at the yield to call until the assumed call date, the investor will hold the bond to the assumed call date, and the issuer will call the bond on the assumed call date.*

- *The yield to worst is the lowest yield from among all possible yield to calls, yield to puts, and the yield to maturity.*

- *For mortgage-backed and asset-backed securities, the cash flow yield based on some prepayment rate is the interest rate that equates the present value of the projected principal and interest payments to the price plus accrued interest.*

- ❑ *The cash flow yield assumes that all cash flows (principal payments and interest payments) can be reinvested at the calculated yield and that the prepayment rate will be realized over the security's life.*
- ❑ *For floating-rate securities, instead of a yield measure, margin measures (i.e., spread above the reference rate) are computed.*
- ❑ *Two margin measures commonly used are spread for life and discount margin.*
- ❑ *The discount margin assumes that the reference rate will not change over the life of the security and that there is no cap or floor restriction on the coupon rate.*
- ❑ *The theoretical spot rate is the interest rate that should be used to discount a default-free cash flow.*
- ❑ *Default-free spot rates can be derived from the Treasury yield curve by a method called bootstrapping.*
- ❑ *The basic principle underlying the bootstrapping method is that the value of a Treasury coupon security should be equal to the value of the package of zero-coupon Treasury securities that duplicates the coupon bond's cash flows.*
- ❑ *The nominal spread is the difference between the yield for a non-Treasury bond and a comparable-maturity Treasury coupon security.*
- ❑ *The nominal spread fails to consider the term structure of the spot rates and the fact that for bonds with embedded options future interest rate volatility may alter the cash flows.*
- ❑ *The zero-volatility spread or Z-spread is a measure of the spread that the investor would realize over the entire Treasury spot rate curve if the bond is held to maturity, thereby recognizing the term structure of interest rates.*
- ❑ *Unlike the nominal spread, the Z-spread is not a spread off one point on the Treasury yield curve but is a spread over the entire spot rate curve.*
- ❑ *For bullet bonds, unless the yield curve is very steep, the nominal spread will not differ significantly from the Z-spread; for securities where principal is repaid over time rather than just at maturity, there can be a significant difference, particularly in a steep yield curve environment.*
- ❑ *The option-adjusted spread (OAS) converts the cheapness or richness of a bond into a spread over the future possible spot rate curves.*
- ❑ *An OAS is said to be option adjusted because it allows for future interest rate volatility to affect the cash flows.*
- ❑ *The OAS is a product of a valuation model, and when comparing the OAS of dealer firms, it is critical to check on the volatility assumption employed in the valuation model.*

- *The cost of the embedded option is measured as the difference between the Z-spread and the OAS.*

- *Investors should not rely on the nominal spread for bonds with embedded options since it hides how the spread is split between the OAS and the option cost.*

Chapter 4

U.S. Treasury Securities

Treasury securities are issued by the U.S. Department of the Treasury and are backed by the full faith and credit of the U.S. government. Market participants view Treasury securities as having no credit risk. Consequently, interest rates on Treasury securities are the benchmark interest rates throughout the U.S. economy as well as in international capital markets. Interest income from Treasury securities is subject to federal income taxes but is exempt from state and local income taxes.

TYPES OF TREASURY SECURITIES

There are two types of Treasury securities (or "Treasuries"): discount and coupon securities. Treasury coupon securities come in two forms: fixed-rate and variable-rate securities.[1]

Treasury Bills

There are Treasury securities that are issued at a discount to par value, have no coupon rate, and mature at par value. The current practice of the Department of the Treasury is to issue all securities with a maturity of 1 year or less as discount securities. These securities are called *Treasury bills* and are issued on a regular basis with initial maturities of 4 weeks, 13 weeks, and 26 weeks.[2] The latter two bills are more popularly referred to as the 3-month and 6-month Treasury bills, respectively. Because of holidays, at issuance the number of days to maturity for a 4-week, 3-month, and 6-month Treasury bill will differ based on the number of holidays in the period. For example, a 3-month Treasury bill can have 90 or 91 days to maturity.

At irregular intervals the Treasury also issues *cash management bills* with maturities ranging from a few days to about 6 months. They are occasionally

---

[1] The Department of the Treasury also issues State and Local Government Series (SLGS) securities. These securities are only offered for sale to issuers of state and local government tax-exempt debt. Their purpose is to assist these issuers in complying with yield restriction or arbitrage rebate provisions of the Internal Revenue Code. Basically, these securities are deposit-type securities. The state and local government may invest in either a time deposit or demand deposit. The interest rate offered on the time deposit securities is 5 basis points below the current estimated Treasury borrowing rate for a security of comparable maturity. The interest rate on SLGS demand deposit securities is based on an adjustment of the average yield in the most recent auction of the 13-week Treasury bills.

[2] The 4-week Treasury bills are reopenings of existing 13- and 26-week bills. The 13-week Treasury bills are reopenings of existing 26-week Treasury bills.

issued a few days or weeks before a large tax payment is due in March, April, June, and September to tide the Treasury over a brief period of cash shortfall.

As discount securities, Treasury bills do not pay coupon interest. Instead, Treasury bills are issued at a discount from their maturity value; the return to the investor is the difference between the maturity value and the purchase price. The minimum face value for a Treasury bill is $1,000 and sold in multiples of $1,000.

Fixed-Rate Treasury Notes and Bonds

All Treasury securities with initial maturities of 2 years or more are issued as coupon securities. Coupon securities are issued at approximately par and mature at par value. Treasury coupon securities issued with original maturities of more than 2 years and no more than 10 years are called *Treasury notes*. Treasury coupon securities with original maturities greater than 10 years are called *Treasury bonds*.

Treasury coupon securities are currently auctioned on a regular basis with initial maturities of 2 years, 5 years, 10 years, and 30 years. On quote sheets, an "n" is used to denote a Treasury note. No notation typically follows an issue to identify it as a bond.

None of the currently issued Treasury coupon securities is callable. The 30-year bonds issued through November 1984 were callable, but issues since then all have been noncallable. Outstanding callable Treasury bonds are callable 5 years prior to their maturity date and identified by two dates: when the bond is first callable and the maturity date. The call price is par value. There are currently only 16 callable Treasury bond issues outstanding.

Auction Process

Treasury securities are all issued on an auction basis. For coupon securities, there are monthly 2-year note and 5-year note auctions and quarterly auctions for the 10-year note and 30-year bond (the "refunding" auction). Occasionally an outstanding issue is "reopened" (i.e., the amount of an outstanding note is increased) at an auction instead of a new issue auctioned. In recent years, the Department of the Treasury has reopened the 10-year note several times. Starting in 1999, the U.S. Treasury has reduced its issuance of Treasury bonds and has pursued a program of buying back outstanding bond issues.

The auction for Treasury securities is conducted on a competitive bid basis. There are actually two types of bids that may be submitted: noncompetitive bid and competitive bid. A noncompetitive bid is submitted by an entity that is willing to purchase the auctioned security at the yield that is determined by the auction process. Typically, individual investors purchase Treasury securities at the auction by submitting noncompetitive bids, as do smaller institutional investors. All noncompetitive bids from the public up to $1 million for bills and $5 million for coupon securities are accepted. When a noncompetitive bid is submitted, the bidder only specifies the quantity sought. A competitive bid specifies both the quantity sought and the yield at which the bidder is willing to purchase the auctioned security.

The auction results are determined by first deducting the total noncompetitive tenders and nonpublic purchases (such as purchases by the Federal Reserve itself) from the total securities being auctioned. The remainder is the amount to be awarded to the competitive bidders. The bids are then arranged from the lowest yield bid to the highest yield bid. (This is equivalent to arranging the bids from the highest price to the lowest price.) Starting from the lowest yield bid, all competitive bids are accepted until the amount to be distributed to the competitive bidders is completely allocated. The highest yield accepted by the Treasury is referred to as the *stop yield*, and bidders at that yield are awarded a percentage of their total tender offer. Bidders higher in yield than the stop yield are not distributed any of the new issue.

All U.S. Treasury auctions are single-price auctions. In a single-price auction, all bidders are awarded securities at the highest yield of accepted competitive tenders (i.e., the stop yield). This type of auction is called a "Dutch auction."

Competitive bids must typically be submitted by 1:00 p.m. eastern time on the day of the auction. Noncompetitive bids must typically be submitted by noon on the day of the auction. The results of the auction are announced within an hour following the 1:00 p.m. auction deadline. When the results of the auction are announced, the Treasury provides the following information: the stop-out yield, the associated price, and the proportion of securities awarded to those investors who bid exactly the stop-out yield, the quantity of noncompetitive tenders, the median-yield bid, and the bid-to-cover ratio. The bid-to-cover ratio is the total par amount of competitive and noncompetitive bids by the public divided by the total par amount of the securities awarded to the public. Some market observers consider this ratio to be an indicator of the bidding interest and, consequently, some barometer of the success of the auction.

Buybacks

In January 2000, the Treasury Department began a program of redeeming outstanding unmatured Treasury securities by purchasing them in the secondary market through reverse auctions. This is referred to as the Treasury's buyback program. The Treasury typically announces the buyback of an outstanding issue on the third and fourth Wednesdays of each month. The reverse auction is conducted the next day.

Price Quotes

Treasury coupon securities are quoted on a dollar price basis in price units of $\frac{1}{32}$ of 1% of par (par is taken to be \$100). For example, a quote of 92-14 refers to a price of 92 and $\frac{14}{32}$. On the basis of \$100,000 par value, a change in price of 1% equates to \$1,000, and $\frac{1}{32}$ of 1% equates to \$31.25. A plus sign following the number of 32nds means that $\frac{1}{64}$ is added to the price. For example, 92-14+ refers to a price of 92 and $\frac{29}{32}$ or 92.453125% of par value.

Secondary Market

The secondary market for Treasury securities is an over-the-counter market where a group of U.S. government securities dealers offer continuous bid and ask prices on issues. There is virtual 24-hour trading of securities. The three primary trading locations are New York, London, and Tokyo. The normal settlement period for Treasury securities is the business day after the transaction day ("next-day" settlement).

On-the-Run and Off-the-Run Issues The most recently auctioned issue is referred to as the *on-the-run issue* or the *current issue*. For example, in May 1999, the on-the-run 30-year Treasury issue was the 5.25s of 2/15/2029. Securities that are replaced by the on-the-run issue are called *off-the-run issues*. For example, prior to the issuance of the 5.25s of 2/15/2029, the on-the-run 30-year Treasury issue was the 5.25s of 11/15/2028 and in May 1999 became an off-the run issue. At a given point in time there may be more than one off-the-run issue with approximately the same remaining maturity as the on-the-run issue. Issues that have been replaced by several on-the-run issues are said to be "well off-the-run issues." For example, in May 1999, the 30-year 6.5% coupon issued in November 1996 and due in May 2026 was a well off-the-run issue.

Primary Dealers Any firm can deal in government securities, but in implementing its open market operations, the Federal Reserve will deal directly only with dealers that it designates as *primary dealers* or *recognized dealers*. Basically, the Federal Reserve wants to be sure that firms requesting status as primary dealers have adequate capital relative to positions assumed in Treasury securities and do a reasonable amount of volume in Treasury securities. Primary dealers include diversified and specialized securities firms, money center banks, and foreign-owned financial entities.

Interdealer Brokers Treasury dealers trade with the investing public and with other dealer firms. When they trade with each other, it is through intermediaries known as *interdealer brokers*. The following interdealer brokers handle the bulk of daily trading volume: BrokerTec, eSpeed, Garban-Intercapital, Hilliard Farber, and Tullett & Tokyo Liberty.

Dealers use interdealer brokers because of the speed and efficiency with which trades can be accomplished. They keep the names of the dealers involved in trades confidential. The quotes provided on the government dealer screens represent prices in the "inside" or "interdealer" market. Historically, primary dealers have resisted attempts to allow the general public to have access to them. However, as a result of government pressure, GovPX Inc. was formed to provide greater public disclosure. GovPX is a joint venture of five of the six interdealer brokers and the primary dealers in which information on best bids and offers, size, and trade price are distributed via Bloomberg, Reuters, and Knight-Ridder. In addition, some dealers have developed an electronic trading system that allows

trading between them and investors via Bloomberg. One example is Deutsche Morgan Grenfell's AutoBond System.

When-Issued Securities Treasury securities are traded prior to the time they are issued. This component of the Treasury secondary market is called the *when-issued market*, or *wi market*. When-issued trading for both bills and coupon securities extends from the day the auction is announced until the issue day.

Inflation-Protected Treasury Notes and Bonds

The U.S. Department of the Treasury issues notes and bonds that adjust for inflation. These securities are popularly referred to as *Treasury inflation protection securities* (TIPS) or *Treasury inflation indexed securities* (TIIS). First issued in January 1997, TIPS work as follows. The coupon rate on an issue is set at a fixed rate. That rate is determined via the auction process described earlier. The coupon rate is called the "real rate," since it is the rate that the investor ultimately earns above the inflation rate. The inflation index that the government has decided to use for the inflation adjustment is the nonseasonally adjusted U.S. City Average All Items Consumer Price Index for All Urban Consumers (CPI-U).

The adjustment for inflation is as follows. The principal that the Treasury Department will base both the dollar amount of the coupon payment and the maturity value on is adjusted semiannually. This is called the *inflation-adjusted principal*. For example, suppose that the coupon rate for a TIPS is 3.5% and the annual inflation rate is 3%. Suppose further that an investor purchases on January 1 $100,000 of par value (principal) of this issue. The semiannual inflation rate is 1.5% (3% divided by 2). The inflation-adjusted principal at the end of the first 6-month period is found by multiplying the original par value by the semiannual inflation rate. In our example, the inflation-adjusted principal at the end of the first 6-month period is $101,500. This inflation-adjusted principal is the basis for computing the coupon interest for the first 6-month period. The coupon payment is then 1.75% (one-half the real rate of 3.5%) multiplied by the inflation-adjusted principal at the coupon payment date ($101,500). The coupon payment is therefore $1,776.25

Let's look at the next 6 months. The inflation-adjusted principal at the beginning of the period is $101,500. Suppose that the semiannual inflation rate for the second 6-month period is 1%. Then the inflation-adjusted principal at the end of the second 6-month period is the inflation-adjusted principal at the beginning of the 6-month period ($101,500) increased by the semiannual inflation rate (1%). The adjustment to the principal is $1,015 (1% times $101,500). So, the inflation-adjusted principal at the end of the second 6-month period (December 31 in our example) is $102,515 ($101,500 + $1,015). The coupon interest that will be paid to the investor at the second coupon payment date is found by multiplying the inflation-adjusted principal on the coupon payment date ($102,515) by one-half the real rate (i.e., one-half of 3.5%). That is, the coupon payment will be $1,794.01.

As can be seen, part of the adjustment for inflation comes in the coupon payment since it is based on the inflation-adjusted principal. However, the U.S. government has decided to tax the adjustment each year. This feature reduces the attractiveness of TIPS as investments in accounts of tax-paying entities.

Because of the possibility of disinflation (i.e., price declines), the inflation-adjusted principal at maturity may turn out to be less than the initial par value. However, the Treasury has structured TIPS so that they are redeemed at the greater of the inflation-adjusted principal and the initial par value.

An inflation-adjusted principal must be calculated for a settlement date. The inflation-adjusted principal is defined in terms of an index ratio, which is the ratio of the reference CPI for the settlement date to the reference CPI for the issue date. The reference CPI is calculated with a 3-month lag. For example, the reference CPI for May 1 is the CPI-U reported in February. The U.S. Department of the Treasury publishes and makes available on its Web site (www.publicdebt.treas.gov) a daily index ratio for an issue.

YIELD CALCULATIONS

In Chapter 3, we explained how the yield on a coupon security is calculated and introduced some of the market conventions for calculating yield. Here we look at how yields are calculated for Treasury securities. There are different yield calculations for discount and coupon securities.

Treasury Bill Yield Calculations

As discount securities, Treasury bills do not pay coupon interest. Instead, Treasury bills are issued at a discount from their maturity value; the return to the investor is the difference between the maturity value and the purchase price. Treasury bills pay interest based on a 360-day basis.

Yield on a Bank Discount Basis

The convention in the Treasury bill market is to calculate a Treasury bill's *yield on a discount basis*. This yield is determined by three variables:

1. the settlement price (denoted by P)
2. the maturity value (denoted by M)
3. the number of days to maturity, which is calculated as the number of days between the settlement date and the maturity date (denoted by N)

The yield on a discount basis (denoted by d) is calculated as follows:

$$d = \frac{M - P}{M} \times \frac{360}{N}$$

As an example, a Treasury bill with 100 days (N) to maturity, a maturity value of $100,000 ($M$), and a settlement price of $98,500 ($P$) would be quoted at 5.40% on a discount basis:

$$d = \frac{\$100{,}000 - \$98{,}500}{\$100{,}000} \times \frac{360}{100} = 5.40\%$$

The price of a Treasury bill can be calculated given the yield on a discount basis, the maturity value, and number of days from settlement to maturity. The price is calculated using the following formula:

$$P = M - (d \times M \times N/360)$$

For example, the price of an 80-day Treasury bill with a maturity value of $100,000 that is quoted at 5% on a discount basis is:

$$P = \$100{,}000 - (0.05 \times \$100{,}000 \times 80/360) = \$98{,}888.89$$

The quoted yield on a discount basis is not a meaningful measure of the return from holding a Treasury bill for two reasons. First, the measure is based on a maturity value investment rather than on the actual dollar amount invested. Second, the yield is annualized according to a 360-day year rather than a 365-day year, making it difficult to compare yields on Treasury bills with Treasury notes and bonds, which pay interest on a 365-day basis. The use of 360 days for a year is a convention for money market instruments, however. Despite its shortcomings as a measure of return, this is the method dealers have adopted to quote Treasury bills.

Annualized Percentage Rate

The yield on a discount basis can be converted to a 365-day basis and related to the settlement price rather than the maturity value. The calculated measure is called the *annualized percentage rate* (denoted by APR) and is found as follows:

$$APR = \frac{365d}{360 - (N \times d)}$$

For example, for the hypothetical 100-day Treasury bill with a maturity value of $100,000, a settlement price of $98,500, and offering a yield on a discount basis of 5.40%, the APR is:

$$APR = \frac{365(0.054)}{360 - (100 \times 0.0540)}$$

Bond-Equivalent Yield

The APR can also be expressed in terms of a bond-equivalent yield (explained in Chapter 3) to provide a benchmark comparison to reward measures of other Treasury

securities. A key difference between bills and coupon securities is that the latter pay interest semiannually, thereby allowing for the compounding of interest. Bills, however, do not pay interest until maturity and therefore do not offer the opportunity to reinvest coupon payments. Restating the yield on a discount basis requires a downward adjustment of the APR to reflect the absence of a reinvestment opportunity.

A downward adjustment is only necessary for bills with terms-to-maturity greater than 6 months. Bills with terms-to-maturity less than or equal to 6 months offer the same compounding opportunity as coupon securities. Thus, the bond-equivalent yield of a Treasury bill with a term-to-maturity less than or equal to 6 months is equal to the annual percentage rate. That is, denoting the bond-equivalent yield by BEY, then

$$APR = BEY \quad \text{if the term-to-maturity is less than 6 months}$$

Bills with terms-to-maturity greater than 6 months, however, entail the opportunity cost of foregoing reinvestment of any interest payments. Letting DY be the number of days in a year (either 365 or 366), then the bond-equivalent yield for such Treasury bills is:

$$BEY = \frac{\frac{-N}{DY} + \sqrt{\left(\frac{N}{DY}\right)^2 + 4\left(\frac{N}{DY} - 0.25\right)\left(\frac{M-P}{P}\right)}}{(N/DY) - 0.5}$$

For example, for a Treasury bill with 300 days from settlement to maturity (N) with a settlement price of \$94,800 (P) and a maturity value of \$100,000 (M), assuming 365 days in a year (DY) the BEY is:

$$BEY = \frac{\frac{-300}{365} + \sqrt{\left(\frac{300}{365}\right)^2 + 4\left(\frac{300}{365} - 0.25\right)\left(\frac{100,000 - 94,800}{94,800}\right)}}{(300/365) - 0.5}$$

$$= 6.59\%$$

The APR for this 300-day Treasury bill is 6.67%, 8 basis points greater.

The table below compares the yield on a discount basis, APR, and BEY for several bills purchased at some assumed price and assuming a 365-day year and a maturity value of \$100:

Price per \$100 maturity value	\$93.6	\$94.8	\$96.4	\$97.1	\$97.3
Maturity (days)	364	300	210	187	182
Yield on a discount basis	6.33%	6.24%	6.17%	5.58%	5.34%
Annualized percentage rate	6.86%	6.67%	6.49%	5.83%	5.57%
Bond-equivalent yield	6.74%	6.59%	6.46%	5.83%	5.57%

Notice the downward adjustment in the BEY relative to the APR the longer the maturity of the bill. For a bill with 182 days to maturity, the APR is equal to the BEY.

CD-Equivalent Yield

Dealer quote sheets and reporting services sometimes provide another yield measure that attempts to make the quoted yield comparable to that for other money market instruments. The *CD-equivalent yield* (also called the *money market equivalent yield*) makes the quoted yield on a bill more comparable to yield quotations on other money market instruments that pay interest on a 360-day basis. It does this by taking into consideration the price of the bill rather than its maturity value. The formula for the CD-equivalent yield is:

$$\text{CD-equivalent yield} = \frac{360d}{360 - (N \times d)}$$

As an illustration, consider once again the hypothetical 100-day bill with a face value of \$100,000, selling for \$98,500, and offering a yield on a discount basis of 5.40%. Then

$$\text{CD-equivalent yield} = \frac{360(0.0540)}{360 - (100 \times 0.0540)} = 0.0548 = 5.48\%$$

Treasury Coupon Security Yield Calculations

Treasury coupon securities are calculated in a different manner than Treasury bills. They trade on a dollar price basis in price units of $\frac{1}{32}$ of 1% of par (par is taken to be \$100). For example, a quote of 92-14 refers to a price of 92 and $\frac{14}{32}$. On the basis of \$100,000 par value, a change in price of 1% equates to \$1,000, and $\frac{1}{32}$ equates to \$31.25. A plus sign following the number of 32nds means that a 64th is added to the price. For example, 92-14+ refers to a price of 92 and $\frac{29}{64}$ or 92.453125% of par value.

On quote sheets and screens, the price quote is followed by some "yield to maturity" measure. Yield quotes can be based on the *Street method* or the *Treasury method*. The difference between the two yield measures is the procedure used to discount the first coupon payment when it is not exactly 6 months away.[3] From a practical point of view, once a security is issued and traded in the secondary market, investors and traders use the Street method.

---

[3] The Treasury method (also called the "Fed" method) assumes simple interest over the period from the value date to the next coupon payment. The Street method (also called the Securities Industry Association or "SIA" method) assumes compound interest over the period from the value date to the next coupon payment. For example, suppose that the next coupon payment is X days from the value date (or previous coupon date), and W is the number of days between the issuance date (or previous coupon date) and the first coupon date (or next coupon date). Letting K denote the ratio of X to W, the discounting of a coupon payment, $C/2$, for a semiannual yield to maturity, y, is simple interest over the period for the Treasury method computed as follows $(C/2)/(1+Ky)$. For the Street method, compound interest over the period is used. That is, the first coupon payment is calculated using the following formula: $(C/2)/(1+y)^K$.

Exhibit 1: Three Observed Shapes for the Yield Curve

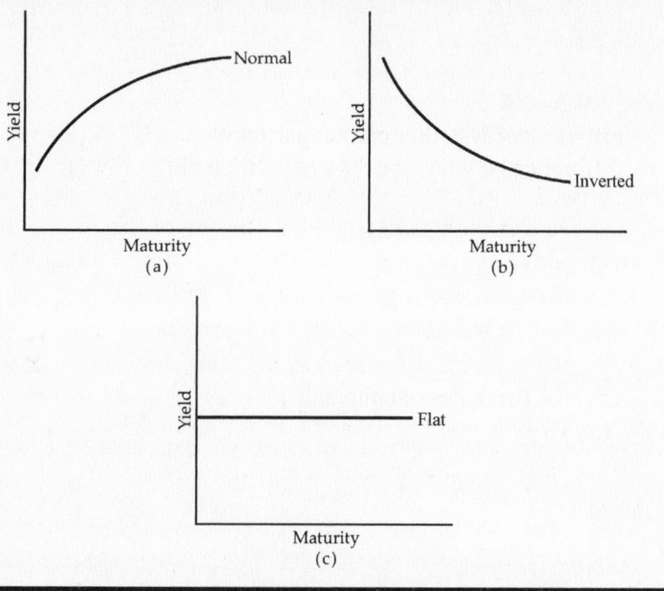

YIELDS ON TREASURY SECURITIES

As explained in Chapter 2, historically the yields offered on Treasury securities represent the base interest rate or minimum interest rate that investors demand if they purchased a non-Treasury security. Therefore, market participants continuously monitor the yields on Treasury securities, particularly the yields on the on-the-run issues.

Term Structure of Interest Rates

Treasuries of different maturities trade at different yield levels. The relationship between the yield on Treasury securities and maturity is called the *term structure of interest rates*. The graphical depiction of this relationship is called the *yield curve*.

Historically, three shapes have been observed for the yield curve. Exhibit 1 shows these three shapes. The most common relationship is a yield curve in which the longer the maturity, the greater the yield. That is, investors are rewarded for holding longer-maturity Treasuries in the form of a higher potential yield. This shape is referred to as a *normal yield curve* or *positively sloped yield curve*. A *flat yield curve* is one in which the yield for all maturities is approximately equal. There have been times when the relationship between maturities and yields were such that the longer the maturity, the lower the yield. Such a downward sloping yield curve is referred to as an *inverted yield curve* or a *negatively sloped yield curve*.

Market participants talk about the difference between long-term Treasury yields and short-term Treasury yields. The spread between these yields for two

maturities is referred to as the *steepness of the yield curve* or *slope of the yield curve*. There is no industrywide accepted definition of the maturity used for the long-end and the maturity for the short-end of the yield curve. Some market participants define the slope of the yield curve as the difference between the 30-year yield and the 3-month yield (i.e., the difference between the longest and shortest Treasury securities issued). Other market participants define the slope of the yield curve as the difference between the 30-year yield and the 2-year yield.

Yield Curve Shifts

A *shift in the yield curve* refers to the relative change in the yield for each Treasury maturity. A *parallel shift in the yield curve* refers to a shift in which the change in the yield for all maturities is the same. A *nonparallel shift in the yield curve* means that the yield for all maturities does not change by the same number of basis points.

Historically, two types of nonparallel yield curve shifts have been observed: a *twist in the slope of the yield curve* and a *change in the humpedness of the yield curve*. All of these shifts are graphically portrayed in Exhibit 2. A twist in the slope of the yield curve refers to a flattening or steepening of the yield curve. A *flattening of the yield curve* means that the slope of the yield curve (i.e., the spread between the yield on a long-term and short-term Treasury) has decreased; a *steepening of the yield curve* means that the slope of the yield curve has increased. The other type of nonparallel shift, a change in the humpedness of the yield curve, is referred to as a *butterfly shift*.

Frank Jones analyzed the types of yield curve shifts that occurred between 1979 and 1990.[4] He found that the three types of yield curve shifts are not independent, with the two most common types of yield curve shifts being (1) a downward shift in the yield curve combined with a steepening of the yield curve and (2) an upward shift in the yield curve combined with a flattening of the yield curve. These two types of shifts in the yield curve are depicted in Exhibit 3. For example, his statistical analysis indicated that an upward parallel shift in the Treasury yield curve and a flattening of the yield curve have a correlation of 0.41. This suggests that an upward shift of the yield curve by 10 basis points is consistent with a 2.5 basis point flattening of the yield curve. Moreover, he finds that an upward shift and flattening of the yield curve is correlated with a positive butterfly (less humpedness), whereas a downward shift and steepening of the yield curve is correlated with a negative butterfly (more humpedness).

STRIPPED TREASURY SECURITIES

The Treasury does not issue zero-coupon notes or bonds. However, because of the demand for zero-coupon instruments with no credit risk and a maturity greater than 1 year, the private sector has created such securities.

---

[4] Frank J. Jones, "Yield Curve Strategies," *Journal of Fixed Income* (September 1991), pp. 43–41.

Exhibit 2: Types of Yield Curve Shifts

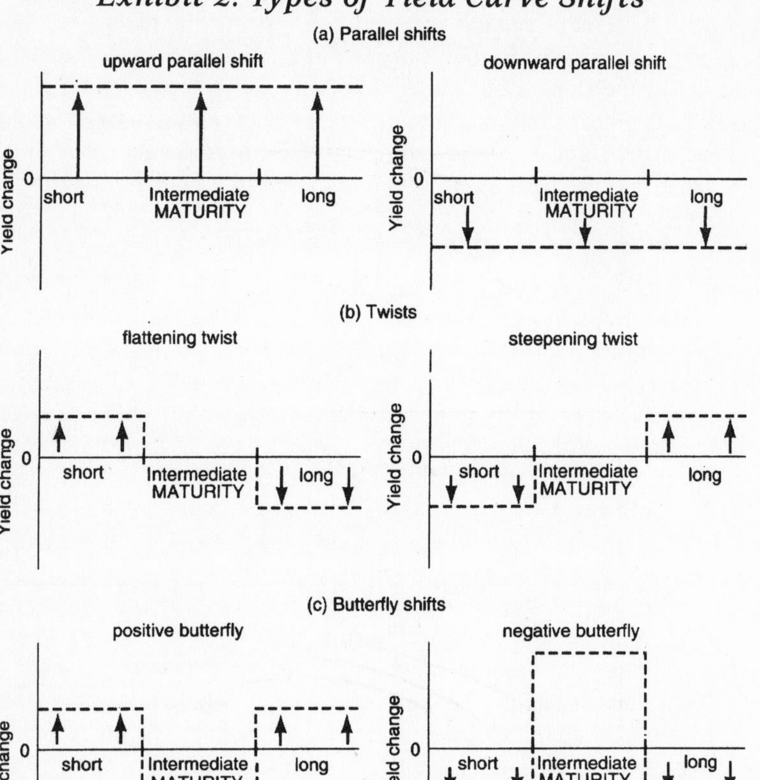

Trademark Products

In August 1982, Merrill Lynch and Salomon Brothers created synthetic zero-coupon Treasury receipts. Merrill Lynch marketed its Treasury receipts as "Treasury Income Growth Receipts" (TIGRs), and Salomon Brothers marketed its as "Certificates of Accrual on Treasury Securities" (CATS). The procedure was to purchase a Treasury coupon security and deposit it in a bank custody account. The firms then issued receipts representing an ownership interest in each coupon payment on the underlying Treasury security in the account and a receipt for ownership of the underlying Treasury security's maturity value. This process of separating each coupon payment, as well as the principal (called the *corpus*), and selling securities against them is referred to as "coupon stripping." Although the receipts created from the coupon stripping process are not issued by the U.S. Treasury, the underlying security deposited in the bank custody account is a debt obligation of the U.S. Treasury, so the cash flows from the underlying security are certain.

Exhibit 3: Combinations of Yield Curve Shifts

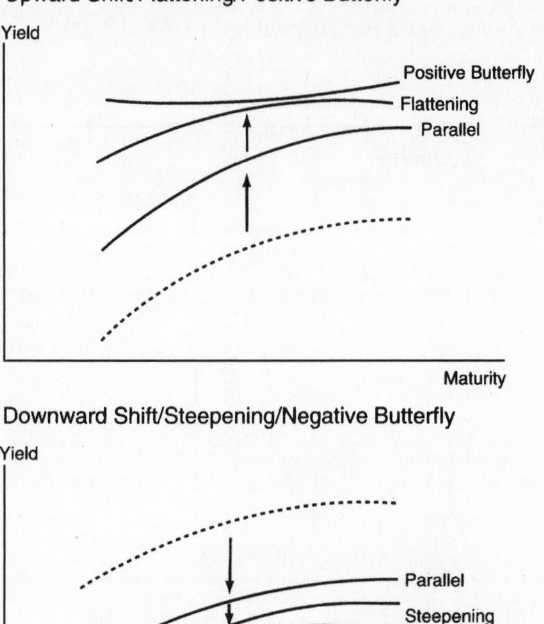

To illustrate the process, suppose $100 million of a Treasury note with a 10-year maturity and a coupon rate of 10% is purchased to create zero-coupon Treasury receipts (see Exhibit 4). The cash flows from this Treasury note are 20 semiannual payments of $5 million each ($100 million times 10% divided by 2) and the repayment of principal (corpus) of $100 million 10 years from now. This Treasury note is deposited in a bank custody account. Receipts are then issued, each with a different single payment claim on the bank custody account. As there are 21 different payments to be made by the Treasury, a receipt representing a single payment claim on each payment is issued, which is effectively a zero-coupon instrument. The amount of the maturity value for a receipt on a particular payment, whether coupon or corpus, depends on the amount of the payment to be made by the Treasury on the underlying Treasury note. In our example, 20 coupon receipts each have a maturity value of $5 million, and one receipt, backed by the corpus, has a maturity value of $100 million. The maturity dates for the receipts coincide with the corresponding payment dates by the Treasury.

Exhibit 4: Coupon Stripping: Creating Zero-Coupon Treasury Securities
Dealer purchases $100 million par of a 10% 10-year Treasury Note

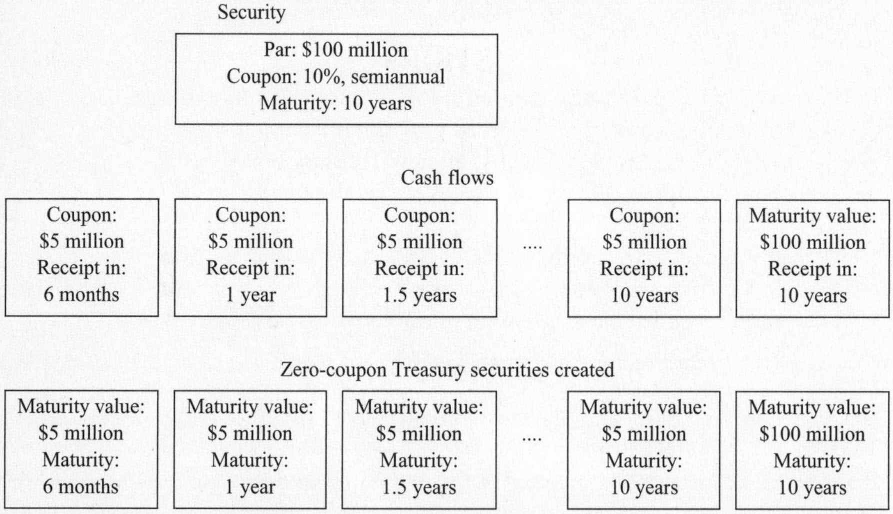

Security

Par: $100 million
Coupon: 10%, semiannual
Maturity: 10 years

Cash flows

Coupon: $5 million Receipt in: 6 months	Coupon: $5 million Receipt in: 1 year	Coupon: $5 million Receipt in: 1.5 years	....	Coupon: $5 million Receipt in: 10 years	Maturity value: $100 million Receipt in: 10 years

Zero-coupon Treasury securities created

Maturity value: $5 million Maturity: 6 months	Maturity value: $5 million Maturity: 1 year	Maturity value: $5 million Maturity: 1.5 years	....	Maturity value: $5 million Maturity: 10 years	Maturity value: $100 million Maturity: 10 years

Other investment banking firms followed suit by creating their own receipts. For example, Lehman Brothers offered "Lehman Investment Opportunities Notes" (LIONs); E.F. Hutton offered "Treasury Bond Receipts" (TBRs); and Dean Witter Reynolds offered "Easy Growth Treasury Receipts" (ETRs). There were also GATORs, COUGARs, and DOGS (Dibs on Government Securities). They all are referred to as *trademark* zero-coupon Treasury receipts because they are associated with particular firms. They are also called "animal products" for obvious reasons. Receipts of one firm were rarely traded by competing dealers, so the secondary market was not liquid for any one trademark. Moreover, the investor was exposed to the risk—as small as it may be—that the custodian bank may go bankrupt.

The motivation for coupon stripping lies in the arbitrage available to government dealers when they can purchase a Treasury security for a price that is less than the aggregate amount that they expect they can sell all the stripped securities for. The theoretical reasons why this can occur are beyond the scope of this chapter.[5]

Treasury Receipts

To broaden the market and improve liquidity of these receipts, a group of primary dealers in the government market agreed to issue generic receipts that would not be directly associated with any of the participating dealers. These generic receipts

[5] An explanation is provided in Chapter 2 in Frank J. Fabozzi, *Valuation of Fixed Income Securities and Derivatives, Third Edition* (New Hope, PA: Frank J. Fabozzi Associates, 1998).

are referred to as "Treasury Receipts" (TRs). Rather than representing a share of the trust as the trademarks do, TRs represent ownership of a Treasury security. A common problem with both trademark and generic receipts was that settlement required physical delivery, which was often cumbersome and inefficient.

STRIPS

In February 1985, the Treasury announced its *Separate Trading of Registered Interest and Principal of Securities* (STRIPS) program to facilitate the stripping of designated Treasury securities. Specifically, all new Treasury bonds and all new Treasury notes with maturities of 10 years and longer are eligible.[6] The inflation-protection bonds may be stripped. The zero-coupon Treasury securities created under the STRIPS program are direct obligations of the U.S. government. Moreover, the securities clear through the Federal Reserve's book-entry system.[7] Creation of the STRIPS program ended the origination of trademarks and generic receipts.

Mechanically, the following occurs as a result of the stripping process. Stripping results in securities created from the interest payments (called *interest strips* or *coupon strips*) and a security created from the principal (called a *principal strip*). All interest strips that are payable on the same day, even when stripped from different securities, are assigned the same generic CUSIP number. For example, if several fixed-rate Treasury notes and bonds that pay interest on May 15 and November 15 are stripped, the interest strips that are payable on the same day are assigned the same CUSIP number. In contrast, the principal strips from each Treasury note or bond have a unique CUSIP number.

There may be confusion when a market participant refers to a "stripped Treasury" or more popularly a *Treasury strip*. Today, a Treasury strip typically means a STRIPS product. However, since there are trademark products and Treasury Receipts still occasionally traded in the market, an investor should clarify what product is the subject of the discussion.

Tax Treatment

A disadvantage of a taxable entity investing in stripped Treasury securities is that accrued interest is taxed each year even though interest is not paid. Thus, these instruments are negative cash flow instruments until the maturity date. They have

---

[6] The Treasury Department allows STRIPS (both interest strips and principal strips) to be reassembled or "reconstituted" into a fully constituted security. To do so, the entity that seeks to reconstitute a security must obtain the appropriate principal component and all unmatured interest components for the security being reconstituted. As explained in Chapter 2, Treasury securities should be priced as a package of zero-coupon Treasury securities (i.e., a package of strips). If they are not, a security will be stripped if a dealer can get a higher price by buying the mispriced security and selling off the strips. However, if a Treasury security is overvalued in the market, an investor can create this security synthetically by putting together the strip components and then sell it off at a higher price than was paid for the strip components. This is more easily accomplished by the Treasury Department facilitating reconstitution of securities.

[7] In 1987, the Treasury permitted the conversion of stripped coupons into book-entry form under its Coupons Under Book-Entry Safekeeping (CUBES) program.

negative cash flow since tax payments on interest earned but not received in cash must be made. A complete discussion of the tax treatment of stripped Treasury securities is provided in Chapter 16.

On dealer quote sheets and vendor screens a distinction is made between strips created from the coupon (interest strips and identified as TINT) and strips created from the principal (principal strips and identified as PRIN). One reason for this distinction is that some foreign buyers have a preference for the STRIPS created from the principal. This preference is due to the tax treatment of the interest in their home country. Some country tax laws treat the interest as a capital gain that receives a preferential tax treatment (i.e., lower tax rate) compared to ordinary interest income if the stripped security was created from the principal.

Yield Spreads to Treasury Securities

There is a yield spread at which STRIPS and Treasury securities trade. The spread varies over time depending on market expectations for future interest rates. Recall that STRIPS eliminate reinvestment risk. Consequently, the yield at the time of purchase on STRIPS is the pretax return that will be realized if an issue is held to maturity. STRIPS trade with a liquidity premium relative to Treasury securities, and there is an adverse tax consequence for taxable entities that purchase these instruments. These disadvantages of STRIPS are reflected in the yield spread.

KEY POINTS

- ❑ *Treasury securities are backed by the full faith and credit of the U.S. government and viewed by market participants as having no credit risk.*
- ❑ *Interest income from Treasury securities is subject to federal income taxes but is exempt from state and local income taxes.*
- ❑ *The Treasury issues two types of securities: discount securities and coupon securities.*
- ❑ *The Treasury issues fixed-rate coupon securities and inflation protection securities that pay an interest rate tied to the rate of inflation (as measured by the CPI).*
- ❑ *Treasury discount securities are called Treasury bills and have a maturity of 1 year or less.*
- ❑ *The Treasury currently issues 4-week, 3-month, and 6-month Treasury bills.*
- ❑ *A Treasury note is a coupon-bearing security that when issued has an original maturity between 2 and 10 years; a Treasury bond is a coupon-bearing security that when issued has an original maturity greater than 10 years.*
- ❑ *Treasury coupon securities are currently issued on a regular basis with initial maturities of 2 years, 5 years, 10 years, and 30 years.*
- ❑ *While there are outstanding Treasury bonds that are callable, the Treasury no longer issues callable bonds.*
- ❑ *The Department of the Treasury auctions securities on a competitive bid basis where all winning bidders are awarded securities at the highest yield of accepted competitive tenders (i.e., the stop yield).*
- ❑ *The most recently auctioned Treasury issue for a maturity is referred to as the on-the-run issue or current coupon issue; off-the-run issues are issues auctioned prior to the current coupon issues and are not as liquid as an on-the-run issue for a given maturity.*
- ❑ *Treasury securities are traded prior to the time they are issued by the Treasury in the when-issued market, where trading is carried on from the day the auction is announced until the issue day.*
- ❑ *The normal settlement period for Treasury securities is the business day after the transaction day ("next-day" settlement).*
- ❑ *The convention in the Treasury bill market is to calculate a bill's yield on a discount basis.*
- ❑ *The quoted yield on a discount basis is not a meaningful measure of the return from holding a bill to maturity because the measure is based on a maturity value investment and the yield is annualized according to a 360-day rather than a 365-day year.*

- ❑ *The annualized percentage rate (APR) converts the yield on a discount basis to a 365-day basis and relates the return to the settlement price rather than the maturity value.*
- ❑ *The APR can be expressed in terms of a bond-equivalent yield to provide a benchmark comparison to reward measures of Treasury coupon securities.*
- ❑ *The CD-equivalent yield is a measure that attempts to make the quoted yield on bills comparable to that of other money market instruments.*
- ❑ *Coupon securities trade on a dollar price basis in price units of 1/32 of 1% of par.*
- ❑ *The relationship between the yield on Treasury securities and maturity is called the term structure of interest rates.*
- ❑ *The yield curve is the graphical depiction of the term structure of interest rates.*
- ❑ *Historically, three shapes have been observed for the yield curve: (1) normal or positively sloped (i.e., the longer the maturity, the higher the yield), (2) flat (i.e., the yield for all maturities is approximately equal), and (3) inverted or negatively sloped (i.e., the longer the maturity, the lower the yield).*
- ❑ *The spread between long-term Treasury yields and short-term Treasury yields is referred to as the steepness or slope of the yield curve.*
- ❑ *Some investors define the slope as the spread between the 30-year yield and the 3-month yield and others as the spread between the 30-year yield and the 2-year yield.*
- ❑ *A shift in the yield curve refers to the relative change in the yield for each Treasury maturity.*
- ❑ *A parallel shift in the yield curve refers to a shift in which the change in the yield on all maturities is the same; a nonparallel shift in the yield curve means that the yield for all maturities does not change by the same number of basis points.*
- ❑ *Historically, the two types of nonparallel yield curve shifts that have been observed are a twist in the slope of the yield curve and a change in the humpedness of the yield curve.*
- ❑ *A flattening of the yield curve means that the slope of the yield curve has decreased; a steepening of the yield curve means that the slope has increased.*
- ❑ *A butterfly shift is the other type of nonparallel shift—a change in the humpedness of the yield curve.*
- ❑ *Historical evidence suggests that the three types of yield curve shifts are not independent, with the two most common types of yield curve shifts being (1) a downward shift in the yield curve combined with a steepening of the yield curve and (2) an upward shift in the yield curve combined with a flattening of the yield curve.*
- ❑ *Zero-coupon Treasury instruments are created by dealers by stripping the coupon payments and principal payment of a Treasury coupon security.*

- ❑ *Stripped securities created from the coupon are called interest strips or coupon strips; those created from the principal are called principal strips.*
- ❑ *While there are three types of stripped Treasury securities outstanding—trademark products, Treasury Receipts, and STRIPS—only STRIPS are issued today and are referred to as Treasury strips.*
- ❑ *A disadvantage of a taxable entity investing in stripped Treasury securities is that accrued interest is taxed each year even though interest is not paid.*

Chapter 5

Federal Agency Securities

Federal agency securities can be classified by the type of issuer—federally related institutions and government-sponsored enterprises. Federal agencies that provide credit for certain sectors of the credit market issue two types of securities: debentures and mortgage-backed/asset-backed securities. Our focus here is on the former securities. We discuss mortgage-backed/asset-backed securities in Chapters 9 to 12.

FEDERALLY RELATED INSTITUTIONS

Federally related institutions are arms of the federal government and generally do not issue securities directly in the marketplace. Federally related institutions include the Export-Import Bank of the United States, the Tennessee Valley Authority, the Commodity Credit Corporation, the Farmers Housing Administration, the General Services Administration, the Government National Mortgage Association, the Maritime Administration, the Private Export Funding Corporation, the Rural Electrification Administration, the Rural Telephone Bank, the Small Business Administration, and the Washington Metropolitan Area Transit Authority.

All federally related institutions are exempt from SEC registration. With the exception of securities of the Tennessee Valley Authority and the Private Export Funding Corporation, the securities are backed by the full faith and credit of the U.S. government. Interest income on securities issued by federally related institutions is exempt from state and local income taxes.

Since the federally related institution that has issued securities in recent years is the Tennessee Valley Authority (TVA), we discuss these securities.

Tennessee Valley Authority

Established by Congress in 1933 primarily to provide flood control, navigation, and agricultural and industrial development, and to promote the use of electric power in the Tennessee Valley region, the TVA is the largest public power system in the United States. The TVA primarily finances its capital requirements through internally generated funds and by issuing debt. The TVA issues a variety of debt securities in U.S. dollars and other currencies (British pounds and German marks). The debt obligations issued by the TVA may be issued only to provide capital for its power program or to refund outstanding debt obligations.

TVA debt obligations are not guaranteed by the U.S. government. However, the securities are rated triple A by Moody's and Standard and Poor's. The

rating is based on the TVA's status as a wholly owned corporate agency of the U.S. government and the view of the rating agencies of the TVA's financial strengths. These strengths include (1) the requirements that bondholders of power bonds are given a first pledge of payment from net power proceeds, and (2) electricity rates charged by the TVA are sufficient to ensure both the full payment of annual debt service and operating and capital costs.

According to the TVA's annual report, as of September 30, 2000, TVA had 36 long-term public debt issues outstanding, totaling $24 billion. There are issues targeted to individual investors (retail debt offerings) and institutional investors (nonretail offerings).

For retail offerings, there are standard callable bonds (2000 Series A through Series E and 1998 Series A Estate Features), with one interesting investment feature. There is an "estate feature" that allows the bonds to be redeemed at par value plus accrued interest upon the death of the bondholder. The Putable Automatic Rate Reset Securities (PARRS) bonds (1999 Series A and 1998 Series D) are noncallable but have two interesting features. First, they have a fixed coupon rate for the first 5 years. Then there is an annual reset provision that provides for a reduction in the issue's coupon rate under certain conditions. The reduction is tied to the 30-year Treasury Constant Maturity (CMT). This is the ratchet feature discussed in Chapter 1. Second, the bondholder has the right to put the bond at par value plus accrued interest if and when the coupon rate is reduced. More recently, the TVA has issued "electronotes." The retail bonds (as well as electronotes) just described are referred to as "power bonds." There are retail bonds that are "subordinated debt." That is, they are subordinated to the power bonds. The only outstanding issue is the 1996 Series A Quarterly Income Debt Securities (QIDS).

For institutional investors, the TVA has global bonds outstanding (e.g., 2001 Series A, 2000 Series G, 1999 Series B, 1998 Series G, and 1998 Series C) that are noncallable and issued in U.S. dollars. There is a global issue denominated in British pounds that is noncallable (1998 Series H) and German marks (1996 Series Global). There are putable issues that may not be called (2000 Series F Put, 1997 Series C Exchange, and 1996 Series A Double Put). There is even one issue that is inflation indexed (1997 Series A Inflation-Indexed VIPS).

GOVERNMENT-SPONSORED ENTERPRISES

Government-sponsored enterprises (GSEs) are privately owned, publicly chartered entities. They were created by Congress to reduce the cost of capital for certain borrowing sectors of the economy deemed to be important enough to warrant assistance. The entities in these privileged sectors include farmers, homeowners, and students. The enabling legislation dealing with a GSE is amended periodically. GSEs issue securities directly in the marketplace. The market for these securities, while smaller than that of Treasury securities, has in recent years become an active and important sector of the bond market. GSEs are also issuers of global bonds.

Today there are six GSEs that currently issue debentures: Federal National Mortgage Association, Federal Home Loan Mortgage Corporation, Federal Agricultural Mortgage Corporation, Federal Farm Credit System, Federal Home Loan Bank System, and Student Loan Marketing Association. The Federal National Mortgage Association, Federal Home Loan Mortgage Corporation, and Federal Home Loan Bank are responsible for providing credit to the housing sectors. The Federal Agricultural Mortgage Corporation provides the same function for agricultural mortgage loans. The Federal Farm Credit Bank System is responsible for the credit market in the agricultural sector of the economy. The Student Loan Marketing Association provides funds to support higher education.

The interest earned on obligations of the Federal Home Loan Bank System, the Federal Farm Credit System, and the Student Loan Marketing Association are exempt from state and local income taxes. In addition to the debt obligations issued by these six GSEs, there are issues outstanding by one-time GSE issuers that have been dismantled. These GSEs include the Financing Corporation, Resolution Trust Corporation, and the Farm Credit Assistance Corporation.

The price quotation convention for GSE securities is the same as that for Treasury securities. That is, the bid and ask price quotations are expressed as a percentage of par plus fractional 32nds of a point. Some GSE issues trade with almost the same liquidity as Treasury securities. Other issues that are supported only by a few dealers trade much like off-the-run corporate bonds.

Types and Features of GSE Securities

In general, GSEs issue two types of debentures: discount notes and bonds. Discount notes are short-term obligations, with maturities ranging from overnight to 360 days. As with Treasury bills, no coupon interest is paid. Instead, the investor earns interest by buying the note at a discount. Bonds have maturities greater than 2 years. There are issues with bullet maturities and those with call provisions. GSEs also issue structured notes.

Description of GSEs and Securities Issued

We briefly describe the six GSEs that currently issue securities and the three GSEs that have outstanding issues as follows.

Federal National Mortgage Association

The residential mortgage debt market in the United States represents the largest debt market in the world. The problem the U.S. government faces is to attract investors to invest in residential mortgages. At one time, savings and loan associations were the primary investors, especially with special inducements the government provided. But since there was not an active market where these debt instruments traded, mortgages were illiquid and financial institutions that invested in them were exposed to liquidity risk.

In the 1930s, Congress figured out a way to handle this problem. It created a federally related institution, the Federal National Mortgage Association, popularly known as "Fannie Mae," which was charged with the responsibility to create a liquid secondary market for mortgages. Fannie Mae was to accomplish this objective by buying and selling mortgages. Fannie Mae needed a funding source in case it faced a liquidity squeeze. Congress provided this by giving Fannie Mae a credit line with the Treasury.

Despite the presence of Fannie Mae, the secondary mortgage market did not develop to any significant extent. During periods of tight money, Fannie Mae could do little to mitigate a housing crisis. In 1968, Congress divided Fannie Mae into two entities: (1) the current Fannie Mae and (2) the Government National Mortgage Association (popularly known as "Ginnie Mae"). Ginnie Mae's function is to use the "full faith and credit of the U.S. government" to support the market for government-insured mortgages. (The mortgage-backed securities guaranteed by Ginnie Mae are discussed in Chapter 9.) While starting out as a federally related institution, today Fannie Mae is a GSE.

Fannie Mae issues Benchmark Bills, Benchmark Notes and Benchmark Bonds, Callable Benchmark Notes, Subordinated Benchmark Notes, Investment Notes, callable securities, and structured notes. Benchmark Notes and Benchmark Bonds are noncallable instruments. The minimum issue size is $4 billion for Benchmark Notes and $2 billion for Benchmark Bonds. Issued quarterly are 2-year or 3-year, 5-year, 10-year, and 30-year maturities.

Fannie Mae's Subordinated Benchmark Notes securities are unsecured subordinated obligations of Fannie Mae that rank junior in right of payment to all of Fannie Mae's existing and future obligations. The payment structure is as follows. Fannie Mae must defer payment of interest on all outstanding Subordinated Benchmark Notes if certain conditions are realized.[1] Deferral of interest is not permitted for more than 5 consecutive years nor beyond the maturity date. Accrual of interest is compounded at the issue's coupon rate. During any deferral period, Fannie Mae may not declare or pay dividends on, or redeem, purchase, or acquire its common stock or its preferred stock. The first offering of Subordinated Benchmark Notes was for $1.5 billion of 10-year securities priced on January 25, 2001, receiving an Aa2 from Moody's Investors Service and AA– from Standard & Poor's.

Callable notes and structured notes are customized based on demand (reverse inquiry) from institutional investors. The structured notes issued have been various floating rate, zero-coupon, and step-up securities; there are securities denominated in U.S. dollars and issues denominated in a wide range of foreign currencies.

---

[1] Specifically, if as of the fifth business day prior to an interest payment on any Subordinated Benchmark Notes: (1) Fannie Mae's "core capital" is determined to be less than 125% of its "critical capital" requirement, *or*, (2) (a) Fannie Mae's "core capital" is below its "minimum capital" requirement *and* (b) the Secretary of the Treasury, acting at Fannie Mae's request, exercises his or her discretionary authority to purchase the company's debt obligations.

Federal Home Loan Mortgage Corporation

In 1970—two years after Congress divided Fannie Mae into the now current Fannie Mae and Ginnie Mae—Congress created the Federal Home Loan Mortgage Corporation (Freddie Mac). The reason for the creation of Freddie Mac was to provide support for conventional mortgages. These mortgages are not guaranteed by the U.S. government.

Freddie Mac issues Reference Bills, discount notes, medium-term notes, Reference Notes, Callable Reference Bonds, and global bonds. Reference Bills and discount notes are issued with maturities of 1 year or less. Reference Notes and Callable Reference Notes have maturities of 2 to 10 years and are the equivalent to Fannie Mae's Benchmark Notes and Callable Benchmark Notes. Freddie Mac will issue and/or reopen Reference Bills, Reference Notes, and 30-year Reference Bonds according to a published issuance calendar. Freddie Mac Reference Notes and Reference Bonds are eligible for stripping. As Fannie Mae has done, Freddie Mac has introduced Subordinated Debt Securities (Freddie SUBS).

Federal Home Loan Bank System

The Federal Home Loan Bank System (FHLBS) consists of the 12 district Federal Home Loan Banks and their member banks. The Federal Home Loan Bank Board was originally responsible for regulating all federally chartered savings and loan associations and savings banks, as well as state-chartered institutions insured by the Federal Savings and Loan Insurance Corporation. These responsibilities have been curtailed since 1989.

The major source of debt funding for the Federal Home Loan Banks is the issuance of consolidated debt obligations, which are joint and several obligations of the 12 Federal Home Loan Banks. Consolidated FHLBS discount notes are issued on a daily basis. Bonds of this GSE are issued monthly.

The Federal Agricultural Mortgage Corporation

The Federal Agricultural Mortgage Corporation (Farmer Mac) provides a secondary market for first mortgage agricultural real estate loans. It was created by Congress in 1998 to improve the availability of mortgage credit to farmers, ranchers, and rural homeowners, businesses, and communities. It does so by purchasing qualified loans from lenders in the same way as Freddie Mac and Fannie Mae.

Farmer Mac raises funds by selling debentures and mortgage-backed securities backed by the loans purchased. The latter securities are called agricultural mortgage-backed securities (AMBS). The debentures that are issued include discount notes and medium-term notes.

Federal Farm Credit Bank System

The purpose of the Federal Farm Credit Bank System (FFCBS) is to facilitate adequate, dependable credit and related services to the agricultural sector of the economy. The Farm Credit System consists of three entities: the Federal Land

Banks, Federal Intermediate Credit Banks, and Banks for Cooperatives. Before 1979, each entity issued securities in its own name. Starting in 1979, they began to issue debt on a consolidated basis as "joint and several obligations" of the FFCBS. All financing for the FFCBS is arranged through the Federal Farm Credit Banks Funding Corporation, which issues consolidated obligations.

Student Loan Marketing Association

Popularly known as "Sallie Mae," the Student Loan Marketing Association provides liquidity for private lenders participating in the Federal Guaranteed Student Loan Program, the Health Education Assistance Loan Program, and the PLUS loan program (a program that provides loans to the parents of undergraduate students).

Sallie Mae issues monthly floating-rate notes that mature in 6 months. In addition, it issues longer-term floating-rate bonds. In 1995, Sallie Mae began issuing floating-rate notes backed by student loans. These securities are called asset-backed securities. In Chapter 12, we describe the general characteristics of asset-backed securities.

Financing Corporation

The deposits of savings and loans were once insured by the Federal Savings and Loan Insurance Corporation (FSLIC), overseen by the Federal Home Loan Bank Board. When difficulties encountered in the savings and loan industry raised concerns about FSLIC's ability to meet its responsibility to insure deposits, Congress passed the Competitive Equality and Banking Act in 1987. This legislation included provisions to recapitalize FSLIC and establish a new government-sponsored agency, the Financing Corporation (FICO), to issue debt in order to provide funding for FICO. FICO issued its first bonds in September 1987—a 30-year noncallable $500 million issue. The principal of these bonds is backed by zero-coupon Treasury securities. The legislation permitted FICO to issue up to $10.825 billion but not more than $3.75 billion in any 1 year. FICO was legislated to be dismantled in 2026, or after all securities have matured, whichever came sooner.

Resolution Trust Corporation

The 1987 legislation that created FICO did not go far enough to resolve the problems facing the beleaguered savings and loan industry. In 1989, Congress passed more comprehensive legislation, the Financial Institutions Reform, Recovery and Enforcement Act (FIRREA). This legislation had three key elements. First, it transferred supervision of savings and loans to a newly created Office of Thrift Supervision. Second, it shifted the FSLIC insurance function to a Savings Association Insurance Fund, placed under the supervision of the Federal Deposit Insurance Corporation. Third, it established the Resolution Trust Corporation (RTC) as a GSE charged with the responsibility of liquidating or bailing out insolvent savings and loan institutions. The RTC obtained its funding from the Resolution Funding Corporation (REFCORP), which was authorized to issue up to $40 bil-

lion of long-term bonds. The principal of this debt is backed by zero-coupon Treasury bonds. REFCORP has issued both 30-year and 40-year bonds.

Farm Credit Financial Assistance Corporation

In the 1980s, the FFCBS faced financial difficulties because of defaults on loans made to farmers. The defaults were caused largely by high interest rates in the late 1970s and early 1980s and by depressed prices on agricultural products. To recapitalize the Federal Farm Credit Bank System, Congress created the Farm Credit Financial Assistance Corporation (FACO) in 1987. This federally sponsored agency was authorized to issue debt to assist the FFCBS. FACO bonds, unlike the debt of other GSEs, are backed by the Treasury.

Credit Risk

With the exception of the securities issued by the Farm Credit Financial Assistance Corporation, GSE securities are not backed by the full faith and credit of the U.S. government, as is the case with Treasury securities. Consequently, investors purchasing GSEs are exposed to credit risk. The yield spread between these securities and Treasury securities of comparable maturity reflects differences in perceived credit risk and liquidity. The spread attributable to credit risk reflects financial problems faced by the issuing GSE and the likelihood that the federal government will allow the GSE to default on its outstanding obligations.

Two examples will illustrate this point. In late 1981 and early 1982, the net income of the Federal National Mortgage Association weakened, causing analysts to report that the securities of this GSE carried greater credit risk than previously perceived. As a result, the yield spread over Treasuries on its debt rose from 91 basis points (on average) in 1981 to as high as 150 basis points. In subsequent years, the Federal National Mortgage Association's net income improved, and its yield spread to Treasuries narrowed. As another example, in 1985 the yield spread on securities of the Farm Credit Bank System rose substantially above those on comparable-maturity Treasuries because of this GSE's financial difficulties. The spread between 1985 and 1986 varied with the prospects of Congressional approval of a bailout measure for the system.

Yield Spreads

Because of credit risk and liquidity, GSEs will trade at a premium to comparable-maturity Treasury securities. The yield spread will differ for each issuing entity, the maturity of the issue, and the call feature. Exhibit 1 shows the yield spread for noncallable GSEs by maturity on July 13, 2001, as reported by Lehman Brothers. To see how the spread can vary over time, the last four columns show the spread for high, low, average, and standard deviation for the prior 12 months. Also shown in the exhibit are the spreads by maturity for the FNMA Benchmarks and FLMC Reference Notes.

Exhibit 1: GSE Spreads versus Benchmark Treasury (July 13, 2001)

		Last 12 Months			
	Current	High	Low	Avg.	St. Dev.
Noncallable					
2-yr	47.0	61.0	38.0	53.0	4.7
3-yr	93.0	93.0	48.0	61.8	8.1
5-yr	75.0	92.0	60.0	79.2	6.5
7-yr	108.0	108.0	85.0	92.4	4.2
10-yr	90.0	126.0	77.0	104.6	13.9
30-yr	95.0	135.0	74.0	108.6	18.0
FNMA Benchmarks					
2-yr	33.5	57.0	28.5	42.8	6.8
3-yr	75.5	76.0	44.5	57.7	8.1
5-yr	67.0	83.5	51.5	70.7	9.6
7-yr	86.0	97.0	55.0	83.9	7.8
10-yr	79.0	114.5	67.0	87.1	13.0
30-yr	83.0	125.0	62.0	88.7	16.0
FHLMC Reference Notes					
2-yr	37.5	56.0	—	38.5	15.2
3-yr	81.5	93.0	44.5	61.0	12.2
5-yr	69.5	84.5	51.5	71.2	9.9
10-yr	80.0	116.5	67.5	88.3	13.1
30-yr	84.0	127.0	64.0	90.2	16.1
Callable					
3-yr(nc 1)	80.0	105.0	68.0	93.9	8.7
5-yr(nc 1)	99.0	147.0	84.0	133.6	15.3
5-yr(nc 2)	91.0	129.0	76.0	115.3	12.5
5-yr(nc 3)	84.0	112.0	67.0	98.9	9.9
10-yr(nc 3)	138.0	177.0	83.0	153.3	20.0
10-yr(nc 5)	121.0	159.0	70.0	129.4	18.4
Callable OAS					
3-yr(nc 1)	60.0	70.0	45.0	61.9	5.4
5-yr(nc 1)	80.0	85.0	65.0	76.5	4.7
5-yr(nc 2)	80.0	85.0	65.0	76.5	4.7
5-yr(nc 3)	80.0	85.0	65.0	76.5	4.8
10-yr(nc 3)	95.0	153.0	70.0	109.6	14.1
FNMA Callable Benchmarks					
5-yr(nc2)	87.0	—	—	—	—
10-yr(nc3)	117.0	—	—	—	—

Source: Lehman Brothers, *Global Relative Value*, Fixed Income Research, July 16, 2001, p. 120.

Callable GSE securities will trade at a higher spread than noncallable securities. This can be seen in Exhibit 1 (see "Callable"). Look at the three 5-year callable securities—5-year (nc1), 5-year (nc3), and 5-year (nc-3). The longer the time before an issue can be called, the less valuable the embedded option. As a result, the longer the noncall period, the lower the spread.

KEY POINTS

- *Federal agencies are categorized as either federally related institutions or government-sponsored enterprises.*

- *Those federal agencies issue debentures and may issue either mortgage-backed securities or asset-backed securities.*

- *Federally related institutions are arms of the federal government and generally do not issue securities directly in the marketplace.*

- *With the exception of securities of the Tennessee Valley Authority and the Private Export Funding Corporation, the securities issued by federally related institutions are backed by the full faith and credit of the U.S. government.*

- *Interest income on securities issued by federally related institutions is exempt from state and local income taxes.*

- *Government-sponsored enterprises (GSEs) are privately owned, publicly chartered entities that were created by Congress to reduce the cost of capital for certain borrowing sectors of the economy deemed to be important enough to warrant assistance.*

- *The six GSEs that issue debentures are the Federal National Mortgage Association, Federal Home Loan Mortgage Corporation, Federal Agricultural Mortgage Corporation, Federal Farm Credit System, Federal Home Loan Bank System, and Student Loan Marketing Association.*

- *In general, GSEs issue two types of debentures: discount notes (short-term obligations with maturities ranging from overnight to 360 days issued on a discount basis) and bonds (which have maturities greater than 2 years).*

- *There are GSE issues with bullet maturities and those with call provisions as well as structured notes.*

- *With the exception of the securities issued by the Farm Credit Financial Assistance Corporation, GSE securities are not backed by the full faith and credit of the U.S. government, and therefore expose investors to credit risk.*

- *Because of credit risk and liquidity, securities issued by GSEs will trade at a yield premium to comparable-maturity Treasury securities.*

Chapter 6

Municipal Securities

Debt obligations are issued by state and local governments and by entities that they establish. Local government units include municipalities, counties, towns and townships, school districts, and special service system districts. Included in the category of municipalities are cities, villages, boroughs, and incorporated towns that received a special state charter. Counties are geographical subdivisions of states whose functions are law enforcement, judicial administration, and construction and maintenance of roads. As with counties, towns and townships are geographical subdivisions of states and perform similar functions as counties. A special-purpose service system district, or simply special district, is a political subdivision created to foster economic development or related services to a geographical area. Special districts provide public utility services (water, sewers, and drainage) and fire protection services. Public agencies or instrumentalities include authorities and commissions.

The number of municipal bond issuers is remarkable. One broker/dealer's estimate places the total at 60,055. Also, Bloomberg Financial Markets' (Bloomberg) database contains 55,000 active issuers. Even more noteworthy is the number of different issues. Interactive Data, a company that provides pricing information for institutional investors, claims that it provides daily prices for more than 1.2 million individual issues in its database. Bloomberg's database contains 1.7 million issues with complete description pages.

In this chapter, we discuss the types of debt obligations issued by states, municipal governments, and public agencies and their instrumentalities. These securities are popularly referred to as *municipal securities*, although they are also issued by states and public agencies and their instruments.

TAX-EXEMPT AND TAXABLE MUNICIPAL SECURITIES

There are both tax-exempt and taxable municipal securities. "Tax-exempt" means that interest on a municipal security is exempt from federal income taxation. The tax-exemption of municipal securities applies to interest income, not capital gains. The exemption may or may not extend to taxation at the state and local levels. Each state has its own rules as to how interest on municipal securities is

---

Parts of this chapter are drawn from various works that I coauthored with Dr. Sylvan G. Feldstein of The Guardian Life Insurance Company.

taxed. The treatment at the state level will be one of the following: (1) exemption of interest from all municipal securities, (2) taxation of interest from all municipal securities, or (3) exemption of interest from municipal securities where the issuer is in the state, but taxation of interest where the issuer is out of state. The interest on taxable municipal securities is taxable at the federal level.

Most municipal securities that have been issued are tax-exempt. Municipal securities are commonly referred to as *tax-exempt securities* although taxable municipal securities have been issued and are traded in the market.

There are other types of tax-exempt bonds. These include bonds issued by nonprofit organizations. Such organizations are structured so that none of the income from the operations of the organization benefit an individual or private shareholder. The designation of a nonprofit organization must be obtained from the Internal Revenue Service. Since the tax-exempt designation is provided pursuant to Section 501(c)(3) of the Internal Revenue Code, the tax-exempt bonds issued by such organizations are referred to as *501(c)(3) obligations*. Museums and foundations fall into this category. Tax-exempt obligations also include bonds issued by the District of Columbia and any possession of the United States—Puerto Rico, the Virgin Islands, and Guam.

TAX PROVISIONS AFFECTING MUNICIPALS

Federal tax rates and the treatment of municipal interest at the state and local levels affect municipal security values and strategies employed by investors. There are provisions in the Internal Revenue Code that investors in municipal securities should recognize. These provisions deal with original issue discounts, the alternative minimum tax, and the deductibility of interest expense incurred to acquire municipal securities.

Treatment of Original-Issue Discount

If at the time of issuance the original-issue price is less than its maturity value, the bond is said to be an *original-issue discount* (OID) *bond*. The difference between the par value and the original-issue price represents tax-exempt interest that the investor realizes by holding the issue to maturity. Such bonds are treated in a special way for tax purposes, and this treatment is discussed in Chapter 16.

For municipal bonds there is a complex treatment that few investors recognize when purchasing OID municipal bonds. The Revenue Reconciliation Act of 1993 specifies that any capital appreciation from the sale of a municipal bond that was purchased in the secondary market after April 30, 1993 could be either (1) free from any federal income taxes, (2) taxed at the capital gains rate, (3) taxed at the ordinary income rate, or (4) taxed at a combination of the two rates.

The key to the tax treatment is the *rule of de minimis* for any type of bond. The rule states that a bond is to be discounted up to 0.25% from the par

value for each remaining year of a bond's life before it is affected by ordinary income taxes. The discounted price based on this rule is called the *market discount cutoff price*. The relationship between the market price at which an investor purchases a bond, the market discount cutoff price, and the tax treatment of the capital appreciation realized from a sale is as follows. If the bond is purchased at a market discount, but the price is higher than the market discount cutoff price, then any capital appreciation realized from a sale will be taxed at the capital gains rate. If the purchase price is lower than the market discount cutoff price, then any capital appreciation realized from a sale may be taxed as ordinary income or a combination of the ordinary income rate and the capital gains rate. (Several factors that determine what the exact tax rate will be in this case.)

The market discount cutoff price changes over time because of the *rule of de minimis*. The price is revised. An investor must be aware of the revised price when purchasing a municipal bond because this price is used to determine the tax treatment.

Alternative Minimum Tax

Alternative minimum taxable income (AMTI) is a taxpayer's taxable income with certain adjustments for specified tax preferences designed to cause AMTI to approximate economic income. For both individuals and corporations, a taxpayer's liability is the greater of (1) the tax computed at regular tax rates on taxable income and (2) the tax computed at a lower rate on AMTI. This parallel tax system, the *alternative minimum tax* (AMT), is designed to prevent taxpayers from avoiding significant tax liability as a result of taking advantage of exclusions from gross income, deductions, and tax credits otherwise allowed under the Internal Revenue Code.

One of the tax preference items that must be included is certain tax-exempt municipal interest. As a result of AMT, the value of the tax-exempt feature is reduced. However, the interest of not all municipal issues is subject to the AMT. Under the current tax code, tax-exempt interest earned on all private activity bonds issued after August 7, 1986 must be included in AMTI. There are two exceptions. First, interest from bonds that are issued by 501(c)(3) organizations (i.e., not-for-profit organizations) is not subject to AMTI. The second exception is interest from bonds issued for the purpose of refunding if the original bonds were issued before August 7, 1986. The AMT does not apply to interest on governmental or nonprivate activity municipal bonds. An implication is that those issues that are subject to the AMT will trade at a higher yield than those exempt from AMT.

Deductibility of Interest Expense Incurred to Acquire Municipals

In Chapter 13, we explain an investment strategy in which securities purchased are used as collateral for a loan. Ordinarily, the interest expense on borrowed funds to purchase or carry investment securities is tax deductible. There is one exception that is relevant to investors in municipal bonds. The Internal Revenue Code speci-

fies that interest paid or accrued on "indebtedness incurred or continued to purchase or carry obligations, the interest on which is wholly exempt from taxes," is not tax deductible. It does not make any difference if any tax-exempt interest is actually received by the taxpayer in the taxable year. In other words, interest is not deductible on funds borrowed to purchase or carry tax-exempt securities.[1]

TYPES OF MUNICIPAL SECURITIES

Municipal securities are issued for various purposes. Short-term notes typically are sold in anticipation of the receipt of funds from taxes or receipt of proceeds from the sale of a bond issue, for example. Proceeds from the sale of short-term notes permit the issuing municipality to cover seasonal and temporary imbalances between outlays for expenditures and inflows from taxes. Municipalities issue long-term bonds as the principal means for financing both (1) long-term capital projects such as schools, bridges, roads, and airports, and (2) long-term budget deficits that arise from current operations.

An *official statement* describing the issue and the issuer is prepared for new offerings. Municipal securities have legal opinions that are summarized in the official statement. The importance of the legal opinion is twofold. First, bond counsel determines if the issue is indeed legally able to issue the securities. Second, bond counsel verifies that the issuer has properly prepared for the bond sale by having enacted various required ordinances, resolutions, and trust indentures and without violating any other laws and regulations.

There are basically two types of municipal security structures: tax-backed debt and revenue bonds. We describe each type as follows, as well as variants.

Tax-Backed Debt

Tax-backed debt obligations are instruments issued by states, counties, special districts, cities, towns, and school districts that are secured by some form of tax revenue. Tax-backed debt includes general obligation debt, appropriation-backed obligations, debt obligations supported by public credit enhancement programs, and short-term debt instruments. We discuss each type as follows.

---

[1] Special rules apply to commercial banks. At one time, banks were permitted to deduct all the interest expense incurred to purchase or carry municipal securities. Tax legislation subsequently limited the deduction first to 85% of the interest expense and then to 80%. The 1986 tax law eliminated the deductibility of the interest expense for bonds acquired after August 6, 1986. The exception to this nondeductibility of interest expense rule is for *bank-qualified issues*. These are tax-exempt obligations sold by small issuers after August 6, 1986 and purchased by the bank for its investment portfolio.

An issue is bank qualified if (1) it is a tax-exempt issue other than private activity bonds, but including any bonds issued by 501(c)3 organizations, and (2) it is designated by the issuer as bank qualified and the issuer or its subordinate entities reasonably does not intend to issue more than $10 million of such bonds. A nationally recognized and experienced bond attorney should include in the opinion letter for the specific bond issue that bonds are bank qualified.

General Obligation Debt

The broadest type of tax-backed debt is *general obligation debt.* There are two types of general obligation pledges: unlimited and limited. An *unlimited tax general obligation debt* (also called an *ad valorem property tax debt*) is the stronger form of general obligation pledge because it is secured by the issuer's unlimited taxing power. The tax revenue sources include corporate and individual income taxes, sales taxes, and property taxes. Unlimited tax general obligation debt is said to be secured by the *full faith and credit of the issuer.* A limited tax general obligation debt (also called a *limited ad valorem tax debt*) is a limited tax pledge because for such debt there is a statutory limit on tax rates that the issuer may levy to service the debt.

Certain general obligation bonds are secured not only by the issuer's general taxing powers to create revenues accumulated in a general fund, but also by certain identified fees, grants, and special charges, which provide additional revenues from outside the general fund. Such bonds are known as *double-barreled* in security because of the dual nature of the revenue sources. For example, the debt obligations issued by special-purpose service systems may be secured by a pledge of property taxes, a pledge of special fees/operating revenue from the service provided, or a pledge of both property taxes and special fees/operating revenues. In the last case, they are double-barreled.

Appropriation-Backed Obligations

Agencies or authorities of several states have issued bonds that carry a potential state liability for making up shortfalls in the issuing entity's obligation. The appropriation of funds from the state's general tax revenue must be approved by the state legislature. However, the state's pledge is not binding. Debt obligations with this nonbinding pledge of tax revenue are called *moral obligation bonds.* Because a moral obligation bond requires legislative approval to appropriate the funds, it is classified as an *appropriation-backed obligation.*

An example of the legal language describing the procedure for a moral obligation bond that is enacted into legislation is as follows:

> In order to further assure the maintenance of each such debt reserve fund, there shall be annually apportioned and paid to the agency for deposit in each debt reserve fund such sum, if any, as shall be certified by the chairman of the agency to the governor and director of the budget as necessary to restore such reserve fund to an amount equal to the debt reserve fund requirement. The chairman of the agency shall annually, on or before December 1, make and deliver to the governor and director of the budget his certificate stating the sum or sums, if any, required to restore each such debt reserve fund to the amount aforesaid, and the sum so certified, if any, shall be apportioned and paid to the agency during the then current state fiscal year.

The purpose of the moral obligation pledge is to enhance the credit worthiness of the issuing entity. The first moral obligation bond was issued by the Housing Finance Agency of the state of New York. Historically, most moral obligation debt has been self-supporting; that is, it has not been necessary for the state of the issuing entity to make an appropriation. In those cases in which state legislatures have been called on to make an appropriation, they have. For example, the states of New York and Pennsylvania did this for bonds issued by their Housing Finance Agency; the state of New Jersey did this for bonds issued by the Southern Jersey Port Authority.

Another type of appropriation-backed obligation is lease-backed debt. There are two types of leases. One type is basically a secured long-term loan disguised as lease. The "leased" asset is the security for the loan. In the case of a bankruptcy, the court would probably rule such an obligation as the property of the user of the leased asset and the debt obligation of the user. In contrast, the second type of lease is a true lease in which the user of the leased asset (called the *lessee*) makes periodic payments to the leased asset's owner (called the *lessor*) for the right to use the leased asset. For true leases, there must be an annual appropriation by the municipality to continue making the lease payments.

Dedicated Tax-Backed Obligations

In recent years, states and local governments have issued increasing amounts of bonds where the debt service is to be paid from so-called dedicated revenues such as sales taxes, tobacco settlement payments, fees, and penalty payments. Many are structured to mimic the asset-backed securities that are discussed in Chapter 12.

Debt Obligations Supported by Public Credit Enhancement Programs

While a moral obligation is a form of credit enhancement provided by a state, it is not a legally enforceable or legally binding obligation of the state. There are entities that have issued debt that carries some form of public credit enhancement that is legally enforceable. This occurs when there is a guarantee by the state or a federal agency or when there is an obligation to automatically withhold and deploy state aid to pay any defaulted debt service by the issuing entity. Typically, the latter form of public credit enhancement is used for debt obligations of a state's school systems.

Here are some examples of state credit enhancement programs. Virginia's bond guarantee program authorizes the governor to withhold state aid payments to a municipality and divert those funds to pay principal and interest to a municipality's general obligation holders in the event of a default. South Carolina's constitution requires mandatory withholding of state aid by the state treasurer if a school district is not capable of meeting its general obligation debt. Texas created the Permanent School Fund to guarantee the timely payment of principal and interest of the debt obligations of qualified school districts. The fund's income is obtained from land and mineral rights owned by the state of Texas.

Short-Term Debt Instruments

Short-term debt instruments include municipal notes, commercial paper, variable-rate demand obligations, and a hybrid of the last two products.

Municipal Notes Usually, municipal notes are issued for a period of 12 months, although it is not uncommon for such notes to be issued for periods as short as 3 months and for as long as 3 years. Municipal notes include *bond anticipation notes* (BANs) and *cash flow notes*. BANs are issued in anticipation of the sale of long-term bonds. The issuing entity must obtain funds in the capital market to pay off the obligation.

Cash flow notes include *tax anticipation notes* (TANs) and *revenue anticipation notes* (RANs). TANs and RANs (also known as TRANs) are issued in anticipation of the collection of taxes or other expected revenues. These are borrowings to even out irregular flows into the treasury of the issuing entity. The pledge for cash flow notes can be either a broad general obligation pledge of the issuer or a pledge from a specific revenue source. The lien position of cash flow noteholders relative to other general obligation debt that has been pledged the same revenue can be either (1) a first lien on all pledged revenue, thereby having priority over general obligation debt that has been pledged the same revenue, (2) a lien that is in parity with general obligation debt that has been pledged the same revenue, or (3) a lien that is subordinate to the lien of general obligation debt that has been pledged the same revenue.

Commercial Paper In Chapter 7, we discuss commercial paper issued by corporations. Commercial paper is also used by municipalities to raise funds on a short-term basis ranging from 1 day to 270 days. There are two types of commercial paper issued, unenhanced and enhanced. *Unenhanced commercial paper* is a debt obligation issued based solely on the issuer's credit quality and liquidity capability. *Enhanced commercial paper* is a debt obligation that is credit enhanced with bank liquidity facilities (e.g., a letter of credit), insurance, or a bond purchase agreement. The role of the enhancement is to reduce the risk of nonrepayment of the maturing commercial paper by providing a source of liquidity for payment of that debt in the event no other funds of the issuer are currently available.

Provisions in the 1986 tax act restricted the issuance of tax-exempt commercial paper. Specifically, the act limited the new issuance of municipal obligations that is tax exempt, and as a result, every maturity of a tax-exempt municipal issuance is considered a new debt issuance. Consequently, very limited issuance of tax-exempt commercial paper exists. Instead, issuers use one of the next two products to raise short-term funds.

Variable-Rate Demand Obligations Variable-rate demand obligations (VRDOs) are floating-rate obligations that have a nominal long-term maturity but have a coupon rate that is reset either daily or every 7 days. The investor has an

option to put the issue back to the trustee at any time with 7 days notice. The put price is par plus accrued interest. There are unenhanced and enhanced VRDOs.

Commercial Paper/VRDO Hybrid The commercial paper/VRDO hybrid is customized to meet the cash flow needs of an investor. As with tax-exempt commercial paper, there is flexibility in structuring the maturity because a remarketing agent establishes interest rates for a range of maturities. Although the instrument may have a long nominal maturity, there is a put provision as with a VRDO. Put periods can range from 1 day to more than 360 days. On the put date, the investor can put back the bonds, receiving principal and interest, or the investor can elect to extend the maturity at the new interest rate and put date posted by the remarketing agent at that time. Thus the investor has two choices when initially purchasing this instrument: the interest rate and the put date. Interest is generally paid on the put date if the date is within 180 days. If the put date is more than 180 days forward, interest is paid semiannually.

Commercial paper dealers market these products under a proprietary name. For example, the Merrill Lynch product is called Unit Priced Demand Adjustable Tax-Exempt Securities, or UPDATES. Lehman Brothers markets these simply as money market municipals. Goldman Sachs refers to these securities as flexible rate notes, and Smith Barney Shearson markets them as BITS (Bond Interest Term Series).

Revenue Bonds

The second basic type of security structure is found in a revenue bond. Revenue bonds are issued for enterprise financings that are secured by the revenues generated by the completed projects themselves, or for general public-purpose financings in which the issuers pledge to the bondholders the tax and revenue resources that were previously part of the general fund. This latter type of revenue bond is usually created to allow issuers to raise debt outside general obligation debt limits and without voter approval.

Revenue bonds can be classified by the type of financing. These include utility revenue bonds, transportation revenue bonds, housing revenue bonds, higher education revenue bonds, health care revenue bonds, seaport revenue bonds, sports complex and convention center revenue bonds, and industrial development revenue bonds. We discuss these revenue bonds as follows. Revenue bonds are also issued by Section 501(c)3 entities (museums and foundations).

Utility Revenue Bonds

Utility revenue bonds include water, sewer, and electric revenue bonds. Water revenue bonds are issued to finance the construction of water treatment plants, pumping stations, collection facilities, and distribution systems. Revenues usually come from connection fees and charges paid by the users of the water systems. Electric utility revenue bonds are secured by revenues produced from electrical

operating plants. Some bonds are for a single issuer who constructs and operates power plants and then sells the electricity. Other electric utility revenue bonds are issued by groups of public and private investor-owned utilities for the joint financing of the construction of one or more power plants.

Also included as part of utility revenue bonds are resource recovery revenue bonds. A resource recovery facility converts refuse (solid waste) into commercially saleable energy, recoverable products, and residue to be landfilled. The major revenues securing these bonds usually are (1) fees paid by those who deliver the waste to the facility for disposal, (2) revenues from steam, electricity, or refuse-derived fuel sold to either an electric power company or another energy user, and (3) revenues from the sale of recoverable materials such as aluminum and steel scrap.

Transportation Revenue Bonds

Included in the category of transportation revenue bonds are toll road revenue bonds, highway user tax revenue bonds, airport revenue bonds, and mass transit bonds secured by farebox revenues. For toll road revenue bonds, bond proceeds are used to build specific revenue-producing facilities such as toll roads, bridges, and tunnels. The pledged revenues are the monies collected through tolls. For highway user tax revenue bonds, the bondholders are paid by earmarked revenues outside of toll collections, such as gasoline taxes, automobile registration payments, and driver's license fees. The revenues securing airport revenue bonds usually come from either traffic-generated sources—such as landing fees, concession fees, and airline fueling fees—or lease revenues from one or more airlines for the use of a specific facility such as a terminal or hangar.

Housing Revenue Bonds

There are two types of housing revenue bonds: *single-family mortgage revenue bonds* and *multifamily housing revenue bonds*. The former revenue bonds are secured by the mortgages and loan repayments on 1-to-4-single-family homes. Security features vary but can include Federal Housing Administration (FHA), Veterans Administration (VA), or private mortgage insurance. Multifamily revenue bonds are usually issued for multifamily housing projects for senior citizens and low-income families. Some housing revenue bonds are secured by mortgages that are federally insured; others receive federal government operating subsidies or interest-cost subsidies. Still others receive only local property tax reductions as subsidies.

Higher Education Revenue Bonds

There are two types of higher education revenue bonds: college and university revenue bonds and student loan revenue bonds. The revenues securing public and private college and university revenue bonds usually include dormitory room rental fees, tuition payments, and sometimes the general assets of the college or univer-

sity. For student loan revenue bonds, student loan repayments are sometimes 100% guaranteed either directly by the federal government or by a state guaranty agency.

Health Care Revenue Bonds

Health care revenue bonds are issued by private, not-for-profit hospitals (including rehabilitation centers, children's hospitals, and psychiatric institutions) and other health care providers such as health maintenance organizations (HMOs), continuing care retirement communities and nursing homes, cancer centers, university faculty practice plans, and medical specialty practices. The revenue for health care revenue bonds usually depends on federal and state reimbursement programs (such as Medicaid and Medicare), third-party commercial payers (such as Blue Cross, HMOs, and private insurance), and individual patient payments.

Seaport Revenue Bonds

The security for seaport revenue bonds can include specific lease agreements with the benefiting companies or pledged marine terminal and cargo tonnage fees.

Sports Complex and Convention Center Revenue Bonds

These bonds usually receive revenues from sporting or convention events held at the facilities and, in some instances, from earmarked outside revenues such as local motel and hotel room taxes.

Industrial Development Revenue Bonds

Generally, industrial development revenue bonds are issued by state and local governments on behalf of individual corporations and businesses. The security for these bonds usually depends on the economic soundness of the particular corporation or business involved.

Special Bond Securities

Some municipal securities have special security structures. These include insured bonds, bank-backed municipal bonds, and refunded bonds. We describe these three special security structures as follows.

Insured Bonds

Insured bonds, in addition to being secured by the issuer's revenue, are also backed by insurance policies written by commercial insurance companies. Insurance on a municipal bond is an agreement by an insurance company to pay the bondholder any bond principal and/or coupon interest that is due on a stated maturity date but that has not been paid by the bond issuer. Once issued, this municipal bond insurance usually extends for the term of the bond issue, and it cannot be canceled by the insurance company.

Because municipal bond insurance reduces credit risk for the investor, the marketability of certain municipal bonds can be greatly expanded. Municipal bonds that benefit most from the insurance would include lower-quality bonds,

bonds issued by smaller governmental units not widely known in the financial community, bonds that have a sound though complex and confusing security structure, and bonds issued by infrequent local-government borrowers that do not have a general market following among investors.

There are two major groups of municipal bond insurers. The first includes the "monoline" companies that are primarily in the business of insuring municipal bonds. Almost all of the companies that are now insuring municipal bonds can be characterized as monoline in structure. The second group of municipal bond insurers includes the "multiline" property and casualty companies that usually have a wide base of business, including insurance for fires, collisions, hurricanes, and health problems. Most new issues in the municipal bond market today are insured by the following monoline insurers: AMBAC Indemnity Corporation (AMBAC); Financial Guaranty Insurance Company (FGIC); Financial Security Assurance, Inc. (FSA); and Municipal Bond Investors Assurance Corporation (MBIA Corp.).

Bank-Backed Municipal Bonds

Since the 1980s, municipal obligations have been increasingly supported by various types of credit facilities provided by commercial banks. The support is in addition to the issuer's cash flow revenues. There are three basic types of bank support: letter of credit, irrevocable line of credit, and revolving line of credit.

A *letter of credit* is the strongest type of support available from a commercial bank. Under this arrangement, the bank is required to advance funds to the trustee if a default has occurred. An *irrevocable line of credit* is not a guarantee of the bond issue, though it does provide a level of security. A *revolving line of credit* is a liquidity-type credit facility that provides a source of liquidity for payment of maturing debt in the event no other funds of the issuer are currently available. Because a bank can cancel a revolving line of credit without notice if the issuer fails to meet certain covenants, bond security depends entirely on the credit worthiness of the municipal issuer.

Refunded Bonds

Although originally issued as either revenue or general obligation bonds, municipals are sometimes refunded. A refunding usually occurs when the original bonds are escrowed or collateralized by direct obligations guaranteed by the U.S. government. By this it is meant that a portfolio of securities guaranteed by the U.S. government are placed in a trust. The portfolio of securities is assembled such that the cash flows from the securities match the obligations that the issuer must pay. For example, suppose that a municipality has a 7% $100 million issue with 12 years remaining to maturity. The municipality's obligation is to make payments of $3.5 million every 6 months for the next 12 years and $100 million 12 years from now. If the issuer wants to refund this issue, a portfolio of U.S. government obligations can be purchased that has a cash flow of $3.5 million every 6 months for the next 12 years and $100 million 12 years from now.

Once this portfolio of securities whose cash flows match those of the municipality's obligation is in place, the refunded bonds are no longer secured as either general obligation or revenue bonds. The bonds are now supported by cash flows from the portfolio of securities held in an escrow fund. Such bonds, if escrowed with securities guaranteed by the U.S. government, have little, if any, credit risk. They are the safest municipal bonds available.

The escrow fund for a refunded municipal bond can be structured so that the refunded bonds are to be called at the first possible call date or a subsequent call date established in the original bond indenture. Such bonds are known as *prerefunded municipal bonds*. While refunded bonds are usually retired at their first or subsequent call date, some are structured to match the debt obligation to the retirement date. Such bonds are known as *escrowed-to-maturity bonds*.

Municipal Derivative Securities

In recent years, a number of municipal products have been created from the basic fixed-rate municipal bonds. This has been done by splitting up cash flows of newly issued bonds as well as bonds existing in the secondary markets. These products have been created by dividing the coupon interest payments and principal payments into two or more bond classes, or *tranches*. The resulting bond classes may have far different yield and price volatility characteristics than the underlying fixed-rate municipal bond from which they were created.

The name *derivative securities* has been attributed to these bond classes because they derive their value from the underlying fixed-rate municipal bond. Much of the development in this market has paralleled that of the taxable market, specifically the mortgage-backed securities market. We give two examples of municipal derivative securities as follows.

Floaters/Inverse Floaters

A common type of derivative security is one in which two classes of securities, a floating-rate security and an inverse floating-rate bond, are created from a fixed-rate bond. Two types of inverse floaters dominate the market: auction rate securities and the Tender Option Bond product.

Initially, inverse floaters took the form of auction rate securities. Salomon Smith Barney's proprietary auction rate product is called ARS (Auction Rate Securities) and IRS (Inverse Rate Securities). Lehman's proprietary product is called RIBS (Residual Interest Bonds) and SAVRS (Select Auction Variable Rate Securities), and Goldman's proprietary product is called PARS (Periodic Auction Rate Securities) and INFLOS, which are inverse floaters.

With these auction rate securities, the coupon rate on the floating-rate security is reset based on the results of a Dutch auction. The auction can take place anywhere between 7 days and 6 months (but the frequency is for a given security). The coupon rate on the floating-rate security changes in the same direction as market rates. The inverse floating-rate bond receives the residual interest;

that is, the coupon interest paid on this bond is the difference between the fixed-rate on the underlying bond and the floating-rate security. Thus the coupon rate on the inverse floating-rate bond changes in the opposite direction of interest rates.

The sum of the interest paid on the floater and inverse floater (plus fees associated with the auction) must always equal the interest paid on the fixed-rate bond from which they were created. A floor (a minimum interest rate) is established on the inverse floater. Typically the floor is zero. As a result, a cap (maximum interest rate) will be imposed on the floater such that the combined floor of zero on the inverse floater and the cap on the floater is equal to the rate on the fixed-rate bond from which they were created.

New issuance of auction-rate derivatives, however, has been largely supplanted by the Tender Offer Bond (TOB) programs as the primary vehicle to create inverse floaters. Functionally, TOBs are similar to the auction-rate product. Both derivatives are inverse floaters. Auction-rate floaters, however, are primarily sold to corporations, whereas TOB floaters are sold to money market funds. Auction floaters are ineligible to be sold to money market funds. When corporations have less use for tax-exempt income, the demand and liquidity in auction-rate securities can substantially decrease. Tax-exempt money market funds, unlike corporations, have a continuous need for tax-exempt interest. This demand provides a more stable buying base for the TOB floaters. To take advantage of this money-market demand, TOBs feature a liquidity facility, which makes these floating-rate derivatives putable and therefore money-market eligible. These liquidity facilities typically last 364 days and are provided by highly rated banks or broker-dealers.

TOBs are created through trusts. Given this structure, certain provisions must exist for the unwinding of a TOB. For example, if the remarketing agent fails to sell out the floating-rate class or the underlying bond falls below a minimum collateral value, a mandatory tender event is triggered. When a mandatory tender event occurs, the liquidity provider pays the floater holder par plus the bonds. The proceeds from this sale are used to first pay par plus accrued interest to the liquidity provider, then any accrued fees. Finally, the inverse floating-rate investor receives the residual value.

Several proprietary programs have been developed to market and sell plain-vanilla TOBs, which are used by mutual bond funds and insurance companies. Additionally, TOBs are used in more exotic combination trades by a few Wall Street structured products areas. Salomon Smith Barney's proprietary program is called "ROCs & ROLs." The short-term certificates are called ROCs or Residual Option Certificates. The inverse floaters are called the "ROLs" or Residual Option Longs. Lehman's is called RIBS and Trust Receipts, and Morgan Stanley's proprietary program is called municipal trust certificates.

Strips

Municipal strip obligations are created when a municipal bond's cash flows are used to back zero-coupon instruments. The maturity value of each zero-coupon

bond represents a cash flow of the underlying security. These are similar to the strips that are created in the Treasury market that we described in Chapter 4. One example of this in the municipal bond market is Merrill Lynch's *M-TIGRS*.

DEBT RETIREMENT STRUCTURE

Municipal securities are issued with one of two debt retirement structures or a combination of both. Either a bond has a *serial maturity structure* or a *term maturity structure*. A serial maturity structure requires a portion of the debt obligation to be retired each year. A term maturity structure provides for the debt obligation to be repaid on a final date.

The various provisions explained in Chapter 1 for paying off an issue prior to maturity—call provisions and sinking fund provisions—are also found in municipal securities. In revenue bonds there is a *catastrophe call provision* that requires the issuer to call the entire issue if the facility is destroyed.

For housing revenue bonds, the repayment of principal is made with each payment by the borrower. More specifically, there is a schedule of principal repayments. We will explain this when we cover mortgage-backed securities in later chapters. Moreover, as will be explained, a borrower has the right to pay off a mortgage prior to the maturity date. As explained in Chapter 1, any principal repayment in excess of the scheduled principal repayment is called a prepayment. As explained in Chapter 8, prepayments occur for a variety of reasons. One important reason is the refinancing of a mortgage loan to take advantage of the opportunity to obtain a lower-cost mortgage. Also, the default of the borrower will result in a prepayment once the property is foreclosed upon and sold. For a single-family housing revenue bond, a specifically identified maturity is designated as one to which all prepayments are used to retire bonds. Such issues are called *super sinkers*. Because of prepayments, the investor in a super sinker cannot be sure that the principal will not be repaid faster than scheduled. This risk is called *prepayment risk*, and we cover this risk when we discuss mortgage-backed securities.

CREDIT RISK

While municipal securities at one time were considered second in safety only to U.S. Treasury securities, today there are concerns about the credit risks of municipal securities. The first concern came out of the New York City billion-dollar financial crisis in 1975. On February 25, 1975, the state of New York's Urban Development Corporation defaulted on a $100 million note issue that was the obligation of New York City; many market participants had been convinced that the state of New York would not allow the issue to default. Although New York City was later able to obtain a $140 million revolving credit line from banks to

cure the default, lenders became concerned that the city would face difficulties in repaying its accumulated debt, which stood at $14 billion on March 31, 1975. This financial crisis sent a loud and clear warning to market participants in general—regardless of supposedly ironclad protection for the bondholder, when issuers such as large cities have severe financial difficulties, the financial stakes of public employee unions, vendors, and community groups may be dominant forces in balancing budgets. This reality was reinforced by the federal bankruptcy law (discussed later) that took effect in October 1979, which made it easier for the issuer of a municipal security to file for bankruptcy.

The second reason for concern about credit risk is the proliferation in the municipal market of innovative financing techniques to secure new bond issues. In addition to the established general obligation bonds and revenue bonds, there are now more non–voter-approved, innovative, and legally untested security mechanisms. These innovative financing mechanisms include moral obligation bonds and commercial bank-backed letters of credit bonds, to name a few. What distinguishes these newer bonds from the more traditional general obligation and revenue bonds is that there is no history of court decisions or other case law that firmly establishes the rights of bondholders and the obligations of issuers. It is not possible to determine in advance the probable legal outcome if the newer financing mechanisms were to be challenged in court. This is illustrated most dramatically by the bonds of the Washington Public Power Supply System (WPPSS), where bondholder rights to certain revenues were not upheld by the highest court in the state of Washington.

The third reason is the impact on the credit worthiness of both general obligation and revenue bonds that the scaling down of federal grants and aid programs have had. At the same time, there has been an increase in federal-mandated services. As an example of the change in federal funding policies, in 1980 then-President Ronald Reagan signed into law an extension of the Clean Water Act of 1970. Among other changes, the new amendments reduced the total federal contribution to local waste-treatment programs from $90 billion projected under the old law to $36 billion. Additionally, after October 1, 1984, the federal matching contribution to local sewerage construction projects declined from 75% to 55% of the costs. For two decades prior, many state and local governments had grown dependent on this and other federal grant programs as direct subsidies to their local economies as well.

The fourth reason for the concern with credit risk is that the U.S. economy is undergoing a fundamental change, which is resulting in a decline of various sectors of the economy. This decline has widespread implications for entire regions of the country. Many general obligations and revenue bond issuers can be expected to undergo significant economic deterioration that could adversely impact their tax collections and wealth indicators, such as personal income, real estate property values, and retail sales.

Finally, there is a concern that financial managers or treasurers of investment funds of municipalities may not be managing those funds prudently. Invest-

ment funds are targeted for short-term operating needs and long-term capital projects. The concern is not that a financial manager is earning a below-market rate using a conservative investment policy; rather, the concern is that the financial manager is pursuing a high-risk investment strategy that can result in a loss of principal that is so large that it jeopardizes the issuer's ability to meet its debt obligations. Such policies were followed by some financial managers as interest rates declined to low levels to generate additional interest income so as to avoid raising taxes. Financial managers who pursued such high-risk investment strategies that benefited from a decline in interest rates did extremely well when interest rates declined. However, when interest rates rose, the losses realized were devastating to some municipalities. Orange County, California, is not only the best-known example of a municipality that defaulted because of the imprudent management of investment funds, but it is also the largest municipal default to date as a result of the losses in its investment portfolio. One of the strategies followed by Orange County's then-treasurer, Robert Citron, is explained in Chapter 15.

Investors rely on the credit ratings that are assigned by the nationally recognized statistical rating organizations, or simply commercial rating companies. While there are four commercial rating companies, the two dominant companies with respect to rating municipal debt obligations are Standard & Poor's and Moody's. We discuss these ratings when we cover corporate debt obligations in Chapter 7.

We discuss the factors that should be considered in assessing the credit risk of an issue as follows.

Tax-Backed Debt

In assessing the credit risk of tax-backed debt, four basic categories should be considered. The first category includes information on the issuer's debt structure to determine the overall debt burden. The debt burden usually is composed of the respective direct and overlapping debts per capita as well as the respective direct and overlapping debts as percentages of real estate valuations and personal incomes.

The second category relates to the issuer's ability and political discipline to maintain sound budgetary policy. The focus of attention here usually is on the issuer's general operating funds and whether it has maintained at least balanced budgets over 3 to 5 years.

The third category involves determining the specific local taxes and intergovernmental revenues available to the issuer, as well as obtaining historical information both on tax collection rates, which are important when looking at property tax levies, and on the dependence of local budgets on specific revenue sources.

The fourth and last category of information necessary to the credit analysis is an assessment of the issuer's overall socioeconomic environment. The determinations that have to be made here include trends of local employment distribution and composition, population growth, real estate property valuation, and personal income, among other economic factors.

Revenue Bonds

Revenue bonds are issued for either project or enterprise financings where the bond issuers pledge to the bondholders the revenues generated by the operating projects financed, or for general public-purpose financings in which the issuers pledge to the bondholders the tax and revenue resources that were previously part of the general fund. While there are numerous security structures for revenue bonds, the underlying principle in rating is whether the project being financed will generate sufficient cash flows to satisfy the obligations due bondholders. In assessing the credit risk of revenue bonds, the trust indenture and legal opinion should provide legal comfort in the following bond-security areas: (1) the limits of the basic security, (2) the flow-of-funds structure, (3) the rate, or user-charge, covenant, (4) the priority-of-revenue claims, (5) the additional-bonds tests, and (6) other relevant covenants.

Limits of the Basic Security

The trust indenture and legal opinion should explain what are the revenues for the bonds and how they realistically may be limited by federal, state, and local laws and procedures. The importance of this is that although most revenue bonds are structured and appear to be supported by identifiable revenue streams, those revenues sometimes can be negatively affected directly by other levels of government.

Flow-of-Funds Structure for Revenue Bonds

For a revenue bond, the revenue of the enterprise is pledged to service the debt of the issue. The details of how revenue received by the enterprise will be disbursed are set forth in the trust indenture. Typically, the flow of funds for a revenue bond is as follows. First, all revenues from the enterprise are put into a revenue fund. From the revenue fund, disbursements for expenses are made to the following funds: *operation and maintenance fund*, *sinking fund*, *debt service reserve fund*, *renewal and replacement fund*, *reserve maintenance fund*, and *surplus fund*.[2]

Operations of the enterprise have priority over the servicing of the issue's debt, and cash needed to operate the enterprise is deposited from the revenue fund into the operation and maintenance fund. The pledge of revenue to the bondholders is a net revenue pledge, "net" meaning after operation expenses, so cash required to service the debt is deposited next into the sinking fund. Disbursements are then made to bondholders as specified in the trust indenture. Any remaining cash is then distributed to the reserve funds.

The purpose of the debt service reserve fund is to accumulate cash to cover any shortfall of future revenue to service the issue's debt. The specific amount that must be deposited is stated in the trust indenture. The function of the

---

2 There are structures in which it is legally permissible for others to tap the revenues of the enterprise prior to the disbursement set forth in the flow-of-funds structure just described. For example, it is possible that the revenue bond could be structured such that the revenue is first applied to the general obligation of the municipality that has issued the bond.

renewal and replacement fund is to accumulate cash for regularly scheduled major repairs and equipment replacement. The function of the reserve maintenance fund is to accumulate cash for extraordinary maintenance or replacement costs that might arise. Finally, if any cash remains after disbursement for operations, debt servicing, and reserves, it is deposited in the surplus fund. The issuer can use the cash in this fund in any way it deems appropriate.

Rate, or User-Charge, Covenants

There are various restrictive covenants included in the trust indenture for a revenue bond to protect the bondholders. A *rate*, or *user-charge, covenant* dictates how charges will be set on the product or service sold by the enterprise. The covenant could specify that the minimum charges be set so as to satisfy both expenses and debt servicing, or to yield a higher rate to provide for a certain amount of reserves.

Priority-of-Revenue Claims

The legal opinion as summarized in the official statement should clearly indicate whether others can legally tap the revenue of the issuer even before they start passing through the issuer's flow-of-funds structure.

Additional-Bonds Test

An *additional-bonds test covenant* indicates whether additional bonds with the same lien may be issued. If additional bonds with the same lien may be issued, the conditions that must first be satisfied are specified. Other covenants specify that the facility may not be sold, the amount of insurance to be maintained, requirements for recordkeeping and for auditing the enterprise's financial statements by an independent accounting firm, and requirements for maintaining the facilities in good order.

Other Relevant Covenants

There are other relevant covenants for the bondholder's protection that the trust indenture and legal opinion should cover. These usually include pledges by the issuer of the bonds to have insurance on the project, to have accounting records of the issuer annually audited by an outside certified public accountant, to have outside engineers annually review the condition of the facility, and to keep the facility operating for the life of the bonds.

TAX RISK

The investor in municipal securities is exposed to *tax risk*. There are two types of tax risk to which tax-exempt municipal security investors are exposed. The first is the risk that the federal income tax rate will be reduced. The higher the marginal tax rate, the greater the value of the tax-exemption feature. As the marginal tax rate

declines, the price of a tax-exempt municipal security will decline. Proposals to reduce the marginal tax rate result in less demand for municipal securities and, as a result, a decline in their price. This occurred most recently in 1995 when there were proposals for a flat tax in which the tax rate would be less than the prevailing rate.

The second type of tax risk is that a municipal bond issued as a tax-exempt issue may be eventually declared by the Internal Revenue Service to be taxable. This may occur because many municipal revenue bonds have elaborate security structures that could be subject to future adverse congressional action and IRS interpretation. A loss of the tax-exemption feature will cause the municipal bond to decline in value in order to provide a yield comparable to similar taxable bonds. As an example, in June 1980, the Battery Park City Authority sold $97.315 million in notes, which at the time of issuance legal counsel advised were exempt from federal income taxation. In November 1980, however, the IRS held that interest on these notes was not exempt. The issue was not settled until September 1981, when the Authority and the IRS signed a formal agreement resolving the matter so as to make the interest on the notes tax-exempt.

SECONDARY MARKET

Municipal bonds are traded in the over-the-counter market supported by municipal bond dealers across the country. Markets are maintained on smaller issuers (referred to as "local credits") by regional brokerage firms, local banks, and by some of the larger Wall Street firms. Larger issuers (referred to as "general market names") are supported by the larger brokerage firms and banks, many of whom have investment banking relationships with these issuers. There are brokers who serve as intermediaries in the sale of large blocks of municipal bonds among dealers and large institutional investors. More recently, municipal bonds are traded via the Internet.

In the municipal bond markets, an odd lot of bonds is $25,000 or less in par value for retail investors. For institutions, anything less than $100,000 in par value is considered an odd lot. Dealer spreads depend on several factors. For the retail investor, the spread can range from as low as one-quarter of one point ($12.50 per $5,000 par value) on large blocks of actively traded bonds to four points ($200 per $5,000 of par value) for odd lot sales of an inactive issue. For institutional investors, the dealer spread rarely exceeds one-half of one point ($25 per $5,000 of par value).

The convention for both corporate and Treasury bonds is to quote prices as a percentage of par value with 100 equal to par. Municipal bonds, however, generally are traded and quoted in terms of yield (yield to maturity or yield to call). The price of the bond in this case is called a *basis price*. The exception is certain long-maturity revenue bonds. A bond traded and quoted in dollar prices (actually, as a percentage of par value) is called a *dollar bond*.

Exhibit 1: Yield Ratio for AAA General Obligation Municipal Bonds to U.S. Treasuries of the Same Maturity (August 16, 1999)

Maturity	Yield on AAA General Obligation	Yield on U.S. Treasury	Yield Ratio
3 months	3.29%	4.93%	0.67
6 months	3.43	5.21	0.66
1 year	3.56	5.55	0.64
2 years	4.03	5.78	0.70
3 years	4.23	5.84	0.72
4 years	4.37	6.00	0.73
5 years	4.46	5.87	0.76
7 years	4.66	6.20	0.75
10 years	4.95	5.99	0.83
15 years	5.33	6.39	0.83
20 years	5.50	6.47	0.85
30 years	5.55	6.26	0.89

Source: Bloomberg Financial Markets

Actual price and trade information for specific municipal bonds is available on a daily basis at no charge actual municipal via the Internet at *www.investinginbonds.com*. This is the homepage of the Bond Market Association. The trade information provided is from the Municipal Securities Rulemaking Board and Standard & Poor's J.J. Kenny. The original source of the trades reported are dealer-to-dealer transactions and dealer-to-institutional customer and retail (individual investor) transactions.

YIELDS ON MUNICIPAL BONDS

Because of the tax-exempt feature of municipal bonds, the yield on municipal bonds is less than that on Treasuries with the same maturity. Exhibit 1 demonstrates this point.

Shown in the exhibit is the yield on AAA general obligation municipal bonds and the yield on same-maturity U.S. Treasuries. The *yield ratio* is the ratio of the municipal yield to the yield of a same-maturity Treasury security. Notice that the yield ratio increases with maturity. The ratio has changed over time. The higher the tax rate, the more attractive the tax-exempt feature and the lower the yield ratio. The yield ratio for 10-year AAA general obligation bonds and 10-year Treasury securities varied in the 1990s from a low of 0.72 on September 30, 1994, to a high of 0.94 on September 30, 1998.

A common yield measure used to compare the yield on a tax-exempt municipal bond with a comparable taxable bond is the *equivalent taxable yield*. The equivalent taxable yield is computed as follows:

$$\text{Equivalent taxable yield} = \frac{\text{Tax-exempt yield}}{1 - \text{Marginal tax rate}}$$

For example, suppose an investor in the 40% marginal tax bracket is considering the acquisition of a tax-exempt municipal bond that offers a yield of 6.5%. The equivalent taxable yield is 10.83%, as shown below:

$$\text{Equivalent taxable yield} = \frac{0.65}{(1 - 0.40)} = 0.1083$$

When computing the equivalent taxable yield, the traditionally computed yield to maturity is not the tax-exempt yield if the issue is selling at a discount because only the coupon interest is exempt from federal income taxes. Instead, the yield to maturity after an assumed tax rate on the capital gain is computed and used in the numerator of the formula above. The yield to maturity after an assumed tax on the capital gain is calculated in the same manner as the traditional yield to maturity as explained in Chapter 3.

Yield Spread Relationships within the Municipal Market

Yield spreads within the municipal bond market are attributable to various factors. Unlike the taxable fixed income market, there is no risk-free interest rate benchmark. Instead, the benchmark interest rate is for a generic triple-A rated general obligation bond or a revenue bond. Thus, the benchmark triple-A rated issue or index is the base rate used in the municipal bond market.

Institutional investors of municipal bonds price their holdings bonds off the MMD scale provided by Thomson Financial. This is a daily index of generic AAA prices covering the full yield curve that is provided to subscriber clients over the Internet. Dealer firms active in the municipal bond market generate a benchmark daily in order to price issues.

Perceived Creditworthiness of Issuer

As explained in Chapter 2, the spread between the yield on a particular issue and a benchmark triple-A rated issue that is identical in all respects except for quality is referred to as a *quality spread* or *credit spread.*

For insured municipal bonds, the insurer has agreed to pay interest and principal on the bonds if the issuer defaults on its bond payments. The rating on the bonds reflects that of the insurer. The spreads on insured bonds depend both on the health of the insurer as well as the credit on the underlying bonds. Prerefunded bonds are triple-A rated bonds when they are backed by an escrow consisting of risk-free bonds. Thus they are perceived as having no credit risk.

The spreads between insured, prerefunded, and noninsured bonds are affected by many factors, including the state of the economy and the relative supply in the market. As the economy deteriorates, the spread between insured or prerefunded and noninsured issues generally widens. This is because investors are

willing to pay up for lower credit risk issues when the economy is in an economic downturn and the expected default rate on municipal bonds rises.

Supply also has an important impact on relative bond spreads. For example, insured bonds generally trade at a lower yield than noninsured bonds. However, because of the large supply of lower credit risk (insured and prerefunded) issues, in recent times these bonds have been noted as trading on top of each other. This is purely a supply effect.

Term to Maturity

As we explained in earlier chapters, there is a term structure of interest rates (graphically portrayed by the yield curve). In the taxable fixed income market, three shapes have been observed for the yield curve: normal (or positively sloped), flat, and inverse (or negatively sloped). For tax-exempt municipal securities, only a positively sloped yield curve has been observed.

Tax Treatment at the State and Local Levels

State and local governments may tax interest income on municipal issues that are exempt from federal income taxes. Some municipalities exempt interest income from all municipal issues from taxation, but others do not. Some states exempt interest income from bonds issued by municipalities within the state but tax the interest income from bonds issued by municipalities outside of the state. The implication is that two municipal securities of the same quality rating and the same maturity may trade at some spread because of the relative demand for bonds of municipalities in different states. For example, in high-income-tax states such as New York and California, the demand for bonds of municipalities will drive down their yield relative to municipalities in a low-income-tax state such as Florida.

Temporary Supply and Demand Imbalances

At any given time, there may be an imbalance between the supply of a particular type of issue (e.g., double-A revenue bond issued by an entity in the state of New York) and the demand for that particular issue. As mentioned earlier, the relatively high supply of insured versus noninsured issues has caused the yield on insured bonds to increase relative to that of noninsured bonds. In addition, in years in which there is a flood of refundings, such as in 1993, there is an increase in supply resulting in an underperformance of municipals relative to the Treasury market.

Certain states or counties, because of credit or other considerations, have high demand relative to supply of like bonds from other municipalities. For example, prerefunded bonds generally outperform non-prerefunded bonds. However, this is not always the case, especially in times of temporary supply/demand imbalances. For example, because the demand for Maryland bonds is high relative to other bonds, the former bonds often outperform prerefunded issues.

In addition, there is a seasonal effect in the municipals market. In December and June, many bonds mature or first become callable. Because of this effect,

new bonds are issued in order to refund existing issues. This is called a *rollover.* Because the supply of municipal bonds increases during these months, the spreads among bonds of different maturities and characteristics are affected and the spread between municipal and Treasury securities widens.

KEY POINTS

- *Municipal securities are debt obligations issued by state governments, local governments (counties, cities, villages, towns, and townships), entities created by local governments (school districts and special service system districts), and public agencies (commissions and authorities).*
- *There are both tax-exempt and taxable municipal securities, where "tax-exempt" means that interest on a municipal security is exempt from federal income taxation.*
- *The tax-exemption of municipal securities applies to interest income, not capital gains, and the exemption may or may not extend to taxation at the state and local levels.*
- *The interest on taxable municipal securities is taxable at the federal level.*
- *Most municipal securities that have been issued are tax-exempt.*
- *Other types of tax-exempt bonds are those issued by nonprofit organizations (501(c)(3) obligations) such as museums and foundations, and obligations of the District of Columbia and any possession of the United States (Puerto Rico, the Virgin Islands, and Guam).*
- *For municipal securities whose interest is subject to the alternative minimum tax, the value of the tax-exempt feature is reduced.*
- *Interest paid or accrued to carry a position in tax-exempt municipal bonds is not tax deductible.*
- *An official statement describing the issue and the issuer is prepared for new municipal offerings.*
- *The legal opinion that is summarized in the official statement is important because (1) it sets forth that bond counsel has determined if the issue is indeed legally able to issue the bonds, and (2) bond counsel verifies that the issuer has properly prepared for the bond sale by having enacted various required ordinances, resolutions, and trust indentures and without violating any other laws and regulations.*
- *There are basically two types of municipal security structures: tax-backed debt and revenue bonds.*
- *Tax-backed debt obligations are instruments issued by states, counties, special districts, cities, towns, and school districts that are secured by some form of tax revenue.*
- *Tax-backed debt includes general obligation debt (the broadest type of tax-backed debt), appropriation-backed obligations, debt obligations supported by public credit enhancement programs, and short-term debt instruments.*
- *Unlimited tax general obligation debt is secured by the issuer's unlimited taxing power where the tax revenue sources include corporate and individual income taxes, sales taxes, and property taxes.*

- ❑ *Unlimited tax general obligation debt is said to be secured by the full faith and credit of the issuer.*

- ❑ *A limited tax general obligation debt is a limited tax pledge because for such debt there is a statutory limit on tax rates that the issuer may levy to service the debt.*

- ❑ *A general obligation bond is said to be double-barreled when it is secured not only by the issuer's general taxing powers to create revenues accumulated in a general fund, but also by certain identified fees, grants, and special charges, which provide additional revenues from outside the general fund.*

- ❑ *Moral obligation bonds and leased-backed debt are examples of appropriation-backed obligations.*

- ❑ *A moral obligation bond is a bond issued by an agency or authority that carries a nonbinding pledge by the state for making up shortfalls in the issuing entity's obligation if approved by the state legislature.*

- ❑ *A public credit enhancement obligation is one in which there is a guarantee by the state or a federal agency or when there is an obligation to automatically withhold and deploy state aid to pay any defaulted debt service by the issuing entity.*

- ❑ *Short-term debt instruments include municipal notes, commercial paper, variable-rate demand obligations, and a hybrid of the last two products.*

- ❑ *Municipal notes include bond anticipation notes (BANs) and cash flow notes [tax anticipation notes (TANs), revenue anticipation notes (RANs), and TRANs)].*

- ❑ *The lien position of cash flow noteholders relative to other general obligation debt that has been pledged the same revenue can be either (1) a first lien on all pledged revenue, thereby having priority over general obligation debt that has been pledged the same revenue, (2) a lien that is in parity with general obligation debt that has been pledged the same revenue, or (3) a lien that is subordinate to the lien of general obligation debt that has been pledged the same revenue.*

- ❑ *There are two types of commercial paper issued by municipalities: unenhanced commercial paper (a debt obligation issued based solely on the issuer's credit quality and liquidity capability) and enhanced commercial paper (a debt obligation that is credit enhanced with bank liquidity facilities, insurance, or a bond purchase agreement).*

- ❑ *Variable-rate demand obligations (VRDOs) are floating-rate obligations that have a nominal long-term maturity but have a coupon rate that is either reset daily or every 7 days with an option to put the issue back to the issuer at any time with 7 days notice.*

- ❑ *Revenue bonds are issued for enterprise financings that are secured by the revenues generated by the completed projects themselves, or for general public-purpose financings in which the issuers pledge to the bondholders the tax and revenue resources that were previously part of the general fund.*

- ❑ *Revenue bonds include utility revenue bonds, transportation revenue bonds, housing revenue bonds, higher education revenue bonds, health care revenue bonds, seaport revenue bonds, sports complex and convention center revenue bonds, and industrial revenue bonds.*

- ❑ *Insured bonds, bank-backed municipal bonds, and refunded bonds are bonds with special security structures.*

- ❑ *Insured bonds, in addition to being secured by the issuer's revenue, are backed by insurance policies written by commercial insurance companies.*

- ❑ *There are three basic types of bank support: letter of credit, irrevocable line of credit, and revolving line of credit.*

- ❑ *Refunded bonds are no longer secured as either general obligation or revenue bonds but are supported by a portfolio of securities held in an escrow fund.*

- ❑ *If escrowed with securities guaranteed by the U.S. government, refunded bonds are the safest municipal bond available.*

- ❑ *A prerefunded municipal bond is one in which the escrow fund is structured so that the bonds are to be called at the first possible call date or a subsequent call date established in the original bond indenture.*

- ❑ *Escrowed-to-maturity bonds are refunded bonds structured to match the debt obligation to the maturity date.*

- ❑ *Municipal derivative securities include inverse floaters, and strips and partial strips.*

- ❑ *Municipal securities are issued with one of two debt retirement structures or a combination of both: a serial maturity structure or a term maturity structure.*

- ❑ *In assessing the credit risk of tax-backed debt, four basic informational categories should be considered: (1) information on the issuer's debt structure to determine the overall debt burden; (2) information on the issuer's ability and political discipline to maintain sound budgetary policy; (3) information on the specific local taxes and intergovernmental revenues available to the issuer; and (4) information on the issuer's overall socioeconomic environment.*

- ❑ *The equivalent taxable yield compares the yield on a taxable security and that of a municipal security.*

- ❑ *Investors in municipal bonds are exposed to tax risk that can take the form of a reduction in the federal marginal tax rate and the potential that a tax-exempt issue may be eventually declared by the Internal Revenue Service to be taxable.*

- ❑ *Municipal bonds generally are traded and quoted in terms of yield (yield to maturity or yield to call) rather than dollar price.*

- ❑ *Because municipal bonds are exempt from federal income taxation, the yield on municipal bonds is less than that on Treasuries with the same maturity.*
- ❑ *For insured municipal bonds, the spread depends both on the health of the insurer as well as the credit on the underlying bonds.*
- ❑ *Since prerefunded bonds are triple-A rated bonds that are backed by an escrow consisting of risk-free bonds, they are perceived as having no credit risk.*
- ❑ *Municipal bond supply has an important impact on yield spreads.*
- ❑ *The municipal bond yield curve has always been normal or positively sloped.*
- ❑ *The tax treatment of interest income at the state and local levels affects spreads.*

Chapter 7

Senior Corporate Instruments: I

Corporations are classified into four general categories by bond information services: (1) utilities, (2) transportations, (3) industrials, and (4) banks and finance companies. Finer breakdowns are often made to create more homogeneous groupings. For example, utilities are subdivided into electric power companies, gas distribution companies, water companies, and communication companies. Transportations are divided further into airlines, railroads, and trucking companies. Industrials are the catchall class and the most heterogeneous of the groupings with respect to investment characteristics. Industrials include all kinds of manufacturing, merchandising, and service companies.

In this chapter and Chapter 8, we look at senior corporate instruments. These instruments are financial obligations of a corporation that have a priority over the claims of common stock in the case of bankruptcy. They include debt obligations and preferred stock. There are four types of corporate debt obligations: bonds, medium-term notes, commercial paper, and bank loans. Preferred stock is a form of equity.

In this chapter we look at the general characteristics of corporate debt and the characteristics of corporate bonds. We begin with an overview of the bankruptcy process and the rights of creditors. We then look at the differences between secured debt and unsecured debt. A detailed look at the indenture for a debt obligation follows. While in Chapter 1 we described sinking fund provisions for bonds in general, here we will look at some of the unique features in corporate bonds. Finally, we look at corporate bond ratings and the rating process.

CORPORATE BANKRUPTCY AND CREDITOR RIGHTS

The holder of a corporate debt instrument has priority over the equity owners in a bankruptcy proceeding. Moreover, there are creditors who have priority over other creditors.

The law governing bankruptcy in the United States is the Bankruptcy Reform Act of 1978. One purpose of the act is to set forth the rules for a corporation to be either liquidated or reorganized. The *liquidation* of a corporation means that all the assets will be distributed to the holders of claims of the corporation and no corporate entity will survive. In a *reorganization*, a new corporate entity

---

This chapter draws from several chapters in Richard W. Wilson and Frank J. Fabozzi, *Corporate Bonds: Structures & Analysis* (New Hope, PA: Frank J. Fabozzi Associates, 1996).

will result. Some security holders of the bankrupt corporation will receive cash in exchange for their claims, others may receive new securities in the corporation that results from the reorganization, and others may receive a combination of both cash and new securities in the resulting corporation.

Another purpose of the bankruptcy act is to give a corporation time to decide whether to reorganize or liquidate and then the necessary time to formulate a plan to accomplish either a reorganization or liquidation. This is achieved because when a corporation files for bankruptcy, the act grants the corporation protection from creditors who seek to collect their claims. The petition for bankruptcy can be filed either by the company itself, in which case it is called a *voluntary bankruptcy*, or by its creditors, in which case it is called an *involuntary bankruptcy*. A company that files for protection under the bankruptcy act generally becomes a "debtor-in-possession," and continues to operate its business under the supervision of the court.

The bankruptcy act comprises 15 chapters, each chapter covering a particular type of bankruptcy. Chapter 7 deals with the liquidation of a company; Chapter 11 deals with the reorganization of a company.

When a company is liquidated, creditors receive distributions based on the "absolute priority rule" to the extent assets are available. The absolute priority rule is the principle that senior creditors are paid in full before junior creditors are paid anything. For secured and unsecured creditors, the absolute priority rule guarantees their seniority to equityholders.

In liquidations, the absolute priority rule generally holds. In contrast, a good body of literature argues that strict absolute priority has not been upheld by the courts or the SEC in reorganizations.[1] Studies of actual reorganizations under Chapter 11 have found that the violation of absolute priority is the rule rather than the exception, occurring about 75% of the time.[2]

SECURED DEBT

A corporate debt issue can be secured or unsecured. Here we look at secured debt. By secured debt it is meant that some form of collateral is pledged to ensure repayment of the debt.

Utility Mortgage Bonds

Debt secured by real property such as plant and equipment is called *mortgage debt*. The largest issuers of mortgage debt are the electric utility companies. Of

---

[1] Thomas H. Jackson, "Of Liquidation, Continuation, and Delay: An Analysis of Bankruptcy Policy and Nonbankruptcy Rules," *American Bankruptcy Law Journal* 60 (1986), pp. 399–428.

[2] See: Julian R. Franks and Walter N. Torous, "An Empirical Investigation of U.S. Firms in Reorganization," *Journal of Finance* (July 1989), pp 747–769; Lawrence A. Weiss, "Bankruptcy Resolution: Direct Costs and Violation of Priority of Claims," *Journal of Financial Economics* (1990), pp. 285–314; and Frank J. Fabozzi, Jane Tripp Howe, Takashi Makabe, and Toshihide Sudo, "Recent Evidence on the Distribution Patterns in Chapter 11 Reorganizations," *Journal of Fixed Income* (Spring 1993), pp. 6–23.

the major electric companies that periodically issue debt, only one—The United Illuminating Company in Connecticut—issues only unsecured debt; all of the others have mortgage debt as the primary debt vehicle in their capital structures. Other utilities, such as telephone companies and gas pipeline and distribution firms, have also used mortgage debt as sources of capital, but generally to a lesser extent than electrics.

Most electric utility bond indentures do not limit the total amount of bonds that may be issued. This is called an *open-ended mortgage*. The mortgage generally is a first lien on the company's real estate, fixed property, and franchises, subject to certain exceptions or permitted encumbrances owned at the time of the execution of the indenture or its supplement. The *after-acquired property clause* also subjects to the mortgage property acquired by the company after the filing of the original or supplemental indenture. For example, the prospectus for Sierra Pacific Power Company's 10⅛% First Mortgage Bonds due 2018 says that the "New Bonds will be secured . . . by a first lien on substantially all properties and franchises owned by the Company at October 31, 1940 [the indenture is dated December 1, 1940] and on property and franchises subsequently acquired which in each case are used or useful in the business of furnishing electricity, water or gas, or in any business incidental thereto or operated in connection therewith, except properties released pursuant to the Mortgage. . . ."

Property that is excepted from the lien of the mortgage may include nuclear fuel (it is often financed separately through other secured loans); cash, securities, and other similar items and current assets; automobiles, trucks, tractors, and other vehicles; inventories and fuel supplies; office furniture and leaseholds; property and merchandise held for resale in the normal course of business; receivables, contracts, leases, and operating agreements; and timber, minerals, mineral rights, and royalties. In Sierra Pacific Power's case, "there are specifically excepted from the lien of the Mortgage certain current assets, securities and other personal property; timber; oil and other minerals; certain other property owned at October 31, 1940; and all property subsequently acquired, not used or useful to the Company in its utility business."

Permitted encumbrances might include liens for taxes and governmental assessments, judgments, easements and leases, certain prior liens, and minor defects, irregularities, and deficiencies in titles of properties and rights-of-way that do not materially impair the use of the property. For example, the mortgage for Indiana & Michigan Electric Company as supplemented in 1987 for the issuance of 9⅛% First Mortgage Bonds due 1997, is "(a) a first lien on substantially all of the fixed physical property and franchises of the Company . . . and (b) a lien, subject to the lien of IMPCo's mortgage, on the fixed physical property acquired in connection with the merger of IMPCo into the Company. . . ." These and other bonds issued after July 1, 1986, were subject to some $24 million of judgment liens, the enforcement of which had been stayed. These judgment liens, according to the prospectus dated June 23, 1987, may have a priority senior to the first mortgage lien of the bonds.

To provide for proper maintenance of the property and replacement of worn-out plant, maintenance fund, maintenance and replacement fund, or renewal and replacement fund provisions were placed in indentures. These clauses stipulate that the issuer spend a certain amount of money for these purposes. Depending on the company, the required sums may be around 15% of operating revenues. As defined in other cases, the figure is based on a percentage of the depreciable property or amount of bonds outstanding. These requirements usually can be satisfied by certifying that the specified amount of expenditures has been made for maintenance and repairs to the property or by gross property additions. They can also be satisfied by depositing cash or outstanding mortgage bonds with the trustee; the deposited cash can be used for property additions, repairs, and maintenance or in some cases—to the concern of holders of high-coupon debt—the redemption of bonds.

Another provision for bondholder security is the *release and substitution of property clause*. If the company releases property from the mortgage lien (such as through a sale of a plant or other property that may have become obsolete or no longer necessary for use in the business, or through the state's power of eminent domain), it must substitute other property or cash and securities to be held by the trustee, usually in an amount equal to the released property's fair value. It may use the proceeds or cash held by the trustee to retire outstanding bonded debt. Certainly, a bondholder would not let go of the mortgaged property without substitution of satisfactory new collateral or adjustment in the amount of the debt because the bondholder should want to maintain the value of the security behind the bond. In some cases the company may waive the right to issue additional bonds.

Although the typical electric utility mortgage does not limit the total amount of bonds that may be issued, certain issuance tests or bases usually have to be satisfied before the company can sell more bonds. New bonds are often restricted to no more than 60% to 66⅔% of the value of net bondable property. This generally is the lower of the fair value or cost of property additions, after adjustments and deductions for property that had previously been used for the authentication and issuance of previous bond issues, retirements of bondable property or the release of property, and any outstanding prior liens. Bonds may also be issued in exchange or substitution for outstanding bonds, previously retired bonds, and bonds otherwise acquired. Bonds may also be issued in an amount equal to the cash deposited with the trustee. Sierra Pacific Power Company's $70 million of 10⅛% First Mortgage Bonds due 2018 were issued against the early retirement of $60 million 15⅜% First Mortgage Bonds due 1991. The remaining $10 million 10⅛s were issued on the basis of unfunded additional property additions at 60%.

A further earnings test found often in utility indentures requires interest charges to be covered by pretax income available for interest charges of at least two times. The Connecticut Light and Power Company prospectus for its 6⅛% First and Refunding Mortgage Bonds, Series B due February 1, 2004, states:

> . . . the Company may not issue additional bonds under the B Provisions unless its net earnings, as defined and as computed without deducting income taxes, for 12 consecutive calendar months during the period of 15 consecutive calendar months immediately preceding the first day of the month in which the application to the Trustee for authentication of additional bonds is made were at least twice the annual interest charges on all the Company's outstanding bonds, including the proposed additional bonds, and any outstanding prior lien obligations.

Mortgage bonds go by many different names. The most common of the senior lien issues are *First Mortgage Bonds* as used by The Cincinnati Gas & Electric Company, Long Island Lighting Company, and Sierra Pacific Power Company, among others. Baltimore Gas & Electric Company has the title of *First Refunding Mortgage Bonds* (First and Refunding Mortgage Bonds for Connecticut Light and Power Company), while Canal Electric Company, a wholesale electric generator, uses *First and General Mortgage Bonds*. The Baltimore issue, subject to a first mortgage lien (with certain exceptions), is also secured by a pledge of 100,000 shares each of Class A stock and Class B stock of Safe Harbor Water Power Corporation, an operator of a hydroelectric plant in Pennsylvania. The Baltimore bonds are also secured by the common stock of other directly owned subsidiaries but not stock of second-level subsidiaries (i.e., subsidiaries of subsidiaries). The Canal Electric lien is broad-based, covering all of its property adjacent to the Cape Cod Canal, after-acquired property, and pledged contracts relating to a couple of its generating units. Texas Utilities Electric Company issues *First Mortgage and Collateral Trust Bonds*. These are secured by Class "A" Bonds held by the trustee, which are first mortgage bonds issued by former subsidiaries (now divisions), and a first mortgage lien on certain other property of the Company. Texas Utilities has also issued Secured Medium-Term Notes as a series of the First Mortgage and Collateral Trust Bonds under the December 1, 1983, Mortgage and Deed of Trust.

There are instances (excluding prior lien bonds as mentioned earlier) when a company might have two or more layers of mortgage debt outstanding with different priorities. This situation usually occurs because the companies cannot issue additional first mortgage debt (or the equivalent) under the existing indentures. Often this secondary debt level is called *General and Refunding Mortgage Bonds* (G&R). In reality, this is mostly second mortgage debt. The mortgage debt issues of Public Service Company of New Hampshire, besides first mortgage bonds and general and refunding mortgage bonds with varying degrees of security, also had third mortgage bonds as well as publicly issued unsecured debt. All in all, there were four levels of claims against the company and its properties.

As stated earlier, electric companies utilize mortgage debt more than other utilities. However, other utilities, such as telephone and gas companies, also have mortgage debt. Among the telephone companies with mortgage bonds are

some of the subsidiaries and affiliates of the GTE Corporation system. Illinois Bell Telephone Company and New York Telephone Company issued first mortgage debt until the early 1970s, when the mortgage was closed and they started issuing unsecured debenture debt. Prior to the Bell System's breakup, the mortgage bonds and debentures of the Bell subsidiaries carried the same rating. For example, the bonds and debentures of New York Telephone and Illinois Bell were rated triple-A by Moody's and Standard & Poor's. After the divestiture, however, Moody's applied different ratings to the secured and unsecured debt, while S&P had the same rating whether the debt was first mortgage or debenture. In early 1994, Illinois Bell's mortgage debt was rated Aaa/AAA and the debentures Aa1/AAA. Similarly, New York Telephone's secured debt was rated A1 and A, while the unsecured carried A2 and A designations.

Gas pipeline companies also use mortgage debt. Here, again, the issuance tests are similar to those for the electric issues, as are the mortgage liens. However, the pipeline companies may have an additional clause subjecting certain gas purchase and sale contracts to the mortgage lien.

Other Mortgage Debt

Nonutility companies do not offer much mortgage debt nowadays; the preferred form of debt financing is unsecured. In the past, railroad operating companies were frequent issuers of mortgage debt. In many cases, a wide variety of secured debt might be found in a company's capitalization. One issue may have a first lien on a certain portion of the right of way and a second mortgage on another portion of the trackage, as well as a lien on the railroad's equipment, subject to the prior lien of existing equipment obligations. Certain railroad properties are not subject to such a lien. Railroad mortgages are often much more complex and confusing to bond investors than other types of mortgage debt.

In the broad classification of industrial companies, only a few have first mortgage bonds outstanding. The steel industry's Inland Steel Company, National Steel Corporation, Youngstown Sheet and Tube Company, and Jones & Laughlin Steel Corporation had mortgage debt. The latter two were part of the bankrupt LTV Steel complex. While electric utility mortgage bonds generally have a lien on practically all of the company's property, steel company mortgage debt has more limited liens. Mortgages may also contain maintenance and repair provisions, earnings tests for the issuance of additional debt, release and substitution of property clauses, and limited after-acquired property provisions. In some cases, shares of subsidiaries might also be pledged as part of the lien.

Some mortgage bonds are secured by a lien on a specific property rather than on most of a company's property, as in the case of an electric utility. For example, Humana Inc. sold a number of small issues of first mortgage bonds secured by liens on specific hospital properties. Although technically mortgage bonds, the basic security is centered on Humana's continued profitable operations. Because the security is specific rather than general, investors are apt to

view these bonds as less worthy or of a somewhat lower ranking than fully secured or general lien issues. As the prospectuses say, the bonds are general obligations of Humana Inc. and also secured by the first mortgage.

Other Secured Debt

Debt can be secured by many different assets. Forstmann & Company, Inc. issued $60 million 11¾% Secured Senior Extendible Notes due April 1, 1998, secured by a first-priority lien on substantially all of its real property, machinery, and equipment, and by a second-priority lien on its inventory, accounts receivables, and intangibles; the first-priority lien on these latter assets is held by General Electric Credit Corporation for its revolving credit loan.

Collateral trust debentures, bonds, and *notes* are secured by financial assets such as cash, receivables, other notes, debentures, or bonds, and not by real property. Collateral trust notes and debentures have been issued by companies engaged in vehicle leasing, such as RLC Corporation, Leaseway Transportation Corporation, and Ryder System, Inc. The proceeds from these offerings were advanced to various subsidiaries in exchange for their unsecured promissory notes which, in turn, were pledged with the trustees as security for the parent company debt. These pledged notes may later become secured by liens or other claims on vehicles. Protective covenants for these collateralized issues may include limitations on the equipment debt of subsidiaries, on the consolidated debt of the issuer and its subsidiaries, on dividend payments by the issuer and the subsidiaries, and on the creation of liens and purchase money mortgages, among other things.

The eligible collateral is held by a trustee and periodically marked to market to ensure that the market value has a liquidation value in excess of the amount needed to repay the entire outstanding bonds and accrued interest. If the collateral is insufficient, the issuer must, within several days, bring the value of the collateral up to the required amount. If the issuer is unable to do so, the trustee would then sell collateral and redeem bonds. Another collateralized structure allows for the defeasance or "mandatory collateral substitution," which provides the investor assurance that it will continue to receive the same interest payments until maturity. Instead of redeeming the bonds with the proceeds of the collateral sale, the proceeds are used to purchase a portfolio of U.S. government securities in such an amount that the cash flow is sufficient to meet the principal and interest payments on the mortgage-backed bond. Because of the structure of these issues, the rating agencies have assigned triple-A ratings to them. The rating is based on the strength of the collateral and the issues' structure, not on the issuers' credit standing.

Equipment Trust Financing: Railroads

Railroads and airlines have financed much of their rolling stock and aircraft with secured debt. The securities go by various names such as *equipment trust certificates* (ETCs), in the case of railroads, and *secured equipment certificates*, *guaranteed loan certificates*, and *loan certificates* in the case of airlines. We look at railroad

equipment trust financing first for two reasons: (1) the financing of railway equipment under the format in general public use today goes back to the late nineteenth century, and (2) it has had a superb record of safety of principal and timely payment of interest, more traditionally known as dividends. Railroads probably comprise the largest and oldest group of issuers of secured equipment financing.

Probably the earliest instance in U.S. financial history in which a company bought equipment under a conditional sales agreement (CSA) was in 1845 when the Schuylkill Navigation Company purchased some barges. Over the years, secured equipment financing proved to be an attractive way for railroads—both good and bad credits—to raise the capital necessary to finance rolling stock. Various types of instruments were devised—*equipment bonds* (known as the New York Plan), *conditional sales agreements* (also known as the New York CSA), lease arrangements, and the Philadelphia Plan equipment trust certificate. The New York Plan equipment bond has not been used since the 1930s. The Philadelphia Plan ETC is the form used for most, if not all, public financings in today's market.

The ratings for equipment trust certificates are higher than on the same company's mortgage debt or other public debt securities. This is due primarily to the collateral value of the equipment, its superior standing in bankruptcy compared with other claims, and the instrument's generally self-liquidating nature. The railroad's actual credit worthiness may mean less for some equipment trust investors than for investors in other rail securities or, for that matter, other corporate paper. However, that is not to say that financial analysis of the issuer should be ignored.

Equipment trust certificates are issued under agreement that provide a trust for the benefit of the investors. Each certificate represents an interest in the trust equal to its principal amount and bears the railroad's unconditional guarantee of prompt payment, when due, of the principal and dividends (the term *dividends* is used because the payments represent income from a trust and not interest on a loan). The trustee holds the title to the equipment, which when the certificates are retired, passes to, or vests in, the railroad, but the railroad has all other ownership rights. It can take the depreciation and can utilize any tax benefits on the subject equipment. The railroad agrees to pay the trustee sufficient rental for the principal payments and the dividends due on the certificates, together with expenses of the trust and certain other charges. The railroad uses the equipment in its normal operations and is required to maintain it in good operating order and repair (at its own expense). If the equipment is destroyed, lost, or becomes worn out or unsuitable for use (i.e., suffers a "casualty occurrence"), the company must substitute the fair market value of that equipment in the form of either cash or additional equipment. Cash may be used to acquire additional equipment unless the agreement states otherwise. The trust equipment is usually clearly marked that it is not the railroad's property.

Immediately after the issuance of an ETC, the railroad has an equity interest in the equipment that provides a margin of safety for the investor. Normally, the ETC investor finances no more than 80% of the cost of the equipment

and the railroad the remaining 20%. The Union Pacific Railroad Company's 8¾% Equipment Trust No. 1 of 1987 issued January 28, 1988, was for $101,200,000, equal to 80% of the original cost of the equipment financed. This equipment consisted of 75 Dash diesel-electric road freight locomotives with a cost of $83,668,950 (cost per locomotive, $1,115,586), 25 diesel-electric road freight locomotives with a cost of $29,357,500 (cost per locomotive, $1,174,300), and 345 center partition bulkhead flat cars costing $13,467,906 ($39,037 each) for a total of $126,494,356. Although modern equipment is longer-lived than that of many years ago, the ETC's length of maturity is still generally the standard 15 years (there are some exceptions noted as follows).

The structure of the financing usually provides for periodic retirement of the outstanding certificates. The most common form of ETC is the serial variety. It is usually issued in 15 equal maturities, each one coming due annually in years 1 through 15. The Atchison, Topeka and Santa Fe Railway Company Equipment Trust, Series AA, dated February 15, 1994, consists of 15 serial maturities of $3,795,000 due each February 15 from 1995 through 2009. The certificates were reoffered at par by J. P. Morgan Securities Inc., the underwriter, in April 1994 at yields ranging from 4.25% for the 1-year piece to 7.57% for the February 15, 2009 maturity. Consolidated Rail Corporation issued its 1988 Equipment Trust Certificates, Series A, with serial maturities of unequal principal amounts due annually October 15, 1991 to October 15, 2004. There are single-maturity (or "bullet maturity") ETCs such as the previously mentioned Union Pacific 8¾% Equipment Trust No. 1 of 1987. This 7-year issue did not have a sinking fund and matured on January 15, 1995. There are also sinking fund equipment trust certificates where the ETCs are retired through the operation of a normal sinking fund, one-fifteenth of the original amount issued per year. Thus the Louisville and Nashville Railroad Company's 12.30% Equipment Trust Certificates, Series 10, due February 1, 1995 (original issue $53,600,000), had an annual sinking fund of $3,575,000, designed to retire 93.4% of the issue prior to maturity.

The standing of railroad or common carrier ETCs in bankruptcy is of vital importance to the investor. Because the equipment is needed for operations, the bankrupt railroad's management will more than likely reaffirm the lease of the equipment because, without rolling stock, it is out of business. One of the first things the trustees of the Penn Central Transportation Company did after the firm filed for bankruptcy on June 21, 1970, was to reaffirm its equipment debt. On August 19, the court issued the required equipment debt assumption orders. There were outstanding about $90.7 million of equipment trust certificates, $442.9 million of conditional sales agreements, and unexpired lease rental payments on other contracts of $594 million. It was not until the end of 1978 that investors and speculators started to recover something from the other Penn Central obligations. Cases of disaffirmation of equipment obligations are very rare indeed, but if equipment debt were to be disaffirmed, the trustee could repossess and then try to release or sell it to others. Any deficiency due the equipment debtholders would

still be an unsecured claim against the bankrupt railway company. Standard-gauge, nonspecialized equipment should not be difficult to release to another railroad.

The Bankruptcy Reform Act of 1978 provides specifically that railroads be reorganized, not liquidated, and subchapter IV of Chapter 11 grants them special treatment and protection. One very important feature found in Section 77(j) of the preceding Bankruptcy Act was carried over to the new law. Section 1168 states that Section 362 (the automatic stay provision) and Section 363 (the use, sale, or lease of property section) are not applicable in railroad bankruptcies. It protects the rights of the equipment lenders while giving the trustee the chance to cure any defaults. Railroad bankruptcies usually do not occur overnight but creep up gradually as the result of steady deterioration over the years. New equipment financing capability becomes restrained. The outstanding equipment debt at the time of bankruptcy often is not substantial and usually has a good equity cushion built in.

Equipment debt of noncommon carriers such as private car leasing lines (Trailer Train, Union Tank Car, General American Transportation, etc.) does not enjoy this special protection under the Bankruptcy Act.

During the twentieth century, losses have been rare and delayed payments of dividends and principal only slightly less so.

Airline Equipment Debt

Airline equipment debt has some of the special status that is held by railroad equipment trust certificates. Of course, it is much more recent, having developed since the end of World War II. Many airlines have had to resort to secured equipment financing, especially since the early 1970s. Like railroad equipment obligations, certain equipment debt of certified airlines, under Section 1110 of the Bankruptcy Reform Act of 1978, is not subject to Sections 362 and 363 of the Act, namely the automatic stay and the power of the court to prohibit the repossession of the equipment. The creditor must be a lessor, a conditional vendor, or hold a purchase money security interest with respect to the aircraft and related equipment. The secured equipment must be new, not used. Of course, it gives the airline 60 days in which to decide to cancel the lease or debt and to return the equipment to the trustee. If the reorganization trustee decides to reaffirm the lease in order to continue using the equipment, it must perform or assume the debtor's obligations, which become due or payable after that date, and cure all existing defaults other than those resulting solely from the financial condition, bankruptcy, insolvency, or reorganization of the airline. Payments resume including those that were due during the delayed period. Thus, the creditor will get either the payments due according to the terms of the contract or the equipment.

The equipment is an important factor. If the airplanes are of recent vintage, well-maintained, fuel efficient, and relatively economical to operate, it is more likely that a company in distress and seeking to reorganize would assume the equipment lease. However, if the outlook for reorganization appears dim from the outset and the airplanes are older and less economical, the airline could very

well disaffirm the lease. In this case, releasing the aircraft or selling it at rents and prices sufficient to continue the original payments and terms to the security holders might be difficult. Of course, the resale market for aircraft is on a plane-by-plane basis and highly subject to supply and demand factors. Multimillion-dollar airplanes have a somewhat more limited market than do boxcars and hopper cars worth only $30,000.

Most of the publicly offered equipment loans in the 1970s financed approximately 70% to 75% of the cost of new aircraft and related parts. The 25% to 30% equity was invested mostly by outside financial institutions. These issues generally had maturities of 15 to 16 years. Some of the equipment deals done in the 1980s had maturities out to 23 or so years. But in many cases the debt portion of the financing amounted to 50% to 60% of the equipment's cost, providing a greater equity cushion. The lease agreement required the airline to pay a rental sufficient to cover the interest, amortization of principal, and a return to the equity participant. The airline was responsible for maintaining and operating the aircraft, as well as providing for adequate insurance. It must also keep the equipment registered and record the ETC and lease under the Federal Aviation Act of 1958.

In the event of a loss or destruction of the equipment, the company may substitute similar equipment of equal value and in as good operating condition and repair and as airworthy as that which was lost or destroyed. It also has the option to redeem the outstanding certificates with the insurance proceeds.

An important point to consider is the equity owner. If the airline runs into financial difficulty and fails to make the required payments, the owner may step in and make the rental payment in order to protect its investment. The carrier's failure to make a basic rental payment within the stipulated grace period is an act of default but is cured if the owner makes payment. Thus, a strong owner lends support to the financing, and a weak one little.

Do not be misled by the title of the issue just because the words secured or equipment trust appear. Investors should look at the collateral and its estimated value based on the studies of recognized appraisers compared with the amount of equipment debt outstanding. Is the equipment new or used? Do the creditors benefit from Section 1110 of the Bankruptcy Reform Act? Because the equipment is a depreciable item and subject to wear, tear, and obsolescence, a sinking fund starting within several years of the initial offering date should be provided if the debt is not issued in serial form. Of course, the ownership of the aircraft is important as just noted. Obviously, one must review the obligor's financials because the investor's first line of defense depends on the airline's ability to service the lease rental payments.

UNSECURED DEBT

We have discussed many of the features common to secured debt. Take away the collateral and we have unsecured debt.

Unsecured debt, like secured debt, comes in several different layers or levels of claim against the corporation's assets. But in the case of unsecured debt, the nomenclature attached to the debt issues sounds less substantial. For example, "General and Refunding Mortgage Bonds" may sound more important than "Subordinated Debentures," even though both are basically second claims on the corporate body. In addition to the normal debentures and notes, there are junior issues; for example, General Motors Acceptance Corporation, in addition to senior unsecured debt, had public issues designated as senior subordinated and junior subordinated notes, representing the secondary and tertiary levels of the capital structure. The difference in a high-grade issuer may be considered insignificant as long as the issuer maintains its quality. But in cases of financial distress, the junior issues usually fare worse than the senior issues. Only in cases of very well-protected junior issues will investors come out whole—in which case, so would the holders of senior indebtedness. Thus, many investors are more than willing to take junior debt of high-grade companies; the minor additional risk, compared to that of the senior debt of lower-rated issuers, may well be worth the incremental income.

Looking at the 14⅜% General Motors Acceptance Corporation's Senior Subordinated Notes that matured April 1, 1991, the prospectus stated that they "are subordinate in right of payment . . . to all indebtedness for borrowed money . . . now outstanding or hereafter incurred, which is not by its terms subordinate to other indebtedness of the Company." The Junior Subordinated Notes, 8⅛% that matured April 15, 1986, stated that they are subordinate and junior, with the remaining wording similar to that of the senior subordinate debt. The junior debt subordination wording further implied that in the event of bankruptcy or insolvency proceedings, liquidation, reorganization, or receivership, all principal, premium (if any), and interest on superior or senior and senior subordinated indebtedness will be paid in full before any payment is made on junior subordinated indebtedness. Many of these legal proceedings actually involve negotiation and compromise among the various classes of creditors. As explained in the next chapter, even junior creditors can receive some consideration, although, under strict application of absolute priority, they normally may be entitled to little or nothing.

Subordination of the debt instrument might not be apparent from the issue's name. This is often the case with bank and bank-related securities. Chase Manhattan Bank (National Association) had some 8¾% Capital Notes due 1986. The term "Capital Notes" would not sound like a subordinated debt instrument to most inexperienced investors unfamiliar with the jargon of the debt world. Yet capital notes are junior securities. The subordination section of the issue's prospectus stated, "The indebtedness . . . evidenced by the Notes . . . is to be subordinate and junior in right of payment to its obligations to depositors, its obligations under banker's acceptances and letters of credit and its obligations to any Federal Reserve Bank and (except as to any Long Term debt as defined ranking on a parity with or junior to the Notes) its obligations to its other creditors. . . ." This issue was debt of the bank and thus had prior claim on the assets of the bank in case of receivership,

conservatorship, or the like, over and above the claim of the Bank's sole shareholder (and the creditors of that shareholder), the Chase Manhattan Corporation.

Credit Enhancements

Some debt issuers have other companies guarantee their loans. This is normally done when a subsidiary issues debt and the investors want the added protection of a third-party guarantee. The use of guarantees makes it easier and more convenient to finance special projects and affiliates, although guarantees are extended to operating company debt. An example of a third-party (but related) guarantee was US West Capital Funding, Inc. 8% Guaranteed Notes that were due October 15, 1996 (guaranteed by US West, Inc.). The principal purpose of Capital Funding was to provide financing to US West and its affiliates through the issuance of debt guaranteed by US West. This guarantee read: "US West will unconditionally guarantee the due and punctual payment of the principal, premium, if any, and interest on the Debt Securities when and as the same shall become due and payable, whether at maturity, upon redemption or otherwise. The guarantees will rank equally with all other unsecured and unsubordinated obligations of US West."

Citicorp has guaranteed the payment of principal and interest on a subordinated basis for some of the debt issues of Citicorp Person-to-Person, Inc., a holding company providing management services to affiliates offering financial and similar services. PepsiCo, Inc. has guaranteed the debt of its financing affiliate, PepsiCo Capital Resources, Inc., and The Standard Oil Company (an Ohio Corporation) has unconditionally guaranteed the debt of Sohio Pipe Line Company. The Seagram Company Ltd., a Canadian corporation, has "unconditionally guarantee[d] the due and punctual payment of principal and interest on the [9.65% Debentures of Joseph E. Seagram & Sons, Inc., an Indiana corporation], when and as the same shall become due and payable, whether at the maturity date, by declaration of acceleration or otherwise."

There are also other types of third-party credit enhancements. Some captive finance subsidiaries of industrial companies enter into agreements requiring them to maintain fixed charge coverage at such a level so that the securities meet the eligibility standards for investment by insurance companies under New York State law. The required coverage levels are maintained by adjusting the prices at which the finance company buys its receivables from the parent company or through special payments from the parent company. These supplemental income maintenance agreements, while usually not part of indentures, are very important considerations for bond buyers.

Another type of support agreement is found in the BellSouth Capital Funding Corporation's 9¼% Notes due January 15, 1998. This support agreement between the company and its parent, BellSouth Corporation, stipulates that the parent (1) agrees to cause BellSouth Capital to maintain a positive tangible net worth in accordance with generally accepted accounting principles; (2) will provide the necessary funds to pay debt service if the subsidiary is unable to meet the

obligations when due; and (3) shall own, directly or indirectly, all of the outstanding voting capital stock of the subsidiary throughout the life of the support agreement. In addition, in case of a default by the parent in meeting its obligations under the default agreement, or in the case of default by the subsidiary in the payment of principal and/or interest, the holders of the securities or the trustee may proceed directly against the parent. However, they do not have any recourse to or against the stock or assets of the parent's telephone subsidiaries.

Another credit-enhancing feature is the letter of credit (LOC) issued by a bank. A LOC requires the bank to make payments to the trustee when requested so that monies will be available for the bond issuer to meet its interest and principal payments when due. Thus the credit of the bank under the LOC is substituted for that of the debt issuer. For example, in February 1988, Holiday Inns, Inc., a subsidiary of Holiday Corporation, issued $200 million each of 8⅝% Notes due 1993 and 9% Notes due 1995. The principal and interest on the notes were payable by drawings under an irrevocable, direct-pay letter of credit issued by The Sumitomo Bank, Limited, acting through its New York City branch. The notes also carried the guarantee of Holiday Corporation. These credit-enhanced securities were rated Aaa by Moody's Investors Service, while Holiday Inns unsecured senior debt is rated B1, hardly investment grade. The adjusted capitalization of Holiday Corporation at the time of the offering showed $250 million of short-term debt, $2,385 million of long-term debt, and a stockholders' deficit of $766 million. The LOC is not given out gratis. In addition to an initial fee for granting the LOC, Holiday Inns must pay an annual fee and a drawing fee for each payment made thereunder. Both Inns and the parent must reimburse the bank for all payments made under the LOC. These reimbursement obligations are secured by first mortgages/deeds of trust on certain hotel/casino properties and first priority interests in certain related properties in Nevada. Sumitomo was also named the trustee of the notes. Interest savings for the company were estimated at a substantial 200 basis points. In other words, the interest rates on the debt would have been around 10⅝% and 11%, respectively, and the total cost increased by $8 million annually or some $48 million over the life of the notes.

Insurance companies also lend their credit standing to corporate debt, both new issues and outstanding secondary market issues. Financial Security Assurance (FSA) has unconditionally and irrevocably guaranteed the scheduled payments on new issues such as Columbus Southern Power Company's 8⅝% First Mortgage Bonds were due in 1996 and County Savings Bank 10.15% Bonds due 1998. In the secondary market, FSA has applied its TAGSS program (Triple-A Guaranteed Secondary Securities) to numerous blocks of bonds issued by Texas Utilities Electric, Commonwealth Edison, and Georgia Power, among others. The ratings on these enhanced securities are Aaa/AAA, not the rating that would be on the securities if they were "stand-alones." FSA usually requires that the issue to be insured must be investment grade on its own merits and also be collateralized so as to reduce the insurer's risk of loss. The investor in these issues gets a greater degree of safety

through the higher rating and protection against the underlying issuer's credit deterioration. In addition, the issue's liquidity could be enhanced because more investment firms may be willing to make a market in the insured bonds. From the new issuers' perspective, the interest savings more than offset the cost of the insurance premium, leading to a lower net interest cost. Certainly, utility rate regulators like to see companies under their supervision take steps to reduce their overall costs.

While a guarantee or other type of credit enhancement may add some measure of protection to a debtholder, caution should not be thrown to the wind. In effect, one's job may become even more complex because an analysis of both the issuer and the guarantor should be performed. In many cases, only the latter is needed if the issuer is merely a financing conduit without any operations of its own. However, if both concerns are operating companies, it may very well be necessary to analyze both because the timely payment of principal and interest ultimately will depend on the stronger party. A downgrade of the enhancer's claims-paying ability reduces the value of the bonds.

Negative Pledge Clause

One of the important protective provisions for unsecured debtholders is the *negative pledge clause*. This provision, found in most senior unsecured debt issues and a few subordinated issues, prohibits a company from creating or assuming any lien to secure a debt issue without equally securing the subject debt issue(s) (with certain exceptions). Designed to prevent other creditors from obtaining a senior position at the expense of existing creditors, "it is not intended to prevent other creditors from sharing in the position of debenture holders."[3] Again, it is not necessary to have such a clause unless the issuer runs into trouble. But like insurance, it is not needed until the time that no one wants arrives.

Negative pledge clauses are not just boiler plate material added to indentures and loan agreements to give lawyers extra work. They have provided additional security for debtholders when the prognosis for corporate survival was bleak. International Harvester Company and International Harvester Credit Company had negative pledge clauses that became operative when they secured sorely needed bank financing.

INDENTURES

As we have seen, corporate debt securities come with an infinite variety of features, yet we have just scratched the surface. While prospectuses may provide most of the needed information, the indenture is the more important document. The indenture sets forth in great detail the promises of the issuer. Here we will

---

[3] *Commentaries on Model Debenture Indenture Provisions 1965 Model All Registered Issues 1967 and Certain Negotiable Provisions Which May Be Included in a Particular Incorporating Indenture* (Chicago, IL: American Bar Foundation, 1971), p. 350.

look at what indentures of corporate debt issues contain. For corporate debt securities to be publicly sold, they must (with some permitted exceptions) be issued in conformity with the Trust Indenture Act of 1939. This act requires that debt issues subject to regulation by the Securities and Exchange Commission (SEC) have a trustee. Also, the trustee's duties and powers must be spelled out in the indenture.

Some corporate debt issues are issued under a *blanket* or *open-ended indenture*; for others a new indenture must be written each time a new series of debt is sold. A blanket indenture is often used by electric utility companies and other issuers of general mortgage bonds, but it is also found in unsecured debt. The initial or basic indenture may have been entered into 30 or more years ago, but as each new series of debt is created, a supplemental indenture is written. For instance, the original indenture for Baltimore Gas and Electric Company is dated February 1, 1919, but it has been supplemented and amended many times since then due to new financings.

A more recent example of an open-ended industrial debenture issue is found in the Eastman Kodak Company debt prospectus dated March 23, 1988 and supplemented October 21, 1988, which says that "the Indenture does not limit the aggregate principal amount of debentures, notes or other evidences of indebtedness ("Debt Securities") which may be issued thereunder and provides that Debt Securities may be issued from time to time in one or more series." The indenture of Fruehauf Finance Company, according to its prospectus dated December 11, 1985, gives the Company the ability to "reopen" a previous issue of securities and to issue additional securities having terms and provisions identical to any such previous issues of debt. PepsiCo, Inc.'s indenture dated December 2, 1993 between the company and The Chase Manhattan Bank (National Association) is closed-end but with another wrinkle. Debt securities issued under this indenture are limited to a maximum of $2,500,000,000. However, the maximum amount can be increased at any time if authorized by PepsiCo's board of directors. An example of an indenture limiting the amount of debt is Harris Corporation's, dated December 1, 1988, which authorizes debt in the amount of $150 million of 10⅜% Debentures due December 1, 2018.

According to the American Bar Foundation, the model debenture indenture has 15 articles and a preamble, or preliminary statement, called *parties and recitals*.[4] The model mortgage bond indenture form has 16 articles and a preliminary statement.[5] Of course, the number of articles depends on the terms of the debt being issued. The consolidated mortgage bonds of Illinois Central Gulf Railroad Company, as supplemented, has 23 articles. The preliminary statements note that the bonds or debentures have been authorized by the corporation's board of directors and that it has the authority to execute the indenture. The introductory

---

[4] Commentaries on Model Debenture Indenture Provisions 1965 Model All Registered Issues 1967 and Certain Negotiable Provisions Which May Be Included in a Particular Incorporating Indenture.

[5] American Bar Foundation, *Mortgage Bond Indenture Form 1981* (Chicago, IL: American Bar Association, 1981).

statements contain granting clauses describing the mortgage property, which is necessary for secured debt.

Definitions, Form of Securities, and Denominations

The first article of an indenture usually includes the definitions of special words and phrases used in the indenture and certain provisions of a general nature or application covering acts of bondholders, notices to the trustee, the company and debtholder, and governing law, among other things. The second article covers the form of the bond or debenture. It spells out what is to appear on the actual security certificate. The third article is called "The Bonds" or "The Debentures," as the case may be. Here the securities' title or series is stated as well as the form (coupon, registered) and denominations. Today, practically all domestically issued corporate bonds are in registered form (i.e., the ownership is registered with the transfer agent (normally the trustee) and a check for the interest payment is sent to the registered holder). In late 1986, a form of registered corporate bond called book-entry appeared. The usual denomination of registered corporate debt is $1,000 (par value) and multiples thereof, although, in some cases, a minimum of $5,000 or $10,000 (and even $100,000 or more) may be required. The third article also sets forth the record dates for interest and the interest payment dates.

Remedies

There are several other articles common to both types of debt, although one may be, for example, article 12 in one indenture and article 8 in the other. Article 9 in the model mortgage indenture (article 5 in the model debenture indenture) concerns *remedies*—the steps available to bondholders in case the company defaults. The trustee is responsible for enforcing the available remedies; while it is only the debtholders' representative, it is ultimately responsible to the majority of the bondholders. In this article, events of default are defined and may include the following: (1) failure to pay interest on the date due or within the grace period (usually 30 days); (2) failure to make a principal payment on the due date; (3) failure to make a sinking fund payment when due; (4) failure to perform any other covenants and the continuation of that failure for a certain period after notice has been given by the trustee to the debtor company; and (5) certain other events of bankruptcy, insolvency, or reorganization that may include defaults of other debt obligations of the company.

If an event of default is continuing, either the trustee or the holders of 25% of the principal amount of the outstanding issue may declare all of the bonds of the particular series immediately due and payable along with unpaid and interest due up to the date of acceleration. This may pressure the corporate issuer to cure the defaults (if it is able to do so) and thus rescind the acceleration or to seek waivers of the defaults while it is trying to find a solution. But such acceleration might force the debtor to seek protection of the bankruptcy courts; it might have been better to work with the debtor and help it on the path to recovery.

The article also provides limits to lawsuits that individual bondholders may bring against the company with a default under the indenture provisions. However, no provision may impair the bondholders' absolute and unconditional right to the timely payment of principal, premium (if any) and interest on the bond, and the right to bring legal action to enforce such payment.

The Trustee

While the rights and duties of the trustee are mentioned in various articles throughout the indenture, articles 6 and 10 in the model indentures contain certain specifics regarding the trustee and its activities, including resignation or removal. Investors should clearly understand that the trustee is paid by the debt-issuing company and can only do what the indenture provides. The article may begin with wording such as: ". . . the Trustee undertakes to perform such duties and only such duties as are specifically set forth in this Indenture, and no implied covenants or obligations shall be read into this Indenture against the Trustee. . . ." Further, ". . . the Trustee shall exercise such of the rights and powers vested in it by this Indenture, and shall use the same degree of care and skill in their exercise, as a prudent man would exercise or use under the circumstances in the conduct of his own affairs," or, "No provision of this Indenture shall be construed to relieve the Trustee from liability for its own negligent action, its own negligent failure to act, or its own willful misconduct. . . ." Of course, certain exceptions are listed.

One of the duties of the indenture trustee as enumerated in this article is the notification to bondholders of a default under the indenture (except in certain cases such as a cured default or provided that the board of directors or "responsible officers" of the trustee, etc., in good faith determine that withholding of the notice is in "their best interests"). Also, the trustee is under no obligation to exercise the rights or powers under the indenture at the request of bondholders unless it has been offered reasonable security or indemnity. This seems reasonable in this age of frivolous lawsuits, but it could possibly be used by the trustee as a reason not to proceed with an action which it ought to do. The trustee is not bound to make investigations into the facts surrounding documents delivered to it, but it may do so if it sees fit.

Another section of the article requires the issuer to pay the trustee reasonable fees for its services, provide reimbursement for reasonable expenses, and to indemnify it for certain losses that might arise from administering the trust. A subsection states that in case of a conflict of interest, the trustee will either eliminate the conflict or resign within 90 days of the date of determining that a conflict of interests exists. Not an uncommon occurrence, one often will see in the financial press legal advertisements of the resignation of a trustee and the appointment of a successor trustee. As there must always be a trustee, no resignation is effective until a new trustee has been secured. Such potential conflicts often occur where the trustee bank is also a creditor of the issuing company. The prospectus for the $600 million May Department Stores offering on June 8, 1988 says that

"the Company maintains deposit accounts with and engages in banking transactions in the ordinary course of business with each [of the trustees]." One bank is a trustee of various employee benefit plans and both trustees have credit agreements with May. In 1984 Citibank, N.A., resigned as trustee for the first mortgage bonds of Long Island Lighting Company, citing a potential conflict of interest between its obligations to bondholders as trustee and as a creditor to LILCO. It cannot very well serve the bondholders' interests and its own creditor interests at the same time. There is also provision for the removal of a trustee, with or without cause, upon the action of a majority of the debtholders.

The prospectus (dated September 14, 1988) for K N Energy's 10 3/4% Sinking Fund Debentures due September 1, 2008 says that the indenture contains "certain limitations on the right of the Trustee, should it become a creditor of the Company, to obtain payment of claims in certain cases, or to realize for its own account on certain property received in respect of any such claim as security or otherwise. The Trustee will be permitted to engage in certain other transactions; however, if it acquires any conflicting interest . . . it must eliminate such conflict or resign."

Reports

The next article (7 and 11 in the model debenture and mortgage indentures, respectively), dealing with debtholders' lists and reports by the trustee and company, is rather short but has caused many investors concern. Under this article, the company is required to furnish the trustee with semiannual lists of bondholders and their addresses and preserve this information until a new list is available. This is to enable the requisite number of bondholders to communicate with other bondholders about their rights under the indenture. The trustee must submit to the bondholders certain brief reports or statements concerning its continued eligibility as a trustee, any advances made by the trustee to the corporation, any other indebtedness owed by the company to the trustee, and any property or funds of the company held by the trustee. An interesting question is how many bondholders have actually received these reports or have even seen them? More than likely, very few; perhaps the many nominees such as stockbrokers and banks have failed to send them to the beneficial owners because of the added (and possibly unreimbursed) costs.

The bone of contention between bondholders and issuers concerns corporate financial reporting. Indentures of public debt issues sold in the United States require an issuing company to file with the trustee copies of annual reports and other reports that it must normally file with the Securities and Exchange Commission. But there is no requirement (unless specifically mentioned) that a company send these reports to debtholders. These reports can be inspected at the SEC or the offices of the trustee, not always convenient for a creditor. Investors desiring such information are often up against the wall, especially when the issuer of public debt securities is privately owned. Companies with fewer than 300 security holders do not have to file regular reports with the SEC.

Consolidation, Merger, Conveyance, and Lease

Common to indentures of secured and unsecured debt are model articles 12 and 8 dealing with consolidation and merger, or the conveyance, transfer, or lease of assets. There might be some indentures that expressly forbid the debtor company to merge or consolidate with another corporation, but most indentures for public debt issues allow corporate mergers, consolidations, and the sale of substantially all of the corporation's assets if certain conditions are satisfied. Transfer or sale of less than substantially all of the corporation's property are usually not subject to control by this article. One such condition is that the company be the surviving party to the merger/consolidation or, if not, that the other party be organized and existing under federal or state law. The new or surviving corporation must assume the terms of the indenture, including the timely payment of principal, interest, and premium (if any) on the subject debt securities, and the successor company is substituted for the predecessor company in the indenture. Of course, if secured, the terms of the transaction (unless waived by bondholders) must provide for the preservation of the security lien and the trustee's rights and powers. The merger, consolidation, or asset sale cannot take place if it would cause an event of default under the indenture's various covenants. Some indentures might place other restrictions on these transactions, including tangible net worth tests of the surviving corporation.

Supplemental Indentures and Covenants

As times change, so may corporate law and practices. An indenture that was satisfactory when entered into many years ago may not be so today. Thus, article 13 in the mortgage indenture and article 9 in the debenture indenture provide for supplemental indentures and the amendments to the original indenture. The most common supplemental indenture is one issued under a blanket indenture for new and additional series or issues of debt securities. The supplemental indenture sets forth the terms and conditions for the issuance of the new securities, including authorized amounts of the new issue, interest rate, maturity, and redemption provisions. It may also include restrictive provisions not found in the basic or blanket indenture but, more often than not, at least nowadays, may contain much less restrictive provisions. Of course, the more restrictive provisions of preceding and still outstanding debt issues remain in force until the debt is extinguished or until the original indenture is changed or amended.

Covenants

Article 14 of the mortgage indenture and article 10 of the debenture indenture are concerned with certain limitations and restrictions on the borrower's activities. Some covenants are common to all indentures, such as (1) to pay interest, principal, and premium, if any, on a timely basis; (2) to maintain an office or agency where the securities may be transferred or exchanged and where notices may be served upon the company with respect to the securities and the indenture; (3) to

pay all taxes and other claims when due unless contested in good faith; (4) to maintain all properties used and useful in the borrower's business in good condition and working order; (5) to maintain adequate insurance on its properties (some indentures may not have insurance provisions since proper insurance is routine business practice); (6) to submit periodic certificates to the trustee stating whether the debtor is in compliance with the loan agreement; and (7) to maintain its corporate existence. These are often called *affirmative covenants* since they call upon the debtor to make promises to do certain things.

Negative covenants require the borrower not to take certain actions. These are usually negotiated between the borrower and the lender or their agents. Setting the right balance between the two parties can be a rather difficult undertaking at times. In public debt transactions, the investing institutions normally leave the negotiating to the investment bankers, although they will often be asked their opinion on certain terms and features. Unfortunately, most public bond buyers are unaware of these articles at the time of purchase and may never learn of them throughout the life of the debt. Borrowers want the least restrictive loan agreement available, while lenders should want the most restrictive, consistent with sound business practices. But lenders should not try to restrain borrowers from accepted business activities and conduct. A company might be willing to include additional restrictions (up to a point) if it can get a lower interest rate on the loan. When companies seek to weaken restrictions in their favor, they are often willing to pay more interest or give other consideration.

An infinite variety of restrictive covenants can be placed on borrowers, depending on the type of debt issue, the economics of the industry and the nature of the business, and the lenders' desires. Some of the more common restrictive covenants include various limitations on the company's ability to incur debt, since unrestricted borrowing can lead a company and its debtholders to ruin. Thus, debt restrictions may include limits on the absolute dollar amount of debt that may be outstanding or may require a *ratio test* (e.g., debt may be limited to no more than 60% of total capitalization or that it cannot exceed a certain percentage of net tangible assets). An example is Jim Walter Corporation's indenture for its 9½% Debentures due April 1, 2016. This indenture restricts senior indebtedness to no more than the sum of 80% of net installment notes receivable and 50% of the adjusted consolidated net tangible assets. The indenture for The May Department Stores Company 7.95% Debentures due 2002 prohibits the company from issuing senior-funded debt unless consolidated net tangible assets are at least 200% of such debt. More recent May Company indentures have dropped this provision.

There may be an *interest* or *fixed-charge coverage test* of which there are two types. One, a *maintenance test*, requires the borrower's ratio of earnings available for interest or fixed charges to be at least a certain minimum figure on each required reporting date (such as quarterly or annually) for a certain preceding period. The other type, a *debt incurrence test*, only comes into play when the company wishes to do additional borrowing. In order to take on additional debt, the

required interest or fixed-charge coverage figure adjusted for the new debt must be at a certain minimum level for the required period prior to the financing. Incurrence tests are generally considered less stringent than maintenance provisions. There could also be *cash flow tests* or *requirements and working capital maintenance provisions*. The prospectus for Federated Department Stores, Inc.'s debentures dated November 4, 1988, has a large section devoted to debt limitations. One of the provisions allows net new debt issuance if the consolidated coverage ratio of earnings before interest, taxes, and depreciation to interest expense (all as defined) is at least 1.35 to 1 through November 1, 1989, 1.45 to 1 through November 1, 1990, 1.50 to 1 through November 1, 1991, and at least 1.60 to 1 thereafter.

Some indentures may prohibit subsidiaries from borrowing from all other companies except the parent. Indentures often classify subsidiaries as restricted or unrestricted. *Restricted subsidiaries* are those considered to be consolidated for financial test purposes; *unrestricted subsidiaries* (often foreign and certain special-purpose companies) are those excluded from the covenants governing the parent. Often, subsidiaries are classified as unrestricted in order to allow them to finance themselves through outside sources of funds.

Limitations on dividend payments and stock repurchases may be included in indentures. Often, cash dividend payments will be limited to a certain percentage of net income earned after a specific date (often the issuance date of the debt and called the "peg date") plus a fixed amount. Sometimes the dividend formula might allow the inclusion of the net proceeds from the sale of common stock sold after the peg date. In other cases, the dividend restriction might be so worded as to prohibit the declaration and payment of cash dividends if tangible net worth (or other measures, such as consolidated quick assets) declines below a certain amount. There are usually no restrictions on the payment of stock dividends. In addition to dividend restrictions, there are often restrictions on a company's repurchase of its common stock if such purchase might cause a violation or deficiency in the dividend determination formulae. Some holding company indentures might limit the right of the company to pay dividends in the common stock of its subsidiaries.

Another part of the covenant article may place restrictions on the disposition and the sale and leaseback of certain property. In some cases, the proceeds of asset sales totaling more than a certain amount must be used to repay debt. This is seldom found in indentures for unsecured debt, but at times some investors may have wished they had such a protective clause. At other times, a provision of this type might allow a company to retire high-coupon debt in a lower interest rate environment, thus causing bondholders a loss of value. It might be better to have such a provision where the company would have the right to reinvest the proceeds of asset sales in new plant and equipment rather than retiring debt, or to at least give the debtholder the option of tendering bonds. Some indentures restrict the investments that a corporation may make in other companies, through either the purchase of stock or loans and advances.

Finally, there may be an absence of restrictive covenants. The shelf registration prospectus of TransAmerica Finance Corporation dated March 30, 1994, forthrightly says:

> The indentures do not contain any provision which will restrict the Company in any way from paying dividends or making other distribution on its capital stock or purchasing or redeeming any of its capital stock, or from incurring, assuming or becoming liable upon Senior Indebtedness or Subordinated Indebtedness or any other type of debt or other obligations. The indentures do not contain any financial ratios or specified levels of net worth or liquidity to which the Company must adhere. In addition, the Subordinated Indenture does not restrict the Company from creating liens on its property for any purpose. In addition, the Indentures do not contain any provisions which would require the Company to repurchase or redeem or otherwise modify the terms of any of its Debt Securities upon a change of control or other events involving the Company which may adversely effect the creditworthiness of the Debt Securities.

If corporate managements and boards of directors viewed themselves as fiduciaries for all of the investors in the company, from stockholders to bondholders, indentures with many restrictive covenants might be unnecessary. But in most instances, that is not the case; they strive to increase shareholder wealth (or their own), not the wealth of the total firm, and often at the expense of the senior security investor. In this age of corporate raiders and management's apparent lack of concern or fiduciary duty towards debt investors, perhaps some consideration ought to be given to the resurrection of good, old-fashioned restrictive provisions. That is, at least until the courts and state legislatures have acted to protect bondholders.

Covenants Change Over Time

Debt covenants can change over the years as companies issue debt under new and more modern indentures. For example, Kansas-Nebraska Natural Gas Company, Inc., now KN Energy, Inc., has issued debt during the past 20 years under three indentures with the same indenture trustee. In each of the indentures there were differences between the various provisions. The 1976 and 1982 issues have provisions limiting dividend payments and share repurchases; the 1988 issue does not. The two earlier issues have a debt issuance test whereby debt cannot exceed 60% of pro forma capitalization; the 1988 issue does not have such a test. The 1976 issue has an interest coverage test for debt issuance, which is not in the 1982 and the 1988 indentures.

SPECIAL CORPORATE SINKING FUND PROVISIONS

A sinking fund is a provision allowing for a debt's periodic retirement or amortization over its life span. In Chapter 1, we discussed the basic sinking fund provision. Here we will look at the sinking fund provisions in corporate bond issues.

A variety of sinking fund types are found in publicly issued corporate debt. The most common is the *mandatory sinking fund*, requiring the periodic redemption of a certain amount of a specific debt issue. A mandatory sinking fund specifies that the issuer may satisfy the provision in whole or in part, by (1) delivering bonds acquired through open-market purchases or other means or (2) paying cash to the trustee who will call bonds for redemption at 100. This type is found in most longer-term industrial issues and some electric utility bonds.

Another type of sinking fund provision that is most prevalent in electric utility company issues is the *nonmandatory sinking fund provision*. This provision allows the issuer to satisfy the sinking fund provision by the utilization of unfunded property additions or improvements at a certain percentage of their cost. This third alternative is referred to as a *property credit*. Property credits so utilized cannot be further employed under the mortgage.

A corporate sinking fund provision may be a specific sinking fund provision or a nonspecific sinking fund provision. A *specific sinking fund* applies to just the named issue. A *nonspecific sinking fund*, also known as a *funnel*, *tunnel*, *blanket*, or *aggregate sinking fund*, is based on the outstanding amount of a company's total bonded indebtedness.

Nonspecific sinking funds are found in the indentures of 17 companies. Three of these—Baltimore Gas & Electric, Ohio Edison, and Pacific Gas & Electric—have mandatory funnel sinking funds. The other 14, including the subsidiaries of the Southern Company and Northeast Utilities, have nonmandatory funnel sinking funds.

In most cases, the redemption price for bonds called under the funnel sinking fund is par, but Pacific Gas & Electric's and Southern California Edison's operate at the general or regular redemption prices. Pacific Gas has usually chosen to retire its low-coupon issues trading at discounts. The funnel sinking fund may be deceptive. Usually 1% of all bonds outstanding, this can amount to a large requirement, especially if the total amount is applied against a single issue. For example, if bonded debt of $3 billion consists of issues ranging in size from $50 million to $200 million, the annual funnel requirement is $30 million; this equals 15% to 60% of any one issue. When interest rates and cash needs are high, companies normally utilize unfunded property additions if they are able to do so. But actual bond retirement provides a way to redeem high-coupon debt (usually at par) when interest rates are down. In some cases, however, a maximum of 1% of a specific issue may be retired in any 1 year if the call is within 5 years of issuance (the refunded protected period). The Southern Company (among others) had to place this restriction in its subsidiaries' indentures after the funnel calls of the early

1970s. Thus, while there is a limit on the amount of the bonds that can be redeemed in the first 5 years, once that period has expired, investors should be careful. An issuer could apply the maximum amount possible to the retirement of the bonds at par and then call any remaining ones at the regular redemption prices.

Because of the risk of exhausting gas supplies, some gas pipeline company indentures provide for the acceleration of the sinking fund in the event that estimates of the reserve lives of the companies' proven gas reserves decline. ANR Pipeline Company (formerly Michigan Wisconsin Pipe Line Company) had such a provision. The prospectus for the 10⅝% First Mortgage Pipe Line Bonds that were due April 15, 1995, stated:

> Indenture will provide in substance that in the event that an independent engineer's certificate of reserve life, which the Company is required to file with the Trustee prior to May 1 of each year, shows a reserve life for the Company's controlled proven gas reserves of less than eight years and a date of exhaustion of reserve life earlier than any sinking fund payment date then in effect, the next two sinking fund installments shall each be increased. . . . However, if the reserve life shown in any such certificate is less than four years, all sinking fund installments falling due subsequent to the year in which such certificate is filed shall become payable on December 31 of such year.

Thus, the sinking fund payments could be increased, but if future certificates subsequently show an improvement in the gas supply, the sinking fund could be adjusted once again.

CORPORATE BOND RATINGS

Professional money managers use various techniques to analyze information on companies and bond issues in order to estimate the ability of the issuer to live up to its future contractual obligations. This activity is known as *credit analysis*.

Some large institutional investors and many investment banking firms have their own credit analysis departments. Few individual investors and institutional bond investors, though, do their own analysis. Instead, they rely primarily on nationally recognized statistical rating organizations that perform credit analysis and issue their conclusions in the form of ratings. The three commercial rating companies are Moody's Investors Service, Standard & Poor's Corporation, and Fitch. The rating systems use similar symbols, as shown in Exhibit 1.

In all systems the term *high grade* means low credit risk, or conversely, high probability of future payments. The highest-grade bonds are designated by Moody's by the symbol Aaa, and by the other two rating systems by the symbol AAA. The next highest grade is denoted by the symbol Aa (Moody's) or AA (the

other two rating systems); for the third grade all rating systems use A. The next three grades are Baa or BBB, Ba or BB, and B, respectively. There are also C grades.

Bonds rated triple A (AAA or Aaa) are said to be *prime*; double A (AA or Aa) are of *high quality*; single A issues are called *upper medium grade*; and triple B are *medium grade*. Lower-rated bonds are said to have speculative elements or be distinctly speculative.

All rating agencies use rating modifiers to provide a narrower credit quality breakdown within each rating category. S&P and Fitch use a rating modifier of plus and minus. Moody's uses 1, 2, and 3 as its rating modifiers.

Exhibit 1: Summary of Corporate Bond Rating Systems and Symbols

Fitch	Moody's	S&P	Summary Description
Investment Grade — High Credit Worthiness			
AAA	Aaa	AAA	Gilt edge, prime, maximum safety
AA+	Aa1	AA+	
AA	Aa2	AA	High-grade, high-credit quality
AA–	Aa3	AA–	
A+	A1	A+	
A	A2	A	Upper-medium grade
A–	A3	A–	
BBB+	Baa1	BBB+	
BBB	Baa2	BBB	Lower-medium grade
BBB–	Baa3	BBB–	
Speculative — Lower Credit Worthiness			
BB+	Ba1	BB+	
BB	Ba2	BB	Low grade, speculative
BB–	Ba3	BB–	
B+	B1		
B	B2	B	Highly speculative
B–	B3		
Predominantly Speculative, Substantial Risk, or in Default			
CCC+		CCC+	
CCC	Caa	CCC	Substantial risk, in poor standing
CC	Ca	CC	May be in default, very speculative
C	C	C	Extremely speculative
		CI	Income bonds—no interest being paid
DDD			
DD			Default
D		D	

Bond issues that are assigned a rating in the top four categories are referred to as *investment-grade bonds*. Issues that carry a rating below the top four categories are referred to as *noninvestment-grade bonds* or *speculative bonds*, or more popularly as *high-yield bonds* or *junk bonds*. Thus, the corporate bond market can be divided into two sectors: the investment-grade and non-investment-grade markets.

A bond issue may be assigned a "dual" rating if there is a feature of the bond that rating agencies believe would alter the credit risk. For example, Standard & Poor's assigns a dual rating to putable bonds. The first rating is the normal rating based on the likelihood of repayment of principal and interest as due in the absence of the put feature. The second rating reflects the ability of the issuer to repay the principal at the put date if the bondholder exercises the put option.

The Rating Process

The rating process involves the analysis of a multitude of quantitative and qualitative factors over the past, present, and future. The past and present are introductions to what the future may hold. Ratings should be prospective because future operations should provide the wherewithal to repay the debt. The ratings apply to the particular issue, not the issuer. While bond analysts rely on numbers and calculate many ratios to get a picture of the company's debt-servicing capacity, a rating is only an opinion or judgment of an issuer's ability to meet all of its obligations when due, whether during prosperity or during times of stress. The purpose of ratings is to rank issues in terms of the probability of default, taking into account the special features of the issue, the relationship to other obligations of the issuer, and current and prospective financial condition and operating performance.

In conducting its examination, the rating agencies consider the four Cs of credit—character, capacity, collateral, and covenants. The first of the Cs stands for *character* of management, the foundation of sound credit. This includes the ethical reputation as well as the business qualifications and operating record of the board of directors, management, and executives responsible for the use of the borrowed funds and repayment of those funds. The next C is *capacity* or the ability of an issuer to repay its obligations. The third C, *collateral*, is looked at not only in the traditional sense of assets pledged to secure the debt, but also to the quality and value of those unpledged assets controlled by the issuer. In both senses the collateral is capable of supplying additional aid, comfort, and support to the debt and the debtholder. Assets form the basis for the generation of cash flow that services the debt in good times as well as bad. The final C is for *covenants*, the terms and conditions of the lending agreement. Covenants lay down restrictions on how management operates the company and conducts its financial affairs. Covenants can restrict management's discretion. A default or violation of any covenant may provide a meaningful early warning alarm enabling investors to take positive and corrective action before the situation deteriorates further. Covenants have value because they play an important part in minimizing risk to

creditors. They help prevent the unconscionable transfer of wealth from debtholders to equityholders.

Character

Character analysis involves the analysis of the quality of management. In discussing the factors it considers in assigning a credit rating, Moody's Investors Service notes the following regarding the quality of management:

> Although difficult to quantify, management quality is one of the most important factors supporting an issuer's credit strength. When the unexpected occurs, it is a management's ability to react appropriately that will sustain the company's performance.[6]

In assessing management quality, the analysts at Moody's, for example, try to understand the business strategies and policies formulated by management. Following are factors that are considered: (1) strategic direction, (2) financial philosophy, (3) conservatism, (4) track record, (5) succession planning, and (6) control systems.[7]

Capacity to Pay

In assessing the ability of an issuer to pay, an analysis of the financial statements is undertaken. In addition to management quality, the factors examined by Moody's, for example, are (1) industry trends, (2) the regulatory environment, (3) basic operating and competitive position, (4) financial position and sources of liquidity, (5) company structure (including structural subordination and priority of claim), (6) parent company support agreements, and (7) special event risk.[8]

In considering industry trends, the rating agencies look at the vulnerability of the company to economic cycles, the barriers to entry, and the exposure of the company to technological changes. For firms in regulated industries, proposed changes in regulations must be analyzed to assess their impact on future cash flows. At the company level, diversification of the product line and the cost structure are examined in assessing the basic operating position of the firm.

The rating agencies must look at the capacity of a firm to obtain additional financing and backup credit facilities. There are various forms of back-up facilities. The strongest forms of backup credit facilities are those that are contractually binding and do not include provisions that permit the lender to refuse to provide funds. An example of such a provision is one that allows the bank to refuse funding if the bank feels that the borrower's financial condition or operating position has deteriorated significantly. (Such a provision is called a "material

---

[6] "Industrial Company Rating Methodology," *Moody's Investor Service: Global Credit Research* (July 1998), p. 6.

[7] "Industrial Company Rating Methodology," p. 7.

[8] "Industrial Company Rating Methodology," p. 3.

adverse change clause.") Noncontractual facilities such as lines of credit that make it easy for a bank to refuse funding are of concern to the rating agency. The rating agency also examines the quality of the bank providing the backup facility.

Other sources of liquidity for a company may be third-party guarantees, the most common being a contractual agreement with its parent company. When such a financial guarantee exists, rating agencies undertake a credit analysis of the parent company.

Collateral

As explained earlier in this chapter, a corporate debt obligation can be secured or unsecured. In our discussion of creditor rights in a bankruptcy, we explained that in the case of a liquidation, proceeds from a bankruptcy are distributed to creditors based on the absolute priority rule. However, in the case of a reorganization, the absolute priority rule rarely holds. That is, an unsecured creditor may receive distributions for the entire amount of his or her claim and common stockholders may receive something, while secured creditors may receive only a portion of their claims because a reorganization requires approval of all the parties. Consequently, secured creditors are willing to negotiate with both unsecured creditors and stockholders in order to obtain approval of the plan of reorganization.

The question is then, what does a secured position mean in the case of a reorganization if the absolute priority rule is not followed? The claim position of a secured creditor is important in terms of the negotiation process. However, because absolute priority is not followed and the final distribution in a reorganization depends on the bargaining ability of the parties, some analysts place less emphasis on collateral compared to the other factors discussed earlier and covenants discussed later.

Covenants

Covenants deal with limitations and restrictions on the borrower's activities. *Affirmative covenants* call upon the debtor to make promises to do certain things. *Negative covenants* are those that require the borrower not to take certain actions. Negative covenants are usually negotiated between the borrower and the lender or their agents. Borrowers want the least restrictive loan agreement available, while lenders should want the most restrictive, consistent with sound business practices. But lenders should not try to restrain borrowers from accepted business activities and conduct. A borrower might be willing to include additional restrictions (up to a point) if it can get a lower interest rate on the debt obligation. When borrowers seek to weaken restrictions in their favor, they are often willing to pay more interest or give other consideration.

Changes in Bond Ratings

Ratings of bonds change over time. Issuers are upgraded when their likelihood of default (as assessed by the rating company) decreases, and downgraded when their

likelihood of default (as assessed by the rating company) increases. The rating companies publish the issues that they are reviewing for possible rating change.

To see how ratings change over time, the rating agencies publish this information periodically in the form of a table. This table is called a *rating transition matrix*. The table is useful for investors to assess potential downgrades and upgrades. A rating transition matrix is available for different holding periods. Exhibit 2 shows a 1-year, 2-year, 5-year, and 10-year rating transition matrix published by Standard & Poor's. Let's use the 1-year rating transition matrix (the first matrix in the exhibit) to explain how to interpret the values.

The rows indicate the rating at the beginning of a year. The columns show the rating at the end of the year. For example, look at the third row. This row shows the transition for A-rated bonds at the beginning of a year. The number 87.94 in the third row means that on average 87.94% of A-rated bonds at the beginning of the year remained A-rated at year end. The value of 2.16 means that on average 2.16% of A-rated bonds at the beginning of the year were upgraded to AA. The value of 4.97 means that on average 4.97% of A-rated bonds at the beginning of the year were downgraded to a BBB rating by the end of the year.

From Exhibit 2, two points are noteworthy. First, for investment-grade bonds the probability of a downgrade is much higher than for an upgrade. Second, the longer the transition period, the lower the probability that an issuer will retain its original rating.

YIELDS

Exhibit 3 shows the spread over Treasuries for corporate bonds issued by industrial, utility, finance, and bank entities as reported by Lehman Brothers. The spreads are for bullet issues (i.e., issues that are noncallable for life). The spreads are based on the bid side for secondary market transactions and are reported by maturity and credit rating. The exhibit shows the 90-day high, low, and average for the week ending July 13, 2001. Basically, it is a term structure of credit spreads. For callable and putable securities, an option-adjusted spread is calculated.

Exhibit 2: Selected Transition Matrices Based on S&P Rated Issues

Average One-Year Transition Rates	Rating at end of first year (%)								
Initial rating	AAA	AA	A	BBB	BB	B	CCC	D	N.R.
AAA	90.34	5.62	0.39	0.08	0.03	0.00	0.00	0.00	3.54
AA	0.64	88.78	6.72	0.47	0.06	0.09	0.02	0.01	3.21
A	0.07	2.16	87.94	4.97	0.47	0.19	0.01	0.04	4.16
BBB	0.03	0.24	4.56	84.26	4.19	0.76	0.15	0.22	5.59
BB	0.03	0.06	0.40	6.09	76.09	6.82	0.96	0.98	8.58
B	0.00	0.09	0.29	0.41	5.11	74.62	3.43	5.30	10.76
CCC	0.13	0.00	0.26	0.77	1.66	8.93	53.19	21.94	13.14
Average Two-Year Transition Rates	Rating at end of second year (%)								
Initial rating	AAA	AA	A	BBB	BB	B	CCC	D	N.R.
AAA	81.51	10.14	1.05	0.18	0.06	0.03	0.00	0.00	7.04
AA	1.18	79.41	11.87	1.07	0.16	0.18	0.01	0.04	6.09
A	0.10	3.86	77.57	8.60	1.07	0.41	0.03	0.11	8.26
BBB	0.10	0.47	8.44	70.48	6.80	1.46	0.33	0.48	11.44
BB	0.03	0.11	0.87	10.79	56.21	10.11	1.61	2.95	17.32
B	0.00	0.14	0.54	0.92	8.88	53.85	3.83	11.01	20.84
CCC	0.14	0.00	0.57	1.72	2.15	11.61	32.09	28.37	23.35
Average Five-Year Transition Rates	Rating at end of fifth year (%)								
Initial rating	AAA	AA	A	BBB	BB	B	CCC	D	N.R.
AAA	60.60	17.32	3.41	0.93	0.14	0.11	0.00	0.11	17.39
AA	2.32	57.01	22.06	3.26	0.53	0.44	0.08	0.24	14.08
A	0.16	6.45	56.74	13.79	2.30	1.12	0.17	0.50	18.78
BBB	0.23	1.25	14.52	44.64	8.47	2.38	0.58	1.76	26.18
BB	0.05	0.30	2.35	15.16	24.23	9.37	1.45	9.14	37.94
B	0.00	0.15	0.87	2.53	10.41	19.42	2.05	19.98	44.59
CCC	0.18	0.00	0.35	2.65	3.36	6.54	7.77	39.22	39.93
Average 10-Year Transition Rates	Rating at end of 10th year (%)								
Initial rating	AAA	AA	A	BBB	BB	B	CCC	D	N.R.
AAA	37.30	20.22	7.84	3.02	0.12	0.00	0.00	0.64	30.85
AA	2.88	33.41	28.09	6.49	0.84	0.24	0.11	0.95	27.00
A	0.37	6.29	37.47	15.23	3.34	1.16	0.11	1.75	34.29
BBB	0.35	1.77	15.71	26.17	6.48	1.57	0.20	4.30	43.45
BB	0.16	0.08	3.44	11.77	7.55	3.32	0.44	18.14	55.12
B	0.00	0.10	0.85	3.07	4.77	3.92	0.38	29.48	57.43
CCC	0.26	0.00	0.26	1.05	3.67	1.83	0.00	46.86	46.07

Source: Table 16 in Leo Brand and Reza Bahar, "Corporate Defaults: Will Things Get Worse Before They Get Better?" Special Report, Standard & Poor's Corporation.

Exhibit 3: Secondary Market Bullet Bid Spreads for 90 Days (in Basis Points) for Corporate Bonds
(July 13, 2001)

	AA			A			BBB		
Maturity	High	Low	Avg.	High	Low	Avg.	High	Low	Avg.
Industrials									
5	77	65	72	116	96	105	169	141	153
10	107	94	100	148	124	134	182	157	168
30	118	107	114	164	144	152	203	174	187
Utilities									
5	125	97	108	143	130	136	183	165	174
10	148	117	127	170	145	154	205	192	198
30	165	127	141	190	158	169	227	213	220
Finance									
3	103	82	89	145	105	120			
5	128	101	111	175	131	148			
10	150	118	133	202	157	174			
Banks									
3	112	94	104	126	98	113			
5	143	120	130	174	138	150			
10	619	329	406	825	710	767			

	BB			B		
	High	Low	Avg.	High	Low	Avg.
High Yield						
10	619	329	406	825	710	767

Source: Lehman Brothers, *Global Relative Value*, Fixed Income Research, July 16, 2001, p. 126.

KEY POINTS

- *The Bankruptcy Reform Act of 1978 governs the bankruptcy process in the United States.*
- *Chapter 7 of the bankruptcy act deals with the liquidation of a company.*
- *Chapter 11 of the bankruptcy act deals with the reorganization of a company.*
- *In theory, creditors should receive distributions based on the absolute priority rule to the extent assets are available.*
- *The absolute priority rule means that senior creditors are paid in full before junior creditors are paid anything.*
- *Generally, the absolute priority rule holds in the case of liquidations and is typically violated in reorganizations.*
- *Senior corporate instruments are financial obligations of a corporation that have a priority claim over its common stock in the case of bankruptcy.*
- *Senior corporate securities include debt obligations (bonds, medium-term notes, commercial paper, and bank loans to corporations) and preferred stock.*
- *A corporate debt issue is said to be secured debt if some form of collateral is pledged to ensure repayment of the debt.*
- *Mortgage debt is debt secured by real property such as plant and equipment, with the largest issuers of such debt being electric utility companies.*
- *An open-ended mortgage is one in which the indenture does not limit the total amount of bonds that may be issued, although certain issuance tests (e.g., earnings coverage test) or bases usually have to be satisfied before the company can sell more bonds.*
- *The after-acquired property clause also subjects to the mortgage property that is acquired by the company after the filing of the original or supplemental indenture.*
- *Maintenance fund, maintenance and replacement fund, or renewal and replacement fund provisions are placed in indentures to provide for proper maintenance of the property and replacement of worn-out plant.*
- *The release and substitution of property clause specifies that if the company releases property from the mortgage lien, it must substitute other property or cash and securities to be held by the trustee, usually in an amount equal to the released property's fair value.*
- *There are instances when a company might have two or more layers of mortgage debt outstanding with different priorities, with the secondary debt often referred to as General and Refunding Mortgage Bonds.*

- ❑ *Today, nonutility companies do not issue much mortgage debt, with the preferred form of debt financing being unsecured debt.*
- ❑ *Collateral trust debentures, bonds, and notes are secured by financial assets such as cash, receivables, other notes, debentures or bonds, and not by real property.*
- ❑ *Railroads and airlines finance much of their rolling stock and aircraft with secured debt in the form of equipment trust certificates.*
- ❑ *The ratings for equipment trust certificates are higher than on the same company's mortgage debt or other public debt securities due primarily to the collateral value of the equipment, its superior standing in bankruptcy compared with other claims, and the instrument's generally self-liquidating nature.*
- ❑ *Unsecured debt, like secured debt, comes in several different layers or levels of claim against the corporation's assets, and subordination of the debt instrument might not be apparent from the issue's name.*
- ❑ *Some debt issues are credit enhanced by having other companies guarantee their loans.*
- ❑ *One of the important protective provisions for unsecured debtholders is the negative pledge clause, which prohibits a company from creating or assuming any lien to secure a debt issue without equally securing the subject debt issue(s) (with certain exceptions).*
- ❑ *While prospectuses may provide most of the needed information, the indenture is the more important document since it sets forth in great detail the promises of the issuer.*
- ❑ *A corporate debt issue can be issued under a blanket or open-ended indenture, or a new indenture must be written each time a new series of debt is sold.*
- ❑ *The model debenture indenture has 15 articles and a preamble, or preliminary statement, called parties and recitals, while the model mortgage bond indenture form has 16 articles and a preliminary statement.*
- ❑ *A debenture indenture includes any covenants that impose certain limitations and restrictions on the borrower's activities.*
- ❑ *Negative covenants are those that require the borrower not to take certain actions.*
- ❑ *An infinite variety of restrictive covenants can be placed on borrowers, depending on the type of debt issue, the economics of the industry and the nature of the business, and the lenders' desires.*
- ❑ *Restrictive provisions on additional borrowings may be based on interest or fixed-charge coverage tests—a maintenance test and debt incurrence test.*
- ❑ *A mandatory specific sinking fund specifies that the issuer may satisfy the sinking fund provision in whole or in part, by (1) delivering bonds acquired through open-market purchases or other means or (2) paying cash to the trustee who will call bonds for redemption at par.*

- ❑ *A nonmandatory sinking fund provision allows the issuer to satisfy the sinking fund provision by the utilization of unfunded property additions or improvements at a certain percentage of their cost.*

- ❑ *A specific sinking provision applies to just the named issue while a nonspecific sinking fund, also known as a funnel, tunnel, blanket, or aggregate sinking fund, is based on the outstanding amount of a company's total bonded indebtedness.*

- ❑ *Because of the risk of exhausting gas supplies, some gas pipeline company indentures provide for the acceleration of the sinking fund in the event that estimates of the reserve lives of the companies' proven gas reserves decline.*

- ❑ *The three nationally recognized statistical rating organizations that rate corporate bonds are Moody's Investors Service, Standard & Poor's Corporation, and Fitch.*

- ❑ *In all rating systems, the term high grade means low credit risk, or conversely, high probability of future payments.*

- ❑ *Bond issues that are assigned a rating in the top four categories are referred to as investment-grade bonds; those rated below the top four ratings are called noninvestment-grade bonds or speculative issues, or more popularly high-yield bonds, or junk bonds.*

- ❑ *The rating of a security is assigned after a thorough analysis of the issuer's and, if applicable, the guarantor's operations and need for funds.*

- ❑ *In conducting a credit rating examination, the analyst considers the four Cs of credit—character, capacity, collateral, and covenants.*

- ❑ *A rating transition matrix shows the percentage of upgrades, downgrades, and no rating change based on historical experience.*

Chapter 8

Senior Corporate Instruments: II

In the previous chapter we looked at the general characteristics of corporate debt and corporate bond ratings. In this chapter, we look at speculative-grade bonds and convertible bonds. Then we discuss three other corporate debt instruments—medium-term notes, commercial paper, and bank loans to corporations—and preferred stock. We conclude this chapter with a look at the historical evidence on default rates and recovery rates on defaulted bonds. In addition, we review the evidence on the extent of violation of the absolute priority rule among claimants.

SPECULATIVE-GRADE BONDS[1]

Speculative-grade bonds are those rated below investment grade by the rating agencies (i.e., BB+ and lower by Duff & Phelps Credit Rating Co., Fitch Investors Service, L.P., and Standard & Poor's Corporation, and Ba1 and less by Moody's Investors Service, Inc.). They may also be unrated, but not all unrated debt is speculative. Also known as *junk bonds*, promoters have given these securities other euphemisms such as high-interest bonds ("HIBS"), high-opportunity debt, and high-yield securities. While some of these terms may be misleading to the uninitiated, they are used throughout the investment world, with "junk" and "high yield" the most popular. We will also use "junk" and "high yield" in this chapter. Speculative-grade bonds may not be high-yielders at all because they may not be paying any interest, and there may be little hope for the resumption of interest payments; even the return expected from a reorganization or liquidation may be low. Some high-yield instruments may not be speculative-grade at all because they may carry investment-grade ratings. The higher yields may be due to fears of premature redemption of high-coupon bonds in a lower interest rate environment. The higher yields may be caused by a sharp decline in the securities markets, which has driven down the prices of all issues, including those with investment merit.

While the term "junk" tarnishes the entire less-than-investment-grade spectrum, it is applicable to some specific situations. Junk bonds are not useless stuff, trash, or rubbish as the term is defined. At times, investors overpay for their speculative-grade securities so they feel that they may have purchased junk or worthless garbage. But this is also the case when they have overpaid for high-

[1] This section is adapted from Richard W. Wilson and Frank J. Fabozzi, *Corporate Bonds: Structures & Analysis* (New Hope, PA: Frank J. Fabozzi Associates, 1996).

grade securities. There are other times when profits may be made from buying junk bonds; certainly then, these bonds are not junk but something that may be quite attractive. Also, not all securities in this low-grade sector of the market are on the verge of default or bankruptcy. Many issuers might be on the fringe of the investment-grade sector. Market participants should be discriminating in the choice of their terminology.

Types of Issuers

Several types of issuers fall into the less-than-investment-grade high-yield category. These include original issuers, fallen angels, and restructuring and leveraged buyouts.

Original issuers may be young, growing corporations lacking the stronger balance sheet and income statement profile of many established corporations, but often with lots of promise. Also called *venture capital situations* or *growth* or *emerging market companies*, the debt is often sold with a story projecting future financial strength. From this we get the term "story bond." There are also the established operating firms with financials neither measuring up to the strengths of investment-grade corporations nor possessing the weaknesses of companies on the verge of bankruptcy. Subordinated debt of investment-grade issuers may be included here. A bond rated at the bottom rung of the investment-grade category (Baa and BBB) or at the top end of the speculative-grade category (Ba and BB) is known as a "businessman's risk."

Fallen angels are formerly companies with investment-grade-rated debt that have come upon hard times with deteriorating balance sheet and income statement financial parameters. An example is CBS Inc., which in November 1995 was downgraded from A to BB by S&P and Baa3 to Ba1 by Moody's. (Companies that have been upgraded to investment-grade status are referred to as *rising stars*.) They may be in default or near bankruptcy. In these cases, investors are interested in the workout value of the debt in a reorganization or liquidation, whether within or without the bankruptcy courts. Some refer to these issues as "special situations." Over the years they have fallen on hard times; some have recovered and others have not. One example of a fallen angel is Navistar International Transportation Company (formerly International Harvester Company). Its senior debt was rated A in 1976, fell to Caa in 1981, then recovered to investment-grade Baa3 in 1989, only to become a fallen angel again in 1992, when it was downgraded to Ba2 and then Ba3. Chrysler Corporation is another issuer making the round trip from investment-grade to noninvestment-grade status and back again. Its senior debt fell from Baa in 1976 to Caa in 1981, and carried the A3 ranking in the fall of 1994. Others that have made the return trip include Long Island Lighting Company and Gulf States Utilities Company.

Restructurings and *leveraged buyouts* are companies that have deliberately increased their debt burden with a view toward maximizing shareholder value. The shareholders may be the existing public group to which the company

pays a special extraordinary dividend, with the funds coming from borrowings and the sale of assets. Cash is paid out, net worth decreased and leverage increased, and ratings drop on existing debt. Newly issued debt gets junk bond status because of the company's weakened financial condition.

In a leveraged buyout (LBO), a new and private shareholder group owns and manages the company. The debt issue's purpose may be to retire other debt from commercial and investment banks and institutional investors incurred to finance the LBO. The debt to be retired is called bridge financing because it provides a bridge between the initial LBO activity and the more permanent financing.

Unique Features of Some Issues

Often actions taken by management that result in the assignment of a noninvestment-grade bond rating result in a heavy interest payment burden. This places severe cash flow constraints on the firm. To reduce this burden, firms involved with heavy debt burdens have issued bonds with *deferred coupon structures* that permit the issuer to avoid using cash to make interest payments for a period of 3 to 7 years. There are three types of deferred coupon structures: (1) deferred-interest bonds, (2) step-up bonds, and (3) payment-in-kind bonds.

Deferred-interest bonds are the most common type of deferred coupon structure. These bonds sell at a deep discount and do not pay interest for an initial period, typically from 3 to 7 years. (Because no interest is paid for the initial period, these bonds are sometimes referred to as zero-coupon bonds.) *Step-up bonds* do pay coupon interest, but the coupon rate is low for an initial period and then increases ("steps up") to a higher coupon rate. Finally, *payment-in-kind (PIK) bonds* give the issuer an option to pay cash at a coupon payment date or give the bondholder a similar bond (i.e., a bond with the same coupon rate and a par value equal to the amount of the coupon payment that would have been paid). The period during which the issuer can make this choice varies from 5 to 10 years.

In late 1987, an issue came to market with a structure allowing the issuer to reset the coupon rate so that the bond will trade at a predetermined price.[2] The coupon rate may reset annually or even more frequently, or reset only one time over the life of the bond. Generally, the coupon rate at the reset date will be the average of rates suggested by two investment banking firms. The new rate will then reflect (1) the level of interest rates at the reset date and (2) the credit spread the market wants on the issue at the reset date. This structure is called an *extendible reset bond.*

Notice the difference between an extendible reset bond and a floating-rate issue as described in Chapter 1. In a floating-rate issue, the coupon rate resets according to a fixed spread over the reference rate, with the index spread specified in the indenture. The amount of the index spread reflects market conditions at the time the issue is offered. The coupon rate on an extendible reset bond, in con-

---

2 Most of the bonds have a coupon reset formula that requires the issuer to reset the coupon so that the bond will trade at a price of $101.

trast, is reset based on market conditions (as suggested by several investment banking firms) at the time of the reset date. Moreover, the new coupon rate reflects the new level of interest rates and the new spread that investors seek.

The advantage to investors of extendible reset bonds is that the coupon rate will reset to the market rate—both the level of interest rates and the credit spread—in principle keeping the issue at par value. In fact, experience with extendible reset bonds has not been favorable during the recent period of difficulties in the high-yield bond market. The sudden substantial increase in default risk has meant that the rise in the rate needed to keep the issue at par value was so large that it would have insured the bankruptcy of the issuer. As a result, the rise in the coupon rate has been insufficient to keep the issue at the stipulated price.

Some speculative-grade bond issues started to appear in 1992, granting the issuer a limited right to redeem a portion of the bonds during the noncall period if the proceeds are from an initial public stock offering. In a few cases, proceeds from a secondary stock offering are also a permissible source of funds. Called "clawback" provisions, they merit careful attention by inquiring bond investors. According to Merrill Lynch's High Yield Securities Research Department, an increasing number of high-yield issues have clawbacks. In the nearly 3-year period ending June 30, 1994, of the almost 700 high-yield issues in its sample, close to 25% came with clawbacks. The percentage of the issue that can be retired with stock proceeds ranges from 20% to 100%, with the clawback period usually limited to the first 3 years after issuance. The redemption prices are around 110% of par, give or take a couple of points. Investors should be forewarned of clawbacks since they can lose bonds at the point in time just when the issuer's finances have been strengthened through access to the equity market. Also, the redemption may reduce the amount of the outstanding bonds to a level at which their liquidity in the aftermarket may suffer.

CONVERTIBLE BONDS

A *convertible bond* is a corporate bond issue that can be converted into common stock at the option of the bondholder. We describe the basic features of convertible bonds and their investment characteristics as follows.

Basic Features of Convertible Bonds

The conversion provision of a bond grants the bondholder the right to convert the security into a predetermined number of shares of common stock of the issuer. An *exchangeable bond* grants the bondholder the right to exchange the security for the common stock of a firm *other* than the issuer of the security. For example, some Ford Motor Credit convertible bonds are exchangeable for the common stock of the parent company, Ford Motor Company. Throughout this chapter, we use the term *convertible bond* to refer to both convertible and exchangeable bonds.

Exhibit 1: Information About General Signal Corporation Convertible Bond 5¾s due June 1, 2002 and Common Stock

Convertible bond:

Market price (as of 10/7/93): $106.50
Issue proceeds: $100 million
Issue date: 6/1/92
Maturity date: 6/1/02
Noncall until 6/1/95

Call price schedule:	
6/1/95	103.59
6/1/96	102.88
6/1/97	102.16
6/1/98	101.44
6/1/99	100.72
6/1/00	100.00
6/1/01	100.00

Coupon rate: 5¾%
Conversion ratio: 25.320 shares of GSX shares per $1,000 par value
Rating: A3/A–

GSX common stock:

Dividend per share: $0.90 per year
Dividend yield (as of 10/7/93): 2.727%
Stock price: $33

In illustrating the various concepts associated with convertible bonds, we use the General Signal Corporation (ticker symbol "GSX") 5¾s convertible issue due June 1, 2002. Information about the issue and the stock of this issuer is provided in Exhibit 1.

Conversion Ratio

The number of shares of common stock that the bondholder will receive from exercising the call option of a convertible bond is called the *conversion ratio*. The conversion privilege may extend for all or only some portion of the security's life, and the stated conversion ratio may change over time. It is always adjusted proportionately for stock splits and stock dividends. For the GSX convertible issue, the conversion ratio is 25.32 shares. This means that for each $1,000 of par value of this issue the bondholder exchanges for GSX common stock, he will receive 25.32 shares.

At the time of issuance of a convertible bond, the issuer effectively grants the bondholder the right to purchase the common stock at a price equal to:

$$\frac{\text{Par value of convertible bond}}{\text{Conversion ratio}}$$

This price is referred to in the prospectus as the *stated conversion price*. Sometimes the issue price of a convertible bond may not be equal to par. In such cases, the stated conversion price at issuance is usually determined by the issue price.

The stated conversion price for the GSX convertible issue is:

$$\text{Stated conversion price} = \frac{\$1,000}{25.32} = \$39.49$$

Call Provisions

Almost all convertible issues are callable by the issuer. This is a valuable feature for issuers who deem the current market price of their stock undervalued enough so that selling stock directly would dilute the equity of current stockholders. The firm would prefer to raise common stock over incurring debt, so it issues a convertible, setting the conversion ratio on the basis of a stock price it regards as acceptable. Once the market price reaches the conversion point, the firm will want to see the conversion happen in view of the risk that the stock price may drop in the future. This gives the firm an interest in forcing conversion, even though this is not in the interest of the owners of the security, whose price is likely to be adversely affected by the call.

Typically there is a noncall period (i.e., a time period from the time of issuance that the convertible bond may not be called). The GSX convertible issue had a noncall period at issuance of 3 years. Some issues have a provisional call feature that allows the issuer to call the issue during the noncall period if the price of the stock reaches a certain price. For example, Whirlpool Corporation zero-coupon convertible bond due 5/14/11 could not be called before 5/14/93 unless the stock price reached $52.35, at which time the issuer had the right to call the issue. In the case of Eastman Kodak zero-coupon convertible bond due 10/15/11, the issuer could not call the issue before 10/15/93 unless the common stock traded at a price of at least $70.73 for at least 20/30 trading days.

The call price schedule of a convertible bond is specified at the time of issuance. Typically, the call price declines over time. The call price schedule for the GSX convertible issue is shown in Exhibit 1. In the case of a zero-coupon convertible bond, the call price is based on an accreted value. For example, for the Whirlpool Corporation zero-coupon convertible, the call price on 5/14/93 was $28.983 and thereafter accretes daily at 7% per annum compounded semiannually. So, if the issue was called on 5/14/94, the call price would have been $31.047 ($28.983 times 1.035^2).

Put Provision

A put option grants the bondholder the right to require the issuer to redeem the issue at designated dates for a predetermined price. Some convertible bonds are putable. For example, Eastman Kodak zero-coupon convertible bond due 10/15/11 is putable. The put schedule is as follows: 32.35 if put on 10/15/94; 34.57 if put on 10/15/95; 36.943 if put on 10/15/96; 51.486 if put on 10/15/01; and 71.753 if put on 10/15/06. The GSX convertible issue is not putable.

Put options can be classified as "hard" puts and "soft" puts. A *hard put* is one in which the convertible bond must be redeemed by the issuer only for cash.

In the case of a *soft put*, the issuer has the option to redeem the convertible bond for cash, common stock, subordinated notes, or a combination of the three.

Traditional Analysis of Convertible Bonds

Minimum Value of a Convertible Bond

The *conversion value* or *parity value* of a convertible bond is the value of the security if it is converted immediately.[3] That is,

Conversion value = Market price of common stock × Conversion ratio

The minimum price of a convertible bond is the greater of

1. Its conversion value, or
2. Its value as a security without the conversion option—that is, based on the convertible bond's cash flows if not converted (i.e., a plain vanilla security). This value is called its *straight value* or *investment value.*

If the convertible bond does not sell for the greater of these two values, arbitrage profits could be realized. For example, suppose the conversion value is greater than the straight value, and the security trades at its straight value. An investor can buy the convertible bond at the straight value and convert it. By doing so, the investor realizes a gain equal to the difference between the conversion value and the straight value. Suppose, instead, the straight value is greater than the conversion value, and the security trades at its conversion value. By buying the convertible at the conversion value, the investor will realize a higher yield than a comparable straight security.

For the GSX convertible issue, the conversion value on 10/7/93 per $1,000 of par value was equal to:

Conversion value = $33 × 25.32 = $835.56

Therefore, the conversion value per $100 of par value was $83.556.

Suppose that the appropriate yield for a straight bond issued by GSX would have been 6.02%. The straight value would be $98.19. Since the minimum value of the GSX convertible issue is the greater of the conversion value and the straight value, the minimum value was $98.19.

Market Conversion Price

The price that an investor effectively pays for the common stock if the convertible bond is purchased and then converted into the common stock is called the *market conversion price* or *conversion parity price*. It is found as follows:

---

3 Technically, the standard textbook definition of conversion value given here is theoretically incorrect because as bondholders convert, the price of the stock will decline. The theoretically correct definition for the conversion value is that it is the product of the conversion ratio and the stock price *after* conversion.

$$\text{Market conversion price} = \frac{\text{Market price of convertible bond}}{\text{Conversion ratio}}$$

The market conversion price is a useful benchmark because once the actual market price of the stock rises above the market conversion price, any further stock price increase is certain to increase the value of the convertible bond by at least the same percentage. Therefore, the market conversion price can be viewed as a breakeven point.

An investor who purchases a convertible bond rather than the underlying stock pays a premium over the current market price of the stock. This premium per share is equal to the difference between the market conversion price and the current market price of the common stock. That is,

$$\text{Market conversion premium per share} = \text{Market conversion price} - \text{Current market price}$$

The market conversion premium per share is usually expressed as a percentage of the current market price as follows:

$$\text{Market conversion premium ratio} = \frac{\text{Market conversion premium per share}}{\text{Market price of common stock}}$$

Why would someone be willing to pay a premium to buy the stock? Recall that the minimum price of a convertible bond is the greater of its conversion value or its straight value. Thus, as the common stock price declines, the price of the convertible bond will not fall below its straight value. The straight value therefore acts as a floor for the convertible bond's price. The straight value at some future date, however, is unknown; the value will change as interest rates in the market change.

The calculation of the market conversion price, market conversion premium per share, and market conversion premium ratio for the GSX convertible issue based on market data as of 10/7/93 is shown below:

$$\text{Market conversion price} = \frac{\$1,065}{25.32} = \$42.06$$

$$\text{Market conversion premium per share} = \$42.06 - \$33 = \$9.06$$

$$\text{Market conversion premium ratio} = \frac{\$9.06}{\$33} = 0.275 \text{ or } 27.5\%$$

Current Income of Convertible Bond Versus Common Stock

As an offset to the market conversion premium per share, investing in the convertible bond rather than buying the stock directly generally means that the investor realizes higher current income from the coupon interest paid than would be received as common stock dividends paid on the number of shares equal to the

conversion ratio. Investors evaluating a convertible bond typically compute the time it takes to recover the premium per share by computing the *premium payback period* (which is also known as the *breakeven time*). This is computed as follows:

$$\frac{\text{Market conversion premium per share}}{\text{Favorable income differential per share}}$$

where the favorable income differential per share is equal to the following for a convertible bond:

$$\frac{\text{Coupon interest} - (\text{Conversion ratio} \times \text{Common stock dividend per share})}{\text{Conversion ratio}}$$

The premium payback period does *not* take into account the time value of money.

For the GSX convertible issue, the market conversion premium per share is \$9.06. The favorable income differential per share is found as follows:

$$\text{Coupon interest from bond} = 0.0575 \times \$1{,}000 = \$57.50$$

$$\text{Conversion ratio} \times \text{Dividend per share} = 25.32 \times \$0.90 = \$22.79$$

Therefore,

$$\text{Favorable income differential per share} = \frac{\$57.50 - \$22.79}{25.32} = \$1.37$$

and

$$\text{Premium payback period} = \frac{\$9.06}{\$1.37} = 6.6 \text{ years}$$

Without considering the time value of money, the investor would recover the market conversion premium per share in about 7 years.

Downside Risk with a Convertible Bond

Investors usually use the straight value as a measure of the downside risk of a convertible bond because the price of the convertible bond cannot fall below this value. Thus, the straight value acts as the *current* floor for the price of the convertible bond. The downside risk is measured as a percentage of the straight value and computed as follows:

$$\text{Premuim over straight value} = \frac{\text{Market price of the convertible bond}}{\text{Straight value}} - 1$$

The higher the premium over straight value, all other factors constant, the less attractive the convertible bond.

Despite its use in practice, this measure of downside risk is flawed because the straight value (the floor) changes as interest rates change. If interest rates rise, the straight value falls, making the floor fall. Therefore, the downside risk changes as interest rates change.

For the GSX convertible issue, since the market price of the convertible bond is \$106.5 and the straight value is \$98.19, the premium over straight value is

$$\text{Premuim over straight value} = \frac{\$106.5}{\$98.19} - 1 = 0.085 \text{ or } 8.5\%$$

The Upside Potential of a Convertible Bond

The evaluation of the upside potential of a convertible bond depends on the prospects for the underlying common stock. Thus, the techniques for analyzing common stocks discussed in books on equity analysis should be employed.

Investment Characteristics of a Convertible Bond

The investment characteristics of a convertible bond depend on the common stock price. If the price is low, so that the straight value is considerably higher than the conversion value, the security will trade much like a straight bond. The convertible bond in such instances is referred to as a *bond equivalent* or a *busted convertible.*

When the price of the stock is such that the conversion value is considerably higher than the straight value, then the convertible bond will trade as if it were an equity instrument; in this case it is said to be a *common stock equivalent.* In such cases, the market conversion premium per share will be small.

Between these two cases, bond equivalent and common stock equivalent, the convertible bond trades as a *hybrid security*, having the characteristics of both a bond and common stock.

The Risk/Return Profile of a Convertible Bond

Let's use the GSX convertible issue to compare the risk/return profile from investing in a convertible issue or the underlying common stock.

Suppose on 10/7/93 an investor is considering the purchase of either the common stock of GSX or the 5¾s convertible issue due 6/1/2002. The stock can be purchased in the market for \$33. By buying the convertible bond, the investor is effectively purchasing the stock for \$42.06 (the market conversion price per share). Let's look at the potential profit and loss, assuming the stock price rises to \$50 and a scenario in which the stock price falls to \$25.

If the stock price rises to \$50, the direct purchase of the stock would generate a profit of \$17 per share (\$50 – \$33), or a return of 34%. If the convertible bond is purchased, the conversion value is \$1,266 per \$1,000 of par value (conversion ratio of 25.32 times \$50). Assuming that the straight value per \$1,000 of par value is unchanged at \$981.90, the minimum value for the convertible bond is \$1,266. Since the initial price of the convertible bond per \$1,000 of par value is \$1,065, the profit is \$201, and the return is 18.9% (\$201/\$1,065). The lower return by buying the convertible bond rather than the stock is because a higher price was effectively paid for the stock. Specifically, by buying the convertible bond, a per-share price of \$42.06 was paid. The profit per share is then \$7.94, which produces the return of 18.9% (\$7.94/\$42.06).

Now let's look at what would happen if the stock price declines to $25. If the stock is purchased, there would be a loss of $8 per share or, equivalently, a return of –24%. For the convertible bond, the conversion value would be $633 (conversion ratio of 25.3 times $25). However, the convertible bond's minimum price is the greater of the convertible bond value and the straight value. Assuming the straight value stays at $981.9, this would be the value of the convertible bond. The loss on the convertible bond is therefore $83.10 or 7.8% ($83.10/$1,065).

One of the critical assumptions in this analysis is that the straight value does not change except for the passage of time. If interest rates rise, the straight value will decline. Even if interest rates do not rise, the perceived credit worthiness of the issuer may deteriorate, causing investors to demand a higher yield.

The illustration clearly demonstrates that there are benefits and drawbacks of investing in convertible bonds. The disadvantage is the upside potential giveup because a premium per share must be paid. An advantage is the reduction in downside risk (as determined by the straight value).

MEDIUM-TERM NOTES

A *medium-term note* (*MTN*) is a corporate debt instrument, with the unique characteristic that notes are offered continuously to investors by an agent of the issuer. Investors can select from several maturity ranges: 9 months to 1 year, more than 1 year to 18 months, more than 18 months to 2 years, and so on up to any number of years. Medium-term notes are registered with the Securities and Exchange Commission under Rule 415 (the shelf registration rule), which gives a corporation the maximum flexibility for issuing securities on a continuous basis. MTNs are also issued by foreign corporations, federal agencies, supranational institutions, and foreign countries. The MTN market is primarily institutional, with individual investors being of little import.

The term "medium-term note" to describe this corporate debt instrument is misleading. Traditionally, the term "note" or "medium-term" was used to refer to debt issues with a maturity greater than 1 year but less than 15 years. Certainly this is not a characteristic of MTNs since they have been sold with maturities from 9 months to 30 years, and even longer. For example, in July 1993, Walt Disney Corporation issued a security with a 100-year maturity off its medium-term note shelf registration.

Borrowers have flexibility in designing MTNs to satisfy their own needs. They can issue fixed- or floating-rate debt. The coupon payments can be denominated in U.S. dollars or in a foreign currency. Earlier in this chapter we described the various security structures. MTNs have been designed with the same features. For example, there are MTNs backed by equipment trust certificates issued by railways and subordinated notes issued by bank holding companies. In Chapter 12, we discuss asset-backed securities. There are asset-backed MTNs as well.

A corporation that wants an MTN program will file a shelf registration with the SEC for the offering of securities. While the SEC registration for MTN offerings are between $100 and $1 billion, once the total is sold, the issuer can file another shelf registration. The registration will include a list of the investment banking firms, usually two to four, that the corporation has arranged to act as agents to distribute the MTNs. The large New York–based investment banking firms dominate the distribution market for MTNs. Not all MTNs are sold on an agency basis; some have been underwritten.

An issuer with an active MTN program will post the rates for the maturity ranges it wishes to sell. Fixed-rate interest payments are typically on a semiannual basis, with the same interest payment dates applicable to all of the notes of a particular series of an issuer. Of course, the final interest payment is made at maturity. Interest on floating-rate MTNs may have more frequent coupon payments. If interest rates are volatile, posted rates may change, sometimes more than once a day. The notes are priced at par, which appeals to many investors; they don't have to be concerned about amortizing premiums and the accretion of discounts. Any change in new rates will not affect the rates on previously issued notes.

The purchaser may usually set the maturity as any business day within the offered maturity range, subject to the borrower's approval. This is a very important benefit of MTNs because it enables a lender to match maturities with its own specific requirements. As they are continuously offered, an investor can enter the market when portfolio needs require and will usually find suitable investment opportunities. With underwritten issues, the available supply, both in the new issue and secondary markets, might not be satisfactory for the portfolio's needs. A particular series of MTNs may have many different maturities, but all will be issued under the same indenture. The bulk of the notes sold have maturities of less than 5 years, with the 2- to 3-year range the most preferred. The notes generally are noncallable for life, although some issuers have leeway to add redemption features to unsold notes.

Structured MTNs

At one time the typical MTN was a fixed-rate debenture that was noncallable. Most have this characteristic. It is common today for issuers of MTNs to couple their offerings with transactions in the derivative markets (options, futures/forwards, swaps, caps, and floors) to create debt obligations with more interesting risk/return features than are available in the corporate bond market. These are called *structured notes*. An inverse floater, which we described in Chapter 1, is an example of a structured note.

Structured notes allow institutional investors who are restricted to investing in investment-grade debt issues the opportunity to participate in other asset classes to make a market play. For example, an investor who buys an MTN whose coupon rate is tied to the performance of the S&P 500 is participating in the equity market without owning common stock. If the coupon rate is tied to a for-

eign stock index, the investor is participating in the equity market of a foreign country without owning foreign common stocks.

COMMERCIAL PAPER

Commercial paper is a short-term unsecured promissory note that is issued in the open market and represents the obligation of the issuing corporation. Typically, commercial paper is issued as a zero-coupon instrument.

The minimum round-lot transaction is $100,000, though some issuers will sell commercial paper in denominations of $25,000. There is very little secondary trading of commercial paper. Typically, an investor in commercial paper is an entity that plans to hold it until maturity. This is understandable since an investor can purchase commercial paper in a direct transaction with the issuer, which will issue paper with the specific maturity the investor desires.

In the United States, the maturity of commercial paper is typically less than 270 days, and the most common maturity range is 30 to 50 days or less. There are reasons for this. First, the Securities Act of 1933 requires that securities be registered with the SEC. Special provisions in the 1933 act exempt commercial paper from registration so long as the maturity does not exceed 270 days.[4]

To pay off holders of maturing paper, issuers generally use the proceeds obtained by selling new commercial paper. This process is often described as "rolling over" short-term paper. The risk that the investor in commercial paper faces is that the issuer will be unable to issue new paper at maturity. As a safeguard against this "rollover risk," commercial paper is typically backed by unused bank credit lines.

Corporate issuers of commercial paper can be divided into financial companies and nonfinancial companies. There are three types of financial companies: captive finance companies, bank-related finance companies, and independent finance companies. Captive finance companies are subsidiaries of equipment manufacturing companies. Their primary purpose is to secure financing for the customers of the parent company. For example, the major automobile manufacturers in the world have captive finance companies. A bank holding company may have a subsidiary that is a finance company that provides loans to enable individuals and businesses to acquire a wide range of products. Independent finance companies are those that are not subsidiaries of equipment manufacturing firms or bank holding companies.

---

[4] Hence to avoid the costs associated with registering issues with the SEC, firms rarely issue commercial paper with maturities exceeding 270 days. Another consideration in determining the maturity is whether the commercial paper would be eligible collateral for a bank that wanted to borrow from the Federal Reserve Bank's discount window. In order to be eligible, the maturity of the paper may not exceed 90 days. Since eligible paper trades at a lower cost than paper that is not eligible, issuers prefer to issue paper whose maturity does not exceed 90 days.

Exhibit 2: Ratings of Commercial Paper

	Fitch	Moody's	S&P
Superior	F1+/F1	P1	A1+/A1
Satisfactory	F2	P2	A2
Adequate	F3	P3	A3
Speculative	F4	NP	B, C
Defaulted	F5	NP	D

While the issuers of commercial paper typically have high credit ratings, smaller and less well-known companies with lower credit ratings were able to issue paper in the 1980s. They have been able to do so by means of credit support from a firm with a high credit rating or by collateralizing the issue with high-quality assets. The former type of commercial paper is called *asset-backed commercial paper*, and the latter type is called *credit-supported commercial paper.* An example of credit-supported commercial paper is one supported by a letter of credit. The terms of a letter of credit specify that the bank issuing the letter guarantees that if the issuer fails to pay off the paper when it comes due, the bank will do so. The bank will charge a fee for the letter of credit. Commercial paper issued with this credit enhancement is referred to as *LOC paper*. The credit enhancement may also take the form of a surety bond from an insurance company.[5]

Commercial paper is classified as either *direct paper* or *dealer paper.* Direct paper is sold by the issuing firm directly to investors without the help of an agent or an intermediary. A large majority of the issuers of direct paper are financial companies. These entities require continuous funds in order to provide loans to customers. As a result, they find it cost-effective to establish and maintain a sales force to sell their commercial paper directly to investors. Direct issuers post rates at which they are willing to sell commercial paper with financial information vendors such as Bloomberg, Reuters, and Telerate. With dealer-placed commercial paper, the issuer uses the services of an agent to sell its paper.

Investors in commercial paper are exposed to credit risk. The three rating agencies, Standard & Poor's, Moody's, and Fitch rate commercial paper. Their rating classification system is summarized in Exhibit 2. The commercial paper market is divided into tiers according to credit risk ratings. The "top top tier" consists of paper rated A1+/P1/F1+. "Top tier" is paper rated A1/ P1, F1. Next, "split tier" issues are rated either A1/P2 or A2/P1. The "second tier" issues are rated A2/P2/F2. Finally, "third tier" issues are rated A3/P3/F3.[6]

---

[5] A surety bond is a policy written by an insurance company to protect another party against loss or violation of a contract.

[6] These ratings are used by money market mutual funds in determining the amount of commercial paper that they are permitted to hold. The SEC requirements establish two categories of eligible commercial paper: first-tier paper and second-tier paper. In general, to be categorized as first-tier paper, the SEC requires that two of the rating companies rate the issue as "1." To be categorized as second-tier paper, the SEC requires that one rating company rate the issue as "1" and at least one other rate it as "2" or two companies rate it at "2." It is the second-tier paper that is considered medium-grade and for which there are restrictions on the amount that can be held by money market mutual funds.

The risk that the investor faces is that the borrower will be unable to issue new paper at maturity. This risk is referred to as "rollover risk." As a safeguard against rollover risk, commercial paper issuers secure backup lines of credit sometimes called "liquidity enhancement." Most commercial issuers maintain 100% backing because the rating agencies usually require a bank line of credit as a precondition for a rating. However, some large issues carry less than 100% backing. Backup lines of credit typically contain a "material adverse change" provision that allows the bank to cancel the credit line if the financial condition of the issuing firm deteriorates substantially. Historically, defaults on commercial paper are relatively rare.[7]

The yield on commercial paper is higher than that on Treasury bills for several reasons. First, commercial paper exposes an investor to credit risk. Second, interest earned from investing in Treasury bills is exempt from state and local income taxes. As a result, commercial paper has to offer a higher yield to offset this tax advantage. Finally, commercial paper is far less liquid than Treasury bills. The liquidity premium demanded is probably small, however, because commercial paper investors typically follow a buy-and-hold strategy and so are less concerned with liquidity.

For the period January 1, 1987 to December 31, 2000, the average spread between the yield on 3-month commercial paper and Treasury bills was 54.5 basis points, with a minimum of 12 basis points and a maximum of 221 basis points.[8] The yield spread between commercial paper rates and Treasury bill rates widens considerably in times of financial crises. For example, in August 1998 when the Russian government defaulted on its debt and devalued the ruble, the "paper-bill" spread for highly rated nonfinancial companies widened from 45 basis points at the beginning of July (pre-crisis) to more than 140 basis points in October.[9]

CORPORATE BANK LOANS

As an alternative to the issuance of securities, a corporation can raise funds by borrowing from a single bank or a group of banks, called a *syndicate of banks*. While at one time, bank loans were held in the loan portfolio of the bank that made the loan, in recent years a market has developed to sell off these loans to other banks and nonbank entities. In 1995, Moody's and Standard & Poor's began to rate floating-rate corporate bank debt, taking into consideration the seniority of the debt, the collateral, and the covenants of the individual loans.

---

[7] As of mid-2001, the last default of any consequence occurred on January 31, 1997, when Mercury Finance Co. defaulted on $17 million in commercial paper.

[8] I am grateful to Steven Mann for providing this information.

[9] Marc R. Saidenberg and Philip E. Strahan, "Are Banks Still Important for Financing Large Businesses?" *Current Issues in Economics and Finance*, Federal Reserve Bank of New York, August 1999, pp. 1–6.

Syndicated Bank Loans

A *syndicated bank loan* is one in which a group of banks provides funds to the borrower. The need for a group of banks arises because the amount sought by a borrower may be too large for any one bank to be exposed to the credit of that borrower. Therefore, the syndicated bank loan market is used by borrowers who seek to raise a large amount of funds in the loan market rather than through the issuance of securities.

A syndicated loan is arranged by either a bank or a securities house. The arranger then lines up the syndicate. Each bank in the syndicate provides the funds for which it has committed. The banks in the syndicate have the right to subsequently sell their parts of the loan to other banks.

Characteristics of Bank Loans to Corporations

There are two types of corporate loans: revolving lines of credit ("revolvers") and term loans. *Revolvers* are basically commercial paper backstops to high-grade corporations (concentrated in the triple A to single A sector). *Term loans* traditionally are to lower-quality corporations (concentrated in the double B to single B sector), they are fully funded, and fully drawn. They are amortizing and prepayable.[10] Revolvers are more common in the syndicated loan market.

Bank loans have a priority position over subordinated lenders (bondholders) with respect to repayment of interest and principal. They have covenants and collateral. Most loans are secured by all of the borrower's material assets. This collateral is important because of the more favorable status relative to other creditors in bankruptcy. Unlike corporate bonds, investors in a bank loan have access to private borrower information. Moreover, protective covenants in a bank loan allow the lender to monitor and adjust the behavior of corporate management. A common covenant is that prepayments are required from proceeds realized from asset sales, debt issuance, and equity issuance as well as 50% to 70% of excess cash flows. As a result of this covenant, prepayment of a significant amount of the loan may be prepaid prior to default. For example, in January 1995 when Grand Union filed for Chapter 11, it had prepaid $170 million of its $210 million term loan.[11]

Most corporate bonds have a fixed rate. In contrast, the interest rate on a bank loan is almost always floating. The loan rate is periodically reset at the reference rate plus a spread. The reference rate is typically LIBOR, although it could be the prime rate (i.e., the rate that a bank charges its most creditworthy customers), the Treasury bill rate, or the rate on certificates of deposits. The spread depends on market conditions, the unique structure of the transaction, and the borrower's credit rating. The spread may step up (increase) and step down (decrease) if the borrower's credit profile changes. The investor in a bank loan may also realize an upfront loan fee. In the case of revolving loans, there is a commitment fee.

---

[10] Elliot Asarnow, "The Asset Class of Corporate Loans," *Journal of Portfolio Management* (Summer 1996), p. 93.

[11] Sam DeRosa-Farag, Reade A. Frank, Peter D. Acciavatti, and Jonathan S. Blau, *1995 High Yield Market Review* (NY: Chase Securities Inc., 1996), p. 52.

Distribution of Loans

Senior loans are distributed by two methods—assignments and participations. Each method has its advantages and relative disadvantages, with the method of assignment being the more desirable of the two.

When the holder of a loan is interested in selling his portion, he can do so by passing his interest in the loan by method of *assignment*. In this procedure, the seller transfers all his rights completely to the holder of the assignment, now called the *assignee*. The assignee is said to have *privity of contract* with the borrower. Because of the clear path between the borrower and assignee, the assignment is the more desirable choice of transfer and ownership.

A *participation* involves a holder of a loan "participating out" a portion of his holding in that particular loan. The holder of the participation does not become a party to the loan agreement. His relationship is not with the borrower but with the seller of the participation. Unlike an assignment, a participation does not confer privity of contract on the holder of the participation. However, the holder of the participation has the right to vote on certain legal matters concerning amendments to the loan agreement. These matters include changes regarding maturity, interest rate, and issues concerning the loan collateral.

Because syndicated loans can be sold in the manner described above, they have become marketable. In response to the large amount of bank loans issued in the 1980s and their strong credit protection, some commercial banks and securities houses have shown a willingness to commit capital and resources to facilitate trading as broker-dealers.

The further development of the senior bank loan market will no doubt eventually erode the once-important distinction between a security and a loan: a security has long been seen as a marketable financial asset, while a loan was not viewed as marketable. Interestingly, the trading of these loans is not limited to *performing loans*, which are loans whose borrowers are fulfilling contractual commitments. There is also a market for nonperforming loans (i.e., loans in which borrowers have defaulted).

PREFERRED STOCK

Preferred stock is a class of stock, not a debt instrument, but it shares characteristics of both common stock and debt. Like the holder of common stock, the preferred stockholder is entitled to dividends. Unlike those on common stock, however, dividends are a specified percentage of par or face value. The percentage is called the *dividend rate*; it need not be fixed, but may float over the life of the issue.

Almost all preferred stock limits the securityholder to the specified amount. Historically, there have been issues entitling the preferred stockholder to participate in earnings distribution beyond the specified amount (based on some formula). Preferred stock with this feature is referred to as *participating preferred stock*.

Failure to make preferred stock dividend payments cannot force the issuer into bankruptcy. Should the issuer not make the preferred stock dividend payment, usually made quarterly, one of two things can happen, depending on the terms of the issue. The dividend payment can accrue until it is fully paid. Preferred stock with this feature is called *cumulative preferred stock.* If a dividend payment is missed and the securityholder must forgo the payment, the preferred stock is said to be *noncumulative preferred stock.* Failure to make dividend payments may result in imposition of certain restrictions on management. For example, if dividend payments are in arrears, preferred stockholders might be granted voting rights.

Preferred stock has some important similarities with debt, particularly in the case of cumulative preferred stock: (1) the returns to preferred stockholders promised by the issuer are fixed, and (2) preferred stockholders have priority over common stockholders with respect to dividend payments and distribution of assets in the case of bankruptcy. (The position of noncumulative preferred stock is considerably weaker.) Because of this second feature, preferred stock is called a *senior security.* It is senior to common stock. On a balance sheet, preferred stock is classified as equity.

Almost all preferred stock has a sinking fund provision, and some preferred stock is convertible into common stock. Preferred stock may be issued without a maturity date. This is called *perpetual preferred stock.*

Some preferred stock is convertible into the common stock of the issuer. The features and investment characteristics of convertible preferred stock are the same as discussed earlier in this chapter for convertible bonds.

As with corporate debt instruments, preferred stock is rated. The four nationally recognized statistical rating organizations that rate corporate bonds also rate preferred stock.

Historically, utilities have been the major issuers of preferred stock, accounting for more than half of each year's issuance. Since 1985, major issuers have become financially oriented companies—finance companies, banks, thrifts, and insurance companies. Utilities now account for less than 30% of annual preferred stock issuance.

Tax Treatment of Dividends

Unlike debt, payments made to preferred stockholders are treated as a distribution of earnings. This means that they are not tax deductible to the corporation under the current tax code. Interest payments are tax deductible, not dividend payments. While this raises the after-tax cost of funds if a corporation issues preferred stock rather than borrowing, there is a factor that reduces the cost differential: a provision in the tax code exempts 70% of qualified dividends from federal income taxation if the recipient is a qualified corporation. For example, if Corporation A owns the preferred stock of Corporation B, for each $100 of dividends received by A, only $30 will be taxed at A's marginal tax rate. The purpose of this provision is to mitigate the effect of double taxation of corporate earnings.

There are two implications of this tax treatment of preferred stock dividends. First, the major buyers of preferred stock are corporations seeking tax-advantaged investments. Second, the cost of preferred stock issuance is lower than it would be in the absence of the tax provision because the tax benefits are passed through to the issuer by the willingness of corporate investors to accept a lower dividend rate.

Types of Preferred Stock

There are three types of preferred stock: (1) fixed-rate preferred stock, (2) adjustable-rate preferred stock, and (3) auction and remarketed preferred stock. With fixed-rate preferred stock, the dividend rate is fixed as long as the issue is outstanding. Prior to 1982, all publicly issued preferred stock was fixed-rate preferred stock.

For *adjustable-rate preferred stock* (ARPS), the dividend rate is reset quarterly based on a predetermined spread from the highest of three points on the Treasury yield curve. The predetermined spread is called the *dividend reset spread*. The three points on the yield curve (called the *benchmark rate*) to which the dividend reset spread is either added or subtracted is the highest of (1) the 3-month Treasury bill rate, (2) the 2-year constant maturity rate, or (3) a 10-year or 30-year constant maturity rate.[12] The motivation for linking the dividend rate to the highest of the three points on the Treasury yield curve is to provide the investor with protection against unfavorable shifts in the yield curve.

Most ARPS are perpetual, with a floor and ceiling imposed on the dividend rate of most issues. Because most ARPS are not putable, however, ARPS can trade below par if after issuance the spread demanded by the market to reflect the issuer's credit risk is greater than the dividend reset spread.

The popularity of ARPS declined when instruments began to trade below their par value because the dividend reset rate is determined at the time of issuance, not by market forces. In 1984, a new type of preferred stock, *auction preferred stock* (APS), was designed to overcome this problem, particularly for corporate treasurers who sought tax-advantaged short-term instruments to invest excess funds.[13] The dividend rate on APS is reset periodically, as with ARPS, but the dividend rate is established through an auction process. Participants in the auction consist of current holders and potential buyers. The dividend rate that participants are willing to accept reflects current market conditions.

In the case of *remarketed preferred stock*, the dividend rate is determined periodically by a remarketing agent, who resets the dividend rate so that any preferred stock can be tendered at par and be resold (remarketed) at the original offering price. An investor has the choice of dividend resets every 7 days or every 49 days.

---

[12] The Treasury constant maturity rate is reported in the *Federal Reserve Report H.15(519)*. It is based on the closing market bid yields on actively traded Treasury securities.

[13] Each investment bank developed its own trademark name for APS. The instrument developed by then Shearson Lehman/American Express was called Money Market Preferred (MMP). Salomon Brothers called it Dutch Auction Rate Transferable Securities (DARTS).

DEFAULT AND RECOVERY STATISTICS

There is a good deal of research published on default rates by both rating agencies and academicians.[14] From an investment perspective, default rates by themselves are not of paramount significance: it is perfectly possible for a portfolio of corporate bonds to suffer defaults and to outperform Treasuries at the same time, provided the yield spread of the portfolio is sufficiently high to offset the losses from default. Furthermore, because holders of defaulted bonds typically recover a percentage of the face amount of their investment, the *default loss rate* can be substantially lower than the default rate. The default loss rate is defined as follows:

$$\text{default loss rate} = \text{default rate} \times \text{recovery rate}$$

For instance, a default rate of 5% and a recovery rate of 30% means a default loss rate of only 3.5% (70% of 5%).

Therefore, focusing exclusively on default rates merely highlights the worst possible outcome that a diversified portfolio of corporate bonds would suffer, assuming all defaulted bonds would be totally worthless.

Default Rates

First, let's look at what research has found for the default rate experience of corporate bonds. We begin with a discussion of the experience for high-yield corporate bonds. We do this because what will be apparent is that there are various ways to define default rates that are clearly illustrated by these studies of high-yield corporate bonds.

In their 1987 study, Altman and Nammacher found that the annual default rate for low-rated corporate debt was 2.15%, a figure that Altman has updated since to 2.40%. The firm of Drexel Burnham Lambert (DBL), a major issuer of high-yield

---

[14] See, for example, Edward I. Altman, "Measuring Corporate Bond Mortality and Performance," *Journal of Finance* (September 1989), pp. 909–922; Edward I. Altman, "Research Update: Mortality Rates and Losses, Bond Rating Drift," unpublished study prepared for a workshop sponsored by Merrill Lynch Merchant Banking Group, High Yield Sales and Trading, 1989; Edward I. Altman and Scott A. Nammacher, *Investing in Junk Bonds* (New York: John Wiley, 1987); Paul Asquith, David W. Mullins, Jr., and Eric D. Wolff, "Original Issue High Yield Bonds: Aging Analysis of Defaults, Exchanges, and Calls," *Journal of Finance* (September 1989), pp. 923–952; Marshall Blume and Donald Keim, "Risk and Return Characteristics of Lower-Grade Bonds 1977–1987," Working Paper (8-89), Rodney L. White Center for Financial Research, Wharton School, University of Pennsylvania, 1989; Marshall Blume and Donald Keim, "Realized Returns and Defaults on Lower-Grade Bonds," Rodney L. White Center for Financial Research, Wharton School, University of Pennsylvania, 1989; Bond Investors Association, "Bond Investors Association Issues Definitive Corporate Default Statistics," press release dated August 15, 1989; Gregory T. Hradsky and Robert D. Long, "High Yield Default Losses and the Return Performance of Bankrupt Debt," *Financial Analysts Journal* (July-August 1989), pp. 38–49; "Historical Default Rates of Corporate Bond Issuers 1970–1988," *Moody's Special Report*, July 1989 (New York: Moody's Investors Service); "High-Yield Bond Default Rates," Standard & Poor's *Creditweek* (August 7, 1989), pp. 21–23; David Wyss, Christopher Probyn, and Robert de Angelis, "The Impact of Recession on High-Yield Bonds," DRI-McGraw-Hill (Washington, D.C.: Alliance for Capital Access, 1989); and the 1984–1989 issues of *High Yield Market Report: Financing America's Futures* (New York and Beverly Hills: Drexel Burnham Lambert, Incorporated).

bonds at one time, also estimated default rates of about 2.40% per year. Asquith, Mullins, and Wolff, however, found that nearly one out of every three high-yield corporate bonds defaults. The large discrepancy arises because the studies use three different definitions of "default rate"; even if applied to the same universe of bonds (which they are not), all three results could be valid simultaneously.[15]

Altman and Nammacher define the default rate as the par value of all high-yield bonds that defaulted in a given calendar year, divided by the total par value outstanding during the year. Their estimates (2.15% and 2.40%) are simple averages of the annual default rates over a number of years. DBL took the cumulative dollar value of all defaulted high-yield bonds, divided by the cumulative dollar value of all high-yield issuance, and further divided by the weighted average number of years outstanding to obtain an average annual default rate. Asquith, Mullins, and Wolff use a cumulative default statistic. For all bonds issued in a given year, the default rate is the total par value of defaulted issues as of the date of their study, divided by the total par amount originally issued to obtain a cumulative default rate. Their result (that about one in three high-yield bonds default) is not normalized by the number of years outstanding.

Although all three measures are useful indicators of bond default propensity, they are not directly comparable. Even when restated on an annualized basis, they do not all measure the same quantity. The default statistics from all studies, however, are surprisingly similar once cumulative rates have been annualized. Exhibit 3 shows the default rates by year for the period 1971 to 1997 as reported in a study by Altman and Kishore.[16] The bottom of the exhibit reports that the arithmetic average default rate for the entire period was 2.6%, and the weighted average default rate (i.e., weighted by the par value of the amount outstanding for each year) was 3.3%. For a more recent time period, 1985 to 1997, the arithmetic average default rate was higher, 3.7%.

Historical Recovery Rates

Next let's look at the historical loss rate realized by investors in high-yield corporate bonds. This rate, referred to earlier as the default loss rate, is reported in the last column of Exhibit 3. The methodology for computing the default loss rate by Altman and Kishore is as follows. First, the *default loss of principal* is computed by multiplying the default rate for the year by the average loss of principal. The average loss of principal is computed by first determining the recovery per $100 of par value. They quantify the recovery per $100 of par value using the weighted average price of all issues after default. The difference between par value of 100 and the recovery of principal is the default loss of principal.

---

15 As a parallel, we know that the mortality rate in the United States is currently less than 1% per year, but we also know that 100% of all humans (eventually) die.

16 Edward I. Altman and Vellore M. Kishore, "Defaults and Returns on High Yield Bonds," Chapter 14 in Frank J. Fabozzi (ed.), *The Handbook of Corporate Debt Instruments* (New Hope, PA: Frank J. Fabozzi Associates, 1998).

Exhibit 3: Default Rates and Default Losses for High-Yield Corporate Bonds: 1978–1997

Year	Par Value Outstanding* ($ Millions)	Par Value Defaults ($ Millions)	Default Rates (%)	Weighted Price After Default ($)	Weighted Coupon (%)	Default Loss (%)
1997	$335,400	4,200	1.25	54.2	11.87	0.65
1996	271,000	3,336	1.23	51.9	8.92	0.65
1995	240,000	4,551	1.90	40.6	11.83	1.24
1994	235,000	3,418	1.45	39.4	10.25	0.96
1993	206,907	2,287	1.11	56.6	12.98	0.56
1992	163,000	5,545	3.40	50.1	12.32	1.91
1991	183,600	18,862	10.27	36.0	11.59	7.16
1990	181,000	18,354	10.14	23.4	12.94	8.42
1989	189,258	8,110	4.29	38.3	13.40	2.93
1988	148,187	3,944	2.66	43.6	11.91	1.66
1987	129,557	7,486	5.78	75.9	12.07	1.74
1986	90,243	3,156	3.50	34.5	10.61	2.48
1985	58,088	992	1.71	45.9	13.69	1.04
1984	40,939	344	0.84	48.6	12.23	0.48
1983	27,492	301	1.09	55.7	10.11	0.54
1982	18,109	577	3.19	38.6	9.61	2.11
1981	17,115	27	0.16	12.0	15.75	0.15
1980	14,935	224	1.50	21.1	8.43	1.25
1979	10,356	20	0.19	31.0	10.63	0.14
1978	8,946	119	1.33	60.0	8.38	0.59

Default Rate Summary

		Default Rates (%)	Standard Deviation
Arithmetic Average Default Rate	1971 to 1997	2.613	2.554
	1978 to 1997	2.849	2.808
	1985 to 1997	3.745	3.059
Weighted Average Default Rate**	1971 to 1997	3.311	3.452
	1978 to 1997	3.342	3.066
Median Annual Default Rate	1971 to 1997	1.500	

* As of mid-year.

** Weighted by par value of amount outstanding for each year.

Default Loss Rate Summary

	Default Rate (%)	Weighted Price After Default ($)	Weighted Coupon (%)	Default Loss (%)
Arithmetic Average 1978–1997	2.85	42.9	11.48	1.83
Weighted Average 1978–1997	3.34			2.18

Sources: Adapted from Exhibits 5 and 6 in Edward I. Altman and Vellore M. Kishore, "Defaults and Returns on High Yield Bonds," Chapter 14 in Frank J. Fabozzi (ed.), *The Handbook of Corporate Debt Instruments* (New Hope, PA: Frank J. Fabozzi Associates, 1998).

For example, in 1997 the weighted average price after default per $100 par value was $54.2, as reported in the fifth column of Exhibit 3. The recovery of principal was therefore $54.2, and the default loss of principal for 1997 was therefore $45.8. The default loss from principal for 1997 is then the product of the default rate for 1997 of 1.25% (fourth column of Exhibit 3) and the default loss of principal of $45.8. The product is 0.573%. Next the default loss of coupon interest is computed. This is found by multiplying the default rate by the weighted average coupon rate divided by 2 (because the coupon payments are semiannual). Again, looking at 1997, the weighted average coupon is shown in the next-to-the-last column in the exhibit to be 11.87%. The default loss of coupon is then the product of the default rate of 1.25% and one-half of 11.87%, or 0.074%. The default loss rate is then the sum of the default loss rate of principal and the default loss rate of principal. For 1997, it was 0.65%.

Several studies have found that the recovery rate is closely related to the bond's seniority. Altman and Kishore computed the weighted average recovery rate for 777 bond issues that defaulted between 1978 and 1997 for the following bond classes: (1) senior secured, (2) senior unsecured, (3) senior subordinated, (4) subordinated, and (5) discount and zero coupon.[17] The recovery rate for senior-secured bonds averaged 59% of face value, compared with 49% for senior-unsecured, 35% for senior-subordinated, and 32% for subordinated bonds.

THE RIGHTS OF CREDITORS: THEORY VERSUS PRACTICE

As explained in the previous chapter, when a company is liquidated, creditors receive distributions based on the "absolute priority rule" to the extent assets are available. This means that senior creditors are paid in full before junior creditors are paid anything. In liquidations, the absolute priority rule generally holds. In contrast, studies of actual reorganizations under Chapter 11 have found that the violation of absolute priority is the rule rather than the exception.[18]

Explanations for Divergence from Absolute Priority

There are several possible explanations suggested as to why in a reorganization the distribution made to claimholders will diverge from that required by the absolute priority principle. The first explanation is that the longer the negotiation process among the parties, the greater the bankruptcy costs and the smaller the amount to be distributed to all parties. This is because the longer the negotiation process

---

[17] Altman and Kishore, "Defaults and Returns on High Yield Bonds."

[18] See Julian R. Franks and Walter N. Torous, "An Empirical Investigation of U.S. Firms in Reorganization," *Journal of Finance* (July 1989), pp. 747–769; Lawrence A. Weiss, "Bankruptcy Resolution: Direct Costs and Violation of Priority of Claims," *Journal of Financial Economics* (1990), pp. 285–314; and Frank J. Fabozzi, Jane Tripp Howe, Takashi Makabe, and Toshihide Sudo, "Recent Evidence on the Distribution Patterns in Chapter 11 Reorganizations," *Journal of Fixed Income* (Spring 1993), pp. 6–23.

among the parties, the more likely that the company will be operated in a manner that is not in the best interest of the creditors and, as a result, the smaller the amount to be distributed to all parties. Since all impaired classes including equityholders generally must approve the plan of reorganization, creditors often convince equityholders to accept the plan by offering to distribute some value to them.

A second explanation is that the violation of absolute priority reflects a recontracting process between stockholders and senior creditors that gives recognition to the ability of management to preserve value on behalf of stockholders.[19] According to this view, creditors are less informed than management about the true economic operating conditions of the firm. Because the distribution to creditors in the plan of reorganization is based on the valuation by the firm, creditors without perfect information easily suffer the loss.[20] Managers generally have a better understanding than creditors or stockholders about a firm's internal operations, while creditors and stockholders can have better information about industry trends. Management may therefore use its superior knowledge to present the data in a manner that reinforces its position.[21]

The essence of another explanation is that the increasing complexity of firms that declare bankruptcy will accentuate the negotiating process and result in an even higher incidence of violation of the absolute priority rule. The likely outcome is further supported by the increased number of official committees in the reorganization process, as well as the increased number of financial and legal advisors.

There are some who argue that creditors will receive a higher value in reorganization than they would in liquidation in part because of the costs associated with liquidation.[22] These additional costs include commissions and Chapter 7–specific costs. The commissions associated with liquidation can be significant. The commission charged on the sale of a particular asset could be as high as 20% of the gross proceeds from the asset. Total liquidation costs can be significant.

Finally, the lack of symmetry in the tax system (negative taxes are not permitted, although loss deductions may be carried forward) results in situations in which the only way to use all current loss deductions is to merge.[23] The tax system may encourage continuance or merger and discourage bankruptcy.

---

[19] Douglas G. Baird and Thomas H. Jackson, "Bargaining After the Fall and the Contours of the Absolute Priority Rule," *University of Chicago Law Review*, 55, 1988, pp. 738–789.

[20] L.A. Bebchuk, "A New Approach to Corporate Reorganizations," *Harvard Law Review*, 101, 1988, pp. 775–804.

[21] Karen Hooper Wruck, "Financial Distress, Reorganization, and Organizational Efficiency," *Journal of Financial Economics*, 27, 1990, pp. 419–444.

[22] Michael C. Jensen, "Eclipse of the Public Corporation," *Harvard Business Review*, 89, 1989, pp. 61–62; and Wruck, "Financial Distress, Reorganization, and Organizational Efficiency."

[23] J.I. Bulow and J.B. Shoven, "The Bankruptcy Decision," *Bell Journal of Economics*, 1978. For a further discussion of the importance of NOLs and the current tax law, see Frank J. Fabozzi, Jane Tripp Howe, Takashi Makabe, and Toshihide Sudo, "Recent Evidence on the Distribution Patterns in Chapter 11 Reorganizations," *Journal of Fixed Income* (Spring 1993), pp. 6–23.

Evidence on Divergence from Absolute Priority

A study by Fabozzi, Howe, Makabe, and Sudo (FHMS hereafter) examined the extent of violation of the absolute priority rule for 26 publicly traded companies that emerged from Chapter 11 between September 1, 1988 and April 1, 1990.[24] The firms included in the study are listed in Exhibit 4. FHMS examined three broad groups of securityholder—secured creditors, unsecured creditors, and equity holders—as well as various types of debt and equity securities. They also provided evidence on which asset class bears the cost of violations of absolute priority and an initial estimate of total distributed value relative to liquidation value.

For all 26 firms, they found that the sum of distributed value to all claimants (secured and unsecured creditors, and old equityholders) was greater than the liquidation value under Chapter 7. It makes sense that the distributions to the sample exceed liquidation value for legal as well as economic reasons. For example, the Bankruptcy Code requires that the distributions under a reorganization to impaired claimants and holders of interests will at least equal the distributions under a liquidation; economics dictates that the distributions under a reorganization should be greater than under a liquidation. The requirement is dictated by Section 1129 (a)(7) of the Bankruptcy Code. Pursuant to this section, the Bankruptcy Court must independently determine that each impaired creditor or interest will receive at least as much value under the reorganization as it would under a liquidation.

To describe the distribution to different classes of creditors and interest holders, all claimants were classified into three groups: secured creditors, unsecured creditors, and equityholders. Then each firm was assigned to one of three classes according to the distribution among the three groups as shown at the top of Exhibit 4.[25] The exhibit presents a summary of bankruptcy resolution for the sample firms. Absolute priority was maintained in only 4 of the 26 cases (15.4%). In the remaining 22 cases, absolute priority was violated. In 12 of these 22 cases of violation, priority held only for secured creditors. In the remaining 10 cases, priority did not hold for even secured creditors. Thus, one can conclude from this study that violation of absolute priority is not an exception but a rule. These results are consistent with an earlier study by Weiss, who found that absolute priority was maintained in only 22% of his sample (8 of 37 cases).[26]

When the priority for secured creditors is maintained, claimants usually receive cash (including deferred payments) or a cash-equivalent note. In terms of present value, the claim was not always fully recovered because of an extension of maturity or a reduction of the interest rate. In contrast, when priority was violated, secured creditors received cash or a cash-equivalent note and equity securities or equity warrants.

---

[24] Fabozzi, Howe, Makabe, and Sudo,"Recent Evidence on the Distribution Patterns in Chapter 11 Reorganizations."

[25] The classification system used by FHMS was first introduced by Lawrence A. Weiss, "Bankruptcy Resolution: Direct Costs and Violation of Priority of Claims."

[26] Weiss, "Bankruptcy Resolution: Direct Costs and Violation of Priority of Claims."

Exhibit 4: Summary of Bankruptcy Resolution

Classification System:

Class 1: Absolute priority holds
Secured: 100% Unsecured: 100% Equity: > 0%
or Secured: 100% Unsecured: balance Equity: 0%

Class 2: Absolute priority is violated; priority held only for secured creditors
Secured: 100% Unsecured: < 100% Equity: > 0%

Class 3: Absolute priority is violated, priority did not hold for secured creditors
Secured: < 100% Unsecured: > 0% Equity: ≥ 0%

Outcome:

Class/Description	Number of cases	Percent of total
1. absolute priority holds	4	15.39%
2. absolute priority is violated; priority held only for secured creditors	12	46.15
3. absolute priority is violated: priority did not hold for secured creditors	10	38.46
Total	26	100.00%

The 26 firms included in the study are Allis Chalmers, All Seasons Resorts, American Healthcare, BASIX Corp., Beker Industries, Bercor, Buttes Gas & Oil, Cardis Corp., Coleco (reorganized as Ranger Industries), DeltaUS, Global Marine, Heck's, Kaiser Steel, Manville (filed for protection from product liability-related law suit), McLean Industries, Melridge, Inc., Newbery Corp., Pengo Industries, Pettibone, Po Folks, Radice, Ramtek, UNR Industries (filed for protection from product liability-related law suit), Western Co., Worlds of Wonder, and Zenith Labs (filed for protection from product liability-related law suit).

Source: Adapted from Frank J. Fabozzi, Jane Tripp Howe, Takashi Makabe, and Toshihide Sudo, "Recent Evidence on the Distribution Patterns in Chapter 11 Reorganizations," *Journal of Fixed Income* (Spring 1993), pp. 6–23.

Within the unsecured creditors classes, absolute priority was seldom found to hold. In two cases, all unsecured claims were aggregated and treated equally. In two other cases, unsecured claims were aggregated into only two classes: convenience (small) claims and general unsecured claims (the rest). Of the 26 sample firms, 13 established a convenience claim class and distributed cash equal to approximately 24% to 100% of the allowed claims in the class. This treatment was granted to make the administration of small claims easier. Although the distribution generally equalled 24% to 100% of the allowed claim, the actual distribution as a percent of the original par value was often lower.

The establishment of several classes of unsecured creditors did not alter the violation of absolute priority because absolute priority did not hold among the classes of unsecured creditors. Where more than one class of unsecured creditor was established, the more senior classes tended to receive a higher payout percentage. However, all the unsecured classes received something even though a senior unsecured claim was not satisfied in full. Later we will discuss the treatment of bonds and debentures with different seniority.

In five cases (19%), equityholders received no distribution and the equities were cancelled. This is consistent with the study by Weiss, who found that equityholders received no distribution in 19% of the cases. There was one case in which equityholders received cash while the old equity was cancelled. Of the remaining 20 cases, there was only one case in which equityholders retained their rights, and in other cases old equityholders received new shares of the emerged companies.

Among equity classes (both preferred and common), the absolute priority rule seldom held. In the sample, 13 firms had both preferred stock and common stock. In three cases (23%), the preferred stock and common stock were treated equally. In the other 10 cases, the preferred stock was treated favorably compared to the common stock. For example, in the Kaiser case preferred stockholders received common stock of the reorganized company but common stockholders received no distribution. At the time of its filing, Kaiser had two issues of preferred outstanding. The Series A had a redemption value of $13 per share while the Series B had a redemption value of $17 per share. These issues were treated differently in the plan, with the Series A receiving 0.035 shares of new common per preferred share while the Series B received 0.045 new common per preferred share.

The resolution of bankruptcy indicates that equityholders in more than 75% of the firms in the study received some distribution in violation of absolute priority.

Focusing on the treatment of debtholders, FHMS also look at the type and value of what was received in exchange for the old debt securities. (By "old debt securities" it is meant the securities of the bankrupt firm that were outstanding at the time of filing.) Holders of old debt securities of all types most often received new common stock of the reorganized firm in exchange for the old debt securities. The second most frequent distribution was cash. In four cases, holders of old debt received new debt securities.

The mean recovery (in cents per dollar of claim amount) of holders of all debt securities (including secured bonds) was 26.2% of the claim amount. The mean recovery of holders of secured bonds, senior subordinated debentures, subordinated debentures, and convertible subordinated debentures was 80.3%, 19.7%, 17.2%, and 8.8% of the claim amount, respectively.

There were five old senior subordinated debentures in the FHMS study. In three cases, creditors of senior subordinated debentures received new common stock of the reorganized firm. In the BASIX Corp. case, holders of senior subordinated debentures received new preferred stock. In the Global Marine case, they received new common stock and new warrants. Only Manville had old debentures and old notes. Holders of both types of securities were treated equally and received a combination of cash, new notes, new debentures, new common stock, and new warrants. In five cases out of eight, old subordinated debenture holders received new common stock of the reorganized firm. In the Coleco case, they received cash and new common stock. In the McLean Industries, Inc. reorganization, holders of subordinated debentures and subordinated notes were treated equally and received new preferred and new common stock. In the Pettibone case,

subordinated debenture holders received new notes and new common stock. There were seven old convertible subordinated debentures. In two cases, holders of the old convertible subordinated debentures received new common stock. In the Coleco case, they received cash, new common stock, and warrants to buy Hasbro common stock. (Hasbro acquired essentially all of Coleco's assets, which were associated with the operation of its toy and game businesses.) In the Global Marine case, new common stock and new warrants were distributed. In the Pettibone case, they received new notes and new common stock. In the Po Folks case, they received cash and new notes. In the Worlds of Wonder case, they received cash and new preferred stock. On average, the unsecured debenture holders received 21.5% of the claim amount.

For four firms in the study, there was more than one kind of old debenture and/or note of different seniority. In each case, the debtor-in-possession had both senior subordinated debentures and junior debentures outstanding. In three cases out of four, holders of senior subordinated debentures received more than junior debenture holders and maintained their seniority relative to the junior debenture holders. In the Global Marine case, holders of senior subordinated debentures received the same amount as holders of convertible subordinated debentures. The average return for senior subordinated debentures was 21.8% of their claims, compared with an 18.5% recovery for the holders of junior debentures.

In four of the sample firms, the debtor-in-possession had two kinds of old debentures, notes, subordinated debentures, or convertible subordinated debentures outstanding with the same seniority. In all cases, the holders were treated equally. This treatment is in accordance with the seniority rule.

The absolute priority rule among debt securities was violated. The junior creditors often received something before the senior creditors obtained 100% of their claims. When a firm had more than one kind of old debentures or notes with different seniorities, all debenture holders were sometimes treated equally. However, in most cases, the senior holders received more than the junior creditors. In comparing the recovery ratio of each bond, the senior creditors tended to receive a higher percentage of their claims than the junior creditors in the plan of reorganization.

Looking at the preferred stockholders, in 13 of 26 cases, debtors-in-possession had old preferred stock. In seven of these cases, old preferred stockholders received only new common stock of the reorganized firm. In three cases, they received only cash. In the Allis Chalmers case, holders of preferred stock received cash and new common stock. In the Global Marine case, they received new common stock and new warrants. In the Manville case, they received new preferred stock and new common stock of the reorganized firm. In only one case, Pettibone, did holders of preferred stock receive a distribution equal to the liquidation preference. (The liquidation value of the Pettibone preferred stock was low.) In other cases, preferred stockholders received much less than the liquidation value.

In 10 of 13 cases, holders of preferred stock received a higher recovery per share than holders of common stock. In three cases, preferred stockholders

were treated equally with common stockholders. (In the Coleco case, each preferred stock was converted to one common stock and treated equally.)

In summary, the FHMS study suggests that unsecured creditors bear a disproportionate cost of reorganization, and that more senior unsecured creditors may bear a disproportionate cost relative to the junior unsecured creditors, while equityholders often benefit from violations of absolute priority.

KEY POINTS

- *Speculative-grade bonds are those rated below investment grade by the rating agencies.*
- *Speculative-grade bonds are either original-issue speculative-grade bonds or bonds that have been downgraded to speculative-grade status because the issuer voluntarily significantly increased its debt as a result of a change in the capital structure or have been downgraded for other reasons.*
- *Complex bond structures issued in the speculative-grade sector of the corporate bond market include deferred-coupon bonds (deferred-interest bonds, step-up bonds, and payment-in-kind bonds) and extendible reset bonds.*
- *Convertible and exchangeable bonds can be converted into shares of common stock, the conversion ratio specifying the number of common stock shares that the holder may receive upon converting.*
- *All convertible bonds are callable and some are putable.*
- *The conversion value is the value of the convertible bond if it is immediately converted into the common stock, and the premium paid for the common stock is measured by the market conversion premium per share and market conversion premium ratio.*
- *The minimum value of a convertible bond is the greater of the conversion value and the straight value (i.e., its value if there was no conversion feature).*
- *A bond-equivalent (or a busted convertible) refers to the situation where the straight value is greater than the conversion value so that the security will trade much like a straight bond.*
- *A common stock equivalent refers to the situation where the conversion value is greater than the straight value so that the convertible bond trades as if it were an equity instrument.*
- *A hybrid equivalent refers to the situation where the convertible bond trades with characteristics of both a bond and a common stock instrument.*
- *The advantage of buying a convertible bond rather than the stock is the reduction in downside risk, but the disadvantage is the upside potential giveup because a premium per share must be paid.*
- *While the downside risk of a convertible bond usually is estimated by calculating the premium over straight value, the limitation of this measure is that the straight value (the floor) declines when interest rates rise.*
- *Medium-term notes are corporate debt obligations offered on a continuous basis and are offered through agents.*
- *The rates posted for medium-term notes are for various maturity ranges, with maturities as short as 9 months to as long as 30 years.*

- ❑ *MTNs have been issued simultaneously with transactions in the derivatives market to create structured MTNs allowing issuers greater flexibility in creating MTNs that are attractive to investors who seek to hedge or undertake a market play that they might otherwise be prohibited from doing.*

- ❑ *Commercial paper is a short-term unsecured promissory note issued in the open market that represents the obligation of the issuing entity.*

- ❑ *Commercial paper is sold on a discount basis.*

- ❑ *The maturity of commercial paper is less than 270 days.*

- ❑ *Direct paper is sold by the issuing firm directly to investors without using a securities dealer as an intermediary; with dealer-placed commercial paper, the issuer uses the services of a securities firm to sell its paper.*

- ❑ *There is little liquidity in the commercial paper market.*

- ❑ *The two types of corporate bank loans are revolving lines of credit and term loans, with the former being more common.*

- ❑ *Revolvers are basically commercial paper backstops to high-grade corporations, and term loans traditionally are to lower-quality corporations that are fully funded and fully drawn.*

- ❑ *Bank loans to corporations have a priority position over subordinated lenders (bondholders) with respect to repayment of interest and principal, have covenants and collateral, and typically have a floating rate.*

- ❑ *Preferred stock is a class of stock, not a debt instrument, with the holder entitled to receive dividends.*

- ❑ *Cumulative preferred stock specifies that a missed dividend accrues, while for noncumulative preferred stock it is lost.*

- ❑ *The two characteristics that cumulative nonparticipating preferred stock shares with debt instruments and that results in such preferred stock being classified as a fixed income security are that the returns to preferred stockholders promised by the issuer are fixed and preferred stockholders have priority over common stockholders with respect to dividend payments and distribution of assets in the case of bankruptcy.*

- ❑ *Preferred stock issued without a maturity date is called perpetual preferred stock.*

- ❑ *Because of the tax treatment of preferred stock dividends, the major buyers of these securities are corporations seeking tax-advantaged investments.*

- ❑ *The three types of preferred stock are fixed-rate preferred stock, adjustable-rate preferred stock, and auction and remarketed preferred stock.*

- *The three rating organizations that rate corporate bonds also rate MTNs, commercial paper, corporate bank loans, and preferred stock.*
- *Investors in corporate bonds are interested in default rates and, more importantly, default loss rates or recovery rates.*
- *A default rate can be measured in terms of the number of issuers defaulting (issuer default rate) or the par amount defaulting (dollar default rate).*
- *There is ample evidence to suggest that the lower the credit rating, the higher the probability of a corporate issuer defaulting.*
- *The extensive studies focusing on default rates for speculative-grade issuers place the annual dollar default rates for all original-issue high-yield bonds between 3% and 4%.*
- *The default loss rate is defined as the product of the default rate and the recovery rate.*
- *Studies of recovery rates found that senior-secured bonds averaged 59% of face value, compared with 49% for senior-unsecured, 35% for senior-subordinated, and 32% for subordinated bonds.*
- *Studies of actual reorganizations under Chapter 11 have found that the violation of absolute priority is the rule rather than the exception.*
- *A study of the extent of violation of the absolute priority rule found that when priority was violated, secured creditors received cash or a cash-equivalent note and equity securities or equity warrants and that within the unsecured creditors classes, absolute priority was seldom found to hold.*
- *Among equity classes (both preferred and common), a study found that absolute priority rule seldom held and that equityholders in more than 75% of the firms studied received some distribution in violation of absolute priority.*
- *A study suggests that unsecured creditors bear a disproportionate cost of reorganization, and that more senior unsecured creditors may bear a disproportionate cost relative to the junior unsecured creditors, while equityholders often benefit from violations of absolute priority.*

Chapter 9

Agency Mortgage Passthrough Securities

Mortgage-backed securities are securities backed by a pool (collection) of mortgage loans. While any type of mortgage loans, residential or commercial, can be used as collateral for a mortgage-backed security, most are backed by residential mortgages. Mortgage-backed securities include the following securities: (1) mortgage passthrough securities, (2) collateralized mortgage obligations, and (3) stripped mortgage-backed securities. The latter two mortgage-backed securities are referred to as *derivative mortgage-backed securities* because they are created from mortgage passthrough securities. In this chapter we describe mortgage passthrough securities and stripped mortgage-backed securities. More specifically, we look at those securities either guaranteed by the full faith and credit of the U.S. government or guaranteed by a government-sponsored enterprise. Such mortgage-backed securities are called *agency mortgage-backed securities*. In Chapter 11, we look at nonagency mortgage-backed securities.

MORTGAGES

We begin our discussion with the raw material for a mortgage-backed security (MBS)—the mortgage loan. A *mortgage loan*, or simply mortgage, is a loan secured by the collateral of some specified real estate property, which obliges the borrower to make a predetermined series of payments. The mortgage gives the lender the right if the borrower defaults (i.e., fails to make the contracted payments) to "foreclose" on the loan and seize the property in order to ensure that the debt is paid off. The interest rate on the mortgage loan is called the *mortgage rate* or *contract rate*. Our focus is on residential mortgage loans.

When the lender makes the loan based on the credit of the borrower and on the collateral for the mortgage, the mortgage is said to be a *conventional mortgage*. The lender also may take out mortgage insurance to guarantee the fulfillment of the borrower's obligation. Some borrowers can qualify for mortgage insurance, which is guaranteed by one of three U.S. government agencies: the Federal Housing Administration (FHA), the Veteran's Administration (VA), and the Rural Housing Service (RHS). There are also private mortgage insurers.

There are many types of mortgage designs available in the United States. A *mortgage design* is a specification of the interest rate, term of the mortgage, and

manner in which the borrowed funds are repaid. We describe the three most popular mortgage designs: (1) the fixed-rate, level-payment, fully amortized mortgage, (2) the adjustable-rate mortgage, and (3) the balloon mortgage as follows.

Fixed-Rate, Level-Payment, Fully Amortized Mortgage

The basic idea behind the design of the fixed-rate, level-payment, fully amortized mortgage is that the borrower pays interest and repays principal in equal installments over an agreed-upon period of time, called the *maturity* or *term* of the mortgage. The frequency of payment is typically monthly. Each monthly mortgage payment for this mortgage design is due on the first of each month and consists of:

1. interest of ¹⁄₁₂th of the annual interest rate times the amount of the outstanding mortgage balance at the beginning of the previous month, and
2. a repayment of a portion of the outstanding mortgage balance (principal).

The difference between the monthly mortgage payment and the portion of the payment that represents interest equals the amount that is applied to reduce the outstanding mortgage balance. The monthly mortgage payment is designed so that after the last scheduled monthly payment of the loan is made, the amount of the outstanding mortgage balance is zero (i.e., the mortgage is fully repaid or amortized).

To illustrate this mortgage design, consider a 30-year (360-month) $100,000 mortgage with a mortgage rate of 8.125%. The monthly mortgage payment would be $742.50. Exhibit 1 shows for selected months how each monthly mortgage payment is divided between interest and repayment of principal. At the beginning of month 1, the mortgage balance is $100,000, the amount of the original loan. The mortgage payment for month 1 includes interest on the $100,000 borrowed for the month. Since the interest rate is 8.125%, the monthly interest rate is 0.0067708 (0.08125 divided by 12). Interest for month 1 is therefore $677.08 ($100,000 times 0.0067708). The $65.42 difference between the monthly mortgage payment of $742.50 and the interest of $677.08 is the portion of the monthly mortgage payment that represents repayment of principal. The $65.42 in month 1 reduces the mortgage balance.

The mortgage balance at the end of month 1 (beginning of month 2) is then $99,934.58 ($100,000 minus $65.42). The interest for the second monthly mortgage payment is $676.64, the monthly interest rate (0.0067708) times the mortgage balance at the beginning of month 2 ($99,934.58). The difference between the $742.50 monthly mortgage payment and the $676.64 interest is $65.86, representing the amount of the mortgage balance paid off with that monthly mortgage payment. Notice that the last mortgage payment in month 360 is sufficient to pay off the remaining mortgage balance.

As Exhibit 1 clearly shows, *the portion of the monthly mortgage payment applied to interest declines each month, and the portion applied to reducing the*

mortgage balance increases. The reason for this is that as the mortgage balance is reduced with each monthly mortgage payment, the interest on the mortgage balance declines. Since the monthly mortgage payment is fixed, an increasingly larger portion of the monthly payment is applied to reduce the principal in each subsequent month.

Exhibit 1: Amortization Schedule for a Fixed-Rate, Level-Payment, Fully Amortized Mortgage

Mortgage loan: $100,000
Mortgage rate: 8.125%
Monthly payment: $742.50
Term of loan: 30 years (360 months)

Month	Beginning mortgage balance ($)	Monthly payment ($)	Monthly interest ($)	Scheduled principal repayment ($)	Ending mortgage balance ($)
1	100,000.00	742.50	677.08	65.42	99,934.58
2	99,934.58	742.50	676.64	65.86	99,868.72
3	99,868.72	742.50	676.19	66.31	99,802.41
25	98,301.53	742.50	665.58	76.91	98,224.62
26	98,224.62	742.50	665.06	77.43	98,147.19
27	98,147.19	742.50	664.54	77.96	98,069.23
74	93,849.98	742.50	635.44	107.05	93,742.93
75	93,742.93	742.50	634.72	107.78	93,635.15
76	93,635.15	742.50	633.99	108.51	93,526.64
141	84,811.77	742.50	574.25	168.25	84,643.52
142	84,643.52	742.50	573.11	169.39	84,474.13
143	84,474.13	742.50	571.96	170.54	84,303.59
184	76,446.29	742.50	517.61	224.89	76,221.40
185	76,221.40	742.50	516.08	226.41	75,994.99
186	75,994.99	742.50	514.55	227.95	75,767.04
233	63,430.19	742.50	429.48	313.02	63,117.17
234	63,117.17	742.50	427.36	315.14	62,802.03
235	62,802.03	742.50	425.22	317.28	62,484.75
289	42,200.92	742.50	285.74	456.76	41,744.15
290	41,744.15	742.50	282.64	459.85	41,284.30
291	41,284.30	742.50	279.53	462.97	40,821.33
321	25,941.42	742.50	175.65	566.85	25,374.57
322	25,374.57	742.50	171.81	570.69	24,803.88
323	24,803.88	742.50	167.94	574.55	24,229.32
358	2,197.66	742.50	14.88	727.62	1,470.05
359	1,470.05	742.50	9.95	732.54	737.50
360	737.50	742.50	4.99	737.50	0.00

Servicing Fee and the Cash Flows

Every mortgage loan must be serviced. Servicing of a mortgage loan involves collecting monthly payments and forwarding proceeds to owners of the loan; sending payment notices to mortgagors; reminding mortgagors when payments are overdue; maintaining records of principal balances; administering an escrow balance for real estate taxes and insurance purposes; initiating foreclosure proceedings if necessary; and furnishing tax information to mortgagors when applicable.

The servicing fee is a portion of the mortgage rate. If the mortgage rate is 8.125% and the servicing fee is 50 basis points, then the investor receives interest of 7.625%. The interest rate that the investor receives is said to be the *net interest* or *net coupon*. The servicing fee is commonly called the *servicing spread*.

The dollar amount of the servicing fee declines over time as the mortgage amortizes. This is true for not only the mortgage design that we have just described, but for all mortgage designs.

Prepayments and Cash Flow Uncertainty

Our illustration of the cash flows from a fixed-rate, level-payment, fully amortized mortgage assumes that the homeowner does not pay off any portion of the mortgage balance prior to the scheduled due date. But homeowners do pay off all or part of their mortgage balance prior to the maturity date. Payments made in excess of the scheduled principal repayments are called *prepayments*. We'll look more closely at the factors that affect prepayment behavior later in this chapter.

The effect of prepayments is that the amount and timing of the cash flows from a mortgage are not known with certainty. This risk is referred to as *prepayment risk*. For example, all that the investor in a $100,000, 8.125% 30-year FHA-insured mortgage knows is that as long as the loan is outstanding, interest will be received and the principal will be repaid at the scheduled date each month; then at the end of the 30 years, the investor would have received $100,000 in principal payments. What the investor does not know—the uncertainty—is for how long the loan will be outstanding, and therefore what the timing of the principal payments will be. This is true for all mortgage loans, not just fixed-rate, level-payment, fully amortized mortgages.

Adjustable-Rate Mortgages

An *adjustable-rate mortgage* (ARM) is a loan in which the mortgage rate is reset periodically in accordance with some appropriately chosen reference rate. Outstanding ARMs call for resetting the mortgage rate every month, 6 months, 1 year, 2 years, 3 years, or 5 years. In recent years ARMs typically have had reset periods of 6 months, 1 year, or 5 years. The mortgage rate at the reset date is equal to a reference rate plus an index spread. The index spread varies with market conditions.

Two categories of reference rates have been used in ARMs: (1) market-determined rates and (2) calculated cost of funds for thrifts. The reference rate

will have an important impact on the performance of an ARM and how it is priced. The most popular reference is a market-determined rate—the weekly average yield of constant maturity 1-year Treasuries. About 60% of ARMs are indexed to this reference rate. Other market-determined rates are 6-month LIBOR, 1-month LIBOR, and 6-month certificate of deposit rates.

The cost of funds index for thrifts is calculated based on the monthly weighted average interest cost for liabilities of thrifts. The most popular is the Eleventh Federal Home Loan Bank Board District Cost of Funds Index (COFI). About 25% of ARMs are indexed to this reference rate. The Eleventh District includes the states of California, Arizona, and Nevada. The cost of funds is calculated by first computing the monthly interest expenses for all thrifts included in the Eleventh District. The interest expenses are summed and then divided by the average of the beginning and ending monthly balance. The index value is reported with a 1-month lag. For example, June's Eleventh District COFI is reported in July. The mortgage rate for a mortgage based on the Eleventh District COFI is usually reset based on the previous month's reported index rate. For example, if the reset date is August, the index rate reported in July will be used to set the mortgage rate. Consequently, there is a 2-month lag by the time the average cost of funds is reflected in the mortgage rate. This obviously is an advantage to the borrower when interest rates are rising and a disadvantage to the investor. The opposite is true when interest rates are falling.

The monthly mortgage payments of an ARM are affected by other features. These features are periodic caps and lifetime rate caps and floors. Periodic caps limit the amount that the mortgage rate may increase or decrease at the reset date. The periodic rate cap is expressed in percentage points. The most common rate cap on annual reset loans is 2%. Most ARMs have an upper limit on the mortgage rate that can be charged over the life of the loan. This lifetime loan cap is expressed in terms of the initial rate, the most common lifetime cap being 5% to 6%. For example, if the initial mortgage rate is 7% and the lifetime cap is 5%, the maximum interest rate that the lender can charge over the life of the loan is 12%. Many ARMs also have a lower limit (floor) on the interest rate that can be charged over the life of the loan.

Balloon Mortgages

A variant of the adjustable-rate mortgage is the *balloon mortgage*. The primary difference between a balloon mortgage design and an ARM is that the mortgage rate is reset less frequently. In this mortgage design the borrower is given long-term financing by the lender, but at specified future dates the mortgage rate is renegotiated. Thus, the lender is providing long-term funds for what is effectively a short-term borrowing, how short depending on the frequency of the renegotiation period. Effectively, it is a short-term balloon loan in which the lender agrees to provide financing for the remainder of the term of the mortgage. The balloon payment is the original amount borrowed less the amount amortized.

Growing-Equity Mortgage

A variation of the GPM that does not have negative amortization is the *growing-equity mortgage* (GEM), which has a fixed-rate mortgage whose monthly mortgage payments increase over time. Rather, the higher monthly mortgage payments serve to pay down the principal faster and shorten the term of the mortgage. For example, a 30-year, $100,000 GEM loan with a contract rate of 9.5% might call for an initial monthly payment of $840.85. However, the GEM payment would gradually increase, and the GEM might be fully paid in only 15 years.

Thus, a GEM effectively shortens the life of a mortgage. The advantage of this mortgage design for the borrower is that because it has a shorter life than a level-payment mortgage, in an upward-sloping yield curve environment a lender will be willing to provide a lower mortgage rate than for a level-payment mortgage. As the borrower's income grows over time, the borrower can afford to make the higher payments that lead to the shorter life for the mortgage.

Reverse Mortgages

Reverse mortgages are designed for senior homeowners who want to convert their home equity into cash. Fannie Mae for instance offers two types of reverse mortgages for senior borrowers. "The Home Keeper Mortgage" is an adjustable-rate conventional reverse mortgage for borrowers who are at least 62 years of age and who either own the home outright or have a very low amount of unpaid principal balance. The maximum amount that can be borrowed is based on the homeowner's age, the property's value, and the interest rate. The borrower will not have to repay the loan until he or she no longer occupies the home as their principal residence and cannot be forced to sell or vacate the home to pay off the loan as long as the property is maintained. The other type of reverse mortgage, "Home Keeper for Home Purchase," enables senior borrowers to buy a new home with a combination of personal funds and calculated amount of reverse mortgage that is based on the borrower's age, number of borrowers, the adjusted property value, and the equity share option chosen.

Prepayment Penalty Mortgages

The majority of mortgages outstanding do not penalize the borrower from prepaying any part or all of the outstanding mortgage balance. In recent years, mortgage originators have begun originating *prepayment penalty mortgages* (PPMs).

The basic structure of a PPM is as follows.[1] There is a specified time period where prepayments are not permitted. This time period is called the *lockout*

---

[1] The laws and regulations governing the imposition of prepayment penalties are established at the federal and state levels. Usually, the applicable laws for fixed-rate mortgages are specified at the state level. There are states that do not permit prepayment penalties on fixed-rate mortgages with a first lien. There are states that do permit prepayment penalties but restrict the type of penalty. For some mortgage designs, such as adjustable-rate and balloon mortgages, there are federal laws that override state laws. For a discussion of these laws and regulations, see Anand K. Bhattacharya, "Prepayment Penalty MBS," Chapter 4 in Frank J. Fabozzi (ed.), *The Handbook of Mortgage-Backed Securities: Fifth Edition* (New York, NY: McGraw Hill Publishing Company, 2001). The information in this section draws from that chapter.

period. Typically this period is either 3 years or 5 years. Depending on the structure, a certain amount of prepayments may be made during the lockout period without the imposition of a prepayment penalty. The common prepayment penalty structure is one that allows partial prepayments up to 20% of the original loan amount in any consecutive 12-month period without a prepayment penalty. When a prepayment penalty is imposed, it is typically as follows:[2]

- If there is a 3-year lockout period, the prepayment penalty is the lesser of 2% of any prepayment amount within 3 years that is greater than 20% of the original mortgage, or 6 months of interest on the portion of the prepayment amount that exceeds 20% of the original principal balance.
- If there is a 5-year lockout period, the prepayment penalty is 6 months interest on any prepayment amount in the first 5 years that is greater than 20% of the original principal balance.

For example, suppose that a borrower with a PPM that has a mortgage rate of 8.5%, original principal balance of $150,000, and a lockout period of 5 years refinances within the first 5 years and prepays the entire balance. The prepayment penalty will be 6 months of interest on the amount prepaid in excess of the 20% of the original principal balance. Since 20% of the original principal balance of $150,000 is $120,000 and interest for 1 year at 8.5% is $10,200 (8.5% times $120,000), the prepayment penalty is 6-months' interest, $5,100.

The motivation for the PPM is that it reduces prepayment risk for the lender during the lockout period. It does so by effectively making it more costly for the borrower to prepay in order to take advantage of a decline in mortgage rates. In exchange for this reduction in prepayment risk, the lender will offer a mortgage rate that is less than that of an otherwise comparable mortgage loan without a prepayment penalty.

MORTGAGE PASSTHROUGH SECURITIES

Investing in mortgages exposes an investor to default risk and prepayment risk. A more efficient way is to invest in a *mortgage passthrough security*. This is a security created when one or more holders of mortgages form a pool (collection) of mortgages and sell shares or participation certificates in the pool. A pool may consist of several thousand or only a few mortgages. When a mortgage is included in a pool of mortgages that is used as collateral for a mortgage passthrough security, the mortgage is said to be *securitized*.

The cash flows of a mortgage passthrough security depend on the cash flows of the underlying mortgages. As explained in the previous section, the cash

[2] The prepayment penalty structures are explained in Bhattacharya and Want, "Prepayment Penalty MBS."

flows consist of monthly mortgage payments representing interest, the scheduled repayment of principal, and any prepayments.

Payments are made to securityholders each month. Neither the amount nor the timing, however, of the cash flows from the pool of mortgages is identical to that of the cash flows passed through to investors. The monthly cash flows for a passthrough are less than the monthly cash flows of the underlying mortgages by an amount equal to servicing and other fees. The other fees are those charged by the issuer or guarantor of the passthrough for guaranteeing the issue. The coupon rate on a passthrough, called the *passthrough coupon rate*, is less than the mortgage rate on the underlying pool of mortgage loans by an amount equal to the servicing fee and guarantee fee. The latter is a fee charged by an agency for providing one of the guarantees discussed later.

The timing of the cash flows is also different. The monthly mortgage payment is due from each mortgagor on the first day of each month, but there is a delay in passing through the corresponding monthly cash flow to the securityholders. The length of the delay varies by the type of passthrough security.

Not all of the mortgages that are included in a pool of mortgages that are securitized have the same mortgage rate and the same maturity. Consequently, when describing a passthrough security, a weighted average coupon rate and a weighted average maturity are determined. A *weighted average coupon rate*, or WAC, is found by weighting the mortgage rate of each mortgage loan in the pool by the amount of the mortgage balance outstanding. A *weighted average maturity*, or WAM, is found by weighting the remaining number of months to maturity for each mortgage loan in the pool by the amount of the mortgage balance outstanding.

FEATURES OF AGENCY PASSTHROUGHS

Features of agency passthroughs vary not only by agency but also by program offered. The key features of a passthrough will have an impact on its investment characteristics (particularly its prepayment characteristics). These general features, summarized as follows and discussed further when we review the various agency programs, can be classified into five groups: (1) the type of guarantee, (2) the numbers of lenders whose mortgage loans are permitted in a pool, (3) the mortgage design of the loans, (4) the characteristics of the mortgage loans in a pool, and (5) the payment procedure.

Type of Guarantee

An agency can provide two types of guarantee. One type is the timely payment of both interest and principal, meaning the interest and principal will be paid when due, even if any of the mortgagors fail to make their monthly mortgage payments. Passthroughs with this type of guarantee are referred to as *fully modified passthroughs*. The second type guarantees both interest and principal payments;

however, it only guarantees the timely payment of interest. The scheduled principal is passed through as it is collected, with a guarantee that the scheduled payment will be made no later than a specified date. Passthroughs with this type of guarantee are called *modified passthroughs*.

Number of Lenders Permitted in a Pool

A pool may consist of mortgages originated by a single lender or multiple lenders. A single-lender pool may have mortgage loans concentrated in one geographical area or a few states. In multiple-lender pools, the underlying mortgage loans have greater geographical diversification of borrowers.

Mortgage Design of the Loans

Earlier we described different types of mortgage designs. Agency passthroughs have pools of loans with various mortgage designs.

Characteristics of the Mortgage Loans in the Pool

Not all mortgage loans are permitted in a pool that collateralizes a passthrough. The underwriting standards established by the agency specify the permissible loans. The key underwriting standards are summarized as follows.

Mortgage Loans Permitted in the Pool

Mortgage loans can be classified as government-insured loans and conventional loans.

Maximum Size of a Loan

For agency securities, the loan limits are reset annually.

Amount of Seasoning Permitted

The seasoning of a mortgage loan refers to the time that has passed since the loan was originated.

Assumability of Mortgages

If a mortgage loan may be taken over by another borrower, the loan is said to be *assumable*.

Maturity

Programs are available with mortgage loans of different maturities. For example, a pool can have a stated maturity of 30 years, even though not all of the mortgage loans in the pool have a maturity of 30 years, since seasoned loans may be included.

Servicing Spread Permitted

As explained earlier, for an individual mortgage loan the servicing spread is the difference between the coupon rate paid by the homeowner and the interest rate

received by the investor. A maximum servicing spread permitted in an agency passthrough is specified.

Payment Procedure

Differences in payment procedures involve payment delays and the method of payment.

Payment Delays

Payment delays for passthroughs occur for two reasons. First, monthly payments made by homeowners are made in arrears. That is, the payment for the funds borrowed in, say, March are due on the first of the month of April, the normal delay when investing in mortgage loans. When the payments are received by the trustee, they must be processed and the checks mailed to passthrough investors. The actual delay for passthrough investors (i.e., the number of days that payment is delayed beyond the normal delay) varies with the agency and agency program. The "stated delay" of a passthrough is the normal delay plus the actual delay. If the payment is made on the 15th of the month, then the actual delay is 14 days, since the monthly payment would have been due on the first of the month. If the stated delay for a passthrough is 44 days, then the actual delay is 14 days.

Method of Payment

By method of payment, we mean how many monthly checks an investor who owns several pools of an agency will receive. There can be either one check for all pools or multiple checks.

TYPES OF AGENCY MORTGAGE PASSTHROUGH SECURITIES

There are three types of agency passthrough securities backed by residential mortgages. Each agency has different programs.

Government National Mortgage Association MBS

Government National Mortgage Association ("Ginnie Mae") passthroughs are guaranteed by the full faith and credit of the U.S. government. Therefore, Ginnie Mae passthroughs are viewed as risk-free in terms of default risk, just like Treasury securities. The security guaranteed by Ginnie Mae is called a *mortgage-backed security* (MBS). Ginnie Mae MBSs are issued under one of two programs: GNMA I (established in 1970) and GNMA II (established in 1983).

Type of Guarantee

All Ginnie Mae MBSs are fully modified passthroughs.

Number of Lenders Permitted in a Pool

Only single-lender pools are permitted under the GNMA I program; both single-lender and multiple-lender pools are allowed in the GNMA II program. Single-lender pools issued under the GNMA II program are called *custom pools*; multiple-lender pools are called *jumbo pools*.

Mortgage Design of the Loans

Under the two programs, passthroughs with different types of mortgage designs are issued. The large majority of GNMA MBSs are backed by single-family mortgages, where a single-family mortgage is a loan for a 1-to-4-family primary residence with a fixed-rate, level-payment mortgage. A Ginnie Mae MBS of this type is referred to as a "GNMA SF MBS."

Mortgage-backed securities backed by adjustable-payment mortgages (APMs) are issued under the GNMA II program. For an APM the monthly mortgage payment changes periodically, based on some reference rate. An example of an adjustable-payment mortgage is the adjustable-rate mortgage (ARM). Not all ARMs qualify for inclusion in the pools that collateralize Ginnie Mae APM mortgage-backed securities.

Characteristics of the Mortgage Loans in the Pool

The key underwriting standards for the mortgage loans are summarized as follows.

Mortgage Loans Permitted in the Pool Only mortgage loans insured or guaranteed by either the Federal Housing Administration, the Veterans Administration, or the Rural Housing Service can be included in a mortgage pool guaranteed by Ginnie Mae.

Maximum Size of a Loan The maximum loan size is set by Congress, based on the maximum amount that the FHA, VA, or RHS may guarantee. The maximum for a given loan varies with the region of the country and type of residential property.

Amount of Seasoning Permitted In both programs, only newly originated mortgage loans may be included in a pool. These are defined as mortgage loans that have been seasoned less than 24 months.

Assumability of Mortgages Assumable mortgages are permitted in the pool.

Maturity Within the single-family MBS, there are pools that consist of 30-year or 15-year mortgages that collateralize the security. The 15-year pools are commonly referred to as "midgets."

Servicing Spread In the GNMA I program, the servicing spread is 50 basis points; for the GNMA II program, the servicing spread may vary from 50 to 150 basis points.

Payment Procedure

The stated delay for GNMA I and II programs are 45 and 50 days, respectively. Thus, corresponding actual delays are 14 and 19 days, respectively.

The method of payment also differs between the two programs. In the GNMA I program, payments are made by the individual servicers. In the GNMA II program, payments from all pools owned by an investor are consolidated and paid in one check by the central paying agent.

Federal Home Loan Mortgage Corporation PC

The Federal Home Loan Mortgage Corporation (also known as Freddie Mac) is a government-sponsored enterprise that issues a passthrough security that is called a *participation certificate* (PC). Although a guarantee of Freddie Mac is not a guarantee by the U.S. government, most market participants view Freddie Mac PCs as similar, although not identical, in credit worthiness to Ginnie Mae passthroughs.

Freddie Mac has two programs from which it creates PCs: the Cash Program and the Guarantor/Swap Program. The underlying loans for both programs are conventional mortgages. In the cash program, the mortgages that back the PC include individual conventional 1- to 4-family mortgage loans that Freddie Mac purchases from mortgage originators, pools, and then sells. Under the Guarantor/Swap Program, Freddie Mac allows originators to swap pooled mortgages for PCs backed by those mortgages. For example, a thrift may have $50 million of mortgages. It can swap these mortgages for a Freddie Mac PC whose underlying mortgage pool is the $50 million mortgage pool the thrift swapped for the PC. The PCs created under the first program are called *Cash PCs* or *Regular PCs*; under the second program they are called *Swap PCs*.

Type of Guarantee

There are both modified passthroughs and fully modified passthroughs. Non-Gold PCs that have been issued as part of its Cash program and almost all that have been issued as part of the Guarantor/Swap program are modified passthroughs. There are a very small number of non-Gold PCs in the latter program that are fully modified passthroughs. All Gold PCs issued are fully modified passthroughs.

For modified PCs issued by Freddie Mac, the scheduled principal is passed through as it is collected, with Freddie Mac only guaranteeing that the scheduled payment will be made no later than 1 year after it is due.

Number of Lenders Permitted in a Pool

There are only multiple-lender pools in the Cash Program. In the Guarantor/Swap program, there are both single-lender and multiple-lender pools.

Mortgage Design of the Loans

There are pools with fixed-rate, level-payment, fully amortized mortgage loans, adjustable-rate mortgage loans, and balloon mortgage loans. A wide variety of ARM PCs are issued under both the Cash and Guarantor/Swap programs. There

are Treasury-indexed ARM pools and cost-of-funds-indexed ARM pools. The latter includes the Eleventh District Cost of Funds, as well as the National Cost of Funds and the Federal Home Loan Bank Contract Rate.

For an ARM to be included in a PC, there are restrictions on the annual cap. There are both Cash ARM PCs and Swap ARM PCs with a 1% annual cap and with a 2% annual cap.

Characteristics of the Mortgage Loans in the Pool

The key underwriting standards for the mortgage loans are summarized as follows.

Mortgage Loans Permitted in the Pool The majority of PCs are backed by conventional mortgage loans. A small portion of PCs are backed by FHA and VA guaranteed mortgage loans.

Maximum Size of a Loan The maximum loan size is set each year based on the annual percentage change in the average price of conventionally financed homes as determined by the Federal Home Loan Bank Board. The maximum loan for a 1-to-4-family residence depends on the number of units.

Amount of Seasoning Permitted There are no limits on seasoning for either program.

Assumability of Mortgages No assumable mortgages are permitted in a pool.

Maturity There are 30-year and 15-year Freddie Mac Regular and Swap PCs. The 15-year Regular PCs are called "gnomes" and Swap PCs are called "non-gnomes."

Net Interest Spread Permitted In general, the net interest spread can be 50 to 250 basis points for both programs.

Payment Procedure

The stated delay and actual delay for non-Gold PCs issued as part of either program is 75 and 44 days, respectively. The Gold PCs have a shorter payment delay; the stated delay is 45 days, the actual delay 14 days. One monthly check is received in both programs for all pools an investor owns.

Federal National Mortgage Association MBS

The passthroughs issued by the Federal National Mortgage Association (also known as Fannie Mae) are called *mortgage-backed securities* (MBSs). Like a Freddie Mac PC, a Fannie Mae MBS is not the obligation of the U.S. government since Fannie Mae is a government-sponsored enterprise. Fannie Mae also has a swap program similar to that of Freddie Mac, through which it issues most of its MBSs.

There are four standard MBS programs established by Fannie Mae, which we discuss as follows. In addition to its regular programs, Fannie Mae issues secu-

rities known as "boutique" securities. These securities are issued through negotiated transactions and not backed by one of the mortgage loan types in its regular program.

Type of Guarantee

All Fannie Mae MBSs are fully modified passthroughs.

Number of Lenders Permitted in a Pool

There are only multiple-lender pools in the Cash program. In this program, Fannie Mae purchases mortgage loans from various lenders and then creates a pool to collateralize the MBS. In Fannie Mae's Guarantor/Swap program there are both single-lender and multiple-lender pools.

Mortgage Design of the Loans Three of the four standard programs have pools backed by mortgage loans that are fixed-rate, level-payment, fully amortized mortgages. The fourth standard program is an MBS collateralized by adjustable-rate mortgage loans. These ARMs are adjusted to the 1-year Treasury index and have a 2% annual adjustment cap and a lifetime cap of 6%.

Characteristics of the Mortgage Loans in the Pool

The key underwriting standards for the mortgage loans are summarized as follows.

Mortgage Loans Permitted in the Pool Two of the four standard programs are backed by conventional mortgages. One is backed by FHA-insured or VA-guaranteed mortgages. Securities issued from the two programs backed by conventional mortgages are called *Conventional MBSs*. The MBSs that are backed by FHA-insured or VA-guaranteed mortgages are called *Government MBSs*.

Maximum Size of a Loan The maximum loan size is the same as for Freddie Mac PCs.

Amount of Seasoning Permitted There are no limits on seasoning.

Assumability of Mortgages No assumable mortgages are permitted in a pool.

Maturity The securities issued from the two programs backed by conventional mortgages are 30-year and 15-year MBS, commonly referred to as the *Conventional Long-Term* and *Conventional Intermediate-Term MBS*, respectively. The 15-year MBSs are also known as "dwarfs." The MBSs that are backed by 30-year FHA-insured or VA-guaranteed mortgages are called *Government Long-Term MBSs*.

Net Interest Spread Permitted In general, the net interest spread can be 50 to 250 basis points for both programs.

Payment Procedure The stated delay is 55 days, and the actual delay is 24 days.

PREPAYMENT CONVENTIONS AND CASH FLOWS

In order to value a passthrough security, it is necessary to project its cash flows. The difficulty is that the cash flows are unknown because of prepayments. The only way to project cash flows is to make some assumptions about the prepayment rate over the life of the underlying mortgage pool. The prepayment rate is sometimes referred to as the *speed*. Two conventions have been used as a benchmark for prepayment rates: conditional prepayment rate and Public Securities Association prepayment benchmark.

Conditional Prepayment Rate

One convention for projecting prepayments and the cash flows of a passthrough assumes that some fraction of the remaining principal in the pool is prepaid each month for the remaining term of the mortgage. The prepayment rate assumed for a pool, called the *conditional prepayment rate* (CPR), is based on the characteristics of the pool (including its historical prepayment experience) and the current and expected future economic environment.

The CPR is an annual prepayment rate. To estimate monthly prepayments, the CPR must be converted into a monthly prepayment rate, commonly referred to as the *single-monthly mortality rate* (SMM). A formula can be used to determine the SMM for a given CPR:

$$\text{SMM} = 1 - (1 - \text{CPR})^{1/12}$$

Suppose that the CPR used to estimate prepayments is 6%. The corresponding SMM is:

$$\begin{aligned}\text{SMM} &= 1 - (1 - 0.06)^{1/12} \\ &= 1 - (0.94)^{0.08333} = 0.005143\end{aligned}$$

An SMM of $w\%$ means that approximately $w\%$ of the remaining mortgage balance at the beginning of the month, less the scheduled principal payment, will prepay that month. That is,

$$\begin{aligned}&\text{Prepayment for month } t = \text{SMM} \\ &\quad \times (\text{Beginning mortgage balance for month } t \\ &\qquad - \text{Scheduled principal payment for month } t)\end{aligned}$$

For example, suppose that an investor owns a passthrough in which the remaining mortgage balance at the beginning of some month is $290 million. Assuming that the SMM is 0.5143% and the scheduled principal payment is $3 million, the estimated prepayment for the month is:

$$0.005143 \times (\$290{,}000{,}000 - \$3{,}000{,}000) = \$1{,}476{,}041$$

Exhibit 2: Graphical Depiction of 100 PSA

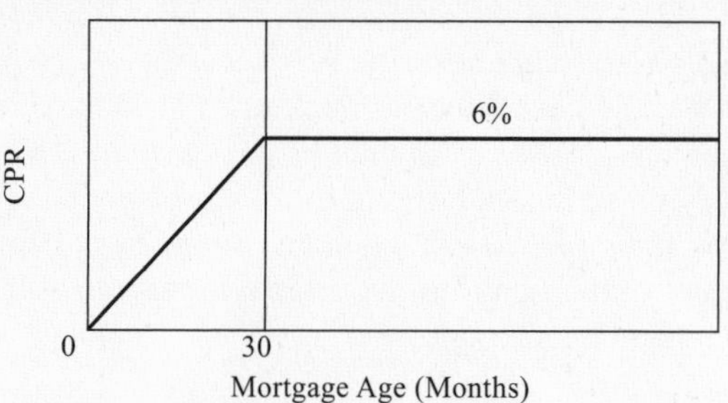

PSA Prepayment Benchmark

The Public Securities Association (PSA) prepayment benchmark is expressed as a monthly series of CPRs.[3] The PSA benchmark assumes that prepayment rates are low for newly originated mortgages and then will speed up as the mortgages become seasoned.

The PSA benchmark assumes the following prepayment rates for 30-year mortgages:

(1) a CPR of 0.2% for the first month, increased by 0.2% per year per month for the next 30 months when it reaches 6% per year, and
(2) a 6% CPR for the remaining years.

This benchmark, referred to as "100% PSA" or simply "100 PSA," is graphically depicted in Exhibit 2. Mathematically, 100 PSA can be expressed as follows:

$$\text{if } t \leq 30 \text{ then CPR} = \frac{6\%\ t}{30}$$

$$\text{if } t > 30 \text{ then CPR} = 6\%$$

where t is the number of months since the mortgage originated.

Slower or faster speeds are then referred to as some percentage of PSA. For example, 50 PSA means one-half the CPR of the PSA benchmark prepayment rate; 150 PSA means 1.5 times the CPR of the PSA benchmark prepayment rate; 300 PSA means three times the CPR of the benchmark prepayment rate. A prepayment rate of 0 PSA means that no prepayments are assumed.

The CPR is converted to an SMM using the formula given above. For example, the SMMs for month 5, month 20, and months 31 through 360 assuming 100 PSA are calculated as follows:

---

[3] This benchmark is commonly referred to as a *prepayment model*, suggesting that it can be used to estimate prepayments. Characterization of this benchmark as a prepayment model is inappropriate. It is simply a market convention describing the behavior pattern of prepayments.

for month 5:

$$CPR = 6\% \, (5/30) = 1\% = 0.01$$
$$SMM = 1 - (1 - 0.01)^{1/12}$$
$$= 1 - (0.99)^{0.083333} = 0.000837$$

for month 20:

$$CPR = 6\% \, (20/30) = 4\% = 0.04$$
$$SMM = 1 - (1 - 0.04)^{1/12}$$
$$= 1 - (0.96)^{0.083333} = 0.003396$$

for months 31 to 360:

$$CPR = 6\%$$
$$SMM = 1 - (1 - 0.06)^{1/12}$$
$$= 1 - (0.94)^{0.083333} = 0.005143$$

The SMMs for month 5, month 20, and months 31 through 360 assuming 165 PSA are computed as follows:

for month 5:

$$CPR = 6\% \, (5/30) = 1\% = 0.01$$
$$165 \text{ PSA} = 1.65 \, (0.01) = 0.0165$$
$$SMM = 1 - (1 - 0.0165)^{1/12}$$
$$= 1 - (0.9835)^{0.083333} = 0.001386$$

for month 20:

$$CPR = 6\% \, (20/30) = 4\% = 0.04$$
$$165 \text{ PSA} = 1.65 \, (.04) = 0.066$$
$$SMM = 1 - (1 - 0.066)^{1/12}$$
$$= 1 - (0.934)^{0.083333} = 0.005674$$

for months 31 to 360:

$$CPR = 6\%$$
$$165 \text{ PSA} = 1.65 \, (0.06) = 0.099$$
$$SMM = 1 - (1 - 0.099)^{1/12}$$
$$= 1 - (0.901)^{0.083333} = 0.00865$$

Notice that the SMM assuming 165 PSA is not just 1.65 times the SMM assuming 100 PSA. It is the CPR that is a multiple of the CPR assuming 100 PSA.

Illustration of Monthly Cash Flow Construction

We now show how to construct a monthly cash flow for a hypothetical passthrough given a PSA assumption. For the purpose of this illustration, the underlying mortgages for this hypothetical passthrough are assumed to be fixed-rate, level-pay-

ment, fully amortized mortgages with a weighted average coupon (WAC) rate of 8.125%. It will be assumed that the passthrough rate is 7.5% with a weighted average maturity (WAM) of 357 months.

Exhibit 3 shows the cash flow for selected months assuming 100 PSA. The cash flow is broken down into three components: (1) interest (based on the passthrough rate), (2) the regularly scheduled principal repayment, and (3) prepayments based on 100 PSA.

Let's walk through Exhibit 3 column by column.

Column 1: This is the month.

Column 2: This column gives the outstanding mortgage balance at the beginning of the month. It is equal to the outstanding balance at the beginning of the previous month reduced by the total principal payment in the previous month.

Column 3: This column shows the SMM for 100 PSA. Two things should be noted in this column. First, for month 1, the SMM is for a passthrough that has been seasoned 3 months. That is, the CPR is 0.8% for the first month. This is because the WAM is 357. Second, from month 27 on, the SMM is 0.00514, which corresponds to a CPR of 6%.

Column 4: The total monthly mortgage payment is shown in this column. Notice that the total monthly mortgage payment declines over time as prepayments reduce the mortgage balance outstanding. There is a formula to determine what the monthly mortgage balance will be for each month given prepayments.[4]

Column 5: The monthly interest paid to the passthrough investor is found in this column. This value is determined by multiplying the outstanding mortgage balance at the beginning of the month by the passthrough rate of 7.5% and dividing by 12.

Column 6: This column gives the regularly scheduled principal repayment. This is the difference between the total monthly mortgage payment [the amount shown in column (4)] and the gross coupon interest for the month. The gross coupon interest is 8.125% multiplied by the outstanding mortgage balance at the beginning of the month, then divided by 12.

Column 7: The prepayment for the month is reported in this column. The prepayment is found as follows:

$$\text{SMM} \times (\text{Beginning mortgage balance for month } t \\ - \text{Scheduled principal payment for month } t)$$

---

[4] The formula is presented in Chapter 20 of Frank J. Fabozzi, *Fixed Income Mathematics: Analytical and Statistical Techniques* (Chicago: Probus Publishing, 1993).

Exhibit 3: Monthly Cash Flow for a $400 Million Passthrough with a 7.5% Passthrough Rate, a WAC of 8.125%, and a WAM of 357 Months Assuming 100 PSA

(1) Month	(2) Outstanding Balance	(3) SMM	(4) Mortgage Payment	(5) Net Interest	(6) Scheduled Principal	(7) Prepayment	(8) Total Principal	(9) Cash Flow
1	$400,000,000	0.00067	$2,975,868	$2,500,000	$267,535	$267,470	$535,005	$3,035,005
2	399,464,995	0.00084	2,973,877	2,496,656	269,166	334,198	603,364	3,100,020
3	398,861,631	0.00101	2,971,387	2,492,885	270,762	400,800	671,562	3,164,447
4	398,190,069	0.00117	2,968,399	2,488,688	272,321	467,243	739,564	3,228,252
5	397,450,505	0.00134	2,964,914	2,484,066	273,843	533,493	807,335	3,291,401
6	396,643,170	0.00151	2,960,931	2,479,020	275,327	599,514	874,841	3,353,860
7	395,768,329	0.00168	2,956,453	2,473,552	276,772	665,273	942,045	3,415,597
8	394,826,284	0.00185	2,951,480	2,467,664	278,177	730,736	1,008,913	3,476,577
9	393,817,371	0.00202	2,946,013	2,461,359	279,542	795,869	1,075,410	3,536,769
10	392,741,961	0.00219	2,940,056	2,454,637	280,865	860,637	1,141,502	3,596,140
11	391,600,459	0.00236	2,933,608	2,447,503	282,147	925,008	1,207,155	3,654,658
12	390,393,304	0.00254	2,926,674	2,439,958	283,386	988,948	1,272,333	3,712,291
13	389,120,971	0.00271	2,919,254	2,432,006	284,581	1,052,423	1,337,004	3,769,010
14	387,783,966	0.00288	2,911,353	2,423,650	285,733	1,115,402	1,401,134	3,824,784
15	386,382,832	0.00305	2,902,973	2,414,893	286,839	1,177,851	1,464,690	3,879,583
16	384,918,142	0.00322	2,894,117	2,405,738	287,900	1,239,739	1,527,639	3,933,378
17	383,390,502	0.00340	2,884,789	2,396,191	288,915	1,301,033	1,589,949	3,986,139
18	381,800,553	0.00357	2,874,992	2,386,253	289,884	1,361,703	1,651,587	4,037,840
19	380,148,966	0.00374	2,864,730	2,375,931	290,805	1,421,717	1,712,522	4,088,453
20	378,436,444	0.00392	2,854,008	2,365,228	291,678	1,481,046	1,772,724	4,137,952
21	376,663,720	0.00409	2,842,830	2,354,148	292,503	1,539,658	1,832,161	4,186,309
22	374,831,559	0.00427	2,831,201	2,342,697	293,279	1,597,525	1,890,804	4,233,501
23	372,940,755	0.00444	2,819,125	2,330,880	294,005	1,654,618	1,948,623	4,279,503
24	370,992,132	0.00462	2,806,607	2,318,701	294,681	1,710,908	2,005,589	4,324,290
25	368,986,543	0.00479	2,793,654	2,306,166	295,307	1,766,368	2,061,675	4,367,841
26	366,924,868	0.00497	2,780,270	2,293,280	295,883	1,820,970	2,116,852	4,410,133
27	364,808,016	0.00514	2,766,461	2,280,050	296,406	1,874,688	2,171,094	4,451,144
28	362,636,921	0.00514	2,752,233	2,266,481	296,879	1,863,519	2,160,398	4,426,879
29	360,476,523	0.00514	2,738,078	2,252,978	297,351	1,852,406	2,149,758	4,402,736
30	358,326,766	0.00514	2,723,996	2,239,542	297,825	1,841,347	2,139,173	4,378,715
100	231,249,776	0.00514	1,898,682	1,445,311	332,928	1,187,608	1,520,537	2,965,848
101	229,729,239	0.00514	1,888,917	1,435,808	333,459	1,179,785	1,513,244	2,949,052
102	228,215,995	0.00514	1,879,202	1,426,350	333,990	1,172,000	1,505,990	2,932,340
103	226,710,004	0.00514	1,869,538	1,416,938	334,522	1,164,252	1,498,774	2,915,712
104	225,211,230	0.00514	1,859,923	1,407,570	335,055	1,156,541	1,491,596	2,899,166
105	223,719,634	0.00514	1,850,357	1,398,248	335,589	1,148,867	1,484,456	2,882,703
200	109,791,339	0.00514	1,133,751	686,196	390,372	562,651	953,023	1,639,219
201	108,838,316	0.00514	1,127,920	680,239	390,994	557,746	948,740	1,628,980
202	107,889,576	0.00514	1,122,119	674,310	391,617	552,863	944,480	1,618,790
203	106,945,096	0.00514	1,116,348	668,407	392,241	548,003	940,243	1,608,650
204	106,004,852	0.00514	1,110,607	662,530	392,866	543,164	936,029	1,598,560
205	105,068,823	0.00514	1,104,895	656,680	393,491	538,347	931,838	1,588,518

Exhibit 3 (Concluded)

(1)	(2)	(3)	(4)	(5)	(6)	(7)	(8)	(9)
Month	Outstanding Balance	SMM	Mortgage Payment	Net Interest	Scheduled Principal	Prepayment	Total Principal	Cash Flow
300	$32,383,611	0.00514	$676,991	$202,398	$457,727	$164,195	$621,923	$824,320
301	31,761,689	0.00514	673,510	198,511	458,457	160,993	619,449	817,960
302	31,142,239	0.00514	670,046	194,639	459,187	157,803	616,990	811,629
303	30,525,249	0.00514	666,600	190,783	459,918	154,626	614,545	805,328
304	29,910,704	0.00514	663,171	186,942	460,651	151,462	612,113	799,055
305	29,298,591	0.00514	659,761	183,116	461,385	148,310	609,695	792,811
350	4,060,411	0.00514	523,138	25,378	495,645	18,334	513,979	539,356
351	3,546,432	0.00514	520,447	22,165	496,435	15,686	512,121	534,286
352	3,034,311	0.00514	517,770	18,964	497,226	13,048	510,274	529,238
353	2,524,037	0.00514	515,107	15,775	498,018	10,420	508,437	524,213
354	2,015,600	0.00514	512,458	12,597	498,811	7,801	506,612	519,209
355	1,508,988	0.00514	509,823	9,431	499,606	5,191	504,797	514,228
356	1,004,191	0.00514	507,201	6,276	500,401	2,591	502,992	509,269
357	501,199	0.00514	504,592	3,132	501,199	0	501,199	504,331

Note: Since the WAM is 357 months, the underlying mortgage pool is seasoned an average of 3 months. Therefore, the CPR for month 27 is 6%.

For example, in month 100, the beginning mortgage balance is $231,249,776, the scheduled principal payment is $332,298, and the SMM at 100 PSA is 0.00514301 (only 0.00514 is shown in the exhibit to save space). Therefore, the prepayment is:

$$0.00514301 \times (\$231{,}249{,}776 - \$332{,}928) = \$1{,}187{,}608.$$

Column 8: The total principal payment, which is the sum of columns (6) and (7), is shown in this column.

Column 9: The projected monthly cash flow for this passthrough is shown in this last column. The monthly cash flow is the sum of the interest paid to the passthrough investor [column (5)] and the total principal payments for the month [column (8)].

Exhibit 4 shows selected monthly cash flow for the same passthrough assuming 165 PSA.

FACTORS AFFECTING PREPAYMENT BEHAVIOR

The factors that affect prepayment behavior are (1) prevailing mortgage rate, (2) characteristics of the underlying mortgage pool, (3) seasonal factors, and (4) general economic activity.

Exhibit 4: Monthly Cash Flow for a $400 Million Passthrough with a 7.5% Passthrough Rate, a WAC of 8.125%, and a WAM of 357 Months Assuming 165 PSA

(1) Month	(2) Outstanding Balance	(3) SMM	(4) Mortgage Payment	(5) Net Interest	(6) Scheduled Principal	(7) Prepayment	(8) Total Principal	(9) Cash Flow
1	$400,000,000	0.00111	$2,975,868	$2,500,000	$267,535	$442,389	$709,923	$3,209,923
2	399,290,077	0.00139	2,972,575	2,495,563	269,048	552,847	821,896	3,317,459
3	398,468,181	0.00167	2,968,456	2,490,426	270,495	663,065	933,560	3,423,986
4	397,534,621	0.00195	2,963,513	2,484,591	271,873	772,949	1,044,822	3,529,413
5	396,489,799	0.00223	2,957,747	2,478,061	273,181	882,405	1,155,586	3,633,647
6	395,334,213	0.00251	2,951,160	2,470,839	274,418	991,341	1,265,759	3,736,598
7	394,068,454	0.00279	2,943,755	2,462,928	275,583	1,099,664	1,375,246	3,838,174
8	392,693,208	0.00308	2,935,534	2,454,333	276,674	1,207,280	1,483,954	3,938,287
9	391,209,254	0.00336	2,926,503	2,445,058	277,690	1,314,099	1,591,789	4,036,847
10	389,617,464	0.00365	2,916,666	2,435,109	278,631	1,420,029	1,698,659	4,133,769
11	387,918,805	0.00393	2,906,028	2,424,493	279,494	1,524,979	1,804,473	4,228,965
12	386,114,332	0.00422	2,894,595	2,413,215	280,280	1,628,859	1,909,139	4,322,353
13	384,205,194	0.00451	2,882,375	2,401,282	280,986	1,731,581	2,012,567	4,413,850
14	382,192,626	0.00480	2,869,375	2,388,704	281,613	1,833,058	2,114,670	4,503,374
15	380,077,956	0.00509	2,855,603	2,375,487	282,159	1,933,203	2,215,361	4,590,848
16	377,862,595	0.00538	2,841,068	2,361,641	282,623	2,031,931	2,314,554	4,676,195
17	375,548,041	0.00567	2,825,779	2,347,175	283,006	2,129,159	2,412,164	4,759,339
18	373,135,877	0.00597	2,809,746	2,332,099	283,305	2,224,805	2,508,110	4,840,210
19	370,627,766	0.00626	2,792,980	2,316,424	283,521	2,318,790	2,602,312	4,918,735
20	368,025,455	0.00656	2,775,493	2,300,159	283,654	2,411,036	2,694,690	4,994,849
21	365,330,765	0.00685	2,757,296	2,283,317	283,702	2,501,466	2,785,169	5,068,486
22	362,545,596	0.00715	2,738,402	2,265,910	283,666	2,590,008	2,873,674	5,139,584
23	359,671,922	0.00745	2,718,823	2,247,950	283,545	2,676,588	2,960,133	5,208,083
24	356,711,789	0.00775	2,698,575	2,229,449	283,338	2,761,139	3,044,477	5,273,926
25	353,667,312	0.00805	2,677,670	2,210,421	283,047	2,843,593	3,126,640	5,337,061
26	350,540,672	0.00835	2,656,123	2,190,879	282,671	2,923,885	3,206,556	5,397,435
27	347,334,116	0.00865	2,633,950	2,170,838	282,209	3,001,955	3,284,164	5,455,002
28	344,049,952	0.00865	2,611,167	2,150,312	281,662	2,973,553	3,255,215	5,405,527
29	340,794,737	0.00865	2,588,581	2,129,967	281,116	2,945,400	3,226,516	5,356,483
30	337,568,221	0.00865	2,566,190	2,109,801	280,572	2,917,496	3,198,067	5,307,869
100	170,142,350	0.00865	1,396,958	1,063,390	244,953	1,469,591	1,714,544	2,777,933
101	168,427,806	0.00865	1,384,875	1,052,674	244,478	1,454,765	1,699,243	2,751,916
102	166,728,563	0.00865	1,372,896	1,042,054	244,004	1,440,071	1,684,075	2,726,128
103	165,044,489	0.00865	1,361,020	1,031,528	243,531	1,425,508	1,669,039	2,700,567
104	163,375,450	0.00865	1,349,248	1,021,097	243,060	1,411,075	1,654,134	2,675,231
105	161,721,315	0.00865	1,337,577	1,010,758	242,589	1,396,771	1,639,359	2,650,118
200	56,746,664	0.00865	585,990	354,667	201,767	489,106	690,874	1,045,540
201	56,055,790	0.00865	580,921	350,349	201,377	483,134	684,510	1,034,859
202	55,371,280	0.00865	575,896	346,070	200,986	477,216	678,202	1,024,273
203	54,693,077	0.00865	570,915	341,832	200,597	471,353	671,950	1,013,782
204	54,021,127	0.00865	565,976	337,632	200,208	465,544	665,752	1,003,384
205	53,355,375	0.00865	561,081	333,471	199,820	459,789	659,609	993,080

Exhibit 4 (Concluded)

(1)	(2)	(3)	(4)	(5)	(6)	(7)	(8)	(9)
Month	Outstanding Balance	SMM	Mortgage Payment	Net Interest	Scheduled Principal	Prepayment	Total Principal	Cash Flow
300	$11,758,141	0.00865	$245,808	$73,488	$166,196	$100,269	$266,465	$339,953
301	11,491,677	0.00865	243,682	71,823	165,874	97,967	263,841	335,664
302	11,227,836	0.00865	241,574	70,174	165,552	95,687	261,240	331,414
303	10,966,596	0.00865	239,485	68,541	165,232	93,430	258,662	327,203
304	10,707,934	0.00865	237,413	66,925	164,912	91,196	256,107	323,032
305	10,451,827	0.00865	235,360	65,324	164,592	88,983	253,575	318,899
350	1,235,674	0.00865	159,202	7,723	150,836	9,384	160,220	167,943
351	1,075,454	0.00865	157,825	6,722	150,544	8,000	158,544	165,266
352	916,910	0.00865	156,460	5,731	150,252	6,631	156,883	162,614
353	760,027	0.00865	155,107	4,750	149,961	5,277	155,238	159,988
354	604,789	0.00865	153,765	3,780	149,670	3,937	153,607	157,387
355	451,182	0.00865	152,435	2,820	149,380	2,611	151,991	154,811
356	299,191	0.00865	151,117	1,870	149,091	1,298	150,389	152,259
357	148,802	0.00865	149,809	930	148,802	0	148,802	149,732

Note: Since the WAM is 357 months, the underlying mortgage pool is seasoned an average of 3 months. Therefore, the CPR for month 27 is 1.65 × 6%.

Prevailing Mortgage Rate

The single most important factor affecting prepayments because of refinancing is the current level of mortgage rates relative to the borrower's contract rate. The more the contract rate exceeds the prevailing mortgage rate, the greater the incentive to refinance the mortgage loan. For refinancing to make economic sense, the interest savings must be greater than the costs associated with refinancing the mortgage. These costs include legal expenses, origination fees, title insurance, and the value of the time associated with obtaining another mortgage loan. Some of these costs, such as title insurance and origination points, will vary proportionately with the amount to be financed. Other costs, such as the application fee and legal expenses, are typically fixed.

Historically, it has been observed that when mortgage rates fall to more than 200 basis points below the contract rate, prepayment rates increase. However, the creativity of mortgage originators in designing mortgage loans such that the refinancing costs are folded into the amount borrowed has changed the view that mortgage rates must drop dramatically below the contract rate to make refinancing economic. Moreover, mortgage originators now do an effective job of advertising to make homeowners cognizant of the economic benefits of refinancing.

The historical pattern of prepayments and economic theory suggests that it is not only the level of mortgage rates that affects prepayment behavior but also the path that mortgage rates take to get to the current level.

To illustrate why, suppose the underlying contract rate for a pool of mortgage loans is 11% and that 3 years after origination, the prevailing mortgage rate declines to 8%. Let's consider two possible paths of the mortgage rate in getting to the 8% level. In the first path, the mortgage rate declines to 8% at the end of

the first year, then rises to 13% at the end of the second year, and then falls to 8% at the end of the third year. In the second path, the mortgage rate rises to 12% at the end of the first year, continues its rise to 13% at the end of the second year, and then falls to 8% at the end of the third year.

If the mortgage rate follows the first path, those who can benefit from refinancing will more than likely take advantage of this opportunity when the mortgage rate drops to 8% in the first year. When the mortgage rate drops again to 8% at the end of the third year, the likelihood is that prepayments because of refinancing will not surge; those who can benefit by taking advantage of the refinancing opportunity will have done so already when the mortgage rate declined the first time. This prepayment behavior is referred to as *refinancing burnout* (or simply, *burnout*).

In contrast, the expected prepayment behavior when the mortgage rate follows the second path is quite different. Prepayment rates are expected to be low in the first 2 years. When the mortgage rate declines to 8% in the third year, refinancing activity and therefore prepayments are expected to surge. Consequently, burnout is related to the path of mortgage rates.

Our focus so far has been on the factors that affect prepayments caused by refinancing. Prepayments also occur because of housing turnover. The level of mortgage rates affects housing turnover to the extent that a lower rate increases the affordability of homes.

Characteristics of the Underlying Mortgage Loans

The following characteristics of the underlying mortgage loans affect prepayments: (1) the contract rate, (2) whether the loans are FHA/VA-guaranteed or conventional, (3) the amount of seasoning, (4) the type of loan (e.g., a 30-year level-payment mortgage, 5-year balloon mortgage, etc.), and (4) the geographical location of the underlying properties.

Seasonality

There is a well-documented seasonal pattern in prepayments. This pattern is related to activity in the primary housing market, with home buying increasing in the spring and gradually reaching a peak in the late summer. Home buying declines in the fall and winter. Mirroring this activity are the prepayments that result from the turnover of housing as home buyers sell their existing homes and purchase new ones. Prepayments are low in the winter months and begin to rise in the spring, reaching a peak in the summer months. However, probably because of delays in passing through prepayments, the peak may not be observed until early fall.

Macroeconomic Factors

Economic theory would suggest that general economic activity affects prepayment behavior through its effect on housing turnover. The link is as follows: a growing economy results in a rise in personal income and in opportunities for worker migration; this increases family mobility and as a result increases housing turnover. The opposite holds for a weak economy.

PREPAYMENT MODELS

A prepayment model is a statistical model that is used to forecast prepayments. It begins by modeling the statistical relationships among the factors that are expected to affect prepayments. The four factors discussed previously explain most of the prepayment activity. These factors are then combined into one model.

Wall Street firms report their projections for different types of passthroughs in their publications. Exhibit 5 is an example. The projections are for Ginnie Mae and Fannie Mae passthroughs that appeared in UBS Warburg's *Mortgage Strategist* (July 24, 2001 issue). There are not only projections by coupon but also by year of origination (referred to as "vintage"). For example, for the 6.5% Fannie Mae, there are projections for passthroughs originated in 1993, 1998, and 2000. Historical prepayments are reported for the past month and the past 3 months. The prepayments are short-term projections in terms of CPR — 1-month projections for the next 3 months (August, September, and October) and 1-year projections.

In addition to reports to their clients, MBS dealers provide their prepayment projections to sources such as Bloomberg, Reuters, and Telerate.

YIELD

Given the projected cash flows based on some prepayment speed and the market price of a passthrough, its yield can be calculated. The yield is the interest rate that will make the present value of the expected cash flows equal to the price. A yield computed in this manner is called a *cash flow yield*.[5]

The Wall Street Journal reports the cash flow yield on passthrough securities of all three agencies. However, there is no information about what prepayment assumption is made. (We are told that the Salomon Brothers' prepayment model is used.) Any cash flow yield must be qualified by an assumption concerning prepayments. Without information about the prepayment speed, the cash flow yield is meaningless.

Exhibit 6 shows for selected passthrough securities the cash flow yield (simply referred to as yield ("Yld") in the exhibit). The projected PSA used to derive the yield is shown. For these securities, three spread measures are reported: (1) static spread, (2) zero-volatility spread, and (3) option-adjusted spread (OAS). In Chapter 3, we indicated that the terms *static spread* and *zero-volatility spread* are used interchangeably. However, Lehman Brothers appears to use the two terms in a different way. Static spread as reported appears to be what was referred to as the nominal spread in Chapter 3. The number of years after the static spread

---

5 For a passthrough, the yield that makes the present value of the cash flows equal to the price is a monthly interest rate. The convention to annualize the monthly interest rate is to calculate an effective 6-month rate and then double it. As explained in Chapter 3, the resulting cash flow yield is called a bond-equivalent yield. Supposedly, this allows an investor to compare the yield on a mortgage passthrough and the yield on a Treasury or corporate bond.

reported is the maturity of the Treasury benchmark issue used to obtain the spread. For example, for the 30-year GNMA 6.5% coupon, the static spread is 135 basis points using the yield on the 10-year Treasury as the benchmark. The maturity of the Treasury benchmark is based on the projected average life of the passthrough security. We discuss the average life measure as follows.

Exhibit 5: FNMA and GNMA – Short-Term Prepayment Projections

					Historical		1-mo Projected CPR			Proj
Cpn	Yr	WAC	WAM	WALA	1-mo	3-mo	Aug	Sep	Oct	1-yr
FNMA										
6.0	98	6.69	316	35	13.3	12.4	13.2	13.3	10.6	8.6
	93	6.69	250	92	13.3	11.4	13.0	13.1	10.4	8.4
6.5	00	7.15	331	21	12.5	11.4	11.2	11.7	11.8	8.0
	98	7.20	314	37	18.7	18.1	17.2	17.6	17.5	12.9
	93	7.07	249	93	16.5	15.7	14.7	15.0	14.7	10.5
7.0	00	7.71	342	14	21.9	24.0	18.9	20.2	20.2	14.5
	98	7.49	309	39	24.6	24.1	21.0	22.1	22.1	16.4
	93	7.51	245	96	20.1	19.8	16.5	17.5	17.1	12.9
7.5	00	8.12	343	13	44.0	48.0	39.4	40.7	39.0	31.8
	97	8.03	297	50	32.7	34.4	28.5	29.7	30.4	24.2
	93	7.95	243	99	25.0	25.2	22.1	22.1	21.8	17.1
8.0	00	8.57	342	13	54.1	57.5	49.5	49.9	47.6	34.6
	97	8.47	296	51	36.6	35.7	33.0	33.2	31.0	24.2
	95	8.58	273	73	36.0	33.9	32.8	32.4	29.7	22.4
	92	8.53	232	109	32.5	30.9	30.2	29.6	28.6	19.8
8.5	00	9.07	341	14	54.7	56.8	49.8	50.1	47.9	35.0
	95	9.06	271	75	34.8	34.1	29.6	29.3	28.9	20.7
	92	8.94	232	111	36.2	34.1	31.9	31.2	28.6	20.2
GNMA										
6.5	00	7.00	335	20	16.7	14.2	11.8	11.7	11.5	9.4
	98	7.00	317	36	17.3	16.9	15.8	16.3	16.2	12.8
	93	7.00	255	93	16.4	16.3	14.6	14.9	14.6	14.3
7.0	00	7.50	344	12	13.8	13.2	11.4	12.5	12.5	7.9
	98	7.50	316	37	24.1	23.7	21.2	21.9	21.9	16.1
	93	7.50	251	96	21.1	20.2	18.2	18.9	18.6	16.4
7.5	00	8.00	346	12	32.8	34.8	29.1	30.6	30.6	15.8
	97	8.00	304	49	30.9	29.7	27.6	28.4	28.9	18.1
	93	8.00	249	97	28.0	26.5	25.7	25.5	25.2	19.9
8.0	00	8.50	345	13	48.9	52.9	44.1	44.4	43.3	31.7
	97	8.50	303	49	31.9	31.2	28.3	28.6	26.5	19.8
	95	8.50	279	71	32.3	30.9	29.2	28.9	26.2	21.7
	92	8.50	237	109	29.2	27.9	26.9	26.4	25.5	18.6
8.5	00	9.00	344	13	53.9	56.6	48.5	48.9	47.0	32.3
	95	9.00	275	74	30.8	31.4	25.6	25.4	25.1	20.2
	92	9.00	236	110	29.8	28.8	25.4	24.9	22.4	18.7

Source: Table 2, "Prepayment Outlook," in *Mortgage Strategist*, UBS Warburg, July 24, 2001, p. 2.

Exhibit 6: Spreads and Other Measures for Selected Passthrough Securities

(July 13, 2001, July Settlement)

	WAM		Projected			Zero Vol.	OAS		90-day OAS			OA Dur.
	(mos)	Price	%PSA	Yld.(%)	Static Sprd.	Spread	Curr.	1-wk.Chg.	High	Low	Avg.	(yrs)
30-yr GNMA												
6.5	357	99-25	137	6.58	135/10yr	113	68	0	83	58	70	5.2
7.0	356	101-21	216	6.71	195/5yr	136	76	0	92	66	79	4.3
7.5	351	103-03	236	6.86	210/5yr	161	88	0	108	76	93	3.1
8.0	352	104-05	443	6.65	188/5yr	182	100	-1	126	88	107	2.1
9.0	349	105-00	664	6.59	241/3yr	228	157	1	162	143	152	1.6
30-yr FHLMC Gold												
6.5	358	99-09	183	6.67	144/10yr	128	76	0	81	63	72	4.7
7.0	356	101-07	372	6.69	192/5yr	149	79	-1	86	65	77	3.3
7.5	353	102-21	670	6.31	213/3yr	160	76	-3	95	67	82	2.0
8.0	352	103-30	698	6.16	197/3yr	155	69	-7	98	60	79	1.3
9.0	349	104-29	962	5.71	162/2yr	154	85	-4	108	84	95	0.9
15-yr FHLMC Gold												
6.0	175	99-10	202	6.19	142/5yr	102	78	1	79	60	70	3.9
6.5	175	101-00	274	6.24	148/5yr	116	82	0	83	63	72	3.3
7.0	170	102-12	539	5.97	179/3yr	125	74	-4	81	59	70	2.1
7.5	168	103-11	650	5.78	169/2yr	134	77	-3	92	66	78	1.5
8.0	164	104-17	602	5.68	159/2yr	136	82	-5	91	72	81	1.3
7-yr FNMA Balloons												
6.0	340	101-00	232	5.63	145/3yr	86	70	4	87	50	69	2.8
6.5	355	101-20	412	5.91	173/3yr	112	82	5	92	60	77	2.6
7.0	354	102-02	687	5.97	179/3yr	142	101	3	104	82	94	1.9
7.5	353	102-18	890	5.92	183/2yr	157	112	1	113	97	106	1.3

Source: Lehman Brothers, *Global Relative Value*, Fixed Income Research, July 16, 2001, p. 124.

The exhibit provides information on the 90-day high, low, and average OAS for each passthrough security. The "OA duration" reported in Exhibit 5 is the option-adjusted (OA) duration. As explained in Chapter 2, this measure is also referred to as *effective duration*.

Limitations of Cash Flow Yield

In fact, even with specification of the prepayment assumption, the yield number is meaningless in terms of the potential return from investing in a passthrough. For an investor to realize the cash flow yield based on some PSA assumption, a number of conditions must be met: (1) the investor must reinvest all the cash flows at the calculated yield, (2) the investor must hold the passthrough security until all the mortgages have been paid off, and (3) the assumed prepayment rate must actually occur over the life of the passthrough. We highlighted the limitations of any yield measure due to the first two conditions in Chapter 3. The third condition is unique to a mortgage-backed security.

What can be stated with a high degree of confidence is that the yield that an investor will realize will *not* be the cash flow yield calculated at the time of purchase.

Comparison to Treasuries

While we have explained that it is not possible to calculate a yield with certainty, it has been stated that passthrough securities offer a higher yield than Treasury securities. Typically, the comparison is between Ginnie Mae passthrough securities and Treasuries, for both are free of default risk. Presumably, the difference between the two yields primarily represents compensation for prepayment risk.

When we speak of comparing the yield of a mortgage passthrough security to a comparable Treasury, what does "comparable" mean? The stated maturity of a mortgage passthrough security is an inappropriate measure because of principal repayments over time. Instead, market participants calculate an average life for a mortgage-backed security.

The *average life* of a mortgage-backed security is the average time to receipt of principal payments (scheduled principal payments and projected prepayments), weighted by the amount of principal expected. Specifically, the average life is found by first calculating:

$$
\begin{aligned}
& \ 1 \times (\text{Projected principal received in month 1}) \\
& + 2 \times (\text{Projected principal received in month 2}) \\
& + 3 \times (\text{Projected principal received in month 3}) \\
& \quad \cdots \\
& + T \times (\text{Projected principal received in month } T) \\
\hline
& \text{Weighted monthly average of principal received}
\end{aligned}
$$

where T is the last month that principal is expected to be received.

Then the average life is found as follows:

$$\text{Average life} = \frac{\text{Weighted monthly average of principal received}}{12(\text{Total principal to be received})}$$

The average life of a passthrough depends on the PSA prepayment assumption. To see this, the average life is shown below for different prepayment speeds for the passthrough we used to illustrate the cash flows for 100 PSA and 165 PSA in Exhibits 3 and 4:

PSA speed	50	100	165	200	300	400	500	600	700
Average life	15.11	11.66	8.76	7.68	5.63	4.44	3.68	3.16	2.78

A CLOSER LOOK AT PREPAYMENT RISK

An investor who owns passthrough securities does not know what the cash flows will be because that depends on prepayments. As noted earlier, this risk is called *prepayment risk.*

Contraction Risk and Extension Risk

To understand the significance of prepayment risk, suppose an investor buys a 10% coupon Ginnie Mae at a time when mortgage rates are 10%. Let's consider what will happen to prepayments if mortgage rates decline to, say, 6%. There will be two adverse consequences. First, a basic property of fixed income securities is that the price of an option-free bond will rise. But in the case of a passthrough security, the rise in price will not be as large as that of an option-free bond because a fall in interest rates will give the borrower an incentive to prepay the loan and refinance the debt at a lower rate. Thus, the upside price potential of a passthrough security is truncated because of prepayments. The second adverse consequence is that the cash flows must be reinvested at a lower rate. These two adverse consequences when mortgage rates decline are referred to as *contraction risk.*

Now let's look at what happens if mortgage rates rise to 15%. The price of the passthrough, like the price of any bond, will decline. But again it will decline more because the higher rates will tend to slow down the rate of prepayment, in effect increasing the amount invested at the coupon rate, which is lower than the market rate. Prepayments will slow down because homeowners will not refinance or partially prepay their mortgages when mortgage rates are higher than the contract rate of 10%. Of course this is just the time when investors want prepayments to speed up so that they can reinvest the prepayments at the higher market interest rate. This adverse consequence of rising mortgage rates is called *extension risk.*

Therefore, prepayment risk encompasses contraction risk and extension risk. Prepayment risk makes passthrough securities unattractive for certain individuals and financial institutions to hold for purposes of accomplishing their investment objectives. Some individuals and institutional investors are concerned with

extension risk and others with contraction risk when they purchase a passthrough security. Is it possible to alter the cash flows of a passthrough to reduce the contraction risk and extension risk for institutional investors? This can be done, as explained in the next chapter.

Prepayments: Friend Or Foe?

The investor does not know precisely what the monthly prepayments will be when purchasing a passthrough security. A certain prepayment speed is assumed when a passthrough is purchased. Actual prepayments will usually differ from prepayments that were anticipated at the time of purchase.

Prepayments above or below the amount anticipated may be good or bad depending on the purchase price. If an investor purchases a passthrough at a premium above par value, then actual prepayments greater than anticipated prepayments will hurt the investor for two reasons. First, there will be a loss since only par is returned, and second, the proceeds must be reinvested at a lower rate. The opposite is true for an investor who purchases a passthrough at a discount. The investor realizes a gain (since par is received but less than par was paid), and the investor can reinvest the proceeds at a higher rate.

TRADING AND SETTLEMENT PROCEDURES FOR AGENCY PASSTHROUGHS

Agency passthroughs are identified by a pool prefix and pool number provided by the agency. The prefix indicates the type of passthrough. For example, a pool prefix of "20" for a Freddie Mac PC means that the underlying pool consists of conventional mortgages with an original maturity of 15 years. A pool prefix of "AR" for a Ginnie Mae MBS means that the underlying pool consists of adjustable-rate mortgages. The pool number indicates the specific mortgages underlying the passthrough and the issuer of the passthrough.

There are specific rules established by the Bond Market Association (formerly the Public Securities Association) for the trading and settlement of mortgage-backed securities. Our discussion here is limited to agency passthrough securities.

Many trades occur while a pool is still unspecified, and therefore no pool information is known at the time of the trade. This kind of trade is known as a "TBA" (to be announced) trade. In a TBA trade, the two parties agree on the agency type, the agency program, the coupon rate, the face value, the price, and the settlement date. The actual pools underlying the agency passthrough are not specified in a TBA trade. However, this information is provided by the seller to the buyer before delivery, as explained as follows. There are trades where more specific requirements are established for the securities to be delivered (e.g., a Freddie Mac Gold with a coupon rate of 8.5% and a WAC between 9.0% and 9.2%). There are also *specified pool trades* wherein the actual pool numbers to be delivered are specified.

Passthroughs are quoted in the same manner as U.S. Treasury coupon securities. A quote of 94-05 means 94 and 5⁄32nds of par value, or 94.15625% of par value. The price that the buyer pays the seller is the agreed-upon sale price plus accrued interest. Given the par value, the dollar price (excluding accrued interest) is affected by the amount of the pool mortgage balance outstanding. The *pool factor* indicates the percentage of the initial mortgage balance for the pool still outstanding. So, a pool factor of 90 means that 90% of the original mortgage pool balance is outstanding. The pool factor is reported by the issuing agency each month.

The dollar price paid for just the principal is found as follows given the agreed-upon price, par value, and the month's pool factor provided by the issuing agency:

$$\text{price} \times \text{par value} \times \text{pool factor}$$

For example, if the parties agree to a price of 92 for $1 million par value for a passthrough with a pool factor of 85, then the dollar price paid by the buyer in addition to accrued interest is:

$$0.92 \times \$1{,}000{,}000 \times 0.85 = \$782{,}000$$

Trades settle according to a delivery schedule established by the BMA. This schedule is published quarterly by the BMA with information regarding delivery for the next 6 months. Each agency and program settles on a different day of the delivery month. There is also a distinction made in the delivery schedule by coupon rate.

By 3 p.m. eastern standard time two business days before the settlement date, the seller must furnish information to the buyer about pools that will be delivered. This is called the *48-hour rule.* The date that this information must be given is called the *notification date* or *call-out date.* Two parties can agree to depart from BMA guidelines and settle at any time.

When an investor purchases, say, $1 million GNMA 8s on a TBA basis, the investor can receive up to three pools. Three pools can be delivered because the BMA has established guidelines for standards of delivery and settlement of mortgage-backed securities,[6] under which our hypothetical TBA trade permits three possible pools to be delivered. The option of what pools to deliver is left to the seller, as long as selection and delivery satisfy the BMA guidelines.

There are many seasoned issues of the same agency with the same coupon rate outstanding at a given point in time. For example, there are more than 30,000 pools of 30-year Ginnie Mae MBSs outstanding with a coupon rate of 9%. One passthrough may be backed by a pool of mortgage loans in which all the properties are located in California, while another may be backed by a pool of mortgage loans in which all the properties are in Minnesota. Yet another may be backed by a

---

[6] Bond Market Association, *Uniform Practices for the Clearance and Settlement of Mortgage-Backed Securities.* More specifically, the requirement for good delivery permits a maximum of three pools per $1 million traded, or a maximum of four pools per $1 million for coupons of 12% or more.

pool of mortgage loans in which the properties are from several regions of the country. So which pool is a dealer referring to when that dealer talks about Ginnie Mae 9s? The dealer is not referring to any specific pool but instead to a generic security, although the prepayment characteristics of passthroughs with underlying pools from different parts of the country are different. Thus, the projected prepayment rates for passthroughs reported by dealer firms are for generic passthroughs. A particular pool purchased may have a materially different prepayment speed from the generic. Moreover, when an investor purchases a passthrough without specifying a pool number, the seller can deliver the worst-paying pools as long as the pools delivered satisfy good delivery requirements.

STRIPPED MORTGAGE-BACKED SECURITIES

A mortgage passthrough security distributes the cash flow from the underlying pool of mortgages on a pro rata basis to the securityholders. A *stripped mortgage-backed security* is created by altering that distribution of principal and interest from a pro rata distribution to an unequal distribution. The result is that the securities created will have a price/yield relationship that is different from the price/yield relationship of the underlying passthrough security.

In the most common type of stripped mortgage-backed securities, all the interest is allocated to one class (called the *interest only* or *IO class*) and all the principal to the other class (called the *principal only* or *PO class*). The IO class receives no principal payments.

Principal-Only Securities

The PO security, also called a *principal-only mortgage strip*, is purchased at a substantial discount from par value. The return an investor realizes depends on the speed at which prepayments are made. The faster the prepayments, the higher the investor's return. For example, suppose there is a mortgage pool consisting only of 30-year mortgages, with $400 million in principal, and that investors can purchase POs backed by this mortgage pool for $175 million. The dollar return on this investment will be $225 million. How quickly that dollar return is recovered by PO investors determines the actual return that will be realized. In the extreme case, if all homeowners in the underlying mortgage pool decide to prepay their mortgage loans immediately, PO investors will realize the $225 million immediately. At the other extreme, if all homeowners decide to remain in their homes for 30 years and make no prepayments, the $225 million will be spread out over 30 years, which would result in a lower return for PO investors.

Let's look at how the price of the PO would be expected to change as mortgage rates in the market change. When mortgage rates decline below the contract rate, prepayments are expected to speed up, accelerating payments to the PO holder. Thus, the cash flow of a PO improves (in the sense that principal repay-

ments are received earlier). The cash flow will be discounted at a lower interest rate because the mortgage rate in the market has declined. The result is that the PO price will increase when mortgage rates decline. When mortgage rates rise above the contract rate, prepayments are expected to slow down. The cash flow deteriorates (in the sense that it takes longer to recover principal repayments). Couple this with a higher discount rate, and the price of a PO will fall when mortgage rates rise.

Exhibit 7 shows various measures for PO and IO securities for several trusts on July 12, 2001, as reported by Lehman Brothers. The characteristics of the collateral for these trusts are also shown. For each trust, the yield (which is the cash flow yield), zero-volatility spread (ZV), option-adjusted spread (OAS), option-adjusted duration (OAD), and option-adjusted spread duration (OA Spread Dur) are shown. The negative values for the OAS for the POs shown in Exhibit 7 are because the PO buyer benefits from the prepayment option. Notice that for the PO, the option-adjusted duration (which is the effective duration) is positive for all the trusts.

Interest-Only Securities

An IO, also called an *interest-only mortgage strip*, has no par value. In contrast to the PO investor, the IO investor wants prepayments to be slow because the IO investor receives interest only on the amount of the principal outstanding. When prepayments are made, less dollar interest will be received as the outstanding principal declines. In fact, if prepayments are too fast, the IO investor may not recover the amount paid for the IO even if the security is held to maturity.

Let's look at the expected price response of an IO to changes in mortgage rates. If mortgage rates decline below the contract rate, prepayments are expected to accelerate. This would result in a deterioration of the expected cash flow for an IO. While the cash flow will be discounted at a lower rate, the net effect typically is a decline in the price of an IO. If mortgage rates rise above the contract rate, the expected cash flow improves, but the cash flow is discounted at a higher interest rate. The net effect may be either a rise or fall for the IO.

Thus, we see an interesting characteristic of an IO: its price tends to move in the same direction as the change in mortgage rates (1) when mortgage rates fall below the contract rate and (2) for some range of mortgage rates above the contract rate. Both POs and IOs exhibit substantial price volatility when mortgage rates change. The greater price volatility of the IO and PO compared to the passthrough from which they were created is because the combined price volatility of the IO and PO must be equal to the price volatility of the passthrough.

An average life for a PO can be calculated based on some prepayment assumption. However, an IO receives no principal payments, so technically an average life cannot be computed. Instead, for an IO a "cash flow average life" is computed, using the projected interest payments in the average life formula instead of principal.

Exhibit 7: Spreads and Other Measures for Stripped Mortgage-Backed Securities

(Based on prices as of 7/12/01)

IOs/POs		IO						PO					
Coupon	Trust	Price	Yield	ZV	OAS	OAD	OA Spread Dur	Price	Yield	ZV	OAS	OAD	OA Spread Dur
6.0	FHT-197	25-17+	10.94	625	310	−11.0	3.9	71-25+	5.12	−133	−84	11.2	4.8
	FNT-293	26-00	8.37	346	104	−8.3	3.9	72-02+	5.76	−52	−13	9.3	4.4
6.5	FHT-192	24-10	12.78	826	399	−17.3	3.6	75-13+	4.69	−171	−113	12.0	4.3
	FNT-249	25-11+	10.01	529	202	−12.9	3.7	74-23+	5.35	−92	−44	10.0	4.1
7.0	FHT-183	22-14	15.35	1141	568	−24.6	3.2	79-02	4.25	−212	−146	12.4	3.8
	FNT-240	23-30+	13.07	801	351	−18.9	3.3	78-02+	4.61	−148	−91	10.7	3.8
7.5	FNT-284	22-01	6.42	1065	455	−31.3	3.2	81-05+	6.33	−201	−132	12.6	3.3
	FNT-252	23-17	8.30	868	277	−28.4	3.3	79-24	5.87	−146	−62	12.1	3.3
8.0	FHT-186	21-01+	9.29	1060	603	−26.9	3.0	83-11+	5.51	−188	−154	10.4	3.1
	FNT-264	21-04	8.80	1028	572	−25.7	3.0	83-12	5.56	−178	−141	9.9	3.1
	FNT-251	23-11+	8.61	751	348	−22.3	3.2	81-08+	5.74	−114	−72	9.8	3.1
8.5	FNT-267	21-00+	15.90	1259	901	−20.1	2.7	84-24	4.02	−215	−206	8.5	3.3
	FHT-169	22-25	17.56	1238	733	−20.0	2.8	83-18+	3.82	−206	−164	8.7	3.3

Exhibit 7 (Continued)

		Collateral Characteristics								
					Prc Spd Over TBA	Settle	Historical CPR			Forecast Long-Run
Coupon	Trust	WALA	WAM	WAC	(32nds)	Date	1-Mo	6-Mo	12-Mo	PSA
6.0	FHT-197	40	308	6.76	12	7/16	15	12	9	160
	FNT-293	91	251	6.69	38	7/16	12	11	8	167
6.5	FHT-192	43	304	7.22	12	7/16	26	20	12	183
	FNT-249	93	249	7.07	26	7/16	17	16	10	183
7.0	FHT-183	54	292	7.62	6	7/16	32	25	15	208
	FNT-240	95	246	7.47	26	7/16	21	20	13	192
7.5	FNT-284	51	297	8.06	19	7/16	31	35	20	355
	FNT-252	97	246	7.92	22	7/16	22	22	14	287
8.0	FHT-186	51	297	8.48	18	7/16	46	41	24	340
	FNT-264	86	260	8.48	24	7/16	32	31	20	336
	FNT-251	103	241	8.46	28	7/16	29	29	18	294
8.5	FNT-267	82	264	8.90	20	7/16	36	34	21	275
	FHT-169	108	235	8.97	34	7/16	34	34	21	229

On-the-run Treasuries							
3 Mo	6 Mo	1 Yr	2 Yr (Y/P)	5 Yr (Y/P)	10 Yr (Y/P)	30 Yr (Y/P)	1 Mo
3.595	3.554	3.490	4.033/99-22+	4.744/99-15+	5.238/98-07	5.651/96-01+	3.830

Source: Adapted from Lehman Brothers, "MBS Derivatives," *MBS & ABS Weekly Outlook*, Fixed Income Research, July 14, 2001.

Exhibit 7 shows the cash flow yield, zero volatility spread, option-adjusted spread, option-adjusted duration, and option-adjusted spread duration for selected IO trusts. Notice that the OAS is positive for each trust and the option-adjusted duration is negative for each trust. This negative value means that the value of the trust changes in the same direction as the change in interest rates.

Trading and Settlement Procedures

The trading and settlement procedures for stripped mortgage-backed securities are similar to those set by the Public Securities Association for agency passthroughs described in the previous section. The specifications are in the types of trades (TBA versus specified pool), calculations of the proceeds, and the settlement dates.

IOs and POs are extreme premium and discount securities and consequently are very sensitive to prepayments, which are driven by the specific characteristics (WAC, WAM, geographic concentration, average loan size) of the underlying loans. The TBA delivery option on IOs and POs is of too great an economic value, and this value is hard to quantify. Therefore, almost all secondary trades in IOs and POs are on a specified pool basis rather than on a TBA basis.

All IOs and POs are given a trust number. Since the transactions are on a specified trust basis, they are also done based on the original face amount. For example, suppose a portfolio manager agrees to buy $10 million original face of Trust 23 PO for August settlement. At the time of the transaction, the August factor need not be known; however, there is no ambiguity in the amount to be delivered because the seller does not have any delivery option. The seller has to deliver $3 million current face amount if the August factor turns out to be 0.30, and the seller needs to deliver $2.5 million current face amount if the August factor turns out to be 0.25.

The total proceeds of a PO trade are calculated the same way as with a passthrough trade except that there is no accrued interest. For example, suppose a buyer and a seller agree to trade $10 million original face of Trust 23 PO at 75-08 for settlement on August 25. The proceeds for the trade are calculated as follows assuming an August trust factor of 0.25:

75.08 ×	$10,000,000 ×	0.25	= $1,881,250
price	original face value	pool factor	proceeds

The market trades IOs based on notional principal. The proceeds include the price on the notional amount and the accrued interest. For example, suppose a buyer and a seller agree to trade $10 million original notional face of Trust 23 IO at 33-20 for settlement on August 25. The proceeds for the trade are calculated as follows assuming an August factor of 0.25:

(0.33625 +	0.10 ×	24 days/360 days) ×	$10,000,000 ×	0.25	= $857,292
price	coupon	days accrued interest	orig. notional	factor	proceeds

As explained earlier, agency passthrough trades settle according to a delivery schedule established by the BMA. Stripped mortgage-backed securities

trades follow the same delivery schedule according to their underlying mortgages. Any other nonstandard settlement dates can be agreed upon between the buyer and the seller.

FEDERAL AGRICULTURAL MORTGAGE CORPORATION

The Federal Agricultural Mortgage Corporation (Farmer Mac) is the newest GSE that issues mortgage-backed securities. The securities are backed by mortgage loans secured by agricultural real estate. These securities are referred to as *agricultural mortgage-backed securities* or AMBS. All the characteristics that we described for agency passthrough securities apply to AMBS.

There is a Farmer Mac I Program and a Farmer Mac II Program. Under the former program the pools consist of mortgage loans secured by first liens on agricultural real estate. The securities issued under this program are guaranteed by Farmer Mac with respect to the timely payment of principal and interest (i.e., fully modified passthroughs). In the Farmer Mac II Program, the securities are backed by portions ("guaranteed portions") of farm ownership and farm operating loans, rural business and community development loans, and certain other loans guaranteed by the U.S. Department of Agriculture. Farmer Mac guarantees the timely payment of principal and interest on securities issued under this program.

KEY POINTS

- ❑ *A mortgage loan is a loan secured by the collateral of some specified real estate property that obliges the borrower to make a predetermined series of payments.*
- ❑ *The three most popular mortgage designs are the fixed-rate, level-payment, fully amortized mortgage; the adjustable-rate mortgage; and the balloon mortgage.*
- ❑ *In a mortgage loan, the portion of the monthly mortgage payment applied to interest declines each month and the portion applied to reducing the mortgage balance increases.*
- ❑ *Prepayments are mortgage payments made in excess of the scheduled principal repayments.*
- ❑ *A mortgage passthrough security is created when one or more holders of mortgages form a pool (collection) of mortgages and sell shares or participation certificates in the pool.*
- ❑ *One government agency—the Government National Mortgage Association ("Ginnie Mae")—and two government-sponsored enterprises—Federal Home Loan Mortgage Corporation ("Freddie Mac") and Federal National Mortgage Association ("Fannie Mae")—guarantee or issue securities referred to as agency passthrough securities.*
- ❑ *Ginnie Mae passthroughs are guaranteed by the full faith and credit of the U.S. government, while Fannie Mae and Freddie Mac passthroughs are not.*
- ❑ *The cash flows of a mortgage passthrough security depend on the cash flows of the underlying mortgages and include the aggregate monthly mortgage payments representing interest net of servicing fees and guarantee fees, the scheduled repayment of principal, and any prepayments.*
- ❑ *The key features of a passthrough are the type of guarantee, the number of lenders whose mortgage loans are permitted in a pool, the mortgage design of the loans, the characteristics of the mortgage loans in the pool, and the payment procedure.*
- ❑ *A projection of prepayments is necessary to determine the cash flows of a passthrough security.*
- ❑ *The only way to project cash flows is to make some assumption about the prepayment rate over the life of the underlying mortgage pool.*
- ❑ *Two conventions have been used as a benchmark for prepayment rates: conditional prepayment rate and Public Securities Association prepayment benchmark.*
- ❑ *The PSA prepayment benchmark is a series of conditional prepayment rates and is simply a market convention that describes in general the pattern of prepayments.*
- ❑ *The four factors that affect prepayments are the prevailing mortgage rate, characteristics of the underlying mortgage pool, seasonal factors, and general economic activity.*
- ❑ *A prepayment model is a statistical model that is used to forecast prepayments.*

- ❑ *Given the projected cash flows based on some prepayment speed and the market price of a passthrough, a cash flow yield can be determined.*
- ❑ *A cash flow yield is subject to all the drawbacks of a yield calculation, plus it assumes that the prepayments are correctly forecasted over the life of the passthrough.*
- ❑ *A measure commonly used to estimate the life of a passthrough is its average life.*
- ❑ *Unanticipated prepayments are beneficial if a passthrough is purchased at a discount and harmful if a passthrough is purchased at a premium.*
- ❑ *The prepayment risk associated with investing in mortgage passthrough securities can be decomposed into contraction risk and extension risk.*
- ❑ *There are specific rules established by the Public Securities Association for the trading and settlement of agency passthrough securities.*
- ❑ *In a TBA trade, the two parties agree on the agency type, the agency program, the coupon rate, the face value, the price, and the settlement date.*
- ❑ *Trades settle according to a delivery schedule established by the PSA.*
- ❑ *A particular pool purchased may have a materially different prepayment speed from the generic passthrough quoted by a dealer.*
- ❑ *A stripped mortgage-backed security is a derivative mortgage-backed security that is created by redistributing the interest and principal payments to two different classes, and the securities exhibit substantial price volatility.*
- ❑ *A principal-only mortgage strip benefits from declining interest rates and fast prepayments.*
- ❑ *An interest-only mortgage strip benefits from rising interest rates and a slowing of prepayments; the investor in an interest-only mortgage strip may not realize the amount invested even if the security is held to maturity.*
- ❑ *The passthroughs guaranteed by Farmer Mac are secured by agricultural real estate and are called agricultural mortgage-backed securities.*

Chapter 10

Agency Collateralized Mortgage Obligations

Agency passthrough securities can be used as collateral to create a collateralized mortgage obligation (CMO). Most investors who follow the bond market have read about this product, and, more than likely, the statements about the product have been unfavorable. CMO products have been responsible for many reported (and unreported) financial debacles. It is not uncommon, for example, for reporters to state that CMOs are the riskiest type of mortgage-backed securities product while mortgage passthrough securities are the safest. This statement, however, is incorrect, as we shall see in this chapter as we explore the world of CMOs.

THE BASIC PRINCIPLE OF CMOS

As explained in the previous chapter, an investor in a mortgage passthrough security is exposed to prepayment risk. Furthermore, prepayment risk can be divided into extension risk and contraction risk. Some investors are concerned with extension risk and others with contraction risk when they invest in a passthrough. An investor may be willing to accept one form of prepayment risk but seek to avoid the other. For example, an investor who seeks a short-term security is concerned with extension risk. An investor who seeks a long-term security, and wants to avoid reinvesting unexpected principal prepayments should interest rates drop, is concerned with contraction risk.

By redirecting how the cash flows of passthrough securities are paid to different bond classes that are created, securities can be created that have different exposure to prepayment risk. When the cash flows of mortgage-related products are redistributed to different bond classes, the resulting securities are called *collateralized mortgage obligations*. The creation of a CMO cannot eliminate prepayment risk; it can only redistribute the two forms of prepayment risk among different classes of bondholders.

The basic principle is that redirecting cash flows (interest and principal) to different bond classes, called *tranches*, mitigates different forms of prepayment risk. It is *never* possible to eliminate prepayment risk. If one tranche in a CMO structure has less prepayment risk than the mortgage passthrough securities that

are collateral for the structure, then another tranche in the same structure has greater prepayment risk than the collateral. Consequently, the statement that CMOs have greater prepayment risk than passthroughs is incorrect.

CMOs are referred to as *paythroughs* or *multiclass passthroughs*. (As will be explained later in this chapter, CMOs are also referred to as REMICs.) A security structure in which collateral is carved into different bond classes is not uncommon. We will see similar paythrough or multiclass passthrough structures when we cover asset-backed securities in Chapter 11.

AGENCY CMOS

Issuers of CMOs are the same three entities that issue agency passthrough securities: Freddie Mac, Fannie Mae, and Ginnie Mae. There has been little issuance of Ginnie Mae CMOs. However, Freddie Mac and Fannie Mae have used Ginnie Mae passthroughs as collateral for their own CMOs. CMOs issued by any of these entities are referred to as *agency CMOs*.

When an agency CMO is created, it is structured so that even under the worst circumstances regarding prepayments, the interest and principal payments from the collateral will be sufficient to meet the interest obligation of each tranche and pay off the par value of each tranche.[1] Defaults are ignored because the agency that has issued the passthroughs used as collateral is expected to make up any deficiency. Thus, the credit risk of agency CMOs is minimal. However, as noted in the previous chapter, the guarantee of a government-sponsored enterprise does not carry the full faith and credit of the U.S. government. Fannie Mae and Freddie Mac CMOs created from Ginnie Mae passthroughs effectively carry the full faith and credit of the U.S. government.

CMO STRUCTURES

There is a wide range of CMO structures. We review these structures as follows. Rather than just provide a definition, it is useful to see how the various types of CMOs are created. In an actual CMO structure, the information regarding the rules for distributing interest and principal to the bond classes is set forth in the prospectus.

Sequential-Pay Tranches

The first CMO was structured so that each class of bond would be retired sequentially. Such structures are referred to as *sequential-pay* CMOs.

---

[1] There are exceptions for some CMO deals that are created from a package of CMO tranches of other deals. In such structures, called re-REMICs, it is possible there will be an interest shortfall for a floating-rate tranche.

Exhibit 1: FAF-01: A Hypothetical Four-Tranche Sequential-Pay Structure

Tranche	Par Amount	Coupon Rate (%)
A	$194,500,000	7.5
B	36,000,000	7.5
C	96,500,000	7.5
D	73,000,000	7.5
Total	$400,000,000	

Payment rules:
1. *For payment of periodic coupon interest:* Disburse periodic coupon interest to each tranche on the basis of the amount of principal outstanding at the beginning of the period.
2. *For disbursement of principal payments:* Disburse principal payments to tranche A until it is completely paid off. After tranche A is completely paid off, disburse principal payments to tranche B until it is completely paid off. After tranche B is completely paid off, disburse principal payments to tranche C until it is completely paid off. After tranche C is completely paid off, disburse principal payments to tranche D until it is completely paid off.

To illustrate a sequential-pay CMO, we discuss FAF-01,[2] a hypothetical deal made up to illustrate the basic features of the structure. The collateral for this hypothetical CMO is a hypothetical passthrough with a total par value of $400 million and the following characteristics: (1) the passthrough coupon rate is 7.5%, (2) the weighted average coupon (WAC) is 8.125%, and (3) the weighted average maturity (WAM) is 357 months. This is the same passthrough that we used in the previous chapter to describe the cash flows of a passthrough based on some PSA assumption.

From this $400 million of collateral, four bond classes or tranches are created. Their characteristics are summarized in Exhibit 1. The total par value of the four tranches is equal to the par value of the collateral (i.e., the passthrough security). In this simple structure, the coupon rate is the same for each tranche and also the same as the collateral's coupon rate. There is no reason why this must be so, and, in fact, typically the coupon rate varies by tranche.

Now remember that a CMO is created by redistributing the cash flow—interest and principal—to the different tranches based on a set of payment rules. The payment rules at the bottom of Exhibit 1 set forth how the monthly cash flow from the passthrough (i.e., collateral) is to be distributed to the four tranches. There are separate rules for the payment of the coupon interest and the payment of principal, the principal being the total of the regularly scheduled principal payment and any prepayments.

In FAF-01, each tranche receives periodic coupon interest payments based on the amount of the outstanding balance. The disbursement of the principal, however, is made in a special way. A tranche is not entitled to receive principal until the entire principal of the tranche before it has been paid off. More specifically, tranche A receives all the principal payments until the entire principal amount

[2] All CMO structures are given a name. In our illustration we use FAF.

owed to that bond class, $194,500,000, is paid off; then tranche B begins to receive principal and continues to do so until it is paid the entire $36,000,000. Tranche C then receives principal, and when it is paid off, tranche D starts receiving principal payments.

While the payment rules for the disbursement of the principal payments are known, the precise amount of the principal in each period is not. This will depend on the cash flow, and therefore principal payments, of the collateral, which depends on the actual prepayment rate of the collateral. An assumed PSA speed allows the monthly cash flow to be projected. Exhibit 4 in the previous chapter shows the monthly cash flow (interest, regularly scheduled principal repayment, and prepayments) assuming 165 PSA. Assuming that the collateral does prepay at 165 PSA, the cash flows available to all four tranches of FAF-01 will be precisely the cash flows shown in Exhibit 4 of the previous chapter.

To demonstrate how the payment rules for FAF-01 work, Exhibit 2 shows the cash flow for selected months assuming the collateral prepays at 165 PSA. For each tranche, the exhibit shows (1) the balance at the end of the month, (2) the principal paid down (regularly scheduled principal repayment plus prepayments), and (3) interest. In month 1, the cash flow for the collateral consists of a principal payment of $709,923 and interest of $2.5 million (0.075 times $400 million divided by 12). The interest payment is distributed to the four tranches based on the amount of the par value outstanding. So, for example, tranche A receives $1,215,625 (0.075 times $194,500,000 divided by 12) of the $2.5 million. The principal, however, is all distributed to tranche A. Therefore, the cash flow for tranche A in month 1 is $1,925,548. The principal balance at the end of month 1 for tranche A is $193,790,076 (the original principal balance of $194,500,000 less the principal payment of $709,923). No principal payment is distributed to the three other tranches because there is still a principal balance outstanding for tranche A. This will be true for months 2 through 80.

After month 81, the principal balance will be zero for tranche A. For the collateral the cash flow in month 81 is $3,318,521, consisting of a principal payment of $2,032,196 and interest of $1,286,325. At the beginning of month 81 (end of month 80), the principal balance for tranche A is $311,926. Therefore, $311,926 of the $2,032,196 of the principal payment from the collateral will be disbursed to tranche A. After this payment is made, no additional principal payments are made to this tranche because the principal balance is zero. The remaining principal payment from the collateral, $1,720,271, is disbursed to tranche B. According to the assumed prepayment speed of 165 PSA, tranche B then begins receiving principal payments in month 81.

Exhibit 2 shows that tranche B is fully paid off by month 100, when tranche C now begins to receive principal payments. Tranche C is not fully paid off until month 178, at which time tranche D begins receiving the remaining principal payments. The maturity (i.e., the time until the principal is fully paid off) for these four tranches assuming 165 PSA is 81 months for tranche A, 100 months for tranche B, 178 months for tranche C, and 357 months for tranche D.

Exhibit 2: Monthly Cash Flow for Selected Months for FAF-01 Assuming 165 PSA

	Tranche A			Tranche B		
Month	Balance	Principal	Interest	Balance	Principal	Interest
1	194,500,000	709,923	1,215,625	36,000,000	0	225,000
2	193,790,077	821,896	1,211,188	36,000,000	0	225,000
3	192,968,181	933,560	1,206,051	36,000,000	0	225,000
4	192,034,621	1,044,822	1,200,216	36,000,000	0	225,000
5	190,989,799	1,155,586	1,193,686	36,000,000	0	225,000
6	189,834,213	1,265,759	1,186,464	36,000,000	0	225,000
7	188,568,454	1,375,246	1,178,553	36,000,000	0	225,000
8	187,193,208	1,483,954	1,169,958	36,000,000	0	225,000
9	185,709,254	1,591,789	1,160,683	36,000,000	0	225,000
10	184,117,464	1,698,659	1,150,734	36,000,000	0	225,000
11	182,418,805	1,804,473	1,140,118	36,000,000	0	225,000
12	180,614,332	1,909,139	1,128,840	36,000,000	0	225,000
75	12,893,479	2,143,974	80,584	36,000,000	0	225,000
76	10,749,504	2,124,935	67,184	36,000,000	0	225,000
77	8,624,569	2,106,062	53,904	36,000,000	0	225,000
78	6,518,507	2,087,353	40,741	36,000,000	0	225,000
79	4,431,154	2,068,807	27,695	36,000,000	0	225,000
80	2,362,347	2,050,422	14,765	36,000,000	0	225,000
81	311,926	311,926	1,950	36,000,000	1,720,271	225,000
82	0	0	0	34,279,729	2,014,130	214,248
83	0	0	0	32,265,599	1,996,221	201,660
84	0	0	0	30,269,378	1,978,468	189,184
85	0	0	0	28,290,911	1,960,869	176,818
95	0	0	0	9,449,331	1,793,089	59,058
96	0	0	0	7,656,242	1,777,104	47,852
97	0	0	0	5,879,138	1,761,258	36,745
98	0	0	0	4,117,880	1,745,550	25,737
99	0	0	0	2,372,329	1,729,979	14,827
100	0	0	0	642,350	642,350	4,015
101	0	0	0	0	0	0
102	0	0	0	0	0	0
103	0	0	0	0	0	0
104	0	0	0	0	0	0
105	0	0	0	0	0	0

The *principal pay down window* for a tranche is the time period between the beginning and the ending of the principal payments to that tranche. So, for example, for tranche A, the principal pay down window would be month 1 to month 81 assuming 165 PSA. For tranche B it is from month 81 to month 100. The window is also specified in terms of the length of the time from the beginning of the principal pay down window to the end of the principal pay down window. For tranche A, the window would be stated as 81 months, for tranche B 20

months. In confirmation of trades involving CMOs, the principal pay down window is specified in terms of the initial month that principal is expected to be received to the final month that principal is expected to be received.

Exhibit 2 (Concluded)

	Tranche C			Tranche D		
Month	Balance	Principal	Interest	Balance	Principal	Interest
1	96,500,000	0	603,125	73,000,000	0	456,250
2	96,500,000	0	603,125	73,000,000	0	456,250
3	96,500,000	0	603,125	73,000,000	0	456,250
4	96,500,000	0	603,125	73,000,000	0	456,250
5	96,500,000	0	603,125	73,000,000	0	456,250
6	96,500,000	0	603,125	73,000,000	0	456,250
7	96,500,000	0	603,125	73,000,000	0	456,250
8	96,500,000	0	603,125	73,000,000	0	456,250
9	96,500,000	0	603,125	73,000,000	0	456,250
10	96,500,000	0	603,125	73,000,000	0	456,250
11	96,500,000	0	603,125	73,000,000	0	456,250
12	96,500,000	0	603,125	73,000,000	0	456,250
95	96,500,000	0	603,125	73,000,000	0	456,250
96	96,500,000	0	603,125	73,000,000	0	456,250
97	96,500,000	0	603,125	73,000,000	0	456,250
98	96,500,000	0	603,125	73,000,000	0	456,250
99	96,500,000	0	603,125	73,000,000	0	456,250
100	96,500,000	1,072,194	603,125	73,000,000	0	456,250
101	95,427,806	1,699,243	596,424	73,000,000	0	456,250
102	93,728,563	1,684,075	585,804	73,000,000	0	456,250
103	92,044,489	1,669,039	575,278	73,000,000	0	456,250
104	90,375,450	1,654,134	564,847	73,000,000	0	456,250
105	88,721,315	1,639,359	554,508	73,000,000	0	456,250
175	3,260,287	869,602	20,377	73,000,000	0	456,250
176	2,390,685	861,673	14,942	73,000,000	0	456,250
177	1,529,013	853,813	9,556	73,000,000	0	456,250
178	675,199	675,199	4,220	73,000,000	170,824	456,250
179	0	0	0	72,829,176	838,300	455,182
180	0	0	0	71,990,876	830,646	449,943
181	0	0	0	71,160,230	823,058	444,751
182	0	0	0	70,337,173	815,536	439,607
183	0	0	0	69,521,637	808,081	434,510
184	0	0	0	68,713,556	800,690	429,460
185	0	0	0	67,912,866	793,365	424,455
350	0	0	0	1,235,674	160,220	7,723
351	0	0	0	1,075,454	158,544	6,722
352	0	0	0	916,910	156,883	5,731
353	0	0	0	760,027	155,238	4,750
354	0	0	0	604,789	153,607	3,780
355	0	0	0	451,182	151,991	2,820
356	0	0	0	299,191	150,389	1,870
357	0	0	0	148,802	148,802	930

Exhibit 3: Average Life for the Collateral and the Four Tranches of FAF-01

Prepayment	Average life for				
speed (PSA)	Collateral	Tranche A	Tranche B	Tranche C	Tranche D
50	15.11	7.48	15.98	21.02	27.24
100	11.66	4.90	10.86	15.78	24.58
165	8.76	3.48	7.49	11.19	20.27
200	7.68	3.05	6.42	9.60	18.11
300	5.63	2.32	4.64	6.81	13.36
400	4.44	1.94	3.70	5.31	10.34
500	3.68	1.69	3.12	4.38	8.35
600	3.16	1.51	2.74	3.75	6.96
700	2.78	1.38	2.47	3.30	5.95

Let's look at what has been accomplished by creating the CMO. First, in the previous chapter we saw that the average life of the passthrough is 8.76 years, assuming a prepayment speed of 165 PSA. Exhibit 3 reports the average life of the collateral and the four tranches, assuming different prepayment speeds. Notice that the four tranches have average lives that are both shorter and longer than the collateral, thereby attracting investors who have a preference for an average life different from that of the collateral.

There is still a major problem: there is considerable variability of the average life for the tranches. We'll see how this can be tackled later on. However, there is some protection provided for each tranche against prepayment risk. This is because prioritizing the distribution of principal (i.e., establishing the payment rules for principal) effectively protects the shorter-term tranche A in this structure against extension risk. This protection must come from somewhere, so it comes from the three other tranches. Similarly, tranches C and D provide protection against extension risk for tranches A and B. At the same time, tranches C and D benefit because they are provided protection against contraction risk, the protection coming from tranches A and B.

Accrual Tranches

In FAF-01, the payment rules for interest provide for all tranches to be paid interest each month. In many sequential-pay CMO structures, at least one tranche does not receive current interest. Instead, the interest for that tranche would accrue and be added to the principal balance. Such a bond class is commonly referred to as an *accrual tranche* or a *Z bond* (because the bond is similar to a zero-coupon bond). The interest that would have been paid to the accrual bond class is then used to speed up pay down of the principal balance of earlier bond classes.

To see this, consider FAF-02, a hypothetical CMO structure with the same collateral as FAF-01 and with four tranches, each with a coupon rate of 7.5%. The difference is in the last tranche, Z, which is an accrual tranche. The structure for FAF-02 is shown in Exhibit 4.

Exhibit 4: FAF-02: A Hypothetical Four-Tranche Sequential-Pay Structure with an Accrual Bond Class

Tranche	Par Amount	Coupon rate (%)
A	$194,500,000	7.5
B	36,000,000	7.5
C	96,500,000	7.5
Z (Accrual)	73,000,000	7.5
Total	$400,000,000	

Payment rules:

1. *For payment of periodic coupon interest:* Disburse periodic coupon interest to tranches A, B, and C on the basis of the amount of principal outstanding at the beginning of the period. For tranche Z, accrue the interest based on the principal plus accrued interest in the previous period. The interest for tranche Z is to be paid to the earlier tranches as a principal pay down.

2. *For disbursement of principal payments:* Disburse principal payments to tranche A until it is completely paid off. After tranche A is completely paid off, disburse principal payments to tranche B until it is completely paid off. After tranche B is completely paid off, disburse principal payments to tranche C until it is completely paid off. After tranche C is completely paid off, disburse principal payments to tranche Z until the original principal balance plus accrued interest is completely paid off.

Exhibit 5 shows the cash flow for selected months for tranches A and B. Let's look at month 1 and compare it to month 1 in Exhibit 2. Both cash flows are based on 165 PSA. The principal payment from the collateral is $709,923. In FAF-01, this is the principal pay down for tranche A. In FAF-02, the interest for tranche Z, $456,250, is not paid to that tranche but instead is used to pay down the principal of tranche A. So, the principal payment to tranche A in Exhibit 5 is $1,166,173, the collateral's principal payment of $709,923 plus the interest of $456,250 that was diverted from tranche Z.

The expected final maturity for tranches A, B, and C has shortened as a result of the inclusion of tranche Z. The final payout for tranche A is 64 months rather than 81 months; for tranche B it is 77 months rather than 100 months; and for tranche C it is 112 months rather than 178 months.

The average lives for tranches A, B, and C are shorter in FAF-02 compared to FAF-01 because of the inclusion of the accrual bond. For example, at 165 PSA, the average lives are as follows:

Structure	Tranche A	Tranche B	Tranche C
FAF-02	2.90	5.86	7.87
FAF-01	3.48	7.49	11.19

The reason for the shortening of the nonaccrual tranches is that the interest that would be paid to the accrual tranche is being allocated to the other tranches. Tranche Z in FAF-02 will have a longer average life than tranche D in FAF-01.

Thus, shorter-term tranches and a longer-term tranche are created by including an accrual bond. The accrual bond has appeal to investors who are concerned with reinvestment risk. Since there are no coupon payments to reinvest, reinvestment risk is eliminated until all the other tranches are paid off.

Exhibit 5: Monthly Cash Flow for Selected Months for Tranches A and B of FAF-02 Assuming 165 PSA

	Tranche A			Tranche B		
Month	Balance	Principal	Interest	Balance	Principal	Interest
1	194,500,000	1,150,965	972,500	36,000,000	0	195,000
2	193,349,035	1,265,602	966,745	36,000,000	0	195,000
3	192,083,433	1,379,947	960,417	36,000,000	0	195,000
4	190,703,486	1,493,906	953,517	36,000,000	0	195,000
5	189,209,581	1,607,383	946,048	36,000,000	0	195,000
6	187,602,197	1,720,286	938,011	36,000,000	0	195,000
7	185,881,911	1,832,519	929,410	36,000,000	0	195,000
8	184,049,392	1,943,990	920,247	36,000,000	0	195,000
9	182,105,402	2,054,604	910,527	36,000,000	0	195,000
10	180,050,798	2,164,271	900,254	36,000,000	0	195,000
11	177,886,528	2,272,897	889,433	36,000,000	0	195,000
12	175,613,631	2,380,393	878,068	36,000,000	0	195,000
60	16,303,583	3,079,699	81,518	36,000,000	0	195,000
61	13,223,884	3,061,796	66,119	36,000,000	0	195,000
62	10,162,088	3,044,105	50,810	36,000,000	0	195,000
63	7,117,983	3,026,624	35,590	36,000,000	0	195,000
64	4,091,359	3,009,352	20,457	36,000,000	0	195,000
65	1,082,007	1,082,007	5,410	36,000,000	1,910,280	195,000
66	0	0	0	34,089,720	2,975,428	184,653
67	0	0	0	31,114,292	2,958,773	168,536
68	0	0	0	28,155,519	2,942,321	152,509
69	0	0	0	25,213,198	2,926,071	136,571
70	0	0	0	22,287,128	2,910,020	120,722
71	0	0	0	19,377,107	2,894,169	104,959
72	0	0	0	16,482,938	2,878,515	89,283
73	0	0	0	13,604,423	2,863,057	73,691
74	0	0	0	10,741,366	2,847,794	58,182
75	0	0	0	7,893,572	2,832,724	42,757
76	0	0	0	5,060,849	2,817,846	27,413
77	0	0	0	2,243,003	2,243,003	12,150
78	0	0	0	0	0	0
79	0	0	0	0	0	0
80	0	0	0	0	0	0

Floating-Rate Tranches

A floating-rate tranche can be created from a fixed-rate tranche by creating a floater and an inverse floater. We illustrate the creation of a floating-rate and an inverse floating-rate bond class using the hypothetical CMO structure FAF-02, which is a four-tranche sequential-pay structure with an accrual bond. We can select any of the tranches from which to create a floating-rate and an inverse floating-rate tranche. In fact, we can create these two securities for more than one of the four tranches or for only a portion of one tranche.

Exhibit 6: FAF-03: A Hypothetical Five-Tranche Sequential-Pay Structure with Floater, Inverse Floater, and Accrual Bond Classes

Tranche	Par amount	Coupon rate
A	$194,500,000	7.50%
B	36,000,000	7.50%
FL	72,375,000	1-mo. LIBOR + 0.50
IFL	24,125,000	28.50 – 3 × (1-mo. LIBOR)
Z (Accrual)	73,000,000	7.50%
Total	$400,000,000	

Payment rules:

1. *For payment of periodic coupon interest:* Disburse periodic coupon interest to tranches A, B, FL, and IFL on the basis of the amount of principal outstanding at the beginning of the period. For tranche Z, accrue the interest based on the principal plus accrued interest in the previous period. The interest for tranche Z is to be paid to the earlier tranches as a principal pay down. The maximum coupon rate for FL is 10%; the minimum coupon rate for IFL is 0%.

2. *For disbursement of principal payments:* Disburse principal payments to tranche A until it is completely paid off. After tranche A is completely paid off, disburse principal payments to tranche B until it is completely paid off. After tranche B is completely paid off, disburse principal payments to tranches FL and IFL until they are completely paid off. The principal payments between tranches FL and IFL should be made in the following way: 75% to tranche FL and 25% to tranche IFL. After tranches FL and IFL are completely paid off, disburse principal payments to tranche Z until the original principal balance plus accrued interest is completely paid off.

In this case, we create a floater and an inverse floater from tranche C. The par value for this tranche is $96.5 million, and we create two tranches that have a combined par value of $96.5 million. We refer to this CMO structure with a floater and an inverse floater as FAF-03. It has five tranches, designated A, B, FL, IFL, and Z, where FL is the floating-rate tranche and IFL is the inverse floating-rate tranche. Exhibit 6 describes FAF-03. Any reference rate can be used to create a floater and the corresponding inverse floater. The reference rate selected for setting the coupon rate for FL and IFL in FAF-03 is 1-month LIBOR.

The amount of the par value of the floating-rate tranche will be some portion of the $96.5 million. There are an infinite number of ways to cut up the $96.5 million between the floater and inverse floater, and final partitioning will be driven by the demands of investors. In the FAF-03 structure, we made the floater from $72,375,000, or 75% of the $96.5 million. The coupon rate on the floater is set at 1-month LIBOR plus 50 basis points. So, for example, if LIBOR is 3.75% at the coupon reset date, the coupon rate on the floater is 3.75% + 0.5%, or 4.25%. There is a cap on the coupon rate for the floater (discussed later).

Unlike a floating-rate note whose principal is unchanged over the life of the instrument, the floater's principal balance declines over time as principal repayments are made. The principal payments to the floater are determined by the principal payments from the tranche from which the floater is created. In our CMO structure, this is tranche C.

Since the floater's par value is $72,375,000 of the $96.5 million, the balance is the inverse floater. Assuming that 1-month LIBOR is the reference rate, the coupon reset formula for an inverse floater takes the following form:

$$K - L \times (\text{1-month LIBOR})$$

In FAF-03, K is set at 28.50% and L at 3. Thus, if 1-month LIBOR is 3.75%, the coupon rate for the month is:

$$28.50\% - 3 \times (3.75\%) = 17.25\%$$

K is the cap or maximum coupon rate for the inverse floater. In FAF-03, the cap for the inverse floater is 28.50%.

The L or multiple in the coupon reset formula for the inverse floater is called the *coupon leverage*. The higher the coupon leverage, the more the inverse floater's coupon rate changes for a given change in 1-month LIBOR. For example, a coupon leverage of 3 means that a 1 basis point change in 1-month LIBOR will change the coupon rate on the inverse floater by 3 basis points.

As in the case of the floater, the principal pay down of an inverse floater will be a proportionate amount of the principal pay down of tranche C.

Because 1-month LIBOR is always positive, the coupon rate paid to the floating-rate tranche cannot be negative. If there are no restrictions placed on the coupon rate for the inverse floater, however, it is possible for the coupon rate for that tranche to be negative. To prevent this, a floor, or minimum, can be placed on the coupon rate. In many structures, the floor is set at zero. Once a floor is set for the inverse floater, a cap or ceiling is imposed on the floater. In FAF-03, a floor of zero is set for the inverse floater. The floor results in a cap or maximum coupon rate for the floater of 10%.

Planned Amortization Class Tranches

A *planned amortization class* (PAC) bond is one in which a schedule of principal of payments is set forth in the prospectus. The PAC bondholders have priority over all other bond classes in the structure with respect to the receipt of the scheduled principal payments. While there is no assurance that the principal payments will be actually realized so as to satisfy the schedule, a PAC bond is structured so that if prepayment speeds are within a certain range, the collateral will throw off sufficient principal to meet the schedule of principal payments.

The greater certainty of the cash flow for the PAC bonds comes at the expense of the non-PAC classes, called the *support* or *companion* bonds. These tranches absorb the prepayment risk. Because PAC bonds have protection against both extension risk and contraction risk, they are said to provide *two-sided prepayment protection.*

To illustrate how to create a PAC bond, we will use as collateral the $400 million passthrough with a coupon rate of 7.5%, an 8.125% WAC, and a

WAM of 357 months. From this collateral a PAC bond with a par value of $243.8 million will be created. The second column of Exhibit 7 shows the principal payment (regularly scheduled principal repayment plus prepayments) for selected months assuming a prepayment speed of 90 PSA, and the next column shows the principal payments for selected months assuming that the passthrough prepays at 300 PSA.

The last column of Exhibit 7 gives the *minimum* principal payment if the collateral speed is 90 PSA or 300 PSA for months 1 to 349. (After month 349, the outstanding principal balance will be paid off if the prepayment speed is between 90 PSA and 300 PSA.) For example, in the first month, the principal payment would be $508,169.52 if the collateral prepays at 90 PSA and $1,075,931.20 if the collateral prepays at 300 PSA. Thus, the minimum principal payment is $508,169.52, as reported in the last column of Exhibit 7. In month 103, the minimum principal payment is also the amount if the prepayment speed is 90 PSA, $1,446,761, compared to $1,458,618.04 for 300 PSA. In month 104, however, a prepayment speed of 300 PSA would produce a principal payment of $1,433,539.23, which is less than the principal payment of $1,440,825.55 assuming 90 PSA. So, $1,433,539.23 is reported in the last column of Exhibit 7. In fact, from month 104 on, the minimum principal payment is the one that would result assuming a prepayment speed of 300 PSA.

Actually, if the collateral prepays at *any* speed between 90 PSA and 300 PSA, the minimum principal payment would be the amount reported in the last column of Exhibit 7. For example, if we had included principal payment figures assuming a prepayment speed of 200 PSA, the minimum principal payment would not change: from month 11 through month 103, the minimum principal payment is that generated from 90 PSA, but from month 104 on, the minimum principal payment is that generated from 300 PSA.

This characteristic of the collateral allows for the creation of a PAC bond, assuming that the collateral prepays over its life at a constant speed between 90 PSA and 300 PSA. A schedule of principal repayments that the PAC bondholders are entitled to receive before any other tranche in the CMO is specified. The monthly schedule of principal repayments is as specified in the last column of Exhibit 7, which shows the minimum principal payment. While there is no assurance that the collateral will prepay at a constant rate between these two speeds, a PAC bond can be structured assuming that it will.

Exhibit 8 shows a CMO structure, FAF-04, created from the $400 million 7.5% coupon passthrough with a WAC of 8.125% and a WAM of 357 months. There are just two tranches in this structure: a 7.5% coupon PAC bond created assuming 90 to 300 PSA with a par value of $243.8 million and a support bond with a par value of $156.2 million. The two speeds used to create a PAC bond are called the *initial PAC collars* (or *initial PAC bands*). For FAF-04, 90 PSA is the lower collar and 300 PSA the upper collar.

Exhibit 7: Monthly Principal Payment for $400 Million Par 7.5% Coupon Passthrough with an 8.125% WAC and a 357 WAM Assuming Prepayment Rates of 90 PSA and 300 PSA

	Principal payment		Minimum principal payment
Month	At 90% PSA	At 300% PSA	PAC schedule
1	$508,169.52	$1,075,931.20	$508,169.52
2	569,843.43	1,279,412.11	569,843.43
3	631,377.11	1,482,194.45	631,377.11
4	692,741.89	1,683,966.17	692,741.89
5	753,909.12	1,884,414.62	753,909.12
6	814,850.22	2,083,227.31	814,850.22
7	875,536.68	2,280,092.68	875,536.68
8	935,940.10	2,474,700.92	935,940.10
9	996,032.19	2,666,744.77	996,032.19
10	1,055,784.82	2,855,920.32	1,055,784.82
11	1,115,170.01	3,041,927.81	1,115,170.01
12	1,174,160.00	3,224,472.44	1,174,160.00
13	1,232,727.22	3,403,265.17	1,232,727.22
14	1,290,844.32	3,578,023.49	1,290,844.32
15	1,348,484.24	3,748,472.23	1,348,484.24
16	1,405,620.17	3,914,344.26	1,405,620.17
17	1,462,225.60	4,075,381.29	1,462,225.60
18	1,518,274.36	4,231,334.57	1,518,274.36
101	1,458,719.34	1,510,072.17	1,458,719.34
102	1,452,725.55	1,484,126.59	1,452,725.55
103	1,446,761.00	1,458,618.04	1,446,761.00
104	1,440,825.55	1,433,539.23	1,433,539.23
105	1,434,919.07	1,408,883.01	1,408,883.01
211	949,482.58	213,309.00	213,309.00
212	946,033.34	209,409.09	209,409.09
213	942,601.99	205,577.05	205,577.05
346	618,684.59	13,269.17	13,269.17
347	617,071.58	12,944.51	12,944.51
348	615,468.65	12,626.21	12,626.21
349	613,875.77	12,314.16	3,432.32
350	612,292.88	12,008.25	0
351	610,719.96	11,708.38	0
352	609,156.96	11,414.42	0
353	607,603.84	11,126.28	0
354	606,060.57	10,843.85	0
355	604,527.09	10,567.02	0
356	603,003.38	10,295.70	0
357	601,489.39	10,029.78	0

Exhibit 8: FAF-04 CMO Structure with One PAC Bond and One Support Bond

Tranche	Par amount	Coupon rate (%)
P (PAC)	$243,800,000	7.5
S (Support)	156,200,000	7.5
Total	$400,000,000	

Payment rules:
1. *For payment of periodic coupon interest:* Disburse periodic coupon interest to each tranche on the basis of the amount of principal outstanding at the beginning of the period.
2. *For disbursement of principal payments:* Disburse principal payments to tranche P based on its schedule of principal repayments. Tranche P has priority with respect to current and future principal payments to satisfy the schedule. Any excess principal payments in a month over the amount necessary to satisfy the schedule for tranche P are paid to tranche S. When tranche S is completely paid off, all principal payments are to be made to tranche P regardless of the schedule.

Exhibit 9: Average Life for PAC Bond and Support Bond in FAF-04 Assuming Various Prepayment Speeds

Prepayment rate (PSA)	PAC Bond (P)	Support Bond (S)
0	15.97	27.26
50	9.44	24.00
90	7.26	18.56
100	7.26	18.56
150	7.26	12.57
165	7.26	11.16
200	7.26	8.38
250	7.26	5.37
300	7.26	3.13
350	6.56	2.51
400	5.92	2.17
450	5.38	1.94
500	4.93	1.77
700	3.70	1.37

Exhibit 9 reports the average life for the PAC bond and the support bond in FAF-04 assuming various *actual* prepayment speeds. Notice that between 90 PSA and 300 PSA, the average life for the PAC bond is stable at 7.26 years. However, at slower or faster PSA speeds, the schedule is broken and the average life changes, lengthening when the prepayment speed is less than 90 PSA and shortening when it is greater than 300 PSA. Even so, there is much greater variability for the average life of the support bond.

Creating a Series of PAC Bonds

Most CMO PAC structures have more than one class of PAC bonds. Exhibit 10 shows six PAC bonds created from the single PAC bond in FAF-04. We will refer to this CMO structure as FAF-05. Information about this CMO structure is pro-

vided in Exhibit 10. The total par value of the six PAC bonds is equal to $243.8 million, which is the amount of the single PAC bond in FAF-04.

Exhibit 11 shows the average life for the six PAC bonds and the support bond in FAF-05 at various prepayment speeds. From a PAC bond in FAF-04 with an average life of 7.26, we have created six PAC bonds with an average life as short as 2.58 years (P-A) and as long as 16.92 years (P-F) if prepayments stay within 90 PSA and 300 PSA.

Exhibit 10: FAF-05 CMO Structure with Six PAC Bonds and One Support Bond

Tranche	Par amount	Coupon rate (%)
P-A	$85,000,000	7.5
P-B	8,000,000	7.5
P-C	35,000,000	7.5
P-D	45,000,000	7.5
P-E	40,000,000	7.5
P-F	30,800,000	7.5
S	156,200,000	7.5
Total	$400,000,000	

Payment rules:

1. *For payment of periodic coupon interest:* Disburse periodic coupon interest to each tranche on the basis of the amount of principal outstanding at the beginning of the period.

2. *For disbursement of principal payments:* Disburse principal payments to tranches P-A to P-F based on their respective schedules of principal repayments. Tranche P-A has priority with respect to current and future principal payments to satisfy the schedule. Any excess principal payments in a month over the amount necessary to satisfy the schedule for tranche P-A are paid to tranche S. Once tranche P-A is completely paid off, tranche P-B has priority, then tranche P-C, etc. When tranche S is completely paid off, all principal payments are to be made to the remaining PAC tranches in order of priority regardless of the schedule.

Exhibit 11: Average Life for the Six PAC Bonds in FAF-05 Assuming Various Prepayment Speeds

Prepayment rate (PSA)	PAC Bonds					
	P-A	P-B	P-C	P-D	P-E	P-F
0	8.46	14.61	16.49	19.41	21.91	23.76
50	3.58	6.82	8.36	11.30	14.50	18.20
90	2.58	4.72	5.78	7.89	10.83	16.92
100	2.58	4.72	5.78	7.89	10.83	16.92
150	2.58	4.72	5.78	7.89	10.83	16.92
165	2.58	4.72	5.78	7.89	10.83	16.92
200	2.58	4.72	5.78	7.89	10.83	16.92
250	2.58	4.72	5.78	7.89	10.83	16.92
300	2.58	4.72	5.78	7.89	10.83	16.92
350	2.58	4.72	5.94	6.95	9.24	14.91
400	2.57	4.37	4.91	6.17	8.33	13.21
450	2.50	3.97	4.44	5.56	7.45	11.81
500	2.40	3.65	4.07	5.06	6.74	10.65
700	2.06	2.82	3.10	3.75	4.88	7.51

As expected, the average lives are stable if the prepayment speed is between 90 PSA and 300 PSA. Notice that even outside this range the average life is stable for several of the PAC bonds. For example, PAC P-A is stable even if prepayment speeds are as high as 400 PSA. For the PAC P-B, the average life does not vary when prepayments are between 90 PSA and 350 PSA. Why is it that the shorter the PAC, the more protection it has against faster prepayments?

To understand why this is so, remember that there are $156.2 million in support bonds that are protecting the $85 million of PAC P-A. Thus, even if prepayments are faster than the initial upper collar, there may be sufficient support bonds to assure the satisfaction of the schedule. In fact, as can be seen from Exhibit 11, even if prepayments are at 400 PSA over the life of the collateral, the average life is unchanged.

Now consider PAC P-B. The support bonds are providing protection for both the $85 million of PAC P-A and $93 million of PAC P-B. As can be seen from Exhibit 11, prepayments could be 350 PSA and the average life is still unchanged. From Exhibit 11, it can also be seen that the degree of protection against extension risk increases the shorter the PAC. Thus, while the initial collar may be 90 to 300 PSA, the *effective collar* is wider for the shorter PAC tranches.

Effective Collars and Actual Prepayments

As we have emphasized, the creation of a mortgage-backed security cannot make prepayment risk disappear. This is true for both a passthrough and a CMO. Thus, the reduction in prepayment risk (both extension risk and contraction risk) that a PAC offers must come from somewhere.

Where does the prepayment protection come from? It comes from the support bonds. The support bonds forego principal payments if the collateral prepayments are slow; support bonds do not receive any principal until the PAC bonds receive the scheduled principal repayment. This reduces the risk that the PAC bonds will extend. Similarly, the support bonds absorb any principal payments in excess of the scheduled principal payments that are made. This reduces the contraction risk of the PAC bonds. *Thus, the key to the prepayment protection offered by a PAC bond is the amount of support bonds outstanding. If the support bonds are paid off quickly because of faster-than-expected prepayments, then there is no longer any protection for the PAC bonds.* In fact, in FAF-05, if the support bond is paid off, the structure is effectively reduced to a sequential-pay CMO. In such cases, the schedule is unlikely to be maintained, and the structure is referred to as a *busted PAC*.

The support bonds can be thought of as bodyguards for the PAC bondholders. When the bullets fly (i.e., prepayments occur), the bodyguards get killed first. The bodyguards are there to absorb the bullets. Once all the bodyguards are killed off (i.e., the support bonds paid off with faster-than-expected prepayments), the PAC bonds must fend for themselves: they are exposed to all the bullets.

With the bodyguard metaphor for the support bonds in mind, let's consider two questions asked by CMO buyers:

1. Will the schedule of principal repayments be satisfied if prepayments are faster than the initial upper collar?
2. Will the schedule of principal repayments be satisfied as long as prepayments stay within the initial collar?

Let's address the first question. The initial upper collar for FAF-04 is 300 PSA. Suppose that actual prepayments are 500 PSA for 7 consecutive months; will this disrupt the schedule of principal repayments? The answer is: it depends!

There are two pieces of information we will need to answer this question. First, when does the 500 PSA occur? Second, what has been the actual prepayment experience up to the time that prepayments are 500 PSA? For example, suppose 6 years from now is when the prepayments reach 500 PSA, and also suppose that for the past 6 years the actual prepayment speed has been 90 PSA every month. What this means is that there are more bodyguards (i.e., support bonds) around than was expected when the PAC was structured at the initial collar. In establishing the schedule of principal repayments, it was assumed that the bodyguards would be killed off at 300 PSA, but the actual prepayment experience results in them being killed off at only 90 PSA. Thus, 6 years from now when the 500 PSA is assumed to occur, there are more bodyguards than expected. Thus, a 500 PSA for 7 consecutive months may have no effect on the ability of the schedule of principal repayments to be met.

In contrast, suppose that the actual prepayment experience for the first 6 years is 300 PSA (the upper collar of the initial PAC collar). In this case, there are no extra bodyguards around. As a result, any prepayment speeds faster than 300 PSA, such as 500 PSA in our example, jeopardize satisfaction of the principal repayment schedule and increase contraction risk. This does not mean that the schedule will be "busted"—the term used in the CMO market when a PAC schedule is broken. What it does mean is that the prepayment protection is reduced.

It should be clear from these observations that the initial collars are not particularly useful in assessing the prepayment protection for a seasoned PAC bond. This is most important to understand because it is common for CMO buyers to compare prepayment protection of PACs in different CMO structures and conclude that the greater protection is offered by the one with the wider initial collars. This approach is inadequate because actual prepayment experience determines the degree of prepayment protection going forward, as well as the expected future prepayment behavior of the collateral.

The way to determine this protection is to calculate the effective collar for a PAC bond. An effective collar for a PAC is the lower and the upper PSA that can occur in the future and still allow maintenance of the schedule of principal repayments.

Exhibit 12: Average Life 2 Years from Now for PAC Bond of FAF-04 Assuming Prepayments of 300 PSA for First 24 Months

PSA from Year 2 on	Average Life
95	6.43
105	6.11
115	6.01
120	6.00
125	6.00
300	6.00
305	5.62

The effective collar changes every month. An extended period over which actual prepayments are below the upper range of the initial PAC collar will result in an increase in the upper range of the effective collar. This is because there will be more bodyguards around than anticipated. An extended period of prepayments slower than the lower range of the initial PAC collar will raise the lower range of the effective collar. This is because it will take faster prepayments to make up the shortfall of the scheduled principal payments not made plus the scheduled future principal payments.

The PAC schedule may not be satisfied even if the actual prepayments never fall outside of the initial collar. This may seem surprising since our previous analysis indicated that the average life would not change if prepayments are at either extreme of the initial collar. However, recall that all of our previous analysis has been based on a single PSA speed for the life of the structure.

If we vary the PSA speed over time rather than keep it constant over the life of the CMO, we can see what happens to the effective collar if the prepayments are at the initial upper collar for a certain number of months.[3] Exhibit 12 shows the average life 2 years from now for the PAC bond in FAF-04, assuming that prepayments are 300 PSA for the first 24 months. Notice that the average life is stable at 6 years if the prepayments for the following months are between 115 PSA and 300 PSA. That is, the effective PAC collar is no longer the initial collar. Instead, the lower collar has shifted upward. This means that the protection from year 2 on is for 115 to 300 PSA, a narrower band than initially, even though the earlier prepayments did not exceed the initial upper collar.

Providing Greater Prepayment Protection for PACs

There are two ways to provide greater protection for PAC bonds: lockouts and reverse PAC structures. One obvious way to provide greater protection for PAC bonds is to issue fewer PAC bonds relative to support bonds. In FAF-05, for example, rather than creating the six PAC bonds with a total par value of $243.8 million, we could use only $158.8 million of the $400 million of collateral to cre-

[3] When an analysis is performed by varying the PSA speed, it is referred to as *vector analysis*.

ate these bonds by reducing the amount of each of the six PAC bonds. An alternative is not to issue one of the PAC bonds, typically the shorter-term one. For example, suppose that we create only the last five of the six PAC bonds in FAF-05. The $85 million for PAC P-A is then used to create more support bonds. Such a CMO structure with no principal payments to a PAC bond in the earlier years is referred to as a *lockout structure*.

A lockout structure provides greater prepayment protection to all PAC bonds in the CMO structure. One way to provide greater prepayment protection to only some PAC bonds is to alter the principal payment rules for distributing principal once all the support bonds have been paid off.

In FAF-05, for example, once the support bond in this structure is paid off, the structure effectively becomes a sequential-pay structure. For PAC P-A this means that while there is protection against extension risk, because this tranche receives principal payments before the other five PAC bonds, there is no protection against contraction. To provide greater protection to PAC P-A, the payment rules set forth in the prospectus can specify that after all support bonds have been paid off, any principal payments in excess of the scheduled amount will be paid to the last PAC bond, P-F in FAF-05. Thus, PAC P-F is exposed to greater contraction risk, which provides the other five PAC bonds with more protection against contraction risk. The principal payment rules would also specify that once the support bonds and PAC P-F bond are paid off, then all principal payments in excess of the scheduled amount to earlier tranches are to be paid to the next-to-the-last PAC bond, PAC P-E in our example.

A CMO structure requiring any excess principal payments to be made to the longer PAC bonds after all support bonds are paid off is called a *reverse PAC structure*.

Other PAC Tranches

Earlier we described how the collateral can be used to create a CMO with accrual bonds and floater and inverse floater bonds. These same types of bond classes can be created from a PAC bond. The difference between the bond classes described and those created from a PAC bond is simply the prepayment protection offered by the PAC structure.

Targeted Amortization Class Bonds

A *targeted amortization class*, or TAC, bond resembles a PAC bond in that both have a schedule of principal repayment. The difference between a PAC bond and a TAC bond is that the former has a wide PSA range over which the schedule of principal repayment is protected against contraction risk and extension risk. A TAC bond, in contrast, has a single PSA rate from which the schedule of principal repayment is protected. As a result, the prepayment protection afforded the TAC bond is considerably less than that for a PAC bond.

The PSA rate used to generate the schedule of principal repayments is such that it results in protection against contraction risk but not extension risk. Thus, while PAC bonds are said to have two-sided prepayment protection, TAC bonds have one-sided prepayment protection. Such a bond would not be acceptable to an investor who seeks protection against extension risk.

Some investors are interested in protection against extension risk but are willing to accept contraction risk. This is the opposite protection from that sought by the buyers of TAC bonds. A TAC structure can be created to provide such protection. The TAC created is called a *reverse TAC bond*.

Very Accurately Determined Maturity Bonds

Accrual or Z-bonds have been used in CMO structures as support for bonds called *very accurately determined maturity* (VADM) or *guaranteed final maturity bonds*. In this case, the interest accruing (i.e., not being paid out) on a Z-bond is used to pay the interest and principal on a VADM bond. This effectively provides protection against extension risk even if prepayments slow down, since the interest accruing on the Z-bond will be sufficient to pay off the scheduled principal and interest on the VADM bond. Thus, the maximum final maturity can be determined with a high degree of certainty. However, if prepayments are high, resulting in the supporting Z-bond being paid off faster, a VADM bond can shorten.

A VADM is similar in character to a reverse TAC. For structures with similar collateral, however, a VADM bond offers greater protection against extension risk. Moreover, most VADMs will not shorten significantly if prepayments speed up. Thus, they offer greater protection against contraction risk compared to a reverse TAC with the same underlying collateral. Compared to PACs, VADM bonds have greater absolute protection against extension risk. While VADM bonds do not have as much protection against contraction risk, the structures that have included these bonds are such that contraction risk is generally not significant.

As an illustration of a plain vanilla CMO structure with a VADM, consider FAF-06 in Exhibit 13. The speed assumed is 165 PSA. There are four tranches: V, B, C, and Z. The interest accruing to the Z-bond, or accrual bond, is used to pay down tranche V, the VADM bond. Exhibit 14 shows the outstanding balance for the first 31 months assuming 165 PSA. The final maturity is in month 30. The maximum extension can be determined by finding the mortgage balance assuming no prepayment (i.e., 0 PSA). The final maturity in this case would be 83 months.

Exhibit 15 shows a VADM created from a PAC structure. There are five tranches in this structure FAF-07: V, B, C, Z, and S. Tranches V, B, C, and Z are the PAC bonds, and tranche S is the support bond. The VADM bond is tranche V, and the accrual bond from which the interest will be used to pay down the VADM is tranche Z. The PAC bonds are created with a PAC band of 90 to 300 PSA. The corresponding mortgage balances for selected months for each PAC tranche if the prepayment speed is between 90 and 300 PSA are shown in Exhibit 16. The final maturity for the VADM can be seen to be 7 years (84 months).

Exhibit 13: FAF-06 CMO Sequential-Pay Structure with a VADM

Tranche	Par amount	Coupon rate (%)
V (VADM)	$77,000,000	7.5
B	88,000,000	7.5
C	165,000,000	7.5
Z (Accrual)	70,000,000	7.5
Total	$400,000,000	

Payment rules:

1. *For payment of periodic coupon interest:* Disburse periodic coupon interest to tranches V, B, and C based on the amount of principal outstanding at the beginning of the period. The interest earned by tranche Z is to be paid to tranche V as a pay down of principal and accrued as interest to tranche Z.
2. *For disbursement of principal payments:* Disburse principal payments to tranche V until it is completely paid off. The interest from tranche Z is to be paid to tranche V as a pay down of principal. After tranche V is completely paid off, disburse principal payments to tranche B until it is completely paid off. After tranche B is completely paid off, disburse principal payments to tranche C until it is completely paid off. After tranche C is completely paid off, disburse principal payments to tranche Z until the original mortgage balance plus accrued interest is completely paid off.

Exhibit 14: Mortgage Balance for Months 1–31 for FAF-06 Assuming 165 PSA

	Tranche			
Month	V (VADM)	B	C	Z (Accrual)
1	77,000,000	88,000,000	165,000,000	70,000,000
2	75,852,577	88,000,000	165,000,000	70,437,500
3	74,590,446	88,000,000	165,000,000	70,877,734
4	73,213,901	88,000,000	165,000,000	71,320,720
5	71,723,325	88,000,000	165,000,000	71,766,475
6	70,119,198	88,000,000	165,000,000	72,215,015
7	68,402,095	88,000,000	165,000,000	72,666,359
8	66,572,684	88,000,000	165,000,000	73,120,524
9	64,631,727	88,000,000	165,000,000	73,577,527
10	62,580,078	88,000,000	165,000,000	74,037,387
11	60,418,685	88,000,000	165,000,000	74,500,120
12	58,148,586	88,000,000	165,000,000	74,965,746
27	12,024,369	88,000,000	165,000,000	82,309,747
28	8,225,769	88,000,000	165,000,000	82,824,183
29	4,452,903	88,000,000	165,000,000	83,341,834
30	705,500	88,000,000	165,000,000	83,862,721
31	0	84,983,291	165,000,000	84,386,863

Exhibit 17 shows the same information assuming no prepayments (i.e., 0 PSA). As can be seen from this exhibit, the VADM has a final maturity of 7 years if no prepayments are made. If the prepayment speed is outside the upper PAC band, the VADM's final maturity will be less than 7 years. The average life for all five tranches assuming a wide range of prepayment scenarios is shown in Exhibit 18. Note the stability of the average life of the VADM bond.

Exhibit 15: FAF-07 CMO PAC Structure with a VADM

Tranche	Par amount	Coupon rate (%)
V (VADM)	$75,000,000	7.5
B	92,800,000	7.5
C	10,000,000	7.5
Z (Accrual)	66,000,000	7.5
S	156,200,000	7.5
Total	$400,000,000	

Payment rules:

1. *For payment of periodic coupon interest:* Disburse periodic coupon interest to tranches V, B, C, and S on the basis of the amount of principal outstanding at the beginning of the period. The interest earned by tranche Z is to be paid to tranche V as a pay down of principal and accrued as interest to tranche Z.

2. *For disbursement of principal payments:* Disburse principal payments to tranches V, B, C, and Z based on their respective schedules of principal repayments. Tranches V, B, C, and Z have priority with respect to current and future principal payments to satisfy the schedule. Any excess principal payments in a month over the amount necessary to satisfy the schedule for tranche V are paid to tranche S. Once tranche V is completely paid off, tranche B has priority, then tranche C, etc. When tranche S is completely paid off, all principal payments are to be made to the remaining classes with a schedule in order of priority regardless of the schedule.

Exhibit 16: Mortgage Balance for Selected Months for FAF-07 Assuming 90 to 300 PSA

	Tranche			
Month	V (VADM)	B	C	Z (Accrual)
1	75,000,000	92,800,000	10,000,000	66,000,000
2	74,319,965	92,559,365	10,000,000	66,412,500
3	73,635,541	92,258,868	10,000,000	66,827,578
4	72,946,698	91,898,661	10,000,000	67,245,250
5	72,253,409	91,478,925	10,000,000	67,665,533
6	71,555,645	90,999,871	10,000,000	68,088,443
7	70,853,377	90,461,736	10,000,000	68,513,996
8	70,146,575	89,864,789	10,000,000	68,942,208
9	69,435,211	89,209,324	10,000,000	69,373,097
10	68,719,255	88,495,666	10,000,000	69,806,679
11	67,998,676	87,724,168	10,000,000	70,242,971
12	67,273,447	86,895,209	10,000,000	70,681,989
71	15,059,365	4,060,751	10,000,000	102,083,716
72	13,992,276	2,837,012	10,000,000	102,721,740
73	12,918,294	1,623,114	10,000,000	103,363,750
74	11,837,374	419,042	10,000,000	104,009,774
75	10,749,472	0	9,224,783	104,659,835
76	9,654,543	0	8,040,323	105,313,959
77	8,552,541	0	6,865,651	105,972,171
78	7,443,420	0	5,700,752	106,634,497
79	6,327,135	0	4,545,615	107,300,963

Exhibit 16 (Continued)

	Tranche			
Month	V (VADM)	B	C	Z (Accrual)
80	5,203,639	0	3,400,228	107,971,594
81	4,072,884	0	2,264,578	108,646,416
82	2,934,825	0	1,138,655	109,325,456
83	1,789,415	0	22,447	110,008,740
84	636,604	0	0	109,612,237
85	0	0	0	108,683,625
86	0	0	0	107,124,919
87	0	0	0	105,572,694
345	0	0	0	55,873
346	0	0	0	42,272
347	0	0	0	29,003
348	0	0	0	16,059
349	0	0	0	3,432
350	0	0	0	0

Exhibit 17: Mortgage Balance for Selected Months for FAF-07 Assuming No Prepayments (0 PSA)

	Tranche			
Month	V (VADM)	B	C	Z (Accrual)
1	75,000,000	92,800,000	10,000,000	66,000,000
2	74,319,965	92,800,000	10,000,000	66,412,500
3	73,635,541	92,800,000	10,000,000	66,827,578
4	72,946,698	92,800,000	10,000,000	67,245,250
5	72,253,409	92,800,000	10,000,000	67,665,533
6	71,555,645	92,800,000	10,000,000	68,088,443
7	70,853,377	92,800,000	10,000,000	68,513,996
8	70,146,575	92,800,000	10,000,000	68,942,208
9	69,435,211	92,800,000	10,000,000	69,373,097
10	68,719,255	92,800,000	10,000,000	69,806,679
11	67,998,676	92,800,000	10,000,000	70,242,971
12	67,273,447	92,800,000	10,000,000	70,681,989
80	5,203,639	92,800,000	10,000,000	107,971,594
81	4,072,884	92,800,000	10,000,000	108,646,416
82	2,934,825	92,800,000	10,000,000	109,325,456
83	1,789,415	92,800,000	10,000,000	110,008,740
84	636,604	92,800,000	10,000,000	110,696,295
85	0	92,276,346	10,000,000	111,388,147
86	0	91,108,593	10,000,000	112,084,323

Exhibit 17 (Continued)

	Tranche			
Month	V (VADM)	B	C	Z (Accrual)
146	0	5,302,864	10,000,000	162,891,520
147	0	3,573,053	10,000,000	163,909,592
148	0	1,832,059	10,000,000	164,934,027
149	0	79,811	10,000,000	165,964,864
150	0	0	8,316,236	167,002,145
151	0	0	6,541,260	168,045,908
152	0	0	4,754,809	169,096,195
153	0	0	2,956,810	170,153,046
154	0	0	1,147,188	171,216,503
155	0	0	0	171,612,472
156	0	0	0	170,856,168
157	0	0	0	170,094,742
158	0	0	0	169,328,161
346	0	0	0	42,272
347	0	0	0	29,003
348	0	0	0	16,059
349	0	0	0	3,432
350	0	0	0	0

Exhibit 18: Average Life of Each Tranche of FAF-07 Assuming 0 to 700 PSA

	Average Life				
PSA	V	B	C	Z	S
0	3.83	9.88	12.61	19.52	27.26
50	3.83	5.10	8.59	13.80	24.00
90	3.83	3.35	6.51	11.54	20.06
100	3.83	3.35	6.51	11.54	18.56
150	3.83	3.35	6.51	11.54	12.57
165	3.83	3.35	6.51	11.54	11.16
200	3.83	3.35	6.51	11.54	8.38
250	3.83	3.35	6.51	11.54	5.37
300	3.83	3.35	6.51	11.54	3.13
350	3.60	3.41	6.26	10.27	2.51
400	3.26	3.39	5.70	9.24	2.17
450	2.98	3.30	5.24	8.38	1.94
500	2.74	3.19	4.85	7.65	1.77
700	2.16	2.71	3.76	5.64	1.37

Exhibit 19: FAF-08 A Hypothetical Five-Tranche Sequential-Pay with an Accrual Tranche, an Interest-Only Tranche, and a Residual Class

Tranche	Par amount	Coupon rate (%)
A	$194,500,000	6.00
B	36,000,000	6.50
C	96,500,000	7.00
Z	73,000,000	7.25
IO	52,566,667 (Notional)	7.50
Total	$400,000,000	

Payment rules:

1. *For payment of periodic coupon interest:* Disburse periodic coupon interest to tranches A, B, and C on the basis of the amount of principal outstanding at the beginning of the period. For tranche Z, accrue the interest based on the principal plus accrued interest in the previous period. The interest for tranche Z is to be paid to the earlier tranches as a principal pay down. Disburse periodic interest to the IO tranche based on the notional amount at the beginning of the period.
2. *For disbursement of principal payments:* Disburse principal payments to tranche A until it is completely paid off. After tranche A is completely paid off, disburse principal payments to tranche B until it is completely paid off. After tranche B is completely paid off, disburse principal payments to tranche C until it is completely paid off. After tranche C is completely paid off, disburse principal payments to tranche Z until the original principal balance plus accrued interest is completely paid off.
3. *No principal is to be paid to the IO tranche:* The notional amount of the IO tranche declines based on the principal payments to all other tranches.

Notional IOs

In our previous illustrations, we used a CMO structure in which all the tranches have the same coupon rate (7.5%) and that coupon rate is the same as the collateral. In practice, the same coupon rate would not be given to each tranche. Instead, the coupon rate would depend on the term structure of interest rates and the average life of the tranche, among other things.

In the earlier CMO deals, all of the excess interest between the coupon rate on the tranches and the coupon interest on the collateral was paid to an equity class referred to as the *CMO residual.* This is no longer the practice today. Instead, a tranche is created that receives the excess coupon interest. This tranche is called a *notional interest-only class*, *notional IO* or *structured IO.*

To see how a notional IO is created, consider the CMO structure shown in Exhibit 19, FAF-08. This is the same structure as FAF-02 except that the coupon rate varies by tranche and there is a class denoted "IO," which is the class of interest to us.

Notice that for this structure the par amount for the IO class is shown as $52,566,667, and the coupon rate is 7.5%. Since this is an IO class there is no par amount. The amount shown is the amount upon which the interest payments will be determined, not the amount that will be paid to the holder of this bond. Therefore, it is called a *notional amount.*

Let's look at how the notional amount is determined. Consider first tranche A. The par value is $194.5 million and the coupon rate is 6%. Since the collateral's coupon rate is 7.5%, the excess interest is 150 basis points (1.5%). Therefore, an IO with a 1.5% coupon rate and a notional amount of $194.5 million can be created from tranche A. But this is equivalent to an IO with a notional amount of $38.9 million and a coupon rate of 7.5%. Mathematically, this notional amount is found as follows:

$$\text{Notional amount for 7.5\% IO} = \frac{\text{Tranche's par value} \times \text{Excess interest}}{0.075}$$

where

$$\text{Excess interest} = \text{Collateral coupon rate} - \text{Tranche coupon rate}$$

For example, for tranche A:

$$\text{Excess interest} = 0.075 - 0.060 = 0.015$$

$$\text{Tranche's par value} = \$194{,}500{,}000$$

$$\text{Notional amount for 7.5\% IO} = \frac{\$194{,}500{,}000 \times 0.015}{0.075} = \$38{,}900{,}000$$

Similarly, from tranche B with a par value of $36 million, the excess interest is 100 basis points (1%), and therefore an IO with a coupon rate of 1% and a notional amount of $36 million can be created. But this is equivalent to creating an IO with a notional amount of $4.8 million and a coupon rate of 7.5%. This procedure is shown below for all four tranches:

Tranche	Par amount	Excess interest (%)	Notional amount for a 7.5% coupon rate IO
A	$194,500,000	1.50	$38,900,000
B	36,000,000	1.00	4,800,000
C	96,500,000	0.50	6,433,333
Z	73,000,000	0.25	2,433,334
	Notional amount for 7.5% IO		$52,566,667

Support Bonds

The support bonds—or bodyguards—are the bonds that provide prepayment protection for the PAC tranches. *Consequently, support tranches expose investors to the greatest level of prepayment risk.* Because of this, investors must be particularly careful in assessing the cash flow characteristics of support bonds to reduce the likelihood of adverse portfolio consequences due to prepayments.

The support bond typically is divided into different bond classes. All the bond classes we have discussed earlier are available, including sequential-pay support bond classes, floater and inverse floater support bond classes, and accrual support bond classes.

Exhibit 20: FAF-09 CMO Structure with a PAC I Bond, a PAC II Bond, and a Support Bond Class without a Principal Repayment Schedule

Initial PAC collar for the PAC I: 90 PSA to 300 PSA
Initial PAC collar for the PAC II: 100 PSA to 225 PSA

Tranche	Par amount ($)	Coupon rate (%)
P-I (PAC I)	$243,800,000	7.50
P-II (PAC II)	50,330,000	7.50
S	105,870,000	7.50
Total	$400,000,000	

Payment rules:

1. *For payment of periodic coupon interest:* Disburse periodic coupon interest to each tranche based on the amount of principal outstanding at the beginning of the period.
2. *For disbursement of principal payments:* Disburse principal payments to tranche P-I based on its schedule of principal repayments. Tranche P-I has priority with respect to current and future principal payments to satisfy the schedule. Any excess principal payments in a month over the amount necessary to satisfy the schedule for tranche P-I are paid to tranches P-II and S. Priority is given to tranche P-II to satisfy its schedule of principal repayments. Any excess principal payments in a month are paid to tranche S. When tranche S is completely paid off its original balance, then any excess is to be paid to tranche P-II regardless of its schedule. After tranche P-II is completely paid off its original mortgage balance, any excess is paid to tranche P-I regardless of its schedule.

The support bond can even be partitioned to create support bond classes with a schedule of principal payments. That is, support bond classes that are PAC bonds can be created. In a structure with a PAC bond and a support bond with a PAC schedule of principal payments, the former is called a *PAC I bond* or *Level I PAC bond* and the latter a *PAC II bond* or *Level II PAC bond*. While PAC II bonds have greater prepayment protection than the support bond classes without a schedule of principal repayments, the prepayment protection is less than that provided PAC I bonds.

To illustrate this concept, the CMO structure shown in Exhibit 20 was created, FAF-09, for the par amounts shown. There is the same PAC bond as in FAF-04 with an initial PAC collar of 90 PSA to 300 PSA. That bond is now labeled P-I, and it is called a PAC I. The support bond in FAF-04 has been split into a support bond with a schedule, labeled P-II, and a support bond without a schedule, labeled S. P-II is a PAC II bond that was created with an initial PAC collar of 100 PSA to 225 PSA.

Exhibit 21 indicates the average life for all the bond classes in FAF-09 under various prepayment scenarios. Also shown in the exhibit is the average life for the support bond in FAF-04. The PAC I enjoys the same prepayment protection in the structure with a PAC II as it does in the structure without a PAC II. The PAC II has considerably more average life variability than the PAC I but less variability than the support bond class S. Comparison of the support bond class S in FAF-09 with the support bond in FAF-04 shows that the presence of a PAC II increases the average life variability. Now the support bond class is providing protection for not only a PAC I but also a support bond with a schedule.

Exhibit 21: Average Life for FAF-09 for Various Assumed Prepayment Rates

Prepayment	Average life			
rate	PAC I bond	PAC II bond	Bond S	Support bond in FAF-04
0	15.973	25.44	28.13	27.26
50	9.44	20.32	25.77	24.00
90	7.26	15.69	22.14	20.06
100	7.26	13.77	20.84	18.56
150	7.26	13.77	12.00	12.57
165	7.26	13.77	9.91	11.16
200	7.26	13.77	5.82	8.38
225	7.26	13.77	3.42	6.75
250	7.26	10.75	2.81	5.37
300	7.26	5.07	2.20	3.13
350	6.56	3.85	1.88	2.51
400	5.92	3.24	1.66	2.17
450	5.38	2.85	1.51	1.94
500	4.93	2.58	1.39	1.77
700	3.70	1.99	1.08	1.37

There is more that can be done with the PAC II bond. A series of PAC IIs can be created just as we did with the PACs in FAF-05. PAC IIs can also be used to create any other type of bond class, such as a PAC II inverse floater or accrual bond, for example.

The support bond without a principal repayment schedule can be used to create any type of bond class. In fact, a portion of the non-PAC II support bond can be given a schedule of principal repayments. This bond class would be called a *PAC III bond* or a *Level III PAC bond.* While it provides protection against prepayments for the PAC I and PAC II bonds and is therefore subject to considerable prepayment risk, such a bond class has greater protection than the support bond class without a schedule of principal repayments.

TAX CONSIDERATIONS IN CMO STRUCTURING

The issuer of a CMO wants to be sure that the trust created to pass through the interest and principal payments is not treated as a taxable entity. A provision of the Tax Reform Act of 1986, called the Real Estate Mortgage Investment Conduit (REMIC), specifies the requirements that an issuer must fulfill so that the legal entity created to issue a CMO is not taxable. Most CMOs today are created as REMICs. While it is common to hear market participants refer to a CMO as a REMIC, not all CMOs are REMICs.

Since 1993, a good number of CMO deals were created whose underlying collateral are tranches from existing CMOs. These deals are called *re-REMICs* because

they use parts of previously issued REMICs to create another REMIC. Through the first three quarters of 1996, about 25% of the CMO deals that were issued were re-REMICs.

YIELD STRUCTURE

The cash flow yield for a CMO is calculated in the same way as that for a mortgage passthrough security. Consequently, the cash flow yield depends on the prepayment speed assumed.

The offered yield on a particular CMO tranche depends on the market's perceived prepayment risk for that tranche. For a given CMO deal, a PAC tranche would be offered at a lower yield than that of a support bond. In a PAC I/PAC II/support without a schedule CMO deal, the PAC II would be offered at a yield that is greater than the PAC I but less than the support bond without a schedule.

Exhibit 22 shows information on PACs and sequential-pay CMO tranches in the secondary market and on new issues on July 14, 2001, as reported by Lehman Brothers. For each tranche, the coupon rate, collateral, price, average life, zero-volatility spread (ZV), option-adjusted spread (OAS), option-adjusted duration (OAD), and option-adjusted spread duration (OAS Spr Dur) are reported. The effective PAC bands are shown for the PAC tranches (Effect. Bands). The spread measure shown in the column "Spread(bp)@PSA" is the nominal spread based on the cash flow yield where the cash flow yield is computed based on the prepayment speed indicated after the right-most slash in the column.

Exhibit 22: Spreads and Other Measures for PAC and Sequential-Pay CMOs

(Based on prices as of 7/12/01)

Mty	Security	Cpn	Collat.	Effect. Bands	Spread(bp) @PSA	Price	Avg Life	Option-Adjusted Analysis			
								ZV	OAS	OAD	OAS SprDur
Secondary CMOs											
PACS:											
2-YR	FHR-2081 PA	6.00	FH30 6.5s	132-274	+100/c/180	101-21+	1.9	66	52	1.5	1.7
4-YR	FHR-2081 PH	6.00	FH30 6.5s	132-274	+107/c/180	101-23+	3.1	82	63	2.3	2.7
6-YR	FHR-2081 PB	6.25	FH30 6.5s	164-254	+120/c/180	101-11+	5.1	108	73	3.4	4.0
9-YR	FHR-2081 PC	6.25	FH30 6.5s	158-251	+138/c/180	99-05	8.1	118	73	4.6	5.7
20-YR	FHR-2081 PD	6.50	FH30 6.5s		+121/30yr/175	97-10+	14.6	119	84	6.8	7.9
SEQUENTIALS:											
4.6-YR	FHR-2056 AC	6.00	FH30 6.0s		+145/c/160	100-09	3.8	102	66	3.0	3.0
12-YR	FHR-2056 B	6.00	FH30 6.0s		+143/c/160	96-18+	8.9	111	70	6.5	6.0
20-YR	FHR-2046 C	6.00	FH30 6.0s		+118/30yr/163	93-19	12.9	118	88	7.8	7.4
4-YR	FHR-2083 A	6.50	FH30 6.5s		+165/c/180	101-15	3.0	124	79	2.0	2.3
10-YR	FNR98-40 B	6.50	FN30 6.5s		+160/c/180	99-27+	7.2	136	81	5.3	4.9
20-YR	FNR98-40 D	6.50	FN30 6.5s		+131/30yr/180	96-11+	15.1	124	78	7.8	7.5
New Issue CMOs											
PACs:											
2-YR	FH65PACRES P2	6.00	FH30 6.5s	100-295	+108/c/181	101-22+	2.9	81	63	2.1	2.5
5-YR	FH65PACRES P5	6.00	FH30 6.5s	100-255	+120/c/181	99-30	5.9	107	73	3.7	4.4
8-YR	FH65PACRES P8	6.50	FH30 6.5s	100-245	+142/c/181	99-31	8.9	123	79	4.5	5.7
11-YR	FH65PACRES P11	6.50	FH30 6.5s	95-245	+144/c/181	98-22+	11.9	114	71	5.6	6.9
20-YR	FH65PACRES P20	6.50	FH30 6.5s	90-245	+121/30yr/181	97-03	17.2	112	74	7.4	8.4
SEQUENTIALS:											
2-YR	FH65SEQRES C2	6.00	FH30 6.5s		+150/c/181	100-18+	3.0	113	71	2.2	2.2
6-YR	FH65SEQRES C6	6.50	FH30 6.5s		+160/c/181	100-01	6.9	133	75	5.4	4.7
8-YR	FH65SEQRES C8	6.50	FH30 6.5s		+163/c/181	98-19	8.9	130	73	6.7	5.6
10-YR	FH65SEQRES C10	6.50	FH30 6.5s		+160/c/181	97-23	10.9	123	67	7.3	6.2
20-YR	FH65SEQRES C20	6.50	FH30 6.5s		+131/30yr/181	96-02	18.0	118	67	8.3	8.0

Source: Adapted from Lehman Brothers, "Secondary CMOs," *MBS & ABS Weekly Outlook*, Fixed Income Research, July 14, 2001.

KEY POINTS

- ❑ *Collateralized mortgage obligations are bond classes created by redirecting the cash flows of passthroughs.*
- ❑ *The creation of a CMO cannot eliminate prepayment risk; it can only transfer the various forms of this risk (contraction and extension) among different classes of bonds called tranches.*
- ❑ *In a CMO there are rules for the distribution of interest and principal from the collateral to the bond classes.*
- ❑ *CMOs are also called paythroughs and multiclass passthroughs.*
- ❑ *An agency CMO is one that is issued by Fannie Mae, Freddie Mac, or Ginnie Mae.*
- ❑ *In a sequential-pay CMO structure the tranches are retired in sequence.*
- ❑ *The principal pay down window for a tranche is the time period between the beginning and the ending of the principal payments to that tranche.*
- ❑ *An accrual bond is one in which the interest for that tranche accrues and is added to the principal balance.*
- ❑ *A floating-rate tranche is created from a fixed-rate tranche, and, unlike a floating-rate note whose principal is unchanged over the life of the instrument, the floater tranche's principal balance declines over time as principal payments are made.*
- ❑ *A floating-rate CMO tranche has a cap.*
- ❑ *An inverse floater is a tranche that has a coupon rate that changes every month in the opposite direction of the change in the reference rate.*
- ❑ *A planned amortization class (PAC) bond has a principal schedule that must be met monthly before any other tranche in the structure may receive principal payments.*
- ❑ *A planned amortization class tranche has reduced average life variability, the better prepayment protection provided by the support tranches.*
- ❑ *If the support bonds of a CMO structure are fully paid off, the PAC bonds no longer have prepayment protection.*
- ❑ *An effective collar for a PAC is the lower and the upper PSA that can occur in the future and still allow maintenance of the schedule of principal payments.*
- ❑ *The effective collar for a PAC differs from its initial collar as the amount of the support bonds change over time.*
- ❑ *Most CMO PAC structures have more than one class of PAC bonds.*

- ❑ *A reverse PAC structure is one in which any excess principal payments are made to the longer PAC bonds after all support bonds are paid off.*
- ❑ *A targeted amortization class (TAC) bond has a schedule of principal payments that provides protection against contraction risk but not against extension risk.*
- ❑ *A reverse TAC bond has a schedule of principal payments that provides protection against extension risk but not against contraction risk.*
- ❑ *A very accurately determined maturity (VADM) bond provides protection against extension risk.*
- ❑ *The key role of support bonds in a CMO structure is to provide prepayment protection for the PAC tranches.*
- ❑ *A notional IO is created by stripping the excess coupon interest from one or more tranches.*
- ❑ *Support bonds expose investors to the greatest level of prepayment risk.*
- ❑ *Support bonds can be partitioned to create support bond classes with a schedule of principal payments.*
- ❑ *While support bonds with a schedule have greater prepayment protection than support bond classes without a schedule of principal payments, the prepayment protection is less than that provided by PAC I bonds.*
- ❑ *A REMIC is tax election for a CMO structure to obtain favorable tax treatment.*
- ❑ *A re-REMIC is a CMO structure in which the underlying collateral is tranches from other REMIC deals.*
- ❑ *A cash flow yield can be calculated for a CMO tranche.*
- ❑ *Dealers report generic spreads for PAC bonds and sequential-pay bonds by average life.*

Chapter 11

Nonagency Mortgage-Backed Securities

In the previous two chapters, we looked at agency mortgage-backed securities (MBSs) in which the underlying mortgages are 1- to 4-single-family residential mortgages. The mortgage-backed securities market includes other types of securities. These securities are called *nonagency mortgage-backed securities* (referred to as *nonagency securities* hereafter). The underlying mortgage loans for nonagency securities can be for any type of real estate property. There are securities backed by 1- to 4-single-family residential mortgages with a first lien on the mortgaged property. There are nonagency securities backed by other types of single family residential loans. These include home equity loan-backed securities and manufactured housing loan-backed securities. Commercial mortgage-backed securities are nonagency securities in which the underlying collateral is a pool of commercial mortgage loans. Commercial mortgage loans include loans for apartment buildings (multifamily housing), shopping centers, office buildings, warehouses, hotels, and nursing homes.

Our focus in this chapter is on nonagency securities in which the underlying loans are first-lien mortgages for 1- to 4-single-family residential properties. In the next chapter, we focus on asset-backed securities. In that chapter we look at nonagency securities in which other residential mortgage loans are the underlying collateral, as well as securities backed by commercial real estate loans.

COLLATERAL FOR NONAGENCY MBS

Mortgage loans used as collateral for an agency security are *conforming loans*. That is, they must meet the underwriting standards of the agency. The collateral for a nonagency MBS consists of *nonconforming loans* (i.e., loans that do not conform to the underwriting standards of the agency). A loan may be nonconforming for one or more of the following reasons:

1. The mortgage balance exceeds the amount permitted by the agency.
2. The borrower characteristics fail to meet the underwriting standards established by the agency.
3. The loan characteristics fail to meet the underwriting standards established by the agency.

4. The applicant fails to provide full documentation as required by the agency.

There are alternative lending programs for borrowers seeking nonconforming loans for any of the aforementioned reasons.

A mortgage loan that is nonconforming merely because the mortgage balance exceeds the maximum permitted by the agency guideline is called a *jumbo loan.*

With respect to the characteristics of the borrower, a loan may fail to qualify because the borrower's credit history does not meet the underwriting standards or the payment-to-income (PTI) ratio exceeds the maximum permitted. Borrowers who do satisfy the underwriting standards with respect to borrower characteristics are referred to as *A credit borrowers* or *prime borrowers*. *Alternative A loans* (Alt-A loans) are made to borrowers whose qualifying mortgage characteristics do not conform to the underwriting criteria established by the agencies but whose borrower characteristics do. For instance, the borrower may be self-employed and may not be able to provide all the necessary documentation for income verification. In such respects, Alt-A loans allow reduced or alternate forms of documentation to qualify for the loan. An Alt-A loan borrower, however, should not be confused with borrowers with blemished credits (discussed next). The typical Alt-A borrower will have an excellent credit rating—referred to as an "A" rating, and hence the loan is referred to as an Alt-A loan—which is especially important to the originator since the credit quality of the borrower must compensate for the lack of other necessary documentation. What is appealing to borrowers about the Alt-A program is the flexibility that the program offers in terms of documentation, and borrowers are willing to pay a premium for the privilege. Typically, rates on Alt-A loans range between 75 to 125 basis points above the rate on otherwise comparable standard mortgage rates.

B and C borrowers or *subprime borrowers* are borrowers who fail to satisfy the underwriting standards of the agencies because of borrower characteristics. These characteristics include credit history and maximum PTI. Borrowers who apply for subprime loans vary from those who have or had credit problems due to difficulties in repayment of debt brought on by an adverse event, such as job loss or medical emergencies, to those that continue to mismanage their debt and finances. The distinguishing feature of a subprime mortgage is that the potential universe of subprime mortgagors can be divided into various risk grades, ranging from B through D. The risk gradation is a function of past credit history and the magnitude of credit blemishes existing in the history. (The loans are actually scaled by originators from B to D. Every originator establishes its own profiles for classifying a loan into a risk category.) Additionally, some of the higher grades in this loan category have also been labeled as "fallen angels" to indicate the fact that the creditworthiness of such borrowers was hampered by a life event, such as job loss or illness. Since such borrowers tend to pose greater credit risk, subprime mortgages command a pricing premium over standard mortgages.

A characteristic that may result in a loan failing to meet the underwriting standards is that the loan-to-value (LTV) ratio exceeds the maximum established by the agency or the loan is not a first-mortgage lien. There are lenders who specialize in loans that exceed the maximum LTV. These lending programs are sometimes referred to as *high LTV* or *125 LTV* programs because the lender may be willing to lend up to 125% of the appraised or market value of the property. Basically, the lender is making a consumer loan based on the credit of the borrower to the extent that the loan amount exceeds the appraised or market value. For this reason, lenders with high LTV programs have limited these loans to A credit borrowers. Mortgage-related products in which the underlying loans are 125 LTV loans are considered part of the ABS market and are discussed in the next chapter.

There are deals in which the underlying collateral is mixed with various types of mortgage-related loans. That is, the collateral backing a deal may include collateral that is a combination of first-lien mortgages, home equity loans, manufactured housing loans, and home improvement loans. The Securities Data Corporation (SDC) has established criteria for classifying a mortgage product with mixed collateral as either a "nonagency MBS" or an "asset-backed security" (ABS), which we discuss in the next chapter. The purpose of the classification is not to aid in the analysis of these securities, but rather to construct the so-called league tables for ranking investment banking firms by deal type. The SDC's rules for classifying a deal as either a nonagency MBS or an ABS are as follows. If at issuance more than 50% of a deal consists of either manufactured housing loans, home equity loans, second mortgage loans, or home improvement loans, then the deal is classified as an ABS. For deals in which more than 50% of the loans are first liens, the SDC uses a size test to classify the deal. If more than 50% of the aggregate principal balance of the loans have a loan balance of more than $200,000, the deal is classified as a nonagency MBS. A deal in which 50% of the loans are first liens, but more than 50% of the aggregate principal balance of the loans is less than $200,000, is classified as an ABS.

DIFFERENCES BETWEEN AGENCY AND NONAGENCY SECURITIES

Nonagency securities can be either passthroughs or CMOs. In the agency market, CMOs are created from pools of passthrough securities. In the nonagency market, a CMO can be created from either a pool of passthroughs or unsecuritized mortgage loans. It is uncommon for nonconforming mortgage loans to be securitized as passthroughs and then the passthroughs carved up to create a CMO. Instead, in the nonagency market a CMO is typically carved out of mortgage loans that have not been securitized as passthroughs. Since a mortgage loan is commonly referred to as a "whole loan," nonagency CMOs are also referred to as *whole-loan CMOs*.

The major differences between agency and nonagency securities have to do with guarantees, servicer advances, and compensating interest. We discuss each as follows.

Guarantees

With a nonagency security there is no explicit or implicit government guarantee of payment of interest and principal as there is with an agency security. The absence of any such guarantee means that the investor in a nonagency security is exposed to credit risk. The nationally recognized statistical rating organizations rate nonagency securities.

Servicer Advances

When there is a delinquency by the homeowner, the investor in a nonagency security may or may not be affected. This depends on whether a servicer is required to make advances. Thus, the financial capacity of the servicer to make advances is critical. Typically, a backup servicer is used just in case the master servicer cannot meet its obligation with respect to advances. The servicer recovers advances when delinquent payments are made or the property is foreclosed and proceeds received.

There are three different forms of advancing: (1) mandatory advancing, (2) optional advancing, and (3) limited advancing. The strongest form from the investor's perspective is *mandatory advancing*, wherein failure to advance by a servicer is an event of default. However, a servicer need not advance if it can show that there is not a strong likelihood of recovery of the amount advanced when the property is ultimately disposed of. In an *optional* or a *voluntary advancing*, the servicer is not legally obligated to advance, so that failure to do so is not an event of default. In a *limited advancing*, the issuer is obligated to advance, but the amount it must advance is limited.

Compensating Interest

Mortgage passthroughs and CMOs pay principal and interest on a monthly basis. While homeowners may prepay their mortgage on any day throughout the month, the agencies guarantee and pay investors a full month of interest as if all the prepayments occur on the last day of the month. This guarantee does not apply to nonagency securities. For example, if a homeowner pays off a mortgage on the tenth day of the month, he or she will stop paying interest for the rest of the month. Because of the payment delay (e.g., 25 days), the investor will receive full principal but only 10 days of interest on the 25th of the following month.

This phenomenon is known as payment interest shortfall or *compensating interest* and is handled differently by each issuer. Some issuers will pay up to only a specified amount and some will not pay at all. Actually, it is the servicers who will pay any compensating interest. The servicer obtains the shortfall in interest from the servicing spread. The shortfall that will be made up to the investor may be limited to the entire servicing spread or part of the servicing spread.

Thus, while an investor has protection against the loss of a full month's interest, the protection is limited.

For a nonagency security in which there is compensating interest, typically prepayments of the entire outstanding balance are covered. Curtailments (i.e., partial prepayments) are not covered.

In an agency CMO and nonagency CMO, the interest is paid to each tranche on the basis of the distribution rules for interest. In a nonagency CMO, as explained as follows, there are tranches within credit classes. When there is a shortfall in the full month's interest, typically the shortfall is prorated among the credit classes based on the outstanding principal balance. Then, for each tranche within a credit class, the shortfall is prorated based on the interest that would be due.

In a nonagency CMO structure, the economic value of compensating interest depends on the speed of prepayment and the type of CMO tranche. Generally, the faster the prepayments and the higher the coupon for the tranche, the higher the economic value of compensating interest.

PREPAYMENTS

Dealers involved in the underwriting and market making of nonagency mortgage-backed securities have developed prepayment models for these loans. Several firms have found that the key difference between the prepayment behavior of borrowers of nonconforming mortgages and conforming mortgages is the important role played by the credit characteristics of the borrower.

Borrower characteristics and the seasoning process must be kept in mind when trying to assess prepayments for a particular deal. In the prospectus of an offering, a base-case prepayment assumption is made—the initial speed and the amount of time until the collateral is seasoned. Thus, the prepayment benchmark is issuer specific. The benchmark speed in the prospectus is called the *prospectus prepayment curve* or PPC. As with the PSA benchmark described in the previous chapter, slower or faster prepayment speeds are a multiple of the PPC. For example, the PPC for a particular nonagency deal might state the following:

> . . . a 100% Prepayment Assumption assumes conditional prepayment rates of 1.5% per annum of the then-outstanding principal balance of the mortgage loans in the first month of the life of the loans and an additional 0.5% per annum in each month thereafter until month 20. Beginning in month 20, 100% Prepayment Assumption assumes a conditional prepayment rate of 11% per annum each month.

For this deal, 100% PPC, 80% PPC, and 150% PPC would then be as follows for the first 20 months:

Month	100% PPC (%)	80% PPC (%)	150% PPC (%)
1	1.5	1.2	2.3
2	2.0	1.6	3.0
3	2.5	2.0	3.8
4	3.0	2.4	4.5
5	3.5	2.8	5.3
6	4.0	3.2	6.0
7	4.5	3.6	6.8
8	5.0	4.0	7.5
9	5.5	4.4	8.3
10	6.0	4.8	9.0
11	6.5	5.2	9.8
12	7.0	5.6	10.5
13	7.5	6.0	11.3
14	8.0	6.4	12.0
15	8.5	6.8	12.8
16	9.0	7.2	13.5
17	9.5	7.6	14.3
18	10.0	8.0	15.0
19	10.5	8.4	15.8
20	11.0	8.8	16.5

Unlike the PSA prepayment benchmark, the PPC is not generic. By this it is meant that the PPC is issuer specific. In contrast, the PSA prepayment benchmark applies to any type of collateral issued by an agency for any type of loan design. This feature of the PPC is important for an investor to keep in mind when comparing the prepayment characteristics and investment characteristics of the collateral between issuers and issues (new and seasoned).

PSA STANDARD DEFAULT ASSUMPTION BENCHMARK

With the increase in nonagency security issuance, a standardized benchmark for default rates was introduced by the then Public Securities Association (now called the Bond Market Association). The *PSA standard default assumption (SDA) benchmark* gives the annual default rate for a mortgage pool as a function of the seasoning of the mortgages. The PSA SDA benchmark, or 100 SDA, specifies the following:

1. The default rate in month 1 is 0.02% and increases by 0.02% up to month 30 so that in month 30 the default rate is 0.60%.
2. From month 30 to month 60, the default rate remains at 0.60%.
3. From month 61 to month 120, the default rate declines from 0.60% to 0.03%.
4. From month 120 on, the default rate remains constant at 0.03%.

As with the PSA prepayment benchmark, multiples of the benchmark are found by multiplying the default rate by the assumed multiple. A "0 SDA" means that no defaults are assumed.

CREDIT ENHANCEMENTS

All nonagency securities are credit enhanced. That means that credit support is provided for one or more bondholders in the structure. Typically a double A or triple A rating is sought for the most senior tranche in a deal. The amount of credit enhancement necessary depends on rating agency requirements and is referred to as "sizing" the transaction. There are two general types of credit enhancement structures: external and internal. We describe each type as follows.

External Credit Enhancements

External credit enhancements come in the form of third-party guarantees that provide for first loss protection against losses up to a specified level, for example, 10%. The most common forms of external credit enhancement are (1) a corporate guarantee, (2) a letter of credit, (3) pool insurance, and (4) bond insurance.

Pool insurance policies cover losses resulting from defaults and foreclosures. Policies are typically written for a dollar amount of coverage that continues in force throughout the life of the pool. However, some policies are written so that the dollar amount of coverage declines as the pool seasons as long as two conditions are met: (1) the credit performance is better than expected, and (2) the rating agencies that rated the issue approve. Since only defaults and foreclosures are covered, additional insurance must be obtained to cover losses resulting from bankruptcy (i.e., court-mandated modification of mortgage debt—"cramdown"), fraud arising in the origination process, and special hazards (i.e., losses resulting from events not covered by a standard homeowner's insurance policy).

Bond insurance provides the same function as in municipal bond structures. Typically, bond insurance is not used as the primary protection but to supplement other forms of credit enhancement.

A nonagency security with external credit support is subject to the credit risk of the third-party guarantor. If the third-party guarantor is downgraded, the issue itself could be subject to downgrade even if the structure is performing as expected.

External credit enhancements do not materially alter the cash flow characteristics of a CMO structure except in the form of prepayment. In case of a default resulting in net losses within the guarantee level, investors will receive the principal amount as if a prepayment has occurred. If the net losses exceed the guarantee level, investors will realize a shortfall in the cash flows.

Internal Credit Enhancements

Internal credit enhancements come in more complicated forms than external credit enhancements and may alter the cash flow characteristics of the loans even in the absence of default. The most common forms of internal credit enhancements are reserve funds, overcollateralization, and senior-subordinated structures.

Reserve Funds

Reserve funds come in two forms: cash reserve funds and excess servicing spread. *Cash reserve funds* are straight deposits of cash generated from issuance proceeds. In this case, part of the underwriting profits from the deal are deposited into a fund, which typically invests in money market instruments. Cash reserve funds are typically used in conjunction with some form of external credit enhancement.

Excess servicing spread accounts involve the allocation of excess spread or cash into a separate reserve account after paying out the net coupon, servicing fee, and all other expenses on a monthly basis. For example, suppose that the gross weighted average coupon (gross WAC) is 7.75%, the servicing and other fees are 0.25%, and the net weighted average coupon (net WAC) is 7.25%. This means that there is excess servicing of 0.25%. The amount in the reserve account will gradually increase and can be used to pay for possible future losses.

The excess servicing spread is analogous to the guarantee fee paid to the issuer of an agency mortgage-backed security except that this is a form of self-insurance. This form of credit enhancement relies on the assumption that defaults occur infrequently in the very early life of the loans but gradually increase in the following 2 to 5 years.

Overcollateralization

The total par value of the tranches is the liability of the structure. So, if a structure has two tranches with a par value of $300 million, then that is the amount of the liability. The amount of the collateral backing the structure must be at least equal to the amount of the liability. If the amount of the collateral exceeds the amount of the liability of the structure, the deal is said to be *overcollateralized*. The amount of overcollateralization represents a form of internal credit enhancement because it can be used to absorb losses. For example, if the liability of the structure is $300 million and the collateral's value is $320 million, then the structure is overcollateralized by $20 million. Thus, the first $20 million of losses will not result in a loss to any of the tranches.

Senior-Subordinated Structure

In a senior-subordinated structure there is a *senior tranche* and at least one *junior* or *subordinated tranche*. For example, suppose a deal has $300 million as collateral (i.e., a pool of loans). The structure may look as follows:

senior tranche	$270 million
subordinated tranche	$ 30 million

This means that the first $30 million of losses are absorbed by the subordinated tranche.

There is no reason why there must be only one subordinated tranche. The structure can have more than one subordinated tranche. For example, the structure could be as follows:

senior tranche	\$270 million
subordinated tranche 1	\$22 million
subordinated tranche 2	\$8 million

In this structure, the subordinated tranches 1 and 2 are called the *nonsenior tranches*. The senior tranche still has protection up to \$30 million as in the previous structure with only one subordinated tranche. In the second structure, the first \$8 million of losses is absorbed by the subordinated tranche 2. Hence, this tranche is referred to as the *first-loss tranche*. Subordinated tranche 1 has protection of up to \$8 million in losses, the protection provided by the first-loss tranche.

Shifting Interest Mechanism The basic concern in the senior-subordinated structure is that while the subordinated tranches provide a certain level of credit protection for the senior tranche at the closing of the deal, the level of protection changes over time due to prepayments. The objective after the deal closes is to distribute any prepayments such that the credit protection for the senior tranche does not deteriorate over time.

There is a well-developed mechanism used to address this concern called the *shifting interest mechanism*. Here is how it works. The percentage of the principal balance of the subordinated tranche to that of the principal balance for the entire deal is called the *level of subordination* or the *subordinate interest*. The higher the percentage, the greater the level of protection for the senior tranches. The subordinate interest changes after the deal is closed due to prepayments. That is, the subordinate interest shifts (hence the term "shifting interest"). The purpose of a shifting interest mechanism is to allocate prepayments so that the subordinate interest is maintained at an acceptable level to protect the senior tranche. In effect, by paying down the senior tranche more quickly, the amount of subordination is maintained at the desired level.

The percentage of prepayments distributed to the senior tranche is determined as follows:

$$\text{Senior prepayment percentage} = \text{Senior interest} + \text{Shifting interest percentage} \times \text{Subordinate interest}$$

where

$$\text{Senior interest} = \frac{\text{Principal of senior tranches}}{\text{Principal of senior plus subordinate tranches}}$$

$$\text{Subordinate interest} = \frac{\text{Principal of subordinate tranches}}{\text{Principal of senior plus subordinate tranches}}$$

The prospectus will provide the shifting interest percentage schedule. A commonly used shifting interest percentage schedule is as follows:

Year after issuance	Shifting interest percentage
1-5	100
6	70
7	60
8	40
9	20
after year 9	0

The dollar amount of the prepayments allocated to the senior tranches is then

Prepayments × Senior prepayment percentage

To illustrate the calculation, suppose that the senior interest is 80% in some month and prepayments in that month are $1 million. Then we know that

Senior interest = 0.80
Subordinate interest = 1 – 0.80 = 0.20

Suppose further that the month in which prepayments are made is sometime in the first 5 years. In that case, assuming the above schedule for the shifting interest percentage,

Shifting interest percentage = 1.00

Then

Senior prepayment percentage = 0.80 + 1.00 × 0.20 = 1.00

That is, all of the prepayments ($1 million) are made to the senior tranche.

Suppose instead that the prepayment occurs in the seventh year after issuance, then

Shifting interest percentage = 0.60

and

Senior prepayment percentage = 0.80 + 0.60 × 0.20 = 0.92

Then the amount of prepayments distributed to the senior tranches is

$1,000,000 × 0.92 = $920,000

The balance of the prepayments, $80,000, is distributed to the subordinate tranches.

The shifting interest percentage schedule given in the prospectus is the "base" schedule. The schedule can change over time depending on the performance of the collateral. If the performance is such that the credit protection for the senior tranche has deteriorated because credit losses have reduced the subor-

dinated tranches, the base shifting interest percentage schedule is overridden and a higher percentage allocation of prepayments is made to the senior tranche.

Performance analysis of the collateral is undertaken by the trustee for determining whether to override the base schedule. The performance analysis is in terms of tests, and if the collateral fails any of the tests, this will trigger an override of the base schedule.

It is important to understand that the presence of a shifting interest mechanism results in a tradeoff between credit risk and contraction risk for the senior tranche. The shifting interest mechanism reduces the credit risk to the senior tranche. However, because the senior tranche receives a larger share of any prepayments, contraction risk increases.

NAS and PAC Tranches Tranches have been structured to give some senior tranches greater prepayment protection than other senior tranches. The two types of structures that do this are the planned amortization class (PAC) tranche discussed in the previous chapter and the *nonaccelerating senior* (NAS) tranche. An NAS tranche receives principal payments according to a schedule. The schedule is not a dollar amount. Rather, it is a principal schedule that shows for a given month the share of pro rata principal that must be distributed to the NAS tranche. A typical principal schedule for an NAS tranche is as follows:

Months	Share of pro rata principal (%)
1 through 36	0
37 through 60	45
61 through 72	80
73 through 84	100
After month 84	300

The average life for the NAS tranche is stable for a large range of prepayments because for the first 3 years all prepayments are made to the other senior tranches. This reduces the risk of the NAS tranche contracting (i.e., shortening) due to fast prepayments. After month 84, 300% of its pro rata share is paid to the NAS tranche, thereby reducing its extension risk.

YIELD SPREADS

Nonagency MBSs trade at a positive spread (as measured by the OAS) to a comparable agency MBS benchmark. This can be seen in Exhibit 1 as reported by Lehman Brothers for July 12, 2001. Agency passthroughs are shown as the benchmark. The OAS for the 30-year benchmark agency passthroughs is shown. The nonagency MBSs reported in the exhibit are backed by 30-year jumbo loans and 30-year Alternative-A loans. The OAS is shown along with the difference between the OAS of the benchmark agency passthrough and the OAS of the jumbo and Alternative-A deals.

Exhibit 1: Benchmark Nonagency Passthroughs

		30-Year Agency		30-Year Jumbo		30-Year Alternative-A	
Date	Coupon	10-Year	OAS	OAS	Diff*	OAS	Diff
8/31/00	7.75	5.73	108	120	12	128	20
9/7/00	7.75	5.76	109	120	11	128	19
9/14/00	7.75	5.79	101	113	12	121	20
9/21/00	7.75	5.88	95	109	14	116	21
9/28/00	7.75	5.82	91	106	15	114	23
10/5/00	7.50	5.86	92	106	14	115	23
10/12/00	7.50	5.81	97	113	16	121	24
10/19/00	7.50	5.66	87	108	21	115	28
10/26/00	7.50	5.68	87	108	21	114	27
11/2/00	7.50	5.74	86	106	20	113	27
11/9/00	7.50	5.81	88	107	19	115	27
11/16/00	7.50	5.67	89	111	22	117	28
11/24/00	7.50	5.63	94	115	21	120	26
11/30/00	7.50	5.63	98	120	22	123	25
12/7/00	7.25	5.31	76	97	21	108	32
12/14/00	7.25	5.18	82	112	30	118	36
12/21/00	7.00	5.03	80	110	30	118	38
12/28/00	7.00	5.12	83	112	29	120	37
1/4/01	7.00	5.02	72	109	37	115	43
1/11/01	7.00	5.13	67	99	32	108	41
1/18/01	7.00	5.10	76	107	31	116	40
1/25/01	7.00	5.27	73	100	27	109	36
2/1/01	7.00	5.08	69	96	27	103	34
2/8/01	7.00	5.10	83	104	21	113	30
2/15/01	7.00	5.19	82	102	20	114	32
2/22/01	7.00	5.15	86	107	21	118	32
3/1/01	6.75	4.86	83	99	16	103	20
3/8/01	6.75	4.89	85	96	11	100	15
3/15/01	6.75	4.89	83	101	18	106	23
3/22/01	6.50	4.71	78	94	16	101	23
3/29/01	6.50	4.97	84	99	15	106	22
4/5/01	6.50	4.98	82	95	13	102	20
4/11/01	6.50	5.11	76	95	19	102	26
4/19/01	6.50	5.25	70	86	16	95	25
4/26/01	6.50	5.19	77	91	14	102	25
5/3/01	6.50	5.20	70	92	22	102	32
5/10/01	6.75	5.28	73	100	27	105	32
5/17/01	6.75	5.44	64	88	24	100	36
5/24/01	6.75	5.50	64	86	22	98	34
5/31/01	6.75	5.40	69	92	23	102	33
6/7/01	6.75	5.30	69	90	21	101	32
6/14/01	6.75	5.22	71	93	22	107	36
6/21/01	6.75	5.19	76	98	22	110	34
6/28/01	6.75	5.33	82	100	18	111	29
7/5/01	6.75	5.42	75	93	18	105	30
7/12/01	6.75	5.24	75	94	19	104	29

*Difference to Agency OAS.

Source: Adapted from Lehman Brothers, *MBS & ABS Weekly Outlook,* Fixed Income Research, July 14, 2001.

Exhibit 2: Nonagency Spreads

Pricing Date: Jul-12-01

Benchmark Jumbo Spreads

Sector	PACs	SEQs	Subord. (10-yr) & NAS	
2-Yr.	115	183	NAS	167
3-Yr.	125	198		
4-Yr.	135	195	Aa	177
5-Yr.	145	195	A	197
7-Yr.	155	195	Baa	265
10-Yr.	165	195	Ba	540
30-Yr.	135	160		

Source: Adapted from Lehman Brothers, *MBS & ABS Weekly Outlook,* Fixed Income Research, July 14, 2001.

Exhibit 2 shows the benchmark jumbo spreads for various tranche types. Looking at the PAC and sequential-pay tranches, it can be seen that (1) with the exception of the 30-year sector, the spread increases with average life, and (2) sequential-pay tranches for a given sector have a higher spread than PACs. This second observation is due to the greater prepayment risk of sequential-pay tranches. Also shown in Exhibit 2 are the spreads based on subordinate tranches with different credit ratings.

KEY POINTS

- *Mortgage loans used as collateral for an agency security are conforming loans, which are loans that do meet the underwriting standards of the agency.*
- *The collateral for a nonagency MBS consists of nonconforming loans, which are loans that do not conform to the underwriting standards of the agency.*
- *There are alternative lending programs for nonconforming loans, which include jumbo loans, Alternative-A loans, high LTV loans, and subprime loans.*
- *Subprime borrowers are borrowers who fail to satisfy the underwriting standards of the agencies because of borrower characteristics.*
- *There are deals in which the underlying collateral is mixed with various types of mortgage-related loans, and the Securities Data Corporation (SDC) has established criteria for classifying a mortgage product with mixed collateral as either a nonagency MBS or an asset-backed security.*
- *Nonagency securities can be either passthroughs or CMOs.*
- *A nonagency security is exposed to credit risk because there is no explicit or implicit government guarantee of payment of interest and principal as there is with an agency security.*
- *Nonagency securities are rated by the rating agencies.*
- *There are various forms of advancing in the case of deliquencies: (1) mandatory advancing, (2) optional advancing, and (3) limited advancing.*
- *Unlike agency securities where the investor is guaranteed a full month of interest as if all prepayments occur on the last day of the month, this is not necessarily the case with nonagency securities; compensating interest refers to the compensation of the investor of a full month's interest regardless of when prepayments occur.*
- *Compensating interest is handled differently by each issuer.*
- *Prepayment rate benchmarks for nonagency securities are specific to issuers and are stated in the prospectus; these benchmarks are referred to as the prospectus prepayment curve (PPC).*
- *The PSA standard default assumption (SDA) benchmark gives the annual default rate for a mortgage pool as a function of the seasoning of the mortgages.*
- *All nonagency securities are credit enhanced.*
- *The amount of credit enhancement necessary to obtain a given rating depends on rating agency requirements and is referred to as "sizing" the transaction.*
- *There are two general types of credit enhancement structures: external and internal.*

- ❑ *External credit enhancements come in the form of third-party guarantees that provide for first-loss protection against losses up to a specified level and include a corporate guarantee, a letter of credit, pool insurance, and bond insurance.*
- ❑ *External credit enhancements do not materially alter the cash flow characteristics of a CMO structure except in the form of prepayments.*
- ❑ *Internal credit enhancements may alter the cash flow characteristics of the loans even in the absence of default.*
- ❑ *The most common forms of internal credit enhancements are reserve funds, overcollateralization, and senior-subordinated structures.*
- ❑ *Reserve funds come in two forms: cash reserve funds and excess servicing spread.*
- ❑ *Cash reserve funds are straight deposits of cash generated from issuance proceeds.*
- ❑ *In a senior-subordinated structure, there is a senior tranche and at least one junior or subordinated tranche.*
- ❑ *The basic concern in the senior-subordinated structure is that while the subordinated tranches provide a certain level of credit protection for the senior tranche at the closing of the deal, the level of protection changes over time due to prepayments.*
- ❑ *A shifting interest mechanism is used to prevent prepayments from reducing the credit protection provided by the subordinated tranches.*
- ❑ *While a shifting interest mechanism reduces credit risk for the senior tranches, because a larger share of any prepayments is paid to the senior tranches, contraction risk increases.*
- ❑ *Tranches have been structured to give some senior tranches greater prepayment protection than other senior tranches; the two types of structures are the planned amortization class (PAC) tranche and the nonaccelerating senior (NAS) tranche.*

Chapter 12

Asset-Backed Securities

While the securitization of residential mortgage loans is by far the largest type of asset that has been securitized, securities backed by other assets (consumer and business loans and receivables) have been securitized. The largest sectors of the asset-backed securities (ABS) market in the United States are securities backed by credit card receivables, auto loans, home equity loans, manufactured housing loans, commercial mortgage loans, student loans, Small Business Administration loans, and high-yield bonds and bank loans. Since home equity loans and manufactured housing loans are backed by real estate property, the securities backed by them are referred to as *real estate-backed asset-backed securities*. Other asset-backed securities include securities backed by home improvement loans, health care receivables, agricultural equipment loans, equipment leases, music royalty receivables, movie royalty receivables, and municipal parking ticket receivables. The list is continually expanding. Moreover, asset-backed securities are not limited to the U.S. market. Many countries have developed asset-backed securities backed by a wide range of loans and receivables.

In this chapter, we discuss the basic features of asset-backed securities and then look at several of the more popular types of asset-backed securities. One important type of asset-backed security is the collateralized debt obligation. Because of its importance and unique characteristics, Chapter 13 is devoted to this type of asset-backed security.

FEATURES OF AN ABS

Before we discuss the major types of asset-backed securities, let's first look at the general features of the underlying collateral and the structure.

Credit Enhancement

All asset-backed securities are credit enhanced. As explained in the previous chapter, this means that support is provided for one or more of the bondholders in the structure. Credit enhancement levels are determined relative to a specific rating desired by the issuer for a security by each rating agency. There are two general types of credit enhancement structures: external and internal. We described each type in the previous chapter.

Amortizing versus Nonamortizing Assets

The collateral for an asset-backed security can be classified as either amortizing or nonamortizing assets. Amortizing assets are loans in which the borrower's periodic payment consists of scheduled principal and interest payments over the life of the loan. The schedule for the repayment of the principal is called an *amortization schedule.* The standard residential mortgage loan falls into this category. Auto loans and certain types of home equity loans (specifically, closed-end home equity loans discussed later in this chapter) are amortizing assets. Any excess payment over the scheduled principal payment is called a *prepayment.* Prepayments can be made to pay off the entire balance or a partial prepayment, called a *curtailment.*

In contrast to amortizing assets, nonamortizing assets do not have a schedule for the periodic payments that the individual borrower must make. Instead, a nonamortizing asset is one in which the borrower must make a minimum periodic payment. If that payment is less than the interest on the outstanding loan balance, the shortfall is added to the outstanding loan balance. If the periodic payment is greater than the interest on the outstanding loan balance, then the difference is applied to the reduction of the outstanding loan balance. There is no schedule of principal payments (i.e., no amortization schedule) for a nonamortizing asset. Consequently, the concept of a prepayment does not apply. Credit card receivables and certain types of home equity loans described later in this chapter are examples of nonamortizing assets.

For an amortizing asset, projection of the cash flows requires projecting prepayments. One factor that may affect prepayments is the prevailing level of interest rates relative to the interest rate on the loan. In projecting prepayments it is critical to determine the extent to which borrowers take advantage of a decline in interest rates below the loan rate in order to refinance the loan.

As with nonagency mortgage-backed securities (MBSs) described in the previous chapter, modeling defaults for the collateral is critical in estimating the cash flows of an asset-backed security. Proceeds that are recovered in the event of a default of a loan prior to the scheduled principal repayment date of an amortizing asset represents a prepayment and are referred to as an *involuntary prepayment.* Projecting prepayments for amortizing assets requires an assumption of the default rate and the recovery rate. For a nonamortizing asset, while the concept of a prepayment does not exist, a projection of defaults is still necessary to project how much will be recovered and when.

The analysis of prepayments can be performed on a pool level or a loan level. In *pool-level analysis* it is assumed that all loans comprising the collateral are identical. For an amortizing asset, the amortization schedule is based on the *gross weighted average coupon* (GWAC) and *weighted average maturity* (WAM) for that single loan. Pool-level analysis is appropriate where the underlying loans are homogeneous. *Loan-level analysis* involves amortizing each loan (or group of homogeneous loans).

The maturity of an asset-backed security is not a meaningful parameter. Instead, the average life of the security is calculated. This measure was introduced in Chapter 9 when we discussed agency passthrough securities.

Fixed-Rate versus Floating-Rate

There are fixed-rate and floating-rate asset-backed securities. Floating-rate asset-backed securities are typically created where the underlying pool of loans or receivables pay a floating rate. The most common are securities backed by credit card receivables, home equity line of credit receivables, closed-end home equity loans with an adjustable rate, student loans, Small Business Administration loans, and trade receivables. As demonstrated in Chapter 10, fixed-rate loans also can be used to create a structure that has one or more floating-rate tranches. For example, there are closed-end home equity loans with a fixed rate that can be pooled to create a structure with floating-rate tranches.

Passthrough versus Paythrough Structures

In Chapter 9, we saw how a mortgage passthrough security is created. A pool of mortgage loans is used as collateral and certificates (securities) are issued with each certificate entitled to a pro rata share of the cash flow from the pool of mortgage loans. So, if a $100 million mortgage pool is the collateral for a passthrough security and 10,000 certificates are issued, then the holder of one certificate is entitled to 1/10,000 of the cash flow from the collateral.

The same type of structure, a passthrough structure, can be used for an asset-backed security deal. That is, each certificate holder is entitled to a pro rata share of the cash flow from the underlying pool of loans or receivables. For example, consider the following asset-backed security structure:

senior tranche	$280 million	10,000 certificates issued
subordinated tranche	$20 million	1,000 certificates issued

Each certificate holder of the senior tranche is entitled to receive 1/10,000 of the cash flow to be paid to the senior tranche from the collateral. Each certificate holder of the subordinated tranche is entitled to receive 1/1,000 of the cash flow to be paid to the subordinated tranche from the collateral.

In Chapter 10 we saw how a passthrough security can be used to create a collateralized mortgage obligation (CMO). That is, passthrough securities are pooled and used as collateral for a CMO. Another name for a CMO structure is a *paythrough structure*. In the case of an asset-backed security, the loans are either pooled and issued as a passthrough security or as a paythrough security. That is, unlike in the agency mortgage-backed securities market, a passthrough is not created first and then the passthrough is used to create a paythrough security. This is the same process as with a nonagency mortgage-backed security.

In a paythrough structure, the senior tranches can be simple sequential-pays, just as we described for CMOs in Chapter 10. Or, there could be a PAC

structure with, say, senior tranche 1 being a short average life PAC, senior tranche 2 being a long average life tranche, and the other two senior tranches being support tranches.

It is important to emphasize that the senior-subordinated structure described in the previous chapter is a mechanism for redistributing credit risk from the senior tranche to the subordinated tranches and is referred to as *credit tranching*. When the senior tranche is carved up into tranches with different exposures to prepayment risk in a paythrough structure, prepayment risk can be transferred among the senior tranches as in a nonagency CMO. This is referred to as prepayment tranching or *time tranching*.

Optional Clean-Up Call Provisions

For asset-backed securities there is an *optional clean-up call provision* granted to the trustee. There are several types of clean-up call provisions.

In a *percent of collateral call* the outstanding bonds can be called at par value if the outstanding collateral's balance falls below a predetermined percent of the original collateral's balance. This is the most common type of clean-up call provision for amortizing assets, and the predetermined level is typically 10%.

A *percent of bonds clean-up call provision* is similar to a percent of collateral call except that the percent that triggers the call is the percent of the amount of the bonds outstanding relative to the original amount of bonds issued. In structures where there is more than one type of collateral, such as in home equity loan-backed securities, a percent of tranche clean-up call provision is used.

A *call on or after specified date* operates just like a standard call provision for corporate, agency, and municipal securities. In a *latter of percent or date call* the outstanding bonds can be called if either (1) the collateral outstanding reaches a predetermined level before the specified call date or (2) the call date has been reached even if the collateral outstanding is above the predetermined level. In an *auction call*, common in certain types of home equity loan-backed securities, at a certain date a call will be exercised if an auction results in the outstanding collateral being sold at a price greater than its par value. The premium over par value received from the auctioned collateral is retained by the trustee and eventually paid to the issuer through the residual.

In addition to the above clean-up call provisions, which permit the trustee to call the bonds, there may be an *insurer call*. Such a call permits the insurer to call the bonds if the collateral's cumulative loss history reaches a predetermined level.

REVIEW OF SEVERAL TYPES OF ABS

As noted at the outset of this chapter, the collateral that has been used for creating asset-backed securities is continually expanding. We provide a summary of some of the major sectors of the ABS market as follows.

Home Equity Loan-Backed Securities

A *home equity loan* (HEL) is a loan backed by residential property. At one time, the loan was typically a second lien on property that was already pledged to secure a first lien. In some cases, the lien was a third lien. In recent years, the character of a home equity loan has changed. Today, a home equity loan is often a first lien on property where the borrower has either an impaired credit history and/or the payment-to-income ratio is too high for the loan to qualify as a conforming loan for securitization by Ginnie Mae, Fannie Mae, or Freddie Mac. Typically, the borrower used a home equity loan to consolidate consumer debt using the current home as collateral rather than to obtain funds to purchase a new home.

Home equity loans can be either closed end or open end. Most home equity loan-backed deals have been backed by closed-end HELs. A closed-end HEL is designed the same way as a fully amortizing residential mortgage loan. That is, it has a fixed maturity and the payments are structured to fully amortize the loan by the maturity date.

There are both fixed-rate and variable-rate closed-end HELs. Typically, variable-rate loans have a reference rate of 6-month LIBOR and have periodic caps and lifetime caps. (A periodic cap limits the change in the mortgage rate from the previous time the mortgage rate was reset; a lifetime cap sets a maximum that the mortgage rate can ever be for the loan.) The cash flow of a pool of closed-end HELs is comprised of interest, regularly scheduled principal repayments, and prepayments, just as with mortgage-backed securities. Thus, it is necessary to have a prepayment model and a default model to forecast cash flows. The prepayment speed is measured in terms of a conditional prepayment rate (CPR).

Borrower characteristics and the seasoning process must be kept in mind when trying to assess prepayments for a particular deal. In the prospectus of an offering, a base-case prepayment assumption is made—the initial speed and the amount of time until the collateral is expected to be seasoned. Thus, the prepayment benchmark is issuer specific. As explained in the previous chapter, the benchmark speed in the prospectus is called the *prospectus prepayment curve* or PPC. Slower or faster prepayments speeds are a multiple of the PPC.

The securities backed by the adjustable-rate (or variable-rate) HELs are called *HEL floaters*. Institutional investors who seek securities that better match their floating-rate funding costs are attracted to securities that offer a floating-rate coupon such as HEL floaters. To increase the attractiveness of home equity loan-backed securities to such investors, the securities typically have been created in which the reference rate is 1-month LIBOR. Because of (1) the mismatch between the reference rate on the underlying loans (typically 6-month LIBOR) and that of the HEL floater (1-month LIBOR) and (2) the periodic and life caps of the underlying loans, there is a cap on the coupon rate for the HEL floater. Unlike a typical floater, which has a cap that is fixed throughout the security's life, the effective cap of an HEL floater is variable. The effective cap, referred to as the *available funds cap*, will depend on the amount of funds generated by the net coupon on the principal, less any fees.

As with nonagency MBSs, an HEL-backed deal can include planned amortization class (PAC) and nonaccelerated senior (NAS) tranches.

Manufactured Housing-Backed Securities

Manufactured housing-backed securities are backed by loans for manufactured homes. In contrast to site-built homes, manufactured homes are built at a factory and then transported to a manufactured home community or private land. The loan may be either a mortgage loan (for both the land and the home) or a consumer retail installment loan.

Manufactured housing-backed securities are issued by Ginnie Mae and private entities. The former securities are guaranteed by the full faith and credit of the U.S. government. The manufactured housing loans that are collateral for the securities issued and guaranteed by Ginnie Mae are loans guaranteed by the Federal Housing Administration (FHA) or Veterans Administration (VA). Loans not backed by the FHA or VA are called conventional loans. Manufactured housing-backed securities that are backed by such loans are called *conventional manufactured housing-backed securities*. These securities are issued by private entities.

The typical loan for a manufactured home is 15 to 20 years. The loan repayment is structured to fully amortize the amount borrowed. Therefore, as with residential mortgage loans and HELs, the cash flow consists of net interest, regularly scheduled principal, and prepayments. However, prepayments are more stable for manufactured housing-backed securities because they are not sensitive to refinancing. There are several reasons for this. First, the loan balances are typically small so that there is no significant dollar savings from refinancing. Second, the rate of depreciation of mobile homes may be such that in the earlier years depreciation is greater than the amount of the loan paid off. This makes it difficult to refinance the loan. Finally, borrowers are typically of lower credit quality and therefore find it difficult to obtain funds to refinance.

As with residential mortgage loans and HELs, prepayments on manufactured housing-backed securities are measured in terms of CPR. The payment structure is the same as with nonagency mortgage-backed securities and home equity loan-backed securities.

Commercial Mortgage-Backed Securities

Commercial mortgage-backed securities (CMBSs) are backed by a pool of commercial mortgage loans on income-producing property—multifamily properties (i.e., apartment buildings), office buildings, industrial properties (including warehouses), shopping centers, hotels, and health care facilities (i.e., senior housing care facilities). The basic building block of the CMBS transaction is a commercial loan that was originated either to finance a commercial purchase or to refinance a prior mortgage obligation.

Unlike residential mortgage loans where the lender relies on the ability of the borrower to repay and has recourse to the borrower if the payment terms

are not satisfied, commercial mortgage loans are *nonrecourse loans*. This means that the lender can only look to the income-producing property backing the loan for interest and principal repayment. If there is a default, the lender looks to the proceeds from the sale of the property for repayment and has no recourse to the borrower for any unpaid balance. Basically, this means that the lender must view each property as a stand-alone business and evaluate each property using measures that have been found useful in assessing credit risk.

While fundamental principles of assessing credit risk apply to all property types, traditional approaches to assessing the credit risk of the collateral differs for CMBS than for nonagency MBS discussed earlier and real estate-backed ABS discussed earlier in this chapter. For MBS and ABS backed by residential property, typically the loans are lumped into buckets based on certain loan characteristics and then assumptions regarding default rates are made regarding each bucket. In contrast, for commercial mortgage loans, the unique economic characteristics of each income-producing property in a pool backing a CMBS require that credit analysis be performed on a loan-by-loan basis not only at the time of issuance, but monitored on an ongoing basis.

Regardless of the property type, the two measures that have been found to be key indicators of the potential credit performance is the debt-to-service coverage ratio and the loan-to-value ratio.

The *debt-to-service coverage* (DSC) ratio is the ratio of the property's *net operating income* (NOI) divided by the debt service. The NOI is defined as the rental income reduced by cash operating expenses (adjusted for a replacement reserve). A ratio greater than 1 means that the cash flow from the property is sufficient to cover debt servicing. The higher the ratio, the more likely that the borrower will be able to meet debt servicing from the property's cash flow.

For all properties backing a CMBS deal, a weighted average DSC ratio is computed. An analysis of the credit quality of an issue will also look at the dispersion of the DSC ratios for the underlying loans. For example, one might look at the percentage of a deal with a DSC ratio below a certain value.

Studies of residential mortgage loans have found that the key determinant of default is the loan-to-value (LTV) ratio. The figure used for "value" in this ratio is either market value or appraised value. In valuing commercial property, there can be considerable variation in the estimates of the property's market value. Thus, analysts tend to be skeptical about estimates of market value and the resulting LTVs reported for properties. The lower the LTV, the greater the protection afforded the lender.

Another characteristic of the underlying loans that is used in gauging the quality of a CMBS deal is the prepayment protection provisions. We discuss these provisions later. Finally, there are characteristics of the property that affect quality. Specifically, analysts and rating agencies look at the concentration of loans by property type and by geographical location.

There are three types of CMBS deal structures that have been of interest to bond investors: (1) liquidating trusts, (2) multiproperty single borrower, and (3)

multiproperty conduit. The liquidating or nonperforming trusts are a small segment of the CMBS market. This segment, as the name implies, represents CMBS deals backed by nonperforming mortgage loans. The fastest growing segment of the CMBS is conduit-originated transactions. Conduits are commercial-lending entities that are established for the sole purpose of generating collateral to securitize.

Basic CMBS Structure

As with any structured finance transaction, sizing will determine the necessary level of credit enhancement to achieve a desired rating level. For example, if certain DSC and LTV ratios are needed, and these ratios cannot be met at the loan level, then subordination is used to achieve these levels.

The rating agencies will require that the CMBS transaction be retired sequentially, with the highest-rated bonds paying off first. Therefore, any return of principal caused by amortization, prepayment, or default will be used to repay the highest-rated tranche.

Interest on principal outstanding will be paid to all tranches. In the event of a delinquency resulting in insufficient cash to make all scheduled payments, the transaction's servicer will advance both principal and interest. Advancing will continue from the servicer for as long as these amounts are deemed recoverable.

Losses arising from loan defaults will be charged against the principal balance of the lowest-rated CMBS bond tranche outstanding. The total loss charged will include the amount previously advanced as well as the actual loss incurred in the sale of the loan's underlying property.

The investor must be sure to understand the cash flow priority of any prepayment penalties and/or yield maintenance provisions because this can impact a particular bond's average life and overall performance.

Structural Call Protection

The degree of call protection available to a CMBS investor is a function of the following two characteristics:

1. call protection available at the loan level
2. call protection afforded from the actual CMBS structure

Protection at the Loan Level At the commercial loan level, call protection can take the following forms:

1. prepayment lockout
2. defeasance
3. prepayment penalty points
4. yield maintenance charges

A *prepayment lockout* is a contractual agreement that prohibits any prepayments during a specified period of time, called the *lockout period*. The lockout

period at issuance can be from 2 to 5 years. After the lockout period, call protection comes in the form of either prepayment penalty points or yield maintenance charges. Prepayment lockout and defeasance are the strongest forms of prepayment protection.

With *defeasance*, rather than prepaying a loan, the borrower provides sufficient funds for the servicer to invest in a portfolio of Treasury securities that replicates the cash flows that would exist in the absence of prepayments. Unlike the other call protection provisions discussed next, there is no distribution made to the bondholders when the defeasance takes place. So, since there are no penalties, there is no issue as to how any penalties paid by the borrower are to be distributed amongst the bondholders in a CMBS structure. Moreover, the substitution of the cash flow of a Treasury portfolio for that of the borrower improves the credit quality of the CMBS deal.

Prepayment penalty points are predetermined penalties that must be paid by the borrower if the borrower wishes to refinance. For example, 5-4-3-2-1 is a common prepayment penalty point structure. That is, if the borrower wishes to prepay during the first year, he must pay a 5% penalty for a total of $105 rather than $100 (which is the norm in the residential market). Likewise, during the second year, a 4% penalty would apply, and so on.

When there are prepayment penalty points, there are rules for distributing the penalty among the CMBS bondholders. Prepayment penalty points are not common in new CMBS structures. Instead, the next form of call protection discussed, yield maintenance charges, is more commonly used.

It has been argued that the prepayment penalty points are not an effective means for discouraging refinancing. However, prepayment penalty points may be superior to yield maintenance charges in a rising rate environment.[1] This is because prepayments do occur when rates rise. With yield maintenance, the penalty will be zero (unless there is a yield maintenance floor that imposes a minimum penalty). In contrast, with prepayment penalty points, there will be a penalty even in a rising rate environment.

Yield maintenance charge, in its simplest terms, is designed to make the lender indifferent as to the timing of prepayments. The yield maintenance charge, also called the *make-whole charge*, makes it uneconomical to refinance solely to get a lower mortgage rate. The simplest and most restrictive form of yield maintenance charge ("Treasury flat yield maintenance") penalizes the borrower based on the difference between the mortgage coupon and the prevailing Treasury rate.

Several methods have been used in practice to compute the yield maintenance charge. These methods include the simple model, the bullet model, the single discount factor model, the multiple discount factor model, the interest difference model, and the truncated interest difference model.[2] To provide further

---

[1] Da Cheng, Adrian R. Cooper, and Jason Huang, "Understanding Prepayments in CMBS Deals," Chapter 24 in Frank J. Fabozzi, Chuck Ramsey, and Michael Marz (eds.), *The Handbook of Nonagency Mortgage-Backed Securities: Second Edition* (New Hope, PA: Frank J. Fabozzi Associates, 2000).

protection to lenders, there are often yield maintenance floors that impose a minimum charge.

The purpose of each of the methods for calculating the yield maintenance charge is to make the lender whole. However, when a commercial loan is included as part of a CMBS deal, there must be an allocation of the yield maintenance charge amongst the bondholders. Several methods are used in practice for distributing the yield maintenance charge and, depending on the method specified in a deal, not all bondholders may be made whole. These methods include the principal allocation method, base interest method, bond yield maintenance method, and present value yield loss method.[3]

Structural Protection The other type of call protection available in CMBS transactions is structural. That is, because the CMBS bond structures are sequential-pay (by rating), the AA-rated tranche cannot pay down until the AAA is completely retired, and the AA-rated bonds must be paid off before the A-rated bonds, and so on. However, principal losses due to defaults are impacted from the bottom of the structure upward.

Balloon Maturity Provisions

Many commercial loans backing CMBS transactions are balloon loans that require substantial principal payment at the end of the term of the loan. If the borrower fails to make the balloon payment, the borrower is in default. The lender may extend the loan, and in so doing may modify the original loan terms. During the workout period for the loan, a higher interest rate will be charged, the default interest rate.

The risk that a borrower will not be able to make the balloon payment because either the borrower cannot arrange for refinancing at the balloon payment date or cannot sell the property to generate sufficient funds to pay off the balloon balance is called *balloon risk*. Since the term of the loan will be extended by the lender during the workout period, balloon risk is also referred to as *extension risk*.

Although many investors like the "bullet bond-like" pay down of the balloon maturities, it does present difficulties from a structural standpoint. That is, if the deal is structured to completely pay down on a specified date, an event of default will occur if any delays occur. However, how such delays impact CMBS investors is dependent on the bond type (premium, par, or discount) and whether the servicer will advance to a particular tranche after the balloon default.

Another concern for CMBS investors in multitranche transactions is the fact that all loans must be refinanced to pay off the most senior bondholders. Therefore, the balloon risk of the most senior tranche (i.e., AAA) may be equivalent to that of the most junior bond class (i.e., B).

---

[2] These methods for computing the yield maintenance charge are discussed in Cheng, Cooper, and Huang, "Understanding Prepayments in CMBS Deals."

[3] These methods for allocating the yield maintenance charge among bondholders are discussed in Cheng, Cooper, and Huang, "Understanding Prepayments in CMBS Deals."

Auto Loan-Backed Securities

Auto loan-backed securities are issued by:

1. the financial subsidiaries of auto manufacturers (domestic and foreign)
2. commercial banks
3. independent finance companies and small financial institutions specializing in auto loans

Auto loans can range in maturity from 3 years to 6 years.

The cash flow for auto loan-backed securities consists of regularly scheduled monthly loan payments (interest and scheduled principal repayments) and any prepayments. For securities backed by auto loans, prepayments result from (1) sales and trade-ins requiring full payoff of the loan, (2) repossession and subsequent resale of the automobile, (3) loss or destruction of the vehicle, (4) payoff of the loan with cash to save on the interest cost, and (5) refinancing of the loan at a lower interest cost. While refinancings may be a major reason for prepayments of mortgage loans, they are of minor importance for automobile loans. Moreover, the interest rates for the automobile loans underlying some deals are substantially below market rates since they are offered by manufacturers as part of a sales promotion.

Prepayments for auto loan-backed securities are measured in terms of the *absolute prepayment speed* (ABS). The ABS is the monthly prepayment expressed as a percentage of the original collateral amount. As explained in Chapter 9, the SMM (monthly CPR) expresses prepayments based on the prior month's balance.

There are auto loan-backed deals that are passthrough structures and paythrough structures. In the typical passthrough structure there is a senior tranche and a subordinate tranche. There is also an interest-only class. While more deals are structured as passthroughs, this structure is typically used for smaller deals. Larger deals usually have a paythrough structure.

Student Loan-Backed Securities

Student loans are made to cover college cost (undergraduate, graduate, and professional programs such as medical school and law school) and tuition for a wide range of vocational and trade schools. Securities backed by student loans, popularly referred to as SLABS (student loan asset-backed securities), have similar structural features as the other asset-backed securities we discussed previously.

The student loans that have been most commonly securitized are those that are made under the Federal Family Education Loan Program (FFELP). Under this program, the government makes loans to students via private lenders. The decision by private lenders to extend a loan to a student is not based on the applicant's ability to repay the loan. If a default of a loan occurs and the loan has been properly serviced, then the government will guarantee up to 98% of the principal plus accrued interest.

Loans that are not part of a government guarantee program are called *alternative loans*. These loans are basically consumer loans, and the lender's decision to extend an alternative loan will be based on the ability of the applicant to repay the loan. Alternative loans have been securitized.

Congress created Fannie Mae and Freddie Mac to provide liquidity in the mortgage market by allowing these government-sponsored enterprises to buy mortgage loans in the secondary market. Congress created the Student Loan Marketing Association (nicknamed "Sallie Mae") as a government-sponsored enterprise to purchase student loans in the secondary market and to securitize pools of student loans. Sallie Mae is the major issuer of SLABS, and its issues are viewed as the benchmark issues. Other entities that issue SLABS are either traditional corporate entities (e.g., the Money Store and PNC Bank) or nonprofit organizations (Michigan Higher Education Loan Authority and the California Educational Facilities Authority). The SLABS of the latter typically are issued as tax-exempt securities and therefore trade in the municipal market.

Let's first look at the cash flow for the student loans themselves. There are different types of student loans under the FFELP, including subsidized and unsubsidized Stafford loans, Parental Loans for Undergraduate Students (PLUS), and Supplemental Loans to Students (SLS). These loans involve three periods with respect to the borrower's payments—deferment period, grace period, and loan repayment period. Typically, student loans work as follows. While a student is in school, no payments are made by the student on the loan. This is the deferment period. Upon leaving school, the student is extended a grace period of usually 6 months when no payments on the loan must be made. After this period, payments are made on the loan by the borrower.

Prior to July 1, 1998, the reference rate for student loans originated under FFELP was the 3-month Treasury bill rate plus a margin of either 250 basis points (during the deferment and grace periods) or 310 basis points (during the repayment period). Since July 1, 1998, the Higher Education Act changed the reference rate to the 10-year Treasury note. Specifically, the interest rate is the 10-year Treasury note rate plus 100 basis points. The spread over the reference rate varies with the cycle period for the loan.

Typically, non-Sallie Mae issues have been LIBOR-based floaters. For Sallie Mae issues, there is no government guarantee, but issues are viewed as triple A rated. Sallie Mae has typically issued SLABS indexed to the 3-month Treasury bill rate. However, late in the second quarter of 1999, Sallie Mae issued bonds in which the buyer of the 2-year average life tranche had the choice of receiving either LIBOR plus 8 basis points or the 3-month Treasury bill rate plus 87 basis points. There are available funds caps in SLABS because of the different reference rates for the loans and the securities.

Prepayments typically occur due to defaults or loan consolidation. Even if there is no loss of principal faced by the investor when defaults occur, the investor is still exposed to contraction risk. This is the risk that the investor must

reinvest the proceeds at a lower spread and, in the case of a bond purchased at a premium, the premium will be lost. Studies have shown student loan prepayments are insensitive to the level of interest rates. Consolidation of a loan occurs when the student who has loans over several years combines them into a single loan. The proceeds from the consolidation are distributed to the original lender and, in turn, distributed to the bondholders.

SBA Loan-Backed Securities

The Small Business Administration (SBA) is an agency of the U.S. government empowered to guarantee loans made by approved SBA lenders to qualified borrowers. The loans are backed by the full faith and credit of the government. Most SBA loans are variable-rate loans where the reference rate is the prime rate. The rate on the loan is reset monthly on the first of the month or quarterly on the first of January, April, July, and October. SBA regulations specify the maximum coupon allowable in the secondary market. Newly originated loans have maturities between 5 and 25 years.

The Small Business Secondary Market Improvement Act passed in 1984 permitted the pooling of SBA loans. When pooled, the underlying loans must have similar terms and features. The maturities typically used for pooling loans are 7, 10, 15, 20, and 25 years. Loans without caps are not pooled with loans that have caps.

Most variable-rate SBA loans make monthly payments consisting of interest and principal repayment. The amount of the monthly payment for an individual loan is determined as follows. Given the coupon formula of the prime rate plus the loan's quoted margin, the interest rate is determined for each loan. Given the interest rate, a level payment amortization schedule is determined. This level payment is paid until the coupon rate is reset.

The monthly cash flow that the investor in an SBA-backed security receives consists of:

- the coupon interest based on the coupon rate set for the period
- the scheduled principal repayment (i.e., scheduled amortization)
- prepayments

Prepayments for SBA-backed securities are measured in terms of CPR. Voluntary prepayments can be made by the borrower without any penalty. There are several factors contributing to the prepayment speed of a pool of SBA loans. A factor affecting prepayments is the maturity date of the loan. It has been found that the fastest speeds on SBA loans and pools occur for shorter maturities. The purpose of the loan also affects prepayments. There are loans for working capital purposes and loans to finance real estate construction or acquisition. It has been observed that SBA pools with maturities of 10 years or less made for working capital purposes tend to prepay at the fastest speed. In contrast, loans backed by real estate that are long maturities tend to prepay at a slow speed. All other factors constant, pools that have capped loans tend to prepay more slowly than pools of uncapped loans.

Credit Card Receivable-Backed Securities

A major sector of the ABS market is that of securities backed by credit card receivables. Credit cards are issued by:

1. banks (e.g., Visa and MasterCard)
2. retailers (e.g., JC Penney and Sears)
3. travel and entertainment companies (e.g., American Express)

Credit card deals are structured as a *master trust*. With a master trust the issuer can sell several series from the same trust. For example, consider the following two deals: Sears Credit Account Master Trust II, Series 1995-4 and Standard Credit Card Master Trust I Series 1995-A.

Sears offers several open-end revolving credit plans. From these various plans, Sears generates a portfolio of receivables. As of July 1995, the master trust consisted of $4 billion of principal receivables. These receivables were randomly selected from the entire portfolio of receivables of Sears Roebuck and Co. About 38% of the accounts had credit limits of $1,999 and about 61% were seasoned at least 5 years. All series issued from this Master Trust II share in the cash flow from the pool of receivables that were randomly selected. Information about the specific accounts in the pool selected for Master Trust II was not disclosed; however, because of the random selection process, an investor might expect that the composition did not differ significantly from the entire portfolio of receivables. Each time a new series of securities is issued, more receivables are randomly selected to be added to the trust. The Sears Credit Account Master Trust II, Series 1995-4 was the sixth of a series issued by Group One of Sears Credit Account Master Trust II. Two classes of certificates were offered to the public: Class A Master Trust Certificates and Class B Master Trust Certificates. The principal for the former was $500 million and for the latter $22.5 million.

The Standard Credit Card Master Trust I is a Citibank master trust. The master trust as of May 22, 1995 was comprised of 20,092,662 accounts with principal receivables of approximately $24.3 billion and approximately $290.8 million of finance charge receivables. The average credit limit was $3,282 and the average principal balance of the accounts was $1,210. About 69% of the accounts were seasoned more than 2 years. The SCCMTI Series 1995A was the twenty-second in a series issued by Group One of Standard Credit Card Master Trust I and is a Euro issue. There was only one certificate offered to the public—$300 million of Floating Rate Class A Credit Card Participation Certificates.

Cash Flow

For a pool of credit card receivables, the cash flow consists of finance charges collected, fees, and principal. Finance charges collected represent the periodic interest the credit card borrower is charged based on the unpaid balance after the grace period. Fees include late payment fees and any annual membership fees.

Interest to securityholders is paid periodically (e.g., monthly, quarterly, or semiannually). The interest rate may be fixed or floating—roughly half of the securities are floaters. The floating rate is uncapped.

A credit card receivable-backed security is a nonamortizing security. For a specified period of time, referred to as the *lockout period* or *revolving period*, the principal payments made by credit card borrowers comprising the pool are retained by the trustee and reinvested in additional receivables to maintain the size of the pool. The lockout period can vary from 18 months to 10 years. So, during the lockout period, the cash flow that is paid out to securityholders is based on finance charges collected and fees.

After the lockout period, the principal is no longer reinvested but paid to investors. This period is referred to as the *principal-amortization period*, and the various types of structures are described later.

Performance of the Portfolio of Receivables

Several concepts must be understood in order to assess the performance of the portfolio of receivables and the ability of the issuer to meet its interest obligation and repay principal as scheduled.

We begin with the concept of the *gross portfolio yield*. This yield includes finance charges collected and fees. Charge-offs represent the accounts charged off as uncollectible. *Net portfolio yield* is equal to gross portfolio yield minus charge-offs. The net portfolio yield is important because it is from this yield that the bondholders will be paid. So, for example, if the average yield (WAC) that must be paid to the various tranches in the structure is 5% and the net portfolio yield for the month is only 4.5%, there is the risk that the bondholder obligations will not be satisfied.

Delinquencies are the percentages of receivables that are past due for a specified number of months, usually 30, 60, and 90 days. They are considered an indicator of potential future charge-offs.

The *monthly payment rate* (MPR) expresses the monthly payment (which includes finance charges, fees, and any principal repayment) of a credit card receivable portfolio as a percentage of credit card debt outstanding in the previous month. For example, suppose a $500 million credit card receivable portfolio in January realized $50 million of payments in February. The MPR would then be 10% ($50 million divided by $500 million).

There are two reasons why the MPR is important. First, if the MPR reaches an extremely low level, there is a chance that there will be extension risk with respect to the principal payments on the bonds. Second, if the MPR is very low, then there is a chance that there will not be sufficient cash flows to pay off principal. This is one of the events that could trigger early amortization of the principal (described as follows).

At issuance, portfolio yield, charge-offs, delinquency, and MPR information are provided in the prospectus. Information about portfolio performance is thereafter available from various sources.

Early Amortization Triggers

There are provisions in credit card receivable-backed securities that require early amortization of the principal if certain events occur. Such provisions, which are referred to as either *early amortization* or *rapid amortization*, are included to safeguard the credit quality of the issue. The only way that the principal cash flows can be altered is by triggering the early amortization provision.

Typically, early amortization allows for the rapid return of principal in the event that the 3-month average excess spread earned on the receivables falls to zero or less. When early amortization occurs, the credit card tranches are retired sequentially (i.e., first the AAA bond then the AA rated bond, etc.). This is accomplished by paying the principal payments made by the credit card borrowers to the investors instead of using them to purchase more receivables. The length of time until the return of principal is largely a function of the monthly payment rate. For example, suppose that a AAA tranche is 82% of the overall deal. If the monthly payment rate is 11%, then the AAA tranche would return principal over a 7.5-month period (82%/11%). An 18% monthly payment rate would return principal over a 4.5-month period (82%/18%).

Several services publish monthly each deal's trigger formula and base rate. The trigger formula is the formula that shows the condition under which the rapid amortization will be triggered. The *base rate* is the minimum payment rate that a trust must be able to maintain to avoid early amortization.

CREDIT RISKS ASSOCIATED WITH INVESTING IN ABS

In evaluating credit risk, the rating companies focus on four areas: (1) asset risks, (2) structural risks, (3) legal and regulatory considerations, and (4) third parties to the structure. We discuss each as follows and then discuss how the agencies differ with respect to rating asset-backed securities versus corporate bonds.

Asset Risks

Evaluating asset risks involves the analysis of the credit quality of the collateral. The rating companies will look at the underlying borrower's ability to pay and the borrower's equity in the asset. The latter will be a key determinant as to whether the underlying borrower will default or sell the asset and pay off a loan. The rating companies will look at the experience of the originators of the underlying loans and will assess whether the loans underlying a specific transaction have the same characteristics as the experience reported by the issuer.

The concentration of loans is examined. The underlying principle of asset securitization is that a large number of borrowers in a pool will reduce the credit risk via diversification. If there are a few borrowers in the pool that are significant in size relative to the entire pool balance, this diversification benefit can be lost, resulting in a higher level of default risk. This risk is called *concentration*

risk. In such instances, rating companies will set concentration limits on the amount or percentage of receivables from any one borrower. If the concentration limit at issuance is exceeded, the issue will receive a lower credit rating than if the concentration limit was not exceeded. If after issuance the concentration limit is exceeded, the issue may be downgraded.

The rating agencies will use statistical analysis to assess the most likely loss to an investor in an ABS tranche due to the performance of the collateral. The rating agencies will analyze various scenarios, and from the results of these scenarios they can determine an expected (or weight average) loss for the investor in a tranche and the variability of the loss. The variability is important for the following reason: Suppose that a tranche has protection against a 5% loss in the value of the collateral due to defaults. For simplicity, assume further that a rating agency only evaluates two equally likely scenarios and that in the first scenario the loss is 3% and in the second it is 4%. The expected value for the loss is 3.5% and is less than the protection of 5%. So, based on these two scenarios, it is unlikely that the investor in this tranche will realize a loss. Suppose instead that the outcome of the two scenarios is that the loss is 1% in the first scenario and 6% in the second scenario. While the expected value for the loss is still 3.5%, the variability of the loss is much greater than before. In fact, if the second scenario with a 6% loss occurs, the tranche would realize a loss of 1% (6% loss in the scenario minus the 5% protection).

Structural Risks

As explained earlier in this chapter, the payment structure of an asset-backed deal can be either a passthrough or paythrough structure. The former simply has one senior tranche and the cash flow is distributed on a pro rata basis to the bondholders. In a paythrough structure, the senior tranche is divided into more than one tranche and there are payment rules as to how the cash flows from the collateral are to be distributed amongst the senior tranches.

The decision as to whether a passthrough or paythrough structure is used is made by the issuer. Once selected, the rating agencies examine the extent to which the cash flow from the collateral can satisfy all of the obligations of the ABS deal. The cash flow of the underlying collateral is interest and principal repayment. The cash flow payments that must be made are interest and principal to investors, servicing fees, and any other expenses for which the issuer is liable. The rating companies analyze the structure to test whether the collateral's cash flows match the payments that must be made to satisfy the issuer's obligations. This requires that the rating agency make assumptions about losses and delinquencies and consider various interest rate scenarios after taking into consideration credit enhancements.

In considering the structure, the rating agencies will consider (1) the loss allocation (how losses will be allocated to the tranches in the structure), (2) the cash flow allocation (i.e., in a paythrough structure the priority rules for the distribution of principal and interest), (3) the interest rate spread between the interest

earned on the collateral and the interest paid to the tranches plus the servicing fee, (4) the potential for a trigger event to occur that will cause the rapid amortization of a deal, and (5) how credit enhancement may change over time.

Legal Structure

A corporation issuing an ABS seeks a rating on the securities it issues that is higher than its own corporate rating. This is done by using the underlying loans as collateral for a debt instrument rather than the general credit of the issuer. Typically, however, the corporate entity (i.e., seller of the collateral) retains some interest in the collateral. For example, the corporate entity can retain a subordinated tranche. Because the corporate entity retains an interest, rating companies want to be assured that a bankruptcy of that corporate entity will not allow the issuer's creditors access to the collateral. That is, there is concern that a bankruptcy court could redirect the collateral's cash flows or the collateral itself from the securityholders in an ABS transaction to the creditors of the corporate entity if it became bankrupt.

To solve this problem, a bankruptcy-remote special-purpose vehicle (SPV) is formed. The issuer of the asset-backed security is then the SPV. Legal opinion is needed stating that in the event of bankruptcy of the seller of the collateral, counsel does not believe that a bankruptcy court will consolidate the collateral sold with the assets of the seller.

The SPV is set up as a wholly owned subsidiary of the seller of the collateral. Although it is a wholly owned subsidiary, it is established in such a way that it is treated as a third-party entity relative to the seller of the collateral. The collateral is sold to the SPV, which, in turn, resells the collateral to the trust. The trust holds the collateral on behalf of the investors. The SPV holds the interest retained by the seller of the collateral.

Third-Party Providers

In an ABS deal there are several third parties involved. These include third-party credit enhancers, the servicer, a trustee, issuer's counsel, a guaranteed investment contract provider (this entity insures the reinvestment rate on investable funds), and accountants. The rating agency will investigate all third-party providers. For the thirty-party enhancers, the rating agencies will perform a credit analysis of their ability to pay.

All loans must be serviced. Servicing involves collecting payments from borrowers, notifying borrowers who may be delinquent, and, when necessary, recovering and disposing of the collateral if the borrower does not make loan repayments by a specified time. These responsibilities are fulfilled by a third party to an ABS transaction, the servicer. Moreover, while still viewed as a "third party" in many asset-backed securities transactions, the servicer is likely to be the originator of the loans used as the collateral.

In addition to the administration of the loan portfolio as just described, the servicer is responsible for distributing the proceeds collected from the bor-

rowers to the different bondholders in an ABS transaction according to the payment priorities. Where there are floating-rate securities in the transaction, the servicer will determine the interest rate for the period. The servicer may also be responsible for advancing payments when there are delinquencies in payments (that are likely to be collected in the future), resulting in a temporary shortfall in the payments that must be made to the bondholders.

The role of the servicer is critical in an ABS transaction. Therefore, rating agencies look at the ability of a servicer to perform all the activities that a servicer will be responsible for before they assign a rating to the bonds in a transaction. For example, the following factors are reviewed when evaluating servicers: servicing history, experience, underwriting standard for loan originations, servicing capabilities, human resources, financial condition, and growth/competition/business environment. Based on its analysis, a rating agency determines whether the servicer is acceptable or unacceptable. Transactions including the latter are not rated, or the rating agency may require a backup servicer if there is a concern about the ability of a servicer to perform.

Remember that the issuer is not a corporation with employees. It simply has loans and receivables. The servicer therefore plays an important role in ensuring that the payments are made to the bondholders. Next we will see how the characteristics of the servicer affect the way in which an issue is evaluated in terms of credit quality in comparison to the rating of a corporate bond issue.

Corporate Bond versus ABS Credit Analysis

Let's look at how the rating of an ABS transaction differs from that of a corporate bond issue. To understand the difference, it is important to appreciate how the cash flow that must be generated differs for an ABS transaction and a corporate bond issue.

In a corporate bond issue, management through its operations must undertake the necessary activities that will produce revenues and collect revenues. Management will incur costs in creating products and services. These costs include management compensation, employees' salaries, the costs of raw materials, and financial costs. Consequently, in evaluating the credit risk of a corporate bond issue, an analyst will examine the factors discussed in Chapter 7 regarding the corporation's character and capability to pay.

In contrast, in an ABS transaction, there are assets (loans or receivables) that are to be collected and distributed to bondholders. There are no operating or business risks, such as the competitive environment or existence of control systems, that are needed to assess the cash flow. What is important is the quality of the collateral in generating the cash flow needed to make interest and principal payments. As mentioned earlier, the rating agencies will review the assurance of cash flow based on different scenarios regarding defaults and delinquencies. The greater predictability of the cash flow in an ABS transaction due to the absence of operational risks distinguishes it from a corporate bond issue.

In a "true" ABS transaction, the role of the servicer is to simply collect the cash flow. There is no active management with respect to the collateral as is the case of the management necessary to operate a corporation to generate cash flow to pay bondholders. Standard & Poor's defines a "true" asset ABS transaction (which this rating agency refers to as a "true securitization") as follows:

> In a true securitization, repayment is not dependent on the ability of the servicer to replenish the pool with new collateral or to perform more than routine administrative functions.[4]

There are ABS transactions where the role of the servicer is more than administrative. In these cases, Standard & Poor's, for example, refers to such transactions as "hybrid transactions" because such transactions have elements of an ABS transaction and a corporation performing a service. According to Standard & Poor's:

> In a hybrid transaction, the role of the servicer is akin to that of a business manager. The hybrid servicer performs not only administrative duties, as in a true securitization, but also . . . [other] services that are needed to generate cash flow for debt service.[5]

Moreover, Standard & Poor's notes that:

> Unlike a true securitization, where the servicer is a fungible entity replaceable with few, if any, consequences to the transaction, bondholders depend on the expertise of the hybrid servicer for repayment. . . . Not coincidentally, these are the same attributes that form the basis of a corporate rating of the hybrid servicer. They also explain the rating linkage between the securitization and its hybrid servicer.[6]

Standard & Poor's provides an illustration of the distinction between a true ABS transaction and one requiring a more active role for the servicer.[7] Consider a railcar company that has several hundred leases and the leases are with a pool of diversified, highly rated companies. Suppose that each lease is for 10 years and it is the responsibility of the customers—not the railcar company—to perform the necessary maintenance on the leased railcars. If there is an ABS transaction backed by these leases and the term of the transaction is 10 years, then the role of the servicer is minimal. Since the leases are for 10 years and the securities issued are for 10 years, the servicer is just collecting the lease payments and dis-

---

[4] Standard & Poor's, "Rating Hybrid Securitizations," *Structured Finance* (October 1999), p. 2.

[5] "Rating Hybrid Securitizations," p. 3.

[6] "Rating Hybrid Securitizations," p. 3.

[7] "Rating Hybrid Securitizations," p. 3.

tributing them to the holders of the securities. In such a transaction, it is possible for this issue to obtain a high investment-grade rating as a true ABS transaction.

Suppose we change the assumptions as follows. The securities issued are for 25 years, not 10 years. Also assume that the railcar company, not the customers, are responsible for the servicing. Now the role of the servicer changes. The servicer will be responsible for finding new companies to release the railcars to when the original leases terminate in 10 years. This is necessary because the securities issued have a maturity of 25 years but the original leases only cover payments to securityholders for the first 10 years. It is the releasing of the railcars that is required for the last 15 years. The servicer under this new set of assumptions is also responsible for the maintenance of the railcars leased. Thus, the servicer must be capable of maintaining the railcars or have ongoing arrangements with one or more companies that have the ability to perform such maintenance.

How do rating agencies evaluate hybrid transactions? These transactions are rated both in terms of a standard methodology for rating an ABS transaction and using a "quasi-corporate approach" (in the words of Standard & Poor's), which involves an analysis of the servicer. The relative weight of the evaluations in assigning a rating to an ABS transaction will depend on the involvement of the servicer. The more important the role of the servicer, the more weight will be assigned to the quasi-corporate approach analysis.

YIELDS

ABSs offer a higher yield than comparable-maturity Treasury securities. Exhibit 1 shows the generic spreads for selected ABS products as reported by Lehman Brothers for July 13, 2001. At the bottom of the exhibit is the benchmark off which the spread is calculated. The spreads reported are the nominal spreads.

Note the higher nominal spread for the home equity loan-backed and manufactured housing-backed securities compared to the credit card and auto deals. For example, the 2-year nominal spread for AAA-rated issues is 123 basis points for home equity loan-backed and manufactured housing-backed securities, but only 66 basis points for credit cards and 78 basis points for autos. The reason for the difference in nominal spreads is that the value of the embedded option for the two real estate-backed securities has not been removed. That is, the option-adjusted spread if it had been reported for the two real estate-backed securities would have been more in line with the nominal spread for the credit card and auto securities. The key point of explaining the different spread measures in Chapter 3 was to highlight the pitfall of the nominal spread for bonds with embedded options. An investor who was unaware of this pitfall might conclude that real estate-backed securities offered a better relative value than the other ABS sectors.

Exhibit 1: Generic Asset-Backed Securities Spreads
(As of 7/13/01)

		Princ Pay. Window	(Bid) Static Spread*	1 week Change	3-mo range Wide	3-mo range Tight	Off-the Runs
Credit Cards (Bullets)							
Fixed (AAA)	2-year par	1	66	1	75	62	74
	3-year par	1	85	–3	89	75	85
	5-year par	1	98	–1	99	85	97
	7-year par	1	101	3	101	86	101
	10-year par	1	112	2	118	102	112
(A)	5-year par	1	127	–1	135	113	126
(BBB)	5-year par	1	187	–1	200	177	186
Floating (AAA)	2-year	1	7	0	7	7	
(1 mo. LIBOR)	3-year	1	8	0	9	8	
	5-year	1	13	0	14	13	
	7-year	1	18	0	20	18	
	10-year	1	25	–1	27	25	
(A)	5-year	1	38	0	43	38	
(BBB)	5-year	1	100	0	105	95	
Autos							
Fixed Retail (AAA)	1-year	12	E+8	0	NA	NA	
	2-year	12	78	2	78	62	
	3-year	18	88	–3	92	77	
Student Loans							
Floating (AAA)	2.5 yr (3mo T-Bill)	60	80	0	85	80	
	7.1 yr (3mo T-Bill)	60	108	0	115	108	
Home Equity Loans							
Fixed (AAA)	1-year	23	92	1	94	78	
	2-year	1	123	2	123	100	
	3-year	26	138	–3	142	130	
	5-year	21	168	1	178	163	
	7-year	27	191	–2	199	186	
	11-year	79	200	–1	218	198	
	NAS	178	158	2	158	150	
(AA)	5-year	132	227	2	227	216	
(A)	5-year	117	281	2	289	270	
(BBB)	5-year	93	331	2	344	320	
Floating (AAA)	3.5-year (LIBOR ARMs)	96	25	1	25	24	
	3.5-year (HELOC)	120	24	1	25	23	
Manufactured Housing							
Fixed (AAA)	1-year	22	92	1	94	79	
	2-year	3	123	2	123	103	
	3-year	22	139	–4	144	133	
	5-year	26	169	1	175	164	
	7-year	22	193	–3	206	191	
	10-year	53	202	–3	226	202	
(AA)	11-year	255	255	0	280	255	
(BBB)	7-year	82	460	0	485	460	
(BBB-/Baa3)	16-year	229	900	0	1015	900	

* All spreads quoted to the off-the-runs below except the 2yr, 5yr, and 10yr fixed-rate credit cards, which are quoted to the on-the-runs.

2 yr 6¼ 2/03	3 yr 5⅞ 2/04	5 yr 5⅝ 2/06	7 yr 5½ 2/08	10 yr 6½ 2/10

Source: Adapted from Lehman Brothers, "Generic Asset-Backed Securities Spreads," *MBS & ABS Weekly Outlook*, Fixed Income Research, July 14, 2001.

KEY POINTS

- *The collateral for an asset-backed security can be either amortizing assets (e.g., auto loans and closed-end home equity loans) or nonamortizing assets (e.g., credit card receivables).*
- *For amortizing assets, projection of the cash flow requires projecting prepayments.*
- *For nonamortizing assets, prepayments by an individual borrower do not apply since there is no schedule of principal repayments.*
- *One factor that may affect prepayments is the prevailing level of interest rates relative to the interest rate on the loan.*
- *Since a default is a prepayment (an involuntary prepayment), prepayment modeling for an asset-backed security backed by amortizing assets requires a model for projecting the amount that will be recovered and when it will be recovered.*
- *Cash flow analysis can be performed on a pool level or a loan level.*
- *Since the maturity of an asset-backed security is not a meaningful parameter, the average life of the security is calculated.*
- *Asset-backed securities must be credit enhanced; that is, there must be support from somewhere to absorb a certain amount of losses.*
- *Credit enhancement levels are determined relative to a specific rating desired for a security, and there are two general types of credit enhancement structures: external and internal.*
- *With an asset-backed security, one of the following optional clean-up call provisions may be granted to the trustee: (1) percent of collateral call, (2) percent of bonds, (3) percent of tranche, (4) call on or after specified date, (5) latter of percent or date call, or (6) auction call.*
- *The collateral for a home equity loan is typically a first lien on residential property and the loan fails to satisfy the underwriting standards for inclusion in a loan pool of Ginnie Mae, Fannie Mae, or Freddie Mac because of the borrower's impaired credit history or too high a payment-to-income ratio.*
- *Typically, a home equity loan is used by a borrower to consolidate consumer debt using the current home as collateral rather than to obtain funds to purchase a new home.*
- *The monthly cash flow for a home equity loan-backed security backed by closed-end HELs and a manufactured housing-backed security consists of (1) net interest, (2) regularly scheduled principal payments, and (3) prepayments.*
- *A prospectus prepayment curve is a multiple of the base-case prepayments assumed in the prospectus (i.e., base case is equal to 100% PPC).*
- *To provide stability to the average life of a senior tranche, nonagency MBS or closed-end home equity loan transactions will include either a nonaccelerating senior (NAS) tranche or a planned amortization class (PAC) tranche.*

- ❏ *A NAS tranche receives principal payments according to a schedule based not on a dollar amount for a given month, but instead on a schedule that specifies for each month the share of pro rata principal that must be distributed to the NAS tranche.*

- ❏ *Manufactured housing-backed securities are backed by loans on manufactured homes (i.e., homes built at a factory and then transported to a site).*

- ❏ *Prepayments are more stable for manufactured housing-backed securities because the loans are somewhat insensitive to refinancing.*

- ❏ *Commercial mortgage-backed securities are backed by a pool of commercial mortgage loans—loans on income-producing property.*

- ❏ *Unlike residential mortgage loans where the lender relies on the ability of the borrower to repay and has recourse to the borrower if the payment terms are not satisfied, commercial mortgage loans are nonrecourse loans, and as a result the lender can only look to the income-producing property backing the loan for interest and principal repayment.*

- ❏ *Two measures that have been found to be key indicators of the potential credit performance of a commercial mortgage loan are the debt-to-service coverage ratio (i.e., the property's net operating income divided by the debt service) and the loan-to-value ratio.*

- ❏ *The degree of call protection available to a CMBS investor is a function of (1) call protection available at the loan level and (2) call protection afforded from the actual CMBS structure.*

- ❏ *At the commercial loan level, call protection can be in the form of a prepayment lockout, defeasance, prepayment penalty points, or yield maintenance charges.*

- ❏ *Many commercial loans backing CMBS transactions are balloon loans that require substantial principal payment at the end of the balloon term and therefore the investor faces balloon risk—the risk that the loan will extend beyond the scheduled maturity date.*

- ❏ *The three types of CMBS transactions that have been of interest to bond investors are liquidating trusts, multiproperty single borrowers, and multiproperty conduits.*

- ❏ *The cash flow for auto loan-backed securities consists of regularly scheduled monthly loan payments (interest and scheduled principal repayments) and any prepayments.*

- ❏ *Prepayments on auto loans are not sensitive to interest rates.*

- ❏ *Prepayments on auto loan-backed securities are measured in terms of the absolute prepayment speed (ABS), which measures monthly prepayments relative to the original collateral amount.*

- ❏ *SLABS are asset-backed securities backed by student loans.*

- ❏ *The student loans most commonly securitized are those that are made under the Federal Family Education Loan Program (FFELP), whereby the government makes loans to students via private lenders and the government guaranteeing up to 98% of the principal plus accrued interest.*

- ❑ *Alternative loans are student loans that are not part of a government guarantee program and are basically consumer loans.*
- ❑ *Student loans involve three periods with respect to the borrower's payments—deferment period, grace period, and loan repayment period.*
- ❑ *Small Business Administration (SBA) loans are backed by the full faith and credit of the U.S. government up to a specified amount.*
- ❑ *Most SBA loans are variable-rate loans where the reference rate is the prime rate, with monthly payments consisting of interest and principal repayment.*
- ❑ *Factors contributing to the prepayment speed of a pool of SBA loans are (1) the maturity date of the loan (it has been found that the fastest speeds on SBA loans and pools occur for shorter maturities), (2) the purpose of the loan, and (3) whether there is a cap on the loan.*
- ❑ *Credit card receivable-backed security deals are structured as a master trust.*
- ❑ *For a pool of credit card receivables, the cash flow consists of finance charges collected, fees, and principal.*
- ❑ *The principal repayment of a credit card receivable-backed security is not amortized; instead, during the lockout period, the principal payments made by credit card borrowers are reinvested in additional receivables and after the lockout period (the principal-amortization period), the principal received is no longer reinvested but paid to investors.*
- ❑ *There are provisions in credit card receivable-backed securities that require early amortization of the principal if certain events occur.*
- ❑ *Since for credit card receivable-backed securities the concept of prepayments does not apply, participants look at the monthly payment rate (MPR), which expresses the monthly payment (which includes finance charges, fees, and any principal) of a credit card receivable portfolio as a percentage of debt outstanding in the previous month.*
- ❑ *The MPR for credit card receivable-backed securities is important because (1) if it reaches an extremely low level, there is a chance that there will be extension risk with respect to the principal payments and (2) if the MPR is very low, there is a chance that there will not be sufficient cash flow to pay off principal (which can trigger early amortization of the principal).*
- ❑ *In evaluating the credit risk of an asset-backed security, the rating companies focus on similar areas of analysis: (1) asset risks, (2) structural risks, (3) legal and regulatory considerations, and (4) third parties to the structure.*
- ❑ *A key factor in assessing the quality of the collateral is the amount of equity the borrowers have in the asset.*
- ❑ *To reduce concentration risk in an asset-backed security, rating companies impose concentration limits.*

- *In assessing structural risk, the following factors are examined: (1) the loss allocation among the tranches in the structure, (2) the cash flow allocation, (3) the interest rate spread between the interest earned on the collateral and the interest paid to the tranches plus the servicing fee, (4) the potential for a trigger event to occur that will cause the rapid amortization of a deal, and (5) how credit enhancement may change over time.*

- *Fundamentally, because of the absence of operational risk, an asset-backed security transaction generally has greater certainty about the cash flow than a corporate bond issue.*

- *A true asset-backed security transaction involves minimal involvement by the servicer beyond administrative functions.*

- *In a hybrid asset-backed security transaction, the servicer has more than an administrative function; the greater the importance of the servicer, the more the transaction should be evaluated as a corporate bond issuance.*

Chapter 13

Collateralized Debt Obligations

collateralized debt obligation (CDO) is an asset-backed security backed by a diversified pool of one or more of the following types of debt obligations:

- U.S. domestic high-yield corporate bonds
- U.S. domestic bank loans
- emerging market bonds
- special situation loans and distressed debt
- foreign bank loans
- asset-backed securities
- residential and commercial mortgage-backed securities

When the underlying pool of debt obligations consists of bond-type instruments (high-yield corporate and emerging market bonds), a CDO is referred to as a *collateralized bond obligation* (CBO). When the underlying pool of debt obligations are bank loans, a CDO is referred to as a *collateralized loan obligation* (CLO).

STRUCTURE OF A CDO

In a CDO structure, there is an asset manager responsible for managing the portfolio of debt obligations. There are restrictions imposed (i.e., restrictive covenants) as to what the asset manager may do and certain tests that must be satisfied for the CDO securities to maintain the credit rating assigned at the time of issuance. We'll discuss some of these requirements later.

The funds to purchase the underlying assets (i.e., the bonds and loans) are obtained from the issuance of debt obligations. These debt obligations are referred to as tranches. The tranches are:

- senior tranches
- mezzanine tranches
- subordinate/equity tranche

There will be a rating sought for all but the subordinate/equity tranche. For the senior tranches, at least an A rating is typically sought. For the mezzanine tranches, a rating of BBB but no less than B is sought. Since the subordinate/equity tranche receives the residual cash flow, no rating is sought for this tranche.

The ability of the asset manager to make the interest payments to the tranches and pay off the tranches as they mature depends on the performance of the underlying assets. The proceeds to meet the obligations to the CDO tranches (interest and principal repayment) can come from (1) coupon interest payments from the underlying assets, (2) maturing assets in the underlying pool, and (3) sale of assets in the underlying pool.

In a typical structure, one or more of the tranches is a floating-rate security. With the exception of deals backed by bank loans that pay a floating rate, the asset manager invests in fixed-rate bonds. Now that presents a problem — paying tranche investors a floating rate and investing in assets with a fixed rate. To deal with this problem, the asset manager uses derivative instruments to be able to convert a portion of the fixed-rate payments from the assets into floating-rate cash flow to pay floating-rate tranches. In particular, interest rate swaps are used. This instrument allows investors a market participant to swap fixed-rate payments for floating-rate payments or vice versa. Because of the mismatch between the nature of the cash flows of the debt obligations in which the asset manager invests and the floating-rate liability of any of the tranches, the asset manager must use an interest rate swap. A rating agency will require the use of swaps to eliminate this mismatch.

Arbitrage versus Balance Sheet Transactions

CDOs are categorized based on the motivation of the sponsor of the transaction. If the motivation of the sponsor is to earn the spread between the yield offered on the debt obligations in the underlying pool and the payments made to the various tranches in the structure, then the transaction is referred to as an *arbitrage transaction*. If the motivation of the sponsor is to remove debt instruments (primarily loans) from its balance sheet, then the transaction is referred to as a *balance sheet transaction*. Sponsors of balance sheet transactions are typically financial institutions such as banks seeking to reduce their capital requirements by removing loans due to their higher risk-based capital requirements. Our focus in this chapter in on arbitrage transactions.

ARBITRAGE TRANSACTIONS

The key as to whether it is economically feasible to create an arbitrage CDO is whether a structure can offer a competitive return for the subordinate/equity tranche.

To understand how the subordinate/equity tranche generates cash flows, consider the following basic $100 million CDO structure with the coupon rate to be offered at the time of issuance as follows:

Tranche	Par value	Coupon type	Coupon rate
Senior	$80,000,000	Floating	LIBOR + 70 basis points
Mezzanine	10,000,000	Fixed	Treasury rate + 200 basis points
Subordinated/Equity	10,000,000	—	—

Suppose that the collateral consists of bonds that all mature in 10 years and the coupon rate for every bond is the 10-Treasury rate plus 400 basis points. The asset manager enters into an interest rate swap agreement with another party with a notional principal of $80 million in which it agrees to do the following:

- Pay a fixed rate each year equal to the 10-year Treasury rate plus 100 basis points
- Receive LIBOR

The interest rate agreement is simply an agreement to periodically exchange interest payments. The payments are benchmarked off a notional principal. This amount is not exchanged between the two parties. Rather it is used simply to determine the dollar interest payment of each party. This is all we need to know about an interest rate swap in order to understand the economics of an arbitrage CDO transaction. Keep in mind, the goal is to show how the subordinate/equity tranche can be expected to generate a return.

Let's assume that the 10-year Treasury rate at the time the CDO is issued is 7%. Now we can walk through the cash flows for each year. Look first at the collateral. The collateral will pay interest each year (assuming no defaults) equal to the 10-year Treasury rate of 7% plus 400 basis points. So the interest will be:

Interest from collateral: 11% × $100,000,000 = $11,000,000

Now let's determine the interest that must be paid to the senior and mezzanine tranches. For the senior tranche, the interest payment will be:

Interest to senior tranche: $80,000,000 × (LIBOR + 70 bp)

The coupon rate for the mezzanine tranche is 7% plus 200 basis points. So, the coupon rate is 9% and the interest is:

Interest to mezzanine tranche: 9% × $10,000,000 = $900,000

Finally, let's look at the interest rate swap. In this agreement, the asset manager is agreeing to pay some third party (we'll call this party the "swap counterparty") 7% each year (the 10-year Treasury rate) plus 100 basis points, or 8%. But 8% of what? As explained above, in an interest rate swap payments are based on a notional principal. In our illustration, the notional principal is $80 million. The asset manager selected the $80 million because this is the amount of principal for the senior tranche. So, the asset manager pays to the swap counterparty:

Interest to swap counterparty: 8% × $80,000,000 = $6,400,000

The interest payment received from the swap counterparty is LIBOR based on a notional amount of $80 million. That is,

Interest from swap counterparty: $80,000,000 × LIBOR

Now we can put this all together. Let's look at the interest coming into the CDO:

Interest from collateral	=	$11,000,000
Interest from swap counterparty	=	$80,000,000 × LIBOR
Total interest received	=	$11,000,000 + $80,000,000 × LIBOR

The interest to be paid out to the senior and mezzanine tranches and to the swap counterparty include:

Interest to senior tranche	=	$80,000,000 × (LIBOR + 70 bp)
Interest to mezzanine tranche	=	$900,000
Interest to swap counterparty	=	$6,400,000
Total interest paid	=	$7,300,000 + $80,000,000 × (LIBOR + 70 bp)

Netting the interest payments coming in and going out we have:

Total interest received	=	$11,000,000 + $80,000,000 × LIBOR
– Total interest paid	=	$7,300,000 + $80,000,000 × (LIBOR + 70 bp)
Net interest	=	$3,700,000 – $80,000,000 × (70 bp)

Since 70 bp times $80 million is $560,000, the net interest remaining is $3,140,000 (= $3,700,000 – $560,000). From this amount any fees (including the asset management fee) must be paid. The balance is then the amount available to pay the subordinate/equity tranche. Suppose that these fees are $634,000. Then the cash flow available to the subordinate/equity tranche is $2.5 million. Since the tranche has a par value of $10 million and is assumed to be sold at par, this means that the potential return is 25%.

Obviously, some simplifying assumptions have been made. For example, it is assumed that there are no defaults. It is assumed that all of the issues purchased by the asset manager are noncallable and therefore the coupon rate would not decline because issues are called. Moreover, as explained as follows, after some period the asset manager must begin repaying principal to the senior and mezzanine tranches. Consequently, the interest swap must be structured to take this into account since the entire amount of the senior tranche is not outstanding for the life of the collateral. Despite the simplifying assumptions, the illustration does demonstrate the basic economics of the CDO, the need for the use of an interest rate swap, and how the subordinate/equity tranche will realize a return.

Early Termination

A deal can be terminated early if certain events of default occur. These events basically relate to conditions that are established that would materially adversely impact the performance of the underlying assets. Such events include (1) the failure to comply with certain covenants, (2) failure to meet payments (interest and/

or principal) to the senior tranches, (3) bankruptcy of the issuing entity of the CDO, and (4) departure of the portfolio management team if an acceptable replacement is not found.

CASH FLOW VERSUS MARKET VALUE TRANSACTIONS

Arbitrage transactions can be divided into two types depending on what the primary source of the proceeds from the underlying assets are to come from to satisfy the obligation to the tranches. If the primary source is the interest and maturing principal from the underlying assets, then the transaction is referred to as a *cash flow transaction*. If instead the proceeds to meet the obligations depend heavily on the total return generated from the portfolio (i.e., interest income, capital gain, and maturing principal), then the transaction is referred to as a *market value transaction*.

Cash Flow Transaction

In a cash flow transaction, the objective of the asset manager is to generate cash flow for the senior and mezzanine tranches without the active trading of bonds. Because the cash flows from the structure are designed to accomplish the objective for each tranche, restrictions are imposed on the asset managers. The asset manager is not free to buy and sell bonds. The conditions for disposing of issues held are specified and are usually driven by credit risk management. Also, in assembling the portfolio, the asset manager must meet certain requirements set forth by the rating agency or agencies that rate the deal.

There are three relevant periods. The first is the *ramp-up period*. This is the period that follows the closing date of the transaction where the asset manager begins investing the proceeds from the sale of the debt obligations issued. This period usually lasts from 1 to 2 years. The *reinvestment period* or *revolving period* is where principal proceeds are reinvested and is usually for 5 or more years. In the final period, the portfolio assets are sold and the debtholders are paid off as described as follows.

Distribution of Income

Income is derived from interest income from the underlying assets and capital appreciation. The income is then used as follows. Payments are first made to the trustee and administrators and then to the senior asset manager.[1] Once these fees are paid, then the senior tranches are paid their interest. At this point, before any other payments are made, certain tests must be passed. These tests are called *coverage tests* and are discussed later. If the coverage tests are passed, then interest is

---

[1] There are other management fees that are usually made based on performance, but these fees are made after payments to the mezzanine tranches.

paid to the mezzanine tranches. Once the mezzanine tranches are paid, interest is paid to the subordinate/equity tranche.

In contrast, if the coverage tests are not passed, then payments are made to protect the senior tranches. The remaining income after paying the fees and senior tranche interest is used to redeem the senior tranches (i.e., pay off principal) until the coverage tests are brought into compliance. If the senior tranches are paid off fully because the coverage tests are not brought into compliance, then any remaining income is used to redeem the mezzanine tranches. Any remaining income is then used to redeem the subordinate/equity tranche.

Distribution of Principal Cash Flow

The principal cash flow is distributed as follows after the payment of the fees to the trustees, administrators, and senior managers. If there is a shortfall in interest paid to the senior tranches, principal proceeds are used to make up the shortfall. Assuming that the coverage tests are satisfied, during the reinvestment period the principal is reinvested. After the reinvestment period or if the coverage tests are failed, the principal cash flow is used to pay down the senior tranches until the coverage tests are satisfied. If all the senior tranches are paid down, then the mezzanine tranches are paid off and then the subordinate/equity tranche is paid off.

After all the debt obligations are satisfied in full and if permissible, the equity investors are paid. Typically, there are also incentive fees paid to management based on performance. Usually, a target return for the equity investors is established at the inception of the transaction. Management is then permitted to share on some pro-rated basis once the target return is achieved.

Restrictions on Management

The asset manager must monitor the collateral to ensure that certain tests are being met. There are two types of tests imposed by rating agencies: quality tests and coverage tests.

In rating a transaction, the rating agencies are concerned with the diversity of the assets. Consequently, there are tests that relate to the diversity of the assets. These tests are called *quality tests*. An asset manager may not undertake a trade that will result in the violation of any of the quality tests. Quality tests include (1) a minimum asset diversity score, (2) a minimum weighted average rating, and (3) maturity restrictions. Moreover, for CDOs in which the collateral consists of emerging market bonds, there are restrictions imposed on the concentration of bonds in certain countries or geographical regions.

There are tests to ensure that the performance of the collateral is sufficient to make payments to the various tranches. These tests are called *coverage tests*. There are two types of leverage tests: par value tests and interest coverage ratio. Recall that if the coverage tests are violated, then income from the collateral is diverted to pay down the senior tranches.

Exhibit 1: Illustration of a Hypothetical Market Value Transaction (in millions of dollars)

Capital structure	At closing date	Fully ramped up
Senior facility	$0	$364
Senior note	40	160
Senior-subordinated notes	80	80
Subordinated notes	40	40
Equity	8	160

Market Value Transaction

As with a cash flow transaction, in a market value transaction there are debt tranches and an equity tranche. However, because in a market value transaction the asset manager must sell assets in the underlying pool in order to generate proceeds for interest and repayment of maturing tranches, there is a careful monitoring of the assets and their price volatility. This is done by the frequent marking to market of the assets.

Because a market value transaction relies on the activities of the asset manager to generate capital appreciation and enhanced return to meet the obligations of the tranches in the structure, greater flexibility is granted to the asset manager with respect to some activities compared to a cash flow transaction. For example, while in a cash flow transaction the capital structure is fixed, in a market value transaction the asset manager is permitted to utilize additional leverage after the closing of the transaction.[2] However, the structural covenants imposed on the asset manager in a market value transaction are based on the market value of the underlying assets, not their par value as in the case of cash flow transactions.

Let's illustrate the structure with the hypothetical transaction shown in Exhibit 1. The first column of the exhibit shows the capital structure of the transaction. The capital structure includes a senior facility, senior notes, senior-mezzanine notes, subordinate notes, and equity. The senior facility is a floating-rate revolving loan. This structure has a subordinated tranche as well as an equity tranche. The second column shows the capital structure at the closing date.

During the ramp-up period, the asset manager obtains additional funding based on the target leverage. The additional leverage is provided from the senior borrowing facility and additional amount provided by senior notes. Additional equity is also injected. The last column shows the capital structure when the transaction is fully ramped up.

The order of priority of the principal payments in the capital structure is as follows. Fees are paid first for trustees, administrators, and managers. After these fees are paid, the senior facility and the senior notes are paid. The two classes in the capital structure are treated *pari passu* (i.e., equal in their rights to their claim on cash proceeds from the underlying assets). That is, their payments

[2] The principle of leverage and its advantages and disadvantages are discussed in Chapter 15.

are pro rated if there is a shortfall. If the senior facility or senior notes are amortizing, they would have the next priority on the cash proceeds from the underlying assets with respect to the payment of the principal due. The senior-subordinated notes would be paid, followed by the subordinated notes.

KEY POINTS

- *A collateralized debt obligation is an asset-backed security backed by a diversified pool of debt obligations (high-yield corporate bonds, domestic bank loans, emerging market bonds, and special situation loans and distressed debt).*
- *A collateralized bond obligation is a CDO in which the underlying pool of debt obligations consists of bond-type instruments (high-yield corporate and emerging market bonds).*
- *A collateralized loan obligation is a CDO in which the underlying pool of debt obligations consists of bank loans.*
- *In a CDO there is an asset manager responsible for managing the portfolio of debt obligations.*
- *The tranches in a CDO include senior tranches, mezzanine tranches, and a subordinate/equity tranche.*
- *The senior and mezzanine tranches are rated and the subordinate/equity tranche is unrated.*
- *The proceeds to meet the obligations to the CDO tranches (interest and principal repayment) can come from (1) coupon interest payments of the underlying assets, (2) maturing assets in the underlying pools, and (3) sale of assets in the underlying pool.*
- *CDOs are categorized based on the motivation of the sponsor of the transaction—arbitrage and balance sheet transactions.*
- *The motivation in an arbitrage transaction is for the sponsor to earn the spread between the yield offered on the debt obligations in the underlying pool and the payments made to the various tranches in the structure.*
- *In a balance sheet transaction, the motivation of the sponsor is to remove debt instruments (primarily loans) from its balance sheet.*
- *The key as to whether it is economically feasible to create an arbitrage transaction is whether a structure that offers a competitive return for the subordinate/equity tranche can be accomplished.*
- *Arbitrage transactions can be divided into two types depending on what the primary source of the proceeds from the underlying assets are to come from to satisfy the obligations to the tranches.*
- *In a cash flow transaction, the primary source is the interest and maturing principal from the underlying assets; in a market value transaction, the proceeds to meet the obligations depend heavily on the total return generated from the portfolio.*
- *The three relevant periods in a CDO are the ramp-up period, the reinvestment period or revolving period, and the final period where the portfolio assets are sold and the debt holders are paid off.*

- *In a CDO transaction, senior tranches are protected against a credit deterioration by coverage tests.*
- *A failure of coverage tests results in paying off the senior tranches until the coverage tests are satisfied.*
- *The tests imposed in a cash flow transaction are quality tests and coverage tests.*
- *Quality tests include a minimum asset diversity score, a minimum weighted average rating, and maturity restrictions.*
- *Coverage tests are tests to ensure that the performance of the collateral is sufficient to make payments to the various tranches and include par value tests and interest coverage ratio tests.*
- *In market value transactions, the focus is on monitoring the assets and their price volatility by the frequent marking to market of the assets.*
- *Structural covenants imposed on the asset manager in a market value transaction are based on the market value of the underlying assets, not their par value as in the case of cash flow transactions.*

Chapter 14

International Bonds

In this chapter we will travel the globe and look at international bonds: foreign bonds, Eurobonds, and global bonds. We highlight the debt obligations issued by central governments. The foreign exchange rate risk associated with investing in non-dollar-denominated bonds was explained in Chapter 1. The motivation for investing in international bonds is left for Chapter 18, where we discuss investment strategies. Before describing the markets and instruments, we discuss the foreign exchange market.

FOREIGN EXCHANGE RATES

An *exchange rate* is defined as the amount of one currency that can be exchanged per unit of another currency, or the price of one currency in terms of another currency. For example, let's consider the exchange rate between the U.S. dollar and the Swiss franc. The exchange rate could be quoted in one of two ways:

1. the amount of U.S. dollars necessary to acquire one Swiss franc (i.e., the dollar price of one franc), or
2. the amount of Swiss francs necessary to acquire one U.S. dollar (i.e., the franc price of one dollar).

Exchange rate quotations may be either *direct* or *indirect.* To understand the difference, it is necessary to refer to one currency as a local currency and the other as a foreign currency. For example, from the perspective of a U.S. investor, the local currency would be the U.S. dollar, and any other currency, such as the Swiss franc, would be the foreign currency. From the perspective of a Swiss money manager, the local currency would be the franc, and other currencies, such as the U.S. dollar, the foreign currency.

A *direct quote* is the number of units of a local currency exchangeable for one unit of a foreign currency. An *indirect quote* is the number of units of a foreign currency that can be exchanged for one unit of a local currency. Looking at this from a U.S. money manager's perspective, a quote indicating the number of dollars exchangeable for one unit of a foreign currency is a direct quote. An indirect quote from the same manager's perspective would be the number of units of the foreign currency that can be exchanged for one U.S. dollar. Obviously, from the point of view of a non-U.S. manager, the number of U.S. dollars exchangeable for one unit

of a non-U.S. currency is an indirect quote; the number of units of a non-U.S. currency exchangeable for a U.S. dollar is a direct quote. Given a direct quote, we can obtain an indirect quote (the reciprocal of the direct quote), and vice versa.

Barring any government restrictions, riskless arbitrage will assure that the exchange rate between two countries will be the same in both countries. The theoretical exchange rate between two countries other than the United States can be inferred from their exchange rate with the U.S. dollar.

Dealers in the foreign exchange market are large international banks and other financial institutions that specialize in making markets in foreign exchange, with the former dominating the market. There is no organized exchange where foreign currency is traded, but dealers are linked by telephone and cable, and by various information transfer services. Consequently, the foreign exchange market can best be described as an interbank over-the-counter market. Most transactions between banks are done through foreign exchange brokers.

Dealers quote an exchange rate at which they are willing to buy a foreign currency and one at which they are willing to sell a foreign currency. That is, there is a bid-ask spread. Consequently, a U.S. money manager who has received Japanese yen and wants to exchange those yen into U.S. dollars will request a quote on the bid price for yen. A U.S. money manager who wants to purchase yen in order to buy a bond denominated in that currency will request an ask (or offer) quote.

The *spot exchange rate market* is the market for settlement within 2 business days. Exchange rates between major currencies have been free to float, with market forces determining the relative value of a currency.[1] Thus, each day a currency's price relative to that of another currency may stay the same, increase, or decrease.

A key factor affecting the expectation of changes in a country's exchange rate is the relative expected inflation rate. Spot exchange rates adjust to compensate for the relative inflation rate between two countries. This is the so-called *purchasing power parity* relationship. It says that the exchange rate—the domestic price of the foreign currency—is proportional to the domestic inflation rate and inversely proportional to foreign inflation.

If the number of units of a foreign currency that can be obtained for one U.S. dollar—the price of a U.S. dollar or indirect quotation—rises, the dollar is said to appreciate relative to the foreign currency, and the foreign currency is said to depreciate relative to the dollar. Thus appreciation means a decline in the direct quotation. If the number of units of a foreign currency that can obtained for one U.S. dollar falls, the dollar is said to depreciate relative to the foreign currency and the foreign currency is said to appreciate relative to the dollar.

From the perspective of a U.S. money manager, the cash flows of bonds denominated in a foreign currency expose the manager to uncertainty as to the cash flows in U.S. dollars. The actual U.S. dollars that are received depends on

---

[1] In practice, national monetary authorities can intervene in the foreign exchange market for their currency for a variety of economic reasons, so the current foreign exchange system is sometimes referred to as a "managed" floating-rate system.

the exchange rate between the U.S. dollar and the foreign currency at the time the nondollar cash flow is received and exchanged for U.S. dollars. If the foreign currency depreciates (declines in value) relative to the U.S. dollar (i.e., the U.S. dollar appreciates), the dollar value of the cash flows will be proportionately less. As explained in Chapter 1, this risk is referred to as *foreign exchange risk.*

An investor who purchases a bond whose cash flows are denominated in a currency that is not the medium of exchange of the investor's country faces foreign exchange risk. For example, a French money manager who acquires a yen-denominated Japanese bond is exposed to the risk that the yen will decline in value relative to the French franc.

TRADING BLOCS

Bond markets can be divided into four trading blocs:

1. dollar bloc (the U.S., Canada, Australia, and New Zealand)
2. European bloc
3. Japan
4. emerging markets

The European bloc is subdivided into two groups:

1. *Euro zone market bloc*, which has a common currency (Germany, France, Holland, Belgium, Luxembourg, Austria, Italy, Spain, Finland, and Portugal)
2. *non-Euro zone market bloc*

The United Kingdom often trades more on its own, influenced by both the Euro zone and the United States, as well as its own economic fundamentals.

The trading bloc construct is useful because each bloc has a benchmark market that greatly influences price movements in the other markets. Investors are often focused more on the spread level of, say, Denmark to Germany, than the absolute level of yields in Denmark. Generally speaking, when bond markets are rallying, spreads within each bloc tend to narrow, much as corporate bond spreads tend to tighten in the United States when yields on Treasuries are falling.

TYPES OF INTERNATIONAL BONDS

International bonds can be classified into three categories: foreign bonds, Eurobonds, and global bonds. Within each classification these bonds can be classified by the currency in which the debt obligation is denominated. From the perspective of a U.S. investor, an international bond can be classified as either a *U.S.-pay bond*

if it is denominated in U.S. dollars or a *non-U.S.-pay bond* if it is not denominated in U.S. dollars.

Foreign Bonds

A *foreign bond* is a bond issued in a country's national bond market by an issuer not domiciled in that country and where those bonds are subsequently traded. For example, in the United States a foreign bond is a bond issued by a non-U.S. entity and then subsequently traded in the U.S. bond market. Foreign bonds issued and then traded in the United States are nicknamed *Yankee bonds*. In Japan, a bond issued by a non-Japanese entity and subsequently traded in Japan's bond market is called a *Samurai bond*. Foreign bonds in the United Kingdom are referred to as *Bulldog bonds*, in the Netherlands *Rembrandt bonds*, and in Spain *Matador bonds*.

Regulatory authorities in the country where the bond is issued impose certain rules governing the issuance of foreign bonds. These may include (1) restrictions on the bond structures that may be issued (e.g., unsecured debt, zero-coupon bonds, convertible bonds, etc.), (2) restrictions on the minimum or maximum size of an issue and/or the frequency with which an issuer may come to market, (3) a waiting period before an issuer can bring the issue to market (imposed to avoid an oversupply of issues), (4) a minimum quality standard (credit rating) for the issue or issuer, (5) disclosure and periodic reporting requirements, and (6) restrictions on the types of financial institutions permitted to underwrite issues. The 1980s were characterized by general government relaxation or abolition of these restrictions to open up their bond markets to issuers.

Issuers of foreign bonds include national governments and their subdivisions, corporations (financial and nonfinancial), and supranationals. A *supranational* is an entity that is formed by two or more central governments through international treaties. The purpose for creating a supranational is to promote economic development for the member countries. Two examples of supranational institutions are the *International Bank for Reconstruction and Development*, popularly referred to as the *World Bank*, and the *Inter-American Development Bank*. The general objective of the former is to improve the efficiency of the international financial and trading markets. The objective of the latter supranational is to promote economic growth in the developing countries of the Americas.

An investor in a foreign bond market must understand that country's conventions for quoting yields, calculating accrued interest, and rules for settlement. In some countries, coupon interest is paid semiannually while in others the payment is annual.

Foreign bonds can be denominated in any currency. For example, a foreign bond issued by an Australian corporation in the United States can be denominated in U.S. dollars, Australian dollars, or French francs. From the perspective of a U.S. investor there are *U.S.-pay foreign bonds* and *non-U.S.-pay foreign bonds*.

Foreign bonds can be publicly issued or privately placed. In many countries, foreign bonds have been privately placed. In the United States, one restriction

imposed on privately placed securities is that they may not be resold for 2 years after acquisition. Thus, there is no liquidity in the market for that time period. However, SEC Rule 144A eliminates the 2-year holding period by permitting large institutions to trade securities acquired in a private placement among themselves without having to register these securities with the SEC.

Eurobonds

Eurobonds are bonds that generally have the following distinguishing features: (1) they are underwritten by an international syndicate, (2) at issuance they are offered simultaneously to investors in a number of countries, (3) they are issued outside the jurisdiction of any single country, and (4) they are in unregistered form.

While a general characteristic of a Eurobond is that it is not regulated by the single country whose currency is used to pay bondholders, in practice only the United States and Canada do not place restrictions on U.S. dollar- or Canadian dollar-denominated issues sold outside their country. Regulators of other countries whose currencies are used in Eurobond issues have closely supervised such offerings. Their power to regulate Eurobond offerings comes from their ability to impose foreign exchange and/or capital restrictions.

While Eurobonds are said to be unregistered securities, they are typically registered on a national stock exchange, the most common being the Luxembourg, London, or Zurich exchanges. However, the bulk of all trading is in the over-the-counter market. Listing is purely to circumvent restrictions imposed on some institutional investors who are prohibited from purchasing securities that are not listed on an exchange. Some of the stronger issuers privately place issues with international institutional investors.

Eurobonds are classified based on the currency in which the issue is denominated. For example, when Eurobonds are denominated in U.S. dollars, they are referred to as *Eurodollar bonds*. Eurobonds denominated in Japanese yen are referred to as *Euroyen bonds*.

Securities Issued in the Eurobond Market

The Eurobond market has been characterized by new and innovative bond structures to accommodate particular needs of issuers and investors. There are the "plain vanilla," fixed-rate coupon bonds, referred to as *Euro straights*. Because these are issued on an unsecured basis, they are usually issued by high-quality entities.

Coupon payments are made annually, rather than semiannually, because of the higher cost of distributing interest to geographically dispersed bondholders. There are also zero-coupon bond issues, deferred-coupon issues, and step-up issues, all of which were described in Chapter 1. We discuss several important structures in the Eurobond market—dual-currency bonds, convertible bonds and bonds with warrants, and floating-rate notes—as follows. We also look at Eurocommercial paper and how it differs from commercial paper issued in the United States.

Dual-Currency Bonds There are issues that pay coupon interest in one currency but repay the principal in a different currency. Such issues are called *dual-currency issues*. For the first type of dual-currency bond, the exchange rate that is used to convert the principal and coupon payments into a specific currency is specified at the time the bond is issued. The second type differs from the first in that the applicable exchange rate is the rate that prevails at the time a cash flow is made (i.e, at the spot exchange rate at the time a payment is made). The third type is one that offers to either the investor or the issuer the choice of currency. These bonds are commonly referred to as *option currency bonds*.

Convertible Bonds and Bonds with Warrants A convertible Eurobond is one that can be converted into another asset. Bonds with attached warrants represent a large part of the Eurobond market. A warrant grants the owner of the warrant the right to enter into another financial transaction with the issuer if the owner will benefit as a result of exercising. Most warrants are detachable from the host bond; that is, the bondholder may detach the warrant from the bond and sell it.

There is a wide array of bonds with warrants: *equity warrants*, *debt warrants*, and *currency warrants*. An equity warrant permits the warrant owner to buy the common stock of the issuer at a specified price. A debt warrant entitles the warrant owner to buy additional bonds from the issuer at the same price and yield as the host bond. The debt warrant owner will benefit if interest rates decline because a bond with a higher coupon can be purchased from the same issuer. A currency warrant permits the warrant owner to exchange one currency for another at a set price (i.e., a fixed exchange rate). This feature protects the bondholder against a depreciation of the foreign currency in which the bond's cash flows are denominated. There are also gold warrants, which allow the warrantholder to purchase gold from the issuer of the bond.

Floating-Rate Notes There is a wide variety of floating-rate Eurobond notes. In the Eurobond market, almost all floating-rate notes are denominated in U.S. dollars, with non-U.S. banks being the major issuers. The coupon rate on a Eurodollar floating-rate note is some stated margin over the London Interbank Offered Rate (LIBOR), the bid on LIBOR (referred to as LIBID), or the arithmetic average of LIBOR and LIBID (referred to as LIMEAN). The size of the spread reflects the perceived credit risk of the issuer, margins available in the syndicated loan market, and the liquidity of the issue. Typical reset periods for the coupon rate are either every 6 months or every quarter, with the rate tied to 6-month or 3-month LIBOR, respectively. That is, the length of the reset period and the maturity of the index used to establish the rate for the period are matched.

Many issues have either a minimum coupon rate (or floor) that the coupon rate cannot fall below or a maximum coupon rate (or cap) that the coupon rate cannot rise above. An issue that has both a floor and a cap is said to be *collared*. There are some issues that grant the borrower the right to convert the float-

ing coupon rate into a fixed coupon rate at some time. There are some issues referred to as *drop-lock bonds*, which automatically change the floating coupon rate into a fixed coupon rate under certain circumstances.

A floating-rate note issue will either have a stated maturity date or it may be a *perpetual*, also called *undated*, issue (i.e., with no stated maturity date). The perpetual issue was introduced into the Eurobond market in 1984. For floating-rate notes that do mature, the term is usually greater than 5 years, with the typical maturity being between 7 and 12 years. There are callable and putable floating-rate notes; some issues are both callable and putable.

Eurocommercial Paper As explained in Chapter 8, commercial paper is a short-term unsecured promissory note issued in the open market as an obligation of the issuing entity. Corporations and sovereign entities are issuers of commercial paper. *Eurocommercial paper* is issued and placed outside the jurisdiction of the currency of denomination.

Several differences between U.S. commercial paper and Eurocommercial paper exist with respect to the characteristics of the paper and the market itself. First, commercial paper issued in the United States usually has a maturity of less than 270 days; the most common maturity range is 30 to 50 days or less. The maturity of Eurocommercial paper can be considerably longer. Second, as a safeguard against an issuer being unable to issue new paper at maturity, commercial paper typically is backed by unused bank credit lines. An issuer must have unused bank credit lines in the United States, but it is possible to issue commercial paper without it in the Eurocommercial paper market. Third, U.S. commercial paper can be directly placed or dealer placed; Eurocommercial paper is dealer placed. The fourth distinction is the greater diversity of dealers in the Eurocommercial paper market. In the United States, only a few dealers dominate the market. Finally, because of the longer maturity of Eurocommercial paper than U.S. commercial paper, there is more trading of Eurocommercial paper. In the United States, investors in commercial paper are typically buy-and-hold, thus making the market illiquid.

Comparing Yields on U.S. Bonds and Eurodollar Bonds

Because Eurodollar bonds pay annually rather than semiannually, an adjustment is required to make a direct comparison between the yield to maturity on a U.S. fixed-rate bond and that on a Eurodollar fixed-rate bond. Given the yield to maturity on a Eurodollar fixed-rate bond, its bond-equivalent yield is computed as follows:

$$\text{Bond-equivalent yield of a Eurodollar bond}$$
$$= 2[(1 + ytm \text{ on Eurodollar bond})^{1/2} - 1]$$

For example, suppose that the yield to maturity on a Eurodollar bond is 10%. Then the bond-equivalent yield is:

$$2[(1.10)^{1/2} - 1] = 0.09762 = 9.762\%$$

Notice that the bond-equivalent yield will always be less than the Eurodollar bond's yield to maturity.

To convert the bond-equivalent yield of a U.S. bond issue to an annual-pay basis so that it can be compared to the yield to maturity of a Eurodollar bond, the following formula can be used:

$$\text{Yield to maturity on an annual-pay basis} = \left(1 + \frac{ytm \text{ on a bond-equivalent basis}}{2}\right)^2 - 1$$

For example, suppose that the yield to maturity of a U.S. bond issue quoted on a bond-equivalent yield basis is 10%. The yield to maturity on an annual-pay basis would be:

$$[(1.05)^2 - 1] = 0.1025 = 10.25\%$$

The yield to maturity on an annual basis is always greater than the yield to maturity on a bond-equivalent basis.

Global Bonds

At one time, a global bond was defined as one that was issued and traded in both the U.S. Yankee bond market and the Eurobond market. The first global bond was issued in September 1989 by the World Bank. A few corporations then began to issue global bonds, including offerings of credit card receivable asset-backed securities. Today, a good number of bond issues are labeled "global bonds" or "globals." However, they are not necessarily true global bonds.

The World Bank provides a fair description of the distinguishing characteristics of a global bond.[2] First, the bonds must qualify for issuance in the major bond markets of the world. This makes the bonds available for distribution to a wide range of international investors. Second, to make it easier for investors throughout the world to trade the bonds, they must be easily settled with minimal transaction costs in the home market and via cross-border settlement systems. Third, when the bonds are first offered, the underwriting process must be such that there is an extended period of price discovery dialogue with investors worldwide that results in a fair and reliable offering price. Finally, international syndicates of bond dealers must be used to distribute the issue so that the bonds are issued globally.

CENTRAL GOVERNMENT SECURITIES

In Chapter 4, we covered the securities issued by the U.S. government. The central governments of other countries issue debt obligations that are referred to as

[2] www.worldbank.org/tre/foddr/global.htm

sovereign debt. Many investors who venture into the area of international fixed income investing restrict their holdings to foreign government securities, shunning nongovernment debt obligations by entities in the same country. The reasons for this are the lower credit risk, greater liquidity, and the simplicity of government securities relative to nongovernment debt obligations. While nongovernment markets ("semigovernment," local government, corporate, and mortgage bond markets) provide higher yields, generally they also have greater credit risks, and foreign investors may not be ready to accept alien credit risks and less liquidity.

The institutional settings for government bond markets throughout the world vary considerably, and these variations may affect liquidity and the ways in which strategies are implemented, or, more precisely, they may affect the tactics of investment strategies. For example, in the government bond market different primary market issuance practices may affect the liquidity and the price behavior of specific government bonds in a country. The nature of the secondary market affects the ease and cost of trading. The importance of the benchmark effect in various countries may influence which bonds to trade and hold. In addition, yields are calculated according to different methods in various countries, and these differences will affect the interpretation of yield spreads. Withholding[3] and transfer tax practices also affect global investment strategies.

While the currency denomination of a government security is typically in the currency of the issuing country, a government can issue bonds that are payable in any currency.

Methods of Distribution of New Government Securities

A government can issue securities in its national bond market, which are subsequently traded within that market. Or, a government can issue bonds in the Eurobond market or the foreign sector of another country's bond market. Consequently, a U.S. investor may be able to invest in a non-U.S. government bond of some country by buying a Yankee bond issued by that government, a Eurobond issued by that government, or a bond issued and traded within that government's domestic bond market. In addition to raising funds through the sale of securities, a government can raise funds by borrowing from a bank via a syndicated bank loan. This method of financing is most often used by governments of emerging market countries.

Four methods have been used by central governments to distribute new securities that they issue: (1) regular auction cycle/multiple-price method, (2) regular auction cycle/single-price method, (3) ad hoc auction method, and (4) tap method.

With the *regular auction cycle/multiple-price method* there is a regular auction cycle and winning bidders are allocated securities at the yield (price) they bid. For the *regular auction cycle/single-price method*, there is a regular auction cycle and all winning bidders are awarded securities at the highest yield accepted

---

[3] A country's tax authorities withhold taxes on income derived in their country by nonresident entities. The withholding tax rate may vary, depending on the type of income (dividends or interest). Major trading countries often negotiate tax treaties to reduce the double taxation of income.

by the government (i.e., the stop-out yield). For example, if the highest yield or stop-out yield for an auction is 7.14% and someone bid 7.12%, that bidder would be awarded the securities at 7.14%. In contrast, with the multiple-price method that bidder would be awarded securities at 7.12%. The regular auction cycle/single-price method is used in the United States.

In the *ad hoc auction system*, governments announce auctions when prevailing market conditions appear favorable. It is only at the time of the auction that the amount to be auctioned and the maturity of the security to be offered are announced. This is one of the methods used by the Bank of England in distributing British government bonds. There are two advantages of an ad hoc auction system rather than a regular calendar auction from the issuing government's perspective. First, a regular calendar auction introduces greater market volatility than an ad hoc auction since yields tend to rise as the announced auction date approaches and then fall afterward. Second, there is reduced flexibility in raising funds with a regular calendar auction.

In a *tap system* additional bonds of a previously outstanding bond issue are auctioned. The government announces periodically that it is adding this new supply. The tap system has been used in the United Kingdom and the Netherlands.

Special Structures in Emerging Market Government Bonds

There is a growing interest by institutional investors in emerging market government bonds. The financial markets of Latin America, Asia with the exception of Japan, and Eastern Europe are viewed as emerging markets. Investing in the government bonds of emerging market countries entails considerably more credit risk than investing in the government bonds of major industrialized countries. S&P and Moody's rate emerging market sovereign debt.

Eurobonds

Some emerging market governments have issued Eurobonds denominated in hard currencies (i.e., currencies in which there is international confidence). The bulk of Eurobond issuance is in U.S. dollars. Typically, the issue size is less than $300 million. In normal market conditions the bid-ask spread ranges from 0.5% to 2% of par value; in crisis periods, the bid-ask spread can range from 5% to 7%.[4]

Brady Bonds

The bulk of secondary trading of government debt of emerging market countries is in *Brady bonds*. The bid-ask spreads on these bonds are typically 0.25% of par value and have remained below 1.0% even during major crises.[5] Trading of Brady bonds takes place primarily in New York, followed by London.

Basically, Brady bonds represent a restructuring of nonperforming bank loans of governments into marketable securities. An agreement for the restructuring of nonperforming bank loans was first worked out between Mexico and the United

---

[4] "Emerging Market Debt," Brinson Associates, May 1999, p. 7.

[5] "Emerging Market Debt," p. 7.

States by then Secretary of the Treasury Nicholas Brady—hence, nicknamed Brady bonds. The agreement called for U.S. government and multilateral support to provide relief for principal and interest payments owed to banks outside Mexico if Mexico successfully implemented certain structural reforms. This U.S. government program was then extended to the government debt of other emerging markets. Countries that issue Brady bonds are referred to as "Brady countries."[6] There is a wide range of coupon types: fixed rate, floating, step-up-to-fixed, and step-up-to-floating.

There are two types of Brady bonds. The first type covers the interest due on these loans ("past-due interest bonds"). The second type covers the principal amount owed on the bank loans ("principal bonds"). Principal bonds have maturities at issuance from 25 to 30 years and are bullet bonds. They are more frequently traded than the past-due interest bonds and therefore have better liquidity. The principal bonds fall into two categories: par and discount bonds. Par principal bonds have a fixed rate; discount principal bonds have a floating rate.

Generally, principal bonds are partially collateralized by U.S. Treasury zero-coupon securities. As a result, for many Brady bonds the next two to three coupon payments following a default by the underlying government are guaranteed.

Accrued Interest and Market Conventions

While a year may have 365 days (366 days in a leap year), the bond market in each country has its own way of determining the number of days in a year and the number of days between any two days. As explained in Chapter 2, these are referred to as *day count conventions*. They are important for determining (1) accrued interest and (2) present value calculations when the next coupon payment is less than a full period (either 6 months for a semiannual-pay bond or 1-year for an annual-pay bond). The day count conventions used in international bond markets are discussed later.

Accrued Interest

As explained in Chapters 1 and 2, the price a buyer pays for a bond is the clean price (usually the same as the quoted price) plus accrued interest. If the buyer receives the next coupon, the bond is said to be traded *cum*-coupon (or *cum*-dividend) and the accrued interest is positive (i.e., the buyer pays the seller accrued interest). If the buyer forgoes the next coupon, the bond is said to be traded ex-coupon (or ex-dividend) and the accrued interest is negative (i.e., the seller pays the buyer accrued interest). In some markets (e.g., the United States) bonds are always traded cum-coupon. In other markets, bonds are traded ex-coupon for a certain period before the coupon date.[7]

---

[6] Actually the Brady Plan is more comprehensive than simply the repackaging of nonperforming bank loans into securities. It includes a set of economic policies that the governments of emerging market countries agreed to adopt in order to receive additional international aid to increase the likelihood that the debt obligations will be satisfied.

[7] For comprehensive coverage of this treatment in non-U.S. markets, see Dragomir Krgin, *Handbook of Global Bond Calculations* (New York: John Wiley & Sons, 2002).

As explained in Chapter 1, interest accrues on a bond from and including the date of the previous coupon up to but *excluding* the value date. The value date is usually, but not always, the same as the settlement date. Unlike the settlement date, the value date is not constrained to fall on a business day. The term "value date" is not used consistently across markets—the definition given previously is that used by the International Securities Market Association (ISMA). For example, in some markets the interest accrues up to and *including* the value date.

Accrued Interest Calculation

Accrued interest on a bond traded cum-coupon is the interest that has accrued between the previous coupon date and the value date. Accrued interest on a bond traded ex-coupon is minus the interest that would accrue between the value date and the *next coupon date*. When calculating accrued interest, the coupon payment is assumed to take place on the scheduled date, even if in practice it will be delayed because the scheduled date is a nonbusiness day.

Accrued interest is calculated as follows:

$$AI = \text{Dollar amount of coupon payment} \times \frac{\text{Days}}{AY}$$

where

AI = accrued interest
Days = number of days between the two days
AY = number of days in a year

There are various ways to calculate the number of days between two days (Days) and the number of days in a year (AY). In our discussion, we will let "D1/M1/Y1" denote the previous coupon date and "D2/M2/Y2" denote the value date.

Calculating Number of Days Between Two Days The appendix to Chapter 2 explains the day count conventions in the U.S. bond markets. In government bond markets, one of the following three day count conventions may be used to determine the number of days between two days (Days):

1. *Actual:* Actual number of days between two dates
2. *30*: Assumes 30-day months using the following rules:

- if $D1$ is 31, change to 30
- if $D2$ is 31 and $D1$ is 30 or 31, change $D2$ to 30, otherwise leave at 31.
- Then, the number of days between the two dates is:

$$((Y2 - Y1) \times 360) + ((M2 - M1) \times 30) + (D2 - D1)$$

Thus, there are 29 days between May 1 and May 30 and 30 days between May 1 and May 31.

3. *30E:* Assumes 30-day months using the following rules:
   - if $D1$ is 31, change to 30
   - if $D2$ is 31, change to 30
   - Then the number of days between the two dates is:

$$((Y2 - Y1) \times 360) + ((M2 - M1) \times 30) + (D2 - D1)$$

Thus, with the 30E convention, there are 29 days between May 1 and 30 and 29 days between May 1 and May 31. The 30E method is used in the Euromarkets and some continental domestic markets.

Calculating the Number of Days in a Year For the number of days in a year (AY), one of the following three day count conventions may be used:

1. *365:* Assume a year of 365 days.
2. *Actual:* AY is the number of days in the current coupon period multiplied by the number of coupon payments per year. For a semiannual coupon, the number of days in a coupon period can range from 181 to 184 days so AY can range from 362 to 368 days.
3. *360:* Assume a year of 360 days.

Of the nine possible combinations of Days and AY, only the following five are used in practice: (1) Actual/365, (2) Actual/360, (3) 30/360, (4) 30E/360, and (5) Actual/Actual.

Credit Risk

While U.S. government debt is not rated by any nationally recognized statistical rating organization, the debt of other national governments is rated. These ratings are referred to as *sovereign ratings*. Standard & Poor's and Moody's rate sovereign debt.

The two general categories used by S&P in deriving their ratings are economic risk and political risk. The former category is an assessment of the ability of a government to satisfy its obligations. Both quantitative and qualitative analyses are used in assessing economic risk. Political risk is an assessment of the willingness of a government to satisfy its obligations. A government may have the ability to pay but may be unwilling to pay. Political risk is assessed based on qualitative analysis of the economic and political factors that influence a government's economic policies.

There are two ratings assigned to each national government. The first is a *local currency debt rating* and the second is a *foreign currency debt rating*. The reason for distinguishing between the two types of debt is that historically, the default frequency differs by the currency denomination of the debt. Specifically, defaults have been greater on foreign currency–denominated debt.[8]

---

[8] David T. Beers, "Standard & Poor's Sovereign Ratings Criteria," Chapter 24 in Frank J. Fabozzi (ed.), *The Handbook of Fixed Income Securities*, 5th edition (Burr Ridge, IL: Irwin Professional Publishing, 1997).

The reason for the difference in default rates for local currency debt and foreign currency debt is that if a government is willing to raise taxes and control its domestic financial system, it can generate sufficient local currency to meet its local currency debt obligation. This is not the case with foreign currency–denominated debt. A national government must purchase foreign currency to meet a debt obligation in that foreign currency and therefore has less control with respect to its exchange rate. Thus, a significant depreciation of the local currency relative to a foreign currency in which a debt obligation is denominated will impair a national government's ability to satisfy such obligation.

The implication of this is that the factors both rating agencies analyze in assessing the creditworthiness of a national government's local currency debt and foreign currency debt will differ to some extent. In assessing the credit quality of local currency debt, for example, S&P emphasizes domestic government policies that foster or impede timely debt service. The key factors looked at by S&P are:

- Stability of political institutions and degree of popular participation in the political process.
- Economic system and structure.
- Living standards and degree of social and economic cohesion.
- Fiscal policy and budgetary flexibility.
- Public debt burden and debt service track record.
- Monetary policy and inflation pressures.[9]

The single most important leading indicator according to S&P is the rate of inflation.

For foreign currency debt, credit analysis by S&P focuses on the interaction of domestic and foreign government policies. S&P analyzes a country's balance of payments and the structure of its external balance sheet. The area of analysis with respect to its external balance sheet are the net public debt, total net external debt, and net external liabilities.

[9] Beers, "Standard & Poor's Sovereign Ratings Criteria."

KEY POINTS

- *An exchange rate is defined as the amount of one currency that can be exchanged for another currency.*
- *A direct exchange rate quote is the domestic price of a foreign currency; an indirect quote is the foreign price of the domestic currency.*
- *The spot exchange rate market is the market for settlement within 2 business days.*
- *An investor who purchases a bond whose cash flows are denominated in a currency that is not the medium of exchange of the investor's country faces foreign exchange risk.*
- *International bonds can be classified into three categories: foreign bonds, Eurobonds, and global bonds.*
- *Within each classification, bonds can be classified by the currency in which the debt obligation is denominated.*
- *From the perspective of a U.S. investor, an international foreign bond can be classified as either a U.S.-pay bond if it is denominated in U.S. dollars or a non-U.S.-pay bond if it is not denominated in U.S. dollars.*
- *A foreign bond is a bond issued in a country's national bond market by an issuer not domiciled in that country and where those bonds are subsequently traded.*
- *Yankee bonds are foreign bonds issued and then traded in the U.S. bond market.*
- *Regulatory authorities in the country where the bond is issued impose rules governing the issuance of foreign bonds.*
- *Issuers of foreign bonds include national governments and their subdivisions, corporations (financial and nonfinancial), and supranationals (e.g., the World Bank and the Inter-American Development Bank).*
- *Eurobonds are bonds that generally have the following distinguishing features: (1) they are underwritten by an international syndicate, (2) at issuance they are offered simultaneously to investors in a number of countries, (3) they are issued outside the jurisdiction of any single country, and (4) they are in unregistered form.*
- *Eurobonds are classified based on the currency in which the issue is denominated.*
- *In addition to Euro straights, there are dual-currency bonds, convertible bonds and bonds with warrants, and floating-rate notes issued in the Eurobond market.*
- *Because Eurodollar bonds pay annually rather than semiannually, an adjustment is required to make a direct comparison between the yield to maturity on a U.S. fixed-rate bond and that on a Eurodollar fixed-rate bond.*

- ❑ *A global bond is a debt obligation that is issued simultaneously in several major bond markets and by an international syndicate.*
- ❑ *Sovereign debt is the obligation of a country's central government.*
- ❑ *The institutional settings for government bond markets throughout the world vary considerably, and these variations may affect liquidity and the ways in which strategies are implemented.*
- ❑ *Yields are calculated according to different methods in various countries, and these differences will affect the interpretation of yield spreads.*
- ❑ *There are various methods of distribution that have been used by central governments when issuing securities: regular auction cycle/single-price system, the regular auction cycle/multiple-price system, ad hoc auction system, and the tap system.*
- ❑ *The securities issued by governments of emerging markets are denominated in hard currencies.*
- ❑ *The bulk of secondary trading of government debt of emerging markets is in Brady bonds.*
- ❑ *There are two types of Brady bonds: past-due interest bonds and principal bonds.*
- ❑ *Brady bonds that are principal bonds are either par bonds (which have a fixed rate) or discount bonds (which have a floating rate).*
- ❑ *Generally, principal bonds are partially collateralized by U.S. Treasury zero-coupon securities and for many Brady bonds the next two to three coupon payments following a default by the underlying government are guaranteed.*
- ❑ *Day count conventions vary by country, and they are important for determining accrued interest and present value calculations when the next coupon payment is less than a full period.*
- ❑ *If the buyer receives the next coupon, the bond is said to be traded cum-coupon and the accrued interest is positive (i.e., the buyer pays the seller accrued interest); if the buyer forgoes the next coupon, the bond is said to be traded ex-coupon and the accrued interest is negative (i.e., the seller pays the buyer accrued interest).*
- ❑ *In some markets, bonds are always traded cum-coupon while in other markets, bonds are traded ex-coupon for a certain period before the coupon date.*
- ❑ *Accrued interest on a bond traded cum-coupon is the interest that has accrued between the previous coupon date and the value date.*
- ❑ *In calculating accrued interest, there are various ways to calculate the number of days between two days ("Actual," "30," or "30E") and the number of days in a year ("365," "Actual," or "360").*
- ❑ *Sovereign credits are rated by Standard & Poor's and Moody's.*

- ❑ *In deriving ratings, the two general categories analyzed are economic risk (the ability to pay) and political risk (the willingness to pay).*
- ❑ *There are two ratings assigned to each central government: a local currency debt rating and a foreign currency debt rating.*
- ❑ *Historically, defaults have been greater on foreign currency–denominated debt.*
- ❑ *In assessing the credit quality of local currency debt, S&P, for example, emphasizes domestic government policies that foster or impede timely debt service, with the single most important leading indicator being the rate of inflation.*
- ❑ *For foreign currency debt, S&P analyzes a country's balance of payments and the structure of its external balance sheet.*

Chapter 15

Collateralized Borrowing and Securities Lending

There are investment strategies in which an investor borrows funds to purchase securities. The expectation of the investor is that the return earned by investing in the securities purchased with the borrowed funds will exceed the borrowing cost. There are several sources of funds available to an investor to borrow funds. When securities are to be purchased with the borrowed funds, the most common practice is to use the securities as collateral for the loan. In such instances, the transaction is referred to as a *collateralized loan*.

In this chapter, we look at the common types of collateralized loan in which the collateral is a fixed income security. There are basically two parties in any such transaction: the borrower of the funds and the lender of the funds. For the lender of the funds, a collateralized loan represents an investment. If the maturity of the loan is short term, then a collateralized loan is a short-term investment.

THE PRINCIPLE OF LEVERAGING

The investment principle of borrowing funds in the hope of earning a return in excess of the cost of funds is called *leveraging*. The attractive feature of leveraging is that it magnifies the return that will be realized from investment in a security for a given change in the price of that security. That's the good news. The bad news is that leveraging also magnifies any loss.

To illustrate this point, consider an investor who wants to purchase a 30-year U.S. Treasury bond in anticipation of a decline in interest rates 6 months from now. Suppose that the investor has $1 million to invest. The $1 million is referred to as the investor's *equity*. Assuming that the coupon rate for the 30-year Treasury bond is 8% with the next coupon payment 6 months from now and the bond can be purchased at par value, then the investor can purchase $1 million of par value of an 8% coupon 30-year Treasury bond with the equity available.

Exhibit 1 shows the return that will be realized assuming various yields 6 months from now at which the 8% coupon 30-year Treasury bond will trade. The dollar return consists of the coupon payment 6 months from now and the change in the value of the 30-year Treasury bond. At the end of 6 months, the 30-year Treasury bond is a 29.5-year Treasury bond. The percent return is found by dividing the dollar return by the $1 million equity investment and then annualizing by simply multiplying by 2. Notice that the range for the annualized percent return based on the assumed yields 6 months from now ranges from –29.8% to +63.0%.

Exhibit 1: Annual Return from a $1 Million Investment in a 30-Year 8% Coupon Treasury Bond Held for 6 Months

Assumed yield 6 months from now (%)	Price per $100 par value ($)	Price per $1 million par value ($)	Semiannual coupon payment ($)	Dollar return ($)	Annualized percent return* (%)
10.00	81.12	811,200	40,000	−148,800	−29.8
9.50	85.23	852,300	40,000	−107,700	−21.5
9.00	89.72	897,200	40,000	−62,800	−12.6
8.50	94.62	946,200	40,000	−13,800	−2.8
8.00	100.00	1,000,000	40,000	40,000	8.0
7.50	105.91	1,059,100	40,000	99,100	19.8
7.00	112.41	1,124,100	40,000	164,100	32.8
6.50	119.58	1,195,800	40,000	235,800	47.2
6.00	127.51	1,275,100	40,000	315,100	63.0

* Annualized by doubling semiannual return.

In our illustration, the investor did not borrow any funds. Hence, the strategy is referred to as an "unleveraged strategy." Now let's suppose that the investor can borrow $1 million to purchase an additional $1 million of par value of the 30-year 8% coupon Treasury bond. Assume further that the loan agreement specifies that: (1) the maturity of the loan is 6 months, (2) the annual interest rate is 9%, and (3) $2 million par value of the 30-year 8% coupon Treasury bond is used as collateral. Therefore, the loan is a collateralized loan. The collateral for this loan is the $2 million par value of the 30-year 8% Treasury bond purchased by the investor. The $2 million invested comes from the $1 million of equity and $1 million of borrowed funds. In this strategy, the investor is using leverage. Since the investor has the use of $2 million in proceeds and has equity of $1 million, this amount of leverage is said to be "2-to-1 leverage."

Exhibit 2 shows the annual percent return for this leveraged strategy assuming the same yields at the end of 6 months as in Exhibit 1. The return is measured relative to the $1 million equity investment made by the investor, not the $2 million. The dollar return on the $1 million of equity invested adjusts for the cost of the borrowing.

By using borrowed funds, the range for the annualized percent return is wider (−68.5% to +117.0%) than in the case where no funds are borrowed (−29.8% to 63.0%). This example clearly shows how leveraging is a two-edged sword—it can magnify returns both up and down. Notice that if the market yield does not change at the end of 6 months for the 30-year Treasury bond, then the unleveraged strategy would have generated an 8% annual return. In contrast, the 2-to-1 leveraging strategy would produce only a 7% annual return because while the value of the 30-year Treasury bond did not change, it cost the investor $45,000 to borrow $1 million for 6 months but only earned coupon interest of $40,000 on the $1 million.

Suppose that instead of borrowing $1 million, the investor can find a lender who is willing to lend for 6 months $11 million at an annual interest rate of

9%. The investor can now purchase $12 million of 30-year 8% coupon Treasury bonds—$1 million of equity and $11 million of borrowed funds. The lender requires that the entire $12 million of Treasury bonds be used as collateral for this loan. Since there is $12 million invested and $1 million of equity, this strategy is said to have "12-to-1 leverage."

Exhibit 3 shows the annual return assuming the same yields for the 30-year Treasury 6 months from now as in Exhibits 1 and 2. Notice the considerably wider range for the annual return for the 12-to-1 leverage strategy compared to the 2-to-1 leverage strategy and the unleveraged strategy. In the case where the yield remains at 8%, the 12-to-1 strategy results in an annual return of –3%.

Exhibit 2: Annual Return from a $2 Million Investment in a 30-Year 8% Coupon Treasury Bond Held for 6 Months Using $1 Million of Borrowed Funds

Assumed yield 6 months from now (%)	Price per $100 par value ($)	Price per $2 million par value ($)	Semiannual coupon payment ($)	Dollar return* ($)	Annualized percent return** (%)
10.00	81.12	1,622,400	80,000	–342,600	–68.5
9.50	85.23	1,704,600	80,000	–260,400	–52.1
9.00	89.72	1,794,400	80,000	–170,600	–34.1
8.50	94.62	1,892,400	80,000	–72,600	–14.5
8.00	100.00	2,000,000	80,000	35,000	7.0
7.50	105.91	2,118,200	80,000	153,200	30.6
7.00	112.41	2,248,200	80,000	283,200	56.6
6.50	119.58	2,391,600	80,000	426,600	85.3
6.00	127.51	2,550,200	80,000	585,200	117.0

* After deducting interest expense of $45,000 ($1 million × 9%/2).
** Annualized by doubling semiannual return.

Exhibit 3: Annual Return from a $12 Million Investment in a 30-Year 8% Coupon Treasury Bond Held for 6 Months Using $11 Million of Borrowed Funds

Assumed yield 6 months from now (%)	Price per $100 par value ($)	Price per $11 million par value ($)	Semiannual coupon payment ($)	Dollar return ($)*	Annualized percent return (%)**
10.00	81.12	9,734,400	480,000	–2,228,600	–456.1
9.50	85.23	10,227,600	480,000	–1,787,400	–357.5
9.00	89.72	10,766,400	480,000	–1,248,600	–249.7
8.50	94.62	11,354,400	480,000	–660,600	–132.1
8.00	100.00	12,000,000	480,000	–15,000	–3.0
7.50	105.91	12,709,200	480,000	694,200	138.8
7.00	112.41	13,489,200	480,000	1,474,200	294.8
6.50	119.58	14,349,600	480,000	2,334,600	466.9
6.00	127.51	15,301,200	480,000	3,286,200	657.2

* After deducting interest expense of $495,000 ($11 million × 9%/2).
** Annualized by doubling semiannual return.

Exhibit 4: Annual Return for Various Degrees of Leverage

Assumed yield 6 months from now (%)	Annual return for $1 million of equity and debt of $X million					
	$0	$1	$2	$4	$5	$11
10.00	−29.8%	−68.5%	−107.3%	−146.0%	−223.6%	−456.1%
9.50	−21.5	−52.1	−82.6	−113.2	174.2	−357.5
9.00	−12.6	−34.1	−55.7	−77.2	120.4	−249.7
8.50	−2.8	−14.5	−26.3	−38.0	61.6	−132.1
8.00	8.0	7.0	6.0	5.0	3.0	−3.0
7.50	19.8	30.6	41.5	52.3	73.9	138.8
7.00	32.8	56.6	80.5	104.3	151.9	294.8
6.50	47.2	85.3	123.5	161.6	238.0	466.9
6.00	63.0	117.0	171.1	225.1	333.1	657.2

Exhibit 4 shows the range for different degrees of leverage. The greater the leverage, the wider the range of potential outcomes, and therefore the greater the risk.

Let's look at this from the lender's perspective. The lender is exposed to the risk that the borrower will default. The lender seeks to protect against this risk by requiring that the borrower use the security purchased as collateral for the loan. If the borrower defaults, the lender can sell the collateral and use the proceeds invested to pay off the borrower's debt obligation. In a collateralized loan, the risk is that the security's value will be less than the amount borrowed. In a collateralized loan, the lender can protect against this risk by requiring the frequent marking to market of the collateral. If the collateral's value falls below some level, the lending agreement can specify that additional collateral must be put up by the borrower in the form of cash or additional securities.

REPURCHASE AGREEMENT

A *repurchase agreement* is the sale of a security with a commitment by the seller to buy the same security back from the purchaser at a specified price at a designated future date. The price at which the seller must subsequently repurchase the security is called the *repurchase price*, and the date that the security must be repurchased is called the *repurchase date*. Basically, a repurchase agreement is a collateralized loan, where the collateral is the security sold and subsequently repurchased. The agreement is best explained with an illustration.

Suppose a government securities dealer has purchased $10 million of a particular Treasury security. Where does the dealer obtain the funds to finance that position? Of course, the dealer can finance the position with its own funds or by borrowing from a bank. Typically, however, the dealer uses the repurchase agreement or "repo" market to obtain financing. In the repo market, the dealer can use the $10 million of the Treasury security as collateral for a loan. The term of the loan and the interest rate that the dealer agrees to pay are specified. The inter-

est rate is called the *repo rate*. When the term of the loan is 1 day, it is called an *overnight repo;* a loan for more than one day is called a *term repo*. The transaction is referred to as a repurchase agreement because it calls for the sale of the security and its repurchase at a future date. Both the sale price and the purchase price are specified in the agreement. The difference between the purchase (repurchase) price and the sale price is the dollar interest cost of the loan.

Back to the dealer who needs to finance $10 million of a Treasury security that it purchased and plans to hold overnight. Suppose that a customer of the dealer has excess funds of $10 million. (The customer might be a municipality with tax receipts that it has just collected and has no immediate need to disburse the funds.) The dealer would agree to deliver ("sell") $10 million of the Treasury security to the customer for an amount determined by the repo rate and buy ("repurchase") the same Treasury security from the customer for $10 million the next day. Suppose that the overnight repo rate is 6.5%. Then, as will be explained later, the dealer would agree to deliver the Treasury securities for $9,998,194 and repurchase the same securities for $10 million the next day. The $1,806 difference between the "sale" price of $9,998,194 and the repurchase price of $10 million is the dollar interest on the financing.

The following formula is used to calculate the dollar interest on a repo transaction:

$$\text{Dollar interest} = (\text{Dollar principal}) \times (\text{Repo rate}) \times \text{Repo term}/360$$

Notice that the interest is computed on a 360-day basis. In our example, at a repo rate of 6.5% and a repo term of 1 day (overnight), the dollar interest is $1,805 as shown below:

$$\$9{,}998{,}195 \times 0.065 \times 1/360 = \$1{,}805$$

The advantage to the dealer of using the repo market for borrowing on a short-term basis is that the rate is lower than the cost of bank financing. (The reason for this is explained later.) From the customer's perspective, the repo market offers an attractive yield on a short-term secured transaction that is highly liquid.

While the example illustrates financing a dealer's long position in the repo market, dealers can also use the market to cover a short position. For example, suppose a government dealer sold $10 million of Treasury securities 2 weeks ago and must now cover the position (i.e., deliver the securities). The dealer can do a *reverse repo* (agree to buy the securities and sell them back). Of course, the dealer eventually would have to buy the Treasury security in the market in order to cover its short position. In this case, the dealer is actually making a collateralized loan to its customer. The customer is then using the funds obtained from the collateralized loan to create leverage.

There is a good deal of Wall Street jargon describing repo transactions.[1] To understand it, remember that one party is lending money and accepting a security as

collateral for the loan; the other party is borrowing money and providing collateral to borrow the money. When someone lends securities in order to receive cash (i.e., borrow money), that party is said to be "reversing out" securities. A party that lends money with the security as collateral is said to be "reversing in" securities. The expressions "to repo securities" and "to do repo" are also used. The former means that someone is going to finance securities using the security as collateral; the latter means that the party is going to invest in a repo. Finally, the expressions "selling collateral" and "buying collateral" are used to describe a party financing a security with a repo on the one hand, and lending on the basis of collateral, on the other.

Rather than using industry jargon, investment guidelines should be clear as to what a manager is permitted to do. For example, a client may have no objections to its money manager using a repo as a short-term investment (i.e., the money manager may lend funds on a short-term basis). The investment guidelines will set forth how the loan arrangement should be structured to protect against credit risk. We'll discuss this later. However, if a client does not want a money manager to use the repo agreement as a vehicle for borrowing funds (thereby, creating leverage), it should state so.

While in our illustration we used Treasury securities as the collateral, the collateral in a repo is not limited to government securities. Money market instruments, federal agency securities, and mortgage-backed securities are also used. In some specialized markets, whole loans are used as collateral.

Most repo market participants in the United States use the Master Repurchase Agreement published by the Bond Market Association. In Europe, the Global Master Repurchase Agreement published by the BMA and the International Securities Market Association has become widely accepted.

Credit Risks

Although there may be high-quality collateral underlying a repo transaction, both parties to the transaction are exposed to credit risk. Why does credit risk occur in a repo transaction? Consider our initial example where the dealer uses $10 million of

---

[1] The jargon relating to repo transactions gets even more confusing when we look at the use of this vehicle by the Federal Reserve. The Federal Reserve influences short-term interest rates through its open market operations (i.e., by the outright purchase or sale of government securities). This is not the common practice followed by the Fed, however. It uses the repo market instead to implement monetary policy by purchasing or selling collateral. By buying collateral (i.e., lending funds), the Fed injects money into the financial markets, thereby exerting downward pressure on short-term interest rates. When the Fed buys collateral for its own account, this is called a *system repo*. The Fed also buys collateral on behalf of foreign central banks in repo transactions that are referred to as *customer repos*. It is primarily through system repos that the Fed attempts to influence short-term rates. By selling securities for its own account, the Fed drains money from the financial markets, thereby exerting upward pressure on short-term interest rates. This transaction is called a *matched sale*. Note the language that is used to describe the transactions of the Fed in the repo market. When the Fed lends funds based on collateral, we call it a system or customer repo, not a reverse repo. Borrowing funds using collateral is called a matched sale, not a repo. The terminology can be confusing, which is why we use the expressions "buying collateral" and "selling collateral" to describe what parties in the market are doing.

government securities as collateral to borrow. If the dealer cannot repurchase the government securities, the customer may keep the collateral; if interest rates on government securities increase subsequent to the repo transaction, however, the market value of the government securities will decline, and the customer will own securities with a market value less than the amount it lent to the dealer. If the market value of the security rises instead, the dealer will be concerned with the return of the collateral, which then has a market value higher than the loan.

Repos should be carefully structured to reduce credit risk exposure. The amount lent should be less than the market value of the security used as collateral, thereby providing the lender with some cushion in case the market value of the security declines. The amount by which the market value of the security used as collateral exceeds the value of the loan is called *repo margin* or simply margin. Margin is also referred to as the "haircut." Repo margin is generally between 1% and 3%. For borrowers of lower creditworthiness and/or when less liquid securities are used as collateral, the repo margin can be 10% or more.

Another practice to limit credit risk is to mark the collateral to market on a regular basis. (Marking a position to market means recording the value of a position at its market value.) When market value changes by a certain percentage, the repo position is adjusted accordingly. The decline in market value below a specified amount will result in a *margin deficit*. Paragraph 4(a) of the BMA Master Repurchase Agreement gives the "Seller" (the dealer in our example) the option to cure the margin deficit by either providing additional cash to the "Buyer" or by transferring "additional Securities reasonably acceptable to Buyer."[2] Suppose instead that the market value rises above the amount required for margin. This results in a *margin excess*. In such instances, Paragraph 4(b) grants the "Buyer" the option to give the "Seller" cash equal to the amount of the margin excess or to transfer purchased securities to the "Seller."[3]

---

[2] Paragraph 4(a) reads:

> If at any time the aggregate Market Value of all Purchased Securities subject to all Transactions in which a particular party hereto is acting as Buyer is less than the aggregate Buyer's Margin Amount for all such Transactions (a "Margin Deficit"), then Buyer may by notice to Seller require Seller in such Transactions, at Seller's option, to transfer to Buyer cash or additional Securities reasonably acceptable to Buyer ("Additional Purchased Securities"), so that the cash and aggregate Market Value of the Purchased Securities, including any such Additional Purchased Securities, will thereupon equal or exceed such aggregate Buyer's Margin Amount (decreased by the amount of any Margin Deficit as of such date arising from any Transactions in which such Buyer is acting as Seller).

[3] Paragraph 4(b) reads:

> If at any time the aggregate Market Value of all Purchased Securities subject to all Transactions in which a particular party hereto is acting as Seller exceeds the aggregate Seller's Margin Amount for all such Transactions at such time (a "Margin Excess"), then Seller may by notice to Buyer require Buyer in such Transactions, at Buyer's option, to transfer cash or Purchased Securities to Seller, so that the aggregate Market Value of the Purchased Securities, after deduction of any such cash or any Purchased Securities so transferred, will thereupon not exceed such aggregate Seller's Margin Amount (increased by the amount of any Margin Excess as of such date arising from any Transactions in which such Seller is acting as Buyer).

Since the BMA Master Repurchase Agreement covers all transactions where a party is on one side of the transaction, the discussion of margin maintenance in Paragraph 4 is in terms of "the aggregate Market Value of all Purchased Securities in which a particular party hereto is acting as Buyer" and "the aggregate Buyer's Margin Account for all such Transactions." Thus, maintenance margin is not looked at from an individual transaction or security perspective. However, Paragraph 4(e) permits the "Buyer" and "Seller" to agree to override this provision to apply the margin maintenance requirement to a single transaction.[4]

The price to be used to mark positions to market is defined in Paragraph 2(h)—definition of "Market Value." The price is one "obtained from a generally recognized source agreed to by the parties or the most recent closing bid quotation from such a source." For complex securities that do not trade frequently, there is difficulty in obtaining a price at which to mark a position to market.

One concern in structuring a repo is delivery of the collateral to the lender. The most obvious procedure is for the borrower to deliver the collateral to the lender or to the cash lender's clearing agent. In such instances, the collateral is said to be "delivered out." At the end of the repo term, the lender returns the collateral to the borrower in exchange for the principal and interest payment. This procedure may be too expensive though, particularly for short-term repos, because of costs associated with delivering the collateral. The cost of delivery would be factored into the transaction by a lower repo rate that the borrower would be willing to pay. The risk of the lender not taking possession of the collateral is that the borrower may sell the security or use the same security as collateral for a repo with another party.

As an alternative to delivering out the collateral, the lender may agree to allow the borrower to hold the security in a segregated customer account. Of course, the lender still faces the risk that the borrower may use the collateral fraudulently by offering it as collateral for another repo transaction. If the borrower of the cash does not deliver out the collateral, but instead holds it, then the transaction is called a *hold-in-custody repo* (HIC repo). Despite the credit risk associated with an HIC repo, it is used in some transactions when the collateral is difficult to deliver (such as in whole loans) or the transaction amount is small and the lender of funds is comfortable with the reputation of the borrower of the cash.

Another method is for the borrower to deliver the collateral to the lender's custodial account at the borrower's clearing bank. The custodian then has possession of the collateral that it holds on behalf of the lender. This practice reduces the cost of delivery because it is merely a transfer within the borrower's

---

[4] Paragraph 4(e) reads:

> Seller and Buyer may agree, with respect to any or all Transactions hereunder, that the respective rights of Buyer or Seller (or both) under subparagraphs (a) and (b) of this Paragraph may be exercised only where a Margin Deficit or Margin Excess, as the case may be, exceeds a specified dollar amount or a specified percentage of the Repurchase Prices for such Transactions (which amount or percentage shall be agreed to by Buyer and Seller prior to entering into any such Transactions).

clearing bank. If, for example, a dealer enters into an overnight repo with Customer A, the next day the collateral is transferred back to the dealer. The dealer can then enter into a repo with Customer B for, say, 5 days without having to redeliver the collateral. The clearing bank simply establishes a custodian account for Customer B and holds the collateral in that account. This specialized type of repo arrangement is called a *tri-party repo*. In fact, for some regulated institutions (e.g., federal credit unions), this is the only type of repo arrangement permitted.

There are also *four-party repos*. The difference between a tri-party repo and a four-party repo is that there is a subcustodian that is the custodian for the lender. This arrangement does not provide any additional protection to the lender. Rather, in the rare circumstances that it is used, it is because of legal requirements. For example, the investment guidelines might specify that in a repo the custodian must be a bank in a particular city. If the borrower of fund's custodian in a tri-party repo is not located in that city, a subcustodian in the specified city must be used.

Paragraph 8 ("Segregation of Purchased Securities") of the BMA Master Repurchase Agreement deals with the possession of the collateral. There are special disclosure provisions when the "Seller" retains custody of the collateral. (See Exhibit 5.)

Paragraph 11 ("Events of Default") sets forth the events that will trigger a default of one of the parties and the options available to the nondefaulting party. In the case of a bankruptcy by the borrower, the bankruptcy code in the United States affords the lender of funds in a qualified repo transaction a special status. It does so by exempting certain types of repos from the stay provisions of the bankruptcy law. This means that the lender of funds can immediately liquidate the collateral to obtain cash.

Exhibit 5: Required Disclosure for Transactions in which the Seller Retains Custody of the Purchased Securities from Bond Market Association Master Repurchase Agreement

Seller is not permitted to substitute other securities for those subject to this Agreement and therefore must keep Buyer's securities segregated at all times, unless in this Agreement Buyer grants Seller the right to substitute other securities. If Buyer grants the right to substitute, this means that Buyer's securities will likely be commingled with Seller's own securities during the trading day. Buyer is advised that, during any trading day that Buyer's securities are commingled with Seller's securities, they [will]* [may]** be subject to liens granted by Seller to [its clearing bank]* [third parties]** and may be used by Seller for deliveries on other securities transactions. Whenever the securities are commingled, Seller's ability to resegregate substitute securities for Buyer will be subject to Seller's ability to satisfy [the clearing]* [any]** lien or to obtain substitute securities.

* Language to be used under 17 C.F.R. ß403.4(e) if Seller is a government securities broker or dealer other than a financial institution.

** Language to be used under 17 C.F.R. ß403.5(d) if Seller is a financial institution.

Participants in the Market

Because it is used by dealer firms (investment banking firms and money center banks acting as dealers) to finance positions and cover short positions, the repo market has evolved into one of the largest sectors of the money market. Financial and nonfinancial firms participate in the market as both sellers and buyers, depending on the circumstances they face. Thrifts and commercial banks are typically net sellers of collateral (i.e., net borrowers of funds); money market funds, bank trust departments, municipalities, and corporations are typically net buyers of collateral (i.e., providers of funds).

While a dealer firm uses the repo market as the primary means for financing its inventory and covering short positions, it will also use the repo market to run a "matched book" where it takes on repos and reverse repos with the same maturity. The firm does so to capture the spread at which it enters into the repo agreement (i.e., arrangement to borrow funds) and reverse repo agreement (i.e., arrangement to lend funds). For example, suppose that a dealer enters into a term repo of 10 days with a money market fund and a reverse repo rate with a thrift for 10 days, for which the collateral is identical. This means that the dealer is borrowing funds from the money market fund and lending money to the thrift. If the repo rate on the repo is 7.5% and the repo rate on the reverse repo is 7.55%, the dealer is borrowing at 7.5% and lending at 7.55%, locking in a spread of 0.05% (5 basis points).

Another participant is the repo broker. To understand the role of the repo broker, suppose that a dealer has shorted $50 million of a security. It will then survey its regular customers to determine if it can borrow, via a reverse repo, the security it shorted. Suppose that it cannot find a customer willing to do a repo transaction (repo from the customer's point of view, reverse repo from the dealer's). At that point, the dealer will use the services of a repo broker.

Determinants of the Repo Rate

There is not one repo rate. The rate varies from transaction to transaction depending on a variety of factors: quality of collateral, term of the repo, delivery requirement, availability of collateral, and the prevailing federal funds rate.

The higher the credit quality and liquidity of the collateral, the lower the repo rate. The effect of the term of the repo on the rate depends on the shape of the yield curve. As noted earlier, if delivery of the collateral to the lender is required, the repo rate will be lower. If the collateral can be deposited with the bank of the borrower, a higher repo rate is paid.

The more difficult it is to obtain the collateral, the lower the repo rate. To understand why this is so, remember that the borrower (or equivalently the seller of the collateral) has a security that lenders of cash want, for whatever reason. Such collateral is referred to as *hot* or *special collateral*. (Collateral that does not have this characteristic is referred to as *general collateral*.) The party that needs the hot collateral will be willing to lend funds at a lower repo rate in order to obtain the collateral.

While these factors determine the repo rate on a particular transaction, the federal funds rate determines the general level of repo rates. The repo rate generally will be a rate lower than the federal funds rate because a repo involves collateralized borrowing, while a federal funds transaction is unsecured borrowing.

Hot (Special) Collateral and Arbitrage

Earlier in this chapter, we explained how an investor can use collateralized borrowing to create a leveraged position and the risk associated with a leveraged position. In certain circumstances a borrower of funds via a repo transaction can generate an *arbitrage opportunity.* This occurs when it is possible to borrow funds at a lower rate than the rate that can be earned by reinvesting those funds.

Such opportunities arise when a portfolio includes securities that are hot or special and the manager can reinvest at a rate higher than the repo rate. For example, suppose that a manager has hot collateral in a portfolio, Bond X, that lenders of funds are willing to take as collateral for 2 weeks charging a repo rate of 3%. Suppose further that the manager can invest the funds in a 2-week Treasury bill (the maturity date being the same as the term of the repo) and earn 4%. Assuming that the repo is properly structured so that there is no credit risk, then the manager has locked in a spread of 1% for 2 weeks. This is a pure arbitrage. The manager faces no risk. Of course, the manager is exposed to the risk that Bond X would decline in value, but this risk would exist as long as the manager intended to hold that security in the portfolio anyway.

Risk Arbitrage: The Financial Equivalent of a "Little Pregnant"

The term *arbitrage* in its purest sense means that there is no risk in a strategy but that the strategy offers the opportunity to earn a positive return without investing any funds. The illustration that we just gave is an example of an arbitrage.

Unfortunately, some market participants use the term *arbitrage* in a more cavalier way. Even if there is risk in a strategy, so long as that risk is perceived to be small—small being a quantity defined by the user of the term—the term *arbitrage* is used. Some market participants will qualify the term by using the adjective "risk" (i.e., risk arbitrage). In such a context, arbitrage with no risk is then referred to as "riskless arbitrage."

Let's look at a so-called risk arbitrage that has been used by some money managers. Suppose that a manager buys an adjustable-rate passthrough security backed by Freddie Mae or Fannie Mae, two government-sponsored enterprises. Suppose that the coupon rate is reset monthly based on the following coupon formula:

1-month LIBOR + 80 basis points

with a cap of 9% (i.e., maximum coupon rate of 9%).

Suppose that the manager can use these securities in a repo transaction in which (1) a repo margin of 5% is required, (2) the term of the repo is 1 month, and (3) the repo rate is 1-month LIBOR plus 10 basis points. Also assume that the manager wishes to invest $1 million of his own funds in these securities. The manager can purchase $20 million in par value of these securities since only $1 million of equity is required. The amount borrowed would be $19 million. The leverage is 20-to-1. Thus, the manager realizes a spread of 70 basis points on the $19 million borrowed since LIBOR plus 80 basis points is earned in interest each month (coupon rate) and LIBOR plus 10 basis point is paid each month (repo rate).

This strategy is sometimes referred to as an arbitrage. However, it has two risks. First, the price of the security may decline because the market may require a spread greater than 80 basis points over LIBOR. Thus, there is *price risk* if the security must be sold prior to maturity. Second, there is the risk that the cost of funds may exceed the cap. For example, if 1-month LIBOR is 9.9% in some month, the coupon rate on the security would be capped at 9%. However, the cost of funds would be 10% (1-month LIBOR plus 10 basis points), the borrowing cost not being capped. Thus, the dollar return and percent return for the month would be:

9% coupon on $20 million par value	$1,800,000
10% borrowing cost on $19 million	$1,900,000
Dollar return for month	–$100,000
Return on equity for month	–10%

The risk that the financing cost will exceed the coupon rate due to a restriction on the coupon rate is called *cap risk*.

DOLLAR ROLLS

In the mortgage-backed securities market, a special type of collateralized loan has developed because of the characteristics of these securities and the need of dealers to borrow these securities to cover short positions. This arrangement is called a *dollar roll* because the dealer is said to "roll in" securities borrowed and "roll out" securities when returning the securities to the investor.

As with a repo agreement, it is a collateralized loan that calls for the sale and repurchase of a security. Unlike a repo agreement, the dealer who borrows the securities need not return the identical securities. That is, the dealer need only return "substantially identical securities." This means that the security returned by the dealer who borrows the security must match the coupon rate and security type (i.e., issuer and mortgage collateral). This provides flexibility to the dealer. In exchange for this flexibility, the dealer provides 100% financing. That is, there is no overcollateralization or margin required. Moreover, the financing cost may be cheaper than in a repo because of this flexibility. Finally, unlike in a repo, the dealer keeps the coupon and any principal paid during the period of the loan.

Determination of the Financing Cost

Determination of the financing cost is not as simple as in a repo. The key elements in determining the financing cost *assuming that the dealer is borrowing securities/lending cash* are:

1. the sale price and the repurchase price
2. the amount of the coupon payment
3. the amount of the principal payments due to scheduled principal payments
4. the projected prepayments of the security sold (i.e., rolled in to the dealer)
5. the attributes of the substantially identical security that is returned (i.e., rolled out by the dealer)
6. the amount of under- or overdelivery permitted

Let's look at these elements. In a repo agreement, the repurchase price is greater than the sale price, the difference representing interest, and is called the *drop*. In the case of a dollar roll, the repurchase price need not be greater than the sale price. In fact, in a positively sloped yield curve environment (i.e., long-term rates exceed short-term rates), the repurchase price will be less than the purchase price because of the second element, the coupon payment. The dealer keeps the coupon payment.

The third and fourth elements involve principal repayments. As explained in Chapter 8, where we discuss the cash flows for passthrough securities, the principal payments include scheduled principal and prepayments. As with the coupon payments, the dealer retains the principal payments during the period of the agreement. A gain will be realized by the dealer on any principal repayments if the security is purchased by the dealer at a discount and a loss if purchased at a premium. Because of prepayments, the principal that will be paid is unknown and, as will be seen, represents a risk in the determination of the financing cost.

The fifth element is another risk since the effective financing cost will depend on the attributes of the substantially identical security that the dealer will roll out (i.e., the security it will return to the lender of the securities) at the end of the agreement. Finally, as explained in Chapter 8, there are delivery tolerances. For example, BMA delivery standards permit under- or overdelivery of up to 2.5%. In a dollar roll, the investor and the dealer have the option to under- or overdeliver: the investor when delivering the securities at the outset of the transaction and the dealer when returning the securities at the repurchase date.

To illustrate how the financing cost for a dollar roll is calculated, suppose that an investor enters into an agreement with a dealer in which it agrees to sell $10 million par value (i.e., unpaid aggregate balance) of Ginnie Mae 8s at 101⁷⁄₃₂ and repurchase substantially identical securities a month later at 101 (the repurchase price). The drop is therefore ⁷⁄₃₂. While under- or overdelivery is permitted, we will assume that $10 million par value will be delivered to the dealer by the investor and the same amount of par value will be returned to the investor

by the dealer. Since the sale price is $101\frac{7}{32}$, the investor will receive in cash \$10,121,875 (101.21875 × \$10 million). At the repurchase date, the investor can repurchase substantially identical securities for 101 or \$10,100,000. Therefore, the investor can sell the securities for \$10,121,875 and buy them back for \$10,100,000. The difference, which is the drop, is \$21,875.

To offset this drop, the investor forfeits the coupon interest during the period of the agreement to the dealer. Since the coupon rate is 8%, the coupon interest forfeited is \$66,666 (8% × \$10 million/12). The dealer is also entitled to any principal repayments, both regularly scheduled and prepayments. Since the dealer purchases the securities from the investor at $\$101\frac{7}{32}$, any principal repayments will result in a loss of $\$1\frac{7}{32}$ per \$100 of par value of principal repaid. From the investor's perspective, this is a benefit and effectively reduces the financing cost. While the regularly scheduled amount can be determined, prepayments must be projected based on some PSA speed. In our illustration, for simplicity let's assume that the regularly scheduled principal payment for the month is \$6,500 and the prepayment is projected to be \$20,000 based on some PSA spread. Since $\$1\frac{7}{32}$ is lost per \$100 par value repaid, the dealer loses \$79 due to the regularly scheduled principal payment ($1\frac{7}{32}$ × \$6,500/100) and \$244 from prepayments ($1\frac{7}{32}$ × \$20,000/100).

The monthly financing cost is then:

Lost coupon interest			\$66,666
Offsets			22,198
Drop (gain from repurchase)		21,875	
Principal repayment premium gained		323	
Due to regularly schedule principal	79		
Due to prepayments	244		
Total financing cost			\$44,468
Monthly financing cost			0.00445
Annual financing cost (monthly rate × 12)			5.34%

The financing cost as calculated, 5.34%, must be compared with alternative financing opportunities. For example, funds can be borrowed via a repo agreement using the same Ginnie Mae collateral. In comparing financing costs, it is important that the dollar amount of the cost be compared to the amount borrowed. For example, in our illustration we annualized the cost by multiplying the monthly rate by 12. The convention in other financing markets may be different for annualizing. Moreover, it is not proper to compare financing costs of other alternatives without recognizing the risks associated with a dollar roll.

Before discussing these risks, it is important to note that there is a factor that can reduce the investor's financing cost. When a dollar roll is entered into, the agreement calls for delivery of the securities by the investor to the dealer at some specified future date. The sale price and repurchase price are established prior to the actual delivery. Since the agreement allows the investor to underdeliver by as much as 2.5%, it will do so if the market price of the securities has

increased prior to the delivery date. Similarly, if the market price has fallen, the investor will overdeliver.

Risks in a Dollar Roll from the Investor's Perspective

Because of the unusual nature of the dollar roll transaction as a collateralized borrowing vehicle, it is only possible to estimate the financing cost. From our illustration, it can be seen that when the transaction prices are above par value, then the speed of prepayments affects the financing cost. The maximum financing cost can be determined by assuming no prepayments. In this case, the total financing cost would be $244 greater, or $44,712. This increases the monthly financing cost from 4.45% to 4.47%, or 2 basis points. In practice, an investor can perform sensitivity analysis to determine the effect of prepayments on the financing cost.

In addition to the uncertainty about prepayments, there are two other risks. First, while the right to under- or overdeliver granted to the investor when delivering the securities to the dealer benefits the investor, the reverse is true at the repurchase date. At that time, the dealer will exercise its right to over- or underdeliver based on the prevailing market price. Second, the dealer can select the securities to deliver, as long as they are substantially identical. However, even among substantially identical securities, some pools perform worse than others. The risk is that the dealer will delivery poor-performing pools.

MARGIN BUYING

Investors can borrow cash to buy securities and use the securities themselves as collateral in a standard margin agreement with a brokerage firm. The funds borrowed to buy the additional securities will be provided by the broker, and the broker gets the money from a bank. The interest rate that banks charge brokers for these transactions is known as the *call money rate* (also called the *broker loan rate*). The broker charges the investor the call money rate plus a service charge.

The broker is not free to lend as much as it wishes to the investor to buy securities. The Securities and Exchange Act of 1934 prohibits brokers from lending more than a specified percentage of the market value of the securities. The *initial margin requirement* is the proportion of the total market value of the securities that the investor must pay for in cash. The 1934 act gives the Board of Governors of the Federal Reserve the responsibility to set initial margin requirements, which it does under Regulations T and U. The initial margin requirement varies for stocks and non-government/nonagency bonds and is currently 50%, though it has been below 40%. There are no restrictions on government and government agency securities. The Fed also establishes a *maintenance margin requirement*. This is the minimum amount of equity needed in the investor's margin account as compared to the total market value. If the investor's margin account falls below the minimum maintenance margin, the investor is required to put up additional cash. The investor receives a *margin call*

from the broker specifying the additional cash to be put into the investor's margin account. If the investor fails to put up the additional cash, the securities are sold.

SECURITIES LENDING

A security lending transaction involves two parties. The first is the owner of a security who agrees to lend that security to another party. This party is called the *security lender* or the *beneficial owner*. The second party is the entity that agrees to borrow the security, called the *security borrower.* A security lending transaction is one in which the security lender loans the requested security to the security borrower at the outset and the security borrower agrees to return the *identical* security to the security lender at some time in the future. The loan may be terminated by the security lender upon notice to the security borrower, typically of not more than 5 business days.

To protect against credit risk, the security lender will require that the security borrower provide collateral. Collateral can take the form of (1) cash, (2) a letter of credit, or (3) a security whose value is at least equal in value to the securities loaned. In the United States, the most common form of collateral is cash. Outside the United States, all types of securities have been used as collateral, including common stock and convertible securities. Typically, if the collateral is a security, it is marked to market on a daily basis.

When cash is the collateral, the proceeds are reinvested by the security lender. The security lender faces the risks associated with reinvesting the cash. The income generated from reinvesting the cash is given to the security borrower less an amount retained by the security lender for loaning the security since the fee earned by the security lender is then the difference between the income earned from reinvesting the cash and the amount the security lender agrees to pay the security borrower. The security lender's fee is called an *embedded fee* when there is cash collateral. The agreed-upon amount that the security lender pays to the security borrower is called a *rebate*. The security lender only earns a fee if the amount earned on reinvesting the cash collateral exceeds the rebate. In fact, if the amount earned is less than the rebate, the security lender incurs this cost.

When the collateral is a letter of credit or a security, the security borrower compensates the security lender by a predetermined fee. This fee is called a *borrow fee,* and it is based on the value of the security borrowed. Notice that while the security lender knows what the fee will be in the case of noncash collateral, this is not the case when there is cash collateral. The fee is a function of the performance of the portfolio or security in which the cash collateral is reinvested.

During the period in which the security is loaned to the borrower, there may be an interest payment (dividend payment in the case of stock). The security lender is entitled to a payment from the security borrower equal in amount to any such payment. The payment made by the security borrower to the security lender for this purpose is called a *substitute payment* or *in lieu of payment*.

A party with a portfolio of securities to lend can either (1) lend directly to counterparties that need securities, (2) use the services of an intermediary, or (3) employ a combination of (1) and (2). If a party decides to lend directly, it must have the in-house capability of assessing counterparty risk. When an intermediary is engaged, the intermediary receives a fee for its services. The intermediary could be an agent (i.e., acts on behalf of a security lender but does not take a principal risk position) or a principal (i.e., takes a principal risk position). Possible agents include the current domestic/global custodian of the securities or a third-party specialist in securities lending.[5]

When cash collateral must be reinvested, a securities lender must decide whether it will reinvest the cash or use the services of an external money manager. As noted earlier, securities lenders may realize a return on the cash collateral that is less than the rebate. Reinvesting cash collateral requires an understanding of the risks associated with investing. These risks are described in this book.

Comparison to Repurchase Agreements

It is worthwhile to compare a security lending transaction in which the collateral is cash to a repurchase agreement since both transactions represent a secured borrowing. We will do this with an illustration. The parties are as follows:

- manager X who is the beneficial owner of security A
- manager Y who needs security A to cover a short position

Also suppose that security A is a debt instrument that pays coupon interest.

The following agreement is entered into by manager X and manager Y:

1. Manager X agrees to transfer security A to manager Y.
2. Manager Y agrees to give cash to manager X.
3. At some future date, manager Y agrees to return security A to manager X.
4. Manager X agrees to return the cash to manager Y when manager Y returns security A to manager X.

The economics of this transaction are simple: it is a secured loan of cash with the lender of cash being manager Y and the borrower of cash being manager X. The collateral for this loan is security A. This transaction can be structured as a security lending or a repurchase agreement. No matter what it is called, the economics are unchanged.

If this transaction is structured as a security lending, then:

---

[5] For a discussion of these approaches to securities lending and their relative advantages and disadvantages, see Mark C. Faulkner and Charles L. Stopford Sackville, "Finding a Route to Market: An Institutional Guide to the Securities Lending Labyrinth," Chapter 4 in Frank J. Fabozzi (ed.), *Securities Lending and Repurchase Agreements* (New Hope, PA: Frank J. Fabozzi Associates, 1997).

1. Manager X is the security lender (beneficial owner).
2. Manager Y is the security borrower.
3. Manager X invests the cash received from manager Y and at the end of the transaction rebates part of the income earned to manager Y.
4. The amount earned by manager X from security lending is uncertain and, in fact, can be negative.
5. Manager Y pays manager X any interest income that manager X would have received from the issuer of the security.
6. At some future time, manager X requests return of security A and returns the cash collateral to manager Y.

If this transaction is structured as a repurchase agreement, then:

1. Manager X is the seller of collateral, or equivalently, the borrower of funds using security A as collateral.
2. Manager Y is the buyer of collateral, or equivalently, the lender of funds.
3. Manager X invests the cash received from manager Y and at the repurchase date pays interest to manager Y based on the repo rate.
4. The amount earned by manager X from the repurchase agreement is uncertain and, in fact, can be negative.
5. Manager Y pays manager X any interest income that manager X would have received from the issuer of the security.
6. At the repurchase date, manager X buys back security A from manager Y at the repurchase price (which includes interest).

Whether the transaction is a repo or reverse repo depends on the perspective of the parties as discussed earlier in this chapter.

Notice that unlike a repurchase agreement, which has a repurchase date that can be rolled over, there is no repurchase price in a security lending transaction.

COLLATERALIZED BORROWING WITH TAX-EXEMPT MUNICIPAL BONDS

Ordinarily, interest expense on borrowed funds to purchase or carry securities is tax deductible. There is one exception that is relevant to investors in tax-exempt municipal bonds. The Internal Revenue Service specifies that interest paid or accrued on "indebtedness incurred or continued to purchase or carry obligations, the interest on which is wholly exempt from taxes," is not tax deductible. It does not make any difference if any tax-exempt interest is actually received by the taxpayer in the taxable year. In other words, interest is not deductible on funds borrowed to purchase or carry tax-exempt securities. Hence, this makes leveraging with tax-exempt municipal unappealing.

KEY POINTS

- ❑ *Securities can be used as collateral to borrow funds.*
- ❑ *Leveraging is the investment principle of borrowing funds in the hope of earning a return in excess of the cost of funds.*
- ❑ *Leveraging magnifies the potential gain that will be realized from investing in a security for a given change in the price of that security but also magnifies the potential loss.*
- ❑ *In a collateralized loan, the lender is exposed to the risk that the borrower will default.*
- ❑ *A repurchase agreement is the sale of a security with a commitment by the seller to buy the security back from the purchaser at the repurchase price at the repurchase date.*
- ❑ *The difference between the repurchase price and the sale price is the dollar interest cost of the loan.*
- ❑ *Interest in a repurchase agreement is computed on a 360-day basis.*
- ❑ *In a repurchase agreement, the lender of funds is borrowing securities and is making a short-term investment.*
- ❑ *In a repurchase agreement, the borrower of funds is using the securities to collateralize the loan.*
- ❑ *There is a good deal of Wall Street jargon describing repo transactions, but basically one party is buying collateral (and making a short-term investment) and the other party is selling collateral (and obtaining financing).*
- ❑ *Rather than using industry jargon, investment guidelines should be clear as to what a manager is permitted to do with respect to a repo transaction.*
- ❑ *The collateral in a repo can be a government security, an agency security, money market instruments, federal agency securities, or mortgage-backed securities.*
- ❑ *To reduce credit risk there is overcollateralization of the loan (i.e., there is a repo margin) and the collateral is marked to market on a regular basis.*
- ❑ *When the market value of the collateral declines by a certain percentage, a repo agreement can specify either a margin call or repricing of the repo.*
- ❑ *One concern in structuring a repo is delivery of the collateral to the lender.*
- ❑ *When the borrower must deliver the collateral to the lender or to the cash lender's clearing agent, the collateral is said to be "delivered out" and at the repurchase date the lender returns the collateral to the borrower in exchange for the principal and interest payment.*

- ❑ *If the lender agrees to allow the borrower to hold the security in a segregated customer account, then the transaction is called a hold-in-custody repo and exposes the lender to greater credit risk than delivering out the securities.*
- ❑ *A tri-party repo is an alternative to delivering out the collateral, which requires that the borrower deliver the collateral to the lender's custodial account at the borrower's clearing bank.*
- ❑ *In certain circumstances, a four-party repo is used to satisfy legal requirements, with the fourth party being a subcustodian for the lender.*
- ❑ *In the case of a bankruptcy by the borrower, the bankruptcy code in the United States affords the lender of funds in a qualified repo transaction the right to immediately liquidate the collateral to obtain cash.*
- ❑ *In structuring a repo agreement, most participants in the United States use the Bond Market Association Master Repurchase Agreement.*
- ❑ *In Europe the BMA/ISMA Global Master Repurchase Agreement has become widely accepted.*
- ❑ *The repo rate for a particular transaction will depend on the quality of the collateral, term of the repo, delivery requirement, availability of collateral, and the prevailing federal funds rate.*
- ❑ *Collateral that is highly sought after by dealers is called hot or special collateral and can be used as a cheap source of repo financing.*
- ❑ *Some opportunities employing repo agreements for borrowing mistakenly refer to arbitrage strategies when in fact the strategy does involve risk.*
- ❑ *A dollar roll is a collateralized loan transaction used in the mortgage-backed securities market by dealers to borrow securities that they are short.*
- ❑ *Unlike a repo agreement, the dealer who borrows securities in a dollar roll agreement need only return "substantially identical securities," thereby providing the dealer with flexibility in borrowing securities.*
- ❑ *In a dollar roll, the dealer provides 100% financing; that is, there is no overcollateralization or margin required.*
- ❑ *The financing cost in a dollar roll may be cheaper than in a repo depending on prepayments, the right to under- or overdeliver, and the type of securities returned.*
- ❑ *In a dollar roll, the dealer retains the coupon payments and any principal paid during the period of the loan.*
- ❑ *Investors can borrow cash to buy securities and use the securities themselves as collateral in a standard margin agreement with a brokerage firm.*
- ❑ *The call money rate or broker loan rate is the interest rate that banks charge brokers for a margin transaction, with the broker charging the investor this rate plus a service charge.*

- *The Securities and Exchange Act of 1934 prohibits brokers from lending more than a specified percentage of the market value of nongovernment/nonagency bonds.*
- *There are mandated initial margin and maintenance margin requirements in a margin transaction.*
- *In a security lending transaction, the security lender loans the requested security to the security borrower at the outset and the security borrower agrees to return the identical security to the security lender at some time in the future.*
- *A security lending transaction may be terminated by the security lender upon notice to the security borrower, typically of not more than 5 business days.*
- *In a security lending transaction, the security lender will require that the security borrower provide collateral in the form of either cash, a letter of credit, or a security whose value is at least equal in value to the securities loaned.*
- *In the United States, the most common form of collateral is cash, while outside the United States, all types of securities have been used as collateral.*
- *When cash is the collateral, the proceeds are reinvested by the security lender and the security lender faces the risks associated with reinvesting the cash.*
- *With cash collateral, the fee earned by the security lender is the difference between the income earned from reinvesting the cash and the rebate (i.e., the amount the security lender agrees to pay the security borrower).*
- *With cash collateral, the security lender only earns a fee if the amount earned on reinvesting the cash collateral exceeds the rebate.*
- *When the collateral is a letter of credit or a security, the security borrower compensates the security lender by a predetermined fee called a borrow fee, which is based on the value of the security borrowed.*
- *Because of the nondeductibility of interest to carry a tax-exempt municipal bond position, leveraging these securities is unappealing.*

Chapter 16

Tax Treatment

In this chapter, we look at the key provisions in the federal tax law that pertain to the tax treatment of interest income and the gain or loss resulting from transactions in bonds by individuals.

INCOME DEFINED

Investors often use the term "income" in a very casual way. *The Internal Revenue Code* (IRC), however, sets forth a more precise definition of income. The IRC distinguishes between gross income, adjusted gross income, taxable income, and alternative minimum taxable income.

Gross Income

Gross income is all income that is subject to income tax. For example, interest income is subject to taxation. However, there is a statutory exemption for interest from certain types of debt obligations. For such obligations, interest income is not included in gross income. Gross income for an individual and a corporation are determined in the same manner.

Adjusted Gross Income

For individuals, *adjusted gross income* is gross income minus certain business and other deductions. For example, an important deduction from gross income to arrive at adjusted gross income is the deduction for certain contributions to qualified tax-deferred retirement plans. The concept of adjusted gross income does not apply to corporations. For a corporation, all permissible deductions are treated as business deductions.

Taxable Income

Taxable income is the amount on which the tax liability is determined. For an individual, it is found by subtracting the personal exemption allowance and itemized deductions (other than those deductible in arriving at adjusted gross income) from adjusted gross income.

The concept of adjusted gross income does not apply to corporations. For a corporation, all permissible deductions are treated as business deductions. Therefore, adjusted gross income is meaningless for a corporation.

Alternative Minimum Taxable Income

Alternative minimum taxable income (AMTI) is a taxpayer's taxable income with certain adjustments for specified tax preferences designed to cause AMTI to approximate economic income. For both individuals and corporations, a taxpayer's tax liability is the greater of (1) the tax computed at regular tax rates on taxable income or (2) the tax computed at a lower rate on AMTI. This parallel tax system, the alternative minimum tax, is designed to prevent taxpayers from avoiding significant tax liability by taking advantage of exclusions from gross income, deductions, and tax credits otherwise allowed under the IRC.

TAX BASIS OF A CAPITAL ASSET, CAPITAL GAIN, AND CAPITAL LOSS

The IRC provides for a special tax treatment on the sale or exchange of a capital asset. Bonds qualify as capital assets in the hands of a qualified owner.

Tax Basis

In order to understand the tax treatment of a capital asset, the tax basis of a capital asset must first be defined. In most instances, the *original basis* of a capital asset is the taxpayer's total cost on the date of acquisition. The *adjusted basis* of a capital asset is its original basis increased by capital additions and decreased by capital recoveries (i.e., return of principal). That is,

adjusted basis = original basis + capital additions – capital recoveries

When securities are purchased in a package, it is necessary to unbundle the package in order to determine the basis for each security. The general rule for determining the basis of each security is to allocate the cost of the package based on the total fair market value of the unit immediately after the acquisition. For example, suppose that a unit package containing one bond and one share of preferred stock is purchased for $950. Immediately after the acquisition, the bond sells for $900 and the preferred stock for $85. The total value of the unit is therefore $985. The original basis of the bond is then 91.4% ($900 divided by $985) of the acquisition cost, or $868.30 (0.914 times $950). The original basis of the preferred stock is $81.70 (0.086 times $950).

Capital Gain or Loss

The proceeds received from the sale or exchange of a capital asset are compared to the adjusted basis to determine if the transaction produced a capital gain or capital loss. If the proceeds exceed the adjusted basis, the taxpayer realizes a *capital gain*; a *capital loss* is realized when the adjusted basis exceeds the proceeds received by the taxpayer. The rules are summarized as follows:

Situation	Result
Proceeds > adjusted basis	Capital gain
Proceeds < adjusted basis	Capital loss
Proceeds = adjusted basis	No capital gain or loss

How capital gains and losses are treated for tax purposes is described later in this chapter.

CLASSIFICATION OF TAXPAYERS

For tax purposes, taxpayers are classified as either dealers, traders, or investors. The classification is important because it determines whether capital gain or loss provisions are applicable and the treatment of transaction costs.[1] Traders and investors are entitled to realize capital gains and losses, while dealers, in general, are not. In the case of dealers, the securities held are considered inventory, and any gains or losses are treated as ordinary gains or losses rather than capital gains or losses.[2]

A *dealer* in securities is a merchant of securities who is regularly engaged in the acquisition of securities and subsequent resale to customers with a view to the gains and profits that may be derived as a result of such transactions. A *trader* is a person who buys and sells for his or her own account rather than the account of a customer, and the frequency of such transacting is such that the person may be said to be engaged in such activities as a trade or business. Investors, like traders, transact for their own accounts. However, transactions are occasional and much fewer than required in a trade or business.

INTEREST INCOME

Interest received by a taxpayer is included in gross income, unless a specific statutory exemption indicates otherwise. A portion of the income realized from holding a bond may be in the form of capital appreciation rather than interest income. The tax treatment of the income component that represents capital appreciation differs depending on when the bond was issued. As explained later, the IRC provides for different tax treatment for certain capital gains and losses on the one hand, and ordinary income and losses on the other. For bonds issued after July 18,

---

[1] The classification is also important because it determines whether "wash sale" provisions discussed later are applicable.

[2] To a limited extent, a dealer can buy and sell securities as an investor and therefore receive capital treatment. Dealers can segregate a portion of their holdings in a separate investment account to derive capital gain treatment on the sale or the exchange. To do so a dealer must clearly specify in its books and records on the day it acquires the asset that it is an asset held for investment, and the asset cannot be held primarily for sale to customers. (The "primarily for sale" rule is a facts and circumstances test.) Also, dealers must mark their inventory to market at year end, which results in treating all inventory positions as if they were sold at year end.

1984, part of the capital appreciation will be treated as ordinary income. Under the current tax law, capital gains are taxed at a lower tax rate than ordinary income. Taxpayers get less favorable treatment for capital losses than ordinary losses. Thus, the tax treatment of income from holding a debt instrument may have a major impact on the after-tax return realized by an investor. Because of the potential importance of distinguishing between income in the form of a capital gain (or loss) and interest income, the investor must be familiar with certain rules set forth in the IRC. These rules are summarized as follows.

Unlike debt instruments whose interest payments are taxable, the capital gain portion of a tax-exempt bond is unattractive for an investor who seeks tax-free income because, although the coupon interest received is exempt from federal income taxation, the capital gain portion is subject to taxation. Moreover, as explained later, a portion of market discount may be classified as ordinary income if the issue was purchased after April 30, 1993.

Accrued Interest

Usually, bond interest is paid semiannually. Accrued interest is the interest earned by the seller from holding the bond until the disposal date. For example, if a bond whose issuer promises to pay $60 on June 1 and December 1 for a specified number of years is sold on October 1, the seller is usually entitled to accrued interest of $40 ($60 times 4/6) for the 4 months that the seller held the bond.

Let us look at the tax position of the seller and the buyer, assuming that our hypothetical bond is selling for $900 in the market and that the seller's adjusted basis for this bond is $870. The buyer must pay the seller $940, $900 for the market price plus $40 of accrued interest. The seller must treat the accrued interest of $40 as interest income. The $900 is compared to the seller's adjusted basis of $870 to determine whether the seller has realized a capital gain or capital loss. Obviously, the seller has realized capital appreciation of $30. When the buyer receives the December 1 interest payment of $60, only $20 is included in gross income as interest income. The basis of the bond for the buyer is $900, not $940.

Treatment of Defaulted Bonds and Income Bonds

Not all transactions involving bonds require the payment of accrued interest by the buyer. This occurs when the issuer of the bond is in default of principal or interest, or if the issuer of the bond is contingent on sufficient earnings of the issuer. A bond whose interest is contingent on sufficient earnings by the issuer is called an *income bond*.

Defaulted bonds and income bonds are said to be quoted *flat*. The acquisition price entitles the buyer to receive the principal and unpaid interest for both past scheduled payments due and accrued interest. Generally, for bonds quoted flat, all payments made by the issuer to the buyer are first considered as payments to satisfy defaulted payments or unpaid contingent interest payments and accrued interest before acquisition. Such payments are treated as a return of capital. As

such, the proceeds reduce the cost basis of the bond. On the other hand, accrued interest after the acquisition date is considered interest income when received. For example, suppose the issuer of a corporate bond is in default of two scheduled interest payments of $60 each. The interest payments are scheduled on April 1 and October 1. The bond is sold for $500 on August 1. Assume that on October 1 of the acquisition year the issuer pays the bondholder $120. The buyer would treat the payment as a return of capital of $120, since it represents the two defaulted interest payments. Hence, the adjusted basis of the bond is $380 ($500 minus $120) and the $120 is not considered interest income. Suppose that 2 weeks later the issuer pays an additional $60 to the bondholder. This payment must then be apportioned between accrued interest before the acquisition date of August 1 and accrued interest after the acquisition date. The latter is $20, since the bond was held by the buyer for 2 months. Thus, $40 of the $60 payment reduces the adjusted basis of $380 prior to the second payment to $340 and is not treated as interest income. The $20 of accrued interest since the acquisition date is treated as interest income.

If a bond is sold flat or is redeemed by the obligor for less than the par amount plus accrued interest, the amount realized is apportioned between principal and interest in a manner that reduces somewhat the amount of interest income realized and increases the amount treated as a return of capital (or, if the amount returned exceeds the holder's tax basis, in a manner that increases the holder's capital gain).

Bond Purchased at a Discount

A bond purchased at a price less than its redemption value at maturity is said to be bought at a discount. The tax treatment of the discount depends on whether the discount represents original-issue discount or market discount.

Original-Issue Discount Bonds

When bonds are issued, they may be sold at a price that is less than their redemption value at maturity. The difference between the redemption value and the original-issue price is the *original-issue discount*. Each year a portion of the original-issue discount must be accrued and included in gross income. There is a corresponding increase in the adjusted basis of the bond.

For corporate obligations issued prior to July 2, 1982, the original-issue discount must be amortized on a straight-line basis each month and included in gross income based on the number of months the bond is held in that tax year. Government bonds that were issued prior to July 2, 1982 are not subject to original-issue discount accrual. The difference between the cost basis and sale proceeds is capital gain or loss. Both corporate and government bonds issued after July 1, 1982 are subject to original-issue discount accrual and must use the *constant-yield method* (also called the *effective* or *scientific method*) with annual compounding. Obligations issued after December 31, 1984 must use the constant-yield method with a compounding method that is at least semiannual or consistent with payments on the bond if such payments are more frequent than semiannual.

For obligations issued on or after July 2, 1982, the amount of the original-issue discount amortized is based on the constant-yield method and included in gross income based on the number of days in the tax year that the bond is held. With this method for determining the amount of the original-issue discount to be included in gross income, the interest for the year is first determined by multiplying the adjusted issue price (essentially, the adjusted basis the bond would have in the hands of the first holder of the bond) by the yield to maturity at issuance. From this interest, the coupon interest is subtracted. The difference is the amount of the original-issue discount amortized for the year. The same amount is then added to the adjusted basis.

To illustrate the tax rules for original-issue discount bonds, consider a bond with a 4% coupon rate (interest paid semiannually), maturing in 5 years, that was issued for $7,683, and has a redemption value of $10,000. The yield to maturity for this hypothetical bond is 10%. The original-issue discount is $2,317 ($10,000 – $7,683). Suppose that the bond was purchased by an investor on the day it was issued, January 1, 1995. The constant-yield method is used to determine the amortization and the adjusted basis.[3] The procedure is as follows.

Every 6 months, the investor in this hypothetical bond is assumed to realize for tax purposes interest income (including accrued original-issue discount) equal to 5% of the adjusted-issue price. The 5% represents one-half of the 10% yield to maturity. The original-issue price is the purchase price of $7,683. In the first 6 months the bond is held, the investor realizes for tax purposes interest equal to 5% of $7,683, or $384. The coupon payment for the first 6-month period that the bond is held is $200. Therefore, $184 ($384 – $200) is assumed to be realized (although not received) by the investor. Thus, the amount of interest from holding this bond for 6 months is $200 in coupon interest plus the $184 of the original-issue discount amortized. The adjusted-issue price for the bond at the end of the first 6 months will equal the original-issue price of $7,683 plus the amount of the original-issue discount amortized, $184. Thus, the adjusted-issue price is $7,867. The bondholder's adjusted basis in the bond (used in calculating gain or loss from sale) will also be increased by the amount of accrued original-issue discount. This way, the increase in the value of the bond (as it approaches maturity) that is included in income as accrued original-issue discount is not taxed again as a capital gain.

Let's carry this out for one more 6-month period. If the bond is held for another 6 months, the amount of interest that the investor realizes for tax purposes is 5% of the adjusted-issue price. Since the adjusted-issue price at the beginning of the second 6-month period is $7,867, the interest is $393. The coupon interest for

---

[3] If the obligation was issued prior to July 2, 1982, the investor is required to amortize the original-issue discount of $2,317 on a straight-line monthly basis. Since there are 60 months to maturity, the prorated monthly interest on a straight-line basis is $38.62 ($2,317/60). Since the hypothetical bond is assumed to be purchased on January 1, the annual interest that must be reported from the amortization of the original-issue discount each year is $464 ($38.62 × 12). The total interest reported each year from holding this bond is $464 plus the coupon interest of $400 ($10,000 × 0.04).

the second 6 months is $200. Therefore, the amount of the original-issue discount amortized for the second 6-month period is $193 ($393 – $200). The $393 reported for holding the bond for the second 6 months is $200 in coupon interest and $193 in accrual of the original-issue discount. The adjusted-issue price at the end of the second 6-month period is $8,060—the previous adjusted-issue price of $7,867 plus $193. If this bond, which was assumed to be purchased on January 1, 1995, is sold on December 31, 1995, interest income would be $777, consisting of $400 of coupon interest and $377 of the original-issue discount amortized. If this bond is sold on December 31, 1995 for $8,200, there would be a capital gain of $140, the difference between the sale proceeds of $8,200 and the adjusted basis of $8,060.[4]

Exhibit 1 shows the amount of the original-issue discount that must be reported as gross income for each 6-month period that the bond is held and the adjusted-issue price at the end of the period. Notice that accrual is lower in the earlier years, increasing over the life of the bond on a compounded basis.

Exhibit 1: Amortization Schedule for an Original-Issue Discount Bond Issued After July 2, 1982

Characteristics of hypothetical bond:

Coupon	= 4%	Years to maturity	= 5
Interest payments	= semiannual	Yield-to-maturity	= 10%
Issue price	= $7,683	Original-issue discount	= $2,317
Redemption value	= $10,000	Basis at time of purchase	= $7,683

Amortization based on constant-yield method

		For the period		
Period held (years)	Adjusted-issue price ($)*	Gross income reported ($)**	Coupon interest ($)	Original-issue discount amortized ($)***
0.5	7,867	384	200	184
1.0	8,060	393	200	193
1.5	8,263	403	200	203
2.0	8,476	413	200	213
2.5	8,700	424	200	224
3.0	8,935	435	200	235
3.5	9,182	447	200	247
4.0	9,441	459	200	259
4.5	9,713	472	200	272
5.0	10,000	486	200	286

* Adjusted-issue price at the end of the period. The adjusted-issue price is found by adding the original-issue discount amortized for the period to the previous period's adjusted-issue price.

** The gross income reported is equal to the coupon interest for the period plus the original-issue discount amortized for the period.

*** By the constant-yield method, it is found as follows: (Adjusted-issue price at the end of the previous period × 0.05) – $200.

---

[4] Because it is assumed that the investor purchased the bond at issuance, the bondholder's adjusted basis equals the bond's adjusted-issue price. Had the bondholder purchased the bond in the secondary market, the bondholder's adjusted basis might have been greater or less than the bond's adjusted-issue price.

Holders of original-issue discount tax-exempt bonds need to accrue the original-issue discount using the constant-yield method as well. However, the amount of the original-issue discount accrued is not included as part of gross income (but may be included in alternative minimum taxable income) because all interest is exempt from federal income taxes. As with taxable bonds, the amount of original-issue discount accrued on a tax-exempt bond is added to its adjusted basis.

The original-issue discount rules do not apply to noninterest-bearing obligations such as Treasury bills and many other taxable short-term obligations with no more than 1 year to maturity. When these obligations are held by investors who report for tax purposes on a cash rather than an accrual basis, the discount is not recognized until the issue is redeemed or sold.

In the case of a callable or putable bond, the embedded option is ignored in determining yield unless it would result in a lower yield/cost to the issuer or, in the case of a put option, a higher yield to the initial holder.

There are four more points the investor should be familiar with when dealing with original-issue discount bonds. First, original-issue discount is treated as zero if the discount is less than one-fourth of 1% of the redemption value at maturity multiplied by the number of complete years to maturity. For example, suppose a bond maturing in 20 years is initially sold for $990 for each $1,000 of redemption value at maturity. The discount is $10. The redemption value multiplied by the number of years to maturity is $20,000. The original-issue discount is 0.0005 of $20,000. Since it is less than one-fourth of 1% (0.0025), the original-issue discount is treated as zero; that is, the investor does not have to amortize the discount and report it as gross income. Second, if an original-issue discount bond is sold before maturity, subsequent holders must continue to amortize the original-issue discount. However, if a subsequent holder purchases such a bond at a lower yield than the original holder (i.e., at a price in excess of the adjusted-issue price—called *acquisition premium*), then the amount of original-issue discount included in income is appropriately reduced. The third point to keep in mind is that an investor may have to pay taxes on interest included in gross income but not received in cash. Consequently, original-issue discount obligations are less attractive for portfolios of investors who are subject to taxation than for investors who are not. Finally, stripped coupon/principal obligations are treated slightly differently. The original-issue discount is measured by the difference between the redemption price and the purchase price of the holder, not the adjusted-issue price. The effect of this rule is that it is not possible to have a market discount (discussed as follows) or premium because a stripped obligation is considered issued on the date any investor purchases it.

The tax rules for original-issue discount are summarized in Exhibit 2.

Bond Purchased at a Market Discount with No Original-Issue Discount

When a bond is purchased at a market discount and there is no original-issue discount, the tax treatment depends on when the bond was issued.

Exhibit 2: Tax Rules for Treatment of Original-Issue Discount

Method for calculating accrued interest:

Bond issued prior to July 2, 1982	Bond issued on or after July 2, 1982
Calculate accrued interest using straight-line amortization	Calculate accrued interest using constant-yield method

Treatment of accrued interest and calculation of adjusted basis:

For taxable issues:	For tax-exempt issues:
Include accrued interest in gross income. The basis is adjusted by the amount of accrued interest.	Accrued interest is not included in gross income but may be included in alternative minimum taxable income. The basis is adjusted by the accrued interest.

For *taxable bonds* issued after July 18, 1984, any capital appreciation must be separated into a portion that is attributable to interest income (as represented by the amortization of the market discount with which it is purchased) and a portion that is attributable to capital gain. The portion representing interest income is taxed as ordinary income when the bond is sold. This is called *accrued market discount*. Unlike original-issue discount, the amount of the accrued market discount that represents interest income is not taxed until the bond is sold or, if the principal on the bond is payable in installments prior to maturity, on each such an installment payment.

The taxpayer can elect to include accrued market discount in gross income. The motivation for doing so is that if interest expenses were incurred to finance the purchase of the bond, the interest expenses would be deferred if the accrued market discount is deferred.

Accrued market discount must be determined using the straight-line method unless the taxpayer elects the constant-yield method. The amount of accrued market discount that is included in income as interest is limited to the amount of capital appreciation on the bond.

For taxable bonds issued on or prior to July 18, 1984 and for tax-exempt bonds whenever issued, any capital appreciation is treated as a capital gain. Tax-exempt bonds purchased at a market discount after April 30, 1993 are subject to the same ordinary income reclassification rules as taxable bonds issued after July 18, 1984. Exhibit 3 shows the tax consequences for five assumed selling prices for a hypothetical bond. The results are shown for bonds issued before and after July 18, 1984. The results are also shown for the constant-yield and straight-line methods.

Two implications result from Exhibit 3. First, from a tax perspective, taxable bonds issued before July 18, 1984 and selling at a discount will be more attractive than bonds issued after that date and selling at a discount. This will be reflected in the market price of those bonds. Consequently, investors who are in low marginal tax rates will find that they may be overpaying for bonds issued before July 18, 1984. The second implication is that it is not in the best interest of the investor

to select the straight-line method to compute the accrued market discount because that method will cause the capital gain portion of any gain on sales to be lower (and the interest portion higher) than if the constant-yield method is elected.

Because of the difference in the tax treatment of original-issue discount bonds and market-discount bonds, the investor should check prior to purchase the type of bond and when it was issued.

The tax rules for the treatment of market discount are summarized in Exhibit 4.

Exhibit 3: Tax Treatment of Market Discount Bond for Five Assumed Selling Prices

Characteristics of hypothetical bond:

Coupon	= 4%	Years to maturity	= 5
Interest payments	= semiannual	Yield to maturity	= 1095
Issue price	= $7,683	Original-issue discount	= $2.317
Redemption value	= $10,000	Basis at time of purchase	= $7,683

Amortization based on constant-yield method

Bond issued before July 18, 1994

Sale price ($)	Accrued market discount	Capital gain or loss ($)
9,500	0	1,817
9,000	0	1,317
8,700	0	1,017
7,683	0	0
7,000	0	–683

Bond issued after July 18, 1994, with amortization based on constant-yield method

Sale price ($)	Accrued market discount	Capital gain or loss ($)
9,500	1,017	800
9,000	1,017	300
8,700	1,017	0
7,683	0*	0
7,000	0*	–683

Bond issued after July 18, 1994, with amortization based on straight-line method

Sale price ($)	Accrued market discount	Capital gain or loss ($)
9,500	1161	656
9,000	1161	156
8,700	1017*	0
7,683	0*	0
7,000	0*	–683

* Actual accrued market discount is $1,017 ($1,161 for amortization based on the straight-line method), but the amount required to be included in income is limited to the excess of the sales price over the purchase price.

Exhibit 4: Tax Rules for Treatment of Accrued Market Discount (with no original-issue discount)

For taxable bonds issued on or prior to July 18, 1984 and for tax-exempt bonds whenever issued but purchased prior to May 1, 1993:
Any capital appreciation is treated as a capital gain.

For taxable bonds issued after July 18, 1984:
Accrued market discount taxed as ordinary income, which is taxed when the bond is sold or issue is paid off or currently if the taxpayer elects so.
Accrued market discount can be determined using either the straight-line method or the constant-yield method.

Bond Purchased at a Market Discount with Original-Issue Discount

An original-issue discount bond may sell in the market below its issuance price. As a result, the bond would embody original-issue discount and market discount. For example, consider the original-issue discount bond with a 4% coupon rate maturing in 5 years that we used earlier to describe the original-issue discount rule. The original-issue price is $7,683 and the redemption value is $10,000, so the original-issue discount is $2,317. The yield to maturity for this issue is 10%. If an investor purchases this bond for $7,000 in the secondary market, then the issue has a $2,317 original-issue discount and a $683 market discount. The original-issue discount must be amortized as discussed earlier. The market discount can be deferred until the issue is sold or paid off, or, if elected can be included in gross income.

The tax treatment for tax-exempt bonds is such that the original-issue discount is exempt from federal income taxes; however, the market discount is not. This means that in a period of rising interest rates, a decline in the price of a tax-exempt issue below its original-issue discount price triggers an unfavorable tax consequence because the market discount will be taxed as ordinary income. As a result, the price of a tax-exempt issue will drop more than an otherwise similar tax-exempt issue whose price would not fall below the original-issue price. For managers of portfolios of tax-exempt securities who have sought to model their interest rate risk, this abrupt change in price is not captured by the usual measures of interest rate risk described in Chapter 13.

Bond Purchased at a Premium

When a bond is purchased at a price greater than its redemption value at maturity, the bond is said to be purchased at a premium. For a taxable bond issued after September 27, 1985, and purchased by a nondealer taxpayer, the taxpayer may elect to amortize the premium over the remaining life of the security under a compound

interest method similar to the method of accruing original-issue discount. Premium on a bond issued prior to September 28, 1985 may, however, be amortized on a straight-line basis. An election to amortize bond premium applies to all bonds held when the election is made and to all bonds acquired thereafter. The amount amortized reduces the amount of the interest income that will be included as taxable gross income. In turn, the basis is reduced by the amount of the amortization. For a tax-exempt bond, the premium must be amortized. Although the amount amortized is not a tax-deductible expense because the interest is exempt from taxation, the amortization reduces the original basis.

For example, suppose that on January 1, 1998, a calendar-year taxpayer purchased taxable bonds for $10,500. The bonds have a remaining life of 5 years, pay interest annually each January 1, and have a $10,000 redemption value at maturity. The coupon rate is 10%. The premium is $500 and the bonds have a yield to maturity of 8.7237%. The taxpayer can amortize this premium over the 5-year remaining life. If so, the amount amortized would be $84.01 for the first year (the difference between (i) the coupon of $1,000 and (ii) the product of the holder's basis, $10,500, and the yield, 0.087237).

The bondholder's basis would be reduced by the amortized premium. In the second year, $91.34 of the premium would be amortized: $1,000 – [($10,500 – 84.01) × 0.087237]. Each year the amortized premium would be sufficient to include, in income, interest (net of the amortized premium) at a rate equal to the bond's yield to maturity, and to amortize exactly 100% of the premium by maturity. Exhibit 5 sets out the amortization schedule of this hypothetical bond. If the bond is held until retired by the issuer at maturity, the adjusted basis would be $10,000, and consequently there would be no capital gain or loss realized. If the taxpayer does not elect to amortize the premium, the original basis is not changed. Consequently, at maturity the taxpayer would realize a capital loss of $500.

If our hypothetical bond was a tax-exempt bond, the premium would have to be amortized. The coupon interest of $1,000 would be tax-exempt, and the amortized premium each year would not be a tax-deductible expense. The basis would, however, be adjusted each year.

Exhibit 5: Amortization of Bond Premium on Bond Issued After September 27, 1985

January 1	Basis ($)	Yield (%)	Income ($)	Coupon ($)	Amortized Premium ($)
1998	10,500.00	0.087237	915.99	1,000	84.01
1999	10,415.99	0.087237	908.66	1,000	91.34
2000	10,324.65	0.087237	900.70	1,000	99.30
2001	10,225.35	0.087237	892.03	1,000	107.97
2002	10,117.38	0.087237	882.61	1,000	117.38
2003	10,000.00				

Treatment of Callable Taxable Bond

So far in our illustration we have used the original basis and the remaining number of years to maturity to determine the amount to be amortized. In the case of a callable taxable bond acquired after January 1, 1957, the taxpayer must elect to compute the amortization based on the earlier call date if it results in a lesser amount of amortizable bond premium attributable to the period before the call date. Suppose that in the previous example the bond was callable on January 1, 2002 (4 years after acquisition) for $10,300. The first election the investor must make is whether to amortize the premium. If the investor makes the election, then the investor must elect to base the amount of the amortization on the call price and call date rather than on the redemption value at maturity, if the deduction is less. If the amount amortized is based on the redemption value at maturity, then the amortizable bond premium for 1998 is $84.01 (see Exhibit 5). If the call date and call price are used, the amortizable bond premium would be $43.66 (the coupon of $1,000 minus the product of the basis, $10,500, and the yield, 9.1080%). Thus, the net amount of interest required to be included in income in 1998 will be $956.34 ($1,000 – $43.66).

Should a bond to which an election to amortize bond premium applies be called before its maturity date, any unamortized portion of the premium is treated as an ordinary loss in the year the bond is called. For example, if our hypothetical 5-year bond was callable on January 1, 2000 at par, and if the bond was actually called on that date, an investor who had elected to amortize the premium would be entitled to an additional offset to interest income of $324.65 (the bondholder's then-current basis of $10,324.65 or $10,500 minus the amortized premium for the first 2 years of $84.01 and $91.34, respectively, minus the $10,000 received on the redemption). If the premium is amortized to a call date but the bond is not then called, the remaining premium is amortized to the next call date (or maturity) as if the bond were newly acquired on the call date at a price equal to the holder's then-current basis in the bond.

Treatment of Convertible Bond Premium

No portion of the premium attributable to the conversion feature of a convertible bond may be amortized. For example, suppose a 15-year convertible bond with a 9.5% coupon rate is selling for $1,400. The investor must determine what portion of the premium is due to the conversion value. Suppose that the investor determines that nonconvertible bonds with the same quality rating and years remaining to maturity are selling to yield 8.1%. A 15-year bond priced to yield 8.1% would sell for $1,120.30 per $1,000 of redemption value at maturity. Consequently, the premium that the investor may elect to amortize is based on $1,120.30, not $1,400.

CAPITAL GAIN AND LOSS TREATMENT

Once a capital gain or capital loss is determined for a capital asset, there are special rules for determining the impact on adjusted gross income. Under current

law, the capital gains tax rate for individuals is 20%, less than the 39.6% maximum tax rate on ordinary income. For corporations, the capital gains tax rate is 35%, the same as on ordinary income. That is, corporations do not have a preferential rate for capital gains as individuals do.

Moreover, capital losses are less favorably treated than ordinary losses. Consequently, a basic understanding of the treatment of capital gains and losses is important. The tax treatment for individuals and nondealer corporations is explained as follows.

Capital Gain and Loss Treatment for Individuals

To determine the impact of transactions involving capital assets on adjusted gross income, it is first necessary to ascertain whether the sale or exchange has resulted in a capital gain or loss that is long-term or short-term. The classification depends on the length of time the capital asset is held by the taxpayer. The general rule is that if a capital asset is held for 18 months or less, the gain or loss is a short-term capital gain or loss. An exception to the general rule is wash sales discussed later. A long-term capital gain or loss results when the capital asset is held for 1 day more than 18 months, or longer.

Second, all short-term capital gains and losses are combined to produce either a *net short-term capital gain* or a *net short-term capital loss*. The same procedure is followed for long-term capital gains and losses. Either a *net long-term capital gain* or a *net long-term capital loss* will result.

Third, an overall net capital gain or net capital loss is determined by combining the amounts in the previous step. One of the following will occur:

- overall net short-term capital gain
- overall net long-term capital gain
- overall net short-term capital loss
- overall net long-term capital loss

If an overall net short-term capital gain is realized, the amount is treated as ordinary income and added to gross income. The tax on the overall net short-term capital gain will be based on the taxpayer's ordinary income tax rate.

If an overall net long-term capital gain results, the gain is taxed at either the taxpayer's ordinary income tax rate or the preferential tax rate for capital gains of 20%. The taxpayer pays the lesser of the two in taxes. Consequently, a taxpayer in the 15% marginal tax bracket for ordinary income will pay 15% of the overall net long-term capital gain rather than 20% of this amount. In contrast, a taxpayer facing the maximum marginal tax rate on ordinary income of 39.6% will pay only 20% of the overall net long-term capital gain.

If an overall net capital loss that is either long term or short term results, the loss is deductible from gross income but only to the extent of $3,000 (but $1,500 for married taxpayers filing separate returns). Unused capital losses can be carried over indefinitely until they are all utilized in subsequent tax years.

Capital loss carrybacks or carryforwards are always treated as short-term losses in the year they are eventually utilized. Their original character as long term or short term is irrelevant. These rules are summarized in Exhibit 6.

Capital Gain and Loss Treatment for Corporations

The procedure for determining an overall net capital gain or loss for corporations is the same as that for individuals. The tax treatment of any overall net capital gain or loss differs from that of individuals in the following two ways. First, there is no preferential tax rate on capital gains. Since the corporate income tax rate is 35%, the overall net capital gain is taxed at this rate. Second, no deduction is allowed for an overall net capital loss. However, overall net capital losses can be carried back to the 3 preceding taxable years and carried forward 5 taxable years to offset any overall net capital gains in those years. Although there are exceptions, the general rule is that any unused overall net capital loss after the fifth subsequent year can never be used by a corporate taxpayer. Unlike regular corporations, a regulated investment company cannot carry back capital losses at all; it can carry losses forward up to 8 years.

Exhibit 6: Determination of Net Capital Gain or Loss

1. Determine whether the sale or exchange has resulted in a capital gain or loss that is long term or short term.

    General rule: If a capital asset is held:
    (a) For 18 months or less, the gain or loss is a short-term capital gain or loss.
    (b) For 1 day more than 18 months, the gain or loss is a long-term capital gain or loss.

2. Combine short-term capital gains and losses to get a:
    (a) net short-term capital gain
    (b) net short-term capital loss

3. Combine long-term capital gains and losses to get a:
    (a) net long-term capital gain
    (b) net long-term capital loss

4. Combine the net short-term and net long-term positions to produce:
    (i) an overall net long-term capital gain
    (ii) an overall net short-term capital gain
    (iii) an overall net long-term capital loss
    (iv) an overall net short-term capital loss

5. Tax treatment
    (a) for individual taxpayers
        (i) is taxed at a maximum of 20%
        (ii) is taxed as ordinary income
        (iii) and (iv) are deductible up to $3,000; any unused amount is carried forward
    (b) for corporate taxpayers
        (i) and (ii) are taxed as ordinary income
        (iii) and (iv) can be carried back or forward and treated as short-term capital loss in the year utilized

Wash Sales

An exception to the general rule applies to *wash sales*. A wash sale occurs when "substantially identical securities" are acquired within 30 days before or after a sale of securities at a loss. In such cases, the loss is not recognized as a capital loss. Instead, the loss is added to the basis of the securities that caused the loss. The holding period for the new securities in connection with a wash sale then includes the period for which the original securities were held. The rule is not applicable to a dealer. Noncorporate traders are subject to the wash sale rule for transactions after January 1, 1985.

KEY POINTS

- ❑ *The tax code distinguishes between gross income, adjusted gross income, taxable income, and alternative minimum taxable income.*
- ❑ *The adjusted basis of a capital asset is its original basis increased by capital additions and decreased by capital recoveries.*
- ❑ *The proceeds received from the sale or exchange of a capital asset are compared to the adjusted basis to determine if the transaction produced a capital gain or capital loss.*
- ❑ *Interest received by a taxpayer is included in gross income, unless a specific statutory exemption indicates otherwise.*
- ❑ *The tax treatment of the income component from holding a bond that represents capital appreciation differs depending on when the bond was issued.*
- ❑ *For bonds issued after July 18, 1984, part of the capital appreciation will be treated as ordinary income and taxed at the ordinary income tax rate.*
- ❑ *Under the current tax law, capital gains are taxed at a lower tax rate than ordinary income; taxpayers get less favorable treatment for capital losses than for ordinary losses.*
- ❑ *Only the interest income received from a tax-exempt issue is not taxed; any capital gain is taxed.*
- ❑ *The tax treatment of a bond acquired at a discount depends on whether the discount represents original-issue discount or market discount.*
- ❑ *At issuance, the difference between the redemption value and the issuance price is the original-issue discount.*
- ❑ *Each year a portion of the original-issue discount must be amortized, with the accrued interest added to gross income and added to the original basis.*
- ❑ *Amortization of an original-issue discount requires the use of the constant-yield method for obligations issued on or after July 2, 1982, and the straight-line method for corporate obligations issued prior to that date.*
- ❑ *For taxable bonds issued after July 18, 1984 that are purchased at a market discount and for which there is no original-issue discount, any capital appreciation must be separated into a portion that is attributable to interest income and a portion that is attributable to capital gain.*
- ❑ *The portion representing interest income, called accrued market discount, is taxed as ordinary income only when the bond is sold or matures.*
- ❑ *Accrued market discount can be determined using either the straight-line method or the constant-yield method.*

- ❑ *A taxpayer can elect to have the accrued market interest included in gross income and will elect to do so if there are interest expenses to finance the position that would otherwise have to be deferred.*

- ❑ *The treatment of accrued market discount for taxable bonds issued on or prior to July 18, 1984, and for tax-exempt bonds whenever issued and purchased prior to May 1, 1993, is that any capital appreciation is treated as a capital gain.*

- ❑ *Tax-exempt bonds purchased at a market discount after April 30, 1993 are subject to ordinary income tax treatment on accrued market discount.*

- ❑ *An implication of taxable bonds issued before July 18, 1984 and selling at a discount is that they will be more attractive than bonds issued after that date and selling at a discount.*

- ❑ *For a bond with an original-issue discount and a market discount, each discount is treated accordingly.*

- ❑ *For a taxable bond issued after September 27, 1985 that is purchased at a premium, the taxpayer may elect to amortize the premium over the remaining life of the security under a compound interest method, while for a bond issued prior to September 28, 1985, a straight-line basis may be used.*

- ❑ *No portion of the premium attributable to the conversion feature of a convertible bond may be amortized.*

- ❑ *Capital gains and losses are classified as either long term or short term depending on the length of time the capital asset is held.*

- ❑ *The general classification rule is that if a capital asset is held for 18 months or less, the gain or loss is a short-term capital gain or loss; a long-term capital gain or loss results when the capital asset is held for more than 18 months.*

- ❑ *An exception to the general rule for determining whether a capital loss is classified as long term or short term applies to wash sales.*

- ❑ *A wash sale occurs when "substantially identical securities" are acquired within 30 days before or after a sale of securities at a loss, resulting in the loss not being recognized as a capital loss.*

- ❑ *An overall net long-term capital gain, net short-term capital gain, net long-term capital loss, or net short-term capital loss is determined.*

- ❑ *For individual taxpayers, an overall net long-term capital gain is taxed at a rate no greater than 20%, an overall net short-term capital gain is included in gross income and taxed at the ordinary income tax rate, and an overall net capital loss is deducted against ordinary income up to a maximum of $3,000 with any excess carried forward, and treated as short-term capital loss in the year used regardless of its original classification.*

- ❑ *For corporate taxpayers, an overall net capital gain is taxed as ordinary income and an overall net capital loss is deductible with any unused amount carried back or forward and treated as a short-term loss in the year used.*

Chapter 17

Introduction to Fixed Income Portfolio Management

The previous chapters in this book covered the wide range of fixed income securities. In this chapter we provide an introduction to fixed income portfolio management. We begin with an overview of the investment management process. Next we review the major bond market indexes and their characteristics. We conclude the chapter with a framework for assessing the potential outcome of an investment strategy. In the next chapter we look at various fixed income portfolio strategies.

OVERVIEW OF THE INVESTMENT MANAGEMENT PROCESS

The investment management process involves five steps: (1) setting investment objectives, (2) establishing investment policy, (3) selecting the portfolio strategy; (4) selecting the assets, and (5) measuring and evaluating performance.

Setting Investment Objectives

The specified investment objective will vary by type of financial institution. For institutions such as pension funds, the investment objective is to generate sufficient cash flows from the investment portfolio to satisfy pension obligations. For life insurance companies, the basic objective is to satisfy obligations stipulated in insurance policies and generate a profit. For institutions such as banks and thrifts, funds are obtained from the issuance of certificates of deposit, short-term money market instruments, and floating-rate notes. These funds are then invested in loans and marketable securities. The objective in this case is to earn a return on invested funds that is higher than the cost of acquiring those funds. For these sorts of institutions, investment objectives are dictated essentially by the nature of their liabilities—obligations to pension recipients, policyholders, and depositors. For investment companies (mutual funds), the investment objectives will be set forth in a prospectus. Typically, no specific liabilities must be met. For other money managers, the objective is to outperform a bond market index or a customized index.

Establishing Investment Policy

Establishing policy guidelines for meeting the investment objectives begins with the asset allocation decision; that is, there must be a decision as to how the funds of the institution should be distributed among the major asset classes (cash equivalents, bonds, equities, real estate, and foreign securities).

Client and regulatory constraints are considerations in establishing an investment policy. Examples of constraints that a client might impose are a maximum allocation of funds to one particular issuer or industry, a minimum acceptable credit rating for an issue to be eligible for purchase, and limitations on the use of derivative instruments (i.e., futures, options, swaps, caps, and floors). Regulators of state-regulated institutions such as insurance companies (both life and property and casualty companies) may restrict the amount of funds allocated to certain major asset classes. Even the amount allocated within a major asset class may be restricted, depending on the characteristics of the particular asset. In the case of investment companies, restrictions on asset allocation are set forth in the prospectus when the fund is launched and may be changed only with approval of the fund's shareholders.

Tax and financial reporting implications must also be considered in adopting investment policies. For example, life insurance companies enjoy certain tax advantages that make investing in tax-exempt municipal securities generally unappealing. Because pension funds are exempt from taxes, they also are not particularly interested in tax-exempt municipal securities.

Selecting a Portfolio Strategy

A portfolio strategy that is consistent with the objectives and policy guidelines of the client or institution must be selected. Later in this chapter we present the total return framework that should be used for assessing the potential outcomes of a strategy.

Portfolio strategies can be classified as either *active strategies* or *passive strategies*. These strategies are described in the next chapter. Essential to all active bond portfolio strategies is specification of expectations about the factors that influence bond performance of an asset class.

Selecting Assets

Once a portfolio strategy is specified, the next step is to select the specific assets to be included in the portfolio. This step requires an evaluation of individual securities. In active bond portfolio management, asset selection involves identifying mispriced bonds. The characteristics of a bond (i.e., coupon, maturity, credit quality, and options granted to either the issuer or bondholder) must be carefully examined to determine fair value. A mispriced bond provides the manager with an opportunity to enhance return. A bond whose market value is below the estimated fair value is cheap and should be purchased if it satisfies the investment objectives and is permitted by investment policy; a bond whose market value is above the estimated fair value is rich and, if permitted, should be shorted.

Measuring and Evaluating Performance

While we have listed measurement and evaluation of investment performance as the last of the five steps in the investment management process, in practice it is not the "last" step because investment management is an ongoing process. The first phase of this step is performance measurement. This involves the calculation of the return realized by a manager over some time interval. Given a performance measurement over some evaluation period, the second phase of this step is performance evaluation. This phase is concerned with two issues. The first issue is to determine whether the manager added value by outperforming the established benchmark. The second issue is to determine how the manager achieved the calculated return. The decomposition of performance results to explain the reasons why those results were achieved is called *return attribution analysis*. We discuss the complications associated with performance measurement as follows.

Calculating Rate of Return

The starting point for evaluating the performance of a manager is measuring return. Several important issues must be addressed in developing a methodology for calculating a portfolio's return. Because different methodologies are available and these methodologies can lead to quite disparate results, it is difficult to compare the performance of managers. Consequently, there is a great deal of confusion concerning the meaning of the data provided by managers to their current and prospective clients. This has lead to abuses by some managers in reporting performance results that are better than actual performance. To mitigate this problem, the Committee for Performance Standards of the Association for Investment Management and Research has established standards for calculating performance results and how to present those results. We discuss these standards later.

The dollar return realized on a portfolio for any evaluation period (i.e., a year, month, or week) is equal to the sum of (1) the difference between the market value of the portfolio at the end of the evaluation period and the market value at the beginning of the evaluation period, and (2) any distributions made from the portfolio. It is important that any capital or income distributions from the portfolio to a client or beneficiary of the portfolio be included.

The *rate of return*, or simply return, expresses the dollar return in terms of the amount of the market value at the beginning of the evaluation period. Thus, the return can be viewed as the amount (expressed as a fraction of the initial portfolio value) that can be withdrawn at the end of the evaluation period while maintaining the initial market value of the portfolio intact. In equation form, the portfolio's return can be expressed as follows:

$$R_p = \frac{V_1 - V_0 + D}{V_0}$$

where

R_p = the return on the portfolio

V_1 = the portfolio market value at the end of the evaluation period
V_0 = the portfolio market value at the beginning of the evaluation period
D = the cash distributions from the portfolio to the client during the evaluation period

To illustrate the calculation of a return, assume the following information for an external manager for a pension plan sponsor: the portfolio's market value at the beginning and end of the evaluation period is \$100 million (V_0) and \$112 million (V_1), respectively, and during the evaluation period \$5 million (D) is distributed to the plan sponsor from investment income. Then

$$R_p = \frac{\$112,000,000 - \$100,000,000 + \$5,000,000}{\$100,000,000} = 0.17 = 17\%$$

Assumption in Calculating Returns There are three assumptions in measuring return as given by the rate of return formula presented above. First, it assumes that cash flows into the portfolio from interest income that occur during the evaluation period but are not distributed to the client are reinvested in the portfolio. For example, suppose that during the evaluation period \$7 million is received from interest income. This amount is reflected in the market value of the portfolio at the end of the period.

The second assumption is that if there are distributions from the portfolio, they occur at the end of the evaluation period or are held in the form of cash until the end of the evaluation period. In our example, \$5 million is distributed to the plan sponsor. But when did that distribution actually occur? To understand why the timing of the distribution is important, consider two extreme cases: (1) the distribution is made at the end of the evaluation period, as assumed by the rate of return formula, and (2) the distribution is made at the beginning of the evaluation period. In the first case, the manager had the use of the \$5 million to invest for the entire evaluation period. By contrast, in the second case, the manager loses the opportunity to invest the funds until the end of the evaluation period. Consequently, the timing of the distribution will affect the return, but this is not considered in the calculation.

The third assumption is that there is no contribution made by the client during the evaluation period. For example, suppose that some time during the evaluation period a client gives an additional \$8 million to the manager to invest. Consequently, the market value of the portfolio at the end of the evaluation period, \$112 million in our example, would reflect the contribution of \$8 million. The rate of return formula does not reflect that the ending market value of the portfolio is affected by the client's cash contribution. Moreover, the timing of this contribution will affect the calculated return.

Thus, while the return calculation for a portfolio using the rate of return formula can be determined for an evaluation period of any length of time such as 1 day, 1 month, or 5 years, from a practical point of view, the assumptions dis-

cussed earlier limit its application. The longer the evaluation period, the more likely the assumptions will be violated. For example, it is highly likely that there may be more than one distribution to the client and more than one contribution from the client if the evaluation period is 5 years than if the evaluation period is one quarter. Thus, a return calculation made over a long period of time would not be very reliable because of the assumption underlying the calculation that all cash distributions and contributions are made and received at the end of the period.

Not only does the violation of the assumptions make it difficult to compare the returns of two managers over some evaluation period, but it is also not useful for evaluating performance over different periods. For example, the equation will not give reliable information to compare the performance of a 1-month evaluation period and a 3-year evaluation period. To make such a comparison, the return must be expressed per unit of time, for example, per year.

Subperiod Returns

The way to handle these practical issues is to calculate the return for a short unit of time such as a month or a quarter. We call the return so calculated the *sub-period return.* To get the return for the evaluation period, the subperiod returns are then averaged. So, for example, if the evaluation period is 1 year and 12 monthly returns are calculated, the monthly returns are the subperiod returns and they are averaged to get the 1-year return. If a 3-year return is sought and 12 quarterly returns can be calculated, quarterly returns are the subperiod returns and they are averaged to get the 3-year return. The 3-year return can then be converted into an annual return by the straightforward procedure described later.

Three methodologies have been used in practice to calculate the average of the subperiod returns: (1) the arithmetic average rate of return, (2) the time-weighted rate of return (also called the geometric rate of return), and (3) the dollar-weighted rate of return.

Arithmetic Average Rate of Return The *arithmetic average rate of return* is an unweighted average of the subperiod returns. For example, if the portfolio returns were 12%, 25%, –15%, and –2% in months January, February, March, and April, respectively, the arithmetic average monthly return is 5%. There is a major problem with using the arithmetic average rate of return. To see this problem, suppose the initial market value of a portfolio is $140 million and the market values at the end of the next 2 months are $280 million and $140 million, and assume that there are no distributions to or contributions from the client for either month. Then using the above equation the subperiod return for the first month is 100% and the subperiod return for the second month is –50%. The arithmetic average rate of return is then 25%. Not a bad return! But think about this number. The portfolio's initial market value was $140 million. Its market value at the end of two months is $140 million. The return over this 2-month evaluation period is zero. Yet, the arithmetic average rate of return says it is a whopping 25%.

Thus, it is improper to interpret the arithmetic average rate of return as a measure of the average return over an evaluation period. The proper interpretation is as follows: *It is the average value of the withdrawals (expressed as a fraction of the initial portfolio market value) that can be made at the end of each subperiod while keeping the initial portfolio market value intact.* In our first example in which the average monthly return is 5%, the investor can withdraw 12% of the initial portfolio market value at the end of the first month, can withdraw 25% of the initial portfolio market value at the end of the second month, must add 15% of the initial portfolio market value at the end of the third month, and must add 2% of the initial portfolio market value at the end of the fourth month. In our second example, the average monthly return of 25% means that 100% of the initial portfolio market value ($140 million) can be withdrawn at the end of the first month and 50% must be added at the end of the second month.

Time-Weighted Rate of Return The *time-weighted rate of return* measures the compounded rate of growth of the initial portfolio market value during the evaluation period, assuming that all cash distributions are reinvested in the portfolio. It is also commonly referred to as the *geometric rate of return* since it is computed by taking the geometric average of the portfolio subperiod returns. The general formula is:

$$R_T = [(1 + R_{P1})(1 + R_{P2})\ldots(1 + R_{PN})]^{1/N} - 1$$

where

R_T = time-weighted rate of return
R_{Pk} = the portfolio return for subperiod k, $k = 1, \ldots, N$
N = the number of subperiods in the evaluation period

For example, let us assume the portfolio subperiod returns were 12%, 25%, –15%, and –2% in January, February, March, and April, as in the first example. Then the time-weighted rate of return is:

$$R_T = [(1 + 0.12)(1 + 0.25)(1 + (-0.15))(1 + (-0.02))]^{1/4} - 1$$

$$= [(1.12)(1.25)(0.85)(0.98)]^{1/4} - 1 = 3.92\%$$

Since the time-weighted rate of return is 3.92% per month, $1 invested in the portfolio at the beginning of January would have grown at a rate of 3.92% per month during the 4-month evaluation period. The time-weighted rate of return in the second example is 0%, as expected.

In general, the arithmetic and time-weighted average returns will give different values for the portfolio return over some evaluation period. This is because in computing the arithmetic average rate of return, the amount invested is assumed to be maintained (through additions or withdrawals) at its initial portfolio market value. The time-weighted return, in contrast, is the return on a portfolio that varies in size because of the assumption that all proceeds are reinvested.

In general, the arithmetic average rate of return will exceed the time-weighted average rate of return. The exception is in the special situation where all the subperiod returns are the same, in which case the averages are identical. The magnitude of the difference between the two averages is smaller the less the variation in the subperiod returns over the evaluation period. For example, suppose that the evaluation period is 4 months and that the four monthly returns are as follows:

$$R_{P1} = 0.04, R_{P2} = 0.06, R_{P3} = 0.02, \text{ and } R_{P4} = -0.02$$

The average arithmetic rate of return is 2.5% and the time-weighted average rate of return is 2.46%. Not much of a difference. In our earlier example in which we calculated an average rate of return of 25% but a time-weighted average rate of return of 0%, the large discrepancy is due to the substantial variation in the two monthly returns.

Dollar-Weighted Rate of Return The *dollar-weighted rate of return* is computed by finding the interest rate that will make the present value of the cash flows from all the subperiods in the evaluation period plus the terminal market value of the portfolio equal to the initial market value of the portfolio. The cash flow for each subperiod reflects the difference between the cash inflows due to investment income (i.e., coupon interest) and contribution made by the client to the portfolio and the cash outflows reflecting distributions to the client. Notice that it is not necessary to know the market value of the portfolio for each subperiod to determine the dollar-weighted rate of return.

The dollar-weighted rate of return is simply an internal rate of return calculation and hence it is also called the *internal rate of return*. The general formula for the dollar-weighted return is:

$$V_0 = \frac{C_1}{(1 + R_D)} + \frac{C_2}{(1 + R_D)^2} + \ldots + \frac{C_N + V_N}{(1 + R_D)^n}$$

where

R_D = the dollar-weighted rate of return
V_0 = the initial market value of the portfolio
V_N = the terminal market value of the portfolio
C_k = the cash flow for the portfolio for subperiod k, $k = 1, 2,\ldots, N$

Let's look at how the cash flow (C_k) is defined. A cash withdrawal is treated as a cash inflow. So, in the absence of any cash contribution for a given time period, a cash withdrawal is a positive cash flow for that time period. A cash contribution is treated as a cash outflow. Consequently, in the absence of any cash withdrawal for a given time period, a cash contribution is treated as a negative cash flow for that period. If there are both cash contributions and cash withdrawals for a given time period, then the cash flow is as follows for that time period:

cash withdrawals exceed cash contributions, then there is a positive cash flow
cash withdrawals less than cash contributions, then there is a negative cash flow

There is a simple way of remembering how to handle cash withdrawals: Treat it the same way as you would an ordinary bond. To compute the yield for a bond, the cash flow for the coupon payments (i.e., a cash withdrawal from the investment) is positive. Since a cash withdrawal is a positive cash flow, a cash contribution is a negative cash flow.

To illustrate the dollar-weighted rate of return calculation, suppose that a portfolio has a market value of \$100 million at the beginning of July, capital withdrawals of \$5 million at the end of months July, August, and September, no cash inflows from the client in any month, and a market value at the end of September of \$110 million. Then $V_0 = \$100{,}000{,}000$, $N = 3$, $C_1 = C_2 = C_3 = \$5{,}000{,}000$, and $V_3 = \$110{,}000{,}000$, and R_D is the interest rate that satisfies the following equation:

$$\$100{,}000{,}000 = \frac{\$5{,}000{,}000}{(1+R_D)} + \frac{\$5{,}000{,}000}{(1+R_D)^2} + \frac{\$5{,}000{,}000 + \$110{,}000{,}000}{(1+R_D)^3}$$

It can be verified that the interest rate that satisfies the above expression is 8.1%. This, then, is the dollar-weighted return.

The dollar-weighted rate of return and the time-weighted rate of return will produce the same result if no withdrawals or contributions occur over the evaluation period and all investment income is reinvested. The problem with the dollar-weighted rate of return is that it is affected by factors that are beyond the control of the manager. Specifically, any contributions made by the client or withdrawals that the client requires will affect the calculated return. This makes it difficult to compare the performance of two managers.

Despite this limitation, the dollar-weighted rate of return does provide information. It indicates information about the growth of the fund, which a client will find useful. This growth, however, is not attributable to the performance of the manager because of contributions and withdrawals.

Annualizing Subperiod Returns The evaluation period may be less than or greater than 1 year. Typically, return measures are reported as an average annual return. This requires the annualization of the subperiod returns. The subperiod returns are typically calculated for a period of less than 1 year for the reasons described earlier. The subperiod returns are then annualized using the following formula:

$$\text{Annual return} = (1 + \text{Average period return})^{\text{Number of periods in year}} - 1$$

AIMR Performance Presentation Standards

As just demonstrated, there are subtle issues in calculating the return over the evaluation period. There are also industry concerns as to how managers should

present results to clients and how managers should disclose performance data and records to prospects from whom they are seeking to obtain funds to manage. To address this issue, standards for performance disclosure were developed by the Association for Investment Management and Research (AIMR). These standards, which went into effect in 1993, "are a set of guiding ethical principles intended to promote full disclosure and fair representation by investment managers in reporting their investment results."[1] A secondary objective of the standards is to ensure uniformity in the presentation of results so it is easier for clients to compare the performance of managers. The standards set forth the requirements and mandatory disclosures for compliance and practices recommended.

In our illustrations of the various ways to measure portfolio return, we used the same length of time for the subperiod (e.g., a month or a quarter). The subperiod returns were averaged, with the preferred method being geometric averaging. The AIMR standards require that the return measure minimize the effect of contributions and withdrawals so that cash flows beyond the control of the manager are minimized. If the subperiod return is calculated daily, the impact of contributions and withdrawals will be minimized. The time-weighted return measure can then be calculated from the daily returns.

From a practical point of view, the problem is that calculating a daily return requires that the market value of the portfolio be determined at the end of each day. While this does not present a problem for a mutual fund that must calculate the net asset value of the portfolio each business day, it is a time-consuming administrative problem for other managers. Moreover, there are asset classes in which the determination of daily prices would be difficult (e.g., certain fixed income securities, emerging market securities, and real estate).

An alternative to the time-weighted rate of return has been suggested. This is the dollar-weighted rate of return, which as we noted earlier is less desirable in comparing the performance of managers because of the effect of withdrawals and contributions beyond the control of the manager. The advantage of this method from an operational perspective is that market values do not have to be calculated daily. The effect of withdrawals and contributions is minimized if they are small relative to the length of the subperiod. However, if the cash flow is more than 10% at any time, the AIMR standards require that the portfolio be revalued on that date.[2]

Once the subperiod returns in an evaluation period are calculated, they are compounded. The AIMR standards specify that for evaluation periods of less than 1 year, returns should *not* be annualized. Thus, if the evaluation period is 7 months and the subperiod returns calculated are monthly, an annualized return should not be reported; instead the compounded 7-month return should be reported.

---

[1] *Performance Presentation Standards: 1993* (Charlottesville, VA: Association for Investment Management and Research, 1993).

[2] For a further discussion of the implementation of the AIMR Standards, see Deborah H. Miller, "How to Calculate the Numbers According to the Standards," in *Performance Reporting for Investment Managers: Applying the AIMR Performance Presentation Standards* (Charlottesville, VA: AIMR, 1991).

BOND MARKET INDEXES

The performance of a portfolio manger is evaluated relative to some benchmark. The benchmark could be a bond market index or a set of liabilities. There are several bond indexes by which a manager can be evaluated. In this section, we review bond indexes. These indexes are classified as broad-based U.S. bond market indexes, specialized U.S. bond market indexes, and global and international bond market indexes.

Broad-Based U.S. Bond Market Indexes

The three broad-based U.S. bond market indexes most commonly used by institutional investors are the Lehman Brothers U.S. Aggregate Index, the Salomon Smith Barney (SSB) Broad Investment-Grade Bond Index (BIG), and the Merrill Lynch Domestic Market Index. There are more than 5,500 issues in each index. One study has found that the correlation of annual returns among the three broad-based bond market indexes is around 98%.

The three broad-based U.S. bond market indexes are computed daily and are market-value weighted. This means that for each issue, the ratio of the market value of an issue relative to the market value of all issues in the index is used as the weight of the issue in all calculations. The securities in the SSB BIG index are all trader priced. For the two other indexes, the securities are either trader priced or model priced. Each index has a different way in which it handles intra-month cash flows that must be reinvested. For the SSB BIG index, these cash flows are assumed to be reinvested at the 1-month Treasury bill rate, while for the Merrill Lynch index, they are assumed to be reinvested in the specific issue. There is no reinvestment of intra-month cash flows for the Lehman index.

Each index is broken into sectors. The Lehman index, for example, is divided into the following six sectors: (1) Treasury sector, (2) agency sector, (3) mortgage passthrough sector, (4) commercial mortgage-backed securities sector, (5) asset-backed securities sector, and (6) credit sector. Exhibit 1 shows the percentage composition of the index as of July 6, 2001.

Exhibit 1: Percentage Composition of Lehman Brothers U.S. Aggregate Index as of July 6, 2001

Sector	Percent of market value
Treasury	23.79%
Agency	11.05
Mortgage Passthroughs	34.36
Commercial Mortgage-Backed Securities	1.95
Asset-Backed Securities	1.83
Credit	27.03
Total	100.00%

Source: Lehman Brothers, *Global Relative Value*, Fixed Income Research, July 9, 2001.

The agency sector includes agency debentures, not mortgage-backed or asset-backed securities issued by federal agencies. The mortgage passthrough sector includes agency passthrough securities—Ginnie Mae, Fannie Mae, and Freddie Mac passthrough securities. Thus, agency collateralized mortgage obligations and agency stripped mortgage-backed securities are not included. These mortgage derivatives products are not included because it would be double counting since they are created from agency passthroughs. In constructing the index for the mortgage sector for the Lehman index, for example, Lehman groups more than 800,000 individual mortgage pools with a fixed-rate coupon into generic aggregates. These generic aggregates are defined in terms of agency (i.e., Ginnie Mae, Fannie Mae, and Freddie Mac), program type (i.e., 30-year, 15-year, balloon mortgages, etc.), coupon rate for the passthrough, and the year the passthrough was originated (i.e., vintage). For an issue to be included, it must have a minimum amount outstanding of $100 million and a minimum weighted average maturity of one year. Agency passthroughs backed by pools of adjustable-rate mortgages are not included in the mortgage index.

The credit sector in the Lehman Brothers index includes corporate issues. In the other two U.S. broad-based bond market indexes, this sector is referred to as the *corporate sector.*

Specialized U.S. Bond Market Indexes

The specialized U.S. bond market indexes focus on one sector of the bond market or a subsector of the bond market. Indexes on sectors of the market are published by the three firms that produce the broad-based U.S. bond market indexes. Nonbrokerage firms have created specialized indexes for sectors. For example, Ryan Labs produces a Treasury index. Since none of the broad-based U.S. bond market indexes include noninvestment-grade or high-yield issues, the three that have created the broad-based indexes and the firms of CS First Boston and Donaldson Lufkin and Jenrette have created indexes for this sector. The number of issues included in each high-yield index varies from index to index. The types of issues permitted (e.g., convertible, floating-rate, payment-in-kind) also varies. There are different ways for treating interim income and default issues that are followed by the index creator.

Global and International Bond Market Indexes

The growth in non-U.S. bond investing has resulted in a proliferation of international bond market indexes. Three types of indexes are available that include non-U.S. bonds. The first is an index that includes both U.S. and non-U.S. bonds. Such indexes are referred to as *global bond indexes* or *world bond indexes*. The second type includes only non-U.S. bonds and is commonly referred to as *international bond indexes* or *ex-U.S. bond indexes*. Finally, there are specialized bond indexes for particular non-U.S. bond sectors. Indexes can be reported on a hedged currency basis and/or an unhedged currency basis.

There are two types of global bond indexes (i.e., indexes that include U.S. and non-U.S. bonds). The first type restricts the sector of each country to just government bonds. For example, the components of the Merrill Lynch Government Bond Index include the government sectors of the following countries:

Europe-EMU: Australia, Belgium, Finland, France, Germany, Ireland, Italy, Netherlands, Portugal, and Spain
Europe-Non-EMU: Denmark, Sweden, Switzerland, and U.K.
North America: Canada and U.S.
Japan & Asia/Pacific: Australia, Japan, and New Zealand

Other similar-type indexes are the Salomon World Government Bond Index and the J.P. Morgan Global Bond Index.

An example of a global bond index that includes government and non-government sectors is the Lehman Brothers Global Index (which Lehman also refers to as its "Core Plus Plus" Portfolio). The index is divided into a U.S. dollar sector and a nondollar sector. The U.S. dollar sector includes all the sectors within the Lehman Brothers U.S. Aggregate Index plus high-yield bonds and dollar-denominated emerging market bonds. The nondollar sector includes the following countries: France, Germany, Italy, Spain, Sweden, and the United Kingdom. An index such as the Lehman Brothers Global Index is an appropriate benchmark for a manager who is permitted to invest in both U.S. and non-U.S. bonds.

An international bond index (i.e., a bond index that includes only non-U.S. bonds) is an appropriate benchmark for a manager who is investing only in non-U.S. bonds. There are two types of non-U.S. indexes. The first is an index that includes government and nongovernment sectors. Other indexes include just the government sector of an international bond index. For example, the Salomon Non-U.S. Government Index is a byproduct of the Salomon World Government Bond Index.

The third type of non-U.S. bond index is a specialized bond index. Here are some examples of such indexes published by two investment banking firms:

Lehman Brothers	Merrill Lynch
Eurodollar Index	Pan European Broad Market Index
Emerging Markets Index	EMU Broad Market Index
Pan-European Aggregate Index	European Currencies High Yield Index
Pan-European High-Yield Index	Emerging Europe Index
Euro-Aggregate Index	

TOTAL RETURN FRAMEWORK

In this section we set forth a framework to assess the potential performance of a bond or bond portfolio strategy—total return.

Sources of a Bond's Return

An investor who purchases a bond can expect to receive a *dollar* return from one or more of the following sources: (1) the coupon interest payments made by the issuer; (2) any capital gain (or capital loss—negative dollar return) when the bond matures, is called, is put, is refunded, or is sold; and (3) income from reinvestment of the coupon interest payments and interim principal payments. Any measure of the potential return from holding a bond over some investment horizon should consider these three sources of return. In Chapter 3, we explained why yield measures are limited with respect to assessing the potential performance over some investment horizon.

Total Return

If yield measures offer little insight into the potential performance of a bond or bond portfolio, what measure can be used? The proper measure is one that considers all three sources of potential dollar return over the investor's investment horizon. It is the return (interest rate) that will make the proceeds (i.e., price plus accrued interest) invested grow to the projected total dollar return at the end of the investment horizon. This is referred to as the *total return.*

The total return requires that the investor specify (1) an investment horizon, (2) a reinvestment rate, and (3) a selling price for the bond at the end of the investment horizon (which depends on the assumed yield to maturity for the bond at the end of the investment horizon). More formally, the steps for computing a total return over some investment horizon are as follows:

Step 1: Compute the total coupon payments plus the reinvestment income based on an assumed reinvestment rate. The reinvestment rate is one-half the annual interest rate that the investor assumes can be earned when reinvesting the coupon interest payments.[3]

Step 2: Determine the projected sale price at the end of the investment horizon. We refer to this as the *horizon price.* The horizon price will depend on the projected yield on comparable bonds at the end of the investment horizon. We refer to the yield at the end of the investment horizon as the *horizon yield.*

Step 3: Add the values computed in Steps 1 and 2. The sum is the *total future dollars* that will be received from the investment given the assumed reinvestment rate and projected horizon yield.

Step 4: To obtain the semiannual total return, use the following formula:

$$\left(\frac{\text{Total future dollars}}{\text{Full purchase price of bond}}\right)^{1/\text{length of horizon}} - 1$$

where the full purchase price is sale price plus accrued interest.

[3] An investor can choose multiple reinvestment rates for cash flows over the investment horizon.

Exhibit 2: Graphical Depiction of Total Return Calculation

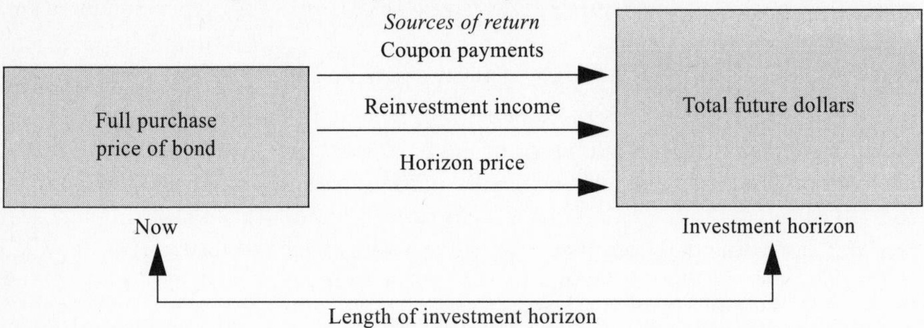

Total return is the interest rate that will make the full purchase price of the bond grow to the total future dollars.

Step 5: For semiannual-pay bonds, double the interest rate found in Step 4. The resulting interest rate is the total return expressed on a bond-equivalent basis. Instead, the total return can be expressed on an effective rate basis by using the following formula:

$$(1 + \text{Semiannual total return})^2 - 1$$

A graphical depiction of the total return calculation is presented in Exhibit 2.

The decision as to whether to calculate the total return on a bond-equivalent basis or an effective rate basis depends on the situation. If the total return is being compared to a benchmark index that is calculated on a bond-equivalent basis, then the total return should be calculated in that way. However, if the bond proceeds are being used to satisfy a liability that is calculated on an effective rate basis, then the total return should be calculated in that way.

To illustrate the computation of the total return, suppose that an investor with a 3-year investment horizon is considering purchasing a 20-year 8% coupon bond for $82.84. The next coupon payment is 6 months from now. The yield to maturity for this bond is 10%. The investor expects that he can reinvest the coupon payments at an annual interest rate of 6% and that at the end of the investment horizon the 17-year bond will be selling to offer a yield to maturity of 7% (i.e., the horizon yield is 7%). The total return for this bond is computed in Exhibit 3.

Total Return to Maturity

In our discussion and illustration, we focused on the total return over some investment horizon shorter than the maturity date. It is useful to calculate a total return to the maturity date to see the relative importance of each source of return. The calculation of the semiannual total return to maturity is

$$\left(\frac{\text{Total future dollars}}{\text{Full purchase price of a bond}}\right)^{1/\text{length of horizon}} - 1$$

Exhibit 3: Illustration of Calculation of Total Return

Assumptions:

Bond: 8%, 20-year bond selling for $82.84 (yield to maturity is 10%)
Reinvestment rate: 6%
Investment horizon: 3 years
Horizon yield: 7%

Calculation:

Step 1: Compute the total coupon payments plus the reinvestment income assuming an annual reinvestment rate of 6%, or 3% every 6 months. The coupon payments are $4 per $100 of par value every 6 months for 3 years or six periods (the length of the investment horizon). The total coupon interest plus reinvestment income is $25.874.

Step 2: The projected sale price at the end of 3 years (i.e., the horizon price) assuming that the required yield to maturity for 17-year bonds (i.e., horizon yield) is 7% is $109.851.

Step 3: Adding the amount in Steps 1 and 2 gives the total future dollars of $135.725.

Step 4: Compute the following:

$$\left(\frac{\$135.725}{\$82.84}\right)^{1/6} - 1 = (1.63840)^{0.16667} - 1$$

$$= 1.0858 - 1 = 0.0858 \text{ or } 8.58\%$$

Step 5: Doubling 8.58% gives a total return of 17.16% on a bond-equivalent basis. On an effective rate basis, the horizon return is

$$(1.0858)^2 - 1 = 1.1790 - 1 = 0.1790 = 17.90\%$$

To illustrate this concept, consider a 4%, 25-year bond selling for $50.594 per $100 par value. The yield to maturity for this bond is 9%. The total coupon payments per $100 par value is $100 ($4 per year times 25 years). The capital gain at the maturity date is $49.406 ($100 – $50.594). To calculate the reinvestment income, a reinvestment rate must be assumed. Assuming a 6% reinvestment rate (3% semiannually), it can be demonstrated that the reinvestment income is $125.5937.

The total future dollars is $325.5937, which is the sum of the total coupon payments ($100), the reinvestment income ($125.5937), and the maturity value ($100). The semiannual total return to maturity is found as follows:

$$\left(\frac{\$325.5937}{\$50.594}\right)^{1/50} - 1 = 0.0379 \text{ or } 3.79\%$$

The bond-equivalent yield is 7.59%, and the total return on an effective rate basis is 7.73%. Thus, if an investor purchases this bond, holds it to maturity, and can reinvest the coupon payments at a 6% yield, the total return to maturity would be 7.59% on a bond-equivalent basis. This is less than the 9% yield to maturity.

The relative importance of each source of return for this bond is summarized below:

Sources of return	Dollars	Percent
Total coupon	\$100.0000	36.36%
Reinvestment income	125.5937	45.67
Capital gain or loss	49.406	17.97
Total future dollars	\$274.9997	100.00%

From the relative contributions, it can be seen how critical the reinvest rate is.

After-Tax Total Return to Maturity

Thus far, we have ignored the impact of taxes on the total return of a bond if it is held to maturity. There are taxes on interest income and any capital gain. As explained in Chapter 16, there may or may not be a preferential tax treatment for the capital gain. Incorporating tax consequences into the total return calculation is fairly straightforward.

Effect of Taxes on Total Dollar Contributions

Taxation of coupon income has three adverse effects. First, it reduces the amount of the coupon income by 1 minus the tax rate. That is, the after-tax semiannual coupon is equal to:

$$\text{Par value} \times (1 - \text{Tax rate on income}) \times (\text{Coupon rate}/2)$$

The total coupon income over the life of the bond is also reduced.

For example, consider a 30-year bond with a coupon rate of 4.2%. Suppose that the tax rate on interest income is 35%. The pretax semiannual coupon is \$2.1. The after-tax semiannual coupon per \$100 of par value is:

$$\$100 \times (1 - 0.35) \times (0.042/2) = \$1.365$$

The total pretax coupon payment is \$126 per \$100 par value; the total after-tax coupon payment is \$81.90.

The second adverse effect of taxation of the coupon income is that there are fewer dollars to reinvest each period. Consequently, the reinvestment income is reduced. The third adverse effect is that the interest earned on the interest income reinvested is reduced since it is taxed.

The total income from coupon interest and reinvestment income is computed as follows:

$$\text{Coupon rate}/2 \times (1 - \text{Tax rate}) \times \text{Par value} \times \frac{[1 + (\text{Reinvestment rate}/2) \times (1 - \text{Tax rate})]^n - 1}{(\text{Reinvestment rate}/2) \times (1 - \text{Tax rate})}$$

where n is the number of semiannual periods to maturity.

For example, consider once again the 4.2% 30-year bond. If the reinvestment rate is assumed to be 6% and the tax rate is 35%, then the total income from coupon interest and reinvestment income is:

$$0.042/2 \times (1 - 0.35) \times \$100 \times \frac{[1 + (0.06/2) \times (1 - 0.35)]^{60} - 1}{(0.06/2) \times (1 - 0.35)} = \$153.0139$$

Since the total after-tax coupon payment is $81.90, this means that the after-tax reinvestment income is $71.1139 ($153.0139 – $81.90).

The effect of taxes on coupon income and reinvestment income for a 4.2% 30-year bond selling at par is shown below:

Source	Tax not considered	35% tax rate
Total coupon payments	$126.0000	$81.9000
Reinvestment income	216.4132	71.1139
Total future dollars	$342.4132	$153.0139

Notice that while the total coupon payments are reduced proportionately by the tax rate, the reinvestment income is reduced more than proportionately. That is, the total coupon payment after reduction for a 35% tax rate is 65% of the total coupon payments ignoring taxes. This is not so for the reinvestment income, which declines by 67% after taxes.

To calculate the total after-tax return to maturity for a bond, the effect of taxes on the capital gain must be considered. In Chapter 14 we explained the tax treatment of bonds purchased at a discount. To illustrate how to incorporate the tax treatment of the capital gain, suppose that a 4.2% 30-year bond is purchased at $75 per $100 of par and that the $25 gain is taxed at a preferential tax treatment of 20%. Then at the maturity date, this amount after the 20% capital gains tax rate will be $20. The total return to maturity for this bond assuming a reinvestment rate of 6% and that coupon income is taxed at 35% is as follows:

	Taxes not considered		Taxes considered	
Source	Dollars	Percent	Dollars	Percent
Total coupon payments	$126.0000	34.3%	$81.9000	47.3%
Reinvestment income	216.4132	58.9	71.1139	41.1
Capital gain	25.0000	6.8	20.0000	11.6
Total future dollars	$342.4132	100.0%	$173.0139	100.0%

Notice that the relative importance of each source has changed once taxes are considered.

Calculation of After-Tax Total Return to Maturity

Given the total future dollars at maturity after accounting for taxes, the after-tax total return to maturity (on a semiannual basis) can be calculated as follows:

$$\left(\frac{\text{Total future dollars at maturity}}{\text{Full purchase price of bond}}\right)^{1/n} - 1$$

where n is the number of periods to maturity. The semiannual rate can then be annualized on a bond-equivalent basis or on an effective rate basis.

For the 4.2% 30-year bond selling at \$75, the after-tax total return to maturity (on a semiannual basis) based on a 35% tax rate on coupon income, 20% capital gains tax rate, and 6% reinvestment rate is:

$$\left(\frac{\$153.0139}{\$75}\right)^{1/60} - 1 = 0.0201 = 2.01\%$$

The bond-equivalent after-tax total return to maturity is 4.02%. On an effective rate basis, the after-tax total return to maturity is 4.07%.

The after-tax yield to maturity for this bond is the interest rate that will make the present value of the after-tax cash flows equal to the proceeds invested. For our hypothetical bonds it is 4.1%. This yield assumes that the after-tax cash flows can be reinvested at 4.1%.

The after-tax total return to maturity is a more appropriate measure for comparing the potential return from holding a taxable bond and the same-maturity tax-exempt municipal bond to the maturity date. For a municipal bond, the coupon payments will not be taxed; however, the capital gain will be.

Portfolio Total Return

To calculate a portfolio's total return, it is first necessary to calculate the total dollars at the end of the investment horizon for each bond in the portfolio. Then the total dollars are summed. This aggregate dollar amount is used in the total return formula. The numerator is the total dollars invested in all the securities.

Scenario Analysis

Total return enables a portfolio manager to analyze the performance of an individual bond or bond portfolio based on different interest rate scenarios for horizon yields and reinvestment rates. This type of analysis, referred to as *scenario analysis*, allows a portfolio manager to see how sensitive the performance of a bond or bond portfolio is to each assumption. A portfolio manager should be more comfortable looking at the total return profile using different interest rate assumptions than blindly relying on the implicit assumptions incorporated into conventional yield measures.

OAS Total Return

In Chapter 3, the option-adjusted spread (OAS) was described. The OAS can be incorporated into a total return analysis to determine the horizon price. This requires a valuation model. At the end of the investment horizon, it is necessary to specify how the OAS is expected to change. The horizon price can be "backed out" of a valuation model. This technique can be extended to the total return framework by making assumptions about the required variables at the horizon date.

Assumptions about the OAS value at the investment horizon reflect the expectations of the portfolio manager. It is common to assume that the OAS at the

horizon date will be the same as the OAS at the time of purchase. A total return calculated using this assumption is sometimes referred to as a *constant-OAS total return*. Alternatively, portfolio managers will make bets on how the OAS will change—either widening or tightening. The total return framework can be used to assess how sensitive the performance of a fixed income security with an embedded option is to changes in the OAS.

KEY POINTS

- ❑ *The first step in the investment management process is setting investment objectives.*
- ❑ *The investment objective depends on the financial institution and, for many institutions, is dictated by the nature of their liabilities.*
- ❑ *The second step in the investment management process is establishing policy guidelines for meeting the investment objectives and begins with the asset allocation decision.*
- ❑ *The third step in the investment management process is selecting a portfolio strategy that is consistent with the objectives and policy guidelines of the client or institution.*
- ❑ *Portfolio strategies can be classified as either active strategies or passive strategies.*
- ❑ *All active bond portfolio strategies are based on expectations about the factors that influence bond performance.*
- ❑ *The fourth step in the investment management process is selecting the specific issues to be included in the portfolio and involves evaluating individual securities in order to identify mispriced securities.*
- ❑ *The measurement and evaluation of investment performance is the fifth step in the investment management process.*
- ❑ *Performance measurement involves the calculation of the return realized by a manager over some evaluation period.*
- ❑ *Performance evaluation is concerned with determining whether the manager added value by outperforming the established benchmark and how the manager achieved the calculated return.*
- ❑ *The rate of return expresses the dollar return in terms of the amount of the initial investment (i.e., the initial market value of the portfolio).*
- ❑ *Three methodologies have been used in practice to calculate the average of the subperiod returns: (1) the arithmetic average rate of return, (2) the time-weighted (or geometric) rate of return, and (3) the dollar-weighted rate of return.*
- ❑ *The arithmetic average rate of return is the average value of the withdrawals (expressed as a fraction of the initial portfolio market value) that can be made at the end of each period while keeping the initial portfolio market value intact.*
- ❑ *The time-weighted rate of return measures the compounded rate of growth of the initial portfolio over the evaluation period, assuming that all cash distributions are reinvested in the portfolio.*
- ❑ *The dollar-weighted rate of return is computed by finding the interest rate that will make the present value of the cash flows from all the subperiods in the evaluation period plus the terminal market value of the portfolio equal to the initial market value of the portfolio.*

- ❑ *The dollar-weighted rate of return is an internal rate of return calculation and will produce the same result as the time-weighted rate of return if (1) no withdrawals or contributions occur over the evaluation period and (2) all dividends are reinvested.*
- ❑ *Because the dollar-weighted rate of return is affected by factors that are beyond the control of the manager (i.e., any contributions made by the client or withdrawals that the client requires), it is difficult to compare the performance of managers.*
- ❑ *The AIMR has adopted standards for the presentation and disclosure of performance results.*
- ❑ *The bond market indexes available can be classified as broad-based U.S. bond market indexes, specialized U.S. bond market indexes, and global and international bond market indexes.*
- ❑ *The three broad-based U.S. bond market indexes most commonly used by institutional investors are the Lehman Brothers U.S. Aggregate Index, the Salomon Smith Barney Broad Investment-Grade Bond Index, and the Merrill Lynch Domestic Market Index.*
- ❑ *The Lehman index is divided into the following six sectors: (1) Treasury sector, (2) agency sector, (3) mortgage passthrough sector, (4) commercial mortgage-backed securities sector, (5) asset-backed securities sector, and (6) credit sector.*
- ❑ *The broad-based U.S. bond market indexes exclude issues that are noninvestment-grade (i.e., below BBB) and issues that have a maturity of 1 year or less.*
- ❑ *The three types of indexes that include non-U.S. bonds are (1) indexes that include both U.S. and non-U.S. bonds ("global bond indexes" or "world bond indexes"), (2) indexes that include only non-U.S. bonds ("international bond indexes" or "ex-U.S. bond indexes"), and (3) specialized bond indexes for particular non-U.S. bond sectors.*
- ❑ *The performance of a money manager is evaluated relative to some benchmark.*
- ❑ *The three sources of potential return from investing in a bond are the coupon interest payments, any capital gain (or capital loss), and reinvestment income.*
- ❑ *The proper measure for assessing potential return is the total return.*
- ❑ *Calculation of the total return requires specification of the reinvestment rate.*
- ❑ *An after-tax total return to maturity can be calculated based on some assumed reinvestment rate and tax rates on coupon interest and capital gains.*
- ❑ *Taxes on coupon income will have a proportionate effect on the total coupon income; the effect will be more than proportionate on reinvestment income.*
- ❑ *Calculation of the total return to an investment horizon that is less than the maturity date requires specification of the horizon yield as well as the reinvestment rate.*

- ❑ *The horizon yield is needed to obtain the horizon price of the bond at the end of the investment horizon.*

- ❑ *Scenario analysis involves calculating the total return under different assumptions regarding the reinvestment rate and horizon yield.*

- ❑ *Option-adjusted spread analysis can be incorporated into a total return analysis by specifying the OAS at the end of the investment horizon.*

- ❑ *When the OAS is not assumed to change from its initial value, the total return is said to be calculated on a constant OAS basis.*

Chapter 18

Overview of Fixed Income Portfolio Strategies

In the previous chapter, we explained the five basic steps in the investment management process and explained how the potential performance of any strategy should be assessed using the total return framework. The use of leverage in a strategy was explained in Chapter 15. In this chapter, we look at the more popular fixed income portfolio strategies. As explained in the previous chapter, strategies can be classified as either active or passive strategies. We begin this chapter with a discussion of how a money manager's or client's view of the pricing efficiency of a market sector affects the selection of a strategy.

PRICING EFFICIENCY AND STRATEGY SELECTION

A *price-efficient market* refers to a market where prices at all times fully reflect all available information that is relevant to the valuation of securities. When a market is price-efficient, strategies pursued to outperform a market index will not consistently produce superior returns after adjusting for risk and transaction costs.

Although many studies have empirically investigated the pricing efficiency of the stock market, there are very few studies of the various sectors of the bond market. The difficulty in testing for price efficiency in the bond market is the lack of good data—a problem not faced by researchers studying the stock market.

Active bond strategies are those that attempt to outperform the market by one or more of the strategies discussed in this chapter. Obviously, the decision to pursue an active strategy must be based on the belief that there is some type of gain from such costly efforts; for there to be a gain, pricing inefficiencies must exist. The particular strategy chosen depends on why the money manager believes this is the case.

If a money manager or client believes that the market is efficient with respect to pricing bonds, then he or she should accept the implication that attempts to outperform the market cannot be successful systematically, except by luck. This does not mean that money managers or their clients should shun the bond market, but rather that they should pursue a structured portfolio strategy, which is one that does not attempt to outperform the bond market or a sector of the bond market. Is there an optimal investment strategy for someone who holds this belief in the pricing efficiency of the bond market? Indeed there is. Its theo-

retical basis is modern portfolio theory and capital market theory. According to modern portfolio theory, the "market" portfolio offers the highest level of return per unit of risk in a market that is price-efficient. A portfolio of financial assets with characteristics similar to those of a portfolio consisting of all bonds or all bonds in a sector of the bond market (i.e., the market portfolio) will capture the pricing efficiency of the market. This strategy is referred to as *bond indexing* and is discussed later in this chapter. Because an increasing number of pension fund sponsors have come to believe that money managers have been unable to outperform the bond market, the amount of funds allocated to be managed using an indexing strategy has increased since the mid-1980s. However, the amount of money indexed is still a small fraction of the amount of bond funds managed.

THE SPECTRUM OF STRATEGIES

A good way to understand the spectrum of bond portfolio strategies and the key elements of each strategy is in terms of the benchmark established by the client. This is depicted in Exhibit 1. The exhibit, developed by Kenneth Volpert of the Vanguard Group, shows the risk and return of a strategy versus a benchmark. Volpert classifies the strategies as follows:[1]

1. pure bond index matching
2. enhanced indexing/ matching primary risk factors
3. enhanced indexing/minor risk factor mismatches
4. active management/larger risk factor mismatches
5. active management/full-blown active

We discuss each of these strategies as follows.

The difference between indexing and active management is the extent to which the portfolio can deviate from the risk factors associated with the index. The primary risk factors associated with an index are:

1. the duration of the index
2. the present value distribution of the cash flows
3. percent in sector and quality
4. duration contribution of sector
5. duration contribution of credit quality
6. sector/coupon/maturity cell weights
7. issuer exposure control

[1] Kenneth E. Volpert, "Managing Indexed and Enhanced Indexed Bond Portfolios," Chapter 4 in Frank J. Fabozzi (ed.), *Fixed Income Readings for the Chartered Financial Analysts Program* (New Hope, PA: Frank J. Fabozzi Associates, 2000).

Exhibit 1: Bond Management Risk Spectrum

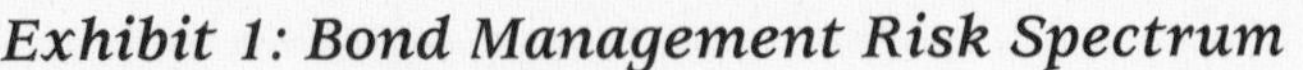

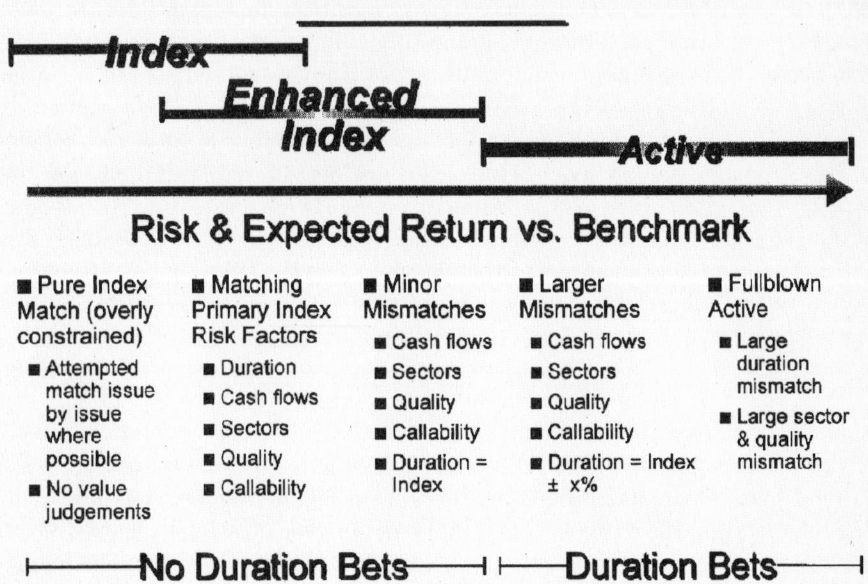

Source: Exhibit 1 in Kenneth E. Volpert, "Managing Indexed and Enhanced Indexed Bond Portfolios," Chapter 4 in Frank J. Fabozzi (ed.), *Fixed Income Readings for the Chartered Financial Analysts Program* (New Hope, PA: Frank J. Fabozzi Associates, 2000), p. 86.

The first primary risk factor deals with the sensitivity of the value of the index to a parallel shift in interest rates. The second factor is important for controlling the yield curve risk associated with an index.

Pure Bond Indexing Strategy

In terms of risk and return, a *pure bond index matching strategy* involves the least risk of underperforming the index. Several factors explain the popularity of bond indexing. First, the empirical evidence suggests that historically the overall performance of active bond managers has been poor. The second factor is the lower advisory management fees charged for an indexed portfolio compared to active management advisory fees. Advisory fees charged by active managers typically range from 15 to 50 basis points. The range for indexed portfolios, in contrast, is 1 to 20 basis points. Some pension plan sponsors have decided to do away with advisory fees and to manage some or all of their funds in-house following an indexing strategy. Lower nonadvisory fees, such as custodial fees, is the third explanation for the popularity of bond indexing.

Critics of indexing point out that while an indexing strategy matches the performance of some index, the performance of that index does not necessarily represent optimal performance. Moreover, matching an index does not mean that

the manager will satisfy a client's return requirement objective. For example, if the objective of a life insurance company or a pension fund is to have sufficient funds to satisfy a predetermined liability, indexing only reduces the likelihood that performance will not be materially worse than the index. The return on the index is not necessarily related to the liability.

The pure bond indexing strategy involves creating a portfolio to replicate the issues comprising the index. This means that the indexed portfolio is a mirror image of the index. However, a manager pursuing this strategy will encounter several logistical problems in constructing an indexed portfolio. First, the prices for each issue used by the organization that publishes the index may not be execution prices available to the manager. In fact, they may be materially different from the prices offered by some dealers. In addition, the prices used by organizations reporting the value of indexes are based on bid prices. Dealer ask prices, however, are the ones that the manager would have to transact at when constructing or rebalancing the indexed portfolio. Thus there will be a bias between the performance of the index and the indexed portfolio that is equal to the bid-ask spread.

Furthermore, there are logistical problems unique to certain sectors in the bond market. Consider first the corporate bond market. There are typically about 4,000 issues in the corporate or credit sector of a broad-based U.S. bond market index. Because of the illiquidity for many of the issues, not only may the prices used by the organization that publishes the index be unreliable, but also many of the issues may not even be available. Next, consider the mortgage sector. There are more than 800,000 agency passthrough issues. As explained in the previous chapter, the organizations that publish indexes aggregate all these issues into a few hundred generic issues. The manager is then faced with the difficult task of finding passthrough securities with the same risk/return profile of these hypothetical generic issues.

Finally, recall that the total return depends on the reinvestment rate available on interim cash flows received prior to month end. If the organization publishing the index regularly overestimates the reinvestment rate, then the indexed portfolio could underperform the index.

To help mitigate these problems that cause underperformance, a manager of an indexed portfolio can pursue a securities lending program using the securities in the portfolio to add return. Securities lending was discussed in Chapter 15.

Enhanced Indexing/Matching Primary Risk Factors Approach

An enhanced indexing strategy can be pursued to construct a portfolio to match the primary risk factors without acquiring each issue in the index. This is a common strategy used by smaller funds because of the difficulties of acquiring all of the issues comprising the index. Generally speaking, the fewer the number of issues used to replicate the index, the smaller the tracking error due to transaction

costs but the greater the tracking error risk because of the difficulties of matching the primary risk factors perfectly. In contrast, the more issues purchased to replicate the index, the greater the tracking error due to transaction costs, but the smaller the tracking error risk due to the mismatch of the primary factors between the indexed portfolio and the index.

While in the spectrum of strategies defined by Volpert this strategy is called an "enhanced strategy," some investors refer to this as simply an indexing strategy. There are three methodologies used to construct a portfolio to replicate an index: the stratified sampling or cellular approach, the optimization approach, and the variance minimization approach. Each approach assumes that the performance of an individual bond depends on a number of systematic factors that affect the performance of all bonds and on a factor unique to the individual issue. This last risk is diversifiable risk. The objective of the three approaches is to construct an indexed portfolio that eliminates this diversifiable risk.[2]

Enhanced Indexing/Minor Risk Factor Mismatches

Another enhanced strategy is one where the portfolio is constructed to have minor deviations from the risk factors that affect the performance of the index. For example, there might be a slight overweighting of issues or sectors where the manager believes there is relative value. However, it is important to point out that the duration of the constructed portfolio is matched to the duration of the index. This is depicted in Exhibit 1, which shows that there are no duration bets for the pure index match strategy and the two enhanced index strategies.

Active Management/Larger Risk Factor Mismatches

Active bond strategies are those that attempt to outperform the market by intentionally constructing a portfolio that will have a greater index mismatch than in the case of enhanced indexing. The decision to pursue an active strategy or to engage a client to request a manager to pursue an active strategy must be based on the belief that there is some type of gain from such costly efforts; for there to be a gain, pricing inefficiencies must exist. The particular strategy chosen depends on why the manager believes this is the case.

Volpert classifies two types of active strategies. In the more conservative of the two active strategies, the manager makes larger mismatches relative to the index in terms of risk factors. This includes minor mismatches of duration. Typically, there will be a limitation as to the degree of duration mismatch. For example, the manager may be constrained to be within +1 of the duration of the index. So, if the duration of the index is 4, the manager may have a duration between 3 and 5. To take advantage of anticipated reshaping of the yield curve, there can be significant differences in the cash flow distribution between the index and the

---

[2] These approaches are discussed in Chapter 15 in Frank J. Fabozzi, *Bond Portfolio Management: Second Edition* (New Hope, PA: Frank J. Fabozzi Associates, 2001).

portfolio constructed by the manager. As another example, if the manager believes that within the corporate sector, A-rated issues will outperform AA-rated issues, the manager may overweight the A-rated issues and underweight AA-rated issues.

Active Management/Full-Blown Active

In the full-blown active management case, the manager is permitted to make a significant duration bet without any constraint. The manager can have a duration of zero (i.e., be all in cash) or can leverage the portfolio to a high multiple of the duration of the index. The manager can decide not to invest in one or more of the major sectors of the broad-based U.S. bond market indexes. The manager can make a significant allocation to sectors not included in the index. For example, there can be a substantial allocation to nonagency mortgage-backed securities.

VALUE-ADDED STRATEGIES

Active portfolio strategies and enhanced indexing/minor risk factor mismatch strategies seek to generate additional return after adjusting for risk. This additional return is popularly referred to as *alpha*. We refer to these strategies as value-added strategies. These strategies can be classified as strategic strategies and tactical strategies.

Strategic strategies, sometimes referred to as top-down *value-added strategies*, involve the following:

1. interest rate expectations strategies
2. yield curve strategies
3. inter- and intra-sector allocation strategies

Tactical strategies, sometimes referred to as *relative value strategies*, are short-term trading strategies. They include:

1. strategies based on rich/cheap analysis
2. yield curve trading strategies
3. return enhancing strategies employing futures and options

We discuss these strategies as follows. To help understand strategic strategies, we use the portfolio recommended by Lehman Brothers to its clients in a July 9, 2001 publication. The recommended portfolio, shown in Exhibit 2, is for a manager whose benchmark is the Lehman Brothers U.S. Aggregate Index.

Exhibit 2: U.S. Aggregate Core Portfolio (July 6, 2001)

	Percent of Market Value by Duration Range													Contribution to						
	0-2		2-4		4-7		7-9		9+		Total		% Over(+)/ Under(–)	OAD			Spread Duration			% Over(+)/ Under(–)
Sector	Index	Rec	Index	Rec	Index	Rec	Index	Rec	Index	Rec	Index	Rec	Weight	Index	Rec	Diff	Index	Rec	Diff	Weight
Treasury	5.74	2.07	5.27	3.71	4.43	0.00	1.14	1.58	7.21	5.41	23.79	12.77	–46	1.39	0.98	–0.41	0.00	0.00	0.00	—
Agency	2.79	0.00	3.46	5.70	2.77	3.48	0.61	1.11	1.41	1.12	11.05	11.42	3	0.50	0.53	0.02	0.50	0.53	0.03	5
Mtg. Pass-throughs	2.12	4.80	19.19	15.07	13.06	16.63	0.00	0.00	0.00	0.00	34.36	36.50	6	1.24	1.31	0.07	1.30	1.41	0.12	9
CMBS	0.03	0.00	0.37	0.18	1.52	1.80	0.03	0.00	0.00	0.00	1.95	1.98	2	0.10	0.11	0.02	0.10	0.11	0.02	17
ABS	0.60	3.46	0.71	2.39	0.45	0.00	0.06	0.00	0.00	0.00	1.83	5.85	220	0.06	0.13	0.08	0.06	0.13	0.08	137
Credit	3.04	2.63	7.69	8.62	9.90	12.14	2.08	3.88	4.33	4.22	27.03	31.49	16	1.47	1.77	0.31	1.47	1.77	0.30	20
Total	14.32	12.96	36.69	35.67	32.12	34.05	3.93	6.57	12.95	10.75	100.00	100.00		4.76	4.84	0.08	3.43	3.96	0.53	16
%Over (+)/ Under(–)Weight		–9		–3		6		67		–17										

Source: Lehman Brothers, "U.S. Aggregate Core Portfolio: July 6, 2001," *Global Relative Value* Fixed Income Research (July 9, 2001), p. 2.

Interest Rate Expectations Strategies

A manager who believes that he or she can accurately forecast the future level of interest rates will alter the portfolio's duration based the forecast.[3] Because duration is a measure of interest rate sensitivity, this involves increasing a portfolio's duration if interest rates are expected to fall and reducing duration if interest rates are expected to rise. For those managers whose benchmark is a bond market index, this means increasing the portfolio duration relative to the benchmark index if interest rates are expected to fall and reducing it if interest rates are expected to rise. The degree to which the duration of the managed portfolio is permitted to diverge from that of the benchmark index may be limited by the client. Interest rate expectations strategies are commonly referred to as "duration strategies."

The key to this active strategy is, of course, an ability to forecast the direction of future interest rates. The academic literature does not support the view that interest rates can be forecasted so that risk-adjusted excess returns can be consistently realized. It is doubtful whether betting on future interest rates will provide a consistently superior return.

While a manager may not pursue an active strategy based strictly on future interest rate movements, there can be a tendency to make an interest rate bet to cover inferior performance relative to a bond market index. For example, suppose a manager holds himself out to a client as pursuing one of the active strategies discussed later in this chapter. Suppose further that the manager is evaluated over a 1-year investment horizon and that 3 months before the end of the investment horizon, the manager is performing below the client-specified benchmark bond index. If the manager believes the account will be lost because of underperformance, there is an incentive to bet on interest rate movements. If the manager is correct, the account will be saved, although an incorrect bet will result in underperforming the index by a greater amount. In this case, the account might probably be lost regardless of the level of underperformance. A client can prevent this type of gaming by a manager by imposing constraints on the degree that the portfolio's duration can vary from that of the index. Also, in the performance evaluation stage of the investment management process, decomposing the portfolio's return into the factors that generated the return will highlight the extent to which a portfolio's return is attributable to changes in the level of interest rates.

Exhibit 2 shows that "option-adjusted duration" for the Lehman Brothers Aggregate Index and the recommended portfolio. The "option-adjusted duration" (OAD) is the term used by Lehman Brothers rather than effective duration. As can be seen in Exhibit 2, the recommended duration for the portfolio was 4.84 versus 4.76 for the index. That is, the recommended portfolio duration was 102% of the index.

---

[3] A portfolio's duration may be altered in the cash market by swapping (or exchanging) bonds in the portfolio for new bonds that will achieve the target portfolio duration. Alternatively, a more efficient means for altering the duration of a bond portfolio is to use interest rate futures contracts. For a discussion of how interest rate futures can be used to alter a portfolio's duration, see Chapter 17 in Fabozzi, *Bond Portfolio Management: Second Edition.*

Yield Curve Strategies

The yield curve for U.S. Treasury securities shows the relationship between maturity and yield. The shape of the yield curve changes over time. A shift in the yield curve refers to the relative change in the yield for each Treasury maturity. A parallel shift in the yield curve refers to a shift in which the change in the yield for all maturities is the same. A nonparallel shift in the yield curve means that the yield for every maturity does not change by the same number of basis points.

A top-down yield curve strategy involves positioning a portfolio to capitalize on expected changes in the shape of the Treasury yield curve. There are three yield curve strategies: (1) bullet strategies, (2) barbell strategies, and (3) ladder strategies. Each of these strategies is depicted in Exhibit 3. In a *bullet strategy*, the portfolio is constructed so that the maturity of the bonds in the portfolio are highly concentrated at one point on the yield curve. In a *barbell strategy,* the maturity of the bonds included in the portfolio is concentrated at two extreme maturities. In a *ladder strategy*, the portfolio is constructed to have approximately equal amounts of each maturity. So, for example, a portfolio might have equal amounts of bonds with 1 year to maturity, 2 years to maturity, and so on.

Each of these strategies will result in different performance when the yield curve shifts. The actual performance will depend on both the type of shift and the magnitude of the shift. Thus, no general statements can be made about the optimal yield curve strategy. The following example illustrates these points. In addition, it will show how to use the total return framework for assessing a portfolio's potential performance, scenario analysis, and the limitations of duration.

Consider the three bonds shown in Exhibit 4. Bond A is the short-term bond, bond B is the long-term bond, and bond C is the intermediate-term bond. Each bond is selling at par, and it is assumed the next coupon payment is 6 months from now. The duration for each bond is shown in the exhibit. Since the bonds are trading at par value, the duration indicates the dollar price change per 100 basis point change in yield.

Suppose that the following two portfolios are constructed. The first portfolio consists of only bond C, a 10-year bond, and is a bullet portfolio. The second portfolio consists of 51.86% of bond A and 48.14% of bond B and is a barbell portfolio.

The duration of the bullet portfolio is 6.50. The duration of the barbell is the weighted average of the dollar duration of the two bonds and is computed below:

$$0.5186\,(4.21) + 0.4814\,(9.90) = 6.50$$

The barbell portfolio's duration is equal to the bullet portfolio's duration. In fact, the barbell portfolio was designed to produce this result.

Duration is just a first approximation of the change in price resulting from a change in interest rates. The convexity measure provides a second approximation. The convexity measure of the two portfolios is not equal. The two convexity measures are reported in the exhibit. The bullet portfolio has a convexity measure that is less than that of the barbell portfolio.

Exhibit 3: Yield Curve Strategies: Bullet, Barbell, and Ladder

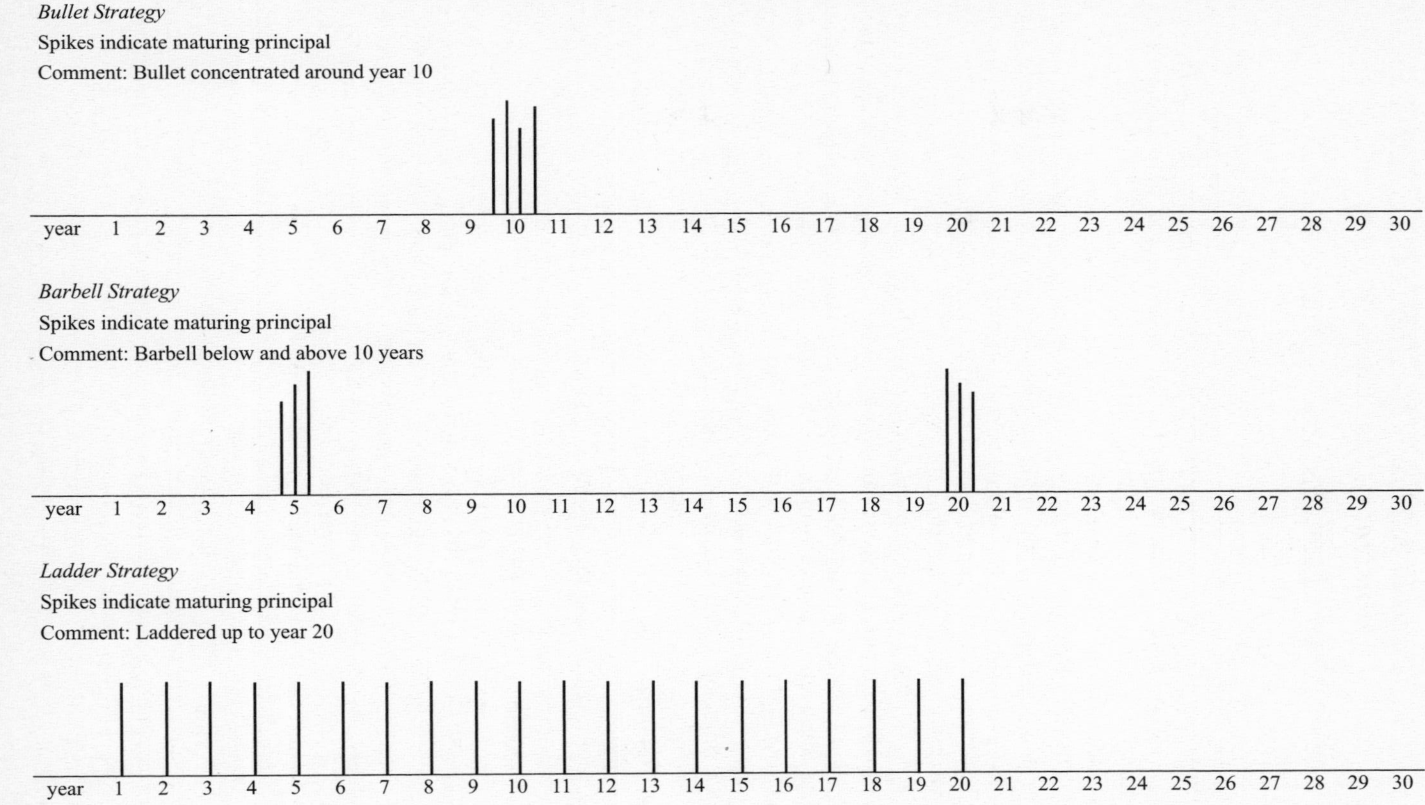

Exhibit 4: Three Hypothetical Bonds to Illustrate Yield Curve Strategies

Bond	Coupon rate	Price	Yield to maturity	Maturity (years)	Duration	Convexity
A	6.5%	100	6.5%	5	4.21	10.68
B	8.0%	100	8.0%	20	9.90	73.64
C	7.5%	100	7.5%	10	6.50	31.10

The "yield" for the two portfolios is not the same. The yield for the bullet portfolio is simply the yield to maturity of bond C, 7.50%. The traditional yield calculation for the barbell portfolio, which is found by taking a weighted average of the yield to maturity of the two bonds included in the portfolio, is 7.22%. This would suggest that the "yield" of the bullet portfolio is 28 basis points greater than the barbell portfolio. Thus, both portfolios have the same duration, but the yield of the bullet portfolio is greater than the yield of the barbell portfolio. However, the convexity of the barbell portfolio is greater than that of the bullet portfolio.

Which is the better portfolio in which to invest? The answer depends on the portfolio manager's investment objectives and investment horizon. Let's assume a 6-month investment horizon. Panel (a) of Exhibit 5 shows the difference in the total return over a 6-month investment horizon for the two portfolios, assuming that the yield curve shifts in a "parallel" fashion. By parallel it is meant that the yield for the short-term bond (A), the intermediate-term bond (C), and the long-term bond (B) change by the same number of basis points, shown in the first column of the exhibit. Note that no assumption is needed for the reinvestment rate since the three bonds shown in Exhibit 4 are assumed to be trading right after a coupon payment has been made and therefore there is no accrued interest. The total return reported in the second column of Exhibit 5 is:

bullet portfolio's total return – barbell portfolio's total return

Thus a positive value in the last column means that the bullet portfolio outperformed the barbell portfolio, while a negative sign means that the barbell portfolio outperformed the bullet portfolio. Which portfolio is the better investment alternative if the yield curve shifts in a parallel fashion *and* the investment horizon is 6 months? The answer depends on the amount by which yields change. Notice in the last column that if yields change by less than 100 basis points, the bullet portfolio will outperform the barbell portfolio. The reverse is true if yields change by more than 100 basis points.

Now let's look at what happens if the yield curve does not shift in a parallel fashion. The last columns of panels (b) and (c) of Exhibit 5 show the relative performance of the two portfolios for a nonparallel shift of the yield curve. Specifically, in panel (b) it is assumed that if the yield on bond C (the intermediate-term bond) changes by the amount shown in the first column, bond A (the short-term bond) will change by the same amount plus 30 basis points, whereas bond B

(the long-term bond) will change by the same amount shown in the first column less 30 basis points. That is, the nonparallel shift assumed is a flattening of the yield curve. For this yield curve shift, the barbell will outperform the bullet for the yield changes assumed in the first column. In panel (c), the nonparallel shift assumes that for a change in bond C's yield, the yield on bond A will change by the same amount less 30 basis points, whereas that on bond B will change by the same amount plus 30 points. That is, it assumes that the yield curve will steepen. In this case, it can be shown that the bullet portfolio would outperform the barbell portfolio for all but a change in yield greater than 250 basis points for bond C.

The key point here is that looking at measures such as yield (yield to maturity or some type of portfolio yield measure), duration, and convexity tells us little about performance over some investment horizon because performance depends on the magnitude of the change in yields and how the yield curve shifts.

Exhibit 5: Performance of Bullet and Barbell Portfolios Over a 6-Month Horizon

Yield change (in b.p.)	Price plus coupon ($)			Total return (%)		
	A	B	C	Bullet	Barbell	Difference[1]
(a) Assuming a Parallel Yield Curve Shift						
-300	115.6407	141.0955	126.7343	53.47	55.79	-2.32
-200	111.3157	126.8082	118.3960	36.79	37.55	-0.76
-150	109.2281	120.4477	114.4928	28.99	29.26	-0.27
-100	107.1888	114.5512	110.7559	21.51	21.47	0.05
-50	105.1965	109.0804	107.1775	14.35	14.13	0.22
0	103.2500	104.0000	103.7500	7.50	7.22	0.28
50	101.3481	99.2780	100.4665	0.93	0.70	0.23
100	99.4896	94.8852	97.3203	-5.36	-5.45	0.09
150	97.6735	90.7949	94.3050	-11.39	-11.28	-0.11
200	95.8987	86.9830	91.4146	-17.17	-16.79	-0.38
300	92.4686	80.1070	85.9857	-28.03	-26.96	-1.06
(b) Assuming a Flattening of the Yield Curve[2]						
-300	114.3218	145.8342	126.7343	53.47	58.98	-5.51
-200	110.0573	130.8648	118.3960	36.79	40.15	-3.36
-150	107.9989	124.2057	114.4928	28.99	31.60	-2.62
-100	105.9879	118.0356	110.7559	21.51	23.58	-2.06
-50	104.0232	112.3139	107.1775	14.35	16.03	-1.67
0	102.1036	107.0033	103.7500	7.50	8.92	-1.42
50	100.2279	102.0699	100.4665	0.93	2.23	-1.30
100	98.3949	97.4829	97.3203	-5.36	-4.09	-1.27
150	96.6037	93.2142	94.3050	-11.39	-10.06	-1.33
200	94.8531	89.2380	91.4146	-17.17	-15.70	-1.47
300	91.4697	82.0718	85.9857	-28.03	-26.11	-1.92

Exhibit 6: Corporate Sector Recommendation in Terms of Spread Duration Contribution (July 6, 2001)

Spread	Aaa-Aa			A			Baa			Total			(%) Over(+)/ Under(−)
Duration	Index	Rec.	Diff.	Index	Rec.	Diff.	Index	Rec.	Diff.	Index	Rec.	Diff.	Wght
0-3	0.04	0.05	0.00	0.05	0.05	0.00	0.03	0.05	0.03	0.12	0.15	0.03	28
3-5	0.10	0.02	−0.08	0.12	0.17	0.05	0.08	0.12	0.03	0.31	0.30	0.00	−1
5-7	0.08	0.15	0.07	0.18	0.32	0.14	0.15	0.14	−0.01	0.42	0.62	0.20	48
7-10	0.05	0.11	0.05	0.09	0.19	0.10	0.10	0.15	0.05	0.25	0.45	0.20	79
10+	0.06	0.05	−0.01	0.18	0.19	0.01	0.13	0.00	−0.13	0.38	0.25	−0.13	−35
Total	0.34	0.37	0.03	0.63	0.93	0.30	0.50	0.46	−0.03	1.47	1.77	0.30	20
%Over(+)/Under(−)Weight			9			48			−7			20	
Industrial	0.09	0.20	0.10	0.34	0.67	0.33	0.33	0.09	−0.24	0.76	0.95	0.20	26
Financial	0.13	0.15	0.02	0.22	0.26	0.04	0.04	0.00	−0.04	0.38	0.42	0.03	9
Utility	0.01	0.00	−0.01	0.04	0.00	−0.04	0.09	0.23	0.15	0.13	0.23	0.10	77
Non-Corp.	0.09	0.02	−0.07	0.05	0.00	−0.05	0.06	0.14	0.09	0.20	0.17	−0.03	−15
Total	0.32	0.37	0.05	0.64	0.93	0.29	0.51	0.46	−0.04	1.47	1.77	0.30	20
%Over(+)/Under(−)Weight			17			45			−9			20	

Source: Lehman Brothers, "Corporate Sector Recommendations: July 6, 2001," *Global Relative Value*, Fixed Income Research (July 9, 2001), p. 3.

Basically, this allocation strategy among sectors is one aimed at benefitting from "spread products"—credit risk and prepayment risk for commercial CMBS, ABS, and credit sectors and prepayment risk for mortgages passthrough securities.

Several duration measures that we discussed in Chapter 2 and reported in Exhibit 2 provide us with information about the level of exposure to spread risk. First is the difference in the spread duration[4] between the index (3.43) and the recommended portfolio (3.96). This is not surprising given the underweighting of the Treasury sector in the recommended portfolio. The second is the difference in the contribution[5] to spread duration for each sector in the index and the corresponding sector in the recommended portfolio.

In an intra-sector allocation strategy, the manager's allocation of funds within a sector differs from that of the index. Exhibit 2 shows for each sector the allocation within each sector in terms of market percentage. Exhibit 6 shows Lehman Brothers' intra-sector allocation recommendation on July 6, 2001, for the corporate sector in terms of contribution to spread duration for each credit quality and by sector (industrial, financial, utility, and Yankee).

On the same date, Exhibit 7 shows the recommended allocation for the mortgage sector in terms of market value and spread duration by program and price. The program classification is for Ginnie Mae (GNMA) passthroughs and conven-

---

4 Spread duration is explained in Chapter 2.

5 Contribution to duration is explained in Chapter 2.

Exhibit 5 (Continued)

Yield change (in b.p.)	Price plus coupon ($)			Total return (%)		
	A	B	C	Bullet	Barbell	Difference[1]
(c) Assuming a Steepening of the Yield Curve[3]						
−300	116.9785	136.5743	126.7343	53.47	52.82	0.65
−200	112.5919	122.9339	118.3960	36.79	35.14	1.65
−150	110.4748	116.8567	114.4928	28.99	27.09	1.89
−100	108.4067	111.2200	110.7559	21.51	19.52	1.99
−50	106.3863	105.9874	107.1775	14.35	12.39	1.97
0	104.4125	101.1257	103.7500	7.50	5.66	1.84
50	102.4839	96.6046	100.4665	0.93	−0.69	1.63
100	100.5995	92.3963	97.3203	−5.36	−6.70	1.34
150	98.7582	88.4758	94.3050	−11.39	−12.38	0.99
200	96.9587	84.8200	91.4146	−17.17	−17.77	0.60
300	93.4812	78.2204	85.9857	−28.03	−27.73	−0.30

[1] A positive sign indicates that the bullet portfolio outperformed the barbell portfolio; a negative sign indicates that the barbell portfolio outperformed the bullet portfolio.
[2] Yield curve shift assumption:
Change in yield of bond C (column 1) results in a change in the yield of bond A plus 30 basis points.
Change in yield of bond C (column 1) results in a change in the yield of bond B minus 30 basis points.
[3] Yield curve shift assumption:
Change in yield of bond C (column 1) results in a change in the yield of bond A minus 30 basis points.
Change in yield of bond C (column 1) results in a change in the yield of bond B plus 30 basis points.

When this strategy is applied by a manager whose benchmark is a broad-based bond market index, there is a mismatching of maturities relative to the index in one or more of the bond sectors. Rather than look at maturity mismatches, the preferred method is to look at duration mismatches as a percentage of market value. This is how the recommendation is expressed in the Lehman Brothers' allocation shown in Exhibit 2.

Inter- and Intra-Sector Allocation Strategies

A manager can allocate funds among the major bond sectors that is different from the allocation in the index. This is referred to as an *inter-sector allocation strategy*. For example, from Exhibit 2 we can see that the Lehman Brothers U.S. Aggregate Index had the following distribution along with Lehman's recommended asset allocation:

Sector	Index	Recommended	Weighting
Treasury	23.79%	12.77%	Underweight
Agency	11.05%	11.42%	Overweight
Mortgage Passthrough	34.36%	36.50%	Overweight
Commercial MBS	1.95%	1.98%	Slight overweight
ABS	1.83%	5.85%	Overweight
Credit	27.02%	31.49%	Overweight

tional passthroughs (Freddie Mac and Fannie Mae). (We referred to these as agency passthroughs in Chapter 9.) The differences in allocation by price reflect differences in prepayment risk exposure. For example, consider the 30-year programs for Ginnie Mae and conventionals. There is an overweighting of premium products (i.e., passthroughs trading above 102% of par value). This suggests that the allocation in the mortgage passthrough sector is such that the expectation is not great that prepayments will accelerate, causing premium products (i.e., high-coupon mortgages) to underperform low-coupon and par-coupon mortgages. In contrast, for the 15-year mortgage products, there is a slight underweighting of premium products.

Exhibit 7: MBS Sector Recommendations in Terms of Spread Duration Contribution

Program & Price		Index		Recommended		Difference		%Over(+)/ Under(−) Weight	
		% Mkt. Val.	% Spread Dur.	% Mkt. Val.	% Spread Dur.	% Mkt. Val.	% Spread Dur.	% Mkt. Val.	% Spread Dur.
GNMA									
30-year	<98	0.59	0.03	0.00	0.00	−0.59	−0.03	N/A	N/A
	98 to <102	3.93	0.18	3.10	0.14	−0.82	−0.04	−21	−24
	102 to <106	2.89	0.10	4.19	0.15	1.30	0.04	45	42
	106+	0.32	0.01	0.00	0.00	−0.32	−0.01	N/A	N/A
15-year									
	<98	0.01	0.00	0.00	0.00	−0.01	0.00	N/A	N/A
	98 to <102	0.15	0.00	0.00	0.00	−0.15	0.00	N/A	N/A
	102 to <106	0.10	0.00	0.00	0.00	−0.10	0.00	N/A	N/A
	106+	0.00	0.00	0.00	0.00	0.00	0.00	N/A	N/A
GNMA Summary		7.99	0.33	7.30	0.28	−0.69	−0.05	−9	−15
Fannie Mae and Freddie Mac									
Conventional 30-year									
	<98	3.14	0.15	6.69	0.35	3.54	0.20	11	136
	98 to <102	12.31	0.49	3.04	0.13	-9.27	−0.36	−75	−73
	102 to <106	5.20	0.15	9.66	0.27	4.46	0.12	86	83
	106+	0.26	0.01	1.35	0.04	1.09	0.03	418	432
Conventional 15-year									
	<98	0.54	0.02	4.30	0.18	3.76	0.16	699	758
	98 to <102	3.67	0.12	3.30	0.13	−0.37	0.01	−10	10
	102 to <106	0.99	0.02	0.86	0.03	−0.13	0.00	N/A	N/A
	106+	0.00	0.00	0.00	0.00	0.00	0.00	N/A	N/A
Conventional Summary		26.11	0.96	29.20	1.13	3.09	0.17	12	18
Balloons		0.26	0.01	0.00	0.00	−0.26	−0.01	N/A	N/A
Total Pass Throughs		34.36	1.30	36.50	1.41	2.14	0.12	6	9
CMBS		1.94	0.10	1.98	0.11	0.04	0.02	2	17
Total		36.31	1.39	38.48	1.53	2.17	0.13	6	10

Source: Lehman Brothers, "MBS Sector Recommendations: July 6, 2001," *Global Relative Value*, Fixed Income Research (July 9, 2001), p. 4.

Considerations in Inter- and Intra-Sector Allocations

In making inter- and intra-sector allocations, a manager is anticipating how spreads will change. Spreads reflect differences in credit risk, call risk (or prepayment risk), and liquidity risk. When the spread for a particular sector or subsector is expected to decline or "narrow," a manager may decide to overweight that particular sector or subsector. It will be underweighted if the manager expects the spread to increase or "widen."

Credit or quality spreads change because of expected changes in economic prospects. Credit spreads between Treasury and non-Treasury issues widen in a declining or contracting economy and narrow during economic expansion. The economic rationale is that in a declining or contracting economy, corporations experience a decline in revenue and cash flow, making it difficult for corporate issuers to service their contractual debt obligations. To induce investors to hold non-Treasury securities, the yield spread relative to Treasury securities must widen. The converse is that during economic expansion and brisk economic activity, revenue and cash flow pick up, increasing the likelihood that corporate issuers will have the capacity to service their contractual debt obligations. Yield spreads between Treasury and federal agency securities will vary depending on investor expectations about the prospects that an implicit government guarantee will be honored.

A manager therefore can use economic forecasts of the economy in developing forecasts of credit spreads. Also, some managers base forecasts on historical credit spreads. The underlying principle is that there is a "normal" credit spread relationship that exists. If the current credit spread in the market differs materially from that "normal" credit spread, then the manager should position the portfolio to benefit from a return to the "normal" credit spread. The assumption is that the "normal" credit spread is some type of average or mean value and that mean reversion will occur. If, in fact, there has been a structural shift in the marketplace, this may not occur because the normal spread may change.

A manager will also look at technical factors to assess relative value. For example, a manager may analyze the prospective supply and demand for new issues on spreads in individual sectors or issuers to determine whether they should be overweighted or underweighted. This commonly used tactical strategy is referred to as *primary market analysis*.

Now let's look at spreads due to call or prepayment risk. Expectations about how these spreads will change will affect the inter-sector allocation decision between Treasury securities (which are noncallable securities except for a few outstanding callable Treasury bonds) and spread products that have call risk. Corporate and agency bonds have callable and noncallable issues, all mortgages are prepayable, and asset-backed securities have products that are callable but borrowers may be unlikely to exercise the call. Consequently, with sectors having different degrees of call risk, expectations about how spreads will change also affect intra-allocation decisions. They affect (1) the allocation between callable and noncallable bonds within the corporate bond sector and (2) within the agency,

corporate, mortgage, and ABS sectors the allocation among premium (i.e., high-coupon), par, and discount (i.e., low-coupon) bonds.

Spreads due to call risk will change as a result of expected changes in (1) the direction of the change in interest rates and (2) interest rate volatility. An expected drop in the level of interest rates will widen the yield spread between callable bonds and noncallable bonds as the prospects that the issuer will exercise the call option increase. The reverse is true: The spread narrows if interest rates are expected to rise. An increase in interest rate volatility increases the value of the embedded call option, and thereby increases the spread between (1) callable bonds and noncallable bonds and (2) premium and discount bonds. Trades where the manager is anticipating better performance due to the embedded options of individual issues or sectors are referred to as *structure trades*.

INTERNATIONAL INVESTING STRATEGIES

Several reasons have been offered for why U.S. money managers or their clients should allocate a portion of their bond portfolio to non-U.S. bonds. The traditional argument in favor of investing in non-U.S. bonds, particularly with the currency hedged, is that they may provide diversification, resulting in a reduction in risk. This is generally demonstrated using modern portfolio theory by showing that investors can realize a higher expected return for a given level of risk (as measured by the standard deviation of return) by adding non-U.S. bonds in a portfolio containing U.S. bonds. These diversification benefits occur as a result of less than perfect positive correlation between U.S. bond returns and the bond returns of other countries.

The potential diversification benefits are demonstrated in Exhibit 8. The exhibit shows the relationship between expected return and risk. The two curves shown in the exhibit indicate that in order to increase the expected return, the risk must be increased. Each point on a curve represents a portfolio that provides the maximum expected return for a given level of risk and is commonly referred to as an *efficient portfolio*. That is, a money manager cannot achieve a higher expected return for a given level of risk. A curve that shows these efficient portfolios is referred to as an *efficient frontier*.[6] For a given universe of assets, it is not possible to get to a point (i.e., create a portfolio) above the efficient frontier—which would represent a higher expected return for a given level of risk.

Look at the efficient frontier that is labeled "U.S. bonds only." By using only U.S. bonds, a money manager can create the risk/return combinations shown on the efficient frontier. The argument for including non-U.S. bonds in a portfolio of bonds is that the efficient frontier labeled "U.S. and non-U.S. bonds" can be achieved. Notice that the efficient frontier with the expanded universe of bonds that includes non-U.S. bonds offers at any given level of risk a higher expected return.

---

6 Because Harry Markowitz was the developer of modern portfolio theory, the efficient frontier is sometimes referred to as the *Markowitz efficient frontier*.

Exhibit 8: Efficient Frontier with and without Non-U.S. Bonds

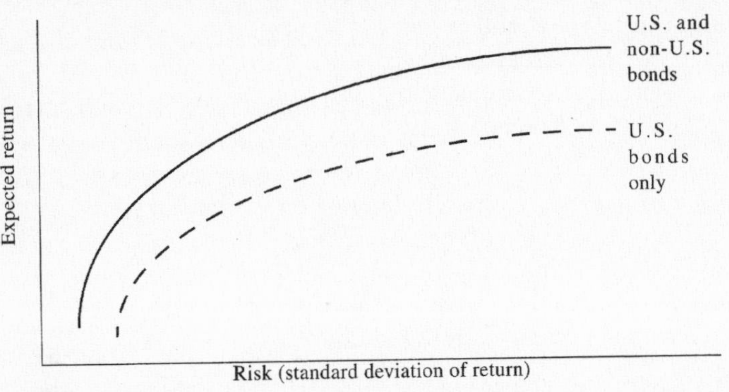

Just how far the efficient frontier can be pushed up by including non-U.S. bonds depends on the correlation between U.S. bond returns and the bond returns of other countries. The lower the correlation, the greater the potential diversification benefits.

Several studies have empirically investigated this question. One of the first studies was by Barnett and Rosenberg, who looked at bond indexes for the period 1973 to 1983.[7] They found that a 30% allocation of a portfolio to non-U.S. bonds reduced the risk of a U.S.-only bond portfolio. These results were supported by a study by Cholerton, Pieraerts, and Solnick covering approximately the same time period.[8] The reduction in risk found by these researchers was due to the low correlation of returns at the time.

As global markets have become better integrated, the correlation between U.S. bond returns and non-U.S. bond returns has increased. Hence, it has been argued, the benefits of diversifying internationally may be reduced significantly.

In contrast to the findings in favor of non-U.S. bond investing to realize diversification benefits, Burik and Ennis argue that the diversification benefits are minor.[9] Rosenberg, whose study in the early 1980s of the benefits of international bond diversification we cited earlier, in 1995 wrote: "The extent of risk reduction from passive international fixed income diversification appears quite modest, so it hardly seems worthwhile."[10] He states that the argument in favor of international bond investing does not rest with risk reduction. Instead, the motiva-

[7] G. Barnett and Michael Rosenberg, "International Diversification in Bonds," *Prudential International Fixed Income Investment Strategy*, Second Quarter 1983.

[8] Kenneth Cholerton, Pierre Pieraerts, and Bruno Solnick, "Why Invest into Foreign Currency Bonds?" *Journal of Portfolio Management* (Summer 1986), pp. 4–8.

[9] Paul Burik and Richard M. Ennis, "Foreign Bonds in Diversified Portfolios: A Limited Advantage," *Financial Analysts Journal* (March-April 1990), pp. 31–39.

[10] Michael R. Rosenberg, "International Fixed Income Investing: Theory and Practice," Chapter 55 in Frank J. Fabozzi (ed.), *The Handbook of Fixed Income Securities* (Burr Ridge, IL: Irwin Professional Publishing, 1997), p. 1113.

tion for international bond investing is the potential for total return enhancement. Litterman, too, suggests that while the diversification benefits may not be as great as in earlier years, a powerful reason for a U.S. money manager to invest in non-dollar bonds is "the increased opportunities to find value that multiple markets provide." [11] But it is hard to quantify such a benefit since it depends on the money manager's talents. As Rosenberg states:

> Foreign bonds offer US investors a unique opportunity to enhance the return on their US fixed income portfolios, but that return enhancement opportunity is available only through successful active management. It is widely recognized that the differences in total-return performance among the competing subsectors of the US domestic bond market are relatively small when compared to the sizable differences in performance that exist between the US and overseas markets. If US fund managers can exploit such differences by correctly shifting their portfolios from US to foreign bonds and then back when conditions warrant, then there will be great interest in the use of foreign bonds, not as a separate asset class for all seasons, but as a tactical asset for selected reasons.[12]

Lee Thomas of PIMCO provides evidence on the potential tactical use of non-U.S. bonds. One tactical strategy is to periodically reallocate funds to countries based on a forecast of relative performance. This is effectively a sector rotation strategy, where a sector is defined as a country. Exhibit 9 shows the potential benefits of a sector rotation strategy. In the exhibit, the country markets with the best and the worst total return (hedged into U.S. dollars) from the Salomon World Government Bond Index are shown for each year from 1987 to 1998. For a given year, the difference in the best- and worst-performing country market is substantial, averaging about 10 percentage points. If currency fluctuations had not been removed, the differential would have been even greater.

An investor who is primarily motivated to invest in non-U.S. bonds because of their diversification benefits must recognize the effect that this has on the investment management process. First, in establishing investment guidelines for its money manager, the investor will want to impose tight limits on the size of positions that its manager may take in individual non-U.S. bond markets relative to the benchmark (i.e., the mismatch between the benchmark and the portfolio). This is necessary because a substantial departure from the benchmark may reduce the benefits of diversifying globally.[13] In contrast, an investor who is motivated

---

[11] Robert Litterman, "Nondollar Bond Markets: Opportunities for U.S. Portfolio Managers," *Fixed Income Research* (New York: Goldman Sachs, April 1992), pp. 2–3.

[12] Rosenberg, "International Fixed Income Investing: Theory and Practice."

[13] Christopher B. Steward, Hank Lynch, and Frank J. Fabozzi, "International Bond Portfolio Management," in *Fixed Income Readings for the Chartered Financial Analysts Program* (New Hope, PA: Frank J. Fabozzi Associates, 2000).

by return enhancement opportunities would either not impose any constraint on the mismatch of any country's bond market relative to the benchmark or would give the manager considerably more latitude in mismatching.

Second, the time horizon over which investment performance is to be measured is also affected by the motivation for investing in non-U.S. bonds. If an investor evaluates a manager using a short-term time horizon such as a calendar quarter, this may encourage a manager to engage in more short-term trading, which could reduce the diversification benefits from global bond investing. Because differences in economic cycles can be prolonged, clients seeking the diversification benefits of global bond investing should use a longer time horizon so that there is sufficient time for a full economic cycle to play out and the diversification benefit to be realized.

Third, the motivation for global bond investing will affect the benchmark that a client would select. In the previous chapter, we discussed the various global/international bond indexes or benchmarks that are available. For example, an index that has only select countries may not provide the diversification benefit expected by the investor.

Finally, the motivation will impact the currency hedging management strategy. For example, a U.S. dollar-based investor whose primary goal is risk reduction might mandate that its manager adopt a hedged or mostly hedged strategy because the diversification benefit has historically been greater from hedged international bonds. In contrast, if an investor seeks to use non-U.S. bonds tactically, then the manager will be allowed to take on greater currency risk exposure.

Exhibit 9: Best and Worst Performing Country Markets 1987 to 1998 (Total Hedged Return in US$)

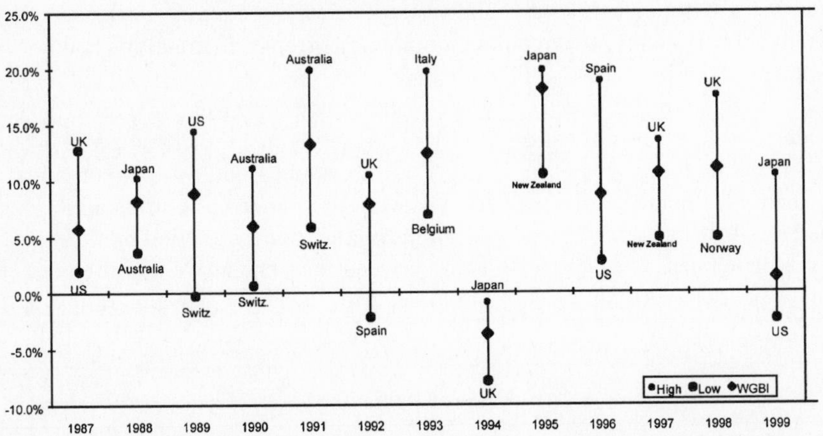

Source: Exhibit 2 in Lee R. Thomas, "Global Bond Investing in the 21st Century: Philosophy and Process," in Frank J. Fabozzi (ed.), *Professional Perspectives on Fixed Income Portfolio Management: Volume 2* (New Hope, PA: Frank J. Fabozzi Associates, 2001), p. 5.

A useful framework for formulating a strategy for international bond investing has been suggested by Rosenberg.[14] A strategy should be broken down into three key decision criteria: currency, market selection, and bond selection. These three key decision criteria determine how the money manager's portfolio will depart from the market capitalization weights in the benchmark index, subject to client constraints. Each of these decisions should be treated separately and then integrated in a portfolio construction context. Each represents an active bet if the allocation departs from the market capitalization weight in the benchmark index.

The currency exposure indicates the degree to which the portfolio is exposed to foreign exchange risk. A currency can be completely hedged, partially hedged, or unhedged. The net currency exposure is the difference between the gross currency position and the currency hedge. The currency exposure will depend on the money manager's expectations about future exchange rates. That is, it represents an active currency play. Rosenberg suggests a summary measure of currency risk that is equal to the ratio of the portfolio's net currency exposure to the benchmark index's market capitalization weight. A currency risk measure greater than 1 indicates that the money manager is willing to take on greater risk for that currency than in the benchmark index.

The market and bond selection decisions are based on the same active management strategies discussed earlier in this chapter applied to each market. The market decision indicates the exposure of the portfolio to each market and market sector (including cash). The interest rate exposure for each market can be calculated and compared to the same exposure for the same market based on the market capitalization in the benchmark index. The degree to which active bond selection strategies are pursued in a particular country's bond market depends on the money manager's belief in the pricing efficiency of that market.

STRUCTURED PORTFOLIO STRATEGIES

In a structured portfolio strategy, the money manager structures the portfolio to match the performance of some predetermined liabilities. The two structured portfolio strategies are immunization and cash flow matching.

Immunization

Immunization is a hybrid strategy having elements of both active and passive strategies. Classical immunization can be defined as the process by which a fixed income portfolio is created having an assured return for a specific time horizon irrespective of interest rate changes.[15] In a concise form, the following are the important characteristics: (1) a specified time horizon; (2) an assured rate of return during the holding period to a fixed horizon date; and (3) insulation from the effects of potential adverse interest rate changes on the portfolio value at the horizon date.

---

[14] Rosenberg, "International Fixed Income Investing: Theory and Practice," pp. 1121–1134.

Exhibit 10: General Principles of Classical Immunization

Goal: Lock in a minimum target rate of return and target investment value regardless of how interest rates change over the investment horizon.

Risk when interest rates change: (1) reinvestment risk, and (2) interest rate or price risk

Principle:

Scenario 1: Interest rates increase

Implications:

1. reinvestment income increases
2. value of bonds in the portfolio with a maturity greater than the investment horizon declines in value

Goal: Gain in reinvestment income ≥ loss in portfolio value

Scenario 2: Interest rates decline

Implications:

1. reinvestment income decreases
2. value of bonds in the portfolio with a maturity greater than the investment horizon increases in value

Goal: Loss in reinvestment income ≤ gain in portfolio value

Assumption: Parallel shift in the yield curve (i.e., all yields rise and fall uniformly)

The fundamental mechanism underlying immunization is a portfolio structure that balances the change in the value of the portfolio at the end of the investment horizon with the return from the reinvestment of portfolio cash flows (coupon payments and maturing securities). That is, immunization requires offsetting interest rate risk and reinvestment risk. To accomplish this balancing act requires controlling duration. By setting the duration of the portfolio equal to the desired portfolio time horizon, the offsetting of positive and negative incremental return sources can be assured. This is a necessary condition for effectively immunized portfolios. Exhibit 10 summarizes the general principles of classical immunization.

How often should the portfolio be rebalanced to adjust its duration? On the one hand, the more frequent rebalancing increases transaction costs, thereby reducing the likelihood of achieving the target return. On the other hand, less frequent rebalancing will result in the portfolio's duration wandering from the target duration, which will also reduce the likelihood of achieving the target return. Thus the money manager faces a tradeoff: Some transaction costs must be accepted to prevent the portfolio duration from wandering too far from its target, but some maladjustment in the portfolio duration must be lived with, or transaction costs will become prohibitively high.

[15] The classical theory of immunization is set forth in F. M. Reddington, "Review of the Principles of Life Insurance Valuations," *Journal of the Institute of Actuaries*, 1952; and Lawrence Fisher and Roman Weil, "Coping with Risk of Interest Rate Fluctuations: Returns to Bondholders from Naive and Optimal Strategies," *Journal of Business* (October 1971), pp. 408–431.

In the actual process leading to the construction of an immunized portfolio, the selection of the universe is extremely important. The lower the credit quality of the securities considered, the higher the potential risk and return. Immunization theory assumes there will be no defaults and that securities will be responsive only to overall changes in interest rates. The lower the credit quality, the greater the possibility that these assumptions will not be met. Further, securities with embedded options such as call features or mortgage-backed prepayments complicate and may even prevent the accurate measure of cash flows and hence duration, frustrating the basic requirements of immunization. Finally, liquidity is a consideration for immunized portfolios because, as just noted, they must be rebalanced over time.

Perhaps the most critical assumption of the classical immunization strategy concerns the assumption regarding the type of interest rate change. A property of a classically immunized portfolio is that the target value of the investment is the lower limit of the value of the portfolio at the horizon date if there is a parallel shift in the yield curve.[16] This would appear to be an unrealistic assumption. According to the theory, if there is a change in interest rates that does not correspond to this shape preserving shift, matching the duration to the investment horizon no longer assures immunization.[17]

A natural extension of classical immunization theory is a technique for modifying the assumption of parallel shifts in the yield curve. One approach is a strategy that can handle any arbitrary interest rate change so that it is not necessary to specify an alternative duration measure. The approach, developed by Fong and Vasicek, establishes a measure of immunization risk against any arbitrary interest rate change.[18] The immunization risk measure can then be minimized subject to the constraint that the duration of the portfolio be equal to the investment horizon resulting in a portfolio with minimum exposure to any interest rate movements.

One way of minimizing immunization risk is shown in Exhibit 11. The spikes in the two panels of the exhibit represent actual portfolio cash flows. The taller spikes depict the actual cash flows generated by matured securities while the smaller spikes represent coupon payments. Both portfolio A and portfolio B are composed of two bonds with a duration equal to the investment horizon. Portfolio A is, in effect, a barbell portfolio—a portfolio comprising short and long maturities and interim coupon payments. For portfolio B, the two bonds mature very close to the investment horizon and the coupon payments are nominal over the investment horizon. As explained earlier in this chapter, a portfolio with this characteristic is called a bullet portfolio.

---

[16] Lawrence Fisher and Roman Weil, "Coping with Risk of Interest Rate Fluctuations," *Journal of Business* (October 1971), pp. 408-431.

[17] For a more complete discussion of these issues, see John C. Cox, Jonathan E. Ingersoll, Jr., and Stephen A. Ross, "Duration and the Measurement of Basis Risk," *Journal of Business* (January 1979), pp. 51-61.

[18] H. Gifford Fong and Oldrich A. Vasicek, "A Risk Minimizing Strategy for Portfolio Immunization," *Journal of Finance* (December 1984), pp. 1541-1546.

Exhibit 11: Immunization Risk Measure

Portfolio A: High-risk immunized portfolio:

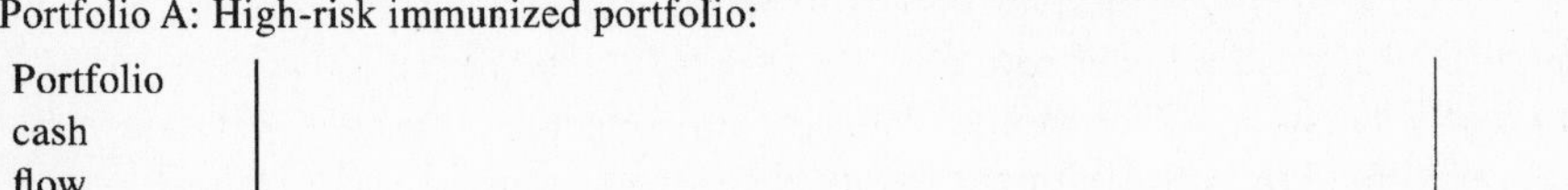

Note: Portfolio duration matches horizon length. Portfolio's cash flow dispersed.

Portfolio B: Low-risk immunized portfolio:

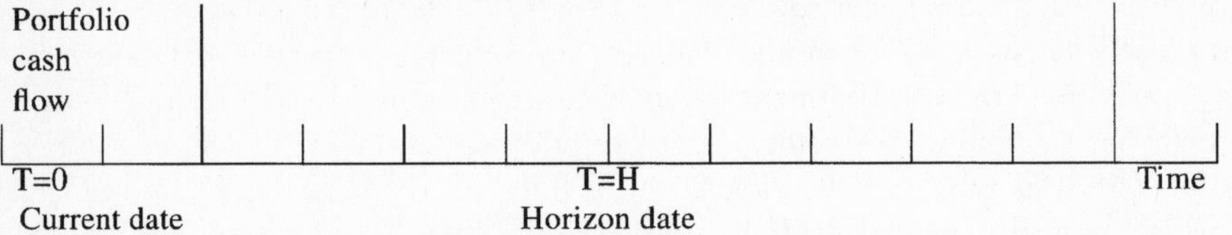

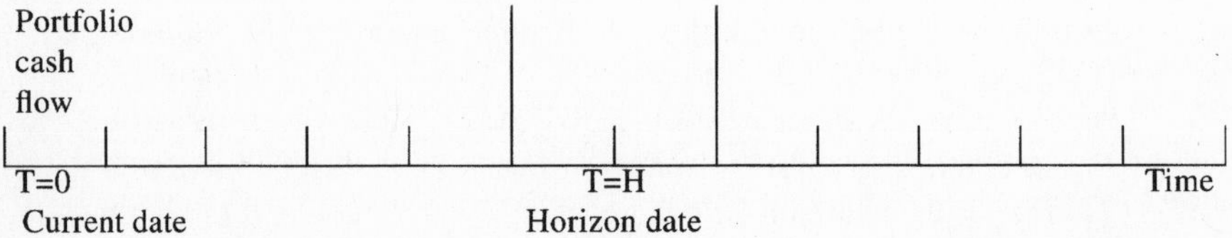

Note: Portfolio duration matches horizon length. Portfolio's cash flow concentrated around horizon dates.

It is not difficult to see why the barbell portfolio should be riskier than the bullet portfolio. Assume that both portfolios have durations equal to the horizon length, so that both portfolios are immune to parallel rate changes. This immunity is attained as a consequence of balancing the effect of changes in reinvestment rates on payments received during the investment horizon against the effect of changes in market value of the portion of the portfolio still outstanding at the end of the investment horizon. When interest rates change in an arbitrary nonparallel way, however, the effect on the two portfolios is very different. Suppose, for instance, that short rates decline while long rates go up. Both portfolios would realize a decline of the portfolio value at the end of the investment horizon below the target investment value, since they experience a capital loss in addition to lower reinvestment rates. The decline, however, would be substantially higher for the barbell portfolio for two reasons. First, the lower reinvestment rates are experienced on the barbell portfolio for longer time intervals than on the bullet portfolio, so that the opportunity loss is much greater. Second, the portion of the barbell portfolio still outstanding at the end of the investment horizon is much longer than that of the bullet portfolio, which means that the same rate increase would result in a much greater capital loss. Thus the bullet portfolio has less exposure to whatever the change in the interest rate structure may be than the barbell portfolio.

It should be clear from the foregoing discussion that immunization risk is the risk of reinvestment. The portfolio that has the least reinvestment risk will have the least immunization risk. When there is a high dispersion of cash flows around the horizon date, as in the barbell portfolio, the portfolio is exposed to higher reinvestment risk. However, when the cash flows are concentrated around the horizon date, as in the bullet portfolio, the portfolio is subject to minimum reinvestment risk.

There are variants of the classical immunization strategy. A *contingent immunization strategy* involves the identification of both the available immunization target rate and a lower *safety net level return* with which the client would be minimally satisfied.[19] The money manager can continue to pursue an active strategy until an adverse investment experience drives the then-available potential return—combined active return (from actual past experience) and immunized return (from expected future experience)—down to the safety net level; at such time the money manager would be obligated to completely immunize the portfolio and lock in the safety net level return. As long as this safety net is not violated, the manager can continue to actively manage the portfolio. Once the immunization mode is activated because the safety net is violated, the manager can no longer return to the active mode unless, of course, the contingent immunization plan is abandoned.

The key considerations in implementing a contingent immunization strategy are (1) establishing accurate immunized initial and ongoing available target returns, (2) identifying a suitable and immunizable safety net, and (3) implementing an effective monitoring procedure to ensure that the safety net is not violated.

Cash Flow Matching

The immunization strategy described previously is used to immunize a portfolio created to satisfy a single liability in the future against adverse interest rate movements. However, it is more common in situations to have multiple future liabilities. One example is the liability structure of pension funds. Another example is a life insurance annuity contract. When there are multiple future liabilities, it is possible to extend the principles of immunization to such situations. However, it is more common in practice to use a *cash flow matching strategy.* This strategy is used to construct a portfolio designed to fund a schedule of liabilities from portfolio return and asset value, with the portfolio's value diminishing to zero after payment of the last liability.

A cash flow matching strategy can be described intuitively as follows. A bond is selected with a maturity that matches the last liability. An amount of principal equal to the amount of the last liability is then invested in this bond. The remaining elements of the liability stream are then reduced by the coupon payments on this bond, and another bond is chosen for the next-to-last liability, adjusted for any coupon payments of the first bond selected. Going backward in time, this sequence is continued until all liabilities have been matched by payments on the securities selected for the portfolio. Exhibit 12 provides a simple illustration of this process for a 5-year liability stream. Optimization techniques can be employed to construct a least-cost cash flow matching portfolio from an acceptable universe of bonds.

---

[19] Martin L. Leibowitz and Alfred Weinberger, "Contingent Immunization—Part 1: Risk Control Procedures," *Financial Analysts Journal* (November-December 1982), pp. 17–31.

Exhibit 12: Illustration of Cash Flow Matching Process

Assume: 5-year liability stream

Cash flow from bonds are annual.

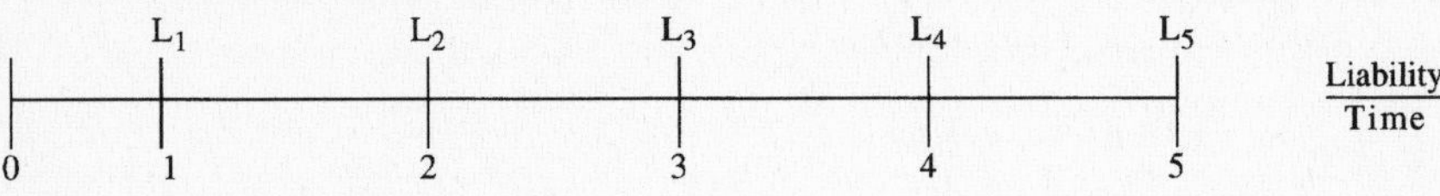

Step 1:

Cash flow from Bond A selected to satisfy L_5

Coupons = A_c; Principal = A_p and $A_c + A_p = L_5$

Unfunded liabilities remaining:

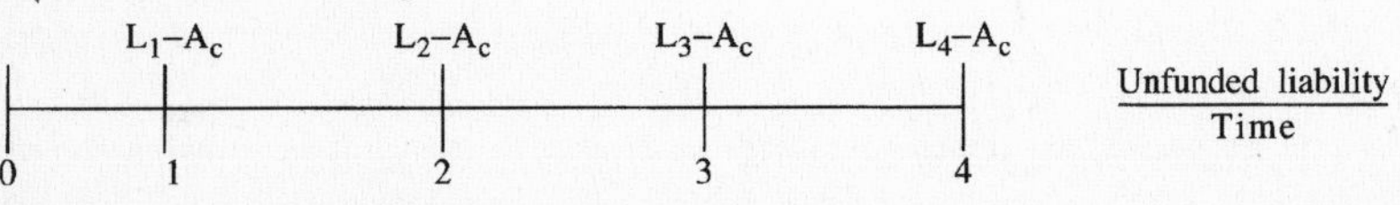

Step 2:

Cash flow from Bond B selected to satisfy L_4

Unfunded liability = $L_4 - A_c$

Coupons = B_c; Principal = B_p and $B_c + B_p = L_4 - A_c$

Unfunded liabilities remaining:

$L_1–A_c–B_c$ $L_2–A_c–B_c$ $L_3–A_c–B_c$

Unfunded liabilty / Time

0 1 2 3

Step 3:

Cash flow from Bond C selected to satisfy L_3

Unfunded liability = $L_3 - A_c - B_c$

Coupons = C_c; Principal = C_p and $C_c + C_p = L_3 - A_c - B_c$

Unfunded liabilities remaining:

$L_1–A_c–B_c–C_c$ $L_2–A_c–B_c–C_c$

Unfunded liabilty / Time

0 1 2

Step 4:

Cash flow from Bond D selected to satisfy L_2

Unfunded liability = $L_2 - A_c - B_c - C_c$

Coupons = D_c; Principal = D_p and $D_c + D_p = L_2 - A_c - B_c - C_c$

Unfunded liabilities remaining:

$L_1–A_c–B_c–C_c–D_c$

Unfunded liabilty / Time

0 1

Step 5:

Select Bond E with a cash flow of $L_1 - A_c - B_c - C_c - D_c$

KEY POINTS

- *Pricing efficiency refers to a market where prices at all times fully reflect all available information that is relevant to the valuation of securities.*
- *If the bond market or a sector of the bond market is price-efficient, active strategies pursued to outperform a market index will not consistently produce superior returns after adjusting for risk and transaction costs.*
- *The decision to pursue an active strategy must be based on the belief that there is some type of pricing inefficiency; if the bond market is price-efficient, a bond indexing strategy should be pursued.*
- *The outcome of an active bond portfolio strategy will depend on how a money manager's expectations differ from that of the market.*
- *Strategies can be classified as follows: (1) pure bond index matching, (2) enhanced indexing/ matching primary risk factors approach, (3) enhanced indexing/minor risk factor mismatches, (4) active management/larger risk factor mismatches, and (5) active management/ full-blown active.*
- *The difference between indexing and active management is the extent to which the portfolio can deviate from the primary risk factors associated with the index.*
- *The primary risk factors associated with an index are (1) the duration of the index, (2) the present value distribution of the cash flows, (3) percent in sector and quality, (4) duration contribution of sector, (5) duration contribution of credit quality, (6) sector/coupon/maturity cell weights, and (7) issuer exposure control.*
- *A pure bond index matching strategy involves the least risk of underperforming the index and involves creating a portfolio to replicate the issues comprising the index.*
- *A manager pursuing a pure index matching strategy will encounter several logistical problems in constructing an indexed portfolio that will cause tracking error.*
- *An enhanced indexing strategy can be pursued to construct a portfolio to match the primary risk factors without acquiring each issue in the index.*
- *Enhanced indexing/minor risk factor mismatches is an enhanced indexing strategy where the portfolio is constructed to have minor deviations from the risk factors that affect the performance of the index but the duration of the constructed portfolio is matched to the duration of the index.*
- *Active bond strategies are those that attempt to outperform the market by intentionally constructing a portfolio that will have a greater index mismatch than in the case of enhanced indexing.*
- *One active bond strategy the manager makes larger mismatches relative to the index in terms of risk factors, including minor mismatches of duration.*

- ❑ *In the full-blown active management case, the manager is permitted to make a significant duration bet without any constraint and can make a significant allocation to sectors not included in the index.*

- ❑ *Value-added strategies are those that seek to enhance return relative to an index and can be strategic or tactical.*

- ❑ *Strategic strategies include interest rate expectations strategies, yield curve strategies, and inter- and intra-sector allocation strategies.*

- ❑ *Tactical strategies are short-term trading strategies that include strategies based on rich/cheap analysis, yield curve trading strategies, and return enhancing strategies employing futures and options.*

- ❑ *Interest rate expectations strategies involve adjusting the duration of the portfolio relative to the index based on expected movements in interest rates.*

- ❑ *Top-down yield curve strategies involve positioning a portfolio to capitalize on expected changes in the shape of the Treasury yield curve following either a bullet strategy, barbell strategy, or ladder strategy.*

- ❑ *An inter-sector allocation strategy involves a manager's allocation of funds among the major bond sectors.*

- ❑ *In making inter- and intra-sector allocations, a manager is anticipating how spreads due to differences in credit risk, call risk (or prepayment risk), and liquidity risk will change.*

- ❑ *The traditional argument in favor of investing in non-U.S. bonds is the risk-reduction opportunities, where risk is defined as the standard deviation of returns.*

- ❑ *Diversification benefits occur as a result of less than perfect positive correlation between U.S. bond returns and the bond returns of other countries.*

- ❑ *Empirical evidence suggests that there are risk-reduction benefits from international bond investing, but some practitioners argue that the benefits from diversification are due to potential return enhancement from active management rather than risk reduction.*

- ❑ *In formulating a global bond investment strategy, the key decision criteria are the currency decision, market selection decision, and bond selection decision, with each decision treated separately; these three key decision criteria determine how the manager's portfolio will deviate from the capitalization weights in the benchmark index.*

- ❑ *In active management, a manager will determine the degree of risk to a particular currency based on expectations about the change in currency rates.*

- ❑ *The net currency exposure can be measured relative to the benchmark index's market capitalization weight.*

- ❏ *The net currency exposure to a market will depend on the money manager's expectations about future exchange rates and can be measured relative to the benchmark index's market capitalization weight.*
- ❏ *In a structured portfolio strategy, the money manager structures the portfolio to match the performance of predetermined liabilities.*
- ❏ *Classical immunization can be defined as the process by which a fixed income portfolio is created having an assured return for a specific time horizon irrespective of interest rate changes.*
- ❏ *The fundamental mechanism underlying immunization theory is a portfolio structure that balances the change in the value of the portfolio at the end of the investment horizon with the return from the reinvestment of portfolio cash flows.*
- ❏ *To immunize a portfolio, a money manager must construct a bond portfolio such that the duration is equal to the investment horizon and the initial present value of the cash flows from the portfolio equals the present value of the future liability.*
- ❏ *An assumption of classical immunization is that the yield curve will shift in a parallel fashion.*
- ❏ *Immunization risk is effectively reinvestment risk.*
- ❏ *In contingent immunization, the money manager pursues an active strategy until an adverse investment experience drives the then-available potential return down to a specified safety net level, at which time the manager must then immunize the portfolio.*
- ❏ *Cash flow matching is used when multiple liabilities must be satisfied regardless of how interest rates change.*

Index

Numerics

A

B

C

D

G

H

I

J

K

L

M

Q

R

S

U

V

W

T